APPROACHES TO MORALITY

Readings in Ethics from
Classical Philosophy to Existentialism

The Harbrace Series in Philosophy

UNDER THE GENERAL EDITORSHIP OF
Jesse A. Mann and Gerald F. Kreyche

REFLECTIONS ON MAN
Readings in Philosophical Psychology from
Classical Philosophy to Existentialism

PERSPECTIVES ON REALITY
Readings in Metaphysics from
Classical Philosophy to Existentialism

APPROACHES TO MORALITY
Readings in Ethics from
Classical Philosophy to Existentialism

APPROACHES TO MORALITY

Readings in Ethics from
Classical Philosophy to Existentialism

UNDER THE GENERAL EDITORSHIP OF

Jesse A. Mann, *Georgetown University*
Gerald F. Kreyche, *DePaul University*

CONTRIBUTING EDITORS:

Francis H. Eterovich, O.P., *DePaul University*
Louis Dupré, *Georgetown University*
Jude P. Dougherty, *Bellarmine College*
Frank Ellis, *St. Mary's College, California*
Wilfrid Desan, *Georgetown University*

Harcourt, Brace & World, Inc.
New York / Chicago / Burlingame

Library of Congress Catalog Card Number: 66-16064

Printed in the United States of America

The experience of past ages, the progress of the sciences, and the treasures hidden in the various forms of human culture, by all of which the nature of man himself is more clearly revealed and new roads to truth are opened, these profit the Church, too. For, from the beginning of her history she has learned to express the message of Christ with the help of the ideas and terminology of various philosophers, and has tried to clarify it with their wisdom, too.

From the text of the Second Vatican Council's Pastoral Constitution on the Church in the Modern World, promulgated December 7, 1965.

The philosophical disciplines are to be taught in such a way that the students are first of all led to acquire a solid and coherent knowledge of man, the world, and of God, relying on a philosophical patrimony which is perennially valid and taking into account the philosophical investigations of later ages. This is especially true of those investigations which exercise a greater influence in their own nations. Account should also be taken of the more recent progress of the sciences. The net result should be that the students, correctly understanding the characteristics of the contemporary mind, will be duly prepared for dialogue with men of their time.

From the text of the Second Vatican Council's Declaration on Priestly Training, promulgated October 28, 1965.

Foreword

Most Christians sooner or later decide that philosophy solves no ultimately important problems by itself.

I hasten to add that only the dullest anti-intellectual, dull to the point of perverse, would be tempted on that account to hold philosophy in anything less than solid esteem. I also add that the Catholic Christian acknowledges that, in principle at least, philosophy could come up with rational solutions to many (theoretically, perhaps, most) of the natural problems which embarrass or intrigue human reason.

The First Vatican Council confirmed what the Apostle Paul had suggested concerning the power of reason (the philosopher's proper and characteristic tool) to solve with considerable certainty even the "problem of God," at least as far as God's existence and some of His essential attributes are concerned. But in the concrete human condition the Christian may well conclude that pure philosophy (to the extent that philosophy can be isolated from the total experience of man made in God's image, fallen from original justice, supernaturally redeemed) raises more questions than it can possibly solve and that, unaided, it solves practically none.

The unbeliever arrives at a like conclusion more often than not, and, if the conclusion be bleak, the unbeliever sometimes expresses it with wistful beauty. Edward Fitzgerald echoes Omar Khayyám:

> *Myself when young did eagerly frequent*
> *Doctor and Saint, and heard great Argument*
> *About it and about: but evermore*
> *Came out by the same Door as in I went.*

But the Christian's conclusion need not be so bleak. His love for philosophy may—indeed, should—be as passionate as that of the unbeliever, but his dependence on it is never more than partial. Not only for salvation hereafter but for sanity here, he has the light of faith to illumine the testimonies of reason and the resources of theology to supply for the inadequacies of philosophy.

For example, he may see no possibility of a satisfactory philosophy of history, as I, for one, see none. However, the Incarnation (which utterly eludes the domain of reason) gives history such meaning as a Christian can bring to his meditations upon it; but the Incarnation is the object of faith and reflection upon it provides the stuff of a theology of history. Philosophy brings cold comfort to the problem of evil; only the Cross (which is, for the philosophers, still the foolishness that Paul confessed it to be) lifts from this mystery the dreadful burden it places on the human heart.

The very "problem of God," mentioned above, illustrates how pathetically inadequate, however certain, are the answers of philosophy to the demands of the devout heart, let alone of the unbelieving mind. The "God of the philosophers," the neat and convenient God who emerges patly as the logical conclusion from lines of cold reasoning much as a mathematical formula emerges, inevitably and inexorably, from a mass of data—this sterile God of the debating halls is by no means to be denied by reason or rejected out of hand by the believer. But He, like reason itself, is only a part of total reality and a meager answer to our total need; He is a poor thing, however logically necessary, beside the God of Abraham, the God of Job, and above all the God of Jesus Christ and His saints.

The Christian perceives a mutual need between philosophy and theology, between reason and revelation, that is satisfied only in the integral wisdom that comes from the interplay of faith asking reason and reason asking faith for their respective witnesses. Hence his special regret when confronted by the excessive mutual exclusions between reason and faith set up by those in whom the method of Descartes speedily resulted in a mood which has permeated our culture to the hurt, the Christian considers, of both philosophy and theology. Hence, too, the special temptation of the devout sometimes to fuse with excessive simplicity the concerns and functions of philosophy and theology. The unity of philosophical experience is an attainable goal for the sophisticated traveler equipped with reliable maps; otherwise, it can be a mirage, a pot of fool's gold at the end of a rainbow that has many broad bands but, in fact, no end. *Myself when young. . . .*

But whatever the abstract power of philosophy in the face of the questions which excite or torment the human spirit, it is not, I submit, the business of philosophy to solve problems. Even in their best efforts to answer the riddles of life, the philosophers make their chief contribution when they succeed, as they have done, in pounding out more clear and pointed statements of the questions. It is probably not the vocation of the philosopher to give *answers,* least of all *final answers;* it is, one suspects, his essential task and his most valuable contribution to uncover, to phrase, and to press the *questions.*

In the present crisis of our culture, this may be of all vocations the most difficult, and one of the most urgent. When Gertrude Stein was dying, she wearily asked the friends clustered about her bed: *What is the answer?* No one replied; no theologian was present. *In that case,* she insisted, *what is the question?* The silence remained unbroken; philosophy, too, was without a representative. It has become the imperative role of philosophers to help us at least to state the question in an age of the dusty answers that "gets the soul when hot for certainties in this, our life."

Herein lies both the justification and great merit for Christian students of the present comprehensive collection of readings from widely differing philosophers. These volumes bring together historic attempts to answer perennial problems which engage human speculation. But the chief value of the publication lies (as it should) not in the enduring worth of any answers suggested, but in the contribution that each tentative answer inevitably makes to the posing of the so elusive questions, to the clarification of the elements of problems—a full answer to which may never be afforded by philosophy but the analysis of which is a built-in demand of the human intellect and an incomparable delight of the human spirit.

No small achievement this, the clarification of the terms of the problems. One suspects that most of the ultimate answers will turn out to be somehow *simple,* with the simplicity that traditional Christian philosophical speculations about God attribute to the Divine Nature. It is the statement of the questions that is tough—that plus, perhaps, the acceptance of the consequences, moral and intellectual, of some of the answers.

And so, if the Church is grateful to the philosophers for stating so many of the questions before which men, in bewilderment, turn to her, it is no less true that the sensitive philosopher is grateful to the Church for the manner in which she, even when lacking specific answers, somehow herself serves as the answer to the master-knots of human fate. She does so by her teaching concerning the Incarnation and the consequent premises for salvation history. She does so by her preaching of Christ, the Alpha and Omega of human experience, and especially of Christ Crucified. She does so supremely in the recollection of the mystery of the Resurrection.

But in all this there is that reciprocity between faith and reason required by the mutual dependencies to which we refer above. The Church, therefore, looks to the philosophers, in varying degrees and with varying profit but to them all without exception, not only for help in stating the questions but for guidance in the phrasing of the articulated responses of the Spirit. This is the clear sense of the Second Vatican Council's Constitution on the Church in the Modern World when it says:

> Just as it is in the world's interest to acknowledge the Church as an historical reality, and to recognize her good influence, so the Church herself knows how richly she has profited by the history and development of humanity.
>
> The experience of past ages, the progress of the sciences, and the treasures hidden in the various forms of human culture, by all of which the nature of man himself is more clearly revealed and new roads to truth are opened, these profit the Church, too. For from the beginning of her history she has learned to express the

message of Christ with the help of ideas and terminology of various philosophers, and has tried to clarify it with their wisdom, too. . . . [And] thus the ability to express Christ's message in its own way is developed in each nation, and at the same time there is fostered a living exchange between the Church and the diverse cultures of people. To promote such exchange, especially in our days, the Church requires the special help of those who live in the world, are versed in different institutions and specialties, and grasp their innermost significance in the eyes of both believers and unbelievers. With the help of the Holy Spirit, it is the task of the entire People of God, especially pastors and theologians, to hear, distinguish and interpret the many voices of our age, and to judge them in the light of the divine word, so that revealed truth can always be more deeply penetrated, better understood and set forth to greater advantage.

The editors of these volumes have acted in response to the implicit plea of the Council's pastoral declaration. That is not the least of the reasons why their work is so welcome.

✠ JOHN WRIGHT
BISHOP OF PITTSBURGH

Epiphany, 1966

Preface

The three text-anthologies in the Harbrace Series in Philosophy—*Approaches to Morality, Reflections on Man,* and *Perspectives on Reality*—offer a genuinely pluralistic approach to the basic issues in Ethics, Philosophy of Man, and Metaphysics. Their publication comes at a time when this approach is being encouraged within the entire Christian world. As His Excellency, Bishop John Wright, has pointed out in the Foreword, the Church "looks to the philosophers, in varying degrees and with varying profit but to them all without exception, not only for help in stating the questions but for guidance in the phrasing of the articulated responses of the Spirit."

An openness to truth wherever it may be found is revealed in various documents promulgated at the Second Vatican Council. In the Declaration on Priestly Training, for example, no one system is singled out for exclusive treatment; rather, seminarians are urged to study the "philosophical patrimony which is perennially valid" and to become acquainted with those investigations that have influenced their own country.

The pluralistic attitude affirmed by the Council has, in recent years, been the dominant approach in many Catholic colleges and universities in the United States. The significance of the *aggiornamento* in philosophy is that the philosophical pluralism initiated by some is now enjoined upon all. Such a positive attitude is in keeping with the demands of the society in which we live. Students of philosophy must know the dynamic currents of thought which are expressed in a free society. It is obvious that valuable insights are to be gained from considering more than one philosophical approach, especially when the pluralism exists within the framework of Christian philosophy itself. The fact that by design Aquinas is systematic and Marcel is unsystematic does not deprive the student from gaining wisdom from both. It is just as true that one can benefit philosophically from a study of philosophies beyond the Christian tradition or even hostile to it. Aquinas did not feel he had to baptize Aristotle before he could study him with profit.

Clearly there is no substitute for reading the philosophers themselves. The great thinkers have a right to be heard on their own; they present their own cases most effectively and are their own best interpreters. The objection is sometimes raised that primary sources are too difficult for the beginning student. This is not the case, however, when the readings have been carefully chosen by specialists in their respective fields and are accompanied by detailed commentary. Such a judicious selection of texts enables the introductory student to read the works of the great philosophers and to study their conception and development in a historical context.

The text-anthologies in this series give the beginning student a substantial introduction to different philosophical perspectives that are relevant to the contemporary American scene. Accordingly, each volume in the series presents materials from Classical and Scholastic Thought, Dialectical Thought, American Naturalist and Pragmatic Thought, Analytic and Positivist Thought, and Existentialist and Phenomenological Thought. A number of other traditions (Cartesian Rationalism and Utilitarianism, for example) have great historical value, but are not directly and dynamically relevant to the contemporary American scene. Although such traditions are not represented in the readings, they are covered in the General Introduction and are discussed in the section introductions where pertinent.

The series has been planned so that one volume does not presuppose the others. There is no fixed order in which the books have to be studied, although in most colleges the courses in Philosophy of Man and Metaphysics are taught to freshmen and sophmores while Ethics is usually a junior- or senior-level course. The five sections of each book have been edited by expert philosophers and teachers, each of whom has worked and written in the subject matter of his field. The Contributing Editors have chosen readings for their respective sections that are both representative of key issues and are within the competence of the beginner. Each selection is an ample, self-contained unit that provides a full argument and an adequate sampling of the philosopher's style. Some of the readings (Brunner's and Husserl's selections in *Reflections on Man* and the sections of the *Vienna Manifesto* in *Perspectives on Reality*) appear in English for the first time, thus making available important works that would be otherwise inaccessible to the vast majority of undergraduate students.

The editors introduce their sections with long essays that discuss the basic issues and place the readings in their historical and philosophical framework. As a further aid to the student's understanding of the subject, the editors provide a glossary of important philosophical terms for each section. No attempt has been made to include all terms or to give exhaustive definitions. The definitions are brief and descriptive, and are intended to serve as a convenient reference for the student as he reads the primary sources. Other editorial aids include headnotes that provide biographical data on each philosopher; footnotes (identified by the initials of the philosopher, editor, translator, or section editor) that clarify references, foreign phrases, or difficult terms; and annotated bibliographies of primary sources and commentaries, selected with the beginning student in mind.

Within each section are questions that test the student's comprehension of the selections he has read. In addition, there are two sets of questions at the end of each section: the first set is for the section as a whole; the second relates the section to other parts of the book. These questions may be used as topics for term papers or as guidelines for those classes conducted in the dialogue or Socratic method; they also are an excellent means of review.

The volumes can be used in the classroom in a variety of ways. Some instructors may want to cover the entire book in the course semester, while others may choose to concentrate on certain sections and assign remaining ones for home study. Because of the extensive editorial aids included, such assignments are feasible. Moreover, the sections do not have to be taken up in the order in which they appear in the books. Most instructors will want to begin with the General Introduction, which explains the nature and historical development of philosophy and analyzes the basic problems, topics, and issues of the particular subject of the volume. Once the student has had this orientation, the teacher may take up any philosophical tradition he chooses. In fact, the pluralistic approach of the volumes makes it possible for teachers with different areas of specialization to collaborate in teaching the course. They can also take advantage of the many excellent films now available that are related to the teaching of philosophy.[1]

The General Editors assume overall responsibility for the three books in the Harbrace Series in Philosophy; their specific responsibility was in writing the General Introduction and Preface for each volume and in coordinating the program of study aids. The Contributing Editors wrote the introductory essays and selected the readings for their respective sections. The series represents a genuinely collaborative effort on the part of seventeen editors to present philosophy as a meaningful enterprise for students. The attitude of pluralistic openness makes it possible for students to enter into the act of philosophizing with initiative, spontaneity, and enthusiasm; it also prevents philosophy from being a subject easily contained in a parcel of memorized formulas. Great philosophers have not been interested in the tidy definition but in a disciplined reflection on the world of truth and value. Students who resist memorized formulas will respond to philosophical materials that have obvious relevance to the world in which they find their problems and project their own solutions. It is precisely such materials that the editors have sought to include in these volumes.

J.A.M.
G.F.K.

January, 1966

---

[1] A very helpful list of films, and their distributors, has been compiled by Caroline E. Schuetzinger of Mercy College, Detroit. This list appeared in *The New Scholasticism*, XXXIX, 2 (April, 1965), 224–29.

Contents

PART I
CLASSICAL AND MEDIEVAL
INTELLECTUALIST THOUGHT:
Plato, Aristotle, Aquinas

EDITED BY Francis H. Eterovich, O.P., *DePaul University*

PART II
DIALECTICAL THOUGHT:
Kant, Fichte, Hegel, Marx, Engels

EDITED BY Louis Dupré, *Georgetown University*

PART III
AMERICAN NATURALISTIC THOUGHT:
James, Dewey, Edel, Hook, Romanell, Dennes

EDITED BY Jude P. Dougherty, *Bellarmine College*

PART IV
ANALYTIC-POSITIVIST THOUGHT:
Moore, Schlick, Ayer, Stevenson, Toulmin, Nowell-Smith

EDITED BY Frank Ellis, *St. Mary's College, California*

PART V
EXISTENTIALIST AND POST-EXISTENTIALIST THOUGHT:
Kierkegaard, Nietzsche, Sartre, Marcel, Camus, Teilhard de Chardin

EDITED BY Wilfrid Desan, *Georgetown University*

General Introduction

BY *Jesse A. Mann* AND *Gerald F. Kreyche*

The main purpose of this book is to present the principal ideas and issues in the area of ethics offered by philosophers from classical to contemporary times. This is the third book in a three-volume series devoted to basic subject matters of philosophy. The first two volumes dealt respectively with the philosophy of man and metaphysics. In metaphysics certain fundamental themes, relevant to all aspects of the philosophic enterprise, were discussed. These themes centered on the basic question of what it is to be or to exist. Involved in being were such realities as causality, change, and contingency, and the foundation of being was seen to be the existence of God. The philosophy of man volume treated such central issues for man as the question of his unity in being, his spiritual nature, his destiny, and the character of his knowledge. These two philosophical sciences are called "speculative" branches of philosophy because their main thrust is toward finding true and satisfactory answers to the questions they raise: "What is it to be?" in metaphysics and "What is it to be a man?" in philosophy of man.

Although the conclusions of speculative sciences will have an indirect effect on the conduct of a man, they do not immediately set themselves to determine what being *should* be or what man *should* be. In the case of ethics, however, there is a practical emphasis, for ethics is a nonspeculative science that seeks normative principles of conduct. Ethics, of course, presupposes some principles from metaphysics and some notion of man's nature from the philosophy of man, but it is mainly concerned with what man should do, with what his action or conduct as a man should be.

More fully expressed, ethics is that practical philosophical study that seeks to find some principle of order for those human actions for which we are freely responsible and over which we have rational control. Such deliberate actions are opposed to countless other *acts of men*—digestion, respiration, the activity of the nervous system—that are our own actions but that are controlled automatically and without need for any choice or direction on our part.

1

The moral philosopher is concerned with "human acts," with those actions in which we are free and responsible. But he is not alone in this concern. The psychiatrist, the theologian, and the psychologist—each in his own way has an interest in deliberative and free human action. The moral philosopher differs from each of them in the point of view that is uniquely his. Unlike the psychiatrist, the moral philosopher is not concerned with the analysis of the subconscious motivation of any one individual or the exposition of the emotions and feelings that accompany the actions of individuals in their lives. The moralist differs from the theologian in that the theologian uses the content of revelation as a source for his normative morality. The psychologist is interested in the measurement and analysis of the emotions and complexes that an individual may have; he is not concerned with establishing a systematic structure of the way men *ought* to act. This latter concern—discovering by reason how men *ought* to act—identifies the precise viewpoint of the moralist.

John Locke, the famous English philosopher, once observed that men thought creatively long before Aristotle wrote his logical treatises on how to think. The same observation can be made about ethics: there were morals long before there was any science of morality.

The student brings to his formal study of ethics his experience of having made, and continuing to make, moral decisions. The very fact of his being human gives him practice in the area of ethics. But the advantage of a continuing experience of moral decision is not enough; moral decisions require analysis on the philosophical level. Every man wants to feel some rational consistency in the kinds of deliberate action he experiences. He is not content to choose to act without reflection; he wants to see whether such choices are warranted or perhaps are the best moral choices he could make.

The philosophers presented in this book have furnished explicit analyses of these moral choices. In keeping with the plan of this series, these analyses reflect a pluralistic approach to morality. However, even with the differences that do exist, certain similarities appear in the key positions considered in each section of the book. Let us then address ourselves to these key issues.

The Key Ethical Issues

Value

The first key topic to be discussed in ethics is the theory of value. Value is sometimes defined as the object of human desire and striving. The technical name for a theory of value is *axiology*. For the classical Greek the life lived according to reason is the value, or the end-in-view proper to human striving. The naturalist feels that the best possible fulfillment of the individual in society is attained through the techniques of the behavioral sciences. The Christian finds value in the good life leading to union with God. For the existentialist value exists in the authenticity of an individual taking his life and his commitments seriously and with full responsibility.

Obligation

We all experience praise and blame in connection with the actions we perform. Obligation is the claim made upon us by reason that some things are to be done and deserve praise whereas others are to be avoided and deserve blame. It is clearly related to the notions of responsibility and freedom: we are responsible for actions when we are ready to account for them to ourselves or to others. Immanuel Kant (1724–1804), a German philosopher of the Enlightenment, stated that the experienced fact of duty or responsibility implies that we are free. In his words, "I ought, therefore I can." The technical name for the part of ethics that deals with obligation is called *deontology*. Kant was a deontologist in that he placed the intuition of moral obligation at the very center of his ethics.

Natural Law

Are all standards of right and wrong conditioned solely by the cultural norms by which one lives? Those who would reply affirmatively are cultural relativists who, like the naturalists, view the emergence of novel situations as a perpetual condition of an evolutionary universe and so cannot grant that any standard based on an unchanging human nature can be adequate. Those who oppose this view, including the Thomists and Aristotelians, call on a natural law theory that states that man himself is capable of setting up a standard of morality based on his own nature.

Virtue

A fourth and final key topic in moral theory concerns virtue, the power for moral action that enables man to act with ease and order in some area of his life. These excellences or good qualities have been given emphasis from classical times to today. The Greek sought wisdom in philosophy and prudence and justice in politics. The existentialist stresses courage in the face of responsibility.

In order to see how these four topics are of central concern to the five perspectives represented in the readings, we will look at them more closely in the context of each of those perspectives.

The Classical-Christian Tradition

The first of our five philosophical perspectives is the one with the longest tradition in the Western world. The statement is frequently made that modern civilization is founded on Greek philosophy, Christian theology, Roman law, and modern science. Within Christian philosophy are included the value of Greek philosophy and the profound religious consciousness of Hebrew civilization.

In our study of moral philosophy, attention must first be given to the extraordinary and brilliant contributions of the Greeks. Socrates (470–399 B.C.), one of the originators of a moral system, declared in the *Apology* that the unexamined life is precisely the life not worth living. He sought in an examination of the values involved in living the good life to determine some kind of definition for key terms such as the good, the just, and the virtues. The significant value of Socrates' contribution is his confidence in the mind's ability to attain a degree of moral wisdom in the conduct of life. In his view man could and should bring his reason to bear on the conduct of the good life. Man should also hope to come up with some standards by which to guide himself on the path of his own fulfillment.

Plato (*c.* 427–347 B.C.), in his dialogues on the *Republic,* the *Laws,* and the *Gorgias,* also made solid contributions to the formation of our moral consciousness. But the Greek masterpiece of moral inquiry is Aristotle's *Nicomachean Ethics,* which treats moral problems in terms of the capacities as well as the potentialities of men to do good. Within this work Aristotle (384–322 B.C.) posited the idea that happiness is the final end of human aspiration and that it can be arrived at only by use of reason. Although not all of Greek civilization could be characterized by a strong devotion to reason, the influence of Socrates, Plato, and Aristotle was so great that today we think of the Greeks as having been more concerned with the function of reason, the need for order, and the value of philosophical analysis than almost any other people.

The Greek perspective is extended and enriched by the philosophy of St. Thomas Aquinas (1225–74), who was clearly impressed by the possibility that reason could achieve solid and respectable results in the field of morality. Aquinas studied the Greek masters and carefully documented them in his writings. He referred to Aristotle as "the Philosopher" and analyzed his ethics in the long and splendid *Commentary on the Nicomachean Ethics.*

Aquinas lived at the height of the "age of faith," but his commitment to faith never diminished his belief in man's power of reason and his obligation to use it fully. By his principles that truth is one and whatever is really true in faith and science will never really conflict, he was able to push his own intellectual pursuits to the very limit. Yet Aquinas was no mere echo of the Greek mind. He informed the Greek mind with the Christian commitment and developed areas in which the Greeks were less explicit—for example, the need for self-love. Since God loves all men, it is important that they imitate him by a proper love of themselves. Divine providence is not operative in Aristotle's moral theory, whereas it is a basic assumption for Aquinas.

Perspectives on the Key Issues

VALUE. What is the supreme value in the classical-Christian tradition? What do these philosophers see as the object toward which human beings strive and that they desire? The Greek and Christian philosophers answered the question of value in two ways. First, they were concerned with finding as a subject that faculty in man that is his highest or most valuable faculty. (By "faculty" they meant the power of acting in some determined or specific way. The eye is the organ or instrument for the faculty of seeing.) The Greeks and most of the Christian philosophers were convinced that the faculty of greatest value in man is his intellect, the power whereby man can engage in reasoning, form ideas or concepts, and make rational judgments.

The second answer concerns the object that will most fulfill the faculty or power of reason. In seeking to establish that the most valuable power of a man is his reason, the Greeks, especially Plato and Aristotle, asked what there is in man that must be satisfied before he can be happy. They generally agreed that man can be properly satisfied only by some object that is proper to his spiritual character. Although they admitted the animal side of man and considered it to be essential to his structure, they did not see the unique function and make-up of man to be accounted for solely by his animal character. Rather they saw man's special satisfaction to be necessarily a fulfillment of what is special in man. This they took to be mind or soul, which represented to them what is best in man. Therefore man's spiritual striving must be satisfied before man is satisfied. Most of the philosophers in this tradition saw the presence of intellect, the power to understand the world and to express that understanding in ideas and sentences, as the appetite or human tendency that is the prime area for human satisfaction, fulfillment, or happiness.

We can summarize this insight of the Greeks by referring to a statement of John Stuart Mill, a utilitarian philosopher of the nineteenth century, who stated that it would be better to be "a sad Socrates than a satisfied pig." In other words, man as a subject simply could not be satisfied without taking into account the perfection of his reason and his power of free choice. To be a man and not exercise responsibility or seek the values of the examined and reasonable life would be to live without exercising one's highest and most distinctive power. The "satisfied pig" would not be aware of his own satisfaction or able to reflect and enjoy it consciously.

Closely related to this intellect is the will, whereby one actively desires the good that one has come to know as the result of the ability of the intellect. Man is ordered to the possession of the true and the good. The Christians concurred with the Greeks in insisting that man cannot be satisfied as man unless his highest seeking, that of his intellect and will, is satisfied. Thus a rational character appears in the ethics of this tradition.

As the Greeks and Christians viewed the world and man, they classified beings in a hierarchical manner. For them the lowest beings in the world of sense experience consist of the minerals, or, in their terms, of the four primary elements of earth, air, fire, and water. These elements lack among other things the essential quality of life, a quality of perfection which plants possess. A being with life is considered more perfect than one without it because of its powers for reproduction of its kind and for growth from a germinal to a mature state, and its ability to engage in nutrition, to master the mineral elements, and to absorb them into its own identity. But even though the plant is considered more perfect than the stone or primary element, it lacks the perfection of life possessed by the sentient animal, which has the greater ability to live because of its powers of locomotion, imagination, instinct, and organic sensation. When the Greeks and Christians viewed man they saw him as possessing the power of abstract reasoning whereby he is able to master technique and gain knowledge that will produce the arts and sciences. This power of reasoning is higher in kind than any possessed by stone, plant, or animal; it is the distinguishing characteristic and essential quality of man.

The next question to consider is what is the nature of objective value. (This differs from the subjective question just mentioned, which concerned what power of man needs to be satisfied before man can be said to be satisfied. The answer has to be that which makes him unique, namely, his intellect.) But what object will satisfy the desires of man? As will be seen, the Greek tradition hints that the object will have to be eternal and unchanging. In metaphysics Plato and Aristotle were concerned with those eternal realities that all other things in the universe either sought or imitated. In Plato this immutability, this eternal character and permanence, is seen in the eternal ideas of justice, truth, goodness, and beauty, though it would be incorrect to think of Plato as naively supposing that these ideas share a kind of spatiotemporal existence in another world. Their realm is spiritual in character. Man reaches his highest value when he is able by an act of direct intuition to see what truth and justice and beauty are in themselves. The steps by which this insight into beauty itself is attained are described by Socrates in the *Symposium*. For Aristotle man's fulfillment is gained by contemplation, but Aristotle did not specify any one object that will itself be the perfect object of contemplation.

OBLIGATION. From the discussion of value, we can see that for classical and Christian philosophers spiritual character, especially possession of intellectual knowledge, is the most valuable subjective power that a man possesses. It is also clear that the object that can most satisfy such a power will have to be one with characteristics of changelessness, perfection, and self-sufficiency. Such qualities are attributed to the Ideas of Plato and the God of Aquinas.

Reason is also emphasized. By the use of it, man sees himself obligated to do certain things—to pay back his debts, to deal fairly with his friends.

Obligation, or the possession of duties, is a moral demand imposed by man's reason in assessing his own life situation. Reason itself does not create this demand, but rather by reason man is able to recognize what is due to others and to himself. Obligation, as described in the readings that follow, treats of rights and duties. A right is a moral power that imposes an obligation on another to respect it. Thus every man who has basic needs for food and survival has a claim on the recognition by others of his needs.

Correlative to the knowledge of obligation is the fact of freedom of choice. One cannot be blamed for doing what he could not avoid under any circumstances. Likewise one cannot claim praise for what was done automatically and without freedom of any kind.

This condition of freedom in the face of obligation is an essential ingredient in the classical and Christian tradition. It is not enough that one *should* act in a specific way; one has to decide whether to follow his reason. Though reason may command, choice of the reasonable deed does not necessarily follow.

The classical tradition also emphasizes the spiritual and interior quality of free assent. Socrates affirmed in the *Phaedo* that his limbs, if left to themselves, would carry him "fast from his prison," but because of his principles he was able to make inner, spiritual, and free commitment to stay there.

In his description of obligation, Aquinas restated in a Christian context much of what was central to the tradition of Socrates, Plato, and Aristotle. For him the ultimate source of all obligation is the eternal law, the divine plan for all creation that proceeds from God. But God chooses to make man such that he can by the use of his reason come to recognize his obligations in life. In the structure of the moral act Aquinas saw another sign of the close way in which the human creature is able to participate in the plan of God. In morality man participates in the eternal law of God by operating his moral life according to reason. Man is not a passive recipient of ready-made laws, but he brings himself to know the law and to formulate it by the power of reason.

NATURAL LAW. Aristotle and Aquinas had confidence that man could discover some objective, universal, and necessary laws of morality. Both considered law as an ordering of some kind whereby the pattern of activities of a being reaches its perfection. They were convinced that the beings below man, such as animals, plants, and minerals, are directed to their perfection, or proper final way of existing, by a principle basic to them. Such a principle of activity is called their substantial form. Thus Aristotle and Aquinas thought of the primary elements (air, earth, fire, and water) as having certain tendencies because of their form—air tended to be dry and light, earth to be dry and heavy, fire to be hot and dry, water to be cold and wet. The primary elements act as they do because of the nature they possess. Similarly, plants and animals are necessitated by their natures, by tropisms and instincts, to act as they do. The natural law for all beings below man is necessarily followed and, so to speak, is built into the basic structure of the beings.

For man, the presence of freedom as a result of reason makes the natural law not an externally imposed necessity; rather, man becomes aware of his nature and the activities proper to him by his autonomous act of reason. For Aquinas, natural law consists of the judgments that man elicits concerning conduct. Aquinas thought that the statement, "Good is to be done and evil avoided," is a statement of law that no man of developed intelligence could deny. The natural law theme in this tradition is closely related to the notion of a standard or norm of morality. Granted that man is to discover the pattern of his morality by the use of his reason, the question remains whether any model or standard exists against which man may rationally measure his action. The response of Aquinas was that the very nature of man presents such a standard.

Man's nature is considered as dependent and contingent on God, who is constantly conserving man in being and is himself the fulfillment of man's striving. The actions of man should reflect reverence toward God as the author and preserver of life. Whereas this first general principle of reverence toward God is found by measuring man's nature in terms of its source and end, a second principle can be found by comparing man to his fellow men. Each man is seen as capable of realizing that all human beings have the same essential needs. An individual should respect in other people the same basic needs that he has in himself. This lateral measurement of man with his peers generates the principle of justice. Justice may be between individuals, between the group and the individual, and between the individual and the group. Justice also pertains to those beings less perfect than man. On these beings man depends for his material and some of his spiritual needs; therefore, the proper virtue for man in their regard is one of prudent care and stewardship. This norm is considered to be an objective norm and in a very special way is seen to reflect the ultimate norm of all morality, divine nature.

VIRTUE. Virtue in the Greek or Christian sense consists of qualities of excellence whereby man is rendered more perfect as man. Aristotle listed many virtues with their extremes in the *Nicomachean Ethics,* Plato used the virtue of justice as the key concept in the *Republic,* and Aquinas devoted a large section of the *Summa Theologica* to a discussion of virtues.

The qualities of excellence enable man to act with ease and order in a given area of human existence. The cardinal virtues—courage, temperance, justice, and prudence—first elaborated by Plato and then taken over by Aristotle and Aquinas, are involved in the reasonable decision made in standard human situations. For example, the man of courage faces danger when it is reasonable to do so. He represents the "mean" which Aristotle declared to be between the extremes of recklessness and cowardice. The reckless man does things because he is unaware of the unreasonableness of exposing himself to unnecessary dangers. The coward refuses to face danger even when reason considers such a confrontation necessary. It is noteworthy that the virtue of courage does not imply, for Aristotle, the lack of fear in the presence of danger. Indeed, it is the vice of the reckless man that he is not aware of the fear that he should have. The virtue of courage then depends on the reasonableness of facing or avoiding danger. The same is true of the other cardinal virtues. Temperance is the exercise of reasonable control over the desires of the body; justice is the reasonable recognition of what is due to others; prudence is reasonableness in decision.

The Dialectical Tradition: Kant, Hegel, Marx

In our second perspective we move from the reasonable world of the Greeks and the God-centered world of the medieval Christians to the subjective moral philosophy developed by Immanuel Kant, G. W. F. Hegel (1770–1831), and Karl Marx (1818–83). Kant not only achieved a radically different solution to the problem, but ushered in an era of critical philosophy and a new approach to the field of morality. An emphasis on subjective analysis, creativity, and human initiative distinguished the critical philosophers from their medieval and ancient predecessors. The Greek and Christian philosophers considered man's main task to be discovering the structure and law that was already present in the world. The human mind was seen essentially as an instrument for copying the world in knowledge. This objective tendency was changed to a subjective one by the critical philosophers. Thus Kant spoke of the moral law as being *within* man.

The philosophies of Kant, Hegel, and Marx reflect the brilliant accomplishments of man in the world of science and technology. At the same time that man was using superb techniques in remaking his world, he was beginning to emphasize his own role in the formation of his knowledge and values.

In Hegel man's confidence in his own ability to construct a completely adequate, systematic understanding of the world is at its highest. In the quest for the system that would rationally explain the Absolute and the world, the nature of history, and the role of the Spirit, Hegel elaborated an intellectual structure that brought him not only serious followers but also dedicated opponents. Marx, too, emphasized the relationship between man and the world and the necessity for man to work and relate himself to the world. The student should see in the writings of these men the beginnings of many of the attitudes that have become essential to modern culture.

Perspectives on Key Issues

VALUE. To all three of these philosophers the dignity and autonomy of the individual person was of paramount importance. In his famous ethical treatise, *Critique of Practical Reason* (1788), Kant viewed the will of the human person as completely autonomous and the value of the person as supreme. We are instructed to treat humanity always as an end in itself, and we are warned against using other persons merely as means to an end. In addition to such democratic themes and values as the dignity of the human person and the inalienable possession of freedom by human beings, Kant's morality also has a distinctively Christian component. The existence of God is postulated as necessary for the moral government of the world, immortality is considered as the destiny of man, and happiness is presented as man's highest good.

Hegel was very much influenced by Kant's moral theory in the formation of his own philosophical theory. He unified his entire philosophy into a comprehensive, rational system of the universe. He saw all reality as the manifestation of an Absolute Spirit that is dynamic in history. Like Kant, he valued the individual and freedom but not to the same extent. For Hegel, the State is a value to which the individual is subordinated; the spiritual is a value in its various manifestations in art, literature, and philosophy.

Karl Marx echoed both Kant and Hegel in his theory of value. In his early writings, which have a distinct humanistic quality, he stressed the dignity of the human person and protested violently against using men as mere commodities whose labor can be bought like any material object. He further stressed the value and dignity of the human person in his doctrine of alienation. Marx lamented the condition of the nineteenth-century factory worker who was rarely able to participate spontaneously and creatively in the making of products. More specifically he regretted the fact that man's labor was bought by the factory owner, and in a real sense man was divorced from a meaningful relationship to the products produced in the factory. As Erich Fromm has pointed out, Marx saw relatedness of man to nature and to his fellow men as a supreme value.

OBLIGATION. In the *Critique of Pure Reason* (1781), Kant analyzed the kind of reason that operates in the sciences and showed that all scientific knowledge is subjective in character even though it retains universality and necessity. In his two major works on ethics, *Critique of Practical Reason* and *Foundations of the Metaphysics of Morals* (1785), Kant was concerned not with pure reason but with practical reason that is applicable to human conduct and practice.

Kant's most important statement on obligation is found in his Categorical Imperative: "Act in conformity with that maxim, and that maxim only, which you can at the same time will to be a universal law." The word "categorical" does not indicate a classification; rather it means unconditional. Accordingly, Kant rigorously insisted that the maxim on which one chooses to act admits of no exceptions before it can be acted on. If, for instance, "lying is forbidden" is taken as a maxim, no exceptions are allowed under any circumstances. Thus the physician is *obligated* to tell the sad truth of impending death to the seriously diseased cancer patient. By "imperative" Kant means a moral command.

Each individual must formulate his own moral imperatives as a result of the felt call to duty that he intuits within himself. Kant, therefore, would have each individual be his own moral legislator. Such personal moral legislation, however, is not egoistic; the law we make for ourselves must be acceptable to all other men in like circumstances. If I were to consider breaking a promise that I had made, I should ask myself whether I would similarly wish all other men to break *their* promises.

The role of the will is central to Kant's theory. For him nothing in the entire universe could be called good without qualification, except a good will. Kant attributed good to the will because the will alone has the right and power to make free choices. He spoke of the autonomy, that is, the self-regulation, of the will as the sole principle of all morality. Kant did not mean that the will operates anarchically but according to its intuition of laws and principles. He added the important qualification that the universal system of laws to which a man subjects himself is that which he imposes upon himself. In contrast to these commands of the autonomous will are those actions that proceed from inclination and emotion. Kant considered such actions amoral, namely, outside the area of moral obligation altogether.

Hegel wrote of ethics mainly in the *Philosophy of Right* (1821). He agreed with Kant that men are conscious of their duty and obligation by their possession of a free will acting in accordance with principles and maxims. But whereas Kant would see each man finding the laws within himself, within *his* will, Hegel postulated a *universal* will present in each man. This universal will is embodied in the laws, institutions, and conventions of the society of which the individual is a member.

Therefore Hegel added another dimension to the theory of obligation that Kant had enunciated. In his view the individual should restrain his sense of what seems right if it conflicts with the wisdom of the community to which he belongs. But it would be a mistake to think that Hegel was preaching mere conformity. He recognized the superiority of an individual who consciously develops his moral values over another individual who unreflectively conforms to convention. His main point was that morality and obligation are not founded on *any* individual will or person. The best embodiment of practical reason is in the State, which is a realization of freedom for all, not a condition of servitude. Although his theory of obligation emphasized the greater wisdom of the collective, it still required the conscious freedom of each individual as an essential element.

The Marxian theory of obligation had to take into account Marx's demand for the abolition of artificial commercial classes and national states, which impose on men obligations and duties that dehumanize them. In his view men are chained and obligated to the very class that treats them as mere objects, and their labor alienates them from themselves and from their world. The obligation of man collectively, then, is to do something about his dismal plight and to emancipate himself from his inhuman role as a purchased commodity.

KANT'S THEORY OF NATURAL LAW. To understand Kant's theory of natural law it is necessary to realize that the ethics of Kant is intuitionistic. This means that the standard of morality will be found only when man recognizes that the moral law is *within*. He cannot look outside himself to find his duty; his call to duty and lawfulness is an inner demand which makes itself clearly heard. Intuitionism implies something more than the immediacy with which man recognizes the law within him. Since moral lawfulness concerns the inner man, morality is not properly a quality of outward behavior. However, the intuitionist advises following the inner dictates of duty without regard for the consequences. Since Kant placed the natural law and the standard of morality within the individual moral agent, he implied that there are no sins but only sinners, no sanctity but only saints.

We must note that the Christian golden rule is an essential part of Kantian ethics. Basic to an understanding of his Categorical Imperative is the realization that Kant translated "Do unto others as you would have others do unto you" into "What is right for one is right for all." Thus moral laws are valid for all men.

Hegel viewed natural law in a different way. He did not share Kant's confidence that the individual could simply follow his own inner directives to the duty that he must perform without regard to consequences. He saw the individual moral agent as needing the organization of the State even to be an autonomous and free individual. The law of man's nature and the standards of his morality come to him imperfectly in his capacity as an individual or as a member of a family. Laws and moral standards are more perfectly embodied in the wisdom of men organized into a state community. One reason for the greater wisdom of the State is that it provides a necessary principle of order and pattern for the freedom of individual citizens.

For Marx the question of natural law and a standard of morality must be viewed in light of the fact that by his "inversion" of Hegelianism he denied the idealistic notion of a developing Absolute Spirit throughout history. Rather, he interpreted man as subject to economic and material forces. Marx was hardly a crude materialist without convictions on the ethical demands and laws that human beings must obey. The selections included in this volume reveal the humanism that he developed in his early writings. The central positive criterion for man as a moral agent can be stated as a demand for relatedness. Man is a species-being; to view him in isolation from his fellow men is to fade out his essential relation to the group and to destroy his meaning and his nature. The greatest unlawfulness is to alienate man from his own need of spontaneous union with his fellow man. But man as a species-being is not only a vitally related member of a group, but he is also essentially ordered to a productive and creative working relationship with the world.

VIRTUE. For Kant the primary human virtue and excellence is *dignity,* the intrinsic worth of the person which results from his status as a rational being. Everything else but man may have a price and be a commodity of exchange. Persons are priceless because they are unique and irreplaceable. Further, man is autonomous: He must make his own laws according to principle. This autonomy is the basis of his dignity.

In a system as complicated as Hegel's it is difficult to isolate any one predominant virtue, but it is possible to indicate some value judgments that are central to the excellence of human life as he conceived it. For instance, Hegel was so convinced of the interrelatedness of all things in an Absolute Spirit that he constantly emphasized the virtue of order. He valued freedom of the individual, but not to the extent that freedom be exercised in disorder, which would occur if in the exercise of my own freedom I destroyed the freedom of others. A related good quality would be sensitivity to the greater wisdom of the human community against that of any one individual.

For Marx the excellence which marks the authentic human being is spontaneous and creative union with one's fellow men and with nature. Opposing this is alienation or separation of man from his own authenticity, from his fellow man, or from nature. Marx also stressed the traditional virtue of courage and demanded that men should oppose and finally overthrow the system that dehumanizes and constantly exploits them.

The Naturalistic Tradition

The third perspective in moral philosophy which has been chosen as a subject for reading in this volume is naturalistic ethics. As a world view, philosophical naturalism claims that the universe does not require any supernatural cause, conservation, or government. Further, naturalism declares that the world is self-existent and capable of its own direction. Some versions of naturalism insist that there is no true purposiveness working in the world and that even the appearance of man in the course of evolution was a completely gratuitous incident. The naturalist also seeks to explain all mental and spiritual life as ordinary operations of nature, without any need for supernatural events or sanctions.

Naturalistic ethics is the moral theory that considers ethics to be essentially an empirical science of human conduct, value, and obligation. The word "empirical" means precisely that the naturalistic moralist seeks to base his claims on relevant findings of the behavioral sciences (sociology, anthropology, and psychology) and the natural sciences (biology, chemistry, and physics).

Considerable stimulation to the perspective of naturalism was provided by the publication of Charles Darwin's *Origin of Species* in 1859. Darwin (1809–82) established his theory of the evolution of man from brute animal ancestors by his principle of natural selection. From this principle some philosophers concluded that the survival of the fittest species by natural selection is a scientific fact that makes the presence of a provident and conserving God no longer necessary. The same principle also stresses the kinship of man with nature and has influenced philosophers to view man totally in terms of nature in this world. Finally, since Darwin saw nature as red in "tooth and claw," many naturalists such as Dewey have stressed the risks man takes in his dealings with a world that cannot always be expected to be friendly and the necessity, therefore, for man to use his intelligence to the utmost.

Although the naturalist stressed the risks, hazards, and appearance of novelty in the universe, he agreed with the Greek and Christian philosophers, who held that there are some stabilities in the world and that through the scientific method some objective knowledge of the world can be gained. What is stable for one age, however, may be outdated for another. Since man and the universe are constantly evolving, the naturalist considered any Hegelian attempt to find out all the secrets of the world once and for all an impossible endeavor.

Although the naturalist will justly insist on the function of reason as an instrument for successful encounter with a world of risk and uncertainty, we must refuse to characterize him as thinking that the world is changing so fast that no stability is possible, no continuity available. For in this tradition the very acquisition of stability and equilibrium is the prize of a reason informed by scientific method. The naturalist is in no sense an irresponsible relativist.

Two of our country's greatest philosophers, John Dewey (1859–1952) and George Santayana (1863–1952), were naturalists. Dewey's naturalistic emphasis can be found in a developed form in such works as *Experience and Nature* (1925) and *The Quest for Certainty* (1929); Santayana's philosophy is well expressed in *The Life of Reason* (5 vols., 1905–06) and *Scepticism and Animal Faith* (1923). Other important American naturalists include Sidney Hook (b. 1902), Abraham Edel (b. 1908), Ernest Nagel (b. 1901), John Herman Randall, Jr. (b. 1899), and Morris R. Cohen (1880–1947).

Perspectives on Key Issues

In the analysis of key positions, we shall concentrate on the naturalism of John Dewey because he expressed the naturalistic temper in a classical manner.

VALUE. Dewey insisted that value proceeds from the reflective analysis of the novelty presented to each generation. Man seeks to transact with nature by intelligence. He increases his own value, as well as that of nature, by the quality of the solutions he brings in answer to the felt needs in his life.

The supreme value is attained when the intellectual mediation of the challenges offered by the world is successful. The good man mediates the conflict between past knowledge and present novelty. Above all he does not flee the problems of this world by looking to another more perfect world, for the answers must be found in this world. The kind of knowledge that will derive the needed answers is known as the scientific method, which, since the time of Galileo, has transformed the world in which we live. Dewey gives his analysis of value in the selection "Reconstruction of Moral Conceptions," a chapter taken from his book *Reconstruction in Philosophy* (1920).

OBLIGATION. In this selection Dewey also speaks of obligation. His general principle is that each man is obligated to action and responsibility in strict proportion to the cultivation of his mind and the power of his reflective intelligence. This is an echo of the Platonic theme that knowledge is virtue. Dewey stresses heavily the need for every man to "grow" to ever greater moral maturity and sense of obligation. He writes: "The good man is the man who no matter how morally unworthy he *has* been is moving to become better. . . . The bad man is the man who no matter how good he *has* been is beginning to deteriorate, to grow less good." For Dewey men are obligated to "the ever-enduring process of perfecting, maturing, refining" their aim in living.

NATURAL LAW. The norm of morality is also given an objective character in the work of Dewey and the other naturalists. Although it has objective reference to the sciences of man, it is not considered impervious to change nor is it binding in the same way on all men. With Dewey the norm and the natural law take on a social character. That action is lawful that will mediate the risks and dangers of situations confronting men and society. It would be inadequate to speak of this as a plea for adjustment; it is more an active solving of a pressing crisis than a fatalistic submission to what are assumed to be insoluble situations. Thus the naturalist insists that no society or individual can gain true moral life without constantly employing intelligent reflection to make the necessary revisions of traditional theory to meet his own requirements and those of society. There is a strong conviction among naturalists that we must avoid the pat answers of past wisdom and be more reflective and experimental in cases of social disorder, such as crime and delinquency. In these problematic areas we are advised to learn from psychology, sociology, and anthropology. It must be remembered that to the naturalist the word "natural" immediately implies change, process, novelty, and risk—not a fixed and final norm whose dictates are timeless.

VIRTUE. From the description of the good man and the bad man in Dewey's *Reconstruction in Philosophy,* it can be seen that the supreme good quality to be found in man is the development of those values that reason itself approves. Related to this, and referred to in the same selection, is an attitude which Dewey calls "meliorism." We must not be foolish optimists and imagine evil can be overcome easily and without intelligence; neither can we be pessimists and assume that evil is overwhelming and that we are powerless before it. The middle attitude of meliorism is the ability to struggle, little by little, to make one's lot and the world itself better.

A final necessary virtue is what Dewey calls "sensitivity to the unique character of every moral situation." This virtue is a kind of flexibility—a recognition of the truth that each situation, each man, or each problem possesses a unique style and structure. Opposed to this virtue is the supposition that all problems are the same, all men are alike, and nothing is new under the sun.

The Analytic Tradition

Analytic ethics, the fourth perspective, describes an attitude toward moral theory that is prevalent today in the United States and Great Britain. The movement includes logical positivism and analytic philosophy, but the distinction between the two is tenuous. The analysts concentrate on the examination of language, whereas the earlier, hard-core positivists are more concerned with the model of the scientific method and the method of verification in the sciences. They have sought to impose this method of verification on philosophy. However, *both* the analysts and the logical positivists are interested in analysis of language as well as in scientific method as a model for philosophy.

The analytic movement is in many ways a continuation of the analytic spirit of David Hume (1711–76), whose clarity of style and logical rigor are considered exemplary by contemporary analysts. The movement really began with the reaction of G. E. Moore (1873–1958) and Bertrand Russell (b. 1872) against the Hegelian idealism current in Great Britain at the turn of the century. Instead of accepting the Hegelian notion of reality as a unity and manifestation of Absolute Spirit, they considered reality as consisting of discrete phenomena and events, each of which must be examined and named. To adapt a metaphor of Russell's, one could say that whereas the universe of Hegel is like a handful of jello that quivers when touched at any spot, the universe of the positive sciences is like a handful of pellets, each of which is distinct from every other. Philosophic language is seen to be an accurate logic whose function is to describe these "atomic facts" that are the substance of all that is real. Russell and Whitehead undertook to provide such a logic in their famous *Principia Mathematica* (1910–13).

As a result of these researches British philosophers became more and more interested in the possibility that language could sometimes be very deceptive and create false issues and problems. A brilliant attempt to state the limits of language with the utmost clarity and completeness was made by Ludwig Wittgenstein (1889–1951) in his *Tractatus Logico-Philosophi-*

cus (1921). At about the same time, A. J. Ayer (b. 1910) was convinced that standard philosophical subjects such as metaphysics are really an abuse of language and ultimately composed of nonsense statements. He came to this conclusion because he could find no way of testing the truth or falsity of many of the statements of idealistic metaphysicians. In his famous verification principle he asserted that before a statement could be considered meaningful there must be some criterion to test its truth or lack of truth. His own description of the verification principle and his reasons for rejecting the scientific character of metaphysical statements are found in his book *Language, Truth, and Logic* (1936).

The distinctive characteristic of analytic philosophy is its insistence that the moral philosopher be constrained to the use of language that has control of its terms and to the use of claims that can be warranted true or false, valid or invalid. This movement considers system-building as not proper for the philosopher and shares with naturalism a respect for and confidence in the scientific method. Like naturalism, it also protests against the idealistic system of Hegel.

Perspectives on Key Issues

Since the analytic philosophers are not primarily concerned with the realities of value, obligation, law, and virtue, it will be necessary to describe the main notions in their ethical theories.

THE "NATURALISTIC FALLACY." The first of these is what G. E. Moore called the "naturalistic fallacy." We commit this fallacy when we derive ethical conclusions from premises that are not ethical or when we attempt to describe ethical notions with terms that are not ethical.

The majority of moralists, according to Moore, make their initial mistake in categorizing the good by reducing it to something else, such as pleasure or utility. Moore was convinced that the good need not be reduced to some other value because it is itself concretely involved in our experience, having the same immediacy as any other quality. What is striking about his view is his claim that the yellow in the tulip and the good of the good deed share the same level of concrete immediacy to the knower. Moore's further elaboration of this claim is included in the selection from *Principia Ethica* (1903).

EMOTIVE LANGUAGE. A second major theme of analytic ethics is the suggestion of A. J. Ayer that ethical language must be sharply distinguished from the use of language in the sciences. Whereas scientific language can be verified concretely and rendered meaningful, ethical language is *emotive*. In other words, any ethical statement merely reflects a personal emotional feeling or attitude that has little more significance than an ejaculation such as "ouch" or "ugh." For Ayer values cannot exist since they are outside the domain of scientific verification and accordingly meaningless. Ayer's own statement of his emotive theory is found in his selection from *Language, Truth, and Logic* in this volume.

THE ROLE OF PERSUASION. Charles L. Stevenson (b. 1908) agrees with Ayer that ethical statements are not scientific and accordingly cannot be verified in any public manner. Stevenson, however, refines the emotive theory by considering moral imperatives as involving an individual's attempt to create an attitude of approval from those who would evaluate his action. He sees the possibility of ethical attitudes and beliefs as properly the area of intelligent discussion, even though they are not subject to public verification as are the experimental sciences. Moral conflicts between the disputants are authentic conflicts that can be dealt with and changed. This is especially true because the *belief* that is one component of the ethical command can be subjected to change or confirmation by *persuasion*. The role of persuasion in dealing with ethical attitudes and belief is of basic importance to Stevenson, and is discussed in detail in the selection from his work studied in this volume.

THE APPROACH OF "ORDINARY LANGUAGE." P. H. Nowell-Smith (b. 1914) represents the "ordinary language" approach to philosophy which developed within the field of analytic philosophy. The ordinary language philosopher retains the desire to analyze philosophical notions with great care, but his special characteristic is that he examines the *use* of a term in a concrete context. Although Nowell-Smith shares some aspects of the emotive theory as it is developed by Ayer and Stevenson, he does not reduce ethical statements to any single pattern. As will be seen in the selection from *Ethics* (1954), he finds such patterns to be richly diversified.

The Existentialist and Post-Existentialist Tradition

Although existentialist philosophers sometimes refuse to define existentialism because they are opposed to thinking of their philosophic posture as an inflexible and rigid doctrine, it is possible to determine the bases of this movement by noting some of its characteristics. Foremost among them is the great emphasis that the existentialists place on the meaning of man's personal freedom. Man is decisive in his own life. In a sense he makes his life what it is by his own free decision. As a corollary, man is subjected to the dread involved in choices, for the consequences of which he has only himself to praise or blame. The authentic man must commit himself. He cannot give his power of choice away without in some way dehumanizing himself and becoming fraudulent or subhuman.

This preoccupation with man's responsibility to himself is a reflection of the very great moral crisis of the 1940s, when so many people despaired of any system of values that mankind would respect. The fearful fact of genocide of the Jews in Germany, the terror of the underground, the betrayal of their country by men who gave in to fraudulent promises, the grim world view of an apparently bankrupt Western culture facing possible atomic annihilation—all these were reasonable grounds for man forever despairing in himself. To this picture of desperation existentialists brought something positive in their insistence on the inescapable freedom that each man as an individual possesses.

Another characteristic of the existentialist movement is its affirmation of the unique individual as opposed to the zero-men or "ciphers" that make up the crowd. The existentialists feel that modern man is doomed to be lost in the crowd and yet, paradoxically, is also lost outside the crowd. Few have expressed this better than the forerunner of existentialism, Søren Kierkegaard (1813–55), who saw the decisive fate of the individual confronted with the option to have religious faith or not. The individual's "leap into faith" and his deep need to decide his fate by a free acceptance of the Christian commitment are the themes of the Kierkegaard selection, "The Task of Becoming Subjective."

Another forerunner of the existentialist movement was the German philosopher Friedrich Nietzsche (1844–1900), who during his lifetime was an ardent critic of the declining status and fraudulent value of the educated middle class of his generation. In addition to his famous analysis of the will to power as a primary motivation of human beings, he anticipated Freud's theory of sublimation with his theory of "overcoming" and made a critical study of the quality of resentment.

Probably the best known of the existentialist thinkers is Jean-Paul Sartre (b. 1905), who, in addition to being a philosopher, is a distinguished literary artist whose plays, novels, and short stories are widely read.

Gabriel Marcel (b. 1883) is another leading member of the school. A convert to Catholicism, he sees no conflict between existentialist value and Christian thought. Marcel's sensitive and probing description of creative fidelity is found in the selection taken from *Man Against Mass Society* (1951). Also included is a selection by Albert Camus (1913–60), a contemporary of Sartre and Marcel. Some of the reasons why Camus is such a moral hero to the younger generation can be seen in the passages from *The Rebel* (1954). Camus' tragic death in an automobile accident a few years ago was a sad loss to contemporary philosophy.

Although Pierre Teilhard de Chardin (1881–1955) is not, properly speaking, an existentialist, he is nonetheless related to the movement as one who reflected the tendency of many serious students of existentialism to move from a study of the individual in his freedom to the study of the collectivity in which every man must exercise his freedom.

Perspectives on Key Issues

The existentialists suspect any philosophical doctrine that purports to be a completely adequate account of existence. They rightly complain that the system-builder can give magnificent and logical accounts as long as he deals with generalities and abstraction. As Kierkegaard noted, however, such intellectual pretentions are dissipated as soon as the system-builder is seen to be incapable of explaining why or how each individual human being comes into existence. Sartre makes the same point by noting how often general moral principles are in conflict and the individual must be left to make his own decision on the basis of the unique moral situation confronting him. This mode of moral decision is sometimes called *situation ethics*.

Since the existentialists are by choice not systematic, it is at best difficult to relate their thought to the four basic notions of ethics: value, obligation, natural law, and virtue. These topics nonetheless are at least implicitly relevant to their thought.

VALUE. The good life is the life of freedom and responsibility. The value of a man is his authenticity and commitment; the end-in-view for man is to make himself by the character of his choices. Man has no previously structured nature that enslaves him to a set range of fulfillments. He must make his life according to the freedom that is his. Unlike the naturalist, the Aristotelian, and the Thomist, the existentialist has no elaborate faith either in reason as an exclusive guide or in systematic philosophy as convenient road map to moral choice.

OBLIGATION. These philosophers are especially concerned with the free character of the human act and the responsibility of the individual for his own life and actions as well as for the effect of his decisions on others. Indeed for those of this group who do not find in religion or science any secure set of values, the very nature of man is freedom and self-obligation. Man is obligated to create and project himself into authentic existing by his moral action. Human free decision and the concomitant obligation and responsibility that it entails are vitally important and constantly stressed. Thus Kierkegaard pointed out the loneliness and anguish that accompany decision-making and Sartre declares that man is condemned to be free. The mood in which obligation is felt and freedom exercised is thus fear and trembling. Abraham, whose agonizing choice must be to obey God at the expense of willing the death of his own son, is the basis for a constant theme of Kierkegaard. Marcel insists on our obligation to resist the pressures against freedom which come to modern life through the leveling and dehumanizing qualities of modern technology. He wishes us to avoid the constant fallacy of trying to manipulate men, who are personal, authentic, and for themselves, by the impersonal and misguiding abstractions taken from the nonhuman sphere of scientific method.

NATURAL LAW. As we have seen in analyzing the notion of natural law in the classical-Christian tradition, law is primarily an ordination of reason. Law is also systematic. Reason and system are both rejected as inadequate for the choices that the existentialists, especially Sartre and Kierkegaard, see us condemned to make. They acknowledge that there are moral principles and maxims, but they insist that these are all too often in conflict. Sartre gives as an example the plight of a young man who is torn between the desire to serve his country by joining the army and the duty he feels of staying with his lonely mother. Since they do not see the natural law of generally accepted moral principles as sufficiently detailed, they seek to solve each moral problem in terms of the concrete situation in which the moral decision must be made. At times even the most painstaking examination of the situation will offer no comfort or clear directive for choice.

VIRTUE. A key human excellence for the existentialist is authenticity, or integrity. We are asked to dare to be the individuals we are. As Kierkegaard said of himself, he would rather be remembered as an *individual*— even eccentric—than simply another zero-man in the crowd.[1] A related virtue is that of responsibility. We are urged to be honest in facing choices as well as their consequences. Above all we are not to deceive ourselves and close our eyes to situations in which we are morally involved. A continuing sense of such responsibility makes up Marcel's key virtue of fidelity.

Conclusion

The distinguished German philosopher, Gottfried Wilhelm Leibniz (1646–1716), once observed that philosophers can usually be taken to be true in what they affirm but false in what they deny. The implication here is that no single philosophical system contains absolute truth or is without some inconsistency, incompleteness, or error. Socrates echoed a similar sentiment in the *Apology* when he declared that God alone is wise. Omniscience and definitive veracity are attributes possessed only by God. No human system of thought, however profound, can make a similar claim. Plato realized this when he stated that his philosophy was really not contained in his classic dialogues but was more like a living flame, a dynamic attitude, to be passed from one generation to another.

Yet all philosophical systems, though admittedly incomplete, do possess their characteristic truth and value. All state some truth. As Aristotle remarked in Book II of his *Metaphysics:*

> Therefore, since the truth seems to be like the proverbial door, which no one can fail to hit, in this respect it must be easy, but the fact that we can have a whole truth and not the particular part we aim at shows the difficulty of it.

For John Dewey, the very function of the philosopher is to rework constantly the truths of traditional systems so that they may help us understand novel and contemporary problems. By such a mediating process of reflective intelligence the past itself is revitalized for us and new knowledge made possible. These insights can be applied particularly to moral philosophy.

---

[1] The statement by Kierkegaard appears in *"That Individual": Two "Notes" Concerning My Work as an Author,* which was published posthumously in 1859, along with *The Point of View.*

Not the least merit of the Greek and Christian tradition is that it includes five of the greatest philosophical geniuses that ever lived: Socrates, Plato, Aristotle, Augustine, and Aquinas. From the first speculations of Thales to the synthesis of Aquinas we have a span of two thousand years of accumulated wisdom. In the seven and a half centuries since the birth of Aquinas this tradition has remained as a vital force in the moral lives of contemporary men.

The Greek component of this tradition is best expressed in the Socratic ideal of the examined life, that is, the life in which reasonable moral action is the human ideal. For Socrates the life not lived according to reason is an inhuman and worthless existence. Plato was so taken with the life of reason that he would not allow that there could be virtue without knowledge or law without reason. Aristotle considered the life according to reason to be divine in character and the necessary condition for happiness. Thus God himself is most happy because the nature of God is "a self-thinking thought."

The Christian tradition also stressed reason. Aquinas sacrificed none of the Greek rational ideal but fused it with the Christian atmosphere of a theocentric universe. Even though God is the Cause of all existing things, the Exemplar of their perfection, and the Final End of their strivings, God allows man to imitate him by participating in the reasonable governing of his own human life and by recognizing and appropriating the law that is natural to him as a man.

Kantian moral philosophy has a distinctive Christian component as well as a background in Greek thought. The Categorical Imperative stresses the Christian motif of taking others into account even when we are legislating for ourselves. Kant likewise saw happiness as the highest value that man can attain, and he reaffirmed the Christian tradition that man is a person in his own right, a possessor of dignity, an end in himself—never to be treated as a mere thing with a price.

Kant brought to his philosophy many explicit statements which confer on it a distinctive democratic flavor. He was a champion of the right of each individual to make his own law—but always according to principle.

The student can also see in the moral philosophy of Kant that growing sense in men of modern times of what it is to be an authentic subject, a dynamic center of responsible action. This constitutes an advance over the Greek and medieval theory, which, though it admitted man's participation in reason, too often neglected the subjective and creative role that man himself portrays in his knowing and in his moral action.

The affirmation of the naturalist is also in the direction of giving a high dignity to the use of reason. Reason is of value to him, however, not as a Platonic storehouse of ready-made ideas by which to structure the world, but as a finely tuned instrument for dealing with the world intelligently. Accordingly, the naturalist insists that the moralist not confuse morality with geometry but seek information from the behavioral and positive sciences. We live in a century that has been profoundly influenced by the discoveries of Freud, and, to the extent that the moralist must assess the responsibility of actions, Freud's findings are relevant, if not indispensable. Such findings from the science of psychology are precisely the kind of information that the naturalist rightly insists on as essential information for the moral philosopher.

The naturalist also correctly advises the moralist not to ignore the extraordinary impact of Darwin's evolutionary theory on traditional theories of morality, which mistakenly assumed an entirely different history for mankind and, more importantly, did not take into account the possibility of a moral evolution of mankind itself. An example of a contemporary Christian moralist who has used evolutionary theory as a central component of his ethics is Teilhard de Chardin, the Jesuit scientist and post-existentialist.

The analytic tradition is to be credited for its demand that the moral philosopher be consciously aware of the kinds of claim he is making and the proper means of backing such claims. The analyst rightly insists on the vast differences between statements of value and statements of fact and properly warns against seeking to verify both kinds by the same method.

Just as the surgeon must examine his instruments before he operates to see that his scalpel is clean and sharp, so too the moral philosopher must analyze with precision the meanings of his terms and statements and reflect deeply on his method of doing moral philosophy. Morris Cohen once remarked that one would not expect a hospital to be a place for the spread of disease; even more one should not expect philosophy to be a source of confusion.

The existentialist tradition emphasizes the nature of human freedom in an age that in many ways is oppressive to freedom. It is a matter of interest that the traditionally Christian value of personal freedom has been most forcefully and stoutly defended by some who are themselves neither Christian nor theistic.

These, then, are the central traditions and topics of moral philosophy. Clearly, each tradition has its own distinctive strengths, and no single approach raises all the questions or gives all the answers. In the pages that follow the moralists speak for themselves through their best writings. The student's task is to search out the elements of moral wisdom contained in those five different points of view that are the most influential and relevant in the world in which he is living his own moral life.

PART ONE

Introduction

Historical Setting

The Problem of the Supreme Good and End

Virtue

Conditions of Moral Responsibility

Individual Moral Virtues

Intellectual Virtues

Natural Moral Law

The Ideal Life: Happiness

Conclusion

Readings

PLATO: *Can Virtue Be Taught?*
On Friendship
Who Is the Happy Man?

ARISTOTLE: *All Human Action Aims at the Good and the Supreme Good*
What Is a Moral Virtue?
Choice and Deliberation
Intellectual Virtues
Friendship
The Problem of Pleasure
Highest Human Happiness: The Contemplative Life

AQUINAS: *Happiness—The Moral Point of View*
Distributive and Commutative Justice
Man's Need of Friends
Happiness and Leisure
The Natural Law

CLASSICAL AND MEDIEVAL INTELLECTUALIST THOUGHT:

Plato
Aristotle
Aquinas

EDITED BY

Francis H. Eterovich, O.P.

DEPAUL UNIVERSITY

CLASSICAL AND MEDIEVAL INTELLECTUALIST THOUGHT:
Plato
Aristotle
Aquinas

Introduction

Historical Setting

The intellectualist tradition in ethics has its principal origins in the Greek thought of Socrates, Plato, and Aristotle. Although Socrates (470–399 B.C.) left no writings, the essence of his thought regarding moral theory was captured in Plato's dialogues. Plato (*c.* 427–347 B.C.) accepted the Socratic ethic and developed it considerably, particularly by applying its principles to the State, for Plato's chief interests lay in political philosophy —an outgrowth of Greek ethics. Although we are indebted to Socrates and Plato for the origins of an intellectualist ethics, we must look to Aristotle (384–322 B.C.) for a definite and systematic exposition. It was he who exerted the lasting influence on moral theory in the Western world.

Aristotle, while owing much to his teacher Plato, was more concerned in his ethical theory with the changeable world than with the immutable, eternal, and perfect Forms or Ideas of his teacher. His concept of nature, and so of human nature, is a dynamic one. In spite of the tremendous influence of Plato, he was a world- and man-centered philosopher.

The main characteristic of his ethics lies in the concept that man, an animal who possesses rational control of his conduct, is supposed to introduce measure, order, and harmony into his complex being and into his social intercourse. Through practical wisdom the well-educated man can discover the right thing to do. It is clear that Aristotle's is an intellectualist ethics.

26

Aristotle in the Middle Ages

Aristotle enjoyed his greatest authority in the days of Albert the Great (1206–80) and his disciple, St. Thomas Aquinas (1225–74), and became in the late Middle Ages an oracle of philosophy. At a time when such outstanding Arabic philosophers as Averroës (1126–98) interpreted Aristotle in a way that threatened to undermine the rational foundations of Christianity, Aquinas courageously seized the occasion to use Aristotle's philosophy as the foundation of his Christian theology. In the Middle Ages philosophy was a handmaid of theology, the sovereign queen of sciences.

The Aristotle whom Albert and Aquinas studied was not the Aristotle of the Greek text and context, historical and cultural; it was an Aristotle translated into Latin word by word and interpreted by three rival groups —the Christian, the Arabic, and the Jewish philosophers—all trying to find in his writings a rational foundation for their religious beliefs. It was an Aristotle expurgated by Pope Urban IV and finally "baptized" by Thomas Aquinas. The enormous contribution of Aquinas must be acknowledged and appreciated; he grasped so much of Aristotle, in spite of all hindrances. Nevertheless, Aristotle as interpreted by the nineteenth- and twentieth-century linguistic and philosophic scholars is incomparably more himself than the one who, in the hands of the schoolmen, became a schoolman himself.

Outstanding among Aquinas' ethical works is his *Commentary on the Nicomachean Ethics*. Two other important works that will be discussed in this essay are his *Summa Theologica* and *Summa Contra Gentiles*. Because both *Summas* present a kind of fusion of theology and philosophy, it is understandable that we should devote primary attention to Aristotle, whom Aquinas called "the Philosopher." Other-worldly and God-centered, Aquinas approached morality in terms of the divine, the revealed, the supernatural, as a theologian must. He neither wrote nor meant to write a philosophical ethical synthesis. An outstanding Thomist, Anton C. Pegis, has recently declared:

> Some one hundred years ago Thomism was reintroduced to the world as a pure philosophy. In the present century, and chiefly between the two great wars, it was discovered to be a Christian philosophy owing many of its ideas to theology, so that as a philosophy it could not be separated from the religious soil in which it grew. . . . the philosophy of St. Thomas was not only Christian in its character and spirit but also theological in its mode of expression and development: it was, in fact, the minister and servant of sacred teaching, forming as such an integral part of the theological whole to which it belonged.[1]

---

[1] *St. Thomas and Philosophy* (Milwaukee: Marquette University Press, 1964), pp. 83–84. For an opposing view, however, see James F. Anderson, "Was St. Thomas a Philosopher?" *The New Scholasticism*, XXXVIII (1964), 435–44; and John A. Osterle, "St. Thomas as a Teacher: A Reply," *Ibid.*, XXXIX (1965), 451–66.

Aquinas took from Aristotle whatever he found to be a fitting rational foundation of supernatural Christian morals. He followed him closely in his *Commentary* and made genuine contributions to Aristotelian ethical thought, drawing as well from Christian and Platonic sources. Aquinas blended these contributions together to serve his purpose.

Implicit in Aquinas' morals is his Christian metaphysics: the existence of a personal and provident God, creator and ruler of the universe and men. The human soul (not only the human intellect) is immortal, and man is a free moral agent under God. Never at home in this world, man's journey leads him back to his creator. Aquinas' Christian moral intellectualism —exemplified by the Beatific Vision—is for him the only real goal of human life.

There is a further reason for our decision to concentrate on Aristotle —namely, those disciples of Aquinas who look for the Aquinas *ethicus* or, generally speaking, for Aquinas the philosopher, lean heavily, as their master did, toward Aristotle. But Aquinas is discussed wherever we thought he had a new ethical insight. Thus, one part of our survey of intellectualist ethics, the problem of natural law, gives primacy to Aquinas, because here his insights are richer and more developed than Aristotle's.

The Problem of the Supreme Good and End

As the sun is to the universe, so the Form of the Good is to the realm of Ideas. For Plato it is a self-subsistent entity, not just a property, but substantial, eternal, unchangeable goodness. The Form of the Good causes the essence and existence of the many imperfect goods we possess, such as pleasure, wealth, honor, and wisdom. These are only reflections, poor copies of the Supreme Good, and are good only in view of their participation in and assimilation of it. Moreover, they are perishable: the Form of the Good transcends them totally and is completely independent of them. It is not in them but external to them, so much so that if all the goods of the world were to perish forever, this tragic event would not affect the existence of the Form of the Good at all.[2]

The highest good of man and consequently his supreme end must be modeled on the Form of the Good. The more men contemplate it and participate in it, the better and the happier they will be. This is the secret of the harmonious development of man's personality as a rational and ethical being.

However, at the outset of his *Nicomachean Ethics,* Aristotle argued against the Platonic "Good in itself" as a separate substance. To him the

[2] See the discussion of the relation between the Form of Good and the many goods in the world in *The Collected Dialogues of Plato, Including the Letters,* ed. and with Introd. by Edith Hamilton and Huntington Cairns (New York: Pantheon Books, 1961). *Republic,* 505a and 509–11.

good is a transcendental property of being possessed analogically by the many goods to a lesser or greater degree. The metaphysical solution to the problem of good is left to metaphysics. As for ethics, Aristotle was convinced that the Platonic Form of the Good was too remote to become a rule of human conduct. He looked for that rule within the tendencies of the human being, for there is a tendency within all things to develop to the fullest extent proper to them.

All Human Action Aims at the Good

In Aristotelian terms one might say: Everything in this vast universe strives to actualize its potentialities or capacities. Omnipresent in Aristotelian ethics is the focus on development or growth, taken originally from the biological sciences with which Aristotle was well acquainted. Growth points to the maturity or fullness of things. This completion of hidden potencies is the good (*agathon*) at which everything aims, be it mineral, plant, or man. Teleology, or purposiveness, rules Aristotelian ethics, although, as we shall see, deontological elements—those pointing to duties —are not absent from it. But moral obligation is only the consequence of the good or virtuous life of man.

The opening sentence of the *Nicomachean Ethics* sets the teleological tenor of Aristotle's ethical inquiry:

> Every art (*technē*) and every investigation (*methodos*), and likewise every practical pursuit (*praxis*) or undertaking (*proairesis*), seems to aim at some good: hence it has been well said, that the good is that at which all things aim.[3]

Aristotle offered this concept of the end (*telos*) in other works: it is "that for the sake of which a thing is done." [4] He listed it among his four causes. For him all change is a process whereby some given underlying substratum (matter) acquires a new specification or perfection (form) through the action of the agent (efficient cause) moved to act by the attraction of some good (the end). Ultimately, the end attracts and leads the agent to fashion a new perfection from the undetermined matter. The end is the supreme cause of action, change, and growth. Such a view of the primacy of ends in the universe makes of our world a place in which all things have their purpose.

This is the *law of teleology or purposiveness*. Each being is so constructed in its nature (*physis*) that it acts only according to a particular pattern or in a certain direction. But this direction presupposes a definite nature or essence from which it starts and a definite action. There is no

---

[3] *Nicomachean Ethics,* Book I, i, 1–1094a 1-4. Most of the quotations found in this essay are taken from *Aristotle: The Nicomachean Ethics,* trans. by H. Rackham (Cambridge: Harvard University Press, 1962). Each quotation gives, besides Rackham divisions of *N.E.,* the standard reference numbers of the Berlin edition of Aristotle.

[4] *The Basic Works of Aristotle,* ed. by Richard McKeon (New York: Random House, 1941) *Physics,* II, iii–194b 3 ss.; *Metaphysics,* V, ii–1013a 33.

random action; every action points to the end or target toward which it aims. Therefore, determined nature produces determined action or function, and this function in turn produces or reaches a determined end. Thus nature, action, and end are correlative terms. Every thing has its function to fulfill, and this fulfillment of its function is its proper end.

Men are not excepted from this universal striving for self-fulfillment; they are filled with potencies, needs, and corresponding desires. The proper role of man's rational faculty (*logos*) and its appetite (*orexis*) is to conduct him from the imperfect state of potency in which he is born to his fullest possible actualization.

The law of teleology, applied to human beings, may be summed up as follows: from human nature springs human action, which in turn leads to the human end. Man's striving for his self-fulfillment is not merely an unconscious impulse; rather, it is a conscious effort. Ethical goodness is rooted in rational human nature and its permanent needs.

Ends and Means

We have seen that all human endeavor aims at the end, but in order to reach his end man must use means. These means are only immediate and intermediate ends, whose real significance cannot be discovered except in terms of the ends to which they aim. Thus, all immediate and intermediate ends receive their meaning from the supreme end of man's action and life, the end in itself, which does not admit of further activity.

Thomas Aquinas gave reasons for Aristotle's seemingly hasty inference about the supreme end. In a series of ends and means, Aquinas wrote, we distinguish the order of planning ("intention") and the order of performing ("execution"). Ends have primacy in both of these. With respect to planning, no thought, choice, or desire would be possible without an end in view; as to performance, no action would start, get its direction, or be completed without an end as its term. But in order to avoid an infinite regress, both orders must reach the ultimate end of human life.

The whole meaning of end consists in the attractive good that it offers to the agent. Both the immediate and intermediate ends aim at further ends, which owe their attraction to the one end that is the highest goal of man's striving. Since all ends receive their goodness and, consequently, their attraction from the last one, there must be a last end—the supreme source of goodness and its attraction—which initiates every other subordinate end in the series of meaningfully connected ends, or there would be no series at all. If there were no last, there could be no first either. Since it is impossible to string out to infinity a series of ends and means, there must be some supreme end of human conduct and life.

What Is the Supreme Good for Man?

The most universal answer to this question is that all men desire to be happy; hence, happiness (*eudaimonia*) would seem to be the supreme good for man. Not all men agree about the meaning or nature of happiness, however. Some equate happiness with pleasure, wealth, health, and honors; but these are only means to happiness.

Aristotle did not see happiness as a feeling, even if the feeling be deep and permanent, refined of gross bodily pleasures; nor did he see it simply as a disposition of temperament. To him happiness is an activity through which a man develops his capacities by living well, and doing and faring well, and so is on the way to reaching his well-being in mind and body. And since "activities are of two kinds, some merely necessary means and desirable only for the sake of something else, others desirable in themselves, it is clear that happiness is to be classed among activities desirable in themselves." [5] Happiness, the activity that is desirable in and for itself, is characterized as something final, self-sufficient, and lasting.

But we must still discover what happiness really is. First, Aristotle took the question of man's function: What kind of function is man designated by nature to fulfill? He answered by searching for what man alone can do. Man shares nutrition and growth with both plants and animals; he shares a sentient life with animals. "There remains therefore what may be called the practical life of the rational part of man." [6] Man is the animal with a rational principle, called *logos,* which understands the end and directs man's acts to it; it is followed by its proper tendency, the *will.* Human well-being or happiness must be found in this rational part of man—thus, the definition of human happiness:

> The good of man is the active exercise of his soul's faculties in conformity with excellence or virtue, or, if there be several human excellencies or virtues, in conformity with the best and most perfect among them.[7]

The two new key terms which have been introduced in this definition —virtue and the best virtue—must be explained before we may fully see the Aristotelian position on human happiness.

Virtue

Socrates and Plato sought to determine how man could become virtuous; but such a question presupposes a knowledge of what virtue is. Although they attempted to define virtue in its universal aspects, rather than to enumerate its particular types, they were unable to formulate an acceptable definition. Nonetheless, Plato left the reader with the distinct impression that virtue is a kind of knowledge or practical wisdom, a concept consistent

---

[5] *N.E.,* X, vi, 2–1176b 1-5.
[6] *Ibid.,* I, vii, 13–1098a 2.
[7] *Ibid.,* vii, 15–1098a 15.

with his view that no man knowingly does evil. Vice implies a kind of ignorance, for if a man knows what is right, he will do what is right.

Aristotle intended to study virtue primarily to find out how to live the good life. To quote from Book II of *Nicomachean Ethics:* "We are not investigating the nature of virtue for the sake of knowing what it is, but in order that we may become good, without which result our investigation would be of no use." Moral virtues are not ingrained in our nature: "Nature gives us the capacity to receive them, and this capacity is brought to maturity by habit." Man becomes virtuous by practicing good acts, which results in the maturity of virtue, in good character, and in the good and consequently happy life. For example: "By acting in dangerous situations and forming a habit of fear or of confidence we become courageous or cowardly." The same holds true for other virtues. Not every action, but the right action in conformity with the right standard, rule, or principle is virtuous action.[8]

Pleasure and Pain: Tests of Virtue

The criteria by which one can judge whether or not one is virtuous are supplied by the tests of pleasure and pain. He who controls his propensity to pleasure and fear of pain is a virtuous man; he who habitually succumbs to the lure of pleasure and avoids pain at the expense of virtue is a vicious man. Aristotle listed several reasons for his theory that pleasure and pain are the tests for virtue and vice in men,[9] a few of which are summarized below:

1. Virtues and vices have to do with actions and feelings, both of which are accompanied by pleasure or pain and both of which virtue must keep in check.
2. The object determines the nature of the habits and acts; the wrong or right pursuit or avoidance of pleasure and pain are decisive factors in the corruption or improvement of man.
3. There are three motives for choosing or avoiding actions according to three kinds of goods: the noble, the expedient, and the pleasant. The last is the best test of the good and bad man, for pleasure tends to lead us on the wrong path in life.
4. Love of pleasure is ingrained in us from birth and is hard to eradicate when it turns to wrong objects. To resist the lure of pleasure is more difficult than to check the impulse to anger, but, after all, the primary concern of virtue is located precisely in that which is difficult to achieve.

It would be wrong to infer that virtue is freedom from both pleasure and pain. The whole point is not to suppress our tendency to pleasure, but to moderate it according to rational rule.

---

[8] This dictum will be discussed at greater length in the section on "Intellectual Virtues."
[9] *N.E.,* II, iii–1104b–1105a 1–15.

Definition of Virtue

There are basic conditions for the acts that flow from virtue (*aretē*); they must be done knowingly and deliberately, and they must spring from a permanent disposition of character. A man must know what he is doing, and he must know that what he is doing is right. Moreover, it is not sufficient just to do a good act; the act must derive from habitually good disposition of character. Virtue is a permanent disposition fixed by steady practice. Its general category (*genus*) is neither emotion nor some faculty of the soul, for these are neither good nor bad in themselves; its distinguishing character (*differentia specifica*) is a mean between excess and defect, that is, between too much and too little in feelings and actions. This mean is determined by the rational part of man which points out what is equitable and suitable in relation to ourselves and others. Thus, Aristotle defined virtue as follows:

> Virtue then is a settled disposition of the mind determining the choice of actions and emotions, consisting essentially in the observance of the mean relative to us, this being determined by principle [*logos*], that is, as the prudent man would determine it.[10]

The Mean of Virtue

The mean of virtue should not be confused with mediocrity. The mean is not simply a middle of the road position, but the most reasonable course of action man can take in a given situation. Avoiding two extremes is the high point of practical wisdom. But to sustain the mean of virtue in all human conduct is an extremely difficult task; it requires using one's judgment habitually and building up the steady moral effort necessary to keep the proper balance between the two extremes.

Aristotle gave three practical rules for achieving the right mean: [11]

1. Avoid first that extreme that is more opposed to the mean. For example, if while driving you must choose between hitting a pedestrian or a fence, choose the fence.

2. Consider your natural inclinations and act accordingly, keeping in mind your strengths and weaknesses. For example, if you are very brave, take care not to behave rashly; if you tend to drink immoderately, avoid drinking altogether.

3. Beware of immoderate pleasures; they are the real test of the virtuous man. For example, Antony's downfall stemmed from overindulgence in sexual pleasure.

Division of Moral Virtues

Virtues are divided into two main groups: intellectual and moral. Intellectual virtues (which will be discussed fully later in this essay) belong to

---

[10] *Ibid.*, II, vi, 15–1107a 1-5.
[11] *Ibid.*, II, ix–1109a 11-35; 1109b 1-25.

the rational part of man, while moral virtues dispose the irrational part of the soul to form a good character. In Book II of the *Nicomachean Ethics,* Aristotle gave the outline of moral virtues according to the feelings to be controlled and actions to be done. Although Aristotle's list of feelings and virtues is far from exhaustive, the important thing for us to know is that for each virtue there are two corresponding vices, or vicious extremes.

1. Division of Moral Virtues According to Feeling (*Pathos*)

Feeling	Virtue	Defect	Excess
Confidence	Courage	Cowardice	Rashness
Fear	Courage	Fearlessness	Cowardice
Pleasures of touch	Self-control	Insensibility	Self-indulgence
Anger	Gentleness	Spiritlessness	Irascibility
Shame	Modesty	Shamelessness	Bashfulness

Aristotle also listed the following:

Feeling: Pain and pleasure felt at the good or bad fortune of others.
Virtue: Righteous joy at the deserved good fortune of others; righteous indignation at the undeserved good fortune of others.
Defect: Malice or rejoicing at the ill-fortune of others.
Excess: Envy or deep sorrow in view of the good fortune of others.

But according to Aristotle, the feelings of shame and of pain and pleasure at the good or bad fortune of others are intermediate states, not pure feelings, and their corresponding virtues are not virtues in the strict sense.

2. Division of Moral Virtues According to Action (*Praxis*)

Action	Virtue	Defect	Excess
Pursuit of money:			
a) Giving and getting money on a modest scale	Liberality	Stinginess	Prodigality
b) Giving money on a large scale	Magnificence	Niggardliness	Vulgarity
Pursuit of honors:			
a) On a modest scale	Proper pride	Lack of ambition	Pride
b) On a large scale	Greatness of soul	Undue humility	Empty vanity
Social intercourse:			
a) Conversation	Truthfulness (sincerity)	Self-deprecation	Boastfulness

Action	Virtue	Defect	Excess
b) Pleasantness in social intercourse	Wittiness	Boorishness	Buffoonery
c) Pleasant companionship	Friendliness	Obsequiousness and flattery [12]	Quarrelsomeness
Exchange of goods:	Justice	Injustice	Injustice

Courage, self-control, friendship, and justice will be taken up later in this essay, but because of space limitations we cannot give detailed explanations of the other moral virtues. We urge the student, however, to read Aristotle's discussion of them in Book IV of his *Nicomachean Ethics.*

Conditions of Moral Responsibility

We have seen in the preceding section that the very essence of moral virtue consists in choosing the right mean between excess and defect in feelings and actions. The nature of such a choice and the moral responsibility for it are the next problems we must consider. Is a man equally responsible for all his actions and passions that concern moral virtues? The human act is performed with knowledge and consent, under the control of man's reason. But not all knowledge is equally clear; man does not consent in all cases in the same degree, nor is he always allowed to make choices of his own. A perfectly intelligent, voluntary, and freely chosen human act involves full knowledge of the intellect and free choice of the will. Whatever destroys or lessens either of these two elements destroys the voluntary character of the action.

Types of Human Action

"Voluntary [or willing] (*hekōn*) act would seem to be an act of which the origin lies in the agent, who knows the particular circumstances in which he is acting." [13] An example would be the student who wants to learn economics; his presence in class is *voluntary.*

The involuntary, or unwilling (*akōn*), act is one done against man's rational part, and, consequently, "it causes the agent pain and regret." If the student is forced to learn economics as part of his required course work, his presence in class is *involuntary.*

A nonvoluntary, or nonwilling (*ouch hekōn*), act is one done in ignorance of its full circumstances and consequences. There is *absence of willing,* that is, no act of will at all, either positive or negative. If the student is

---

[12] The obsequious man has no personal stake in a matter; the flatterer aims at his own interests.

[13] *N.E.,* III, i, 20–1111a 22.

indifferent to the subject of economics, neither wanting to learn nor rejecting learning, his presence in class is *nonvoluntary*.

Mixed actions are partly voluntary, partly involuntary (although strictly speaking, more voluntary than involuntary). A man performs such an action with the clear understanding that it is a reasonable thing to do here and now, but he does it reluctantly in order to avoid a greater evil; a man consents to having his leg amputated in order to save his life.

Deliberate action refers to the means within one's power of reaching the end or ends he has set in his mind after reflecting upon them.

Choice

Choice (*proairesis*) is a voluntary act, but it implies a wider and deeper involvement of an agent. Aristotle ascribed the voluntary act to children and even to animals (for him the will is not exactly an intellectual power) but choice is the truly human act, and it is of crucial importance in moral life. This is the closest Aristotle came to the problem that was later called "freedom of will"; the concept was not completely clear to him in a Greek setting where Nature, Necessity, and Chance seemed to leave little to human freedom.

Choice involves an analysis of the moments through which the fully deliberate human act must pass. These moments in the genesis of the human act must not be considered as separate or isolated; they are psychological elements of a single whole. The whole man acts and every human act is a unit.

The human act ordinarily consists of two phases: *planning* and *performing*. Both have to deal with the end and the means leading to it; both involve intellectual activity preceding the voluntary.

In addition to Aristotle's doctrine, the following outline includes the more elaborate analysis of the human act that Aquinas wrote in his *Summa Theologica*, I–II.[14]

I. Planning Phase

CONCERNING THE END

Intellect	*Will*
1) Perception of the good as end	2) Wish to attain the end
3) Judgment of mind that the end may be attained	4) Intention to attain the end

CONCERNING THE MEANS

5) Deliberation about the means	6) Consent to the means
7) Practical judgment about the means to employ	8) Choice of the means

---

[14] *Basic Writings of St. Thomas Aquinas*, ed. by Anton C. Pegis (New York: Random House, 1945), II, 225–316.

II. *Performing Phase*

CONCERNING THE MEANS

9) Command to carry out the choice   10) Use of powers to fulfill the choice

CONCERNING THE END

11) Perception or contemplation of end attained   12) Enjoyment of the end attained

Two of these steps in the full human act—practical judgment and choice —deserve at least a brief explanation, because they are crucial to a discussion of moral responsibility.

When the mind must determine, here and now, which specific means will best lead it to the end, the crucial moment of the human act has come. This determination constitutes practical judgment, which is the result of practical reasoning.

The will follows the practical judgment of intellect by choosing a proposed means. The awareness of alternatives and the discovery of the most suitable one are functions of the intellect; the power to choose and actual choice are functions of the will. The two functions are so close that they seem to make one act. Surely, the root of choice is found in the intellect, but it belongs to two powers. The basic characteristic of freedom of the will is choice, but choice preceded necessarily by the practical judgment of the intellect. Aristotle defined choice "as voluntary action preceded by deliberation, since choice involves reasoning and some process of thought." [15] He included deliberation as part of the last practical judgment of intellect. Later Aristotle gave an even more condensed definition of choice: "a deliberate desire of things in our power; for we first deliberate, then select, and finally fix our desire according to the result of our deliberation." [16] Choice, then, includes perception or judgment, selection, and actual decision. The following example will clarify the steps in the planning and performing phases in a real situation:

I. *Planning Phase*

CONCERNING THE END

1. A senior high school student understands, at least hazily, that college education is a good thing for him.

2. He likes the idea and wants to go to college when he completes high school.

3. His scholastic record is above average; his parents are willing to help him to meet the expenses. His goal seems attainable.

4. His wish has matured by now into a serious intention to go to college.

---

[15] *N.E.,* III, ii, 17–112a 15.
[16] *Ibid.,* iii, 19–1113a 10.

CONCERNING THE MEANS

5. However, neither want nor intention is enough. Many alternatives must be carefully considered before he enters college: he must see which college best suits his financial resources and intellectual aptitudes; he must consider the geographical location of the college; before matriculating, he may have to take some refresher courses; he might think about taking a part-time job to supplement his parents' contribution; he would be wise to consider what he wants to gain from a college education.

6. When the deliberating process has come to an end (at least for the present) the student agrees to this panorama of presented means, convinced that he has not neglected any important factor.

7. The time has come for him to make up his mind about the college he is going to enter and the particular steps he must take to do so—here and now. This is his last practical judgment.

8. The crucial moment of decision or choice has arrived: he is going to register in the college of his choice.

II. *Performing Phase*

CONCERNING THE MEANS

9. The intellect issues a command (a directive order, not an arbitrary imposition) to the will: carry out your decison—register.

10. The will, a dynamic intellectual power, prompts all other human powers (including intellect) to act in order to make a reality of choice. The result is that our student has become a college freshman.

CONCERNING THE END

11. In spite of some confusion during his first days on the campus, he fully realizes that he has started a new life and that his wish has come true.

12. He is happy to be among those relatively few who have been accepted—and enjoys his new status of college student.

Responsibility

Since choice and the preceding deliberation enter into a human act, it is clear that men are responsible for both their virtuous and vicious actions. Those who argue for the absence of responsibility because of an alleged absence of choice are clearly wrong. This responsibility is assumed by the system of rewards for virtuous and punishment for vicious conduct.

An attempt to escape moral responsibility is sometimes explained by a poor choice of means on the grounds of character or temperament, properties for which men are not responsible. Aristotle answered that each man *is* responsible for his conception of the good; because he has the power of deliberation and choice, he cannot be a blind victim of his bodily constitution and basic emotional disposition. Although Aristotle definitely rejected the Socratic view that no man is willingly bad, he allowed for the debilitating influence of many factors upon man's exercise of his powers of intellect and will.

Obstacles to Voluntary Action

Man is the agent, the efficient cause of his conduct, but in order to judge him we must know the state of his soul at the moment he commits a deed. There are many hindrances to clear knowledge and the power of will to follow intellectual perception, such as ignorance, compulsion, fear, anger, and habit.

Ignorance is not a simple absence of any knowledge, but a lack of the necessary knowledge that a person should have in order to act morally. Ignorance in ethics refers to the object (what is to be done); the subject (or person who is supposed to act); the circumstances of an action (where or place, when or time, how or the way in which the act was done); why an act was done (purpose in the mind of the agent); and the consequences that will or could follow from that action.

If a person deliberately neglects to acquire knowledge that would dispel ignorance, his ignorance is voluntary and he is responsible for his action. If, however, he acts out of ignorance that could not be avoided (such as a hunter killing a friend when he thought he was firing at a deer), his ignorance is nonvoluntary and he is not guilty.

Compulsion

Compulsory action is that action which is exacted of a man against his will through the use of physical force. When a man commits bad acts under the pressure of violence that no one could withstand, he is not guilty because his actions are involuntary. But Aristotle was careful to add here: "Yet there seem to be some acts which a man cannot be compelled to do, and rather than do them he ought to submit to the most terrible death." [17] Such might be the case when a tyrant would try to compel a man to kill his mother.

Fear is not taken here as a simple emotion, but as a generalized anxiety caused by an imminent or future danger. Its origin may be within the agent (sickness) or without (the threat of kidnapping). Its intensity may be serious (fear of death, public disgrace, or financial ruin) or slight, depending on the imminent danger. As for its influence, man acts *from* fear when fear precedes the action and moves the will to act; man acts *with* fear when fear accompanies the action without causing it—for example, a soldier endures battle despite his fear.

Fear may render an act involuntary if the intensity of the emotion

---

[17] *Ibid.*, i, 8–1110a 25.

blocks man's rational control. But not every act done out of fear destroys voluntariness; circumstances are the determining factors.

Anger, like any other strong emotion (love, hate, hope, despair), may modify the voluntariness of the human act. Strong passions can cloud the clear understanding of the intellect and weaken the strength of the will, thereby producing nonvoluntary action. When the passion is not quite so strong, it allows for a degree of voluntariness. When passion has been voluntarily aroused, the action flowing from it is not only voluntary but even more voluntary than it would be had there been no deliberate stimulus. In any case, however, we may say that passions lessen free choice.

Habit is a lasting disposition to a constant way of acting acquired by repetition of the same act. One who deliberately acquires a habit is responsible for it, despite the fact that he cannot easily get rid of it. If a person tries to correct a bad habit willingly, he is no longer responsible for the acts which inadvertently flow from it.

This discussion by no means exhausts the hindrances to man's rational control of his conduct. Abnormal mental states such as mental retardation, neurosis, psychosis, and varieties of psychopathies take some, if not all, rational control from man. In addition, the contemporary inventions of indoctrination and brainwashing aim at total thought control, and ultimately at total destruction of the moral personality. Ethics is deeply concerned with all these matters affecting man's free choice of conduct.

Individual Moral Virtues

Plato gave much thought to the four cardinal virtues: prudence, justice, temperance, and courage. Instead of looking for these in the microscosm —the individual man—Plato analyzed them as manifested in the macrocosm—the State. There the virtues will be "writ large" for all to see; their parallel in the individual will then be examined.

The ideal State will be composed of three classes of citizens: (1) rulers, or guardians; (2) soldiers, or auxiliaries; (3) tradesmen—with the appropriate virtue predominating in each. The ruler should typify prudence; the soldier, courage; the tradesman, temperance. Justice will prevail in the State when there is harmony among these parts.

The individual is similarly composed of three elements: (1) a rational part of the soul, (2) a spirited part that tends to side with reason, (3) an appetitive part that tends to go against reason. Prudence corresponds to the first part; courage to the second; temperance to the third. When all are functioning harmoniously, justice will be found in the individual man. The good man, then, is guided by an informed reason.

Aristotle's discussion concentrated on those outstanding moral virtues that are related to *emotion* (self-control and courage) and to *action* (justice and friendship).

Self-Control (*sophrosynē*)

Self-control is the observance of moderation in relation to pleasures of the body—eating, drinking, and sexual intercourse. Intellectual, esthetic, and religious joys, as well as those experienced in colors, sounds, and perfumes, should have their virtues, but Aristotle did not elaborate on them. The pleasures of food, drink, and sex are, morally speaking, indifferent. Their function is to stimulate us to satisfy natural human needs, which differ markedly in intensity from one man to another.

There is little danger of a defective extreme in this virtue of self-control, except in the case of irrational dieting and abstinence from drink that leads to malnutrition and dehydration. A person is not guilty of a defective extreme if he is naturally inclined to be spare in eating and drinking or is organically impotent in sexual intercourse.

The excessive extreme in bodily pleasures is more likely to occur. Gluttony, drunkenness, and lust are forms of self-indulgence that go beyond the right measure necessary for the natural satisfaction of human needs.

Briefly, "The temperate man desires the right thing in the right way at the right time, which is what principle [*logos*] ordains." [18]

Courage (*andreiā*)

Disgrace, poverty, disease, and lack of friends are among the things men fear, but none of them constitutes the supreme test of courage. Since death is what men fear most, it is the test most befitting the strength of the courageous man. But, men die naturally and violently every day and not all of them are courageous people. Aristotle believed that death in battle is a truly courageous death.

> What form of death then is a test of Courage? Presumably that which is the noblest. Now the noblest form of death is death in battle, for it is encountered in the midst of the greatest and most noble of dangers.[19]

The perils of war, more than any others, expose the courageous man to death. The man of courage faces terrifying dangers because his right principle dictates that he must; above all, he will endure perils for the sake of what is noble (*kalon*) in that heroic deed.

Moreover, courage is also tested by endurance of pain and strain and by abstinence from pleasures that are likely to weaken the endurance of a courageous man. As with other virtues, courage demands that the courageous man follow the right mean—moderation. "The courageous man then is he that endures or fears the right things and for the right purpose and in the right manner and at the right time, and who shows confidence in a similar way." [20]

---

[18] *Ibid.*, xii, 9–1119b 15.
[19] *Ibid.*, vi, 8–1115a 30.
[20] *Ibid.*, vii, 5–1115b 15.

VICES OPPOSED TO COURAGE. When a man cannot control his fear in the face of death for a noble cause he is said to be a coward. But a man who without deliberation rushes into death goes beyond courage; his attitude is irrational because it is excessive. While an excess of confidence results in rashness, lack of confidence may result in cowardice. Aristotle believed that rash men are basically cowards who wish to feign courage. "They make a bold show in situations that inspire confidence, but do not endure terrors." [21] He also believed that courage is lacking in men who willingly kill themselves, for their real motivation is a desire to flee the sorrows of life.

Justice (dikaiosynē)

Aristotle distinguished two kinds of justice:

1. *General justice* or righteousness, taken in the broader sense, means a disposition to do what is good, right, fair, and lawful. Its opposite, injustice, includes all unlawful deeds. The law (*nomos*) is not so much a dry legal formula as it is a principle of reason and a guardian of the virtue and happiness (well-being) of citizens. The law is a custom, written or unwritten, expressing what is right, fair, or just, and so embodying that moral public opinion which has grown from the experience and wisdom of the ages.

We must point out here that Aristotle wrote his *Nicomachean Ethics* in Athens, the city-state where law was not a tyrant's rule, and where judges were not legal specialists but men chosen from the people to judge according to the best customs and opinions prevalent in those times. In Athens being a good citizen could easily be equated with being a good man. But under tyranny a good citizen, that is, one who obeys the tyrannical laws, is not necessarily a good man.

Thus, justice in its general sense includes every virtue; expressed in politico-ethical terms, it is obedience to laws—"the whole of virtue," just as its opposite, injustice, is in a broad sense "the whole of vice." Justice, however, should not simply be combined with the other virtues; justice adds to all of them. Even in this broader sense, it displays and brings into focus the social character of every virtue, for justice is a social virtue. "Justice alone of the virtues is 'the good of others,' because it does what is for the advantage of another, either a ruler or an associate." [22]

2. *Particular justice* is a part of general justice. It can be described as the disposition to do, or wish, or act in accordance with what is equal, fair, and, consequently, due to others. Aristotle assumed that men live freely and equally in a city-state. The mean of justice as a particular moral virtue is that every citizen has a right to his equal share of goods and services. The man who takes more than his due share of wealth, honor, or security and who contributes less than his due share of service to the political community is an injust man.

---

[21] *Ibid.*, vii, 9–1116a 5.
[22] *Ibid.*, V, i, 17–1130a 3.

Particular justice may be divided into distributive and corrective justice. *Distributive justice* is "exercised in the distribution of honor, wealth, and the other divisible assets of the community, which may be allotted among its members in equal or unequal shares." [23] It operates between the state and its citizens. Ideally, there would be an equal share in goods and services for every citizen. But since not all citizens are of equal merit, there will be unequal rewards for the good and punishment for the bad citizens. This does not, however, constitute actual inequality or injustice. The mean of distributive justice will be the proportion between rewards and merits and between punishments and demerits. Strictly speaking, citizens are equal and free with respect to their basic human constituents—body and soul; but they are unequal in their bodily and mental abilities and their proportionate contributions to the community. Hence, distributive justice does not involve an arithmetical proportion, but a proportion of merits.

Corrective justice is concerned with fairness in the private transactions of citizens. It may be based on a voluntary contract between two parties in matters of selling, buying, and lending, and applies when one of the parties breaks the contract; or it may pertain to involuntary transactions made by fraud or force. Corrective justice demands that the damage inflicted be repaired and equality restored.

Before offering further distinctions in justice, Aristotle paused to tell us that it would be wrong to consider justice as being concerned only and exclusively with the external just mean or proportion. Justice is a moral virtue. As such it involves choice. It disposes a man to give to others what is due to them. Consequently, whenever the inner control of one's act is impeded by the obstacles to voluntary choice (ignorance, anger, and fear), neither justice nor injustice is involved. "When, however, an injury is done from choice, the doer is unjust and wicked." [24] Both justice and injustice are evaluated by the deliberate choice that precedes them.

The last important distinction Aristotle made is that between the law and equity (*epieikeiā*). No law can cover all cases; it can only take the majority into consideration. When a case arises in which to act according to law would result in injustice, equity steps in and "corrects" the law. Equity can be defined as "rectification of law where law is defective because of its generality." [25] The equitable is not legally just but it is by nature a corrective of legal justice. The equation that the lawful is the just, or, in other words, that law is justice is not true here. Equity is justice, but it is not a legal justice. In fact, if the lawgiver were present in the case—the lawgiver who declares the laws according to his legislative practical wisdom—he would accept the equitable exception to the law.

---

[23] *Ibid.*, ii, 12–1130b 30.

[24] *Ibid.*, viii, 8–1135b 20.

[25] *Ibid.*, x, 6–1137b 25. Equity is discussed again and more extensively and is illustrated by many examples in Aristotle's *Rhetoric*, Book I, Ch. xiii and part of Ch. xv—1373b 1; 1374a 1; 1374b 1; 1375a 25-1375b 5.

Friendship

Aristotelian ethics extols the good and wise man, for he is the happy man. He is not the stoic man who lives in splendid isolation and gives such absolute primacy to reason that he has only contempt for emotion. The Aristotelian prudent and wise man recognizes his obligations of justice to others; he knows the value of emotions and cultivates them through the series of moral virtues. He realizes that in order to be happy he needs friends. Man is a political animal, as Aristotle defined him, and while justice removes friction and injuries, it is friendship (*philiā*) that binds citizens into many forms of individual, domestic, and political community.

NATURE AND TYPES OF FRIENDSHIP. The love between two human beings is called "friendship" when men feel goodwill for one another, are aware of one another's good will, and base their own good will on a friend's good qualities of mind and body. Friendship, then, is a conscious, reciprocal well-wishing because of the good qualities of friends.

Friendships can be found in various associations of daily life: between husband and wife, parent and child, brothers and relatives, and among citizens. The three kinds of good are the criteria for the different kinds of friendship. There is the friendship of *utility* based on a mutual exchange of benefits; the friendship of *pleasure* based on what friends derive from one another's company; and the friendship of *virtue* based on moral and intellectual qualities possessed and shared by friends. Without excluding the positive elements of the others, Aristotle considered the third type as the best.

PSYCHOLOGY OF FRIENDSHIP. The essence of friendship can be found more in loving than in being loved. A man loves a friend for his friend's sake. However, men are, metaphysically speaking, beggars who are filled with needs and desires in every age of their lives. Hence, the deepest motivation of friendship is self-love, which amounts to self-projection. In loving another, man recognizes his own self in his friend. This operates both ways, because friendship is a conscious, mutual love of two human beings. Self-love is not a selfish or self-centered egoism. In fact, when sacrificing himself for his friend, a man may lose his fortune, health, or even life, but gain a moral nobility—that is what truly matters in the noble love of oneself.

Intellectual Virtues

Since virtue is knowledge, the intellectual virtues mark the climax of Plato's intellectualism. Dialectic, which means philosophy for Plato, leads the human mind from the realm of opinion fashioned from conjectures and beliefs collected in this sensible world and helps it climb toward the intellectual knowledge of Ideas. Both moral and intellectual virtues have their paradigms in the world of Forms (Ideas); and only intellectual contemplation, the act of theoretical wisdom, can intuit Ideas. Theoretical wisdom is the queen of all virtues, moral and intellectual. Philosophers who dedicate their lives to it possess knowledge; non-philosophers, who live in the world of obscure, probable, and unstable opinions, do not possess real knowledge. Consequently, the philosophers must lead the non-philosophers. Plato could not help but make philosophers the rulers or kings in his republic.

Aristotle also considered intellectual virtues not only a fitting subject for ethics, but the essence of ethics. However, to him these virtues are formal causes of moral virtues and, consequently, moral conduct for each individual man.

Moral virtue is a choice according to right rule or principle of the means to an end. This right rule or principle, which determines the mean of moral virtue, is found in the intellect and is exercised by practical wisdom, which is itself an intellectual virtue.

A man may be inclined by nature toward good, but if he lacks prudence to guide him, this natural virtuous inclination will never develop into a proper, fixed virtue and good character. On the other hand, simple prudence without the moral virtues of friendship, justice, courage, and self-control will not produce good character. The fact that we know what is good does not guarantee that we will do the good. Moral virtues dispose the various faculties to cooperate with practical wisdom.

Indeed, Aristotle believed that the intellectual virtues are formal causes of human happiness as well as of moral conduct. If we want to know what happiness is we must study not only the moral but the intellectual virtues to discover which of these two classes is better. There was no doubt in the mind of Aristotle that primacy belongs to the intellectual virtues and, among them, to wisdom. Wisdom is the formal cause of happiness; practical wisdom ensures the right means for attaining happiness while theoretical wisdom produces happiness. It is not surprising then that Aristotle dedicated all of Book VI of his *Nicomachean Ethics* to the intellectual virtues.

Contemplative and Deliberative Intellect

The rational faculty of the soul can be divided into the contemplative or theoretical and the deliberative or calculative intellect. The first contemplates *invariable, necessary,* and *eternal* things, the essences and their transcendental properties and, in particular, truth. The second considers *variable, contingent,* and *temporal* things in their relation to right desire and works out the rules of conduct.

Thought alone does not move us to act, but rather thought motivated by right desire; the result of this combination of thought and desire is moral choice. The three elements in the soul that are relevant to action are sensation (*aisthesis*), desire (*orexis*), and intellect (*nous*).

Sensation does not move to action, by which Aristotle meant distinctly human or moral action. Involved here is Aristotle's distinction between man and animals: Animals respond to sense stimuli but lack reason, which leads to genuine action, deliberate and responsible. Desire alone cannot move to action because it is the irrational part of the soul. Only when desire is deliberate, when it has been determined by reason, does it influence human action.

We see then that the most important factor in human conduct is the intellect presiding over the process of deliberation: "If the choice is to be good, both the principle must be true and the desire right, and that desire must pursue the same things as principle affirms." [26] This principle or intellect is the practical, deliberative, or calculative reason seeking the truth in order to act.

Both the theoretical and the practical intellect seek the truth, the former for its own sake, the latter for the direction of action. "Therefore, their respective virtues are those dispositions which will best qualify them to attain truth." [27]

Virtues of Theoretical Intellect

Science (epistēmē) is concerned with the necessary and invariable and eternal truths. It is "the quality whereby we demonstrate" or give proof by deduction, and it can be communicated by teaching. Teaching always starts with the known and proceeds by induction or deduction. In Aristotle's view, only deduction leads to demonstration and hence to scientific knowledge.

Intellect or intuitive reason (nous) is the faculty of rational intuition whereby we grasp the ultimate principles from which science begins. Intellect proceeds in this task by induction which, for Aristotle, means "the process whereby after experience of a certain number of particular instances, the mind grasps a universal truth which then and afterwards is seen to be self-evident." [28] Theoretical wisdom (sophiā) is a union of intuitive intellect and science directed to the most exalted objects, the most valued, perfect, and absolute truths, namely, those of metaphysics, mathematics, and natural philosophy.

Virtues of Deliberative Intellect

PRUDENCE. Practical wisdom or prudence (phronēsis) is the ability to deliberate well about what is good for oneself and for others. The deliberation is not about particular states such as health and strength, but about what is useful as a means to the good life of man in general. ". . . It is a truth-attaining rational quality, concerned with action in relation to things that are good or bad for human beings." [29] Man must know wherein his happiness lies (it will be shown that it lies in a contemplative life) and then he

---

[26] Ibid., VI, ii, 2–1139a 25.
[27] Ibid., ii, 6–1139b 10.
[28] W. D. Ross, Aristotle, 5th ed. (New York: Barnes & Noble, 1964), p. 217.
[29] N.E., VI, v, 4–1140b 5.

must choose the means to attain it. Since no one deliberates about things that cannot vary, nor about things not within his power to do, practical wisdom thus differs from science. It is also different from theoretical wisdom because its primary realm is that of particular facts, things, and events.

ANALYSIS OF PRUDENT REASONING. A complete prudential judgment is a complex act; its principal ingredient is an act of deliberation, and deliberation is practical reasoning through the practical syllogism. The major premise is the most universal ethical principle: Live in accordance with right reason. The minor premise contains a general moral principle or conclusion that derives immediately from the first moral principle. It can be expressed as follows: "Such and such a kind of action is good." This assertion covers all similar cases of that kind of action and, hence, it has a universal character. It is worth remarking here that there is another implicit minor premise: "This action of mine, here and now, happens to be of such kind." This is, of course, nothing but an application of the universal minor to the particular minor; however, it is a necessary step to a particular conclusion. The conclusion makes a particular judgment about the particular fact and tells us what to do here and now, in this or that case.

The following example should clarify the process of practical reasoning:

Major: Live in accordance with right reason.
Minor: Take care of your health.
(Minor assumed: My reading late into the night hurts my eyes.)

Conclusion: I must stop reading late into the night.

The major premise, containing the universal moral principle, is grasped by the practical intuitive intellect. The practical deliberative intellect extends the general moral principle to all cases included in its minor premise. The conclusion, which is completely particular, is grasped again by the practical intuitive intellect through some kind of direct perception. The principal characteristic of intuitive knowledge is its immediacy or direct contact with the truth of things. This is true for the major premise and for the conclusion. The former is self-evident, while the latter refers to the immediate datum of experience.

This immediacy, however, does not imply intuitionism. The crucial role of practical reasoning consists in linking the middle term of the minor to both the major premise and the conclusion of the practical syllogism.

Not all men, however, will be able to follow the practical syllogism throughout. In fact, most people will reach the right conclusion without consciously passing through a fixed pattern of reasoning. They will do that from long experience and good temperament. On the whole, their moral knowledge is perceived by experience rather than by any deliberative reasoning.

Prudence is not only concerned with the personal affairs of the individual man, but also with the affairs of the family and state. Statesmanship is exercised through the legislative, deliberative, and judicial functions, and practical wisdom is necessary in each one of these.

ART. The second virtue of practical or deliberative intellect is art (*technē*). Man shapes or molds the world around him by mastering its matter and channeling its energies in order to make for himself and his descendants a better place in which to live. Through artistry man is able to embellish his surroundings and refine, enhance, and enrich his life. This enhancement of life is the subject of art in its broad Aristotelian sense; it involves all skills—applied science or technology, fine arts, music, dance, and literature.

Art is concerned with *products* (*ergon*) which are neither necessary nor natural. While practical wisdom is concerned with the man himself and his conduct, art, as an intellectual virtue, is directed exclusively to the product. "It follows that an art is the same thing as a rational quality, concerned with making, that reasons truly." [30]

The underlying question in Book VI—what is the right rule of conduct—is now clear. The right rule is the one reached by the deliberative analysis of the practically wise man; it tells him that the end of human life is best attained by certain actions that are intermediate between extremes. Obedience to such a rule is moral virtue. [31]

Natural Moral Law

The seeds of the natural moral law tradition can be found early in Greek literature. In *Antigone,* Sophocles wrote of "the law that all men have in their hearts." Yet the idea of natural law remained largely undeveloped until the time of Socrates, Plato, and Aristotle. In fact, the Sophists explicitly rejected the natural law and held instead that law is only convention, and morality is simply mores or customs.

To this prevailing Sophist view Plato took sharp exception, holding instead that law is rooted in nature and both are unchangeable. Both have their full reality by virtue of participating in their eternal and immutable counterparts in the realm of Ideas: there, and only there, is to be found the real Man, the real Law, and the real Justice. These can be reached by intellect alone, and only in an imperfect way while it is still in company with the body. Wherein, then, lies the wisdom of the good life? In the soul's detachment from the body as much as possible:

> Surely the soul can best reflect when it is free of all distractions such as hearing or sight or pain or pleasure of any kind—that is, when it ignores the body and becomes as far as possible independ-

---

[30] *Ibid.,* iv, 3–1140a 5.
[31] Ross, p. 221.

ent, avoiding all physical contacts and associations as much as it can, in its search for reality.[32]

Plato's great merit was his emphasis on the intellect and wisdom in ethics. But he neglected man's drives, passions, and ambitions. He disembodied man, taking too negative a view of man's bodily components.

Aristotle, greatly inspired by his teacher, followed Plato's main design of intellectualist ethics but built his ethical theory around man's earthly life. His approach to the natural law problem was not fully developed, but he left insights that enabled his successors to formulate natural law in intellectualist ethics.

From the union of the basic characteristics of Aristotelian ethics— teleology and intellectualism—and from Aristotle's explanation of nature, justice, and law, tradition derives the ethical teaching on natural moral law. The theory that gradually emerged from the Peripatetic school was developed by the Stoics in the third century B.C., eloquently affirmed by Cicero (106–143), and incorporated into the doctrine of eternal law by both Augustine (354–430) and Aquinas, and by the twentieth-century followers of Aquinas. Natural moral law has thus become one of the constituent philosophic elements of our Western culture.

What Is a Man?

Attempts to seek the meaning of the natural moral law, which is supposed to guide human moral conduct, must reach some kind of agreement on these questions: What is a man? What is human nature? Man has been called a microcosm, a small universe, having within his constitution physical, biological, psychosomatic, and mental elements. The great thinkers have reduced this combination to the union of the body (the subject of man's material qualities) and the mind or soul (the subject of man's intellectual qualities). Plato saw man as the incarnate spirit, while Aristotle saw him as the unique animal possessing reason. The nature of the union of mind and body was explained differently by the two great Greeks, and the mind-body relationship has become, since the days of Descartes, one of the most hotly debated problems. Furthermore, man is not only a body-soul unit; he is a person—a self-conscious, self-determined, somehow independent master of his acts and his destiny. Man is a responsible subject of his acts because he is endowed with reason and freedom.

In order to discover real human nature and to formulate the rules of human conduct, reason has to understand the whole of human nature. Man is to be understood, first, in all his *parts*—body and soul; second, in all his *needs* and *drives;* and, third, in all his *natural relations*.

In regard to drives or tendencies, "Aristotle neither praises nor condemns the tendencies inherent in man. They are indifferent in themselves; they become good or bad according as they are subjugated to, or allowed

---

[32] Plato, *Phaedo,* 65c.

to assert themselves against the 'right rule' which our reasonable nature grasps for itself and seeks to impose on them." [33] However, the Stoics were the principal advocates of the natural tendencies of man as the foundation of the natural law. In their view, self-love is most fundamental, followed by love for one's fellow man. From these are derived the precepts of natural law: preserve yourself by providing food, shelter, clothing, and rest to maintain life and health; reproduce your own kind; respect your family and your social ties; and, above all, be reasonable.

Expressing these tendencies and corresponding needs in modern terms, we may list them briefly as follows: *organic,* which involves self-preservation, self-defense, and self-perpetuation in one's offspring; *psychosomatic,* which amounts to sense-knowledge and sense-feeling; *mental,* which includes intellectual striving for truth, moral aiming at the good, esthetic tending to beauty, and religious aspiring to the meeting with divinity; and *social drive,* which is directed toward the family, state, and intermediate social groups in order to find help and companionship and to build up social well-being.

Finally, human nature cannot be fully understood without knowing about man's natural relations, which are built into human nature and cannot be ignored by reason. For example: the relation of man, a contingent being, to God, the necessary being; the relation of man to those around him—his family and friends; the relation of man toward the goods of the earth and the many material and mental products of his labor. Man needs food and liquids, clothing and shelter, work and rest for his body as much as he needs ideas, judgments, and conclusions that satisfy his mind.

Human nature is *given* to us—it is man's structure and the source of his activity as understood in the metaphysical and physical, the static and the dynamic, the other-centered and the self-centered senses. It cannot be the principle of its own guidance, harmony, or order, or of the subordination of all its complex parts, needs, and relations. There must be within human nature a principle that guides it. Reason, a discursive power of intellect, is called upon to illuminate these manifold elements and direct man to his end. This way reason finds out which human acts befit human nature and it formulates the basic and first law of nature: live in accordance with human nature in all its essential aspects.

Definition of the Moral Rule of Human Conduct

When the narrow boundaries of the Greek city-states had become obsolete because of the conquests of Alexander the Great (356–323 B.C.), the philosophers that followed Aristotle had to face a new historical fact: man had become a citizen of the world. The multitude of tribes and nations, different in customs and languages, were united first by Greek, then by Roman, and in the Middle Ages by Christian culture. This new historical setting brought a new philosophical question: Is the particular code of laws

[33] Ross, p. 193.

of each city-state or even of each nation a supreme instance of morality or righteousness? Or is morality itself rooted in some universal law valid for all men? Is there such a thing as the common ethical heritage of all mankind, a natural code of morality to which all individuals and nations could turn in spite of their sociocultural differences?

Aristotle remained faithful all his life to the city-state political and moral frame. But he understood that just as there is a particular and universal justice, there must be a corresponding particular and universal law for all men. It would seem that Aristotle meant by universal law the law of human nature.

For the Stoics, the supreme moral ideal is to live in accordance with Nature. Nature includes everything in the vast universe, and the whole of Nature is penetrated and ruled by Reason. The Reason that keeps the universe in order has different names—a sentient being, a force or even fire, the soul of the world, the wisdom and providence of gods, Fate or Necessity—but they are really alike in that Reason is immanent in all of them.

In spite of this haziness, there is a little doubt that the Stoics gave primacy to Reason in Nature. To say that the moral idea is to act according to Nature is to say "live according to Reason." And this Reason is called Right Reason when it agrees with the order established in the universe. Gods, men, animals, plants, and minerals blend into one single commonwealth ruled by Reason.

Cicero rejected the rationalism of the Stoics, but he approached ethical problems with the probabilistic criterion of the New Academy.[34] However, he saw clearly the universal, or natural human law: "True law is right reason in agreement with nature; it is of universal application, unchanging and everlasting . . . valid for all nations and all times. . . . Whoever is disobedient is fleeing from himself and denying his human nature, and by reason of this very fact he will suffer the worst penalties, even if he escapes what is commonly considered punishment. . . ."[35]

Although St. Augustine stressed that part of the Stoics' natural law which points to divine reason, there is a considerable difference between the two beliefs. The divine reason of the Stoics does not belong to a personal god, but is diffused in nature and immanent in things. The Divine Reason of Augustine belongs to a personal God who transcends nature, although he is present everywhere. Augustine's Christian God is the Creator

---

[34] The New Academy (second and first centuries B.C.): a school of philosophy that succeeded the Old and the Middle Academies—all of them successors to Plato's Academy. The two heads of the New Academy, Carneades of Cyrene (c. 214–129 B.C.) and Philo of Larissa (c. 159–86 B.C.), developed the criterion of probability in matters of conduct in opposition to both extremes: Stoic dogmatism and Middle Academy scepticism. Their opponent, Antiochus of Ascalon (fl. 68 B.C.), returned to the Old Academy criterion of evidence in moral matters. Cicero was strongly influenced by both Philo and Antiochus.

[35] Marcus T. Cicero, *De re publica* III, xxii, 33, quoted by Lactantius, *De institutionibus divinis* VI, 8, 6–9. Also, Cicero, *De Legibus* I, v – II, vii (Cambridge, Mass.: Harvard University Press, 1961), pp. 313–79.

and Lawgiver, the Provider and Governor of the universe. He plans, directs, and executes every thing and every move in nature. His law is found impressed in human reason and so becomes the natural rule or law of man. This law is the highest reason and the ultimate law to which men must submit. It is called *eternal law*.

For the solution to the natural law problem, Augustine, the theologian, looked to God. The philosopher can look for the natural law in the nature of man and of the universe around him. This world is his realm of reality and only through reasoning about it can he reach God indirectly. Nevertheless, Augustine did have a philosophical point, too. The question of the ultimate foundation of the natural law is not an idle one. Since the natural law is inherent in human nature, the question is legitimately raised: How did it come to be there? And who is the ultimate designer of human nature and its rule of conduct? Who is the highest enforcer of this rule?

St. Thomas tried to unite the Augustinian and Aristotelian views of the natural law. As a theologian, he agreed with Augustine that natural law is "a participation of the eternal law." But at the same time he accepted Aristotle's teleology and intellectualism, as well as his definitions of "nature" and "law." From these elements he said, as Aristotle did, that man is destined to fulfill his end or aim guided by his rational nature. By combining the thought of Augustine and Aristotle with his own, Aquinas was able to offer the following explanation of natural law:

> Now among other things, the rational creature is subject to divine providence in a more excellent way, in so far as it itself partakes of a share of providence, by being provident both for itself and for others. Therefore, it has a share of the eternal reason, whereby it has a natural inclination to its proper act and end.[36]

By sharing the eternal reason of God and his Providence, man is able to discover intuitively his natural tendencies, to formulate them into rules of conduct, and to live accordingly, guiding himself to his proper function and destiny. Man becomes, in a way, his own lawgiver and providence.

The content of the natural law is based, according to the Stoic tradition, upon the natural tendencies of man. The presupposition is that whatever is natural to man is good for him, and whatever is unnatural to man is bad for him.

From Aquinas' rudimentary listing of the human natural inclinations [37] and from the further developments of Aquinas' followers up to the present day, we may summarize the basic precept of natural law as follows: Do good and avoid evil. Or, as we would say today: Live in accordance with human nature in all its basic parts, needs, and relations, harmoniously ordered by practical and right reason. The precepts springing from

---

[36] *Summa Theologica*, I–II, 91, 2, in Pegis, II, 750.
[37] *Ibid.*, 94, 2, p. 774. Also, *Summa Contra Gentiles*, III, 129, trans. by Vernon J. Bourke (Garden City, N.Y.: Doubleday & Co., 1956), pp. 162–64.

the numerous natural inclinations or tendencies of man immediately follow. As to these basic rules there is considerable agreement among men of all races, creeds, and cultures. As to the immediate or remote conclusions that involve moral reasoning and, particularly, as to their applications to the individual cases of human conduct, there is considerable disagreement among humans. Human nature is essentially and dynamically the same in all men—hence, the agreement in principles—but that same nature grows in different environments and under various pressures and handicaps. We see a considerable variety among humans in moral customs and traditions and different conclusions and applications of the basic moral insights common to all men.

We may sum up this discussion on the natural law by attempting to give a scientifically acceptable definition of it based on the tradition presented here. Natural law consists of the harmony between natural human tendencies and reason. All virtues, rights, and duties spring from reasonably understood and reasonably satisfied human tendencies with a view to the well-being of the whole man. Natural law comes into play where man's tendencies are humanized, intellectualized, reasonably subordinated, and made habitually well-ruled. Natural law, the true law of human development, is the harmonious union of human drives and moral ideals, worked out by reason and converted into norms of human conduct.

The Ideal Life: Happiness

Pleasure

Ethics is deeply concerned with the problem of pleasure (*hedonē*). Before we can discuss the final problem, happiness, we must touch, at least briefly, on the nature, kinds, and value of pleasure—for most men and not a few philosophers consider happiness and pleasure identical.

For Plato pleasure is a movement parallel to that of human activity. We enjoy it imperfectly and only a little at a time. Pleasure is divided into the unmixed or pure, proper to the intellectual part of the soul, and the mixed or impure, belonging to the body. Men cannot live by pure pleasure alone, because their souls are still united with their bodies. But neither can men live by impure pleasure alone since such a life would be subhuman, or animal, rather than human. However, if the pleasure of the body be innocent and moderate so that it does not impede the intellectual pleasure (insofar as it can be enjoyed in this world), the two kinds of pleasure may be harmoniously blended. Honey, taken as a figure for pleasure, and water, taken as a figure for intelligence and its contemplative life, mixed in due proportion, make a pleasant drink.[38]

According to Aristotle, the pleasure we feel consciously seems com-

---

[38] Plato, *Philebus,* 61c. p. 1143.

plete and satisfactory at any moment of its duration. If we feel it at all, we feel it now as a whole. Thus pleasure cannot be a motion since the latter is characterized by specific parts, specific duration, differing successive movements, and completion only when the end is reached.

The conditions of pleasure are those of activity on every level: perceiving through the senses, imagining, remembering, reasoning, and contemplating—all of which involve a subject, or faculty, and an object. The unimpeded activity of healthy senses, directed to their finest objects, constitutes pleasurable activity. When these proper conditions prevail for the intellect, thought and speculation are also pleasurable.

The role of pleasure is to perfect, stimulate, intensify, and reward activity. Pleasure subsides when activity subsides and ends when it ends; it cannot last forever because activity cannot last forever.

Pleasures, like activities, differ in kind, some being *necessary* (connected with bodily needs such as food, drink, and sex), others simply *desirable* (such as honors, wealth, victory). Aristotle also distinguished *bad pleasures,* unnatural ones stemming from bad habit or disease of some kind and classified as morbid or bestial. Finally, there are *pleasures of the intellect:* reasoning and contemplation.

In order to discover which of these pleasures are truly human and ethical, we must remember that in ethics we are concerned not with pleasure in itself, but with good pleasure, that which completes or perfects the functions proper to man. Although the definition of good pleasure furnishes an objective criterion for judging pleasures, our human weakness renders us less than effective in applying it. Aristotle suggested that we permit the wise man of good character to be the judge; as the bad man's activities are accompanied by bad pleasures, so the good man's activities are accompanied by good pleasures and are a fitting model of ethical action.

Happiness Is an Activity

We may recall from Book I of the *Nicomachean Ethics* that happiness must be an activity desirable for itself. Three kinds of activity that are thought to be desirable for themselves are: actions in conformity with virtue, agreeable amusements, and contemplation. Amusements, however, cannot be regarded as the purpose of life, for they represent relaxation from labors and restoration of lost energies needed to continue working. Aristotle included among amusements both the pleasures of body and the pleasures of mind. He had no doubt that "to make amusement the object of our serious pursuits and our work seems foolish and childish to the excess." On the contrary, he believed that "Anarchasis' motto, 'Play in order that you may work,' is felt to be the right rule." [39]

In Book I Aristotle said that happiness is activity in conformity with virtue, but he distinguished between moral and intellectual virtue. The first, ruled by practical wisdom, engenders in man a disposition to good emo-

---

[39] *N.E.,* X, vi, 6–1176b 32–6.

tions and actions. The life of man as a composite being ruled by practical reason is "the best human life, the completest expression of human nature." [40] This means that every man may reach happiness by living a virtuous life. The just, brave, self-restrained, and prudent man lives a good moral life and is happy on his human level because he is faithful to his composite human nature; he is truly man and is happy. On the other hand, good moral conduct will help him to ascend to the third and highest degree of happiness: contemplation.

Contemplative Life

In *Phaedo* Plato viewed this world as a world of shadow rather than reality. Consequently, in it men possess only an imperfect knowledge of Ideas and, thus, an imperfect happiness. To remedy this situation Plato's wise man spends as much time as he can in contemplating Ideas; hazy though they are, they are the source of his happiness. However, the real bliss in the contemplation of Ideas awaits men only in the afterlife. The first condition for reaching truth and reality is the liberation of the soul from the body. As Plato put it: The philosopher's true study is to learn how to die. And as Socrates said before drinking the hemlock: "Then it is a fact, Simmias, that true philosophers make dying their profession, and that to them of all men death is least alarming."

Regardless of the difficulties of achieving it, for Aristotle the happiness of contemplation is envisioned in the context of this world. Since man is a composite being, his earthly happiness will involve a composite of mental, bodily, and external goods used in conformity with moral virtue. While this moral happiness is purely human, contemplative happiness resembles the divine. Intellect, which grasps and contemplates ideas immediately and intuitively, is set aside from reason, the discursive power of thinking, as well as from all other functions, powers, and emotions of the soul. Being indestructible, it is eternal and will share the life of God after the death of the body.

Nothing else will survive—neither reasoning, remembering, loving, nor hating—since these are all functions of the embodied soul; but the pure and simple exercise of mind, contemplation, will endure. Contemplation is the proper activity of God. He is Pure Form and Pure Act, and this Pure Act is the contemplation of himself. The contemplation of the Pure Form, supreme reality without any matter or potency, is the thinking of the pure thought. Aristotle characterized divine life by saying, "Its thinking is a thinking on thinking." [41]

Similarly, the objects of intellectual contemplation here on earth, and more so after death, will be those that have no matter attached to them. These are intelligible forms that theoretical wisdom offers to the human

---

[40] H. H. Joachim, *Aristotle: The Nicomachean Ethics, A Commentary*, ed. by D. A. Rees (Oxford: Clarendon Press, 1951), p. 287.
[41] *Metaphysics*, XII, 9–1074a 34, in McKeon, p. 885.

mind: metaphysics, offering being *qua* being; mathematics, offering being as abstract quantity; and physics (philosophy of nature), offering being detached from particular and changeable matter. Truth has primacy in the Aristotelian view of contemplation. The good, the beauty, and the unity of things would normally follow truth on a list of transcendental objects grasped by the intellect, but these are not expressly mentioned by Aristotle.[42]

Such a contemplative life requires tranquillity and leisure, but in our world today man is notably deprived of both. Feverish activity, restlessness, and tension, coupled with overcrowded and noisy city life, take from him two elements indispensable for contemplative happiness: silence and solitude. In fact, with many activity has become an obsession and silence and solitude intolerable. In considering the distractions of modern living, the struggle for existence in a competitive society, and the erroneous ideas about the real meaning of human well-being, we cannot wonder that few achieve the contemplative life here, in this life. But the admitted obstacles to its achievement are not enough reason to discard such a sublime concept. We work to earn leisure, and leisure is a happy time for the enrichment of the intellectual or rational part of our selves. The smallest share in the contemplative life exceeds all material wealth.

Conclusion

Looking back at intellectualist ethical theory we may point out these milestones: We started with the study of the good as an end and found that purposiveness is embedded not only in the universe but in human conduct as well. The logical study of ends and means then led us to the supreme good for man, his total well-being or happiness.

Happiness consists in the life lived in conformity with virtue, whose nature Plato identified with knowledge, while Aristotle and Aquinas found it to be the mean between excess and defect in feelings and emotions. Since the very essence of the virtuous life lies in the deliberation and choice of the virtuous mean, they, together with the impediments to and modifiers of choice, were closely examined.

After Aristotle had clarified the issues of human happiness, virtue, and choice, he devoted a great deal of his *Nicomachean Ethics* (just as Plato did in his *Republic* and Aquinas in the whole of his *Summa Theologica*) to the study of individual moral and intellectual virtues. Ethics is the science of the good life: thus Aristotle discussed the variety of virtues exercised in daily life. The study of the principal moral virtues (self-control, courage, justice, and friendship) is necessary since they control emotions and ac-

---

[42] See Joachim, pp. 286–97, for an interesting discussion on the intellect, the contemplative life, as well as the divine life in its sublimity, and the difficulties inherent in Aristotelian doctrine. This is, however, a matter of philosophical psychology.

tions; the study of intellectual virtues is also necessary in order to discover the rule or principle by which the right mean is found in feelings and actions.

After the norm of morality was found to be right reason as it functions in the mind of the prudent man, we deepened our study to discover whether there is in every mature human being a law of nature leading him to his happiness. This law, called the natural moral law, was discussed in the light of post-Aristotelian ethical theory, primarily that of the Stoics and Aquinas.

Happiness, the ultimate end of man's striving, was examined last. We turned first to the problem of pleasure, too often identified with happiness, in order to distinguish the two and clarify their relationship. Although we have seen that Aristotle recognized the great importance of the moral happiness that leads to the contemplative, there is no doubt that he considered contemplation the essence of human happiness. Aristotle's ethics is, in the final analysis, an intellectualist ethics, retaining its ultimate connection with the pure intellectualism in the ethics of his teacher, Plato.

Glossary

(The following key Aristotelian terms are explained by quoting appropriate passages from Aristotle's works. Unless otherwise indicated, the quotations are from the *Nicomachean Ethics*. The numbers are the standard reference to the Berlin edition of Aristotle, the numbering system that is followed in most editions of Aristotle's works. A separate glossary for the ethical terms of Aquinas is not included since he followed Aristotle's meaning whenever he used those terms in a purely philosophical context. Aquinas' corresponding Latin terms are entered after the Greek terms of Aristotle.)

ART (*technē, ars*):
Craftsmanship of any kind, including both fine arts and crafts. "Art, therefore, . . . is a rational quality concerned with making, that reasons truly." (1140a 20.)

CHARACTER (*ethos, mos, moris*):
A fixed pattern of feeling and acting. Men "acquire a particular quality [character] by constantly acting in a particular way." (1114a 7.)

CHOICE (*proairesis, electio*):
Choice is the deliberate decision concerning moral conduct. "As then the object of choice is something within our power which after deliberation we desire, choice will be a deliberate desire of things in our power; . . ." (1113a 10.)

CONTEMPLATION (*theoriā, contemplatio*):
Contemplation is an intuitive act of the intellect, a direct grasp of eternal truths. ". . . among human activities that which is most akin to the divine activity of contemplation will be the greatest source of happiness." (1178b 22.)

COURAGE (*andreiā, fortitudo*):
"Courage is the observance of the mean in relation to things that inspire confidence [excess] or fear [defect]." (1116a 10.)

END (*telos, finis*):
The aim, end of activity. "That for the sake of which a thing is done." (*Physics,* 194b 33.)

GOOD (*agathon, bonum*):
"The good is that at which all things aim." (1094a 1–4). "The good of man is the active exercise of his soul's faculties in conformity with excellence or virtue, . . ." (1098a 15–20.)

HABIT (*hexis, habitus*):
"The dispositions [*hexeis*] are the formed states of character in virtue of which we are well or ill disposed in respect of the emotions [and actions]." (1105b 25.)

HAPPINESS (*eudaimoniā, felicitas*):
That well-being in man that is the result of well-doing. "An activity of the perfect life in accord with perfect virtue, i.e., theoretical wisdom." (*Eudemian Ethics,* 1219a 38–9.) "Happiness, therefore, being found to be something final and self-sufficient, is the End at which all the actions aim." (1097b 20.)

INTELLECT (*nous, intellectus*):
Intuitive rational power. "If then the qualities whereby we attain truth, and are never led into falsehood, whether about things invariable or things variable, are Scientific Knowledge, Prudence, Wisdom, and Intelligence, and if the quality which enables us to apprehend first principles cannot be any one among three of these . . . it remains that first principles must be apprehended by intelligence." (1141a 3–8.) "[Mind] seems to be an independent substance implanted within the soul and to be incapable of being destroyed." (*De Anima,* 408b 15–20.)

INVOLUNTARY (*akōn, involuntarium*):
"[The act] is involuntary only when it causes the agent pain and regret." (1110b 18.)

JUSTICE (*dikaiosynē, iustitia*):
"Justice then in this sense [the general sense] is perfect Virtue, though with a qualification, namely, that it is displayed towards others." (1129b 25–35.) "Justice [in a particular sense] is the virtue through which everybody enjoys his own possessions in accordance with the law." (*Rhetoric,* 1366b 8–10.)

LAW (*nomos, lex*):
". . . law . . . is a rule, emanating from a certain wisdom and intelligence, that has compulsory force." (1180a 12–23.)

MEAN (*mesotēs, medietas*):

Mean of virtue in emotions and actions. "By the mean of the thing I denote a point equally distant from either extreme, which is one and the same for everybody; by the mean relative to us, that amount which is neither too much nor too little, and this is not one and the same for everybody." (1106a 30.)

NATURE (*physis, natura*):

Source of spontaneous self-growth and self-arrest. "Each of them [the things constituted by nature, as opposed to those made by art] has *within itself* a principle of motion and of stationariness . . . ." (*Physics,* 192b 14–16.)

PLEASURE (*hedonē, delectatio*):

Pleasure is intended to perfect the activity of human powers. ". . . It follows that the activity of any of the senses [and more so of intellect] is at its best when the sense-organ being in the best condition is directed to the best of its objects; and this activity will be the most perfect and the pleasantest." (1174a 15–20.)

PRUDENCE (*phronēsis, prudentia*):

Practical wisdom that guides moral virtues. "Prudence is [the knowledge of the] right principle in matters of conduct." (1144b 25.)

RATIONAL ACTION (*praxis, actio*):

Human conduct; acting and doing. "The class of things that admit of variation includes both things made and actions done. But making is different from doing . . . . Hence the rational quality concerned with doing [i.e., prudence] is different from the rational quality concerned with making [i.e., art]." (1140a 1–5.)

RIGHT RULE OR PRINCIPLE (*orthos, logos, recta ratio*):

Right or sound reason is that rational ability which, by the mediation of practical wisdom, fixes for every virtue the right mean in emotions and actions in the right set of circumstances. Moral virtue "is a disposition determined by the right principle; and the right principle is the principle determined by Prudence." (1144b 23.)

SCIENCE (*epistēmē, scientia*):

Scientific, or syllogistic, knowledge is "the quality whereby we demonstrate," i.e., give proof by deduction from first principles and arrive at certain conclusions. (1139b 31–33.)

TEMPERANCE (*sophrosynē, temperantia*):

Self-control; self-restraint. "The temperate man desires the right thing in the right way at the right time, which is what principle (*logos*) ordains." (1119b 15.)

VIRTUE (*aretē, virtus*):

Excellence of character. "Moral virtue is a mean between two vices, one of excess and the other of defect; and it is such a mean because it aims at hitting the middle point in feelings and actions." (1109a 20–23.)

VOLUNTARY (*hekōn, voluntarium*):

"Voluntary act would seem to be an act of which the origin lies in the agent, who knows the particular circumstances in which he is acting." (1111a 22.)

WISDOM (*sophiā, sapientia*):

Theoretical wisdom is a union of intuitive and scientific knowledge. "Wisdom must be a combination of Intelligence and Scientific Knowledge: it must be the consummated knowledge of the most exalted objects." (1141a 15.)

Plato

PLATO (*c.* 427–347 B.C.) was born of a noble Athenian family. His early ambitions were political, but the tyranny and anarchy in Athens which followed her disastrous defeat in the Peloponnesian War dissuaded him from a career in politics. Plato's philosophical outlook was shaped by the teachings of Socrates, and he was greatly affected by Socrates' execution in 399. For several years he traveled extensively in Greece, Egypt, Italy, and Sicily; three times he tried, unsuccessfully, to introduce a rule of law and order into Sicily. Disappointed, he returned to Athens about 387 and founded the famous Academy. Plato is best known for his dialogues, literary masterpieces that have had a profound influence on Western thought. His more technical works are no longer extant.

Can Virtue Be Taught?

MENO: Can you tell me, Socrates—is virtue something that can be taught? 70 Or does it come by practice? Or is it neither teaching nor practice that gives it to a man but natural aptitude or something else?

SOCRATES: Well, Meno, in the old days the Thessalians had a great reputation among the Greeks for their wealth and their horsemanship. Now b it seems they are philosophers as well—especially the men of Larissa, where your friend Aristippus comes from. It is Gorgias who has done it. He went to that city and captured the hearts of the foremost of the Aleuadae for his wisdom—among them your own admirer Aristippus—not to speak of other leading Thessalians. In particular he got you into the c habit of answering any question you might be asked, with the confidence and dignity appropriate to those who know the answers, just as he himself invites questions of every kind from anyone in the Greek world who wishes to ask, and never fails to answer them. But here at Athens, my dear Meno, it is just the reverse. There is a dearth of wisdom, and it looks as if it had migrated from our part of the country to yours. At any rate if you put your 71 question to any of our people, they will all alike laugh and say, You must think I am singularly fortunate, to know whether virtue can be taught or

From pp. 115–57 of Plato, *Meno*, in *Plato: Protagoras and Meno*, translated by W. K. C. Guthrie. © 1956 by Penguin Books Ltd., Harmondsworth, Middlesex. Reprinted by permission of the publisher.

how it is acquired. The fact is that far from knowing whether it can be taught, I have no idea what virtue itself is.

b   That is my own case. I share the poverty of my fellow countrymen in this respect, and confess to my shame that I have no knowledge about virtue at all. And how can I know a property of something when I don't even know what it is? Do you suppose that somebody entirely ignorant who Meno is could say whether he is handsome and rich and wellborn or the reverse? Is that possible, do you think?

MENO: No. But is this true about yourself, Socrates, that you don't
c   even know what virtue is? Is this the report that we are to take home about you?

SOCRATES: Not only that, you may say also that, to the best of my belief, I have never yet met anyone who did know.

MENO: What! Didn't you meet Gorgias when he was here?

SOCRATES: Yes.

MENO: And you still didn't think he knew?

SOCRATES: I'm a forgetful sort of person, and I can't say just now what
d   I thought at the time. Probably he did know, and I expect you know what he used to say about it. So remind me what it was, or tell me yourself if you will. No doubt you agree with him.

MENO: Yes, I do.

SOCRATES: Then let's leave him out of it, since after all he isn't here. What do you yourself say virtue is? I do ask you in all earnestness not to refuse me, but to speak out. I shall be only too happy to be proved wrong if you and Gorgias turn out to know this, although I said I had never met anyone who did.

e   MENO: But there is no difficulty about it. First of all, if it is manly virtue you are after, it is easy to see that the virtue of a man consists in managing the city's affairs capably, and so that he will help his friends and injure his foes while taking care to come to no harm himself. Or if you want a woman's virtue, that is easily described. She must be a good housewife, careful with her stores and obedient to her husband. Then there is another virtue for a child, male or female, and another for an old man, free or slave as you like, and a great many more kinds of virtue, so that no one need be
72   at a loss to say what it is. For every act and every time of life, with reference to each separate function, there is a virtue for each one of us, and similarly, I should say, a vice.

SOCRATES: I seem to be in luck. I wanted one virtue and I find that you have a whole swarm of virtues to offer. But seriously, to carry on this
b   metaphor of the swarm, suppose I asked you what a bee is, what is its essential nature, and you replied that bees were of many different kinds. What would you say if I went on to ask, And is it in being bees that they are many and various and different from one another? Or would you agree that it is not in this respect that they differ, but in something else, some other quality like size or beauty?

MENO: I should say that in so far as they are bees, they don't differ from one another at all.

SOCRATES: Suppose I then continued, Well, this is just what I want you   c to tell me. What is that character in respect of which they don't differ at all, but are all the same? I presume you would have something to say?

MENO: I should.

SOCRATES: Then do the same with the virtues. Even if they are many and various, yet at least they all have some common character which makes them virtues. That is what ought to be kept in view by anyone who answers the question, What is virtue? Do you follow me?   d

MENO: I think I do, but I don't yet really grasp the question as I should wish.

SOCRATES: Well, does this apply in your mind only to virtue, that there is a different one for a man and a woman and the rest? Is it the same with health and size and strength, or has health the same character everywhere, if it is health, whether it be in a man or any other creature?   e

MENO: I agree that health is the same in a man or in a woman.

SOCRATES: And what about size and strength? If a woman is strong, will it be the same thing, the same strength, that makes her strong? My meaning is that in its character as strength, it is no different, whether it be in a man or in a woman. Or do you think it is?

MENO: No.

SOCRATES: And will virtue differ, in its character as virtue, whether it   73 be in a child or an old man, a woman or a man?

MENO: I somehow feel that this is not on the same level as the other cases.

SOCRATES: Well then, didn't you say that a man's virtue lay in directing the city well, and a woman's in directing her household well?

MENO: Yes.

SOCRATES: And it is possible to direct anything well—city or house-   b hold or anything else—if not temperately and justly?

MENO: Certainly not.

SOCRATES: And that means with temperance and justice?

MENO: Of course.

SOCRATES: Then both man and woman need the same qualities, justice and temperance, if they are going to be good.

MENO: It looks like it.

SOCRATES: And what about your child and old man? Could they be good if they were incontinent and unjust?

MENO: Of course not.

SOCRATES: They must be temperate and just?

MENO: Yes.

SOCRATES: So everyone is good in the same way, since they become   c good by possessing the same qualities.

MENO: So it seems.

SOCRATES: And if they did not share the same virtue, they would not be good in the same way.

MENO: No.

SOCRATES: Seeing then that they all have the same virtue, try to remember and tell me what Gorgias and you, who share his opinion, say it is.

d   MENO: It must be simply the capacity to govern men, if you are looking for one quality to cover all the instances.

SOCRATES: Indeed I am. But does this virtue apply to a child or a slave? Should a slave be capable of governing his master, and if he does, is he still a slave?

MENO: I hardly think so.

SOCRATES: It certainly doesn't sound likely. And here is another point. You speak of "capacity to govern." Shall we not add, "justly but not otherwise"?

MENO: I think we should, for justice is virtue.

e   SOCRATES: Virtue, do you say, or *a* virtue?

MENO: What do you mean?

SOCRATES: Something quite general. Take roundness, for instance. I should say that it is a shape, not simply that it is shape, my reason being that there are other shapes as well.

MENO: I see your point, and I agree that there are other virtues besides justice.

74   SOCRATES: Tell me what they are. Just as I could name other shapes if you told me to, in the same way mention some other virtues.

MENO: In my opinion then courage is a virtue and temperance and wisdom and dignity and many other things.

SOCRATES: This puts us back where we were. In a different way we have discovered a number of virtues when we were looking for one only. This single virtue, which permeates each of them, we cannot find.

· · ·

77   MENO: It seems to me then, Socrates, that virtue is, in the words of the poet, "to rejoice in the fine and have power," and I define it as desiring fine things and being able to acquire them.

SOCRATES: When you speak of a man desiring fine things, do you mean it is good things he desires?

MENO: Certainly.

SOCRATES: Then do you think some men desire evil and others good? Doesn't everyone, in your opinion, desire good things?

c   MENO: No.

SOCRATES: And would you say that the others suppose evils to be good, or do they still desire them although they recognize them as evil?

MENO: Both, I should say.

SOCRATES: What? Do you really think that anyone who recognizes evils for what they are, nevertheless desires them?

MENO: Yes.

SOCRATES: Desires in what way? To possess them?

MENO: Of course.

SOCRATES: In the belief that evil things bring advantage to their pos-   d
sessor, or harm?

MENO: Some in the first belief, but some also in the second.

SOCRATES: And do you believe that those who suppose evil things bring
advantage understand that they are evil?

MENO: No, that I can't really believe.

SOCRATES: Isn't it clear then that this class, who don't recognize evils   e
for what they are, don't desire evil but what they think is good, though in
fact it is evil; those who through ignorance mistake bad things for good obviously desire the good?

MENO: For them I suppose that is true.

SOCRATES: Now as for those whom you speak of as desiring evils in the
belief that they do harm to their possessor, these presumably know that
they will be injured by them?

MENO: They must.

SOCRATES: And don't they believe that whoever is injured is, in so far
as he is injured, unhappy?

MENO: That too they must believe.

SOCRATES: And unfortunate?   78

MENO: Yes.

SOCRATES: Well, does anybody want to be unhappy and unfortunate?

MENO: I suppose not.

SOCRATES: Then if not, nobody desires what is evil, for what else is unhappiness but desiring evil things and getting them?

MENO: It looks as if you are right, Socrates, and nobody desires what is   b
evil.

SOCRATES: Now you have just said that virtue consists in a wish for
good things plus the power to acquire them. In this definition the wish is
common to everyone, and in that respect no one is better than his neighbor.

MENO: So it appears.

SOCRATES: So if one man is better than another, it must evidently be in
respect of the power, and virtue, according to your account, is the power of
acquiring good things.

MENO: Yes, my opinion is exactly as you now express it.   c

SOCRATES: Let us see whether you have hit the truth this time. You
may well be right. The power of acquiring good things, you say, is virtue?

MENO: Yes.

SOCRATES: And by good do you mean such things as health and
wealth?

MENO: I include the gaining both of gold and silver and of high and
honorable office in the state.

SOCRATES: Are these the only classes of goods that you recognize?

d   MENO: Yes, I mean everything of that sort.

SOCRATES: Right. In the definition of Meno, hereditary guest-friend of the Great King, the acquisition of gold and silver is virtue. Do you add "just and righteous" to the word "acquisition," or doesn't it make any difference to you? Do you call it virtue all the same even if they are unjustly acquired?

MENO: Certainly not.

SOCRATES: Vice then?

MENO: Most certainly.

SOCRATES: So it seems that justice or temperance or piety, or some

e   other part of virtue, must attach to the acquisition. Otherwise, although it is a means to good things, it will not be virtue.

MENO: No, how could you have virtue without these?

SOCRATES: In fact lack of gold and silver, if it results from failure to acquire it—either for oneself or another—in circumstances which would have made its acquisition unjust, is itself virtue.

MENO: It would seem so.

SOCRATES: Then to have such goods is no more virtue than to lack them. Rather we may say that whatever is accompanied by justice is virtue,

79   whatever is without qualities of that sort is vice.

MENO: I agree that your conclusion seems inescapable.

SOCRATES: But a few minutes ago we called each of these—justice, temperance, and the rest—a part of virtue?

MENO: Yes, we did.

SOCRATES: So it seems you are making a fool of me.

MENO: How so, Socrates?

SOCRATES: I have just asked you not to break virtue up into fragments, and given you models of the type of answer I wanted, but taking no notice of this you tell me that virtue consists in the acquisition of good things with

b   justice, and justice, you agree, is a part of virtue.

MENO: True.

SOCRATES: So it follows from your own statements that to act with a part of virtue is virtue, if you call justice and all the rest parts of virtue. The point I want to make is that whereas I asked you to give me an account of virtue as a whole, far from telling me what it is itself you say that

c   every action is virtue which exhibits a part of virtue, as if you had already told me what the whole is, so that I should recognize it even if you chop it up into bits. It seems to me that we must put the same old question to you, my dear Meno—the question, What is virtue?—if every act becomes virtue when combined with a part of virtue. That is, after all, what it means to say that every act performed with justice is virtue. Don't you agree that the same question needs to be put? Does anyone know what a part of virtue is without knowing the whole?

MENO: I suppose not.

SOCRATES: No, and if you remember, when I replied to you about shape just now, I believe we rejected the type of answer that employs terms which are still in question and not yet agreed upon.

MENO: We did, and rightly.

SOCRATES: Then please do the same. While the nature of virtue as a whole is still under question, don't suppose that you can explain it to anyone in terms of its parts, or by any similar type of explanation. Understand rather that the same question remains to be answered; you say this and that about virtue, but what *is* it? Does this seem nonsense to you?

MENO: No, to me it seems right enough.

SOCRATES: Then go back to the beginning and answer my question. What do you and your friend say that virtue is?

MENO: Socrates, even before I met you they told me that in plain truth you are a perplexed man yourself and reduce others to perplexity. At this moment I feel you are exercising magic and witchcraft upon me and positively laying me under your spell until I am just a mass of helplessness. If I may be flippant, I think that not only in outward appearance but in other respects as well you are exactly like the flat sting ray that one meets in the sea. Whenever anyone comes into contact with it, it numbs him, and that is the sort of thing that you seem to be doing to me now. My mind and my lips are literally numb, and I have nothing to reply to you. Yet I have spoken about virtue hundreds of times, held forth often on the subject in front of large audiences, and very well too, or so I thought. Now I can't even say what it is. In my opinion you are well advised not to leave Athens and live abroad. If you behaved like this as a foreigner in another country, you would most likely be arrested as a wizard.

SOCRATES: You're a real rascal, Meno. You nearly took me in.

MENO: Just what do you mean?

SOCRATES: I see why you used a simile about me.

MENO: Why do you think?

SOCRATES: To be compared to something in return. All goodlooking people, I know perfectly well, enjoy a game of comparisons. They get the best of it, for naturally handsome folk provoke handsome similes. But I'm not going to oblige you. As for myself, if the sting ray paralyzes others only through being paralyzed itself, then the comparison is just, but not otherwise. It isn't that, knowing the answers myself, I perplex other people. The truth is rather that I infect them also with the perplexity I feel myself. So with virtue now. I don't know what it is. You may have known before you came into contact with me, but now you look as if you don't. Nevertheless I am ready to carry out, together with you, a joint investigation and inquiry into what it is.

MENO: But how will you look for something when you don't in the least know what it is? How on earth are you going to set up something you don't know as the object of your search? To put it another way, even if you come right up against it, how will you know that what you have found is the thing you didn't know?

e   SOCRATES: I know what you mean. Do you realize that what you are bringing up is the trick argument that a man cannot try to discover either what he knows or what he does not know? He would not seek what he knows, for since he knows it there is no need of the inquiry, nor what he does not know, for in that case he does not even know what he is to look for.

81   MENO: Well, do you think it a good argument?

SOCRATES: No.

MENO: Can you explain how it fails?

SOCRATES: I can. I have heard from men and women who understand the truths of religion . . .

MENO: What did they say?

SOCRATES: Something true, I thought, and fine.

MENO: What was it, and who were they?

SOCRATES: Those who tell it are priests and priestesses of the sort who
b   make it their business to be able to account for the functions which they perform. Pindar speaks of it too, and many another of the poets who are divinely inspired. What they say is this—see whether you think they are speaking the truth. They say that the soul of man is immortal. At one time it comes to an end—that which is called death—and at another is born again, but is never finally exterminated. On these grounds a man must live all his days as righteously as possible. For those from whom

> Persephone receives requital for ancient doom,
> In the ninth year she restores again
> Their souls to the sun above.
> From whom rise noble kings
c   And the swift in strength and greatest in wisdom,
> And for the rest of time
> They are called heroes and sanctified by men.

Thus the soul, since it is immortal and has been born many times, and has seen all things both here and in the other world, has learned everything that is. So we need not be surprised if it can recall the knowledge of virtue
d   or anything else which, as we see, it once possessed. All nature is akin, and the soul has learned everything, so that when a man has recalled a single piece of knowledge—*learned* it, in ordinary language—there is no reason why he should not find out all the rest, if he keeps a stout heart and does not grow weary of the search, for seeking and learning are in fact nothing but recollection.

We ought not then to be led astray by the contentious argument you
e   quoted. It would make us lazy, and is music in the ears of weaklings. The other doctrine produces energetic seekers after knowledge, and being con-

vinced of its truth, I am ready, with your help, to inquire into the nature of virtue.

. . .

MENO: Quite ready. All the same, I would rather consider the question as I put it at the beginning, and hear your views on it—that is, are we to pursue virtue as something that can be taught, or do men have it as a gift of nature or how?   **86**
    d

SOCRATES: If I were your master as well as my own, Meno, we should not have inquired whether or not virtue can be taught until we had first asked the main question—what it is. But not only do you make no attempt to govern your own actions—you prize your freedom, I suppose—but you attempt to govern mine. And you succeed too, so I shall let you have your way. There's nothing else for it, and it seems we must inquire into a single property of something about whose essential nature we are still in the dark.   **e**
Just grant me one small relaxation of your sway, and allow me, in considering whether or not it can be taught, to make use of a hypothesis—the sort of thing, I mean, that geometers often use in their inquiries. When they are asked, for example, about a given area, whether it is possible for this area to be inscribed as a triangle in a given circle, they will probably reply, "I   **87**
don't know yet whether it fulfills the conditions, but I think I have a hypothesis which will help us in the matter. It is this. If the area is such that, when one has applied it [sc. as a rectangle] to the given line [i.e., the diameter] of the circle, it is deficient by another rectangle similar to the one which is applied, then, I should say, one result follows; if not, the result is different. If you ask me, then, about the inscription of the figure in   **b**
the circle—whether it is possible or not—I am ready to answer you in this hypothetical way."

Let us do the same about virtue. Since we don't know what it is or what it resembles, let us use a hypothesis in investigating whether it is teachable or not. We shall say, "What attribute of the soul must virtue be, if it is to be teachable or otherwise?" Well, in the first place, if it is anything else but knowledge, is there a possibility of anyone teaching it—or, in the language   **c**
we used just now, reminding someone of it? We needn't worry about which name we are to give to the process, but simply ask, Will it be teachable? Isn't it plain to everyone that a man is not taught anything except knowledge?

MENO: That would be my view.

SOCRATES: If on the other hand virtue is some sort of knowledge, clearly it could be taught.

MENO: Certainly.

SOCRATES: So that question is easily settled—I mean, on what condition virtue would be teachable.

MENO: Yes.

SOCRATES: The next point then, I suppose, is to find out whether virtue is knowledge or something different.

d   MENO: That is the next question, I agree.

SOCRATES: Well then, do we assert that virtue is something good? Is that assumption a firm one for us?

MENO: Undoubtedly.

SOCRATES: That being so, if there exists any good thing different from, and not associated with, knowledge, virtue will not necessarily be any form of knowledge. If on the other hand knowledge embraces everything that is good, we shall be right to supect that virtue is knowledge.

e   MENO: Agreed.

SOCRATES: First then, is it virtue which makes us good?

MENO: Yes.

SOCRATES: And if good, then advantageous. All good things are advantageous, are they not?

MENO: Yes.

SOCRATES: So virtue itself must be something advantageous?

MENO: That follows also.

SOCRATES: Now suppose we consider what are the sorts of things that profit us. Take them in a list. Health, we may say, and strength and good looks, and wealth—these and their like we call advantageous, you agree?

MENO: Yes.

88   SOCRATES: Yet we also speak of these things as sometimes doing harm. Would you object to that statement?

MENO: No, it is so.

SOCRATES: Now look here. What is the controlling factor which determines whether each of these is advantageous or harmful? Isn't it right use which makes them advantageous, and lack of it, harmful?

MENO: Certainly.

SOCRATES: We must also take spiritual qualities into consideration. You recognize such things as temperance, justice, courage, quickness of mind, memory, nobility of character, and others?

b   MENO: Yes, of course I do.

SOCRATES: Then take any such qualities which in your view are not knowledge but something different. Don't you think they may be harmful as well as advantageous? Courage, for instance, if it is something thoughtless, just a sort of confidence. Isn't it true that to be confident without reason does a man harm, whereas a reasoned confidence profits him?

MENO: Yes.

SOCRATES: Temperance and quickness of mind are no different. Learning and discipline are profitable in conjunction with wisdom, but without it harmful.

MENO: That is emphatically true.

c   SOCRATES: In short, everything that the human spirit undertakes or suffers will lead to happiness when it is guided by wisdom, but to the opposite, when guided by folly.

MENO: A reasonable conclusion.

SOCRATES: If then virtue is an attribute of the spirit, and one which cannot fail to be beneficial, it must be wisdom, for all spiritual qualities in and by themselves are neither advantageous nor harmful, but become advantageous or harmful by the presence with them of wisdom or folly. If we accept this argument, then virtue, to be something advantageous, must be a sort of wisdom.

    MENO: I agree.

    SOCRATES: To go back to the other class of things, wealth and the like, of which we said just now that they are sometimes good and sometimes harmful, isn't it the same with them? Just as wisdom when it governs our other psychological impulses turns them to advantage, and folly turns them to harm, so the mind by its right use and control of these material assets makes them profitable, and by wrong use renders them harmful.

    MENO: Certainly.

    SOCRATES: And the right user is the mind of the wise man, the wrong user the mind of the foolish.

    MENO: That is so.

    SOCRATES: So we may say in general that the goodness of nonspiritual assets depends on our spiritual character, and the goodness of that on wisdom. This argument shows that the advantageous element must be wisdom, and virtue, we agree, is advantageous; so that amounts to saying that virtue, either in whole or in part, is wisdom.

    MENO: The argument seems to me fair enough.

    SOCRATES: If so, good men cannot be good by nature.

    MENO: I suppose not.

    SOCRATES: There is another point. If they were, there would probably be experts among us who could recognize the naturally good at an early stage. They would point them out to us and we should take them and shut them away safely in the Acropolis, sealing them up more carefully than bullion to protect them from corruption and ensure that when they came to maturity they would be of use to the state.

    MENO: It would be likely enough.

    SOCRATES: Since then goodness does not come by nature, is it got by learning?

    MENO: I don't see how we can escape the conclusion. Indeed it is obvious on our assumption that, if virtue is knowledge, it is teachable.

    SOCRATES: I suppose so. But I wonder if we were right to bind ourselves to that.

    MENO: Well, it seemed all right just now.

    SOCRATES: Yes, but to be sound it has got to seem all right not only "just now" but at this moment and in the future.

    MENO: Of course. But what has occurred to you to make you turn against it and suspect that virtue may not be knowledge?

    SOCRATES: I'll tell you. I don't withdraw from the position that if it is knowledge, it must be teachable, but as for its being knowledge, see

whether you think my doubts on this point are well founded. If anything
—not virtue only—is a possible subject of instruction, must there not be
teachers and students of it?

MENO: Surely.

e   SOCRATES: And what of the converse, that if there are neither teachers
nor students of a subject, we may safely infer that it cannot be taught?

MENO: That is true. But don't you think there are teachers of virtue?

SOCRATES: All I can say is that I have often looked to see if there are
any, and in spite of all my efforts I cannot find them, though I have had
plenty of fellow searchers, the kind of men especially whom I believe to
have most experience in such matters.

·   ·   ·

QUESTIONS FOR STUDY AND DISCUSSION

1. Indicate the major difficulties that follow from the position that virtue is
   teachable or that it is not teachable.
2. What is Socrates' major objection to Meno's definition of virtue?
3. How does Plato tend to resolve the problem of the one and the many with
   respect to virtue?
4. Discuss the statement: "A man cannot knowingly choose that which he fully
   recognizes as contrary to his good."

On Friendship

203 I was walking straight from the Academy to the Lyceum, by the road
which skirts the outside of the walls, and had reached the little gate where
is the source of the Panops, when I fell in with Hippothales, the son of
Hieronymus, Ctesippus the Paeanian, and some more young men, standing
together in a group.

Hippothales, seeing me approach, called out, Ha, Socrates, whither and
b   whence?

From the Academy, I replied, and I am going straight to the Lyceum.

Straight to us, I hope, cried he. Won't you turn in? It will be worth
your while.

Turn in where? said I. And whom do you mean by us?

There, he replied, pointing out to me an enclosure facing the wall, with

From Plato, Lysis, translated by J. Wright. From the book Socratic Discourses by
Plato and Xenophon. Everyman's Library Edition. Reprinted by permission by E. P.
Dutton & Co., Inc., and J. M. Dent and Sons Ltd., London.

a door open. There we are passing our time, he added, we whom you see, and a great many other fine fellows too.

And what's all this, pray? And how are you passing your time?

This is a palaestra that has been lately erected, and we are passing our time principally in conversations, of which we should be very glad to give you a share.   204

You are very kind, I answered. And who is your teacher there?

A friend and admirer of yours, Miccus.

And no ordinary man either, I rejoined, a most competent Sophist.

Won't you come with us, then, he said, to see both him and all our party there too?

Here, where I am, was my reply, I should like first to be informed,   b
what I am to enter for, and who is your prime beauty?

Some think one, and some another, Socrates.

But whom do you think, Hippothales? Tell me this.

He answered only with a blush. So I added, Hippothales, son of Hier-
onymus, there is no longer any need for you to tell me whether you are in love or not, since I am sure you are not only in love, but pretty far gone in it too by this time. For though in most matters I am a poor useless crea-   c
ture, yet by some means or other I have received from heaven the gift of being able to detect at a glance both a lover and a beloved.

On hearing this, he blushed still more deeply than before. Whereupon Ctesippus broke in, It is very fine of you, Hippothales, turning red in this way, and making such a fuss about telling Socrates the name, when he is quite sure, if he stays ever so short a time in your company, to be bored to death by hearing it always repeated. At any rate, Socrates, he has deafened *our* ears for us, and filled them full of Lysis. Nay, if he be but a little tipsy   d
when he talks of him, we can easily fancy, on waking, even the next morn-
ing, that we are still hearing the name of Lysis. But his constant talk about him, bad as it is, is not the worst—nothing like so bad as when he begins to deluge us with his poems and speeches, and worse and worse, to sing a song on his darling in a portentous voice, which we are compelled to listen to with patience.

Your Lysis must be quite a juvenile, I rejoined. I conjecture this from   e
my not knowing the name when you mentioned it.

Why, they don't often call him by his own name, Socrates; he still goes by his father's, the latter being so well known. Still, I am sure, you cannot be a stranger to the boy's appearance; that's quite enough to know him by.

Say, then, whose son he is.

Democrates' of Aexone, his eldest.

Well done, Hippothales, said I. A noble, and in every way a brilliant choice is this which you have made. But come now, go on about him with   205
me, just as you do with your friends here, that I may know what language a lover ought to hold with regard to his favorite, either to his face or before others.

And do you really, Socrates, set any value on what this fellow says?

Do you mean, I asked, absolutely to deny being in love with the person he mentions?

No, not that, he answered, but I do the making verses or speeches on him.

He is out of his senses, doting, mad, cried Ctesippus.

But, I replied, I don't want to hear any of your verses, Hippothales, nor
b any song either that you may have composed upon your darling, but I should like to have an idea of their sense, that I may know how you behave toward your favorite.

Ctesippus will tell you all about it, Socrates, I don't doubt. He must remember it well enough, if it be true, as he says, that I dinned it into his ears till he was deaf.

Oh, I know it, cried Ctesippus, right thoroughly too. It is such a joke, Socrates. The idea of a lover devoting himself exclusively to the object of his love, and yet having nothing of a personal interest to say to him that
c any child might not say—isn't it absurd? But stories that all the city rings with, about Democrates, and Lysis, the boy's grandfather, and all his ancestors—their wealth, their breeds of horses, their victories at the Pythian, Isthmian, Nemean with four steeds and single—all these he works into poem and speech, aye, and stories too, still further out-of-date than these. For in a sort of poem the other day, he gave us the whole account of Hera-
d cles' entertainment, telling us how their ancestor received that hero into his house on the strength of his relationship, being himself son of Zeus, by the daughter of the founder of Aexone. Yes, Socrates, such, among others, are the old wives' tales that our lover here is ever singing and reciting, and condemning us moreover to listen to.

On hearing this, I said to the lover, You ridiculous Hippothales, before you have gained the victory, you compose and sing a hymn of praise on yourself.

It isn't on myself, Socrates, that I either make or sing it.

You fancy not, said I.

How is it so? said he.

e In every way, I replied, these songs have reference to you. If you succeed in winning such a youth as you describe, all that you have said and sung will redound to your honor, and be in fact your hymn of triumph, as if you had gained a victory in obtaining such a favorite. But if he escape your grasp, then the higher the eulogium you have passed on him, the greater will be the blessings which you will seem to have missed, and the greater
206 consequently the ridicule you will incur. All connoisseurs, therefore, in matters of love, are careful of praising their favorites before they have won them, from their doubts as to the result of the affair. Moreover, your beauties, when lauded and made much of, become gorged with pride and arrogance. Don't you think so?

I do, he replied.

And the more arrogant they are, the harder they become to be caught?
It is to be expected, at any rate.

Well, what should you say to a huntsman that frightened the prey he was in chase of, and rendered it harder to be caught?

That he was a very sorry one, certainly.   b

And if by speech and song he renders it wild instead of luring it, he can be no favorite of the Muses, can he?

I think not.

Have a care then, Hippothales, that you do not lay yourself open with your poetry to all these reproaches. And yet I am sure, that to a man who injured himself by his poetry, you would not be willing to accord the title of a good poet, so long as he did himself harm.

No, indeed, that would be too unreasonable, he replied. But it is on this very account, Socrates, that I put myself in your hands, and beg you to give   c
me any advice you may have to bestow, as to the course of conduct or conversation that a lover ought to adopt in order to render himself agreeable to the object of his affection.

That were no such easy matter, I replied. But if you would bring me to speak with Lysis, perhaps I could give you a specimen of what you ought to say to him, in place of the speeches and songs which you are in the habit of treating him with, according to your friends here.

Well, there is no difficulty in that, he rejoined. If you will only go into the palaestra with Ctesippus, and sit down and begin to talk, I have little doubt that he will come to you of his own accord, for he is singularly fond of listening. And, moreover, as they are keeping the Hermaea, boys and men are all mixed up together today. So he is pretty certain to join you.   d
But if he does not, Ctesippus knows him, through his cousin Menexenus, who is Lysis' particular friend. You can get Ctesippus, therefore, to summon him, in case he does not come of himself.

This be our plan, I cried. And taking Ctesippus with me, I walked toward the palaestra, the rest following.   e

On entering we found that the boys had finished their sacrifices, and, the ceremony being now pretty well over, were playing together at knucklebones, all in their holiday dress. The greater part were carrying on their game in the court outside, but some of them were in a corner of the dressing room, playing at odd and even with a number of bones which they drew out of small baskets. Round these were stationed others looking on, among whom was Lysis, and he stood in the midst of boys and youths with a chaplet on his head, unmatched in face or form. You would say he was not   207
beautiful merely, but even of a noble mien. For ourselves, we withdrew to the opposite part of the room, and sitting down, as nothing was going on there, began to talk. While thus engaged, Lysis kept turning round and eyeing us, evidently wishing to join us. For some time though he remained in doubt, not liking to walk up alone. But when Menexenus looked in from his game in the court and on seeing Ctesippus and me came to sit down   b

with us, Lysis also followed at sight of his friend, and took a seat by his side.

There came up, moreover, the rest of our party, among them Hippothales, who, seeing them form into a good-sized group, screened himself behind them in a position where he did not think he could be seen by Lysis —so fearful was he of giving him offense. And thus placed near him, he listened to our conversation.

I began it by turning my eyes on Menexenus, and saying, Son of c Demophon, which of you two is the elder?

It is a disputed point, he replied.

And do you dispute, too, which is the better fellow?

Right heartily, was his answer.

And so too, I suppose, which is the more beautiful?

At this they both laughed.

I will not ask you, I added, which is the wealthier, for you are friends, are you not?

Oh dear, yes! they both cried.

And friends, they tell us, share and share alike; so in this respect, at any rate, there will be no difference between you, if only you give me a true account of your friendship.

To this they both assented.

d I was then proceeding to inquire which of the two excelled in justice, and which in wisdom, when someone came up and carried off Menexenus, telling him that the master of the palaestra wanted him—I presume, on business connected with the sacrifice. Accordingly he left us, and I went on questioning Lysis.

Lysis, said I, I suppose your father and mother love you very dearly?

Very dearly, he answered.

They would wish you then to be as happy as possible.

Of course.

e Do you think a man happy if he is a slave, and may not do anything he wants?

No, that indeed I don't.

Well, if your father and mother love you, and wish you to become happy, it is clear that they try in every way to make you happy.

To be sure they do.

They allow you then, I suppose, to do what you wish, and never scold you, or hinder you from doing what you want to do?

Yes, but they do though, Socrates, and pretty frequently too.

208 How? said I. They wish you to be happy, and yet hinder you from doing what you want. But tell me this. If you wanted to ride on one of your father's chariots, and take the reins during a race, would they not allow you?

No, most assuredly they would not.

Whom would they then? I asked.

There is a charioteer paid by my father.

Paid! cried I. Do they allow a paid servant in preference to you to do what he pleases with the horses, and, what is more, give him money for so doing?

Not a doubt about it, Socrates, he replied.   b

Well, but your pair of mules I am sure they let you drive, and even if you wished to take the whip and whip them, they would allow you.

Allow me, would they? said he.

Would they not? said I. Is there no one allowed to whip them?

Of course there is—the mule driver.

Is he a slave or free?

A slave, he answered.

A slave then, it appears, they think of more account than you, their son; they entrust their property to him rather than to you, and they allow him to do what he pleases, while you they hinder. But answer me further. Do   c they let you rule yourself, or not even allow you this?

Rule myself! I should think not, said he.

You have someone to rule you, then?

Yes, my governor here.

Not a slave?

Yes, but he is, though, ours.

Shocking! I exclaimed. A free man to be ruled by a slave. But how, pray, does this governor exercise his authority?

He takes me to school, of course.

And do you mean to say that they rule you there, too—the schoolmasters?

Most certainly they do.

Very many then, it appears, are the masters and rulers whom your fa- d ther sets over you on purpose. But come now, when you go home to your mother, she, I am sure, lets you do what you please—that you may be as happy as she can make you—either with her wool or her loom, when she is spinning. It cannot possibly be that she hinders you from touching her comb or her shuttle, or any other of her spinning implements.

He burst out laughing. I can assure you, Socrates, he said, she not only hinders me, but would get me a good beating if I did touch them.   e

Beating! cried I. You haven't done your father or mother any wrong, have you?

Not I, he answered.

Whatever is the reason, then, that they hinder you, in this shocking manner, from being happy, and acting as you please, and keep you, all the day long, in a state of bondage to someone or other—and, in a word, of doing hardly anything at all you want to do? So that it seems you get no good whatever from your fortune, large as it is, but all have control over it,

209   rather than you, nor, again, from that beautiful person of yours, for it, too, is under the care and charge of other people, while you, poor Lysis have control over nothing at all, nor do a single thing you wish.

Because I'm not old enough yet, Socrates.

That should be no hindrance, son of Democrates, since there are things, I fancy, which both your father and mother allow you to do, without waiting for you to be old enough. When they wish, for example, to have anything written or read, it is you, I conceive, whom they appoint to the
b   office, before anyone else in the house. Isn't it?

Beyond a question, he replied.

In these matters, then, you are allowed to do as you please; you may write whichever letter you like first, and whichever you like second. And in reading you enjoy the same liberty. And when you take up your lyre, neither father nor mother, I imagine, hinders you from tightening or loosening such strings as you choose, or from playing with your fingers or stick, as you may think proper. Or do they hinder you in such matters?

Oh dear, no! he exclaimed.

What in the world, then, can be the reason, Lysis, that in these matters
c   they don't hinder you, while in the former they do?

I suppose it is, Socrates, because I understand the one, and don't understand the other.

Oh! That's it, is it, my fine fellow? It is not, then, for you to be old enough that your father is waiting in all cases, but on the very day that he thinks you are wiser than he is, he will hand over to you himself and his property.

I shouldn't wonder, said he.

Nor I, said I. But again. Does your neighbor follow the same rule that your father does with regard to you? Do you expect he will hand over to
d   you his house to manage, as soon as he thinks you have a better idea of the management of a house than he has himself, or will he keep it in his own hands?

Hand it over to me, I should think.

And the Athenians? Will they, do you imagine, hand over to you their matters directly they perceive that you are wise enough to manage them?

Yes, I expect so.

But come now, I asked, what will the Great King do? When his meat is cooking, will he allow his eldest son, heir to the throne of Asia, to throw
e   into the gravy whatever he chooses, or us, rather, if we come before him, and prove that we have a better idea than his son has of dressing a dish?

Us, to be sure, said he.

And the prince he won't allow to put in the least morsel even, while with us he would make no difficulty, though we wished to throw in salt by handfuls?

Exactly.

Once more. If his son had something the matter with his eyes, would he

allow him to touch them himself, if he thought him ignorant of the healing   210
art, or rather hinder him?

Hinder him.

But against us, on the other hand, if he conceived us to be skilled in the
art, he would, I imagine, make no objection, even though we wished to
force open the eyes, and sprinkle in ashes, as he would suppose us to be
rightly advised.

True, he would not.

And so, with everything else whatsoever, he would entrust it to us
rather than to himself or his son, if he believed that we knew more about it
than either of them did.

Necessarily he would, Socrates.

You see then, said I, how the case stands, dear Lysis. All matters of
which we have a good idea will be put into our hands by all people,
whether Greeks or barbarians, men or women. We shall act, with regard to   b
them, exactly as we please; no one will intentionally stand in our way. And
not only shall we be free ourselves in these matters, but we shall be lords
over others, and they will be in fact our property, as we shall have the enjoyment of them. With regard to matters, on the other hand, into which we
have acquired no insight, no one will ever allow us to act as we think
proper, but all persons, to the best of their power, will hinder us from med-
dling with them—not only strangers, but even our own father and mother,   c
and if we possess any nearer relation. And we ourselves, in these matters,
shall be subject to others, and they will be, in fact, the property of others,
as we shall derive no advantage from them. Do you allow this to be the
case?

I do.

Will anyone, then, count us his friends, will anyone love us in those
matters in which we are of no use?

Indeed no.

According to this, then, not even you are loved by your own father, nor
is anyone else by anyone else in the world, in so far as you or he is useless?

So it would appear, he said.

If, therefore, you acquire knowledge, my son, all men will be friendly   d
to you, all men will be attached to you, for you will be useful and good. If
not, you will have no friend in anyone, not even in your father or mother,
or any of your own family. Now is it possible, Lysis, for a man to have a
great idea of himself in those matters of which he has yet no idea?

How can he possibly? he replied.

And if you still require, as you do, an instructor, you are still without
ideas.

True, he answered.

It cannot be, then, that you have a great idea of yourself, if as yet you
have no idea.

No, really, Socrates, I don't see how I can.

e On receiving this reply from Lysis, I turned my eyes on Hippothales, and was on the point of making a great blunder. For it came into my head to say, This is the way, Hippothales, that you should talk to your favorite, humbling and checking, instead of puffing him up and pampering him, as you now do. However, on seeing him writhing with agitation at the turn the conversation was taking, I recollected that though standing so near, he didn't wish to be seen by Lysis. So I recovered myself in time, and forbore to address him.

. . .

QUESTIONS FOR STUDY AND DISCUSSION

1. Why does Socrates proceed gradually in talking to Lysis about the nature of friendship instead of offering him an ideal definition?
2. How does Lysis interpret the restrictions his parents impose upon him? Are they a consequence of his youth or his lack of wisdom?
3. The discipline under which Lysis lives moves him to assert that even his slaves are more free than he is himself. Discuss freedom versus licentiousness.
4. In Socrates' opinion, what is the main virtue necessary for true friendship?
5. Should friendly love be blind to a friend's real qualities? Discuss the difference between Socrates' and Hippothales' friendly treatment of Lysis.

Who Is the Happy Man?

. . .

482 CALLICLES: Socrates, it seems to me that you run wild in our talk like a true mob orator, and now you are haranguing us in this way because Polus fell into the very error which he blamed Gorgias for being drawn into by you. Gorgias, he said, was asked by you whether, in case a prospective pupil of rhetoric came to him without a knowledge of justice, he himself would

d teach him, and he was shamed into saying he would do so, because the general conventional view demanded it and men would be vexed if one refused. It was through this admission that he was forced to contradict himself, and that is just what you like. And Polus, in my opinion, was quite right in laughing at you at the time, but now he himself in turn has been caught in the same way. And I do not think much of Polus for the very

From Plato, *Gorgias,* in *Plato Socratic Dialogues,* translated by W. D. Woodhead. Published 1955 by Thomas Nelson and Sons Ltd. Reprinted by permission of the publisher.

reason that he agreed with you that it is more disgraceful to do than to suffer injustice, for it was as a result of this admission that he was caught in the toils of your argument and silenced, because he was ashamed to say what he thought. For, Socrates, though you claim to pursue the truth, you actually drag us into these tiresome popular fallacies, looking to what is fine and noble, not by nature, but by convention. Now, for the most part, these two, nature and convention, are antagonistic to each other. And so, if a man is ashamed and dares not say what he thinks, he is compelled to contradict himself. And you have discovered this clever trick and do not play fair in your arguments, for if a man speaks on the basis of convention, you slyly question him on the basis of nature, but if he follows nature, you follow convention. For example, in our present discussion of doing and suffering wrong, when Polus spoke of what was conventionally the more shameful, you followed it up by appealing to nature. For by nature everything that is worse is more shameful, suffering wrong for instance, but by convention it is more shameful to do it. For to suffer wrong is not even fit for a man but only for a slave, for whom it is better to be dead than alive, since when wronged and outraged he is unable to help himself or any other for whom he cares. But in my opinion those who framed the laws are the weaker folk, the majority. And accordingly they frame the laws for themselves and their own advantage, and so too with their approval and censure, and to prevent the stronger who are able to overreach them from gaining the advantage over them, they frighten them by saying that to overreach others is shameful and evil, and injustice consists in seeking the advantage over others. For they are satisfied, I suppose, if being inferior they enjoy equality of status. That is the reason why seeking an advantage over the many is by convention said to be wrong and shameful, and they call it injustice. But in my view nature herself makes it plain that it is right for the better to have the advantage over the worse, the more able over the less. And both among all animals and in entire states and races of mankind it is plain that this is the case—that right is recognized to be the sovereignty and advantage of the stronger over the weaker. For what justification had Xerxes in invading Greece or his father in invading Scythia? And there are countless other similar instances one might mention. But I imagine that these men act in accordance with the true nature of right, yes and, by heaven, according to nature's own law, though not perhaps by the law we frame. We mold the best and strongest among ourselves, catching them young like lion cubs, and by spells and incantations we make slaves of them, saying that they must be content with equality and that this is what is right and fair. But if a man arises endowed with a nature sufficiently strong, he will, I believe, shake off all these controls, burst his fetters, and break loose. And trampling upon our scraps of paper, our spells and incantations, and all our unnatural conventions, he rises up and reveals himself our master who was once our slave, and there shines forth nature's true justice.

b And it seems to me that Pindar expresses what I am saying in that ode in which he writes,

> Law is the sovereign of all,
> Of mortals and immortals alike,

and it is law, he says, that

> Carries all, justifying the most violent deed
> With victorious hand; this I prove
> By the deeds of Heracles, for without paying the price—

it runs something like that—for I do not know the poem by heart—but it says that he drove off the oxen of Geryon which were neither given to him
c nor paid for, because this is natural justice, that the cattle and all other possessions of the inferior and weaker belong to the superior and stronger.

This is the truth then, and you will realize it if you will now abandon philosophy and rise to greater things. For philosophy, you know, Socrates, is a pretty thing if you engage in it moderately in your youth; but if you continue in it longer than you should, it is the ruin of any man. For if a man is exceptionally gifted and yet pursues philosophy far on in life, he
d must prove entirely unacquainted with all the accomplishments requisite for a gentleman and a man of distinction. Such men know nothing of the laws in their cities, or of the language they should use in their business associations both public and private with other men, or of human pleasures and appetites, and in a word they are completely without experience of men's characters. And so when they enter upon any activity public or pri-
e vate they appear ridiculous, just as public men, I suppose, appear ridiculous when they take part in your discussions and arguments. For what Euripides says is true:

> All shine in that and eagerly pursue it—
> Giving the better part of the day thereto—
> In which they find themselves most excellent,

485 but that in which they are inferior they shun and abuse, praising the other out of partiality to themselves, with the idea that they are thus praising themselves. But to my mind the right course is to partake of both. It is a good thing to engage in philosophy just so far as it is an aid to education, and it is no disgrace for a youth to study it, but when a man who is now
b growing older still studies philosophy, the situation becomes ridiculous, Socrates, and I feel toward philosophers very much as I do toward those who lisp and play the child. When I see a little child, for whom it is still proper enough to speak in this way, lisping and playing, I like it and it seems to me pretty and ingenuous and appropriate to the child's age, and when I hear it talking with precision, it seems to me disagreeable and it vexes my ears and appears to me more fitting for a slave, but when one
c hears a grown man lisping or sees him playing the child, it looks ridiculous and unmanly and worthy of a beating. I feel exactly the same too about

students of philosophy. When I see a youth engaged in it, I admire it and it seems to me natural and I consider such a man ingenuous, and the man who does not pursue it I regard as illiberal and one who will never aspire to any fine or noble deed, but when I see an older man still studying philoso-   d phy and not deserting it, that man, Socrates, is actually asking for a whipping. For as I said just now, such a man, even if exceptionally gifted, is doomed to prove less than a man, shunning the city center and market place, in which the poet said that men win distinction, and living the rest of his life sunk in a corner and whispering with three or four boys, and incapable of any utterance that is free and lofty and brilliant. Now I am quite   e friendly disposed toward you, Socrates, and I suppose I feel much as Zethus, whom I mentioned, felt toward Amphion in Euripides. For I am moved to say to you the same kind of thing as he said to his brother, "You neglect, Socrates, what you most ought to care for, and pervert a naturally noble spirit by putting on a childlike semblance, and you could neither con-   486 tribute a useful word in the councils of justice nor seize upon what is plausible and convincing, nor offer any brilliant advice on another's behalf." And yet, my dear Socrates—and do not be angry with me, for I am saying this out of good will toward you—do you not consider it a disgrace to be in the condition I think you are in, you and the others who advance ever farther into philosophy? For now if anyone should seize you or any others like you and drag you off to prison, claiming you are guilty when you are not, you realize that you would not know what to do, but you   b would reel to and fro and gape openmouthed, without a word to say, and when you came before the court, even with an utterly mean and rascally accuser, you would be put to death, if he chose to demand the death penalty. And yet what wisdom is there in this, Socrates, in "an art which finds a man well-gifted and leaves him worse"—able neither to help himself nor to save from the extremes of danger either himself or anybody else, but fated to be robbed by his enemies of all his property and to live literally   c like one disfranchised in his own city? And such a man, if I may put it somewhat crudely, one may even box on the ears with impunity. But, my good fellow, "cease your questioning, and practice the fairer music of affairs" and try something that will win you a name for good sense, and leave to others "these dainty devices," whether we should call them babblings or follies, "which will set you to dwell in empty mansions." You should not emulate those who investigate these trifling matters but those who enjoy a livelihood and a reputation and many other blessings.   d

. . .

SOCRATES: But please take up the question again from the beginning and   488 tell me what "natural justice" is according to you and Pindar—that the more powerful carries off by force the property of the weaker, the better rules over the worse, and the nobler takes more than the meaner? Have you any other conception of justice than this, or is my memory right?

CALLICLES: No, that is what I said then and still hold to.

SOCRATES: And is it the same man whom you call better and more powerful? I could not grasp at the time, you know, just what you meant. Is

c it the physically stronger that you call more powerful, and must the weaker obey the stronger—as, for example, you seemed to indicate at the time by saying that great cities assail small ones in accordance with natural justice, because they are more powerful and stronger, the more powerful and stronger and better being one and the same thing—or is it possible to be better but weaker and less powerful, or more powerful but more evil? Or

d have you the same definition for the better and the more powerful? Please make your distinction clear, whether you consider the more powerful, the better, and the stronger as the same thing or different.

CALLICLES: Well, I can plainly assure you that they are the same.

SOCRATES: Are not the many more powerful by nature than the one? And it is these who, as you yourself said just now, frame their laws to restrain the one.

CALLICLES: Of course.

SOCRATES: Then the ordinances of the many are those of the more powerful?

CALLICLES: Certainly.

e SOCRATES: And of the better also? For the more powerful are far better, according to you.

CALLICLES: Yes.

SOCRATES: Then their ordinances are naturally noble, since they are those of the more powerful.

CALLICLES: I agree.

SOCRATES: Now do the many hold the opinion, as you just now stated, that justice means equal shares and that it is more shameful to do than to

489 suffer wrong? Is this true or not? And mind that you yourself are not caught this time a victim of modesty. Is it the view of the many, or not, that justice means equal shares, not excess, and that it is more shameful to do than to suffer wrong? Do not grudge me my answer, Callicles; then, if you agree with me, I may now confirm the truth by the admission of one fully competent to decide.

CALLICLES: Well, that is the view of the majority.

SOCRATES: Then it is not by convention only, but also by nature that it

b is more shameful to do than to suffer wrong and true justice to share equally; so apparently what you said previously was not true and you were mistaken in attacking me when you said that convention and nature are opposed and that I have recognized this and do not play fairly in debate, but invoke convention if a man refers to nature, or nature, when he refers to convention.

CALLICLES: Will this fellow never stop driveling? Tell me, Socrates, are you not ashamed to be captious about words at your age, considering it a

godsend if one makes a slip in an expression? Do you imagine that by the   c
more powerful I mean anything else but the better? Did I not tell you long
ago that I identify the better and the more powerful? Do you think I mean
that, if a rabble of slaves and nondescripts who are of no earthly use except
for their bodily strength are gathered together and make some pronouncement, this is law?

SOCRATES: Well, most sage Callicles, is this what you have to say?

CALLICLES: Most certainly.

SOCRATES: Well, my strange friend, I myself guessed long since that you   d
meant something like this by "the more powerful," and I repeat my questions only because I am eager to understand clearly what you mean. For
surely you do not consider that two are better than one or that your slaves
are better than you because they are stronger. But start once again and tell
me what you mean by "the better," since you do not mean the stronger, and,
my admirable friend, lead me on the path of knowledge more gently, that I
may not run away from your school.

CALLICLES: You are ironical, Socrates.   e

SOCRATES: No indeed, Callicles, by that very Zethus of whom you
made use just now to heap your irony upon me, but come, tell me, whom
do you mean by "the better"?

CALLICLES: I mean the nobler.

SOCRATES: You see then that you yourself are playing with words but
revealing nothing. Will you not tell me whether by "the better" and "the
more powerful" you mean the wiser or some other class?

CALLICLES: By heaven, I do mean those, and most emphatically.

SOCRATES: Then according to your account one sensible man is often   490
more powerful than ten thousand fools and it is right that he should rule
and they be subjects and that the ruler should have more than his subjects;
that, I think, is what you mean to say—and I am not trapping you with
words—if the one is more powerful than ten thousand.

CALLICLES: That is what I mean, for natural justice I consider to be
this, that the better and wiser man should rule over and have more than the
inferior.

SOCRATES: Hold there a moment! What is it you mean this time? If   b
many of us are gathered together, as now, in the same place, with plenty of
food and drink in common, and if we are of various kinds, some strong,
some weak, and one of us, being a doctor, is wiser in these matters and, as
is likely, is stronger than some, weaker than others, then surely, being wiser
than we are, he will be better and more powerful in this field.

CALLICLES: Certainly.

SOCRATES: Then must he have a larger portion of the food than we do,   c
because he is better, or in virtue of his authority should he do all the distributing, but in the use and expenditure of it ought he to seek no excessive
portion for his own body, if he is not to suffer for it, but to receive more

than some and less than others? And if he happens to be the weakest of all, then must not the best man get the smallest share of all, Callicles? Is it not so, my good friend?

CALLICLES: You keep talking about food and drink and doctors and
d nonsense. I am not speaking of these things.

SOCRATES: Do you not say the wiser man is the better? Yes or no?

CALLICLES: I do.

SOCRATES: But should not the better have a larger share?

CALLICLES: Not of food or drink.

SOCRATES: I see. Of clothes, perhaps, and the most expert weaver should have the largest cloak and should go around clad in the most numerous and handsome garments?

CALLICLES: Garments indeed!

SOCRATES: Well then, the best and wisest expert in shoes should obvi-
e ously have the advantage in them. The cobbler, I suppose, should have the largest and most numerous shoes in which to walk around.

CALLICLES: Shoes! You keep talking nonsense.

SOCRATES: Well, if that is not what you mean, here it is perhaps. A farmer for instance who is an expert with good sound knowledge about the soil should have a larger share of seed and use the most seed possible on his own land.

CALLICLES: How you keep saying the same things, Socrates!

SOCRATES: Not only that, Callicles, but about the same matters.

491 CALLICLES: By heaven, you literally never stop talking about cobblers and fullers and cooks and doctors, as if we were discussing them.

SOCRATES: Then will you not yourself say in what matters a superiority in wisdom and power justly entitles a man to a larger share? Or will you neither put up with my suggestions nor tell me yourself?

CALLICLES: But I have been telling you for a long time. First of all I mean by the more powerful, not cobblers or cooks, but those who are wise
b in affairs of the state and the best methods of administering it, and not only wise but courageous, being competent to accomplish their intentions and not flagging through weakness of soul.

SOCRATES: You see, my good Callicles, that you do not find the same fault with me as I with you. For you claim that I keep saying the same things, and reproach me with it, but I make the opposite statement of you, that you never say the same things about the same subjects. Previously you defined the better and more powerful as the stronger, and next as the wiser,
c and now you come forward with something else; the better and the more powerful are now described by you as the more courageous. But, my good sir, tell me and have done with it, whom you mean by the better and more powerful, and what is their sphere of action.

CALLICLES: But I told you—those who are wise in the affairs of the state and courageous. It is proper that these should govern states, and this

is the meaning of justice, that these should have more than the others, the   d
rulers than the subjects.

SOCRATES: Tell me, my friend, what is their relation to themselves? Are they rulers or subjects?

CALLICLES: What do you mean?

SOCRATES: I mean that every man is his own master, or is there no need for him to govern himself but only to govern others?

CALLICLES: What do you mean by governing himself?

SOCRATES: Nothing very subtle, but merely the popular notion of being temperate and in control of oneself, and mastering one's own pleasures and appetites.   e

.   .   .

SOCRATES: Back then to our previous admissions. Did you say hunger   496
was pleasant or painful? Actual hunger, I mean.

CALLICLES: Painful, but to satisfy hunger by eating is pleasant.

SOCRATES: I understand. But hunger itself at least is painful, is it not?   d

CALLICLES: I agree.

SOCRATES: And thirst too?

CALLICLES: Most certainly.

SOCRATES: Am I to ask any further then, or do you admit that every deficiency and desire is painful?

CALLICLES: I admit it; you need not ask.

SOCRATES: Very well then, but to drink when thirsty you say is pleasant?

CALLICLES: I do.

SOCRATES: Now in this statement the word "thirsty" implies pain, I presume.

CALLICLES: Yes.   e

SOCRATES: And drinking is a satisfaction of the deficiency and a pleasure?

CALLICLES: Yes.

SOCRATES: Then you say that in drinking there is pleasure?

CALLICLES: Certainly.

SOCRATES: When one is thirsty?

CALLICLES: I agree.

SOCRATES: That is, when in pain?

CALLICLES: Yes.

SOCRATES: Then do you realize the result—that you say a man enjoys pleasure simultaneously with pain, when you say that he drinks when thirsty? Does not this happen at the same time and the same place, whether in body or soul? For I fancy it makes no difference. Is this so or not?

CALLICLES: It is.

SOCRATES: Yes, but you say also that when one is faring well it is impossible for him at the same time to fare ill.

497

CALLICLES: I do.

SOCRATES: But you have agreed it is possible to experience pleasure at the same time as pain.

CALLICLES: Apparently.

SOCRATES: Then pleasure is not the same as faring well, nor pain as faring ill, and so the pleasant is different from the good.

CALLICLES: I do not understand what your quibbles mean, Socrates.

SOCRATES: You understand, Callicles, but you are playing coy. But
b push on a little further, that you may realize how cunning you are, you who admonish me. Does not each one of us cease at the same time from thirsting and from his pleasure in drinking?

CALLICLES: I do not know what you mean.

GORGIAS: Do not behave so, Callicles, but answer for our sakes too, that the arguments may be concluded.

CALLICLES: But Socrates is always the same, Gorgias. He asks these trivial and useless questions and then refutes.

GORGIAS: What difference does that make to you? In any case you do not have to pay the price, Callicles, but suffer Socrates to cross-examine you as he will.

c CALLICLES: Well then, ask these petty little questions, since Gorgias so wishes.

SOCRATES: You are lucky, Callicles, in having been initiated in the Great Mysteries before the Little; I did not think it was permitted. Answer then from where you left off, whether thirst and the pleasure of drinking do not cease for each of us at the same time.

CALLICLES: I agree.

SOCRATES: And does not one cease from hunger and other desires, and from pleasures at the same time?

CALLICLES: That is so.

d SOCRATES: Does he not then cease from pains and pleasures at the same time?

CALLICLES: Yes.

SOCRATES: Yes, but he does not cease from experiencing the good and the ill simultaneously, as you yourself agreed. Do you not agree now?

CALLICLES: I do. What of it?

SOCRATES: Only this, that the good is not the same as the pleasant, my friend, nor the evil as the painful. For we cease from the one pair at the same time, but not from the other, because they are distinct. How then could the pleasant be the same as the good, or the painful as the evil? Let
e us look at it in a different way, if you like, for I think that even here you do not agree. But just consider. Do you not call good people by that name because of the presence in them of things good, just as you call beautiful those in whom beauty is present.

CALLICLES: I do.

SOCRATES: Again, do you call fools or cowards good men? You did not just now, but it was the brave and the wise, or do you not call these good?

CALLICLES: Certainly I do.

SOCRATES: And have you ever seen a silly child enjoying pleasure?

CALLICLES: I have.

SOCRATES: And never seen a silly man enjoying pleasure?

CALLICLES: Yes, I suppose so, but what of it?

SOCRATES: Nothing, just answer.   498

CALLICLES: I have seen.

SOCRATES: And a sensible man experiencing pain or pleasure?

CALLICLES: I have.

SOCRATES: And which feels more pain or pleasure, the sensible or the fool?

CALLICLES: I do not think there is much difference.

SOCRATES: That is quite enough. And have you ever seen a coward in battle?

CALLICLES: Of course.

SOCRATES: Well, which of the two seemed more to rejoice, when the enemy retreated, the cowards or the brave?

CALLICLES: Both equally, I think, or if not, pretty much so.   b

SOCRATES: It makes no difference. At least cowards too feel pleasure?

CALLICLES: Most certainly.

SOCRATES: And fools too, it appears.

CALLICLES: Yes.

SOCRATES: And is it cowards only or the brave too that feel pain at the enemy's approach?

CALLICLES: Both.

SOCRATES: To a like degree?

CALLICLES: Cowards, perhaps, more.

SOCRATES: And they rejoice more at the enemy's retreat?

CALLICLES: Perhaps.

SOCRATES: Then fools and wise, cowards and brave feel pain and pleasure to a like degree, as you say, but the coward more so than the   c
brave?

CALLICLES: I agree.

SOCRATES: But the wise and the brave are good, cowards and fools bad.

CALLICLES: Yes.

SOCRATES: Then the good and the bad feel pleasure and pain to a like degree.

CALLICLES: I agree.

SOCRATES: Now are the good and the bad good and evil to a similar degree? Or are the bad even better than the good?

CALLICLES: Good heavens, I do not understand what you mean.   d

SOCRATES: Do you not understand that according to you the good are good through the presence of good things, and the bad, of evil things, and that—according to you—pleasures are good things, and pains evil?

CALLICLES: I do.

SOCRATES: Then good things, that is, pleasures, are present to those who rejoice, if they rejoice.

CALLICLES: Of course.

SOCRATES: And is it not through the presence of good things that those who rejoice are good?

CALLICLES: Yes.

SOCRATES: Again, evil things, namely pains, are present for those who suffer pain.

CALLICLES: They are present.

e SOCRATES: And it is through the presence of evil things that you claim the evil are evil. Or do you no longer hold to that?

CALLICLES: I do.

SOCRATES: Then those who feel pleasure are good, those who feel pain, bad.

CALLICLES: Certainly.

SOCRATES: More, less, or equally good or bad, according as they feel these things more, less, or equally?

CALLICLES: Yes.

SOCRATES: Now do you not say that the wise and the fool, the brave and the coward feel pleasure and pain to a like degree, or the coward even to a greater degree?

CALLICLES: I do.

SOCRATES: Then reckon up along with me what is the result of our admissions, for they say that it is good to repeat and examine twice and once

499 again what is good. We say the wise and the brave man is good, do we not?

CALLICLES: Yes.

SOCRATES: And the fool and coward is bad?

CALLICLES: Certainly.

SOCRATES: And he who enjoys pleasure is good?

CALLICLES: Yes.

SOCRATES: And he who suffers pain is bad?

CALLICLES: Necessarily so.

SOCRATES: And the good and the bad experience pain and pleasure to a like degree, though perhaps the bad even more so.

CALLICLES: Yes.

SOCRATES: Then the evil man becomes just as bad and good as the

b good man, or even more good. Is not this the result, along with what we said before, if anyone identifies the pleasant and the good? Must not this be so, Callicles?

CALLICLES: I have been listening to you for a long time, Socrates, and agreeing with you, as I reflected that, if one concedes something to you even in play, you gladly seize hold of it like a child. Just as if you really think that I or anyone else does not hold some pleasures to be better and others worse!

SOCRATES: Ho, ho, Callicles! What a rascal you are, treating me like a child and deceiving me by saying the same things are now thus, now different. And yet I did not think at the beginning that you would willingly deceive me, since you are my friend. But now I have been misled, and apparently, as the old proverb goes, I must make the best of the circumstances and take just what you give me. What you now say, it seems, is that some pleasures are good, and some bad. Is it not so?

CALLICLES: Yes.

. . .

SOCRATES: Yes, because Polus and I agreed, if you remember, that all our actions should be for the sake of the good. Do you too share our opinion, that the good is the end of all actions and that everything else should be done for its sake, not the good for the sake of everything else? Do you of the third part add your vote to ours?

CALLICLES: I do.

SOCRATES: Then the pleasant as well as everything else should be done for the sake of the good, not the good for the sake of the pleasant.

CALLICLES: Certainly.

SOCRATES: Now can any and every man choose which pleasures are good and which bad, or do we need an expert in each case?

CALLICLES: We need an expert.

SOCRATES: Let us recapitulate then what I was saying to Polus and Gorgias. I said, if you remember, that there are certain processes aiming at pleasure which secure pleasure alone but know nothing of the better and the worse, and others that know what is good and evil. And among those concerned with pleasures I named cookery, which is a routine, not an art, and among those concerned with the good the medical art. And, by the god of friendship, Callicles, do not fancy that you should play with me, and give me no haphazard answers contrary to your opinion. And do not either take what I say as if I were merely playing, for you see the subject of our discussion—and on what subject should even a man of slight intelligence be more serious?—namely, what kind of life one should live, the life to which you invite me, that of a "real man," speaking in the Assembly and practicing rhetoric and playing the politician according to your present fashion, or the life spent in philosophy, and how the one differs from the other. Perhaps then it is best for us, as I endeavored to do just now, to distinguish between them, and after distinguishing and coming to an agreement together, then, if there are two such lives distinct, to consider in what way they differ from one another and which one should be lived. Now perhaps you do not yet understand what I mean.

CALLICLES: Indeed I do not.

SOCRATES: Well, I will tell you more clearly. Since you and I have agreed that there is a good and there is a pleasant, and that the pleasant is different from the good, and that there is a method of studying and contriving to acquire each of them, one method for pursuing pleasure, another for pursuing the good—but first of all you must either agree with or reject this

e statement. Do you agree?

CALLICLES: It is as you state.

. . .

503   SOCRATES: Yes, if what you previously spoke of as virtue is truly so, namely to satisfy to the full your own appetites and those of others, but if this is not so, but, as in our later argument we were compelled to admit,

d only those desires, the satisfaction of which makes man better, should be indulged, not those which make us worse, and if for this there is a special art—I cannot admit that any of those mentioned satisfied these demands.

CALLICLES: Well, if you make good search, you will find one.

SOCRATES: Then let us just quietly consider whether any of them had this quality. Well now, the good man who speaks for the best surely will

e not say what he says at random but with some purpose in view, just as all other craftsmen do not each choose and apply materials to their work at random, but with the view that each of their productions should have a certain form. Look, for example, if you will, at painters, builders, shipwrights, and all other craftsmen—any of them you choose—and see how each one disposes each element he contributes in a fixed order, and compels one to fit

504   and harmonize with the other until he has combined the whole into something well ordered and regulated. Other craftsmen in general and those we were speaking of just now, who have to do with the body, physical trainers and doctors, give order, I think, and discipline to the body. Do we admit the truth of this or not?

CALLICLES: Let it be granted.

SOCRATES: Then harmony and order will make a building good, but disorder bad.

CALLICLES: I agree.

SOCRATES: Is it not the same too with a ship?

b CALLICLES: Yes.

SOCRATES: And with our bodies also, we say?

CALLICLES: Certainly.

SOCRATES: And what about the soul? Will it be good if disordered, or rather if it achieves a certain order and discipline?

CALLICLES: Here to our previous argument demands that we agree.

SOCRATES: Now what is the name of that bodily quality resulting from order and discipline?

CALLICLES: Health and strength, I suppose you mean.

c SOCRATES: I do. And the effect of order and discipline in the soul? Try to discover and name it, as in the other case.

CALLICLES: Why do you not name it yourself, Socrates?

SOCRATES: Well, if you prefer that, I will do so, and do you, if you think I am right, agree; if not, refute me and do not let me escape. It seems to me that the word healthy is applied to all regularity in the body, and from this come health and general bodily excellence. Is it so or not?

CALLICLES: It is.

SOCRATES: And the words lawfulness and law are applied to all order   d
and regularity of the soul, whence men become orderly and law-abiding, and this means justice and temperance. Yes or no?

CALLICLES: So be it.

SOCRATES: And is it not with his eye on these things that our orator, the good and true artist, will bring to bear upon our souls the words he utters and all his actions too, and give any gift he gives, or take away what he takes—his mind always occupied with one thought, how justice may be implanted in the souls of the citizens and injustice banished, and how temperance may be implanted and indiscipline banished, and how goodness in   e
general may be engendered and wickedness depart? Do you agree or not?

CALLICLES: I agree.

SOCRATES: For what benefit is there, Callicles, when a body is sick and distempered, in giving it abundant food and the most delicious drinks or other such things, which, so far from profiting it, will on the contrary, if the truth be told, do it more harm? Is this true?

CALLICLES: So be it.   505

SOCRATES: For it is not worth while in my opinion for a man to live with a diseased body; in that case he must live a diseased life. Is it not so?

CALLICLES: Yes.

SOCRATES: Now when a man is well, do not the doctors generally allow him to satisfy his appetites, eating as much as he wishes when hungry or drinking when thirsty, but when he is sick, practically never allow him to take his fill of what he craves? Do you and I agree upon this?

CALLICLES: I agree.

SOCRATES: And is it not the same, my good friend, with the soul? So   b
long as it is evil, senseless and undisciplined and unjust and impious, it should be restrained from its desires and suffered to do nothing but what will improve it. Do you agree or not?

CALLICLES: I agree.

SOCRATES: For thus, I suppose, it will be better for the soul itself.

CALLICLES: Certainly.

SOCRATES: And to restrain it from its desires is to discipline it?

CALLICLES: Yes.

. . .

SOCRATES: I assert then that, if the temperate soul is good, then the   507
soul in the opposite condition to the temperate is evil, and this we saw, was the foolish and undisciplined. Certainly. Moreover the sound-minded man would do his duty by gods and men, for he would not be sound of mind if he did what was unfitting. That must necessarily be so. And doing his duty   b
by men, he would be acting justly, and doing it by the gods, piously, and

the doer of just and pious deeds must be just and pious. That is so. And further, he must be brave, for it is not the part of a man of sound mind to pursue or avoid what he should not, but to pursue or avoid what he should, whether it be things, or people, or pleasures, or pains, and to stand his ground, where duty bids, and remain steadfast. So there is every necessity,

c Callicles, that the sound-minded and temperate man, being, as we have demonstrated, just and brave and pious, must be completely good, and the good man must do well and finely whatever he does, and he who does well must be happy and blessed, while the evil man who does ill must be wretched, and he would be the opposite of the temperate man, the undisciplined creature of whom you approve.

This then is the position I take, and I affirm it to be true, and if it is true, then the man who wishes to be happy must, it seems, pursue and

d practice temperance, and each of us must flee from indiscipline with all the speed in his power and contrive, preferably to have no need of being disciplined, but if he or any of his friends, whether individual or city, has need of it, then he must suffer punishment and be disciplined, if he is to be happy. This I consider to be the mark to which a man should look throughout his life, and all his own endeavors and those of his city he should de-

e vote to the single purpose of so acting that justice and temperance shall dwell in him who is to be truly blessed. He should not suffer his appetites to be undisciplined and endeavor to satisfy them by leading the life of a brigand—a mischief without end. For such a man could be dear neither to any other man nor to God, since he is incapable of fellowship, and where there is no fellowship, friendship cannot be. Wise men, Callicles, say that

508 the heavens and the earth, gods and men, are bound together by fellowship and friendship, and order and temperance and justice, and for this reason they call the sum of things the "ordered" universe, my friend, not the world of disorder or riot. But it seems to me that you pay no attention to these things in spite of your wisdom, but you are unaware that geometric equality is of great importance among gods and men alike, and you think we should practice overreaching others, for you neglect geometry. Well, either we must refute this argument and prove that happiness does not come to

b the happy through the possession of justice and temperance, nor does misery come through the possession of wickedness, or, if my argument is true, we must consider the consequences. And the consequences are all those previously mentioned, about which you asked me, Callicles, if I was speaking seriously when I said that a man should accuse himself and his son and his friend, if guilty of any wrong deed, and should employ rhetoric for this purpose, and what you thought Polus admitted through a sense of

c shame is true after all—that it is as much more evil as it is more shameful to do than to suffer wrong, and he who is to become a rhetorician in the right way must after all be a just man with a knowledge of what is just—an admission which Gorgias in turn made, according to Polus, through a sense of shame.

This being so, let us consider whether or not you spoke aright in your reproaches to me, when you said that I am not able to help myself or any of my friends and relations, or to save them from the gravest perils, but like outlawed men am at the mercy of anyone, whether he wishes to box my ears, as you so forcefully expressed it, or rob me of my money, or drive me out of the city, or, worst of all, put me to death, and, according to your view to be in this plight is of all things the most shameful. But as to my own view, though it has often been expressed already, there is no harm in my expressing it once more. I maintain, Callicles, that it is not the most shameful of things to be wrongfully boxed on the ears, nor again to have either my purse or my person cut, but it is both more disgraceful and more wicked to strike or to cut me or what is mine wrongfully, and, further, theft and kidnaping and burglary and in a word any wrong done to me and mine is at once more shameful and worse for the wrongdoer than for me the sufferer. These facts, which were shown to be as I state them some time earlier in our previous discussion, are buckled fast and clamped together —to put it somewhat crudely—by arguments of steel and adamant—at least so it would appear as matters stand. And unless you or one still more enterprising than yourself can undo them, it is impossible to speak aright except as I am now speaking. For what I say is always the same—that I know not the truth in these affairs, but I do know that of all whom I have ever met either before or now no one who put forward another view has failed to appear ridiculous. And so once more I hold these things to be so, and if they are, and if injustice is the greatest of evils to the wrongdoer, and, greatest though it be, it is an even greater evil, if that be possible, to escape punishment when one does wrong, what is that help, the failure to avail himself of which makes a man in very truth ridiculous? Is it not that which will avert from us the greatest harm? This must surely be the help which it is most shameful to be unable to render to oneself and one's friends and relations, and next to this the second most shameful, and after that the third and so with the rest; as is the magnitude of the evil in each case, so too will be the beauty of being able to help oneself to meet such evil and the shame of being unable. Am I right or wrong, Callicles?

CALLICLES: You are right.

.   .   .

QUESTIONS FOR STUDY AND DISCUSSION

1. "The virtuous life is a mere convention, unnatural for man," says Callicles. How do you disprove this claim?
2. Callicles insists that the stronger rightfully rules the weaker, that is, that "might makes right." Discuss the implications of this.
3. Socrates disagrees with Callicles' opinion that happiness is identical with the pleasures of the body. Why?
4. It is better to suffer injustice than to do an injustice. Discuss.
5. Discuss harmony and order (discipline) in moral conduct as opposed to disorder and its consequences for the soul and body.

Aristotle

ARISTOTLE was born in Stagira in 384 B.C., and as a boy lived at the Macedonian court where his father was physician to the king of Macedonia. At seventeen he went to Athens to study at Plato's Academy, and became its most brilliant student. After Plato's death in 348, Aristotle spent some years formulating his own philosophical position; at first he retained strong Platonic elements but eventually developed an original approach. In 342 he became tutor to a young Macedonian later to be known as Alexander the Great. When Alexander embarked on his career of conquest, Aristotle returned to Athens, where he attracted many distinguished pupils to his school, the Lyceum. For twelve years he directed the course of studies at the Lyceum, but in 323 strong anti-Macedonian feeling drove him from Athens, where he feared he would suffer the fate of Socrates. He died one year later in Chalcis. Aristotle wrote many great treatises in philosophy; his principal ethical work is the *Nicomachean Ethics,* which remains a major work in ethics and is a cornerstone of Western ethical thought.

All Human Action Aims at the Good and the Supreme Good

BOOK I

i Every art and every investigation, and likewise every practical pursuit or undertaking, seems to aim at some good: hence it has been well said that
2 the Good is That at which all things aim. (It is true that a certain variety is to be observed among the ends at which the arts and sciences aim: in some cases the activity of practising the art is itself the end,[1] whereas in others the end is some product over and above the mere exercise of the art; and in the arts whose ends are certain things beside the practice of the arts them-
3 selves, these products are essentially superior in value to the activities.) But as there are numerous pursuits and arts and sciences, it follows that

---

[1] Aristotle gives flute-playing as an instance of an art the practice of which is an end in itself, in contrast with the art of building, the end of which is the house built. (*Magna Moralia,* 1211 b 27 ff.) [H.R.]

Reprinted by permission of the publishers, The Loeb Classical Library, from pp. 3–5 of Aristotle, *The Nicomachean Ethics,* Book I, translated by H. Rackham. Cambridge, Mass.: Harvard University Press, 1962.

their ends are correspondingly numerous: for instance, the end of the science of medicine is health, that of the art of shipbuilding a vessel, that of strategy victory, that of domestic economy wealth. Now in cases where 4 several such pursuits are subordinate to some single faculty—as bridle-making and the other trades concerned with horses' harness are subordinate to horsemanship, and this and every other military pursuit to the science of strategy, and similarly other arts to different arts again—in all these cases, I say, the ends of the master arts are things more to be desired than all those of the arts subordinate to them; since the latter ends are only pursued for the sake of the former. (And it makes no difference whether 5 the ends of the pursuits are the activities themselves or some other thing beside these, as in the case of the sciences mentioned.)

If therefore among the ends at which our actions aim there be one ii which we wish for its own sake, while we wish the others only for the sake of this, and if we do not choose everything for the sake of something else (which would obviously result in a process *ad infinitum,* so that all desire would be futile and vain), it is clear that this one ultimate End must be the Good, and indeed the Supreme Good. Will not then a knowledge of this 2 Supreme Good be also of great practical importance for the conduct of life? Will it not better enable us to attain what is fitting, like archers having 3 a target to aim at? If this be so, we ought to make an attempt to determine at all events in outline what exactly this Supreme Good is, and of which of the theoretical or practical sciences it is the object.

. . .

QUESTIONS FOR STUDY AND DISCUSSION

1. How does Aristotle generally characterize the good?
2. Every good is an end, and every end is a good; however, the two terms are not identical. Explain.
3. Every means may be an end, but not every end is a means. Explain.
4. Why should there necessarily be a supreme end of human life?
5. Why does Aristotle begin his ethics with a study of end?

What Is a Moral Virtue?

BOOK II

. . .

We have next to consider the formal definition of virtue. v

A state of the soul is either (1) an emotion, (2) a capacity, or

Reprinted by permission of the publishers, The Loeb Classical Library, from pp. 87–95 of Aristotle, *The Nicomachean Ethics,* Book II, translated by H. Rackham. Cambridge, Mass.: Harvard University Press, 1962.

2   (3) a disposition; virtue therefore must be one of these three things. By the emotions, I mean desire, anger, fear, confidence, envy, joy, friendship, hatred, longing, jealousy, pity; and generally those states of consciousness which are accompanied by pleasure or pain. The capacities are the faculties in virtue of which we can be said to be liable to the emotions, for example, capable of feeling anger or pain[1] or pity. The dispositions are the formed states of character in virtue of which we are well or ill disposed in respect of the emotions; for instance, we have a bad disposition in regard to anger if we are disposed to get angry too violently or not violently enough, a good disposition if we habitually feel a moderate amount of anger; and similarly in respect of the other emotions.

3   Now the virtues and vices are not emotions because we are not pronounced good or bad according to our emotions, but we are according to our virtues and vices; nor are we either praised or blamed for our emotions—a man is not praised for being frightened or angry, nor is he blamed for being angry merely, but for being angry in a certain way—but we are

4   praised or blamed for our virtues and vices. Again, we are not angry or afraid from choice, but the virtues are certain modes of choice, or at all events involve choice. Moreover, we are said to be "moved" by the emotions, whereas in respect of the virtues and vices we are not said to be "moved" but to be "disposed" in a certain way.

5   And the same considerations also prove that the virtues and vices are not capacities; since we are not pronounced good or bad, praised or blamed, merely by reason of our capacity for emotion. Again, we possess certain capacities by nature, but we are not born good or bad by nature: of this however we spoke before.

6   If then the virtues are neither emotions nor capacities, it remains that they are dispositions.

Thus we have stated what virtue is generically.

vi   But it is not enough merely to define virtue generically as a disposition;

2   we must also say what species of disposition it is. It must then be premised that all excellence has a twofold effect on the thing to which it belongs: it not only renders the thing itself good, but it also causes it to perform its function well. For example, the effect of excellence in the eye is that the eye is good *and* functions well; since having good eyes means having good sight. Similarly excellence in a horse makes it a good horse, and also good

3   at galloping, at carrying its rider, and at facing the enemy. If therefore this is true of all things, excellence or virtue in a man will be the disposition which renders him a good man and also which will cause him to perform

4   his function well. We have already indicated [c. ii 8f.] what this means; but it will throw more light on the subject if we consider what constitutes the specific nature of virtue.

---

[1] Probably for "pain" we should read "fear." [H.R.]

Now of everything that is continuous [2] and divisible, it is possible to take the larger part, or the smaller part, or an equal part, and these parts may be larger, smaller, and equal either with respect to the thing itself or relatively to us; the equal part being a mean between excess and defi- 5 ciency.[3] By the mean of the thing I denote a point equally distant from either extreme, which is one and the same for everybody; by the mean rela- tive to us, that amount which is neither too much nor too little, and this is not one and the same for everybody. For example, let 10 be many and 2 6 few; then one takes the mean with respect to the thing if one takes 6; since $6 - 2 = 10 - 6$, and this is the mean according to arithmetical propor- 7 tion.[4] But we cannot arrive by this method at the mean relative to us. Sup- pose that 10 lb. of food is a large ration for anybody and 2 lb. a small one: it does not follow that a trainer will prescribe 6 lb., for perhaps even this will be a large ration, or a small one, for the particular athlete who is to receive it; it is a small ration for a Milo,[5] but a large one for a man just beginning to go in for athletics. And similarly with the amount of running 8 or wrestling exercise to be taken. In the same way then an expert in any art avoids excess and deficiency, and seeks and adopts the mean—the mean, that is, not of the thing but relative to us. If therefore the way in which 9 every art or science performs its work well is by looking to the mean and applying that as a standard to its productions (hence the common remark about a perfect work of art, that you could not take from it nor add to it—meaning that excess and deficiency destroy perfection, while adherence to the mean preserves it)—if then, as we say, good craftsmen look to the mean as they work, and if virtue, like nature, is more accurate and better than any form of art, it will follow that virtue has the quality of hitting the mean. I refer to moral virtue,[6] for this is concerned with emotions and ac- 10 tions, in which one can have excess or deficiency or a due mean. For ex- ample, one can be frightened or bold, feel desire or anger or pity, and expe- rience pleasure and pain in general, either too much or too little, and in

---

[2] I.e., without distinct parts, and so (if divisible at all), divisible at any point, as opposed to what is "discrete" (*diērēmenon*), or made up of distinct parts and only divisible between them. [H.R.]

[3] Greek comparatives, "larger," "smaller," etc., may also mean "too large," "too small," etc.; and there is the same ambiguity in the words translated "excess" and "deficiency." Again "middle" (*meson*) or "mean," is used as a synonym for "moderate" (*metrion*) or of the right amount, and "equal" (*ison*) can mean "equitable." Hence "to take an equal part with respect to the thing itself" means to take a part equal to the part left, viz. a half; "to take an equal part relatively to us," means to take what is a fair or suitable amount. The former is a mean as being exactly in the middle be- tween all and none—if the thing in question is represented by a line, this is bisected at a point equidistant from its two ends; the latter is a mean in the sense of being the right amount for the recipient, and also of lying somewhere between any two other amounts that happen to be too much and too little for him. [H.R.]

[4] We should rather call this an arithmetical progression. [H.R.]

[5] A famous wrestler. [H.R.]

[6] The formula of the mean does not apply to the intellectual virtues. [H.R.]

11 both cases wrongly; whereas to feel these feelings at the right time, on the right occasion, towards the right people, for the right purpose and in the right manner, is to feel the best amount of them, which is the mean
12 amount—and the best amount is of course the mark of virtue. And similarly there can be excess, deficiency, and the due mean in actions. Now feelings and actions are the objects with which virtue is concerned; and in feelings and actions excess and deficiency are errors, while the mean amount is praised, and constitutes success; and to be praised and to be suc-
13 cessful are both marks of virtue. Virtue, therefore, is a mean state in the
14 sense that it is able to hit the mean. Again, error is multiform (for evil is a form of the unlimited, as in the old Pythagorean imagery,[7] and good of the limited), whereas success is possible in one way only (which is why it is easy to fail and difficult to succeed—easy to miss the target and difficult to hit it); so this is another reason why excess and deficiency are a mark of vice, and observance of the mean a mark of virtue:

Goodness is simple, badness manifold.[8]

15 Virtue then is a settled disposition of the mind determining the choice [9] of actions and emotions, consisting essentially in the observance of the mean relative to us, this being determined by principle, that is,[10] as the prudent man would determine it.

QUESTIONS FOR STUDY AND DISCUSSION

1. What is the nature of habit?
2. Explain the necessity of habits for man.
3. Distinguish the objective from the subjective mean in relation to moral virtue. Give examples.
4. Why does virtue consist in a mean?
5. What is the difference between mean and mediocrity? Could one practice the mean to excess? Why or why not?

---

[7] Cf. I. vi. 7. [H.R.]
[8] This verse from an unknown source would come in better just before or just after the last parenthesis. [H.R.]
[9] "Choice" (proairesis) or "purpose," is discussed in III. ii., where see note. [H.R.]
[10] A variant reading gives "determined by principle, or whatever we like to call that by which the prudent man would determine it." (Vide A. E. Taylor, Aristotle [London, 1943], p. 77.) [H.R.]

Choice and Deliberation

BOOK III

. . .

Having defined voluntary and involuntary action, we next have to examine   ii
the nature of Choice.[1] For this appears to be intimately connected with virtue, and to afford a surer test of character than do our actions.

Choice is manifestly a voluntary act. But the two terms are not synony-   2
mous, the latter being the wider. Children and the lower animals as well as
men are capable of voluntary action, but not of choice. Also sudden acts
may be termed voluntary, but they cannot be said to be done by choice.

Some identify Choice with (1) Desire, or (2) Passion, or (3)   3
Wish, or (4) some form of Opinion. These views however appear to be
mistaken.

(1) The irrational animals do not exercise choice, but they do feel de-   4
sire, and also passion. Also a man of defective self-restraint acts from desire but not from choice; and on the contrary a self-restrained man acts   5
from choice and not from desire. Again, desire can run counter to choice,
but not desire to desire.[2] And desire has regard to an object as pleasant or
painful, choice has not.[3]

(2) Still less is choice the same as passion. Acts done from passion   6
seem very far from being done of deliberate choice.

(3) Again, choice is certainly not a wish, though they appear closely   7
akin. Choice cannot have for its object impossibilities: if a man were to say
he chose something impossible he would be thought a fool; but we can wish
for things that are impossible, for instance immortality. Also we may wish   8
for what cannot be secured by our own agency, for instance, that a particu-

---

[1] The writer here examines the operation of the Will, which is regarded as essentially
an act of choosing between alternatives of conduct. The technical term employed,
"choice" or "preference," has appeared in the formal definition of virtue (II. vi. 15).
In the present passage, cf. § 9, it is viewed as directed to means: at the moment of
action we select from among the alternative acts possible (or expressing it more
loosely, among the various things here and now obtainable by our action) the one
which we think will conduce to the end we wish. Elsewhere however (III. i. 15 and
vi. xii. 8) it is used of the selection of ends, and it is almost equivalent to "purpose";
while at VI. xiii. 8 it includes both ends and means. (See also VII. ix. 1.) The writer
returns to the subject in VI. ii. [H.R.]

[2] I.e., you cannot feel two contradictory desires at once (though you can of course
desire two incompatible things: you may want to eat your cake and have it; but
you cannot strictly speaking at the same time both desire to eat the cake and desire
not to eat it). But you can desire to do a thing and choose not to do it. [H.R.]

[3] But as good or bad. [H.R.]

Reprinted by permission of the publishers, The Loeb Classical Library, from pp. 129–
41 of Aristotle, *The Nicomachean Ethics*, Book III, translated by H. Rackham.
Cambridge, Mass.: Harvard University Press, 1962.

lar actor [4] or athlete may win; but no one chooses what does not rest with
himself, but only what he thinks can be attained by his own act. Again, we
wish rather for ends than for means, but choose the means to our end; for
example, we wish to be healthy, but choose things to make us healthy; we
wish to be happy, and that is the word we use in this connexion, but it
would not be proper to say that we choose to be happy; since, speaking
generally, choice seems to be concerned with things within our own control.

(4) Nor yet again can it be opinion. It seems that anything may be
matter of opinion—we form opinions about what is eternal,[5] or impossible, just as much as about what is within our power. Also we distinguish
opinion by its truth or falsehood, not by its being good or bad, but choice is
distinguished rather as being good or bad. Probably therefore nobody actually identifies choice with opinion in general. But neither is it the same as
some particular opinion.[6] For it is our choice of good or evil that determines our character, not our opinion about good or evil. And we choose to
take or avoid some good or evil thing, but we opine what a thing is, or for
whom it is advantageous, or how it is so: [7] we do not exactly form an
opinion to take or avoid a thing. Also we praise a choice rather for choosing the right thing, but an opinion for opining in the right way. And we
choose only things that we absolutely know to be good, we opine things we
do not quite certainly know to be true. Nor do the same persons appear to
excel both at choosing and at forming opinons: some people seem to form
opinions better, but yet to choose the wrong things from wickedness. That
choice is preceded or accompanied by the formation of an opinion is immaterial, for that is not the point we are considering, but whether choice is
the same thing as some form of opinion.

What then are the genus and differentia of Choice, inasmuch as it is not
any of the things above mentioned? It manifestly belongs to the genus voluntary action; but not every voluntary act is chosen. Perhaps we may define it as voluntary action preceded by deliberation, since choice involves
reasoning and some process of thought. Indeed previous deliberation seems
to be implied by the very term *proaireton,* which denotes something *chosen
before* other things.

As for Deliberation, do people deliberate about everything—are all
things possible objects of deliberation—, or are there some things about
which deliberation is impossible? The term "object of deliberation" presumably must not be taken to include things about which a fool or a madman might deliberate, but to mean what a sensible person would deliberate
about.

---

[4] Greek dramas were produced in competitions (and it is noteworthy that in the
Old Comedy at Athens the play itself dramatized a contest or debate). [H.R.]
[5] Cf. c. iii. 3 and note. [H.R.]
[6] I.e., an opinion or belief that so-and-so is good, and is within our power to obtain.
[H.R.]
[7] Perhaps to be emended "how it is to be achieved." [H.R.]

Well then, nobody deliberates about things eternal,[8] such as the order   3
of the universe, or the incommensurability of the diagonal and the side of a
square. Nor yet about things that change but follow a regular process,   4
whether from necessity or by nature [9] or through some other cause: such
phenomena for instance as the solstices and the sunrise. Nor about irregu-   5
lar occurrences, such as droughts and rains. Nor about the results of
chance, such as finding a hidden treasure. The reason [10] why we do not   6
deliberate about these things is that none of them can be effected by our
agency. We deliberate about things that are in our control and are attaina-   7
ble by action (which are in fact the the only things that still remain to be
considered; for Nature, Necessity, and Chance, with the addition of Intelligence and human agency generally, exhaust the generally accepted list of
causes). But we do not deliberate about all human affairs without exception either: for example, no Lacedaemonian deliberates about the best
form of government [11] for Scythia; but any particular set of men deliberates about the things attainable by their own actions. Also there is no room   8
for deliberation about matters fully ascertained and completely formulated
as sciences; such for instance as orthography, for we have no uncertainty
as to how a word ought to be spelt. We deliberate about things in which
our agency operates but does not always produce the same results; for instance about questions of medicine and of business; and we deliberate
about navigation more than about athletic training, because it has been less
completely reduced to a science; and similarly with other pursuits also.   9
And we deliberate more about the arts [12] than about the sciences, because
we are more uncertain about them.

Deliberation then is employed in matters which, though subject to rules   10
that generally hold good, are uncertain in their issue; or where the issue is
indeterminate,[13] and where, when the matter is important, we take others
into our deliberations, distrusting our own capacity to decide.

And we deliberate not about ends, but about means. A doctor does not   11
deliberate whether he is to cure his patient, nor an orator whether he is to

---

[8] The term includes the notion of immutability. [H.R.]

[9] Here and in § 7 "necessity" denotes natural law in the inanimate world, while "nature" or "growth" means natural law as governing animate creatures. Aristotle held
that these agencies, and with them the operation of human intelligence and art,
beside their designed results, produced by their interplay certain by-products in
the shape of undesigned and irregular occurrences, which are referred to in the
next section. These in the natural world he spoke of as due to "spontaneous" (*auto-
maton*); when due to the activity of man he ascribed them to fortune or chance. In
§ 7 chance is made to include "the spontaneous." [H.R.]

[10] In the MSS. the words "The reason why . . . list of causes" come after "But we do
not deliberate . . . Scythia." [H.R.]

[11] Or, "the best line of policy." [H.R.]

[12] A less well attested reading gives "more about our opinions," and Aristotle does
not usually distinguish sharply between the arts and crafts and the practical sciences. (The theoretic sciences cannot here be meant, see §§ 3, 4.) [H.R.]

[13] The text is probably corrupt, and perhaps should be altered to run "and in which
the right means to take are not definitely determined." [H.R.]

convince his audience, nor a statesman whether he is to secure good government, nor does anyone else debate about the end of his profession or calling; they take some end for granted, and consider how and by what means it can be achieved. If they find that there are several means of achieving it, they proceed to consider which of these will attain it most easily and best. If there is only one means by which it can be accomplished, they ask how it is to be accomplished by that means, and by what means that means can itself be achieved, until they reach the first link in the chain of causes, which is the last in the order of discovery. (For when deliberating one seems in the procedure described to be pursuing an investigation or

12 analysis that resembles the analysis of a figure in geometry [14]—indeed it appears that though not all investigation is deliberation, for example, mathematical investigation is not, yet all deliberations is investigation—and

13 the last step in the analysis seems to be the first step in the execution of the design.) Then, if they have come up against an impossibility, they abandon the project—for instance, if it requires money and money cannot be procured; but if on the other hand it proves to be something possible, they begin to act. By possible, I mean able to be performed by our agency—things we do through the agency of our friends counting in a sense as done by ourselves, since the origin of their action is in us.

14 (In practising an art [15]) the question is at one moment what tools to use, and at another how to use them; and similarly in other spheres, we have to consider sometimes what means to employ, and sometimes how exactly any given means are to be employed.

15 It appears therefore, as has been said, that a man is the origin of his actions, and that the province of deliberation is to discover actions within

16 one's own power to perform; and all our actions aim at ends other than themselves. It follows that we do not deliberate about ends, but about means. Nor yet do we deliberate about particular facts, for instance, Is this object a loaf? or, Is this loaf properly baked? for these are matters of direct perception. Deliberation must stop at the particular fact, or it will embark on a process *ad infinitum*.

17 The object of deliberation and the object of choice are the same, except that when a thing is chosen it has already been determined, since it is the thing already selected as the result of our deliberation that is chosen. For a man stops enquiring how he shall act as soon as he has carried back the

18 origin of action to himself, and to the dominant part [16] of himself, for it is this part that chooses. This may be illustrated by the ancient constitutions

---

[14] The reference is to the analytical method of solving a problem: the figure required to be drawn is assumed to have been drawn, and then we analyse it and ask what conditions it implies, until we come down to something that we know how to draw already. [H.R.]

[15] This clause seems implied by the context. [H.R.]

[16] I.e., the intellect or reason, which chooses a line of action for the individual, as the Homeric monarch chose a policy for his kingdom. [H.R.]

represented in Homer: the kings used to proclaim to the people the measures they had chosen to adopt.

As then the object of choice is something within our power which after deliberation we desire, Choice will be a deliberate desire of things in our power; for we first deliberate, then select, and finally fix our desire according to the result of our deliberation. 19

Let this serve as a description in outline of Choice, and of the nature of its objects, and the fact that it deals with means to ends. 20

QUESTIONS FOR STUDY AND DISCUSSION

1. Describe the act of deliberation.
2. Explain Aristotle's definition of choice.
3. What is the distinction between choice and wish? Give an example of each.
4. Is there a relation between deliberation and choice?
5. Why does Aristotle fail to discuss formally the problem of freedom of will?

Intellectual Virtues

BOOK VI

We have already said [1] that it is right to choose the mean and to avoid excess and deficiency, and that the mean is prescribed by the right principle. Let us now analyse the latter notion. i

In the case of each of the moral qualities or dispositions that have been discussed, as with all the other virtues also, here is a certain mark to aim at, on which the man who knows the principle involved fixes his gaze, and increases or relaxes the tension [2] accordingly; there is a certain standard determining those modes of observing the mean which we define as lying between excess and defect, being in conformity with the right principle. This bare statement however, although true, is not at all enlightening. In all departments of human endeavour that have been reduced to a science, it is true to say that effort ought to be exerted and relaxed neither too much nor 2

---

[1] Cf. II. vi., esp. § 15. [H.R.]
[2] The words denote tightening and loosening a bowstring, and also tuning a lyre. The former image is suggested by the preceding words, but the latter perhaps is a better metaphor for that avoidance of the too much and the too little which, according to Aristotle, constitutes right conduct. [H.R.]

Reprinted by permission of the publishers, The Loeb Classical Library, from pp. 325–47 of Aristotle, *The Nicomachean Ethics,* Book VI, translated by H. Rackham. Cambridge, Mass.: Harvard University Press, 1962.

too little, but to the medium amount, and as the right principle decides. Yet a person knowing this truth will be no wiser than before: for example, he will not know what medicines to take merely from being told to take everything that medical science or a medical expert would prescribe. Hence with respect to the qualities of the soul also, it is not enough merely to have established the truth of the above formula; we also have to define exactly what the right principle is, and what is the standard that determines it.[3]

4 Now we have divided the Virtues of the Soul into two groups, the Virtues of the Character and the Virtues of the Intellect. The former, the Moral Virtues, we have already discussed. Our account of the latter must be prefaced by some remarks about psychology.

5 It has been said before [4] that the soul has two parts, one rational and the other irrational. Let us now similarly divide the rational part, and let it be assumed that there are two rational faculties, one whereby we contemplate those things whose first principles are invariable, and one whereby we contemplate those things which admit of variation: since, on the assumption that knowledge is based on a likeness or affinity of some sort between subject and object, the parts of the soul adapted to the cognition of objects that are of different kinds must themselves differ in kind. These two rational faculties may be designated the Scientific Faculty and the Calculative Faculty respectively; since calculation is the same as deliberation, and deliberation is never exercised about things that are invariable, so that the Calculative Faculty is a separate part of the rational half of the soul.

7 We have therefore to ascertain what disposition of each of these faculties is the best, for that will be the special virtue of each.

ii But the virtue of a faculty is related to the special function which that faculty performs. Now there are three elements in the soul which control action and the attainment of truth: namely, Sensation, Intellect,[5] and Desire.

2 Of these, Sensation never originates action, as is shown by the fact that animals have sensation but are not capable of action.[6]

Pursuit [7] and avoidance in the sphere of Desire correspond to affirmation and denial in the sphere of the Intellect. Hence inasmuch as moral vir-

---

[3] Book VI. thus purports to explain further the definition of Moral Virtue (II. vi. 15), while at the same time (§ 4) continuing the analysis of the definition of Happiness (I. vii. 15) by examining the Intellectual Virtues. [H.R.]

[4] I. xiii. 9. [H.R.]

[5] Intellect (*nous*) here bears its usual philosophic sense of the intellect, or rational part of the "soul," as a whole, whose function is thought (*dianoia*) in general. In c. vi. it is given a special and restricted meaning, and this in c. xi. is related to the popular use of the word to denote "good sense" or practical intelligence. [H.R.]

[6] (*Praxis*), rational action, conduct. The movements of animals, Aristotle appears to think, are mere reactions to the stimuli of sensation. [H.R.]

[7] Greenwood points out that the passage would be clearer if § 2 mid.–§ 3, "Pursuit . . . right desire," and § 5, "Thought by itself . . . desire aims," came lower down, after the verse-quotation in § 6. The earlier part of § 6 is a parenthetical note. [H.R.]

tue is a disposition of the mind in regard to choice,[8] and choice is deliberate desire,[9] it follows that, if the choice is to be good, both the principle must be true and the desire right, and that desire must pursue the same things as principle affirms. We are here speaking of practical thinking, and 3 of the attainment of truth in regard to action; with speculative thought, which is not concerned with action or production, right and wrong functioning consist in the attainment of truth and falsehood respectively. The attainment of truth is indeed the function of every part of the intellect, but that of the practical intelligence is the attainment of truth corresponding to right desire.[10]

Now the cause of action (the efficient, not the final cause) is choice,[11] 4 and the cause of choice is desire and reasoning directed to some end. Hence choice necessarily involves both intellect or thought and a certain disposition of character [for doing well and the reverse in the sphere of action necessarily involve thought and character [12]].

Thought by itself however moves nothing, but only thought directed to 5 an end, and dealing with action. This indeed is the moving cause of productive activity [13] also, since he who makes something always has some further end in view: the act of making is not an end in itself, it is only a means, and belongs to something else. Whereas a thing done is an end in itself: since doing well (welfare) is the End, and it is at this that desire aims.

Hence Choice may be called either thought related to desire or desire related to thought; and man, as an originator of action, is a union of desire and intellect.

(Choice is not concerned with anything that has happened already: for 6 example, no one chooses to have sacked Troy; for neither does one deliberate about what has happened in the past, but about what still lies in the future and may happen or not; what has happened cannot be made not to have happened. Hence Agathon is right in saying

This only is denied even to God,
The power to make what has been done undone.)

The attainment of truth is then the function of both the intellectual parts of the soul. Therefore their respective virtues are those dispositions which will best qualify them to attain truth.

Let us then discuss these virtues afresh, going more deeply into the iii matter.

---

[8] II. vi. 15. [H.R.]

[9] III. iii. 19. [H.R.]

[10] I.e., truth about the means to the attainment of the rightly desired End. [H.R.]

[11] Cf. III. ii. 1 note. Here again choice (*proairesis*) seems to mean choice of means, not of ends. [H.R.]

[12] This clause must be rejected as superfluous and logically unsound: the nature of action is explained by that of "choice," not *vice versa*. [H.R.]

[13] For this distinction between making and doing, production and action or conduct, see I. i. 2, 5. [H.R.]

Let it be assumed that there are five qualities through which the mind achieves truth in affirmation or denial, namely Art or technical skill,[14] Scientific Knowledge, Prudence, Wisdom, and Intelligence. Conception and Opinion are capable of error.

2 The nature of Scientific Knowledge (employing the term in its exact sense and disregarding its analogous uses) may be made clear as follows. We all conceive that a thing which we know scientifically cannot vary; when a thing that can vary is beyond the range of our observation, we do not know whether it exists or not. An object of Scientific Knowledge, therefore, exists of necessity. It is therefore eternal, for everything existing of absolute necessity is eternal; and what is eternal does not come into exist-

3 ence or perish. Again, it is held that all Scientific Knowledge can be communicated by teaching, and that what is scientifically known must be learnt. But all teaching starts from facts previously known, as we state in the *Analytics*,[15] since it proceeds either by way of induction, or else by way of deduction. Now induction supplies a first principle or universal, deduction works *from* universals; therefore there are first principles from which deduction starts, which cannot be proved by deduction; therefore

4 they are reached by induction. Scientific Knowledge, therefore, is the quality whereby we demonstrate,[16] with the further qualifications included in our definition of it in the *Analytics,* namely, that a man knows a thing scientifically when he possesses a conviction arrived at in a certain way, and when the first principles on which that conviction rests are known to him with certainty—for unless he is more certain of his first principles than of the conclusion drawn from them he will only possess the knowledge in question accidentally.[17] Let this stand as our definition of Scientific Knowledge.

iv The class of things that admit of variation includes both things made

2 and actions done. But making is different from doing (a distinction we may accept from extraneous discourses [18]). Hence the rational quality concerned with doing is different from the rational quality concerned with making. Nor is one of them a part of the other, for doing is not a form of

3 making, nor making a form of doing. Now architectural skill, for instance, is an art, and it is also a rational quality concerned with making; nor is

---

[14] Art (*technē*), as appears below, stands for *eutechniā* and means here craftsmanship of any kind; it includes skill in fine art, but is not limited to it.[H.R.]

[15] See *An. Post.,* Book I, i. 71a 1 ff. [H.R.]

[16] Demonstration in Aristotle means proof by deduction. [H.R.]

[17] I.e., the conviction may happen to be true, but he will not hold it as Scientific Knowledge in the proper sense of the term. [H.R.]

[18] The "extraneous discourses" (*exōterikoi logoi*) are also mentioned in I, xiii, 9 and six other places in Aristotle (see Ross on *Met.* 1076a 28). In *Pol.* 1323a 22 they are appealed to for the tripartite classification of goods which in I, viii, 2 is ascribed to current opinion "of long standing and generally accepted by students of philosophy." The phrase therefore seems to denote arguments or doctrines (whether familiar in philosophical debates or actually recorded in books) that were not peculiar to the Peripathetic school. [H.R. Note on I, xiii, 9.]

there any art which is not a rational quality concerned with making, nor any such quality which is not an art. It follows that an art is the same thing as a rational quality, concerned with making, that reasons truly. All Art **4** deals with bringing something into existence; and to pursue an art means to study how to bring into existence a thing which may either exist or not, and the efficient cause of which lies in the maker and not in the thing made; for Art does not deal with things that exist or come into existence of necessity, or according to nature, since these have their efficient cause in themselves. But as doing and making are distinct, it follows that Art, being concerned **5** with making, is not concerned with doing. And in a sense Art deals with the same objects as chance, as Agathon says:

> Chance is beloved of Art, and Art of Chance.

Art, therefore, as has been said, is a rational quality, concerned with **6** making, that reasons truly. Its opposite, Lack of Art, is a rational quality, concerned with making, that reasons falsely. Both deal with that which admits of variation.

We may arrive at a definition of Prudence by considering who are the **v** persons whom we call prudent. Now it is held to be the mark of a prudent man to be able to deliberate well about what is good and advantageous for himself, not in some one department, for instance what is good for his health or strength, but what is advantageous as a means to the good life in **2** general. This is proved by the fact that we also speak of people as prudent or wise in some particular thing, when they calculate well with a view to attaining some particular end of value (other than those ends which are the object of an art); so that the prudent man in general will be the man who is good at deliberating in general.

But no one deliberates about things that cannot vary, nor about things **3** not within his power to do. Hence inasmuch as scientific knowledge involves demonstration, whereas things whose fundamental principles are variable are not capable of demonstration, because everything about them is variable, and inasmuch as one cannot deliberate about things that are of necessity, it follows that Prudence is not the same as Science. Nor can it be the same as Art. It is not Science, because matters of conduct admit of variation; and not Art, because doing and making are generically different,[19] since making aims at an end distinct from the act of making, whereas in doing the end cannot be other than the act itself: doing well is in itself the **4** end. It remains therefore that it is a truth-attaining rational quality, concerned with action in relation to things that are good and bad for human beings.

Hence men like Pericles are deemed prudent, because they possess a **5** faculty of discerning what things are good for themselves and for mankind;

---

[19] The words "since . . . itself the end" in the MSS. follow § 4 "for human beings." [H.R.]

and that is our conception of an expert in Domestic Economy or Political Science.

6 (This also accounts for the word Temperance, which signifies "preserving prudence." And Temperance does in fact preserve our belief as to our own good; for pleasure and pain do not destroy or pervert all beliefs, for instance, the belief that the three angles of a triangle are, or are not, together equal to two right angles, but only beliefs concerning action. The first principles of action are the end to which our acts are means; but a man corrupted by a love of pleasure or fear of pain, entirely fails to discern any first principle,[20] and cannot see that he ought to choose and do everything as a means to this end, and for its sake; for vice tends to destroy the sense of principle.[21])

It therefore follows that Prudence is a truth-attaining rational quality, concerned with action in relation to the things that are good for human beings.

7 Moreover, we can speak of excellence in Art,[22] but not of excellence in Prudence. Also in Art voluntary error is not so bad as involuntary, whereas in the sphere of Prudence it is worse, as it is in the sphere of the virtues. It is therefore clear that Prudence is an excellence or virtue, and not an Art.

8 Of the two parts of the soul possessed of reason, Prudence must be the virtue of one, namely, the part that forms opinions;[23] for Opinion deals with that which can vary, and so does Prudence. But yet Prudence is not a rational quality merely, as is shown by the fact that a purely rational faculty can be forgotten, whereas a failure in Prudence is not a mere lapse of memory.[24]

vi Scientific Knowledge is a mode of conception dealing with universals and things that are of necessity; and demonstrated truths and all scientific knowledge (since this involves reasoning) are derived from first principles. Consequently the first principles from which scientific truths are derived cannot themselves be reached by Science; nor yet are they apprehended by Art, nor by Prudence. To be matter of Scientific Knowledge a truth must be demonstrated by deduction from other truths; while Art and Prudence are

---

[20] Or "to one corrupted by pleasure or pain this end does not seem to be a first principle at all." [H.R.]

[21] I.e., to destroy our perception of the true end of life, which constitutes the major premise of the practical syllogism. [H.R.]

[22] Art (techné) is here (as in c. vii. 1) used in a neutral sense, of a systematic procedure for making something, or a body of principles for such a procedure—one may be good at it or bad; whereas Prudence (phronēsis), or practical wisdom, itself denotes an excellence, not a neutral sphere in which one may excel or the reverse. Elsewhere in this book techné has the positive sense of artistic excellence or technical skill. [H.R.]

[23] Called in c. i. 6 the Calculative Faculty. [H.R.]

[24] A loss of Prudence is felt to involve a moral lapse, which shows that it is not a purely intellectual quality. [H.R.]

concerned only with things that admit of variation. Nor is Wisdom the knowledge of first principles either: [25] for the philosopher has to arrive at some things by demonstration.

If then the qualities whereby we attain truth,[26] and are never led into   2 falsehood, whether about things invariable or things variable, are Scientific Knowledge, Prudence, Wisdom, and Intelligence, and if the quality which enables us to apprehend first principles cannot be any one among three of these, namely Scientific Knowledge, Prudence, and Wisdom, it remains that first principles must be apprehended by Intelligence.[27]

The term Wisdom is employed in the arts to denote those men who are   vii the most perfect masters of their art, for instance, it is applied to Pheidias as a sculptor and to Polycleitus as a statuary. In this use then Wisdom merely signifies artistic excellence. But we also think that some people are   2 wise in general and not in one department, not "wise in something else," [28] as Homer says in the *Margites:*

> Neither a delver nor a ploughman him
> The Gods had made, or wise in aught beside.

Hence it is clear that Wisdom must be the most perfect of the modes of   3 knowledge. The wise man therefore must not only know the conclusions that follow from his first principles, but also have a true conception of those principles themselves. Hence Wisdom must be a combination of Intelligence and Scientific Knowledge: [29] it must be a consummated knowledge [30] of the most exalted objects.

For it is absurd to think that Political Science or Prudence is the loftiest kind of knowledge, inasmuch as man is not the highest thing in the world. And as "wholesome" and "good" mean one thing for men and another for   4 fishes, whereas "white" and "straight" mean the same thing always, so everybody would denote the same thing by "wise," but not by "prudent"; for each kind of beings will describe as prudent, and will entrust itself to, one who can discern its own particular welfare; hence even some of the lower animals are said to be prudent, namely those which display a capacity for forethought as regards their own lives.

It is also clear that Wisdom cannot be the same thing as Political Science; for if we are to call knowledge of our own interests wisdom, there

---

[25] I.e., not exclusively: see c. vii. 3. [H.R.]

[26] Cf. c. iii. 1. Art is here omitted from the list. [H.R.]

[27] *Nous* now receives its special sense (see c. ii. 1, note) of a particular virtue of the intellect, viz. that faculty or rational intuition whereby it correctly apprehends (by process of induction, see c. iii. 3) undemonstrable first principles. It is thus a part of *sophiā* (c. vii, 3, 5). [H.R.]

[28] The sense rather requires "wise in some particular thing," but the expression is assimilated to the quotation. [H.R.]

[29] See vi. 1, 2. [H.R.]

[30] Literally "knowledge having as it were a head," a phrase copied from Plato, *Gorgias,* 505 D. [H.R.]

will be a number of different kinds of wisdom, one for each species: there cannot be a single such wisdom dealing with the good of all living things, any more than there is one art of medicine for all existing things. It may be argued that man is superior to the other animals, but this makes no difference: since there exist other things far more divine in their nature than man, for instance, to mention the most visible, the things [31] of which the celestial system is composed.

5   These considerations therefore show that Wisdom is both Scientific Knowledge and Intuitive Intelligence as regards the things of the most exalted [32] nature. This is why people say that men like Anaxagoras and Thales [33] "may be wise but are not prudent," when they see them display ignorance of their own interests; and while admitting them to possess a knowledge that is rare, marvellous, difficult and even superhuman, they yet declare this knowledge to be useless, because these sages do not seek to

6   know the things that are good for human beings. Prudence on the other hand is concerned with the affairs of men, and with things that can be the object of deliberation. For we say that to deliberate well is the most characteristic function of the prudent man; but no one deliberates about things that cannot vary nor yet about variable things that are not a means to some end, and that end a good attainable by action; and a good deliberator in general is a man who can arrive by calculation at the best of the goods attainable by man.

7   Nor is Prudence a knowledge of general principles only: it must also take account of particular facts, since it is concerned with action, and action deals with particular things. This is why men who are ignorant of general principles are sometimes more successful in action than others who know them: for instance,[34] if a man knows that light meat is easily digested and therefore wholesome, but does not know what kinds of meat are light, he will not be so likely to restore you to health as a man who merely knows that chicken is wholesome; and in other matters men of experience are more successful than theorists. And Prudence is concerned with action, so one requires both forms of it, or indeed knowledge of particular facts even more than knowledge of general principles. Here too however there must be some supreme directing faculty.[35]

---

[31] This means apparently the sun, stars, and planets, elsewhere referred to by Aristotle as "the divine bodies that move through the heaven," "the visible divine things," "the heaven and the most divine of visible things." (*Met.* 1074a 30, 1026a 18, *Phys.* 196a 33.) [H.R.]

[32] See § 2, note. [H.R.]

[33] Thales was the first of the Seven Wise Men: Anaxagoras belonged to a later generation. [H.R.]

[34] The words "for instance . . . chicken is wholesome" in the MSS. come after "theorists." [H.R.]

[35] I.e., Political Science (*politikē*) or Statesmanship (cf. I. i., ii.), the relation of which to Prudence is next considered. [H.R.]

QUESTIONS FOR STUDY AND DISCUSSION

1. Distinguish between the contemplative and deliberative intellects.
2. Describe and show the relationship among the following intellectual virtues: science, intellectual intuition, theoretical wisdom.
3. Is there a need for practical wisdom, or prudence, in human moral conduct?
4. Define the virtue of practical wisdom.
5. Which kind of art is referred to in the Aristotelian "virtue of art"?

Friendship

BOOK VIII

Our next business after this will be to discuss Friendship.[1] For friendship is a virtue,[2] or involves virtue; and also it is one of the most indispensable requirements of life. For no one would choose to live without friends, but possessing all other good things. In fact rich men, rulers and potentates are thought especially to require friends, since what would be the good of their prosperity without an outlet for beneficence, which is displayed in its fullest and most praiseworthy form towards friends? and how could such prosperity be safeguarded and preserved without friends? for the greater it is, the greater is its insecurity. And in poverty or any other misfortune men think friends are their only resource. Friends are an aid to the young, to guard them from error; to the elderly, to tend them, and to supplement their failing powers of action; to those in the prime of life, to assist them in noble deeds—

When twain together go [3]—

for two are better able both to plan and to execute. And the affection of parent for offspring and of offspring for parent seems to be a natural instinct, not only in man but also in birds and in most animals; as also is friendship between members of the same species; and this is especially

i

2

3

---

[1] "Friendship" (*philiā*) sometimes rises to the meaning of affection or love, but also includes any sort of kindly feeling, even that existing between business associates, or fellow-citizens. The corresponding verb means both "to like" and "to love"; the adjective is generally passive, "loved," "liked," "dear," but sometimes active "loving," "liking," and so on, as a noun "a friend." [H.R.]

[2] I.e., the social grace of friendliness described in IV. vi.; it is there said to be nameless, but it is called *philiā* at II. vii. 13. [H.R.]

[3] Homer, *Iliad*, X. 224. [H.R.]

Reprinted by permission of the publishers, The Loeb Classical Library, from pp. 451–65 of Aristotle, *The Nicomachean Ethics*, Book VIII, translated by H. Rackham. Cambridge, Mass.: Harvard University Press, 1962.

strong in the human race; for which reason we praise those who love their fellow men. Even when travelling abroad one can observe that a natural

4 affinity and friendship exist between man and man universally. Moreover, friendship appears to be the bond of the state; and lawgivers seem to set more store by it than they do by justice, for to promote concord, which seems akin to friendship, is their chief aim, while faction, which is enmity, is what they are most anxious to banish. And if men are friends, there is no need of justice between them; whereas merely to be just is not enough—a feeling of friendship also is necessary. Indeed the highest form of justice seems to have an element of friendly feeling in it.

5 And friendship is not only indispensable as a means, it is also noble in itself. We praise those who love their friends, and it is counted a noble thing to have many friends; and some people think that a true friend must be a good man.

6 But there is much difference of opinion as to the nature of friendship. Some define it as a matter of similarity; they say that we love those who are like ourselves: whence the proverbs "Like finds his like," "Birds of a feather flock together," and so on. Others on the contrary say that with men who are alike it is always a case of "two of a trade." Some try to find a more profound and scientific explanation of the nature of affection. Euripides writes that "Earth yearneth for the rain" when dried up, "and the majestic Heaven when filled with rain Yearneth to fall to Earth." Heracleitus says, "Opposition unites," and "The fairest harmony springs from difference," and " 'Tis strife that makes the world go on." Others maintain the opposite view, notably Empedocles, who declares that "Like seeks after like."

7 Dismissing then these scientific speculations as not germane to our present enquiry, let us investigate the human aspect of the matter, and examine the questions that relate to man's character and emotions: for instance, whether all men are capable of friendship, or bad men cannot be friends; and whether there is only one sort of friendship or several. Those who hold that all friendship is of the same kind because friendship admits of degree, are relying on an insufficient proof, for things of different kinds also can differ in degree. But this has been discussed before.

ii Perhaps the answer to these questions will appear if we ascertain what sort of things arouse liking or love. It seems that not everything is loved, but only what is lovable, and that this is either what is good, or pleasant, or useful. But useful may be taken to mean productive of some good or of

2 pleasure, so that the class of things lovable as ends is reduced to the good and the pleasant. Then, do men like what is really good, or what is good for them? for sometimes the two may be at variance; and the same with what is pleasant. Now it appears that each person loves what is good for himself, and that while what is really good is lovable absolutely, what is good for a particular person is lovable for that person. Further, each person loves not what is really good for himself, but what appears to him to be

so; however, this will not affect our argument, for "lovable" will mean "what appears lovable."

There being then three motives of love, the term Friendship is not ap- **3** plied to love for inanimate objects, since here there is no return of affection, and also no wish for the good of the object—for instance, it would be ridiculous to wish well to a bottle of wine: at the most one wishes that it may keep well in order that one may have it oneself; whereas we are told that we ought to wish our friend well for his own sake. But persons who wish another good for his own sake, if the feeling is not reciprocated, are merely said to feel goodwill for him: only when mutual is such goodwill termed friendship. And perhaps we should also add the qualification that **4** the feeling of goodwill must be known to its object. For a man often feels goodwill towards persons whom he has never seen, but whom he believes to be good or useful, and one of these persons may also entertain the same feeling towards him. Here then we have a case of two people mutually well-disposed, whom nevertheless we cannot speak of as friends, because they are not aware of each other's regard. To be friends therefore, men must (1) feel goodwill for each other, that is, wish each other's good, and (2) be aware of each other's goodwill, and (3) the cause of their goodwill must be one of the lovable qualities mentioned above.

Now these qualities differ in kind; hence the affection or friendship they **iii** occasion may differ in kind also. There are accordingly three kinds of friendship, corresponding in number to the three lovable qualities; since a reciprocal affection, known to either party, can be based on each of the three, and when men love each other, they wish each other well in respect of the quality which is the ground of their friendship.[4] Thus friends whose affection is based on utility do not love each other in themselves, but in so far as some benefit accrues to them from each other. And similarly with those whose friendship is based on pleasure: for instance, we enjoy the society of witty people not because of what they are in themselves, but because they are agreeable to us. Hence in a friendship based on utility or on **2** pleasure men love their friend for their own good or their own pleasure, and not as being the person loved, but as useful or agreeable. And therefore these friendships are based on an accident since the friend is not loved for being what he is, but as affording some benefit or pleasure as the case may be. Consequently friendships of this kind are easily broken off, in the **3** event of the parties themselves changing, for if no longer pleasant or useful to each other, they cease to love each other. And utility is not a permanent quality; it differs at different times. Hence when the motive of the friendship has passed away, the friendship itself is dissolved, having existed merely as a means to that end.

Friendships of Utility seem to occur most frequently between the old, **4**

---

[4] I.e., they wish each other to become more virtuous, pleasant, or useful as the case may be; so that there is a different species of well-wishing in each case. [H.R.]

as in old age men do not pursue pleasure but profit; and between those persons in the prime of life and young people whose object in life is gain. Friends of this kind do not indeed frequent each other's company much, for in some cases they are not even pleasing to each other, and therefore have no use for friendly intercourse unless they are mutually profitable; since their pleasure in each other goes no further than their expectations of advantage.

With these friendships are classed family ties of hospitality with foreigners.

5   With the young on the other hand the motive of friendship appears to be pleasure, since the young guide their lives by emotion, and for the most part pursue what is pleasant to themselves, and the object of the moment. And the things that please them change as their age alters; hence they both form friendships and drop them quickly, since their affections alter with what gives them pleasure, and the tastes of youth change quickly. Also the young are prone to fall in love, as love is chiefly guided by emotion, and grounded on pleasure; hence they form attachments quickly and give them up quickly, often changing before the day is out.

The young do desire to pass their time in their friend's company, for that is how they get the enjoyment of their friendship.

6   The perfect form of friendship is that between the good, and those who resemble each other in virtue. For these friends wish each alike the other's good in respect of their goodness,[5] and they are good in themselves; but it is those who wish the good of their friends for their friends' sake who are friends in the fullest sense, since they love each other for themselves and not accidentally.[6] Hence the friendship of these lasts as long as they continue to be good; and virtue is a permanent quality. And each is good relatively to his friend as well as absolutely, since the good are both good absolutely and profitable to each other. And each is pleasant in both ways also, since good men are pleasant both absolutely and to each other; for everyone is pleased by his own actions, and therefore by actions that resemble

7   his own, and the actions of all good men are the same or similar.—Such friendship is naturally permanent, since it combines in itself all the attributes that friends ought to possess. All affection is based on good or on pleasure, either absolute or relative to the person who feels it, and is prompted by similarity[7] of some sort; but this friendship possesses all

---

[5] See § 1 above, and note. [H.R.]

[6] I.e., for some accidental, i.e., temporary or not essential, quality: cf. §§ 2, 3. [H.R.]

[7] There is some uncertainty here and elsewhere in these chapters whether "similarity" refers to resemblance between the friends or between the different forms of friendship, friendships based on pleasure or profit being only so called "by way of resemblance," i.e. in an analogical and secondary sense. But the latter consideration seems irrelevant here, and is first developed in the next chapter (§§ 1, 4). It is true that whether similarity between the parties is an element in all friendship (although this is implied by the words "who resemble each other in virtue" in § 6) is nowhere clearly decided, and it can hardly be predicated of some friendships considered below. [H.R.]

these attributes in the friends themselves, for they are alike, *et cetera*,[8] in that way.[9] Also the absolutely good is pleasant absolutely as well; but the absolutely good and pleasant are the chief objects of affection; therefore it is between good men that affection and friendship exist in their fullest and best form.

Such friendships are of course rare, because such men are few. More-   8
over they require time and intimacy: as the saying goes, you cannot get to know a man till you have consumed the proverbial amount of salt in his company; and so you cannot admit him to friendship or really be friends, before each has shown the other that he is worthy of friendship and has   9
won his confidence. People who enter into friendly relations quickly have the wish to be friends, but cannot really be friends without being worthy of friendship, and also knowing each other to be so; the wish to be friends is a quick growth, but friendship is not.

QUESTIONS FOR STUDY AND DISCUSSION

1. In what does true friendship consist?
2. List the major reasons why Aristotle considers friendship necessary and vital to men.
3. Friendship is termed mutual goodwill. Explain.
4. What is a friendship of pleasure? Give some examples.
5. Does virtuous friendship exclude pleasure and usefulness? Explain.

The Problem of Pleasure

BOOK X

.   .   .

We may ascertain the nature and quality of pleasure more clearly if we   iv
start again from the beginning.

Now the act of sight appears to be perfect at any moment of its duration; it does not require anything to supervene later in order to perfect its specific quality. But pleasure also appears to be a thing of this nature. For it is a whole, and one cannot at any moment put one's hand on a pleasure which will only exhibit its specific quality perfectly if its duration be prolonged.

---

[8] I.e., absolutely and relatively good and pleasant: cf. c. iv. 1. [H.R.]
[9] I.e., in themselves, and not accidentally. [H.R.]

Reprinted by permission of the publishers, The Loeb Classical Library, from pp. 591–607 of Aristotle, *The Nicomachean Ethics*, Book X, translated by H. Rackham. Cambridge, Mass.: Harvard University Press, 1962.

2   It follows also that pleasure is not a form of motion.[1] For every motion
or process of change involves duration, and is a means to an end, for instance the process of building a house; and it is perfect when it has effected
its end. Hence a motion is perfect either when viewed over the whole time
of its duration, or at the moment when its end has been achieved. The several motions occupying portions of the time of the whole are imperfect, and
different in kind from the whole and from each other. For instance, in
building a temple the fitting together of the stones is a different process
from the fluting of a column, and both are different from the construction
of the temple as a whole; and whereas the building of the temple is a perfect process, for nothing more is required to achieve the end proposed, laying the foundation and constructing the triglyphs are imperfect processes,
since each produces only a part of the design; they are therefore specifically
different from the construction of the whole, and it is not possible to lay
one's finger on a motion specifically perfect at any moment of the process
of building, but only, if at all, in the whole of its duration.

3   And the same is true of walking and the other forms of locomotion.
For if locomotion is motion from one point in space to another, and if this
is of different kinds, flying, walking, leaping and the like, and not only so,
but if there are also differences in walking itself (for the terminal points of
a racecourse are not the same as those of a portion of the course, nor are
those of one portion the same as those of another; nor is traversing this line
the same as traversing that one,[2] for the runner does not merely travel
along a certain line but travels along a line that is in a certain place, and
this line is in a different place from that)—however, for a full treatment of
the subject of motion I must refer to another work,[3] but it appears that a
motion is not perfect at every moment, but the many movements which
make up the whole are imperfect; and different from each other in kind,
4   inasmuch as the terminal points of a movement constitute a specific quality. The specific quality of pleasure on the contrary is perfect at any moment. It is clear therefore that pleasure is not the same as motion, and that
it is a whole and something perfect.

This may also be inferred from the fact that a movement necessarily
occupies a space of time, whereas a feeling of pleasure does not, for every
moment of pleasurable consciousness is a perfect whole.

These considerations also show that it is a mistake to speak of pleasure
as the result of a motion or of a process of generation. For we cannot so
describe everything, but only such things as are divided into parts and are

---

[1] Motion here has its wider sense of any process of change that actualizes what is
potentially; it includes generation, of which building is an instance. In its proper
sense motion is limited to change of quality, quantity, or place. [H.R.]

[2] The lecturer appears to draw a line representing a racecourse, and divide it into
two parts, representing two sections of the course (not two lines *across* the course).
The motion of traversing one section is not the same as that of traversing the others,
if only because they are in different places. [H.R.]

[3] *Physics*, VI–VIII. [H.R.]

not wholes. Thus an act of sight, a geometrical point, an arithmetical unit are not the result of a process of generation (nor is any of them a motion or process [4]). Pleasure therefore also is not the result of a motion or process; for pleasure is a whole.

Again, inasmuch as each of the senses acts in relation to its object, and 5 acts perfectly when it is in good condition and directed to the finest of the objects that belong to it (for this seems to be the best description of perfect activity, it being assumed to make no difference whether it be the sense itself that acts or the organ in which the sense resides), it follows that the activity of any of the senses is at its best when the sense-organ being in the best condition is directed to the best of its objects; and this activity will be the most perfect and the pleasantest. For each sense has a corresponding pleasure, as also have thought and speculation, and its activity is pleasantest when it is most perfect, and most perfect when the organ is in good condition and when it is directed to the most excellent of its objects; and the pleasure perfects the activity. The pleasure does not however perfect 6 the activity in the same way as the object perceived and the sensory faculty, if good, perfect it; just as health and the physician are not in the same way the cause of being healthy.

(It is clear that each of the senses is accompanied by pleasure, since we 7 apply the term pleasant to sights and sounds; [5] and it is also clear that the pleasure is greatest when the sensory faculty is both in the best condition and acting in relation to the best object; and given excellence in the perceived object and the percipient organ, there will always be pleasure when an object to cause it and a subject to feel it are both present.)

But the pleasure perfects the activity, not as the fixed disposition does, 8 by being already present in the agent, but as a supervening perfection, like the bloom of health in the young and vigorous.

So long therefore as both object thought of or perceived, and subject discerning or judging, are such as they should be, there will be pleasure in the activity; since while both the passive and the active parties to a relationship remain the same in themselves and unaltered in their relation to one another, the same result is naturally produced.

How is it then that no one can feel pleasure continuously? Perhaps it 9 is due to fatigue, since no human faculty is capable of uninterrupted activity, and therefore pleasure also is not continuous, because it accompanies the activity of the faculties. It is for the same reason that some things please us when new, but cease to give so much pleasure later, this is because at first the mind is stimulated, and acts vigorously in regard to the object, as in the case of sight when we look at something intently; but afterwards the activity is less vigorous and our attention relaxes, and consequently the pleasure also fades.

---

[4] This parenthesis is perhaps an interpolation. [H.R.]
[5] As well as to tastes, scents, and contacts, which are more obviously pleasant. [H.R.]

10   It might be held that all men seek to obtain pleasure, because all men desire life. Life is a form of activity, and each man exercises his activity upon those objects and with those faculties which he likes the most: for example, the musician exercises his sense of hearing upon musical tunes, the student his intellect upon problems of philosophy, and so on. And the pleasure of these activities perfects the activities, and therefore perfects

11   life, which all men seek. Men have good reason therefore to pursue pleasure, since it perfects for each his life, which is a desirable thing. The question whether we desire life for the sake of pleasure or pleasure for the sake of life, need not be raised for the present. In any case they appear to be inseparably united; for there is no pleasure without activity, and also no perfect activity without its pleasure.

v   This moreover is the ground for believing that pleasures vary in specific quality. For we feel that different kinds of things must have a different sort of perfection. We see this to be so with natural organisms and the productions of art, such as animals, trees, a picture, a statue, a house, a piece of furniture. Similarly we think that that which perfects one kind of activity

2   must differ in kind from that which perfects another kind. Now the activities of the intellect differ from those of the senses, and from [6] one another, in kind: so also therefore do the pleasures that perfect them.

      This may also be seen from the affinity which exists between the various pleasures and the activities which they perfect. For an activity is augmented by the pleasure that belongs to it; since those who work with pleasure always work with more discernment and with greater accuracy—for instance, students who are fond of geometry become proficient in it, and grasp its various problems better, and similarly lovers of music, architecture or the other arts make progress in their favourite pursuit because they enjoy it. An activity then is augmented by its pleasure; and that which augments a thing must be akin to it. But things that are akin to things of different kinds must themselves differ in kind.

3   A still clearer proof may be drawn from the hindrance that activities receive from the pleasure derived from other activities. For instance, persons fond of the flute cannot give their attention to a philosophical discussion when they overhear someone playing the flute, because they enjoy music more than the activity in which they are engaged; therefore the

4   pleasure afforded by the music of the flute impairs the activity of study. The same thing occurs in other cases when a man tries to do two things at once; the pleasanter activity drives out the other, the more so if it is much more pleasant, until the other activity ceases altogether. Hence, when we enjoy something very much, we can hardly do anything else; and when we find a thing only mildly agreeable, we turn to some other occupation; for

5   instance, people who eat sweets at the theatre do so especially when the

---

[6] A variant reading gives "and these [sc. the activities of the senses] from one another." [H.R.]

acting is bad. And since our activities are sharpened, prolonged and improved by their own pleasure, and impaired by the pleasures of other activities, it is clear that pleasures differ widely from each other. In fact alien pleasures have almost the same effect on the activities as their own pains; [7] since, when an activity causes pain, this pain destroys it, for instance, if a person finds writing or doing sums unpleasant and irksome; for he stops writing or doing sums, because the activity is painful. Activities then are affected in opposite ways by the pleasures and the pains that belong to them, that is to say, those that are intrinsically due to their exercise. Alien pleasures, as has been said, have very much the same effect as pain, for they destroy an activity, only not to the same degree.

Again, since activities differ in moral value, and some are to be 6 adopted, others to be avoided, and others again are neutral, the same is true also of their pleasures: for each activity has a pleasure of its own. Thus the pleasure of a good activity is morally good, that of a bad one morally bad; for even desires for noble things are praised and desires for base things blamed; but the pleasures contained in our activities are more intimately connected with them than the appetites which prompt them, for the appetite is both separate in time and distinct in its nature from the activity, whereas the pleasure is closely linked to the activity, indeed so inseparable from it as to raise a doubt whether the activity is not the same 7 thing as the pleasure. However, we must not regard pleasure as really being a thought or a sensation—indeed this is absurd, though because they are inseparable they seem to some people to be the same.

As then activities are diverse, so also are their pleasures. Sight excels touch in purity, and hearing and smell excel taste; and similarly the pleasures of the intellect excel in purity the pleasures of sensation, while the pleasures of either class differ among themselves in purity.

And it is thought that every animal has its own special pleasure, just as 8 it has its own special function: namely, the pleasure of exercising that function. This will also appear if we consider the different animals one by one: the horse, the dog, man, have different pleasures—as Heracleitus says, an ass would prefer chaff to gold, since to asses food gives more pleasure than gold. Different species therefore have different kinds of pleasures. On the other hand it might be supposed that there is no variety among the pleas- 9 ures of the same species. But as a matter of fact in the human species at all events there is a great diversity of pleasures. The same things delight some men and annoy others, and things painful and disgusting to some are pleasant and attractive to others. This also holds good of things sweet to the taste: the same things do not taste sweet to a man in a fever as to one in good health; nor does the same temperature feel warm to an invalid and to a person of robust constitution. The same holds good of other things as well.

---

[7] I.e., the special pain accompanying a particular activity when it functions badly or in relation to a bad object. [H.R.]

10   But we hold that in all such cases the thing really is what it appears to be to the good man. And if this rule is sound, as it is generally held to be, and if the standard of everything is goodness, or the good man, *qua* good, then the things that seem to him to be pleasures are pleasures, and the things he enjoys are pleasant. Nor need it cause surprise that things disagreeable to the good man should seem pleasant to some men; for mankind is liable to many corruptions and diseases, and the things in question are not really pleasant, but only pleasant to these particular persons, who are in a condition to think them so.

11   It is therefore clear that we must pronounce the admittedly disgraceful pleasures not to be pleasures at all, except to the depraved.

    But among the pleasures considered respectable, which class of pleasures or which particular pleasure is to be deemed the distinctively human pleasure? Perhaps this will be clear from a consideration of man's activities. For pleasures correspond to the activities to which they belong; it is therefore that pleasure, or those pleasures, by which the activity, or the activities, of the perfect and supremely happy man are perfected, that must be pronounced human in the fullest sense. The other pleasures are so only in a secondary or some lower degree, like the activities to which they belong.

QUESTIONS FOR STUDY AND DISCUSSION

1. How does pleasure accompany and perfect human activity?
2. Is it true that fatigue diminishes pleasure? Explain.
3. Give a list of basic pleasures corresponding to the list of basic human activities.
4. What is the hierarchical order among pleasures and what is its basis?
5. Are pleasures evil in themselves? Are they good in themselves? Explain your answer.

Highest Human Happiness: The Contemplative Life

BOOK X

vi   Having now discussed the various kinds of Virtue, of Friendship and of Pleasure, it remains for us to treat in outline of Happiness, inasmuch as we count this to be the End of human life. But it will shorten the discussion if we recapitulate what has been said already.

Reprinted by permission of the publishers, The Loeb Classical Library, from pp. 607–29 of Aristotle, *The Nicomachean Ethics*, Book X, translated by H. Rackham. Cambridge, Mass.: Harvard University Press, 1962.

Now we stated [1] that happiness is not a certain disposition of charac- 2
ter; since if it were it might be possessed by a man who passed the whole of
his life asleep, living the life of a vegetable, or by one who was plunged in
the deepest misfortune. If then we reject this as unsatisfactory, and feel
bound to class happiness rather as some form of activity, as has been said
in the earlier part of this treatise, and if activities are of two kinds, some
merely necessary means and desirable only for the sake of something else,
others desirable in themselves, it is clear that happiness is to be classed
among activities desirable in themselves, and not among those desirable as
a means to something else; since happiness lacks nothing, and is self-
sufficient.

But those activities are desirable in themselves which do not aim at any 3
result beyond the mere exercise of the activity. Now this is felt to be the
nature of actions in conformity with virtue; for to do noble and virtuous
deeds is a thing desirable for its own sake.

But agreeable amusements also are desirable for their own sake; we do
not pursue them as a means to something else, for as a matter of fact they
are more often harmful than beneficial, causing men to neglect their health
and their estates. Yet persons whom the world counts happy usually have
recourse to such pastimes; and this is why adepts in such pastimes stand in
high favour with princes, because they make themselves agreeable in supplying what their patrons desire, and what they want is amusement. So it is
supposed that amusements are a component part of happiness, because
princes and potentates devote their leisure to them.

But (i) perhaps princes and potentates are not good evidence. Virtue 4
and intelligence, which are the sources of man's higher activities, do not
depend on the possession of power; and if these persons, having no taste
for pure and liberal pleasure, have recourse to the pleasures of the body,
we must not on that account suppose that bodily pleasures are the more
desirable. Children imagine that the things they themselves value are actually the best; it is not surprising therefore that, as children and grown men
have different standards of value, so also should the worthless and the virtuous. Therefore, as has repeatedly been said, those things are actually val- 5
uable and pleasant which appear so to the good man; but each man thinks
that activity most desirable which suits his particular disposition, and
therefore the good man thinks virtuous activity most desirable. It follows 6
therefore that happiness is not to be found in amusements.

(ii) Indeed it would be strange that amusement should be our End—
that we should toil and moil all our life long in order that we may amuse
ourselves. For virtually every object we adopt is pursued as a means to
something else, excepting happiness, which is an end in itself; to make
amusement the object of our serious pursuits and our work seems foolish
and childish to excess: Anacharsis's motto, Play in order that you may

---

[1] See I. viii. 9. [H.R.]

work, is felt to be the right rule. For amusement is a form of rest; but we need rest because we are not able to go on working without a break, and therefore it is not an end, since we take it as a means to further activity.

(iii) And the life that conforms with virtue is thought to be a happy life; but virtuous life involves serious purpose, and does not consist in amusement.

7 (iv) Also we pronounce serious things to be superior to things that are funny and amusing; and the nobler a faculty or a person is, the more serious, we think, are their activities; therefore, the activity of the nobler faculty or person is itself superior, and therefore more productive of happiness.

8 (v) Also anybody can enjoy the pleasures of the body, a slave no less than the noblest of mankind; but no one allows a slave any measure of happiness, any more than a life of his own.[2] Therefore happiness does not consist in pastimes and amusements, but in activities in accordance with virtue, as has been said already.

vii But if happiness consists in activity in accordance with virtue, it is reasonable that it should be activity in accordance with the highest virtue; and this will be the virtue of the best part of us. Whether then this be the intellect, or whatever else it be that is thought to rule and lead us by nature, and to have cognizance of what is noble and divine, either as being itself also actually divine, or as being relatively the divinest part of us, it is the activity of this part of us in accordance with the virtue proper to it that will constitute perfect happiness; and it has been stated already[3] that this activity is the activity of contemplation.

2 And that happiness consists in contemplation may be accepted as agreeing both with the results already reached and with the truth. For contemplation is at once the highest form of activity (since the intellect is the highest thing in us, and the objects with which the intellect deals are the highest things that can be known), and also it is the most continuous, for 3 we can reflect more continuously than we can carry on any form of action. And again we suppose that happiness must contain an element of pleasure; now activity in accordance with wisdom is admittedly the most pleasant of the activities in accordance with virtue: at all events it is held that philosophy or the pursuit of wisdom contains pleasures of marvellous purity and permanence, and it is reasonable to suppose that the enjoyment of knowl- 4 edge is a still pleasanter occupation than the pursuit of it. Also the activity of contemplation will be found to possess in the highest degree the quality that is termed self-sufficiency; for while it is true that the wise man equally with the just man and the rest requires the necessaries of life, yet, these

---

[2] Cf. *Politics*, III. ix., 1280a 32, "Slaves and lower animals are not members of the state, because they do not participate in happiness nor in purposeful life." [H.R.]

[3] This does not appear to have been stated exactly, but in Book VI. (see esp. cc. v. 3, xiii. 8) it was shown that *sophiā*, the virtue of the higher part of the intellect, is the highest of the virtues. [H.R.]

being adequately supplied, whereas the just man needs other persons towards whom or with whose aid he may act justly, and so likewise do the temperate man and the brave man and the others, the wise man on the contrary can also contemplate by himself, and the more so the wiser he is; no doubt he will study better with the aid of fellow-workers, but still he is the most self-sufficient of men. Also the activity of contemplation may be held 5 to be the only activity that is loved for its own sake: it produces no result beyond the actual act of contemplation, whereas from practical pursuits we look to secure some advantage, greater or smaller, beyond the action itself. Also happiness is thought to involve leisure; for we do business in order 6 that we may have leisure, and carry on war in order that we may have peace. Now the practical virtues are exercised in politics or in warfare; but the pursuits of politics and war seem to be unleisured—those of war indeed entirely so, for no one desires to be at war for the sake of being at war, nor deliberately takes steps to cause a war: a man would be thought an utterly blood-thirsty character if he declared war on a friendly state for the sake of causing battles and massacres. But the activity of the politician also is unleisured, and aims at securing something beyond the mere participation in politics—positions of authority and honour, or, if the happiness of the politician himself and of his fellow-citizens, this happiness conceived as something distinct from political activity (indeed we are clearly investigating it 7 as so distinct).[4] If then among practical pursuits displaying the virtues, politics and war stand out pre-eminent in nobility and grandeur, and yet they are unleisured, and directed to some further end, not chosen for their own sakes: whereas the activity of the intellect is felt to excel in serious worth,[5] consisting as it does in contemplation, and to aim at no end beyond itself, and also to contain a pleasure peculiar to itself, and therefore augmenting its activity: [6] and if accordingly the attributes of this activity are found to be self-sufficiency, leisuredness, such freedom from fatigue as is possible for man, and all the other attributes of blessedness: it follows that it is the activity of the intellect that constitutes complete human happiness—provided it be granted a complete span of life, for nothing that belongs to happiness can be incomplete.

Such a life as this however will be higher than the human level: [7] not 8 in virtue of his humanity will a man achieve it, but in virtue of something within him that is divine; and by as much as this something is superior to his composite nature, by so much is its activity superior to the exercise of the other forms of virtue. If then the intellect is something divine in comparison with man, so is the life of the intellect divine in comparison with

[4] Probably the sentence should be curtailed to run "or in fact the happiness of himself and his fellow-citizens; and happiness we are clearly investigating as something distinct from the art of politics [whose object it is]." [H.R.]

[5] This should almost certainly be emended to "excel in leisuredness." [H.R.]

[6] A reminder of ch. v. § 2. [H.R.]

[7] This section and c. viii. §§ 7 and 13 interpret I. ix. 3. [H.R.]

human life. Nor ought we to obey those who enjoin that a man should have man's thoughts and a mortal the thoughts of mortality, but we ought so far as possible to achieve immortality, and do all that man may to live in accordance with the highest thing in him; for though this be small in bulk, in power and value it far surpasses all the rest.

9   It may even be held that this is the true self of each,[8] inasmuch as it is the dominant and better part; and therefore it would be a strange thing if a man should choose to live not his own life but the life of some other than himself.

Moreover what was said before will apply here also: that which is best and most pleasant for each creature is that which is proper to the nature of each; accordingly the life of the intellect is the best and the pleasantest life [9] for man, inasmuch as the intellect more than anything else is man; therefore this life will be the happiest.

viii   The life of moral virtue, on the other hand, is happy only in a secondary degree. For the moral activities are purely human: Justice, I mean, Courage and the other virtues we display in our intercourse with our fellows, when we observe what is due to each in contracts and services and in our various actions, and in our emotions also; and all of these things seem
2   to be purely human affairs. And some moral actions are thought to be the outcome of the physical constitution, and moral virtue is thought to have a
3   close affinity in many respects with the passions. Moreover, Prudence is intimately connected with Moral Virtue, and this with Prudence, inasmuch as the first principles which Prudence employs are determined by the Moral Virtues, and the right standard for the Moral Virtues is determined by Prudence. But these being also connected with the passions are related to our composite nature; now the virtues of our composite nature are purely human; so therefore also is the life that manifests these virtues, and the happiness that belongs to it. Whereas the happiness that belongs to the intellect is separate: [10] so much may be said about it here, for a full discussion of the matter is beyond the scope of our present purpose. And such
4   happiness would appear to need but little external equipment, or less than the happiness based on moral virtue.[11] Both, it may be granted, require the mere necessaries of life, and that in an equal degree (though the politician does as a matter of fact take more trouble about bodily requirements and so forth than the philosopher); for in this respect there may be little difference between them. But for the purpose of their special activities their requirements will differ widely. The liberal man will need wealth in order

---

[8] Cf. IX. iv. 3, 4, viii. 6. [H.R.]
[9] Cf. I. viii. 14. [H.R.]
[10] In *De Anima*, III. v. Aristotle distinguishes the active from the passive intellect, and pronounces the former to be "separate or separable (from matter, or the body), unmixed and impassible." [H.R.]
[11] Cf. vii. 4, viii. 9, 10, and I. viii. 15–17. [H.R.]

to do liberal actions, and so indeed will the just man in order to discharge his obligations (since mere intentions are invisible, and even the unjust pretend to wish to act justly); and the brave man will need strength if he is to perform any action displaying his virtue; and the temperate man opportunity for indulgence: otherwise how can he, or the possessor of any other virtue, show that he is virtuous? It is disputed also whether purpose or performance is the more important factor in virtue, as it is alleged to depend on both; now the perfection of virtue will clearly consist in both; but the performance of virtuous actions requires much outward equipment, and the more so the greater and more noble the actions are. But the student, so far as the pursuit of his activity is concerned, needs no external apparatus: on the contrary, worldly goods may almost be said to be a hindrance to contemplation; though it is true that, being a man and living in the society of others, he chooses to engage in virtuous action, and so will need external goods to carry on his life as a human being.

The following considerations also will show that perfect happiness is some form of contemplative activity. The gods, as we conceive them, enjoy supreme felicity and happiness. But what sort of actions can we attribute to them? Just actions? but will it not seem ridiculous to think of them as making contracts, restoring deposits and the like? Then brave actions—enduring terrors and running risks for the nobility of so doing? Or liberal actions? but to whom will they give? Besides, it would be absurd to suppose that they actually have a coinage or currency of some sort! And temperate actions—what will these mean in their case? surely it would be derogatory to praise them for not having evil desires! If we go through the list we shall find that all forms of virtuous conduct seem trifling and unworthy of the gods. Yet nevertheless they have always been conceived as, at all events, living, and therefore living actively, for we cannot suppose they are always asleep like Endymion. But for a living being, if we eliminate action, and *a fortiori* creative action, what remains save contemplation? It follows that the activity of God, which is transcendent in blessedness, is the activity of contemplation; and therefore among human activities that which is most akin to the divine activity of contemplation will be the greatest source of happiness.

A further confirmation is that the lower animals cannot partake of happiness, because they are completely devoid of the contemplative activity. The whole of the life of the gods is blessed, and that of man is so in so far as it contains some likeness to the divine activity; but none of the other animals possess happiness, because they are entirely incapable of contemplation. Happiness therefore is co-extensive in its range with contemplation: the more a class of beings possesses the faculty of contemplation, the more it enjoys happiness, not as an accidental concomitant of contemplation but as inherent in it, since contemplation is valuable in itself. It follows that happiness is some form of contemplation.

9   But the philosopher being a man will also need external well-being, since man's nature is not self-sufficient for the activity of contemplation, but he must also have bodily health and a supply of food and other requirements. Yet if supreme blessedness is not possible without external goods, it must not be supposed that happiness will demand many or great possessions; for self-sufficiency does not depend on excessive abundance,

10   nor does moral conduct, and it is possible to perform noble deeds even without being ruler of land and sea: one can do virtuous acts with quite moderate resources. This may be clearly observed in experience: private citizens do not seem to be less but more given to doing virtuous actions than princes and potentates. It is sufficient then if moderate resources are forthcoming; for a life of virtuous activity will be essentially a happy life.

11   Solon also doubtless gave a good description of happiness,[12] when he said that in his opinion those men were happy who, being moderately equipped with external goods, had performed noble exploits and had lived temperately; for it is possible for a man of but moderate possessions to do what is right. Anaxagoras again does not seem to have conceived the happy man as rich or powerful, since he says that he would not be surprised if he were to appear a strange sort of person in the eyes of the many; for most

12   men judge by externals, which are all that they can perceive. So our theories seem to be in agreement with the opinions of the wise.

     Such arguments then carry some degree of conviction; but it is by the practical experience of life and conduct that the truth is really tested, since it is there that the final decision lies. We must therefore examine the conclusions we have advanced by bringing them to the test of the facts of life. If they are in harmony with the facts, we may accept them; if found to disagree, we must deem them mere theories.[13]

13   And it seems likely that the man who pursues intellectual activity, and who cultivates his intellect and keeps that in the best condition, is also the man most beloved of the gods. For if, as is generally believed, the gods exercise some superintendence over human affairs, then it will be reasonable to suppose that they take pleasure in that part of man which is best and most akin to themselves, namely the intellect, and that they recompense with their favours those men who esteem and honour this most, because these care for the things dear to themselves, and act rightly and nobly. Now it is clear that all these attributes belong most of all to the wise man. He therefore is most beloved by the gods; and if so, he is naturally most happy. Here is another proof that the wise man is the happiest.

---

[12] Solon in his conversation with Croesus (Herodotus, i. 30–32, see I. x. 1, note) says that Tellus the Athenian was the happiest man he ever knew. Tellus was well off; he lived to see his children's children, and he died gloriously in battle. [H.R.]

[13] This section concludes the subject and prepares for the transition to politics in the next chapter; § 13 would come better after § 7: it looks back to I. ix. 1–3. [H.R.]

QUESTIONS FOR STUDY AND DISCUSSION

1. Define human happiness in terms of the virtuous life.
2. Why is it that amusement for the sake of amusement cannot constitute human happiness?
3. According to Aristotle, why does happiness lie in contemplation?
4. Why does one need leisure, tranquillity, and moderate fortune to live the life of contemplation?
5. If contemplative happiness is truly godlike happiness, what would be purely human happiness?

St. Thomas Aquinas

ST. THOMAS AQUINAS was born in 1225 at the castle of Roccasecca in Italy, and as a youth studied the liberal arts in Naples. In 1244 he entered the Dominican order and continued his studies in Paris, where he came under the influence of Albert the Great. As a professor at the University of Paris, Aquinas struggled to introduce philosophical reasoning into theology and, against strong opposition, defended a Christianized interpretation of Aristotle. Aquinas died in 1274 on his way to the General Council at Lyons. His most famous works are the *Summa Theologica,* written to introduce his pupils to Christian theology; the *Summa Contra Gentiles,* designed to help the Dominican missionaries in Moorish Spain; and the *Commentary on the Nicomachean Ethics.*

Happiness — The Moral Point of View

TEXT OF ARISTOTLE

(*B.1095 b 12*)

Chapter 5

Let us return to the subject from which we have digressed. Some seem to think, not without reason, that the supreme good called happiness is a good belonging
55   to this life.

Now, most men, including some very eminent persons, place happiness in
56–57   pleasure and so logically prefer a sensual life.

There are indeed three very prominent types of life: that just mentioned,
58–59   another called public life, and last the contemplative life.

60   The majority of men seem quite bestial in choosing to live a life of pleasure.

They justify their choice on the plea that many in high places share the
61   tastes of Sardanapalus.

Men of superior refinement, however, and those occupied in the active life,
62   place happiness in honor, for honor seems to be nearly the whole purpose of
63   public life.

But this seems too superficial to be the good we are looking for. Honor consists in the action of those rendering it rather than anything in the power of the person honored; while happiness certainly should be a good proper to man
64   and a thing not easily taken from him.

From pp. 26–31 of Book I, Lecture 5, in St. Thomas Aquinas, *Commentary on the Nicomachean Ethics,* vol. I, translated by C. I. Litzinger. © 1964 by Henry Regnery Company. Reprinted by permission of the publisher.

Another reason is that men appear to seek honor to convince themselves of their own good qualities. They strive to be honored by the prudent, by those who know them best and for their virtue. Obviously then, in their opinion, virtue is a better thing than honor. 65

From this someone may conclude that virtue rather than honor is the end of public life. 66

But apparently virtue too is lacking in perfection because a man may have a habit of virtue when he is asleep or when he has no opportunity to exercise its acts for a lifetime. 67

Moreover, he may be subject to evils and very often may be ill-favored by fortune. No one would call such a man happy, unless he were merely defending an argumentative position. Enough has now been said, for we treated the subject sufficiently in the *Encyclis*. *B.1096* 68

Later on we shall investigate the third type of life, the contemplative. 69

As to the accumulator of riches, he lives a life of constraint; 70–71

and riches themselves are not the good we seek, for they are merely useful and sought for the sake of something else. Rather therefore the things previously treated are considered ends, since they are desired for themselves. Yet even these are not the supreme good and happiness, although many arguments have been marshalled to prove this. But these discussions must be terminated now. 72

COMMENTARY OF ST. THOMAS

55. After the Philosopher has recounted the different opinions about happiness, he begins to investigate the truth of these opinions. First he examines the opinion of those discussing happiness from the moral point of view who place happiness in some good of this life. Second [Lect. VI], at "Perhaps it will be better" (B.1096 a 12), he examines the opinion of those who do not discuss happiness from the moral point of view but place it in some separated good. In regard to the first he does two things. He lays down a notion that opinions on this subject have in common; and next, at "Now, most men," he begins to investigate the variety of opinions. Then, because the Philosopher seemed to have made a digression from his principal purpose while he was determining the mode of procedure, he returns to the point whence he had digressed, that is, to the opinions about happiness. He asserts that some seem to think, not without reason, that the final good called happiness is a good belonging to this life on the purely human level. This is the goal of all the works of life. Now, means are proportionate to that end. Hence it is probable that happiness is among the number of goods belonging to this life. But what the truth may be in this matter will be indicated later (60, 64, 65, 70–72).

56. Next, at *"Now, most men,"* he searches for the truth about the things on which the opinions differ. In regard to this he does two things. First he examines the opinions that seem more likely to be true. Second, at "As to the accumulator of riches etc.," he examines an opinion rather remote from the truth. In regard to the first he does three things. First he examines the opinion placing happiness in the things that pertain to a life of pleasure. Second, at "Men of superior refinement etc.," he examines the opinion placing happiness in the things pertaining to public life. Third, at

"Later on we shall investigate etc.," he mentions the contemplative life. In regard to the first he does three things. First, he presents the opinion. Second, at "There are indeed three etc.," he distinguishes three types of life without elaborating on them. Third, at "The majority of men etc.," he examines the truth of the opinion presented.

57. He says then in the first place that some men, from the goods of this life, choose pleasure and place happiness in it. They include not only the majority or the common people who by and large favor pleasure, but also persons eminent either in knowledge and teaching or in uprightness of life. Even the Epicureans, who considered pleasure the highest good, carefully cultivated the virtues. They did so, however, on account of pleasure, that is, for fear their pleasure would be hindered by means of contrary vices. The vice of gluttony, for instance, causes bodily suffering through excessive eating; because of theft a man is thrown into prison. So different vices are an impediment to pleasure in different ways. Since then the ultimate end is exceedingly delectable, they who make pleasure the highest good intensely love the life of pleasure.

58. Then, at *"There are indeed three,"* he distinguishes three types of life: the sensual just mentioned, the public, and the contemplative. These he calls the most prominent types. For evidence of this we must now bear in mind what will later be discussed in the ninth book (1944–1949), that every man thinks his life to be that to which he is most strongly drawn, as the philosopher to philosophizing, the hunter to hunting, and so on. Because man is most strongly drawn to the last end, it is necessary that the types of life be distinguished according to the diversity of the ultimate end. Now the end has the nature of good, and good is threefold: the useful, the pleasurable, and the virtuous or honorable. Two of these, namely, the pleasurable and the virtuous or honorable, have the nature of end because both are desirable for their own sake. That indeed is called virtuous which is good according to reason, and this has pleasure attached to it. Hence the pleasurable, as distinguished from the virtuous, is so called in reference to the senses. Reason, we must remember, is both speculative and practical.

59. Therefore, that life is called sensual which fixes its end in the pleasures of the senses; and that public which fixes its end in the good of the practical reason, for example, in the exercise of virtuous deeds; and that contemplative which fixes its end in the good of the speculative reason or in the contemplation of truth.

60. Next at *"The majority of men,"* he examines the opinion cited above. In regard to this he does two things. First he disproves it. Second, at "they justify their choice etc.," he advances a reason why some are drawn to this life. In regard to the first we must consider that the sensual life, which fixes its end in sense pleasure, necessarily has to place that end in those very intense pleasures following from the natural operations by which the individual is preserved by eating and drinking and the race by sexual intercourse. Now pleasures of this kind are found in both men and beasts.

If follows then that the multitude of men who fix their end in such pleasures seem quite bestial in choosing a life which even the pigs enjoy. If the happiness of man would consist in this, dumb animals enjoying the pleasure of food and sexual intercourse would have to be called happy for the same reason. Assuming that happiness is a characteristically human good, it cannot possibly consist in these things.

61. Then, at *"They justify their choice,"* he gives the reason why some hold this opinion. He says that the reason they offer is that many in high places, like kings and princes who are considered very happy by the common people, share the tastes of a certain Assyrian king named Sardanapalus who was much given to sensuality. On this account it is thought that pleasure is something very good since it is a thing highly esteemed by the great.

62. At *"Men of superior refinement"* he investigates opinions concerning the active or public life. First he does this in regard to honor; and second, at "From this someone etc.," in regard to virtue. This is a reasonable procedure, for the active or public life aims at the honorable good. Now it is called honorable as pertaining to the state of honor. Hence both honor itself and virtue, which is the cause of honor, appear to belong to it. In regard to the first he does three things. First, in presenting the opinion, he notes that persons of superior refinement, namely, the virtuous and those occupied in the active life, place happiness in honor.

63. Second, at *"for honor seems,"* he offers a reason for this: the sole purpose of public life appears to be honor which is rendered as a reward to the politically successful. Therefore, for those engaged in public life happiness probably seems to consist in honor.

64. Third, at *"But this seems,"* he disproves this opinion by two reasons. In the first of these he says that in a way we divine the true nature of happiness, that is, we surmise happiness to be a good proper to the happy man, a thing belonging preeminently to him and taken from him with difficulty. But this is not true of honor which seems rather to consist in the action of the one rendering the honor, and to be in his power rather than in the power of the one honored. Therefore honor is something more extrinsic and superficial than the good we are seeking, which is happiness.

65. He gives the second reason at *"Another reason."* Happiness is some very good thing which is not sought on account of another. But there is something better than honor, namely, that on account of which honor is sought. Men appear to seek honor in order to confirm the solid opinion they have formed of themselves that they are good men and that they may be assured of this by the judgment of others. They look, therefore, for honor from prudent men with correct judgment and from those who know them best and can be better judges. Hence they seek to be honored for their virtue, which is the source of man's good, as will be shown in the second book (307–308). So virtue, for whose sake honor is sought, is a better thing than honor. It follows then that happiness does not consist in honor.

66. Then, at *"From this someone,"* he investigates the opinion of those who place happiness in virtue. In regard to this he does two things. First he states the opinion and says that perhaps someone will think, by reason of what was just said, that virtue rather than honor is the end of public life.

67. Second, at *"But apparently,"* he rejects this for two reasons. The first is that happiness seems to be a most perfect good. But virtue is not of such a nature, for sometimes it is found without the perfection of activity, as we see in those who are asleep and yet have the habit of virtue. It is possible, too, that a man may have the habit of virtue, but for lack of opportunity not perform a single act of a particular virtue during his whole life. This is particularly evident regarding magnanimity and magnificence, virtues perhaps possessed by a poverty-stricken person who is never able to perform great deeds. Therefore virtue is not the same as happiness.

68. He gives the second reason at *"Moreover he may be."* It is this. It happens that one who has the habit of virtue may be ill-favored by fortune. Who will call such a man happy except someone obstinately defending a thesis against the plain truth? Therefore happiness is not the same as virtue. This, he says, is sufficient for his purpose. Enough has been said on the subject in his *Encyclis,* that is, in certain learned verses that Aristotle composed on happiness.

69. Then, at *"Later on we shall investigate,"* he mentions the contemplative life, saying that it will be investigated later on in the tenth book (2086–2125).

70. At *"As to the accumulator of riches,"* he examines another opinion, less probable, which places happiness in a thing which has the nature of a useful good, money. But this is incompatible with the nature of an ultimate end, for a thing is called useful because it is ordered to an end. However, since money has an over-all utility in respect of temporal goods, the opinion that places happiness in money has some probability.

71. But he rejects it for two reasons. The first is that money is acquired under coercion and is parted with under coercion. But this is not in keeping with happiness, which is the goal of voluntary operations. Consequently happiness does not consist in money.

72. He gives the second reason, at *"and riches themselves."* It is this. We look for happiness as a good that is not sought for something else. But money is sought for something beyond itself since it is by its nature a useful good, as was just said (70). Therefore happiness does not consist in money.

73. A further conclusion notes that pleasure, honor, and virtue, all of which were treated above (57–72), can be considered ultimate ends at least in the sense that they are sought for themselves, as was said (57, 61, 63, 70). However, the ultimate end is not to be found in these, as has been shown (57–72), although many arguments have been marshalled by various philosophers to prove that happiness consists in these goods. But these discussions must be terminated.

QUESTIONS FOR STUDY AND DISCUSSION

1. The fact is that the majority of people, both ordinary and eminent, seek their happiness in the physical pleasures of eating, drinking, and sexual intercourse. These pleasures, however, cannot offer specifically human happiness. Why not?
2. Honors, sought particularly by those people engaged in public life, do not fulfill the two conditions of happiness. What are those two conditions?
3. Virtue itself cannot fulfill man's desire for happiness. Why not?
4. Money, by its nature a useful good, cannot make man happy. Why not?
5. Can a man achieve human happiness if the above mentioned goods are completely absent from his life? If so, why? If not, why not?

Distributive and Commutative Justice

TEXT OF ARISTOTLE

(*B.1130 b 30*)

Chapter 2

One species of particular justice—and of the just thing corresponding to it—consists in the distribution of honor, money, and other common goods that are to be apportioned to people sharing in social community, for in these matters one man as compared with another may have an equal or unequal share.   927

Another species gives directions for use in private transactions.   *B.1131*   928

There are two parts of this species, as some types of transaction are voluntary and others involuntary. Examples of the voluntary are selling, buying, bail, loan, deposit, rent. They are called voluntary because the origin of these exchanges is voluntary.   929

Some kinds of involuntary transaction are occult, like theft, adultery, poisoning, procuring, enticement of a slave, assassination, false testimony. Others are done with manifest violence, for example, beating, imprisonment, murder, robbery, despoiling parents of children, reproach, outrage.   930–931

Chapter 3

Since the unjust person is unfair and the unjust thing is unequal, it is clear that there is a mean corresponding to what is unjust. This is the equal, for in operations of this kind where there is more or less, there is also an equal. Therefore, if the unjust thing is the unequal and, the just thing the equal— and this is evident in all situations without need of proof—then the just thing will be the mean since the equal is the mean.   932–933

However, the equal implies at least two things. Therefore, since the just

From pp. 398–403 of Book V, Lecture 4, in St. Thomas Aquinas, *Commentary on the Nicomachean Ethics*, vol. I, translated by C. I. Litzinger. © 1964 by Henry Regnery Company. Reprinted by permission of the publisher.

thing is both a mean and an equal, it necessarily is related to another and pertains to certain matters of equality. As a mean it will be between two things which are more and less. As it is an equal it will be between two things. As it is a just thing it will concern matters in relation to other persons, for justice regards another. Therefore, the just necessarily involves at least four objects, viz., two persons by whom justice is observed and two things about which justice is done. There will be the same equality between persons and between things in such a way that, as things are related to one another, so are persons. If they are not equal they will not have equal shares, and from this source quarrels and complaints will arise when, either persons who are equal do not receive equal shares in distribution, or persons who are not equal do receive

934–935   equal shares.

Moreover, this is clear from the fact that bestowal should be made according to merit, for the just thing in distribution has to be done according to a certain merit. But all do not agree that merit consists in the same thing. People of a democracy place it in a condition of freedom, people of an oligarchy in one's

936–937   riches or nobility of birth, and people of an aristocracy in a state of virtue.

COMMENTARY OF ST. THOMAS

927. After the Philosopher has differentiated particular justice from legal justice, he now begins to investigate particular justice without treating legal justice. He divides the investigation into two parts. In the first part he considers particular justice in a general way by comparison with its proper object, and in the second part [Lect. XI], at "Since someone etc." (B.1134 a 16), he considers it in its application to the subject. In regard to the first part, he does two things. Initially he makes a division of particular justice. Next, at "Since the unjust person etc.," he explains how a mean may be taken in this virtue. He discusses the initial point from three aspects. First he indicates a species of particular justice. He says that one species—the same holds for the unjust thing corresponding to it—consists in the distribution of certain common goods (either honor or money or any other thing belonging to external goods or even to external evils, like labor, expenses and so on) that are to be apportioned among people who share in social community. He proves that this should belong to particular justice because in matters of this kind, equality and inequality—which belong to particular justice and injustice, as was stated before (922)—of one person to another are taken into consideration.

928. Next, at "Another species," he gives a second kind of particular justice. He says that another species establishes a measure of justice in transactions, by which a thing is transferred from one person to another —in the first species the transfer of a thing from the community to the individual was considered.

929. Last, at "There are two parts," he subdivides commutative justice according to the different kinds of transactions, making a twofold division. He says first that there are two parts of commutative justice because there are two kinds of transactions. Some are voluntary, others involuntary. The

voluntary are so-called because the principle of transaction is voluntary in both parties, as is evident *in selling and buying,* by which one man transfers the dominion over his own property to another as compensation for a price received; *in barter,* by which someone gives what is his to another for something of equal value; *in bail,* by which a person voluntarily appoints himself a debtor for another; *in a loan,* by which a man grants the use of his property to another without recompense but reserves ownership of the thing to himself; *in a deposit,* by which one commits something of his to the custody of another; *in rent,* by which a person accepts the use of something belonging to another for a price.

930. Then, at *"Some kinds of involuntary,"* he subdivides the other division of transactions, saying that some involuntary transactions are occult: like theft, by which one takes a thing belonging to another who is unwilling; adultery, by which a man secretly approaches the wife of another for sexual intercourse; poisoning, by which a person poisons another with intent either to kill or injure in some way. Also they are especially called poisoners who by some sorcery bring about murder or harm. *Paragogia* is a derivation or a leading away, for example the occult diversion of a stream belonging to one person to the property of another. The enticement of a slave takes place when someone induces another's slave to flee from his master. Assassination is that slaying which happens from wounds inflicted by trickery. Testimony is false in which a person conceals the truth by lying. Other transactions are involuntary and done by manifest violence. Thus a man may use violence either upon a person by beating, fettering, murdering, or upon things by robbing another of his goods, by despoiling parents of their children through murder. Likewise, a man may use violence through infamy by using reproachful words, or through injury by inflicting outrage.

931. We must consider that the voluntary and involuntary in transactions make a difference in the species of justice because voluntary transactions cause the subtraction of only a thing which must be repaid according to the equality of justice. But involuntary transactions cause a certain injury. Hence the robber is forced not only to return the thing plundered but to undergo punishment because of the affront inflicted. Since the involuntary is twofold, viz., arising from force and from ignorance, he divides involuntary transactions into those which are occult, as it were through ignorance, and those that are done openly through violence.

932. Next, at *"Since the unjust person,"* he shows how a mean is understood in these matters. He discusses this point from two aspects. First, he explains how the just thing is a mean; and then [Lect. X], at "From these discussions etc." (B.1133 b 30), how justice is a mean. He treats the first point in a twofold manner. First he shows in what way the just thing, consisting in a mean according to either justice, may be determined. Next [Lect. VIII], at "Some philosophers seem to think etc."

(B.1132 b 21), he rejects an error. He further discusses the first point in two stages. First he explains how the just thing may be taken as a mean according to distributive justice; and second [Lect. VI], at "There remains another etc." (B.1131 b 25), according to commutative justice. He considers the first point in two ways. First he proves that the mean of distributive justice should be taken according to a certain relationship of proportions. Next [Lect. V], at "Therefore, the just thing etc." (B.1131 a 30), he shows what the nature of that relationship of proportions is. On the initial point he does two things. First he proves the proposition from the very concept of justice; and then, at "Moreover, this is clear etc.," from the concept of merit. He treats the first point under two headings. First, he shows from the very notion of justice that the just thing is a certain mean. Second, at "However, the equal etc.," he explains that the mean is according to a certain relationship of proportions.

933. He says first that, as was said previously (898, 921), the unjust man is one who desires an inequality of good and evil, and the unjust thing is that which consists in an inequality, and concerns both too much and too little. But wherever there is more and less, there the equal must be found, for the equal is the mean between the greater and the less. Hence wherever we find equality, there we find a mean. It is clear then that the unjust thing is a kind of unequal thing, and the just thing is a kind of equal thing. That the just thing is a kind of equal thing is obvious to everyone without any proof. Therefore, since the equal is a mean between more and less, as has been shown (310, 896, 898), it follows that the just thing is a kind of mean.

934. At *"However, the equal"* he explains that the just thing is a mean according to a certain relationship of proportions. To prove this he takes for granted that the equal consists in at least two things between which an equality is considered. Therefore, since the just thing is both a mean and an equal, inasmuch as it is just, it is necessarily a relation to something, i.e., with respect to another, as is evident from what has been indicated (922); but inasmuch as it is an equal it pertains to certain matters in which equality between two persons is taken into account. Thus it is evident that if we consider the just thing precisely as a mean, it will then be a mean between two things that are more and less. But precisely as the just thing is an equal, it must be between two things (as a just thing, of course, it must concern some matters in relation to other persons, because justice regards another person). However, justice insofar as it is a mean, an extrinsic thing, considers more or less; but as something intrinsic it considers two things and two persons in which justice is established. So it is clear that what is just, necessarily consists in at least four objects, viz., two persons by whom justice is observed and two things about which justice is done.

935. In the concept of justice there must be the same equality between persons who practice justice and between things about which justice is done, so that as the things are related to one another, so are the persons.

Otherwise they will not have shares proportional to themselves. But, by reason of this, quarrels and complaints arise as if justice had been neglected because, either persons who are equal do not receive equal shares in the distribution of common goods or persons who are not equal do receive equal shares, for example, if laborers are paid equal wages for doing an unequal amount of work, or are paid unequal wages for doing an equal amount of work. So then it is evident that the mean of distributive justice is taken according to a certain relationship of proportions.

936. Then, at *"Moreover, this is,"* he shows that it is obvious also by reason of merit that the just thing consists in a certain relationship of proportions. In this way a thing is said to be just in distributions inasmuch as allotment is made according to merit as each is worthy to receive. A certain relationship of proportions is designated by this—that as one person is deserving of one thing, so another is deserving of another thing.

937. However, all do not judge merit in distribution in agreement with the same norm. In a democratic state where everyone governs, they judge merit according to a condition of freedom. Because the common people are the equal of others in freedom, therefore they think it proper that equal distribution be made to them. In an oligarchy where some few rule, they measure merit according to a man's riches or according to nobility of birth, so that men who are more eminent by birth or riches should have more of the common goods. In an aristocracy where certain men govern because of their virtue, they measure merit according to a state of virtue, so that a man should have more who practices virtue more perfectly. Thus it is clear that the mean of distributive justice is understood according to a relationship of proportions.

QUESTIONS FOR STUDY AND DISCUSSION

1. Define as clearly as possible both distributive and commutative justice.
2. List some examples of both voluntary and involuntary transactions.
3. How do voluntary and involuntary transactions differ in the way they restore former possessions?
4. What is the mean (proportion, equality) of distributive justice?
5. Describe the mean of commutative justice.
6. In distributing honors and rewards, what criteria do the three types of governments use to judge the merits of citizens?

Man's Need of Friends

TEXT OF ARISTOTLE
(B.1169 b 3)
Chapter 9

1885   Some doubt whether or not a happy man needs friends.

It is said that because happy people are self-sufficient they do not need friends; since they have all good things, being self-sufficing, they need nothing else. Now a friend is looked upon as another self who provides what a man 1886 himself cannot.

1887   Hence the saying: "If fortune favors us, what need of friends?"

There seems to be an inconsistency in attributing to a happy man all goods 1888 but not friends since a friend seems to be the greatest of external goods.

If it is more characteristic of a friend to give than to receive a benefit, more proper to virtue and a virtuous man to do good for others, and better to be kind to friends than strangers, then the virtuous person will need friends whom 1889 he can benefit.

This is why the related question arises: does a man need friends more in prosperity or in adversity? Undoubtedly, the unfortunate man needs them to 1890 help him, and the fortunate man needs friends he can help.

It seems strange indeed to make the happy man a solitary. For no one would choose to have the whole world if he had to live alone, since man is naturally a social animal and fitted by nature to live with others. Therefore, the happy man lives in this way because he has what is naturally good. But obviously it is better to live with friends and virtuous men than with strangers and chance 1891 acquaintances. Therefore the happy man needs friends.

What then are the followers of the first opinion holding, and to what extent is their opinion true? Do they, like the majority, look upon friends as useful people? Certainly the happy man will not need such friends for he has useful goods already; nor will he need those whom one chooses for their pleasantness, except to a slight extent. Indeed the happy man does not require pleasure from the outside, for his life is pleasant in itself. Since then he does not stand in need 1892–1893 of friends of this sort, he seems not to need friends at all.

Certainly this is not true. For we said in the beginning that happiness is an activity; and activity obviously is a coming into being and is not like something in one's possession. But happiness consists in living and doing, and the activity of the good man is virtuous and pleasurable in itself, as we noted earlier; of all pleasures, happiness is proper to a virtuous man. Now we can study our neigh-B.1170 bors better than ourselves and their actions better than our own. Evidently then virtuous persons find pleasure in the actions of friends who are good men, since they have both qualities that are naturally pleasurable. The happy man, there-fore, will need such friends inasmuch as he wants to study actions that are good and his own, and the actions of the virtuous man who is his friend are of this 1894–1896 nature.

From pp. 832–37 of Book IX, Lecture 10, in St. Thomas Aquinas, *Commentary on the Nicomachean Ethics*, vol. II, translated by C. I. Litzinger. © 1964 by Henry Regnery Company. Reprinted by permission of the publisher.

Besides, people think that a happy man should live pleasantly. Now the man who lives alone does have a hard life, since it is not easy to keep up a continuous activity by oneself. But with others and in relation to others it is less difficult. Therefore, his activity will be more continuous and delightful in itself, as it ought to be for the happy man. Indeed the good man, as such, rejoices in virtuous actions but is distressed by those which arise from wickedness; he is like a musician pleased by good music but irritated by bad. 1897–1898

Then too a companionship in virtue results from living with good men, as Theognis remarks. 1899

COMMENTARY OF ST. THOMAS

1885. After the Philosopher has investigated and solved the question that was raised about a person loving himself, he now solves the question that was raised of a person loving another. First he proposes the doubt. Then, at "It is said etc.," he shows that the doubt is reasonable. Finally, at "What then are etc.," he solves it. He notes first that there is a doubt whether or not the happy man needs friends.

1886. Then, at *"It is said,"* he shows that the doubt is reasonable by raising difficulties for both sides. First he objects for the negative; next at "There seems to etc.," for the affirmative. He objects in a two-fold manner for the initial position. First by an argument. Some say that happy people are self-sufficing and do not need friends; they have all good things, and so, being complete in themselves, they seem to need nothing else. But a friend, inasmuch as he is another self, seems to be necessary to provide what a man cannot obtain by himself. So, apparently, a happy person does not need friends.

1887. Second, at *"Hence the saying,"* he offers a pagan proverb in favor of the same view: "When the spirit is benign there is no need of friends." The pagans, especially the Platonists, believed the order of providence was such that human affairs were governed by divine dispensation through intermediary spirits. Some of the spirits, they held, were favorable; others malevolent. Therefore, the proverb says that when a man enjoys the favor of divine providence, as happy people seem to do, he has no need of friends.

1888. At *"There seems to be,"* he objects for the opposite side by three arguments. (He offers the first.) It seems unreasonable to assign all external goods to a happy man, and not assign him friends, since a friend is the greatest of external goods.

1889. He treats the second argument at *"If it is more characteristic,"* handling it in a twofold manner. First he presents the argument. We have pointed out already that it is more characteristic of a friend to give than to receive a benefit. But it is proper to virtue to impart benefits; and happiness consists in virtuous action, as indicated in the first book (127–128). The happy man then is necessarily virtuous and beneficent. But it is better for a man to be good to friends than strangers, other things being equal, because he does this with more pleasure and alacrity. Consequently, since a happy person is virtuous he needs friends whom he can benefit.

1890. Second, at *"This is why,"* he deduces a doubt from the premises: whether a man has need of friends more in adversity than in prosperity. He seems to need friends in both circumstances, for the unfortunate man needs friends to help him, and the fortunate man needs friends he can help. But this doubt will be pursued later (1925–1943).

1891. He presents the third argument at *"It seems strange indeed,"* saying that it appears unreasonable for the happy man to be a solitary; for this is contrary to everyone's choice. No one would choose to live alone all the time, even after he had all other goods, because man is naturally a social animal and fitted by nature to live with others. Since, therefore, the happy person has what is naturally good for man, he should have people to live with. Obviously it is better for him to live with friends and virtuous men than strangers and others. Thus, it is clear that the happy man needs friends.

1892. Next, at *"What then are,"* he solves the preceding doubt. First he shows how those, who deny that a happy man needs friends, may be saying what is true; then, at "Certainly this is not etc.," how they may be saying what is false. He says first that since we have just proved that the happy man does need friends we must consider what the followers of the first opinion are holding, when they deny the happy man's need of friends, and to what extent their opinion may be true.

1893. On this question we should note that most men consider as friends those useful to them in the bestowal of external goods—and these alone are appreciated by the common run of men. Therefore, the happy man does not need friends like this, for the goods he has are enough. Likewise, he does not need friends for pleasantness, except in that minor way —that we need jests for relaxation. Cf. the fourth book (844–845). Indeed, the happy man does not require external pleasure for which such friends are absolutely necessary, for his life is pleasant in itself, as we have indicated in the first book (145). Since then he does not stand in need of these useful and pleasant friends, it seems that he has no need of friends.

1894. Then, at *"Certainly this is not,"* he shows that their statement is not entirely true. First he proves this by moral arguments; next [Lect. XI], at "Looking more profoundly etc." (B.1170 a 13), by a more intrinsic reason. He offers three reasons for the initial point. First it is not true that, if the happy man does not need useful and pleasant friends, he does not therefore need any friends at all, as affirmed previously (1892–1893). For there are virtuous friends whom he does need. The primary reason for this is that happiness is an operation (144, 145, 180, 1267).

1895. It is evident that operation consists in doing; it is not an entity existing in the manner of permanent things, as if it were a possession that, once obtained, a man would be happy without the necessity of doing anything. But happiness consists in continual living and doing. Now the operation of the virtuous man must be good and pleasurable in itself because it is essentially good, as indicated in the first book (156). But among pleasures good operation is the pleasure proper to the virtuous man, for the person who would not delight in virtuous operation would not be virtuous, as we stated in the first book (158).

1896. We can have pleasure only in what we know. But we can examine our neighbors better than ourselves and their actions better than our own because every man is a bad judge of his own case on account of the private affection he has for himself. Evidently then virtuous persons find pleasure in the actions of those who are both virtuous men and friends of theirs; in them are found both qualities pleasurable by nature, namely, the good and the lovable. In this way, therefore, the happy man will need these virtuous friends inasmuch as he seeks to study the virtuous actions of the good man who is his friend. Since a man's friend is another self, so to speak, the friend's actions will be his own in a sense.

1897. He presents the second argument at *"Besides, people think."* It is generally thought, he says, that the happy man should live pleasantly; for pleasure is one of the conditions for happiness—we have noted this in the first book (158). But he who lives by himself experiences a hard and burdensome life; pleasure that he enjoys following upon activity must be interrupted, for it is not easy for a man to be continuously active by himself, i.e., when living alone. But it is easy if he lives with another, since a kind of interchange of activities takes place while they perform good actions for one another. In this way pleasure is continued.

1898. If then a man lives with friends, his virtuous activity delightful in itself will be more continuous. And this ought to be true for the happy man so that he may have uninterrupted pleasure in works of virtue. For the good man as such rejoices in virtuous actions performed either by himself or others. Moreover, he is grieved by contrary actions arising from another's wickedness, like a musician who is pleased by good music but irritated by bad.

1899. He presents the third argument at *"Then too."* Here he observes that because the virtuous person lives on friendly terms with good men there results *ascesis* or a companionship in virtue, as the poet Theognis has remarked. Such an association is advantageous for anyone disposed to virtue, just as other human activities also are more satisfactorily accomplished in partnership.

QUESTIONS FOR STUDY AND DISCUSSION

1. In a sense, a happy man does not need friends. Explain.
2. As a rule, however, the happy man needs friends. What are the three reasons given in the text for this statement?

3. Those who deny that a happy man needs friends say, in effect, that a happy man need not look for two kinds of friends. Which are those two kinds?
4. In order to be happy a man needs virtuous friendship. What are the three reasons given in the text for this statement?
5. What is the distinction between togetherness and friendship?

Happiness and Leisure

TEXT OF ARISTOTLE

(B.1177 b 4)

Chapter 7

And happiness is thought to depend on leisure, for we are busy in order to have leisure, and we wage war in order to attain peace. Now the exercise of the practical virtues is evident in political and military affairs, but actions concerned with these seem to be without leisure. This is completely the case with warlike activity, for no one chooses to wage war or provoke it merely for the sake of fighting. Indeed a man would be considered a murderous character if he turned his friends into enemies for the sake of causing battles and slaughter. But the activity of the statesman is also without leisure, and aims at—apart from participation in politics—positions of power and honor or even the happiness of himself and fellow citizens as something distinct from political activity (and we are investigating it as something distinct). Even if, among the activities of the moral virtues, political and military actions stand out prominent both in nobility and in greatness, they are without leisure, aim at some other end, and are not desirable for their own sakes. On the other hand the activity of the intellect, being contemplative, is thought to be different by reason of serious application, both in desiring no end beyond itself and in possessing a proper pleasure that increases its activity. So contemplation seems to have self-sufficiency, leisureliness, freedom from labor (as far as humanly possible), and all other activities usually assigned to the happy man. Therefore, man's perfect happiness will consist in this activity of the intellect, if a long span of life be added (as nothing belonging to happiness should be incomplete).

2098–2104

Such a life is higher than the human level; and it is not lived by man according to the human mode but according to something divine in him. And so far as this differs from the composite, to that extent its activity differs from the activity flowing from the other kind of virtue. Therefore, if the intellect is divine in comparison with man, so is its life divine in comparison with human life.

2105–2106

Nor ought we to follow the philosophers who advise man to study human things, and mortals to study mortality, but we ought to strive to attain immortality so far as possible and to exert all our power to live according to the best thing in us. For, though this is a small part of us, it far surpasses all else in

From pp. 910–14 of Book X, Lecture 11, in St. Thomas Aquinas, *Commentary on the Nicomachean Ethics*, vol. II, translated by C. I. Litzinger. © 1964 by Henry Regnery Company. Reprinted by permission of the publisher.

power and value; it may seem, even, to be the true self of each, being the **B.1178** principal and better part. Consequently it would be strange if a person were to choose to live not his own life but the life of some other. Moreover, our previous statement is applicable here: what is proper to the nature of each thing is best and most pleasant for it. So then the life of the intellect is best and most pleasant for man since the intellect more than anything else is man. This life, therefore, will be the happiest. **2107–2110**

COMMENTARY OF ST. THOMAS

2098. After Aristotle has presented five reasons to show that happiness consists in the contemplation of truth, he now adds a sixth reason, not previously mentioned, arising from a feature of happiness. Now happiness involves a kind of leisure. For a person is said to have leisure when he has nothing further to do—a condition in which he finds himself on arriving at some goal. For this reason the Philosopher adds that we are busy in order to have leisure, that is, we are active in working—this is being busy—in order to rest at the end, and this is having leisure. And he finds an example of this in soldiers who wage war to obtain a desirable peace.

2099. We should note, as the Philosopher stated before (2077), that rest should be taken for the sake of activity. But there he was speaking of rest which, before attaining the end, suspends activity because of the impossibility of uninterrupted labor—this rest being ordered to activity as an end. On the other hand leisure is rest in the end to which activity is ordered. Thus understood, leisure is a special property of happiness, the ultimate end; it is not found in the activities of the practical virtues. Prominent among these are the virtues dealing with political affairs involving the direction of the common or most divine good and with warfare involving the defense of the common good against enemies; nevertheless in such activities leisure has no part.

2100. In the first place this is entirely clear in military operations since no one chooses to wage war or to provoke it solely for the sake of fighting, which would be to have leisure for warfare. The reason is that if someone were to make his end the waging of war he would be a murderous character turning his friends into enemies so that he could fight and kill.

2101. Second, it is obvious that there is no place for leisure in political activities. But a man wants something besides mere participation in politics, like positions of power and honor; and—since these objectives do not constitute the ultimate end, as was pointed out in the first book (60–72) —it is rather fitting that by means of politics a person should wish to obtain happiness for himself and everyone else; happiness of this kind sought in political life is distinct from political life itself, and in fact we do seek it as something distinct. This is contemplative happiness to which the whole of political life seems directed; as long as the arrangement of political life establishes and preserves peace giving men the opportunity of contemplating truth.

2102. Among the activities of the moral virtues political and military actions stand out preeminent both in nobility (they are most honorable) and in greatness (they concern the greatest good, i.e., the common good), and these actions do not themselves possess leisure but are directed to a further end and are not desirable for their own sakes. Hence perfect happiness will not be found in the activities of the moral virtues.

2103. But the activity of the intellect, which is contemplative, seems to differ from the preceding activities by reason of serious application, since man applies himself to it for its own sake so that he seeks no further end. This activity also contains a proper pleasure proceeding from itself and augmenting it. So then such contemplative activity of the intellect clearly provides for man the attributes customarily assigned to the happy person: self-sufficiency, leisureliness, and freedom from labor. And I say this insofar as it is possible for man living a mortal life in which such things cannot exist perfectly.

2104. Therefore man's perfect happiness consists in contemplation of the intellect, if a long span of life be added. This indeed is necessary for the well-being of happiness, as nothing belonging to happiness should be incomplete.

2105. Then, at *"Such a life,"* he shows how this contemplative life is associated with man. First he explains his proposition. Second, at "Nor ought we etc.," he rejects an error. He says first that the kind of life that has leisure for the contemplation of truth is higher than the human level. Since man is composed of soul and body with a sensitive and intellectual nature, life commensurate to him is thought to consist in this, that he directs by reason his sensitive and bodily affections and activities. But to engage solely in intellectual activity seems proper to the superior substances possessing only an intellectual nature that they participate by their intellect.

2106. For this reason in explaining his statement he adds that man living in this manner, i.e., occupied in contemplation, does not live as man, composed of diverse elements, but as something divine is present in him, partaking in a likeness to the divine intellect. And on that account, as the intellect considered in its purity differs from a composite of soul and body so the contemplative activity differs from the activity following moral virtue, which is properly concerned with human affairs. Therefore, just as the intellect compared to man is something divine, so the contemplative life, which is based upon the intellect, is compared to the life of moral virtue as divine to human life.

2107. Next, at *"Nor ought we,"* he rejects the error of some philosophers who advised man that he must strive to know the things of man, and mortals the things of mortals. This was the advice of the poet Simonides, as appears in the beginning of the *Metaphysics* (Ch. 2, 982 b 30–983 a 4; St. Th., III, 61–63). But the Philosopher calls it false, since we must strive to attain immortality so far as possible, and exert all our power to live according to reason—the best of all the elements in man who is truly divine and immortal. For, though this best element is a small part, being incorporeal and most simple, and consequently lacking greatness, nevertheless it surpasses everything human in the extent of its power and value.

2108. It excels in power by its activities, which are akin to superior beings and have authority over inferior beings, and so in a way it embraces all things. Likewise, it excels in value as regards the excellence of its nature, since the intellect is immaterial and simple, incorruptible and incapable of suffering. Now each human being, i.e., the whole man, seems to be the intellect if it is true—nay rather because it is true—that the intellect is the principal and better part of man.

2109. We have stated in the ninth book (1868, 1872) that each thing is thought to be especially that which constitutes its chief part, since all other parts are its tools, so to speak. And so when man lives in accordance with the activity of the intellect, he lives in accordance with the life most proper to him; for it would be strange if a person were to choose to live not his own life but the life of some other. Hence they give unwise counsel who say that man should not engage in intellectual contemplation. And the statement made in the ninth book (1807, 1847, 1869–1872) that what accords with reason is proper to man is applicable also to our present purpose. For that which is best in each thing's nature is most proper to it. But what is best and proper consequently is most delightful because everyone delights in a good that is pleasing to him. So then, if man is especially his intellect, since this is the principal element in him, evidently life according to the intellect is most delightful and proper to him in the highest degree.

2110. Nor is it contrary to our previous assertion (2106) that this is not on the human level but above man. Indeed it is not on the human level considering man's composite nature, but it is most properly human considering what is principal in man—a thing found most perfectly in superior substances but imperfectly and by participation, as it were, in man. Nevertheless this small part is greater than all the other parts in man. Thus it is clear that the person who gives himself to the contemplation of truth is the happiest a man can be in this life.

QUESTIONS FOR STUDY AND DISCUSSION

1. What is the difference between leisure and rest?
2. Why is there no leisure in political activity?
3. Why do we need leisure?
4. Is the happiness of the contemplative life an attainable human goal? If so, why? If not, why not?
5. Prove that the intellect is the best part of man.

The Natural Law

QUESTION 94: THE NATURAL LAW

We must now consider the natural law, concerning which there are six points of inquiry: (1) What is the natural law? (2) What are the precepts of the natural law? (3) Whether all the acts of the virtues are prescribed by the natural law? (4) Whether the natural law is the same in all? (5) Whether it is changeable? (6) Whether it can be abolished from the mind of man?

ARTICLE 1. Whether the natural law is a habit?

We proceed thus to the First Article:—

Objection 1. It would seem that the natural law is a habit. For, as the Philosopher says, *there are three things in the soul, power, habit and passion.* But the natural law is not one of the soul's powers, nor is it one of the passions, as we may see by going through them one by one. Therefore the natural law is a habit.

Obj. 2. Further, Basil says that the *conscience or synderesis is the law of our mind;* which can apply only to the natural law. But *synderesis* is a habit, as was shown in the First Part. Therefore the natural law is a habit.

Obj. 3. Further, the natural law abides in man always, as will be shown further on. But man's reason, which the law regards, does not always think about the natural law. Therefore the natural law is not an act, but a habit.

On the contrary, Augustine says that *a habit is that whereby something is done when necessary.* But such is not the natural law, since it is in infants and in the damned who cannot act by it. Therefore the natural law is not a habit.

I answer that, A thing may be called a habit in two ways. First, properly and essentially, and thus the natural law is not a habit. For it has been stated above that the natural law is something appointed by reason, just as a proposition is a work of reason. Now that which a man does is not the same as that whereby he does it, for he makes a becoming speech by the habit of grammar. Since, then, a habit is that by which we act, a law cannot be a habit properly and essentially.

Secondly, the term habit may be applied to that which we hold by a habit. Thus *faith* may mean *that which we hold by faith.* Accordingly, since the precepts of the natural law are sometimes considered by reason actu-

From pp. 772–81 of *Summa Theologica,* I–II, in *Basic Writings of St. Thomas Aquinas,* vol. II, edited by Anton C. Pegis. © 1945 by Random House, Inc. Reprinted by permission of Random House, Inc., and Burns and Oates Ltd., London.

ally, while sometimes they are in the reason only habitually, in this way the natural law may be called a habit. So, too, in speculative matters, the indemonstrable principles are not the habit itself whereby we hold these principles; they are rather the principles of which we possess the habit.

Reply Obj. 1. The Philosopher proposes there to discover the genus of virtue; and since it is evident that virtue is a principle of action, he mentions only these things which are principles of human acts, viz., powers, habits and passions. But there are other things in the soul besides these three: e.g., acts, as *to will* is in the one that wills; again, there are things known in the knower; moreover its own natural properties are in the soul, such as immortality and the like.

Reply Obj. 2. *Synderesis* is said to be the law of our intellect because it is a habit containing the precepts of the natural law, which are the first principles of human actions.

Reply Obj. 3. This argument proves that the natural law is held habitually; and this is granted.

To the argument advanced in the contrary sense we reply that sometimes a man is unable to make use of that which is in him habitually, because of some impediment. Thus, because of sleep, a man is unable to use the habit of science. In like manner, through the deficiency of his age, a child cannot use the habit of the understanding of principles, or the natural law, which is in him habitually.

ARTICLE 2. Whether the natural law contains several precepts, or only one?

We proceed thus to the Second Article:—

Objection 1. It would seem that the natural law contains, not several precepts, but only one. For law is a kind of precept, as was stated above. If therefore there were many precepts of the natural law, it would follow that there are also many natural laws.

Obj. 2. Further, the natural law is consequent upon human nature. But human nature, as a whole, is one, though, as to its parts, it is manifold. Therefore, either there is but one precept of the law of nature because of the unity of nature as a whole, or there are many by reason of the number of parts of human nature. The result would be that even things relating to the inclination of the concupiscible power would belong to the natural law.

Obj. 3. Further, law is something pertaining to reason, as was stated above. Now reason is but one in man. Therefore there is only one precept of the natural law.

On the contrary, The precepts of the natural law in man stand in relation to operable matters as first principles do to matters of demonstration. But there are several first indemonstrable principles. Therefore there are also several precepts of the natural law.

I answer that, As was stated above, the precepts of the natural law are to the practical reason what the first principles of demonstrations are to the speculative reason, because both are self-evident principles. Now a thing is said to be self-evident in two ways: first, in itself; secondly, in relation to us. Any proposition is said to be self-evident in itself, if its predicate is contained in the notion of the subject; even though it may happen that to one who does not know the definition of the subject, such a proposition is not self-evident. For instance, this proposition, *Man is a rational being,* is, in its very nature, self-evident, since he who says *man,* says *a rational being;* and yet to one who does not know what a man is, this proposition is not self-evident. Hence it is that, as Boethius says, certain axioms or propositions are universally self-evident to all; and such are the propositions whose terms are known to all, as, *Every whole is greater than its part,* and, *Things equal to one and the same are equal to one another.* But some propositions are self-evident only to the wise, who understand the meaning of the terms of such propositions. Thus to one who understands that an angel is not a body, it is self-evident that an angel is not circumscriptively in a place. But this is not evident to the unlearned, for they cannot grasp it.

Now a certain order is to be found in those things that are apprehended by men. For that which first falls under apprehension is *being,* the understanding of which is included in all things whatsoever a man apprehends. Therefore the first indemonstrable principle is that *the same thing cannot be affirmed and denied at the same time,* which is based on the notion of *being* and *not-being:* and on this principle all others are based, as is stated in *Metaph.* iv. Now as *being* is the first thing that falls under the apprehension absolutely, so *good* is the first thing that falls under the apprehension of the practical reason, which is directed to action (since every agent acts for an end, which has the nature of good). Consequently, the first principle in the practical reason is one founded on the nature of good, viz., that *good is that which all things seek after.* Hence this is the first precept of law, that *good is to be done and promoted, and evil is to be avoided.* All other precepts of the natural law are based upon this; so that all the things which the practical reason naturally apprehends as man's good belong to the precepts of the natural law under the form of things to be done or avoided.

Since, however, good has the nature of an end, and evil, the nature of the contrary, hence it is that all those things to which man has a natural inclination are naturally apprehended by reason as being good, and consequently as objects of pursuit, and their contraries as evil, and objects of avoidance. Therefore, the order of the precepts of the natural law is according to the order of natural inclinations. For there is in man, first of all, an inclination to good in accordance with the nature which he has in common with all substances, inasmuch, namely, as every substance seeks the preservation of its own being, according to its nature; and by reason of this inclination, whatever is a means of preserving human life, and of warding off its obstacles, belongs to the natural law. Secondly, there is in man an inclination to things that pertain to him more specially, according to that nature which he has in common with other animals; and in virtue of this inclination, those things are said to belong to the natural law *which nature has taught to all animals,* such as sexual intercourse, the education of off-spring and so forth. Thirdly, there is in man an inclination to good according to the nature of his reason, which nature is proper to him. Thus man has a natural inclination to know the truth about God, and to live in society; and in this respect, whatever pertains to this inclination belongs to the natural law: e.g., to shun ignorance, to avoid offending those among whom one has to live, and other such things regarding the above inclination.

Reply Obj. 1. All these precepts of the law of nature have the character of one natural law, inasmuch as they flow from one first precept.

Reply Obj. 2. All the inclinations of any parts whatsoever of human nature, e.g., of the concupiscible and irascible parts, in so far as they are ruled by reason, belong to the natural law, and are reduced to one first precept, as was stated above. And thus the precepts of the natural law are many in themselves, but they are based on one common foundation.

Reply Obj. 3. Although reason is one in itself, yet it directs all things regarding man; so that whatever can be ruled by reason is contained under the law of reason.

ARTICLE 3. Whether all the acts of the virtues are prescribed by the natural law?

We proceed thus to the Third Article:—

Objection 1. It would seem that not all the acts of the virtues are prescribed by the natural law. For, as was stated above, it is of the nature of law that it be ordained to the common good. But some acts of the virtues are ordained to the private good of the individual, as is evident especially in regard to acts of temperance. Therefore, not all the acts of the virtues are the subject of natural law.

Obj. 2. Further, every sin is opposed to some virtuous act. If therefore all the acts of the virtues are prescribed by the natural law, it seems to follow that all sins are against nature; whereas this applies to certain special sins.

Obj. 3. Further, those things which are according to nature are common to all. But the acts of the virtues are not common to all, since a thing is virtuous in one, and vicious in another. Therefore, not all the acts of the virtues are prescribed by the natural law.

On the contrary, Damascene says that *virtues are natural.* Therefore virtuous acts also are subject to the natural law.

I answer that, We may speak of virtuous acts in two ways: first, in so far as they are virtuous; secondly, as such and such acts considered in their proper species. If, then, we are speaking of the acts of the virtues insofar as they are virtuous, thus all virtuous acts belong to the natural law. For it has been stated that to the natural law belongs everything to which a man is inclined according to his nature. Now each thing is inclined naturally to an operation that is suitable to it according to its form: e.g., fire is inclined to give heat. Therefore, since the rational soul is the proper form of man, there is in every man a natural inclination to act according to reason; and this is to act according to virtue. Consequently, considered thus, all the acts of the virtues are prescribed by the natural law, since each one's reason naturally dictates to him to act virtuously. But if we speak of virtuous acts, considered in themselves, i.e., in their proper species, thus not all virtuous acts are prescribed by the natural law. For many things are done virtuously, to which nature does not primarily incline, but which, through the inquiry of reason, have been found by men to be conducive to well-living.

Reply Obj. 1. Temperance is about the natural concupiscences of food, drink and sexual matters, which are indeed ordained to the common good of nature, just as other matters of law are ordained to the moral common good.

Reply Obj. 2. By human nature we may mean either that which is proper to man, and in this sense all sins, as being against reason, are also against nature, as Damascene states; or we may mean that nature which is common to man and other animals, and in this sense, certain special sins are said to be against nature: e.g. contrary to sexual intercourse, which is natural to all animals, is unisexual lust, which has received the special name of the unnatural crime.

Reply Obj. 3. This argument considers acts in themselves. For it is owing to the various conditions of men that certain acts are virtuous for some, as being proportioned and becoming to them, while they are vicious for others, as not being proportioned to them.

ARTICLE 4. Whether the natural law is the same in all men?

We proceed thus to the Fourth Article:—

Objection 1. It would seem that the natural law is not the same in all. For it is stated in the *Decretals* that *the natural law is that which is contained in the Law and the Gospel.* But this is not common to all men, because, as it is written (*Rom.* x. 16), *all do not obey the gospel.* Therefore the natural law is not the same in all men.

Obj. 2. Further, *Things which are according to the law are said to be just,* as is stated in *Ethics* v. But it is stated in the same book that nothing is so just for all as not to be subject to change in regard to some men. Therefore even the natural law is not the same in all men.

Obj. 3. Further, as was stated above, to the natural law belongs everything to which a man is inclined according to his nature. Now different men are naturally inclined to different things,—some to the desire of pleasures, others to the desire of honors, and other men to other things. Therefore, there is not one natural law for all.

On the contrary, Isidore says: *The natural law is common to all nations.*

I answer that, As we have stated above, to the natural law belong those things to which a man is inclined naturally; and among these it is proper to man to be inclined to act according to reason. Now it belongs to the reason to proceed from what is common to what is proper, as is stated in *Physics* i. The speculative reason, however, is differently situated, in this matter, from the practical reason. For, since the speculative reason is concerned chiefly with necessary things, which cannot be otherwise than they are, its proper conclusions, like the universal principles, contain the truth without fail. The practical reason, on the other hand, is concerned with contingent matters, which is the domain of human actions; and, consequently, although there is necessity in the common principles, the more we descend towards the particular, the more frequently we encounter defects. Accordingly, then, in speculative matters truth is the same in all men, both as to principles and as to conclusions; although the truth is not known to all as regards the conclusions, but only as regards the principles which are called *common notions.* But in matters of action, truth or practical rectitude is not the same for all as to what is particular, but only as to the common principles; and where there is the same rectitude in relation to particulars, it is not equally known to all.

It is therefore evident that, as regards the common principles whether of speculative or of practical reason, truth or rectitude is the same for all, and is equally known by all. But as to the proper conclusions of the speculative reason, the truth is the same for all, but it is not equally known to all. Thus, it is true for all that the three angles of a triangle are together equal to two right angles, although it is not known to all. But as to the proper conclusions of the practical reason, neither is the truth or rectitude the same for all, nor, where it is the same, is it equally known by all. Thus, it is right and true for all to act according to reason, and from this principle it follows, as a proper conclusion, that goods entrusted to another should be restored to their owner. Now this is true for the majority of cases. But it may happen in a particular case that it would be injurious, and therefore unreasonable, to restore goods held in trust; for instance, if they are claimed for the purpose of fighting against one's country. And this principle will be found to fail the more, according as we descend further towards the particular, e.g., if one were to say that goods held in trust should be restored with such and such a guarantee, or in such and such a way; because the greater the number of conditions added, the greater the number of ways in which the principle may fail, so that it be not right to restore or not to restore.

Consequently, we must say that the natural law, as to the first common principles, is the same for all, both as to rectitude and as to knowledge. But as to certain more particular aspects, which are conclusions, as it were, of those common principles, it is the same for all in the majority of cases, both as to rectitude and as to knowledge; and yet in some few cases it may fail, both as to rectitude, by reason of certain obstacles (just as natures subject to generation and corruption fail in some few cases because of some obstacle), and as to knowledge, since in some the reason is perverted by passion, or evil habit, or an evil disposition of nature. Thus at one time theft, although it is expressly contrary to the natural law, was not considered wrong among the Germans, as Julius Cæsar relates.

Reply Obj. 1. The meaning of the sentence quoted is not that whatever is contained in the Law and the Gospel belongs to the natural law, since they contain many things that are above nature; but that whatever belongs to the natural law is fully contained in them. Therefore Gratian, after saying that *the natural law is what is contained in the Law and the Gospel,* adds at once, by way of example, *by which everyone is commanded to do to others as he would be done by.*

Reply Obj. 2. The saying of the Philosopher is to be understood of things that are naturally just, not as common principles, but as conclusions drawn from them, having rectitude in the majority of cases, but failing in a few.

Reply Obj. 3: Just as in man reason rules and commands the other powers, so all the natural inclinations belonging to the other powers must needs be directed according to reason. Therefore it is universally right for all men that all their inclinations should be directed according to reason.

ARTICLE 5. Whether the natural law can be changed?

We proceed thus to the Fifth Article:—

Objection 1. It would seem that the natural law can be changed. For on *Ecclus.* xvii. 9 (*He gave them instructions, and the law of life*) the *Gloss* says: *He wished the law of the letter to be written, in order to correct the law of nature.* But that which is corrected is changed. Therefore the natural law can be changed.

Obj. 2. Further, the slaying of the innocent, adultery and theft are against the natural law. But we find these things changed by God: as when God commanded Abraham to slay his innocent son (*Gen.* xxii. 2); and when He ordered the Jews to borrow and purloin the vessels of the Egyptians (*Exod.* xii. 35); and when He commanded Osee to take to himself *a wife of fornications* (*Osee* i. 2). Therefore the natural law can be changed.

Obj. 3. Further, Isidore says that *the possession of all things in common, and universal freedom, are matters of natural law.* But these things are seen to be changed by human laws. Therefore it seems that the natural law is subject to change.

On the contrary, It is said in the *Decretals: The natural law dates from the creation of the rational creature. It does not vary according to time, but remains unchangeable.*

I answer that, A change in the natural law may be understood in two ways. First, by way of addition. In this sense, nothing hinders the natural law from being changed, since many things for the benefit of human life have been added over and above the natural law, both by the divine law and by human laws.

Secondly, a change in the natural law may be understood by way of subtraction, so that what previously was according to the natural law, ceases to be so. In this sense, the natural law is altogether unchangeable in its first principles. But in its secondary principles, which, as we have said, are certain detailed proximate conclusions drawn from the first principles, the natural law is not changed so that what it prescribes be not right in most cases. But it may be changed in some particular cases of rare occurrence, through some special causes hindering the observance of such precepts, as was stated above.

Reply Obj. 1. The written law is said to be given for the correction of the natural law, either because it supplies what was wanting to the natural law, or because the natural law was so perverted in the hearts of some men, as to certain matters, that they esteemed those things good which are naturally evil; which perversion stood in need of correction.

Reply Obj. 2. All men alike, both guilty and innocent, die the death of nature; which death of nature is inflicted by the power of God because of original sin, according to I *Kings* ii. 6: *The Lord killeth and maketh alive.* Consequently, by the command of God, death can be inflicted on any man, guilty or innocent, without any injustice whatever.—In like manner, adultery is intercourse with another's wife; who is allotted to him by the law emanating from God. Consequently intercourse with any woman, by the command of God, is neither adultery nor fornication.—The same applies to theft, which is the taking of another's property. For whatever is taken by the command of God, to Whom all things belong, is not taken against the will of its owner, whereas it is in this that theft consists.—Nor is it only in human things that whatever is commanded by God is right; but also in natural things, whatever is done by God is, in some way, natural, as was stated in the First Part.

Reply Obj. 3. A thing is said to belong to the natural law in two ways. First, because nature inclines thereto: e.g., that one should not do harm to another. Secondly, because nature did not bring with it the contrary. Thus, we might say that for man to be naked is of the natural law, because nature did not give him clothes, but art invented them. In this sense, *the possession of all things in common and universal freedom* are said to be of the natural law, because, namely, the distinction of possessions and slavery were not brought in by nature, but devised by human reason for the benefit of human life. Accordingly, the law of nature was not changed in this respect, except by addition.

ARTICLE 6. Whether the natural law can be abolished from the heart of man?

We proceed thus to the Sixth Article:—

Objection 1. It would seem that the natural law can be abolished from the heart of man. For on *Rom.* ii. 14 (*When the Gentiles who have not the law,* etc.) the *Gloss* says that *the law of justice, which sin had blotted out, is graven on the heart of man when he is restored by grace.* But the law of justice is the law of nature. Therefore the law of nature can be blotted out.

Obj. 2. Further, the law of grace is more efficacious than the law of nature. But the law of grace is blotted out by sin. Much more, therefore, can the law of nature be blotted out.

Obj. 3. Further, that which is established by law is proposed as something just. But many things are enacted by men which are contrary to the law of nature. Therefore the law of nature can be abolished from the heart of man.

On the contrary, Augustine says: *Thy law is written in the hearts of men, which iniquity itself effaces not.* But the law which is written in men's hearts is the natural law. Therefore the natural law cannot be blotted out.

I answer that, As we have stated above, there belong to the natural law, first, certain most common precepts that are known to all; and secondly, certain secondary and more particular precepts, which are, as it were, conclusions following closely from first principles. As to the common principles, the natural law, in its universal meaning, cannot in any way be blotted out from men's hearts. But it is blotted out in the case of a particular action, in so far as reason is hindered from applying the common principle to the particular action because of concupiscence or some other passion, as was stated above.—But as to the other, i.e., the secondary precepts, the natural law can be blotted out from the human heart, either by evil persuasions, just as in speculative matters errors occur in respect of necessary conclusions; or by vicious customs and corrupt habits, as, among some men, theft, and even unnatural vices, as the Apostle states (*Rom.* i. 24), were not esteemed sinful.

Reply Obj. 1. Sin blots out the law of nature in particular cases, not universally, except perchance in regard to the secondary precepts of the natural law, in the way stated above.

Reply Obj. 2. Although grace is more efficacious than nature, yet nature is more essential to man, and therefore more enduring.

Reply Obj. 3. This argument is true of the secondary precepts of the natural law, against which some legislators have framed certain enactments which are unjust.

QUESTIONS FOR STUDY AND DISCUSSION

1. How do we discover first moral principles? Are they inborn, habitually possessed, or acquired through reasoning or simple intuition?
2. What is the relationship between precepts of the natural moral law and man's natural inclinations?
3. If man reveals both good and bad natural inclinations, would the natural law incline him to both the good and the bad?

4. Does the natural moral law include virtues in their developed state? Give reasons for your answer.
5. Account for the fact that the basic principles of the natural moral law are the same in all civilizations but, at the same time, its remote conclusions and practical applications differ considerably from one to another.

TOPICS FOR DISCUSSION AND TERM PAPERS

A

1. What do you think are the greatest weaknesses and strengths of the intellectualist ethical theory?
2. Essentially virtue consists in a deliberate choice of the mean; practically, however, it consists in excellence or in the best moral conduct. Reconcile this apparent opposition.
3. Compare the Platonic and Aristotelian theories of virtue.
4. Describe in your own words the relationship between practical wisdom and the virtuous life.
5. How is the meaning of the natural law discovered by practical right reason?
6. If the natural law is universal and supposedly found in all men, how can one account for the many disagreements with respect to (a) its reality, (b) its conclusions, and (c) its applications to particular situations?
7. We seek refreshment, stimulation, and compensation in pleasure. Is this a sign of immaturity or normality? Justify your answer.
8. Compare the Platonic and Aristotelian theories of friendship.
9. How can one reconcile the obligation to obey all true laws—natural and civil—with the obligation to retain the deliberate choice essential to the human act?
10. Consider honestly, carefully, and clearly your own particular desire in regard to happiness. Now, to what extent does your desire approximate the intellectualist view of happiness? How do you explain any discrepancy between the two?

B.

1. Cite some basic agreements between an intellectualist ethics and

   a) Marxism
   b) Existentialism
   c) Positivism
   d) Naturalism

2. Name some ways in which intellectualist ethics poses serious problems for the ethical system of

   a) Marxism
   b) Existentialism
   c) Positivism
   d) Naturalism

3. Conversely, what serious problems for an intellectualist ethics are presented by these ethical systems?
4. Name at least one contribution that could be made to the intellectualist ethics by each of the other philosophies discussed in this volume.
5. Which aspects or areas in moral philosophy need further development, that is, which ones leave us unsatisfied by the inability of philosophy to explain these to our full satisfaction?

RECOMMENDED READINGS

Primary Sources

Aristotle. *Basic Works of Aristotle,* Ed. by Richard McKeon. New York: Random House, 1941. The translation of the *Nicomachean Ethics* is that of W. D. Ross. The Introduction to all works of Aristotle emphasizes particularly the method of Aristotelian philosophy.

―――. *Complete Works.* 19 vols. Cambridge, Mass.: The Loeb Classical Library, Harvard University Press. The works of Aristotle important for the study of ethics are *Eudemian Ethics, Nicomachean Ethics, Magna Moralia, Politics, Rhetoric.* The *Nicomachean Ethics* in this series was translated by H. Rackham, first printed in 1926 and reprinted in 1962. Quotations in the Introduction and the Glossary as well as selected readings were taken from this translation.

―――. *Nicomachean Ethics.* Trans. by Martin Ostwald. New York: Liberal Arts Press, 1962. Pocket edition. A short bibliography, pp. xxv–xxvi, as well as a Glossary of technical terms at the end of the book are helpful tools for a better understanding of the Aristotelian ethical teaching.

―――. *The Oxford Translation of Aristotle.* Trans. under the editorship of W. D. Ross and J. A. Smith. 12 vols. Oxford: Clarendon Press, 1928–52. The first complete English translation of the works of Aristotle. This is a monumental work for which all the findings of nineteenth-century textual and philosophical Aristotelian scholarship have been utilized.

Plato. *The Collected Dialogues of Plato, Including the Letters.* Ed. and with Introd. and Pref. Notes by Edith Hamilton and Huntington Cairns. New York: Pantheon Books, 1961. In this complete edition of Plato's works, the editors have made a judicious selection of translators for different dialogues. Short Introductions to the dialogues are particularly helpful in alerting the reader to the principal ideas contained in each one. The excellent Index will be of great value to the student.

―――. *Complete Works and Letters.* 10 vols. Cambridge, Mass.: The Loeb Classical Library, Harvard University Press. Greek text with English translation. The classical Greek works in this series are, as a rule, the best such editions published in the United States. For Plato's ethical ideas, the following dialogues are of particular interest: *Republic, Laws, Stateman, Meno, Gorgias, Lysis, Philebus, Laches.*

―――. *The Dialogues of Plato,* 4th ed. rev. Trans. by B. Jowett. 4 vols. Oxford: Clarendon Press, 1953. The shortened edition of the five-volume work published in 1892. Excellent Introductions and analyses for each dialogue.

St. Thomas Aquinas. *Basic Writings of St. Thomas Aquinas.* Ed., annot., and with Introd. by Anton C. Pegis. 2 vols. New York: Random House, 1945. Volume II contains those parts of the two *Summas* that cover moral matters. Questions 1–5 of I–II (on the problem of happiness) are not included. Though not complete, this edition is the best English translation of the two *Summas* available.

―――. *Commentary on the Nicomachean Ethics.* Trans. by C. I. Litzinger. 2 vols. Chicago: Henry Regnery Co., 1964. Aquinas' comments on the *Nicomachean Ethics* following the literal Latin translation of William of Moerbeke. This is the best medieval commentary on the *Nichomachean Ethics,* considering the state of Aristotelian scholarship in that era. The alphabetical indexes of "Subjects" in vol. I and of "Names" in vol. II are very useful to the student.

St. Thomas Aquinas. *On the Truth of the Catholic Faith (Summa Contra Gentiles)*, vol. III, *Providence*. Trans. by Vernon J. Bourke. Garden City, N.Y.: Doubleday & Co., 1956. Parts I and II deal with moral matters in general.

———. *Summa Theologica*. Trans. by the English Dominican Fathers. 3 vols. New York: Benzinger Bros., 1947–48. This is a complete edition of the *Summa Theologica*. A more recent translation which contains extensive descriptive notes and discussions is now being published in several volumes. (Ed. by Thomas Gilby and P. K. Meagher. New York: McGraw-Hill, 1964–   .)

Commentaries

Copleston, Frederick. *A History of Philosophy*. Garden City, N.Y.: Doubleday & Co., 1962. Volume I, *Greece and Rome*. See Part II, pp. 74–91, for a clear, substantial, and fair presentation of Aristotelian ethical ideas. Volume II, *Medieval Philosophy*. Part II, pp. 20–155, contains an excellent exposition of Aquinas' teachings. Chapter 39, pp. 118–37, is particularly related to ethics.

Deferrari, Roy J. *A Latin-English Dictionary of St. Thomas*. Boston: St. Paul Editions, 1960. Based on the *Summa Theologica* and selected passages of his other works. One of the best dictionaries in the field, it explains Aquinas' medieval Latin terminology. Because it is principally based on the theocentric world view of the *Summa Theologica,* this dictionary would seem to be more useful to the theologian than to the philosopher.

Gilson, Etienne. *History of Christian Philosophy in the Middle Ages*. New York: Random House, 1955. This is the best history of medieval philosophy. See especially the chapter on St. Thomas, pp. 361–81.

———. *Moral Values and Moral Life: The Ethical Theory of St. Thomas Aquinas*. Hamden, Conn.: Shoe String Press, 1961. The great historian of medieval philosophy here gives a unified view of the ethical doctrines of Aquinas.

Jaeger, Werner. *Aristotle: Fundamentals of the History of His Development*, 2nd ed. Trans. by R. Robinson. Oxford: Oxford University Press, 1948. This classic work presents the development of Aristotelian philosophical thought. See Chs. 4 and 9 for the development or Aristotle's ethical ideas.

Joachim, H. H. *Aristotle: The Nicomachean Ethics, A Commentary*. Ed. by D. A. Rees. Oxford: Clarendon Press, 1951. A solid and oftentimes brilliant commentary for students wishing to delve into the meaning of particularly difficult passages in the *Nicomachean Ethics*.

Kiernan, Thomas P., ed. *Aristotle Dictionary*. New York: Philosophical Library, 1962. This work contains a long Introduction, pp. 7–162, that presents an exposition of the content of Aristotle's writings. The dictionary gives a description and definition of Aristotelian terms, quoting the place in his writings from which the definition has been taken.

Maritain, Jacques. *Moral Philosophy: An Historical and Critical Survey of the Great Systems*. New York: Charles Scribner's Sons, 1964. This is the first volume of three planned. Here the author presents Aquinas' moral teachings; in subsequent volumes he intends to give us Aquinas' ethical synthesis.

Ross, W. D. *Aristotle*, 5th ed. New York: Barnes & Noble, 1964. The most complete presentation in English of Aristotle's philosophy. Chapter 7 presents Aristotelian ethics.

Sidgwick, Henry. *Outlines of the History of Ethics for English Readers.* Boston: Beacon Press, 1960. See especially pp. 51–70 for a brief and reliable account of Aristotelian ethics.

Veatch, Henry B. *Rational Man: A Modern Interpretation of Aristotelian Ethics.* Bloomington, Ind.: Indiana University Press, 1962. An appeal, interestingly written, for the restoration of *logos* in ethics. The author insists that norms of conduct are more important for ethics than the linguistic analysis of its terms.

PART TWO

DIALECTICAL THOUGHT:

Kant

Fichte

Hegel

Marx

Engels

EDITED BY

Louis Dupré
GEORGETOWN UNIVERSITY

DIALECTICAL THOUGHT:

Kant

Fichte

Hegel

Marx

Engels

Introduction

The Dialectical Philosophers:
From Idealism to Materialism

It would be difficult to think of even one basic thesis on which the philosophers discussed in this section all agree. They are grouped here under the title "dialectical philosophers," but even the term "dialectic" cannot be considered a common denominator, for it has a different meaning for each author. To Immanuel Kant (1724–1804) it is almost a derogatory term, referring to the process of thinking insofar as it reaches beyond the limits set to strict science. For G. W. F. Hegel (1770–1831) dialectic coincides with rational thought; it is the self-development of a spirit that is both mind and reality, subject and object. One might almost say the same about Johann Gottlieb Fichte (1762–1814), except that his concept of mind is purely subjective and the dialectic, therefore, consists in the process by which this subjective spirit develops and produces objective reality. In the early writings of Karl Marx (1818–83) dialectic indicates the dynamic relation between man and his environment, whereas for Friedrich Engels (1820–95) it describes the evolution of a material world process in which the mind is more a determined than a determining factor.

Yet despite such basic differences, their thought has a common origin. It represents an intellectual development that started with Kant and reached completion in Marx and Engels. This does not imply, however, that no other course of thought could have been followed. There are several seminal ideas in the philosophy of Kant; neopositivist and analytic philosophers may

164

claim him as their ancestor with as much right as idealists. Still, one logical end of his philosophy can be found in the idealism of Fichte and Hegel. Similarly, several trends of thinking originated in Hegel, ranging from neo-Hegelianism to Kierkegaard's dialectic of existence. But one of these trends led logically to Marx.

Kant's position that the truth of an object is to be found in the subject and its ethical application that morality is entirely determined by the intention of the subject were further developed in Fichte's philosophy, which places the subject at the origin of all reality. Hegel fully accepted the reduction of reality to Spirit implicit in this position, but he no longer identified spirit with subject. He was able to adopt an *objective* system of ethics without abandoning the Kantian primacy of the mind. The ethical life is the life of freedom, but freedom expresses itself objectively in the entire social order. So Hegel returned to the ancient definition of the perfect life as life in the perfect State. Marx maintained Hegel's social objectivism but dropped the idealist presupposition that this social, objective reality is a creation of the spirit. For him the humanization process takes place in a dialogue between man and his environment. In Engels the dialectical struggle seems to be replaced more and more by an economic determinism. Yet the dialectical nature of this economic reality itself still lifts Engels' philosophy above pure materialism.

Kant: Principle of Moral Autonomy

In the Introduction to *Critique of Pure Reason* (1781), Immanuel Kant announced a revolution in philosophy comparable to the one that Copernicus had accomplished in astronomy. As the heliocentric theory had solved a number of previously insoluble problems by simply reversing the relationship between the sun and the earth, philosophy was to achieve the same result by reversing the traditional relation between knower and known object. Whereas in the past philosophy had held cognition to be a conformity of the mind to the external object, Kant assumed that it was rather the object that must be made conform to the mind. The representation of an object is entirely determined by the structure of man's cognitive apparatus. From this fact Kant concluded to the dependence of the object on the subject.

The same dependence is to be seen in man's moral life. The morality of an act is determined not by the object, the external aspect of the act, but by the intention of the acting subject, just as truth is to be found solely in the knowing subject. Kant's position is based upon the nature of the will. As a part of reason, it must follow the most basic law of reason which, in a Kantian perspective, is self-determination. Only by rejecting all extrinsic determinations and by accepting its own rational nature as sole motive of action can the will be rational and good. But this restricts moral goodness to the intention of the agent, for the intention is the one stage of the act over which the agent has full control and which can be entirely determined by reason. The *good will* alone, that is, the pure intention to act in accordance with Reason, is impervious to corruption. On the contrary, even the loftiest achievements may be morally spoiled by selfishness and pride in the intention. Furthermore, these achievements depend too much on natural talents and dispositions, factors beyond man's control. Moral goodness is determined by man's free contribution, which consists entirely in his *good will*. "Even though by some special disfavor of fortune or because of the meager provision of a stepmotherly nature this will was entirely lacking in ability to carry out its intentions . . . it would still sparkle like a jewel by itself." [1] The moral law, then, is restricted to the intentions; it never descends into the confused arena of man's external actions.

But if the act cannot be a norm for morality, what is to determine the intention itself? How can the rational will be its own purpose and motive of action? Kant answered: By accepting no other motive of action than the moral law itself, that is, by pursuing duty for duty's sake. Yet the very fact that freedom proposes its ends in the form of a duty, a law, requires some justification. Kant explained this obligatory character of morality by the basic ambiguity of human nature. Man is both rational and empirical, and the latter part of his nature stands in a certain tension to the former. That is why he never *possesses* the moral good but only *strives* for it. The good is proposed to him in the form of an imperative, an "ought."

Human life is full of "oughts," for the satisfaction of every desire requires that one follow certain rules. *If* I want a particular object, I *must* go about it in a certain way. All these conditions in the exercise of freedom are imperatives. But they are hypothetical; their necessity follows exclusively from the necessary relationship between means and end. The end itself is never proposed as an absolute imperative. One can take it or leave it. The moral obligation, however, is not conditioned by any further empirical end; it is an end in itself which therefore commands in a *categorical* way.

Kant's categorical imperative has been the object of much criticism, a good deal of which is unfair or irrelevant. The solidity of Kant's position depends entirely on his ability to make the categorical imperative a *concrete* norm of action. How can an order to act for duty's sake ever tell me which acts are to be done and which are to be omitted? According to Kant, the notion of duty itself provides a sufficient criterion, for it implies that one must act in such a way that one's line of action can be adopted by all men. If an act is not universally acceptable, it is definitely not in conformity with the rational will, for a rational obligation is per se universal. This obviously rules out certain acts such as murder, robbery, and adultery, for one cannot reasonably wish that all people would commit them.

---

[1] Immanuel Kant, *The Fundamental Principles of the Metaphysic of Ethics,* trans. by Otto Manthey-Zorn (New York: Appleton-Century-Crofts, 1938), p. 9.

Similarly, because of its rational character the will must always be treated as an end, never as a means. Kant therefore concluded, "Act so that in your own person as well as in the person of every other you are treating mankind also as an end, never merely as a means." This attitude excludes all acts that man has traditionally considered to be immoral, because in one way or another they all conflict with the dignity of the human person. Kant had no difficulty showing that not only are murder, mutilation, and fraud irreconcilable with human dignity, but that this dignity requires all of one's acts to be done for the advancement of humanity in himself and in others.

Yet this concretization of the categorical imperative does not solve the basic difficulty resulting from the separation of moral intention and empirical act. Kant never bridged the gap between a moral but purely interior intention on the one hand, and an empirical but amoral external act on the other. All his efforts to give the formal imperative a concrete, moral content are doomed to failure, for any content will have to include empirical elements if it is to be practical at all. Yet the "pure," that is, the non-empirical character of the categorical imperative, excludes all empirical elements. Indeed, the essential demand of Kant's morality is that freedom remain *autonomous*; it must reject any determination that does not originate in its own rational character. Morality therefore can never accept empirical motives. Precisely for that reason Kant had to make the rational character of the will itself into the only norm of morality. No appeal to empirical elements of happiness or well-being is needed, he claimed, for any action conflicting with the moral imperative appears to be self-contradictory and is thus intrinsically irrational. Not to return money that I have received in deposit destroys respect for private property and leads to the contradiction that property is non-property. No empirical element, Kant claimed, has been used; the sheer force of reason brings out the immoral character of this behavior.

Yet, as Hegel pointed out, this is true only if we assume that property is necessarily implied in man's rational nature. As long as this intrinsic necessity has not been established, dishonesty proves merely that non-property is non-property, which is not contradictory and could, at least theoretically, be made into a universal law of man. To support his position Kant has surreptitiously introduced empirical elements (proving on a *de facto* basis that property is necessary for man) into the pure and universal form of his categorical imperative. No one would object to this solution if it did not conflict with Kant's own principles.

In spite of this obvious weakness, Kant's moral system has had a lasting impact on all subsequent moral philosophy because of its introduction of the principle of moral autonomy and its emphasis on the subjective element of the moral act.

Fichte: Philosophy of the Moral Obligation

The Kantian principle of morality is developed to its ultimate, idealist conclusions in the philosophy of Johann Gottlieb Fichte, in which the "ought" of the moral imperative is made into the basis of an entire philosophy. In the unshakable certainty of the moral obligation man knows that he himself, not the phenomenal world about him, must be the determining principle of his actions. Therefore, instead of having regarded man as only one link in nature's deterministic chain of cause and effect, Fichte saw nature as essentially subjected to human freedom. Not only is our knowledge of the world determined by the structure of the human mind, as Kant had pointed out, but the world becomes a *reality* only insofar as it is an object of man's free activity. Whereas Kant's philosophy still admits of a modicum of realism in postulating a *thing in itself* (reality insofar as it is beyond knowledge), Fichte eliminated this independent reality by reducing the entire world to an object of human freedom. True enough, the world imposes certain restrictions upon this freedom, but these are simply limitations that freedom imposes upon itself. The existence of an outside world is a necessary condition for the existence of a self which needs such a world in order to exercise its essential activity. As Josiah Royce put it:

> The deepest truth, then, is a practical truth. I *need* something not myself, in order to be active, that is, in order to exist. My very existence is practical; it is self-assertion.[2]

In *The Vocation of Man* (1800) Fichte drew the ethical conclusions inherent in this position. Man's task is to become free by overcoming the resistance of nature. As he conquers nature, man will conquer himself. To control himself he must first control his self-imposed resistance. Fichte foresaw the time when man will have spiritualized nature so completely that manual labor will be reduced to the minimum necessary for physical health. Fichte's contemporaries must have felt very sceptical in reading this. But we who live in the age of cybernetics no longer consider it a philosophical pipe dream.

Yet the resistance of nature is not the hardest obstacle for man to overcome in his struggle for freedom. It is much more difficult for him to outgrow his own moral immaturity, which makes him turn against himself the very intentions of his conquering spirit. Here again, Fichte anticipated what we see under our eyes: the threat of total destruction that modern man has brought upon himself by his inability to make morality keep pace with scientific progress. Fichte mentioned not only international conflicts, but, even more, social injustice and man-made poverty. Some of his descriptions read like the more rhapsodic passages of Karl Marx. Similarly in Marxist fashion he predicted that this social injustice will eventually give rise to its own

---

[2] *Spirit of Modern Philosophy* (New York: George Braziller, 1955), p. 157.

remedy. Oppression will lead to revolt, revolt will create a new ideal of man, and the new man will establish new conditions of peace and brotherhood.

> From the establishment of a just eternal organization and of peace between individuals, there will necessarily result integrity in the external relations of nations toward each other, and universal peace among them. But the establishment of this just eternal organization, and the emancipation of the first nation that shall be truly free, arises as a necessary consequence from the ever-growing oppression exercised by the ruling classes toward the subjects, which gradually becomes insupportable—a progress which may be safely left to the passions and the blindness of these classes, even though warned of the result.[3]

The necessity with which this ideal will be realized is not due to physical or economic determinism; it is the necessity of man's inextinguishable striving for freedom. Nor is the scope of man's striving restricted to this world. If it were, every individual's efforts would serve future generations more than himself, and some heroic actions, thwarted by the course of history, would serve no purpose at all. But in the spiritual world no step is ever lost, and freedom is realized primarily on a spiritual level.

> I pursue the earthly purpose not for its own sake alone or as a final aim, but only because my true final aim, obedience to the law of conscience, does not present itself to me in this world in other shape than as a commandment to promote this purpose in my own place. . . . In this life I must *will* to promote it because I must obey; whether it be *actually* promoted by the deed that follows my will thus fittingly directed is not my concern: I am responsible only for the will . . . but not for the result.[4]

This is Fichte's version of the distinction between the noumenal world of the moral intention and the phenomenal world of nature. Yet the two are no longer separated as they were in Kant. For to become actual, freedom must have a real impact upon the material world. Without a true, causal influence upon this world, freedom will never be actualized. On the other hand, freedom will never gain complete control over this world; the real will always resist the ideal and partly escape it. We must conclude that what man does is definitely effective in this world, but it may not have the full effect that the free action *intends*. On man's spiritual life, however, the free action cannot fail to have its full effect. This effect may be invisible now, but it will appear in a future life. Fichte strongly stressed the continuity between man's present spiritual life and his afterlife. By resolving to obey the laws of reason man becomes immortal in this life, because by this

---

[3] Johann Gottlieb Fichte, *The Vocation of Man,* ed. and with Introd. by Roderick M. Chisholm (New York: Liberal Arts Press, 1956), p. 111.
[4] *Ibid.,* pp. 120–21.

act he places himself above all empirical causes and his existence ceases to depend upon contingent sources.

Fichte reconciled Kant's morality of a good will residing entirely in the intention with a revolutionary theory of action capable of changing the aspect of the world. The moral life combines the indifference to empirical phenomena, which results from the autonomous character of the rational will, with a deep involvement in the empirical world, where the moral obligation is to be executed. On the supersensual level the will is entirely self-sufficient; it is both act and effect. On this level the will is in rapport with the invisible community of all rational beings of which a divine will is the spiritual bond. It is this divine will that renders the finite will effective in the spiritual realm.

> It has results because it is immediately and infallibly perceived by another will to which it is related, which is its own accomplishment and the only leveling principle of the spiritual world; *in Him* it has its first results and *through Him* it acquires an influence on the whole spiritual world, which throughout is only a product of that Infinite Will.[5]

The relation between the finite and the infinite will is rather vague in Fichte's philosophy, and it is not too surprising that his contemporaries accused him of pantheism and even atheism (an attack which he rightly rejected, but which cost him his chair at the University of Jena). More difficult to refute was the charge of subjectivism—Fichte defined reality entirely in terms of the acting ego. Even his early followers, Schelling and Hegel, eventually rejected this philosophy which reduces the entire universe to a battlefield for moral strivings. Reality has an objective aspect, an *in itself,* which is just as real as the determinations of freedom.

Hegel: Christian Morality in His Early Writings

G. W. F. Hegel's first training in theology had a lifelong impact upon his work. Throughout his works the Gospel always remained the ultimate criterion of the good life. But his philosophical interpretation of the evangelic ideal developed considerably over the years. For a while it took the form of Kantian morality. An early essay describes Jesus as a teacher of moral integrity whose entire doctrine consisted of the precept to follow the law of reason. Whatever Christianity later added to this content was a deviation from the original message. It contaminated Jesus' universal, ethical doctrine with "positive" elements, that is, it made salvation dependent upon the faithful acceptance of certain historical events rather than upon the sole observance of the moral law.

Probably under the influence of German romanticism, Hegel gradually

---

[5] *Ibid.,* p. 134.

abandoned this Kantian moral ideal, which he came to see as too rationalistic and altogether too far away from the main stream of life. If life has any meaning at all, it cannot be as diametrically opposed to reason's "ought" as Kant's philosophy seemed to imply. Nor can one claim the moral law as the highest expression of human freedom if it constantly thwarts man's natural inclinations. In fact, Kant's purely interior moral law restricts freedom as much as any exterior command could ever do.

> Between the Shaman of the Tungus, the European prelate who rules Church and State, the Voguls and the Puritans, on the one hand, and the man who listens to his own command of duty, on the other, the difference is not that the former make themselves slaves, while the latter is free, but that the former have the lord outside themselves, while the latter carries his lord in himself, yet at the same time is his own slave.[6]

Law and reason in this view are too far removed from inclination and nature: the opposition between *is* and *ought* constantly denies life as it is actually lived. Kant's moral *autonomy* is in fact a *heteronomy* of life, far worse than any positive law. Kant rejected the Jewish law because it reduces man's morality to a set of positive prescriptions, but his own theory of morality is hardly less legalistic. As to the morality of the Gospel which Kant claimed for himself, it is at least as much opposed to his doctrine as to the Jewish law.

The real revolution in ethics, which Kant seems to have missed altogether, was accomplished by Jesus' teaching of religious love.

> Up against commands which required a bare service of the Lord, a direct slavery, an obedience without joy . . . Jesus set their precise opposite, a human urge and so a human need. Religious practice is the most holy, the most beautiful, of all things; it is our endeavor to unify the discords necessitated by our development and our attempt to exhibit the unification in the *ideal* as fully *existent,* as no longer opposed to reality, and thus to confirm it in a deed.[7]

In Christian religions the opposition between *ought* and *is* disappears completely, and thus there can be no religious "commands" in the strict sense of the word. What Jesus taught was not a new *ought* but a new *is,* a transformation of *life itself.* True, the way to this new life is often indicated in terms of commands, but this is only because life cannot be expressed in thought without being put forth in the same conceptual form as the precepts of reason. The expression here is opposed to the content of life, while Kant's moral imperative is a concept and a command in *essence,* and not merely in expression. Because he failed to see this distinction, Kant interpreted the ethics of Christianity as a new sort of *command,* the interior

---

[6] G. W. F. Hegel, *The Spirit of Christianity,* in *On Christianity: Early Theological Writings,* trans. by T. M. Knox (New York, Harper & Row, 1961), p. 211.
[7] *Ibid.,* p. 206.

command of the moral law. What Christ teaches in the Sermon on the Mount however is *love,* a new kind of *life* in which man's inclination is united with the law in such a way that the law loses the form of law. Through love, the universality of the law of reason is channeled into the personal life and inclinations of the individual. Man thus identifies himself with the universal to the point that it ceases to be law and becomes life.

This new ethical attitude is at once easier and more demanding. It is easier, for love always follows its own inclinations. It is more demanding, for whereas the Commandments merely forbid certain external acts, the Gospel indicts the very disposition towards these acts. Instead of simply proscribing murder, the Gospel excludes whatever conflicts with charity; instead of forbidding divorce, the Gospel teaches love as the "fulfillment" of the law against divorce. The new ethics transforms man's entire attitude, not merely his external acts. That is why he should never be self-complacent about having done his duty. Much less should he seek the approval of others, for this indicates that he has never integrated the universal law with his individual life; he still feels that in being moral he raises himself above himself and all others insofar as they are less than universal. As long as man is conscious of duty and law, he has not reached the height of Christian morality. That is also the reason why Jesus tells his followers not to judge. For he who judges sets himself up as a law, even though he may also subject himself to the norms that he applies to others. The distinction between a universal law and an individual "application" is altogether excluded by the ethics of love.

Hegel's interpretation of the ethics of the Gospel is debatable from both a moral and an exegetical point of view.[8] But it is useless to criticize it in detail, since Hegel later changed his position and admitted that the notion of law can never be completely eliminated from the ethical order. Yet, the basic insight that ethics must never separate what *is* from what *ought* to be is retained and strengthened in the *Philosophy of Right.*

Hegel: Social Ethics in the *Philosophy of Right*

This work of Hegel's mature age is a philosophy of freedom considered in all its expressions. The title is narrower than the content since it covers not only the juridical order but the entire ethical order, which includes private morality and the social institutions of family, economic community, and State.

Hegel agreed with Kant on a very substantial point: the will is essentially rational; it is reason in its practical aspect. But whereas for Kant reason is static, fully completed from the beginning like Minerva stepping out

---

[8] It is interesting to note that it anticipates a present-day trend of "situation ethics" which, in the name of Christian love, denies the existence of universal imperatives.

of Jupiter's head, for Hegel reason is a *process* in which freedom is the power moving it from one stage to another. No single moment in this process is final, yet each one is necessary and prepares for the next. It is important to keep this connection in mind when considering the various stages of freedom; otherwise one might be tempted to consider only the final stage as the expression of freedom. For Hegel, the truth is in the totality, and the first stage of freedom, the juridical order, is just as necessary as the later stages of morality or "ethics" (the social institutions).

But this does not imply that one stage smoothly turns into another. Freedom is a struggle: it develops in a dialectical fashion, that is, by way of opposition and reconciliation. It becomes *real* only by opposing itself to itself, by losing itself in an unfree world. According to Kant, freedom can remain pure only by enclosing itself in the interiority of the intention. For Hegel, on the contrary, freedom can become real only by venturing out into the world, by losing itself or by "alienating" itself. Hegel rejected Kant's dichotomy between an internal order of freedom and an external order of compulsion.

The juridical order, which rules man's behavior in society and which, for Kant, is ruled by compulsion, should be seen as an initial, objective expression of freedom. Positive law preserves the extrinsic aspect of man's freedom, his social and economic relations with others. That is why Hegel called the law "the external existence of freedom." This is not to deny that the individual often experiences the law as a restriction of his freedom and that he accepts its external obligations merely because it guarantees him an equal number of rights. In the juridical order freedom appears exclusively in its universal and external aspect; the law is the same for all, and everyone must obey its external orders.

Against Kant, Hegel stressed that this objective exteriority is an essential part of freedom. But it is not all of it, and if the juridical order is isolated from the more internal aspects of freedom, it turns into pure compulsion. Yet in Hegel the internal and the external are not isolated from each other: they are complementary aspects—"moments"—of one ethical totality.

In the sphere of right, freedom is merely *in itself,* pure substance, and is not aware of itself as freedom. In order to gain self-consciousness freedom must withdraw from its objective works and return into itself. In this movement of introspection freedom experiences itself as being *for itself.* Through moral consciousness man learns that he is able to fashion his life without outside determination. As he progresses in freedom, his desire to preserve this independence grows stronger. The internal intention becomes all important, while the external act is relegated to the world of positive laws. This is the morality of *good will* which Kant described.

> So far as right in the strict sense was concerned, it was of no importance what my intention or my principle was. This question about the self-determination and motive of the will, like the ques-

tion about its purpose, now enters at this point in connexion with morality. Since man wished to be judged in accordance with his own self-determined choices, he is free in this relation to himself whatever the external situation may impose upon him. No one can break in upon this inner conviction of mankind, no violence can be done to it, and the moral will, therefore, is inaccessible. Man's worth is estimated by reference to his inward action and hence the standpoint of morality is that of freedom aware of itself.[9]

But here the question arises: To what extent can I, in my intention, claim the objective action as *mine?* Hegel's answer is that the action is my own insofar as I can reasonably be expected to foresee its consequences. These consequences are partly objective, the changes that my action will work in the outside world, and partly subjective, the personal satisfaction that I pursue in and through my act and its objective consequences. It is not true, as Kant claimed, that the pursuit of a particular, subjective satisfaction beyond the universal, objective good of the action perverts the morality of the act.

Since the subjective satisfaction of the individual himself (including the recognition which he receives by way of honour and fame) is also part and parcel of the achievement of ends of absolute worth, it follows that the demand that such an end alone shall appear as willed and attained, like the view that, in willing, objective and subjective ends are mutually exclusive, is an empty dogmatism of the abstract Understanding. And this dogmatism is more than empty, it is pernicious if it passes into the assertion that because subjective satisfaction is present, as it always is when any task is brought to completion, it is what the agent intended in essence to secure and that the objective end was in his eyes only a means to that.—What the subject is, is the series of his actions. If these are a series of worthless productions, then the subjectivity of his willing is just as worthless. But if the series of his deeds is of a substantive nature, then the same is true also of the individual's inner will.

The right of the subject's particularity, his right to be satisfied, or in other words the right of subjective freedom, is the pivot and centre of the difference between antiquity and modern times. This right in its infinity is given expression in Christianity and it has become the universal effective principle of a new form of civilization. Amongst the primary shapes which this right assumes are love, romanticism, the quest for the eternal salvation of the individual. . . .

Now this principle of particularity is, to be sure, one moment of the antithesis, and in the first place at least it is just as much identical with the universal as distinct from it. Abstract reflection, however, fixes this moment in its distinction from and opposition to the universal and so produces a view of morality as nothing but

---

[9] Hegel, *Philosophy of Right,* trans. and with notes by T. M. Knox (Oxford: Clarendon Press, 1942), No. 106, addition, p. 248. This and following excerpts from *Philosophy of Right* are reprinted by permission of the publisher.

a bitter, unending struggle against self-satisfaction, as the command: "Do with abhorrence what duty enjoins."

It is just this type of ratiocination which adduces that familiar psychological view of history which understands how to belittle and disparage all great deeds and great men by transforming into the main intention and operative motive of actions the inclinations and passions which likewise found their satisfaction from the achievement of something substantive, the fame and honour, &c., consequential on such actions, in a word their particular aspect, the aspect which it has decreed in advance to be something in itself pernicious. Such ratiocination assures us that, while great actions and the efficiency which has subsisted through a series of them have produced greatness in the world and have had as their consequences for the individual agent power, honour, and fame, still what belongs to the individual is not the greatness itself but what has accrued to him from it, this purely particular and external result; because this result is a consequence, it is therefore supposed to have been the agent's end and even his sole end. Reflection of this sort stops short at the subjective side of great men, since it itself stands on purely subjective ground, and consequently it overlooks what is substantive in this emptiness of its own making. This is the view of those valet psychologists "for whom there are no heroes, not because there are no heroes, but because these psychologists are only valets." [10]

The *particular* end of one's personal well-being is a perfectly legitimate goal, as long as it does not conflict with the universal content of an action, that is, with that which the action is in itself, regardless of the intention of the agent.

My particularity, however, like that of others, is only a right at all in so far as I am a free entity. Therefore, it may not make claims for itself in contradiction to this its substantive basis, and an intention to secure my welfare or that of others (and it is particularly in this latter case that such an intention is called "moral") cannot justify an action which is wrong.

It is one of the most prominent of the corrupt maxims of our time to enter a plea for the so-called "moral" intention behind wrong actions and to imagine bad men with well-meaning hearts, i.e. hearts willing their own welfare and perhaps that of others also. This doctrine is rooted in the "benevolence" of the pre-Kantian philosophers and constitutes, e.g., the quintessence of well-known touching dramatic productions; but today it has been resuscitated in a more extravagant form, and inner enthusiasm and the heart, i.e. the form of particularity as such, have been made the criterion of right, rationality, and excellence. The result is that crime and the thoughts that lead to it, be they fancies however trite and empty, or opinions however wild, are to be regarded as right, rational, and excellent, simply because they issue from men's hearts and enthusiasms.[11]

[10] *Ibid.,* No. 124, pp. 83–84.
[11] *Ibid.,* No. 126, p. 85.

But if the intention alone cannot justify an act, what does make an act good? Hegel answered that the good consists in the unity of the particular will with the universal. To be good, the will must raise itself to universality, that is, to rationality. As Professor Stace remarks:

> So far as my will is reasonable it is not merely my will but is universal; for reason *is* the universal; it is common to all rational beings, whereas my self-will and my whims are merely my own. Hence when I will reasonably my will coincides with the universal will; it coincides with its notion, and is, therefore, good. When it wills merely private ends, which are unreasonable, it is evil.[12]

Yet, even so, the good remains abstract and the will never becomes identical with it; it is merely related dynamically to it. The will experiences the good as that which *is to be done,* as an obligation, a duty that transcends the will.

> It [the will] stands in a *relation* to the good, and the relation is that the good *ought* to be substantive for it, i.e. it ought to make the good its aim and realize it completely, while the good on its side has in the subjective will its only means of stepping into actuality.[13]

To do the good is to do what is rational, to do my duty. But what is my duty? What is rational? At this stage we are unable to answer this question and it was Kant's mistake to expect an answer from the notion of moral duty alone.

> However essential it is to give prominence to the pure unconditioned self-determination of the will as the root of duty, and to the way in which knowledge of the will, thanks to Kant's philosophy, has won its firm foundation and starting-point for the first time owing to the thought of its infinite autonomy, still to adhere to the exclusively moral position, without making the transition to the conception of ethics, is to reduce this gain to an empty formalism, and the science of morals to the preaching of duty for duty's sake. From this point of view, no immanent doctrine of duties is possible; of course, material may be brought in from outside and particular duties may be arrived at accordingly, but if the definition of duty is taken to be the absence of contradiction, formal correspondence with itself— which is nothing but abstract indeterminacy stabilized—then no transition is possible to the specification of particular duties nor, if some such particular content for acting comes under consideration, is there any criterion in that principle for deciding whether it is or is not a duty. On the contrary, by this means any wrong or immoral line of conduct may be justified.
>
> Kant's further formulation, the possibility of visualizing an action as a universal maxim, does lead to the more concrete visualization

---

[12] W. T. Stace, *The Philosophy of Hegel: A Systematic Exposition* (New York: Dover Publications, 1955), p. 401.

[13] Hegel, *Philosophy of Right,* No. 131, p. 87.

of a situation, but in itself it contains no principle beyond abstract identity and the "absence of contradiction" already mentioned.

The absence of property contains in itself just as little contradiction as the non-existence of this or that nation, family, &c., or the death of the whole human race. But if it is already established on other grounds and presupposed that property and human life are to exist and be respected, then indeed it is a contradiction to commit theft or murder; a contradiction must be a contradiction of something, i.e. of some content presupposed from the start as a fixed principle. It is to a principle of that kind alone, therefore, that an action can be related either by correspondence or contradiction. But if duty is to be willed simply for duty's sake and not for the sake of some content, it is only a formal identity whose nature it is to exclude all content and specification.[14]

Ethics in the proper sense brings together the juridical and the moral order which are separately only abstract, one-sided expressions of freedom: one is almost exclusively objective, the other predominantly subjective. It is true that the moral order also has an objective aspect, the *good* of the moral obligation, but this remains separated from the subjective aspect of *conscience*. Conscience is that which *ought* to be good, but which never fully is. Man's particular will is related to the universal objectives of reason; it is never *identical* to them. The good remains forever an ideal, separated from reality, since no particular will can fully actualize it. In the sphere of ethics, however, the remote ideal of the good is replaced by actually existing institutions—the family, the economic community that Hegel called the "civil society," and the State. At first this may seem to be a simple reappearance of the exteriority of abstract right. But this is by no means the case. Society is objective indeed, but at the same time it is totally subjective, for it can exist only if actively accepted by its members. The bond of love is the subjective fundament of the family relationship; loyalty and self-sacrifice are the subjective support of the State.

On the other hand, the subjective aspect of the ethical order is identical with the objective institution. "Ethical life is: subjective disposition, but one which is imbued with what is inherently right." [15]

> This ethical substance and its laws and powers are on the one hand an object over against the subject, and from this point of view they are—"are" in the highest sense of self-subsistent being. This is an absolute authority and power infinitely more firmly established than the being of nature.
>
> The sun, the moon, mountains, rivers, and the natural objects of all kinds by which we are surrounded, are. For consciousness they have the authority not only of mere being but also of possessing a particular nature which it accepts and to which it adjusts itself in

---

[14] *Ibid.*, No. 135, pp. 89–90.
[15] *Ibid.*, No. 141, pp. 103–04.

dealing with them, using them, or in being otherwise concerned with them. The authority of ethical laws is infinitely higher, because natural objects conceal rationality under the cloak of contingency and exhibit it only in their utterly external and disconnected way.

On the other hand, they are not something alien to the subject. On the contrary, his spirit bears witness to them as to his own essence, the essence in which he has a feeling of his selfhood, and in which he lives as in his own element which is not distinguished from himself. The subject is thus directly linked to the ethical order by a relation which is more like an identity than even the relation of faith or trust.[16]

The institutions of family, civil society, and State, incarnate the true self of the individual. Through these institutions he becomes *free*. Almost all social philosophers from Hobbes to Kant saw the highest realization of human freedom in the private well-being of the individual and, therefore, subordinated social institutions, particularly the State, to the needs of the individual. In Hegel's ethics the State is not a means but the highest end of the individual—it is the supreme realization of his freedom. The restrictions that social institutions, particularly the State, seem to impose upon man's freedom and that all predecessors of Hegel so vividly described, are in reality not restrictions of freedom, but rather of license and arbitrariness.

The truth is . . . that in duty the individual finds his liberation; first, liberation from dependence on mere natural impulse and from the depression which as a particular subject he cannot escape in his moral reflections on what ought to be and what might be; secondly, liberation from the indeterminate subjectivity which, never reaching reality or the objective determinacy of action, remains self-enclosed and devoid of actuality. In duty the individual acquires his substantive freedom.[17]

Because the social institutions make man's freedom *real,* the good life is the life within these institutions. Only in society can man fully develop himself, and that is precisely the goal of ethics. Hegel did not exclude moral greatness independent of, or even opposed to, society. But such individualistic heroism ignores the social aspect of morality, and is therefore in constant danger of turning into ruthlessness and egotism. The "virtue" of the Renaissance *condotierre* or of the Western gunslinger is at best a substitute for ethical life when no rationally organized society exists. Daring individualism displays a flourish and bravura compared to a righteous life in a good society which seems dull and uninspired. At the same time, the "heroic" life is shallow; it is not rooted in rational conviction but in the irrational gifts of nature.

---

[16] *Ibid.,* Nos. 146, 147, pp. 105–06.
[17] *Ibid.,* No. 149, p. 107.

Virtue is the ethical order reflected in the individual character so far as that character is determined by its natural endowment. When virtue displays itself solely as the individual's simple conformity with the duties of the station to which he belongs, it is rectitude.

In an ethical community, it is easy to say what man must do, what are the duties he has to fulfil in order to be virtuous: he has simply to follow the well-known and explicit rules of his own situation. Rectitude is the general character which may be demanded of him by law or custom. But from the standpoint of morality, rectitude often seems to be something comparatively inferior, something beyond which still higher demands must be made on oneself and others, because the craving to be something special is not satisfied with what is absolute and universal; it finds consciousness of peculiarity only in what is exceptional.

The various facets of rectitude may equally well be called virtues, since they are also properties of the individual, although not specially of him in contrast with others. Talk about virtue, however, readily borders on empty rhetoric, because it is only about something abstract and indeterminate; and furthermore, argumentative and expository talk of the sort is addressed to the individual as to a being of caprice and subjective inclination. In an existing ethical order in which a complete system of ethical relations has been developed and actualized, virtue in the strict sense of the word is in place and actually appears only in exceptional circumstances or when one obligation clashes with another. The clash, however, must be a genuine one, because moral reflection can manufacture clashes of all sorts to suit its purpose and give itself a consciousness of being something special and having made sacrifices.

It is for this reason that the phenomenon of virtue proper is commoner when societies and communities are uncivilized, since in those circumstances ethical conditions and their actualization are more a matter of private choice or the natural genius of an exceptional individual. For instance, it was especially to Hercules that the ancients ascribed virtue. In the states of antiquity, ethical life had not grown into this free system of an objective order self-subsistently developed, and consequently it was by the personal genius of individuals that this defect had to be made good.[18]

Hegel's description of virtue implies that ethics is the science of what *is* rather than what *ought* to be, of actual customs rather than of abstract norms. Wherever man lives in society, he leads, at least to some extent, an ethical life. Hegel fully admitted that there are good societies and bad ones, but even in the worst there is something left of the "good life" which man attains only in society.

When individuals are simply identified with the actual order, ethical life (*das Sittliche*) appears as their general mode of conduct, i.e. as

---

[18] *Ibid.*, No. 150, p. 107.

custom (*Sitte*), while the habitual practice of ethical living appears as a second nature which, put in the place of the initial, purely natural will, is the soul of custom permeating it through and through, the significance and the actuality of its existence. It is mind living and present as a world, and the substance of mind thus exists now for the first time as mind.

Education is the art of making men ethical. It begins with pupils whose life is at the instinctive level and shows them the way to a second birth, the way to change their instinctive nature into a second, intellectual, nature, and makes this intellectual level habitual to them. At this point the clash between the natural and the subjective will disappears, the subject's internal struggle dies away. To this extent, habit is part of ethical life as it is of philosophic thought also, since such thought demands that mind be trained against capricious fancies, and that these be destroyed and overcome to leave the way clear for rational thinking.[19]

However, Hegel did not emphasize the ethical role of society at the expense of the individual's subjective aspirations; he saw it as the satisfaction of his particular impulses and inclinations. In the civil society, for instance, the individual enjoys all the satisfaction of working for his own interests while at the same time fulfilling the needs of society.

The right of individuals to be subjectively destined to freedom is fulfilled when they belong to an actual ethical order, because their conviction of their freedom finds its truth in such an objective order, and it is in an ethical order that they are actually in possession of their own inner universality.

. .

The right of individuals to their *particular* satisfaction is also contained in the ethical substantial order, since particularity is the outward appearance of the ethical order.[20]

But prior to the civil society comes the family, man's first and immediate social institution. In the love for his wife and children man satisfies the universal and particular ends of freedom. Yet this harmonization is still unreflective; it is primarily by instinct rather than by rational insight that husband and wife love each other and their children.

The beautiful but nonreflective union of the family is bound to perish. The parents grow old and the children leave the home to found families of their own and to make their way in the world. In his struggle for life man joins the civil society; he learns a trade or chooses a profession. All this fulfills the demands of society, even though the individual heeds only his particular interest. For to secure his private interest, the individual must become a member of an economic group, and the group's interest in turn must be protected by even larger groups until an integrated economic system, uniting all particular endeavors, prevails in the commonwealth.

---

[19] *Ibid.*, No. 151, p. 108, and No. 151, addition, p. 260.
[20] *Ibid.*, Nos. 153–54, p. 109.

In the course of the actual attainment of selfish ends . . . , there is formed a system of complete inter-dependence, wherein the livelihood, happiness, and legal status of one man is interwoven with the livelihood, happiness, and rights of all. On this system, individual happiness, &c., depend, and only in this connected system are they actualized and secured.[21]

From an economic point of view, society is exclusively a means for the attainment of particular interests. But this first and selfish contact with an open society allows man to break out of the unsophisticated state of nature of a closed, family-styled society. Freedom requires a certain level of sophistication, and the task of economic striving is precisely to provide this.

The end [of private interest] is *mediated* through the universal which thus *appears* as a *means* to its realization. Consequently, individuals can attain their ends only in so far as they themselves determine their knowing, willing, and acting in a universal way and make themselves links in this chain of social connexions. In these circumstances, the interest of the Idea—an interest of which these members of civil society are as such unconscious—lies in the process whereby their singularity and their natural conditions are raised, as a result of the necessities imposed by nature as well as of arbitrary needs, to formal freedom and formal universality of knowing and willing—the process whereby their particularity is educated up to subjectivity.

The idea that the state of nature is one of innocence and that there is a simplicity of manners in uncivilized (*ungebildeter*) peoples, implies treating education (*Bildung*) as something purely external, the ally of corruption. Similarly, the feeling that needs, their satisfaction, the pleasures and comforts of private life, and so forth, are absolute ends, implies treating education as a mere means to these ends. Both these views display lack of acquaintance with the nature of mind and the end of reason. Mind attains its actuality only by creating a dualism within itself, by submitting itself to physical needs and the chain of these external necessities, and so imposing on itself this barrier and this finitude, and finally by maturing (*bildet*) itself inwardly even when under this barrier until it overcomes it and attains its objective reality in the finite. The end of reason, therefore, is neither the manners of an unsophisticated state of nature, nor, as particularity develops, the pleasure for pleasure's sake which education procures. On the contrary, its end is to banish natural simplicity, whether the passivity which is the absence of the self, or the crude type of knowing and willing, i.e. immediacy and singularity, in which mind is absorbed.[22]

The highest stage of ethics is the State which Hegel defined as "the actuality of the ethical." "Idea" means the synthesis of the real and

---

[21] *Ibid.*, No. 183, p. 123.
[22] *Ibid.*, No. 187, pp. 124–25.

the ideal, the reality that has become fully rational. On the level of the State, the particular interests of the citizens are no longer separated from the universal interests of the community as they are in law and morality, nor are they merely united by instinct or unintended effect as in the family and the civil society. As a citizen man for the first time becomes fully aware that the universal aims of the State (the concrete realization of mankind as a whole) are also his own aims, and that his subjective inclinations find their true fulfillment only through objective institutions.

The State is much more than a protector of particular rights (especially property), which it had been in most political philosophies since John Locke (1632–1704). Such a "liberal" State is merely an extension of what Hegel called the civil society; it remains a public means for a private end. Hegel's State, however, is an "unmoved end in itself in which freedom comes into its supreme right."

In pursuing his particular ends in family and civil society, the individual unknowingly works himself up to the point where he is able to see the universal *as his own,* where law and institutions are no longer felt as external compulsions but as concrete realizations of his freedom. As a citizen man learns that a person is more than an individual, and that to be a person in the full sense of the word he must unite his particular inclinations with the concrete realization of his universal nature.

> The State is absolutely rational inasmuch as it is the actuality of the substantial will which it possesses in the particular self-consciousness once that consciousness has been raised to consciousness of its universality. This substantial unity is an absolute unmoved end in itself, in which freedom comes into its supreme right. On the other hand this final end has supreme right against the individual, whose supreme duty is to be a member of the State.
>
> If the State is confused with civil society, and if its specific end is laid down as the security and protection of property and personal freedom, then the interest of the individuals as such becomes the ultimate end of their association, and it follows that membership of the State is something optional. But the State's relation to the individual is quite different from this. Since the State is mind objectified, it is only as one of its members that the individual himself has objectivity, genuine individuality, and an ethical life. Unification pure and simple is the true content and aim of the individual, and the individual's destiny is the living of a universal life. His further particular satisfaction, activity, and mode of conduct have this substantive and universally valid life as their starting point and their result.
>
> Rationality, taken generally and in the abstract, consists in the thorough-going unity of the universal and the single. Rationality, concrete in the state, consists (a) so far as its content is concerned, in the unity of objective freedom (i.e. freedom of the universal or substantial will) and subjective freedom (i.e. freedom of everyone in his knowing and in his volition of particular ends); and conse-

quently, (b) so far as its form is concerned, in self-determining action on laws and principles which are thoughts and so universal. This Idea is the absolutely eternal and necessary being of mind.[23]

Hegel's ethical theory culminates in his philosophy of the State. The State is the highest end for the individual. This does not mean that the individual becomes subordinated to a superhuman institution, but that he consents to subordinate his arbitrary whims and idiosyncrasies to more universal values. Freedom is never sacrificed but remains the single end of the State.

In spite of all these restrictions, one feels somewhat uncomfortable in the face of the enormous ethical power which Hegel ascribed to the State, for all too easily it could justify political totalitarianism. National socialism and communism claim to find in this philosophy the ideological support which they could not find elsewhere. Yet Hegel must not be held responsible for political systems that admit of no spiritual values above society. When freedom had completed its objective course, Hegel moved on to the higher level [24] where the mind reaches its full potential in art, religion, and philosophy. These values to a certain extent depend upon society, but they transcend society as such. In Hegel's philosophy it never becomes clear how they fit into man's ethical life, since the ethical sphere ends with the State.

Hegel's ideal of the State as apex of man's ethical life can be traced to his early infatuation with the Greek city-state which, indeed, was the dispenser and inspirer of all human values. In his earliest systematic writings on ethics, Hegel mentioned no sphere of life beyond the State; he felt that there was no need for any other sphere since all values came through the State. As he grew older he partly abandoned this ancient ideal and placed the highest spiritual values above the State. Yet he never rethought the basic framework of his ethical system which terminates in the philosophy of the State.

Marx: Theory of Man's Alienation

Although Karl Marx was one of the first to criticize the narrowness of Hegel's ethical system, he agreed with Hegel to an extent which few people realize. Like Hegel, he saw man as a dynamic being liberating himself in a dialectical process. The basic principle of Marx's ethics, as well as of Hegel's, is that man creates himself through a process of alienation and reassertion. Freedom must lose itself in order to find itself on a higher level. In *The Economic and Philosophical Manuscripts* of 1844, Marx wrote:

---

[23] *Ibid.,* No. 258, pp. 155–56.
[24] This is called the Absolute Spirit, as opposed to the Objective Spirit, which is described in the *Philosophy of Right.*

> The outstanding achievement of Hegel's *Phenomenology*—the dialectic of negativity as the moving and creating principle—is, first, that Hegel grasps the self-creation of man as a process, objectification as loss of the object, as alienation and transcendence of this alienation, and that he therefore grasps the nature of *labor,* and conceives objective man (true, because real man) as the result of his *own labor.*[25]

But according to Marx, Hegel reduced the essence of man to pure consciousness so that any relation to an object estranges man from himself. Yet if man's alienation is his involvement with the external world, then his entire humanization consists simply in the process from consciousness of the object to self-consciousness. For Marx man is part of nature, and to be involved with the material world belongs to his essence; it is precisely in his relation to the world that he becomes himself. Consequently, man's relation to nature, rather than his alienation from it, is the basis of his salvation. Man is alienated only when his relation to nature is no longer the right one, that is, when he comes to stand in a thing-like relation to nature.

Marx agreed with Hegel on the social character of ethics, but went even further by stating that there are no ethical principles beyond what the good of society requires. His criticism of Hegel was directed not against the social nature of ethics but against the asocial character of Hegel's society. Hegel simply took it for granted that present-day society allows man to lead a truly social life, but this assumption is entirely false according to Marx.

In 1843, Marx started writing a critical commentary on Hegel's philosophy of the State. The work was abandoned after a while and remained unpublished until 1927. In it Marx attacked Hegel for regarding the State as the end of the civil society, whereas in fact it is the civil society that is the basis and meaning of the State. As good as the civil society is, so will be the State. But it does not take much insight to see that today's civil society is inhumanly selfish and asocial, and the State, far from lifting man up to the perfect ethical life, merely provides legal protection to the civil society's individualism. Marx agreed with Hegel that man can become human only in society, but only a human society, one based upon respect for human dignity, can have a humanizing effect. A society geared toward material production exploits and dehumanizes man, which is precisely what capitalist society does. As Marx showed in *The Economic and Philosophical Manuscripts,* the aim of capitalist society is the production of material goods rather than the production of man. The worker is a mere instrument in a material production process. What he produces is not his own humanity, but a *thing* hostile to himself. His labor is absorbed by an external opposition, independent of himself, and is consumed by a stranger. Man becomes estranged from the product of his own work. In-

---

[25] Erich Fromm, *Marx's Concept of Man* (New York: Frederick Ungar Publishing Co., 1961), pp. 176–77.

stead of making it into an extension of himself, he becomes an extension of an inhuman product.

Such production enslaves man, rather than liberating him. The more he produces, the more his personal value decreases. For his value consists entirely in his contribution to the production of external goods, and these goods devaluate as their number increases.

> The worker becomes poorer the more wealth he produces and the more his production increases in power and extent. The worker becomes an ever cheaper commodity the more goods he creates. The *devaluation* of the human world increases in direct relation with the *increase in value* of the world of things. Labor does not only create goods; it also produces itself and the worker as a *commodity,* and indeed in the same proportion as it produces goods.[26]

Nature provides man with his means of subsistence. But the more the worker appropriates nature, the less he receives for it. He is reduced to the bare minimum that is necessary to keep him active in the process of production. Whatever exceeds the satisfaction of his most immediate needs is a waste of production capital.

The division of labor estranges man from his producing activity even more than from the results of it. The worker's activity is no longer determined by his personal benefit (his self-creation), but by his physical or mental dispositions for the benefit of the objective product. Labor, instead of being man's self-realization, becomes his self-negation. "The worker therefore feels himself at home only during his leisure time, whereas at work he feels homeless. His work is not voluntary but imposed, *forced labor.*" [27] The more man works the less human he becomes. As a result, he is comfortable only in the animal functions of eating, drinking, and procreating. Labor has reduced him to an animal.

A third aspect of capitalist society is the estrangement of man from his fellow man. As a conscious being, man in his creative activity goes beyond the mere satisfaction of immediate, physical needs. Consciousness enables him to stand at a remove from his object. As a result, he produces beyond the immediate requirements of his subsistence, and the entire world becomes a possible object of his activity. In producing beyond individual needs, man produces with and for the entire human race. Any cultural production is a common enterprise made possible and shared by the entire community. Unlike the animal man produces as a *species-being.*

In capitalist society, however, the very labor through which man is to become a universal being is deprived of its universal character. Work is restricted to a mere means for the satisfaction of individual, physical needs. Man's activity, as that of the animal, is entirely determined by the requirements for bare subsistence.

---

[26] *Ibid.,* p. 95.
[27] *Ibid.,* p. 98.

> Just as alienated labor transforms free and self-directed activity into a means, so it transforms the species-life of man into a means of physical existence. . . . Thus alienated labor turns *the species-life* of man, and also nature as his mental species-property, into an *alien* being and into a *means* for his *individual existence.*[28]

The alleged social aspect of capitalist economy, the division of labor, is merely the social form of man's alienation by which the diversity of man's abilities are exploited for the benefit of an individualistic production process.

As Marx's thought developed, he replaced the philosophical terminology of his early writings by economic terms. In *The German Ideology* (1845–46), the word *alienation* is mentioned only in a critical fashion. Instead, Marx used the term *division of labor,* which at that time he considered to be the cause of all social evil. Private property, which was criticized so much in *The Economic and Philosophical Manuscripts,* is now seen as a result rather than as the cause of the division of labor.

> The various stages of development in the division of labor are just so many different forms of ownership, i.e. the existing stage in the division of labor determines also the relations between individuals to one another with reference to the material instrument, and product of labor.[29]

Division of labor and private property are two aspects of the same thing: one refers to the activity, the other to the product of this activity.

What leads men to adopt division of labor in their producing activity? One might think that it follows from the intrinsically social character of this activity, but it does not. Although the social nature of human labor implies some form of cooperation, the division of labor, in its present form, follows exclusively from the individualistic desire to produce and exchange as much as possible. Far from promoting man's social interests, the division of labor brings out "the contradiction between the interest of the separate individual or the individual family and the communal interest of all individuals who have intercourse with one another." Yet, these communal interests are real, and to ignore them can lead only to an inhuman way of producing.

In a sense, human production is always a social activity. Even for the attainment of his most private goals man depends on others. Capitalist society may disregard the social objectives (the communal interests) of human production but it cannot ignore its social character altogether. In fact, in the division of labor, it exploits this social character as a means for its own selfish ends. It even pays some lip service to man's social interests by assigning them a special sphere of life. In the State, capitalism creates

---

[28] *Ibid.,* p. 103.
[29] Karl Marx and Friedrich Engels, *The German Ideology,* trans. by R. Pascal (New York: International Publishers, 1960), p. 9.

an illusion of social life. But in reality the State merely provides the sanction of law and institution to socially organized selfishness.

The only social group that capitalism recognizes is the class, a group based not on the social character of man's activity but on the production requirements of the material thing. In the class, man uses the social powers of his producing activity exclusively for private interests. The State is the social illusion; the class, the social reality of an individualistic society. Man remains a social being, but a frustrated one.

A society whose structure originates in individualistic drives will necessarily have conflicts among its social groups. Such conflicts are always *class struggles,* since there are no other real groups. The political conflicts which receive all the attention of the historians merely cover the deeper, apolitical oppositions among the classes.

Each class, in its struggle to dominate other classes, tries first to conquer the State, the political power, "in order to represent its interest as the general interest." But the "general" interest of the State is no more than the interest of one particular class. That is why every intervention of the State appears to all nonruling classes "not as their own united power but as an alien force existing outside them."

We may summarize Marx's dialectic as follows: The division of labor leads to private property, and this in turn creates social inequality, class struggles, and the erection of political structures.

Marx: Concept of the Liberation of Man

The reason we have given so much attention thus far to the alienation of man is that according to Marxist ethics the sickness of capitalism produces its own remedy and is the only way to reach the freedom of the communist society.

Marx's notion of freedom is far removed from Kant's pure autonomy. His freedom so much depends upon man's material environment that, at first, Marx's theory may impress one as pure sociological determinism. Human history, as Marx saw it, is determined by social relations which in turn are determined by the material conditions of production. Whenever these material conditions change, the existing social patterns must in some way be readjusted to the new conditions of production. Yet where the extreme division of labor, necessitated by the machine industry, has transformed the means of production into a hostile power reducing most people to the level of bare subsistence, a mere readjustment, which leaves the basic structure of society unchanged, is no longer sufficient. More and more people are cast into a class for which the production forces fail to provide even the minimum comfort of a human life and which embodies the complete dehumanization of modern society: the proletariat. For them, a revolutionary reappropriation of the production forces has become an inescapable necessity. This proletarian revolution will be different from all previous revolutions: other classes have freed themselves by subjugating the rest of society; the proletariat, which suffers from the evils of *all* classes at once, can emancipate itself only by emancipating the entire society.

If this description may seem deterministic, Marx pointed out that the communist revolution, inevitable as it is, is not simply the outcome of a material, economic process. Capitalism has not only created the need and the necessary conditions for the revolution; it has also created the class that will accomplish the revolution. Without the proletariat, which is *aware* of its situation and *determined* to end it, there can be no revolution. The revolutionary consciousness of the proletariat and its decision to revolt are the final but indispensable factors needed to bring the process of capitalism to completion. Insofar as it is revolutionary this consciousness goes obviously beyond the existing social structures—it is destructive of the past and creative of the future.

This should not be understood to mean that the revolutionary consciousness is a purely ideal element that could originate independently of socioeconomic conditions. Nothing could be further from the truth, since any form of consciousness depends intrinsically upon the socioeconomic structure of society. The proletarian consciousness is an ideal expression of the destructive forces presently at work in this society. Nor is the communist society a *future ideal* set up by the party and to be realized by the revolution. Communism is not an ideal; it is a future reality necessarily resulting from events that are taking place in the present. It would be presumptuous to predict what the communist man or his code of ethics will be as long as the social structures that will create him have not come into existence.

It is obvious that Marx's concept of freedom differs from that of his German predecessors. Freedom is not an independent force; it is one factor in a chain of necessary events. Yet this factor is so essential and so different from all others that without it, history would not exist. Marx by no means eliminated human freedom, but he tightened the bond between man (as free being) and nature (as physical determinism). One cannot be without the other. That is why history is both necessary and free. That also is why the Communist Party must work hard to awaken the proletariat while realizing at the same time that the revolution is inevitable.

Engels: Social Relativism

The balance between freedom and necessity in communism is a very delicate one. According to many authors, particularly some French existentialists, Marx's own position drifted in his later years toward a socioeconomic determinism in which there was no room for real freedom. His lifelong friend and collaborator, Friedrich Engels, has often been blamed for this evolution. But even if one does not admit that there is a substantial difference between Marx's early and his later work, Engels' position still comes undeniably closer to materialism than the one described in Marx's early writings. It is this more materialistic interpretation of "Marxism" that has prevailed in the Communist world, perhaps because it possesses a clarity and a simplicity that the more nuanced thought of Marx's early writings lacks.

In *Anti-Dühring* (1878) Engels defended dialectical materialism against the criticism of Eugen Dühring, a German socialist. No one today is still interested in Dühring's position, but its refutation has been the occasion for defining the position of dialectical materialism on a number of issues. In Chapters 9–11, Engels attacked Dühring's thesis that there are eternal moral truths. According to Engels no eternal truth is possible in the historical sciences to which morality belongs. Morality, religion, and art are ideological *superstructures* of man's social conditions, and they change as the conditions change.

Although it is obvious that the socioeconomic situation is in constant flux and moral systems vary, there is nevertheless a remarkable similarity among these systems. The reason for this, according to Engels, is that the basic structure of society has remained unchanged almost since the beginning of historical times. It is characterized by private property, division of labor, and a social class system. As a result, all moral systems of the past have been class moralities; they have rationalized such behavior as serves the domination and interests of the ruling class. But true morality must transcend all class antagonisms and can therefore originate only in a classless society. In this society, which the communist revolution will bring about, many of the moral rules that men live by today will be abolished because the social structure which they protect will have ceased to exist. Engels mentioned only the precept to respect property, but the same would apply to many other rules of bourgeois morality.

From this basic thesis it follows that a purely a priori method, which deduces moral conclusions from an abstract concept of man, is worthless in moral philosophy. If morality is the outcome and justification of socioeconomic conditions, the only proper way to understand a moral system is by an empirical study of the socioeconomic conditions that produced it. Engels did not deny that there are some constant characteristics in human nature, but he felt that they seem to be particularly irrelevant for defining the rules of man's behavior in a certain society. These characteristics are usually invoked after a society has decided which course of action it must take to preserve itself—and they are applied only *to the extent* that they coincide with this course of action. The statement that all men share in a common humanity, and therefore must be equal, never had any impact upon the creation of social or political equality. For people are not equal in many other respects. Concrete action will depend on which aspect is given preference—equality or inequality—and this in turn depends entirely on the existing sociological structure. In a society where slavery has existed since time immemorial, the *basic* equality of men is not denied; it is simply thought to be entirely irrelevant for ruling people's actual behavior.

Even the Christian idea of equality based upon a common vocation of all men (which Engels, strangely enough, described as sharing in the same sin rather than in the same redemption) is unable to abolish the inequality among men. In fact, it adds some inequalities of its own, like the one between priest and layman. In contrast with these ideologies, some socioeconomic changes, particularly the rise of the bourgeoisie, make the notion of equality acceptable on a practical level.

The social revolution built up the ideology of equality for its own stabilization. It had to present it on the broadest possible basis, as a conclusion drawn directly from the nature of man. But beyond the limits of its social basis the ideology is completely impotent, as is shown in the case of the American Constitution, which, on the one hand, proclaimed equality as a basic human right and, on the other hand, recognized the slavery of the Negro. The ideology, although presented in a universal form in order to find general acceptance, could not be stretched beyond the existing social structure. Morality, like any other ideology, remains subordinate to the society for the protection of which it was invented. Engels concluded: "The idea of equality, both in its bourgeois and in its proletarian form, is itself a historical product, the creation of which required definite historical conditions which in turn themselves presupposed a long previous historical development." [30]

Engels' exposition makes the dividing line between sociology and ethics seem extremely thin. He himself was aware of the fact that his socioeconomic determinism is irreconcilable with the traditional notion of freedom, but rather than give it up, he preferred to redefine freedom as "the appreciation of necessity." He thus reached a position similar to Spinoza's in which freedom consists exclusively in understanding what is necessary. The conclusion that such a position excludes any kind of true morality is refuted by both Spinoza's life and work.

Yet, even if Engels' position could be shown to be consistent on freedom, it still remains open to a number of objections, in particular, his attack on the a priori method. If Marxists do not *deduce* from a static concept of human nature, they certainly *predict,* on the basis of their dialectic of history, with an assurance unequaled by the natural law moralists. This certitude is not obtained by means of empirical observation and analysis. But this problem is not purely ethical—it is inherent in any philosophy that claims to be both empirical and a priori.

---

[30] Friedrich Engels, *Anti-Dühring* (London: Lawrence and Wishart, 1959), p. 121.

Glossary

ALIENATION:
The dynamic opposition between the two first movements of the dialectic, which leads to a reconciliation on a higher level.

AUTONOMY:
The quality that Kant attributed to the free will by which it rejects any external determination and accepts only itself as supreme law.

CATEGORICAL IMPERATIVE:
The unconditioned ought of the moral obligation.

CIVIL SOCIETY:
The economic community in which the individual, while pursuing his private interests, unknowingly promotes the common good. Hegel placed it as a social institution between the family and the State.

DIALECTIC:
According to Hegel, the process of thought and reality, in which thought becomes more and more real and reality more and more ideal by a constant and dynamic negation of the original opposition between the two terms. Briefly, the self-development of thought that is also the self-development of reality.

HETERONOMY:
Characteristic of a moral command that has not been issued by the will itself and that therefore is to be rejected, according to Kant's moral system.

IDEA:
The final stage of the Hegelian dialectic in which the concrete identity of truth and reality is achieved.

IDEALISM:
Trend in philosophy that reduces reality to a predicate of consciousness. Is opposed to realism in which reality maintains an existence independent of consciousness.

IDEOLOGY:
Engels defines ideology as "occupation with thoughts as with independent entities, developing independently and subject only to their own laws." (*Ludwig Feuerbach.*)

MOMENT:
Stage in a dialectical development, which intrinsically refers to its opposite and, mediately, to all other stages of the development.

NOUMENAL:
What lies entirely beyond sense experience and is therefore unknowable by a human being, according to Kant. (See *Phenomenal.*)

OBJECT:

1. What is present to knowledge and distinct from the knowing *subject*.
2. What is realized through the action of a free subject.

PARTICULAR:

What does not belong to the totality as such, as opposed to universal. (See *Universal.*)

PHENOMENAL:

What is object of possible experience and must therefore be given in space and time, according to Kant. (See *Noumenal.*)

SUBJECT:

Conscious being considered as the most essential condition of knowledge that unifies a variety of data into a single *object* or as the spontaneous source of action. It roughly coincides with the philosophical Ego.

THING IN ITSELF:

In Kant, reality insofar as it lies entirely beyond human knowledge.

UNIVERSAL:

That state of the dialectical development in which reality is considered in its *totality*. It is concrete insofar as all particular determinations are already implicitly present in it. The universal is opposed to the *particular,* as is shown in Hegel's social theory, where the collective will and interests are clearly distinct from the particular will and interests of each member. Only in the highest stage of ethics, the State, are both united.

Immanuel Kant

IMMANUEL KANT was born in Königsberg, East Prussia, in 1724 and spent his entire life in this small provincial capital. He was educated at the University of Königsberg and, after a brief period as a private tutor, went back to the University in 1755. There he remained as professor of Logic and Metaphysics until his death in 1804. One of the most powerful and original thinkers in the history of philosophy, Kant is best known for his critical trilogy on knowledge, morality, and esthetics: *Critique of Pure Reason* (1781), *Critique of Practical Reason* (1788), and *Critique of Judgment* (1790). His emphasis on the role of the subject in knowledge and morality was the basis of subsequent German idealism.

The Moral Law — The Categorical Imperative

All philosophy in so far as it has its basis in experience may be called *empirical,* but that which derives its doctrines solely from *a priori* principles may be termed *pure* philosophy. When the latter is merely formal it is called *logic,* but when it is limited to definite objects of reasoning it is called *metaphysic.*

Thus there arises the idea of a two-fold metaphysic: a *metaphysic of nature* and a *metaphysic of ethics.* Consequently physics will have its empirical but also its rational part. The same is true of ethics, though the empirical part in this case may be designated more especially as *practical anthropology,* the rational part however being *morality* proper.

All trades, crafts and arts have profited by the division of labor, according to which all things are not done by one person but each restricts himself to a definite kind of work whose treatment is noticeably different from other kinds, so as to provide greater perfection and ease of execution. Wherever labor is not thus differentiated and divided, where each man is a jack-of-all-trades, there very barbarous conditions still prevail. It may be a worthy subject of speculation to ask whether pure philosophy in all its parts should not also require its specialists, and whether the whole of the

From pp. 2–4, 8–19, 29–33, and 37–51 of *The Fundamental Principles of the Metaphysic of Ethics* by Immanuel Kant. Translated by Otto Manthey-Zorn. Copyright 1938 by D. Appleton-Century Company, Inc. Reprinted by permission of Appleton-Century-Crofts, Division of Meredith Publishing Company.

learned profession would not be better off if those who are accustomed to sell the empirical together with the rational, adjusted to public taste and mixed in all sorts of proportions which they themselves do not understand, and who call themselves independent thinkers while they designate as hair-splitters those who prepare the rational part only; had better be warned not to carry on two jobs at once, each of which demands a special talent and whose combination in one person merely produces bunglers. However, I shall merely inquire whether the nature of the science does not demand at all times carefully to separate the empirical from the rational element and to preface the real (empirical) physics by a metaphysic of nature, but the practical anthropology by a metaphysic of ethics which must have been cleared carefully of everything empirical in order to know how much pure reason can accomplish in both cases and from what sources it derives its teachings *a priori*. The last occupation incidentally may be undertaken by all the moralists (whose name is legion) or by the few only who feel a calling for it.

Since my present concern is really with moral philosophy I shall narrow the proposed problem to the question whether it is not of the utmost necessity for once to prepare a pure moral philosophy which has been thoroughly cleared of all that is empirical only and belongs to anthropology. That there is such a thing is self-evident from the general idea of duty and the moral laws. Everyone must admit that a law in order to be considered moral, that is to say a basis of obligation, must contain absolute necessity; that, for example, the commandment: "Thou shalt not lie" cannot be valid merely for men whereas all other rational beings need not concern themselves with it. The same is true of all other real moral laws. Consequently it is evident that the basis of obligation is not to be sought for in the nature of man or the circumstances in which he is placed, but *a priori* solely in the concepts of pure reason; and that every other precept which is founded on principles of mere experience, even a precept that may in a certain sense be called universal, but in its smallest detail, perhaps only in respect to a motive, is founded on empirical grounds, may be called a practical rule, but never a moral law.

Consequently in the entire realm of practical knowledge the moral laws together with their principles not only differ in essence from all knowledge that contains anything empirical, but all moral philosophy rests wholly upon its pure part. Applied to man it does not derive the least thing from a knowledge of man himself (anthropology) but it supplies him as a rational being with laws *a priori*. These laws, to be sure, demand human judgment sharpened by experience in order that man may distinguish in what cases they are to be applied and also to enable them to enter into his will and to give them the emphasis necessary for their execution. For man, being of himself susceptible to so many inclinations, is capable of the idea of a practical pure reason, to be sure, but does not easily have the ability to make it concretely applicable in his conduct of life.

Thus a metaphysic of ethics is indispensable, not only because of the need of speculation in order to investigate the source of the practical principles which lie *a priori* in our reason, but because the morals themselves are subject to all kinds of corruptions as long as that elementary direction and highest norm has not been properly evaluated. For, if a thing is to be morally good, it is not enough that it be done *in accordance* with the moral law but it must be done *for its sake*. Otherwise the conformity is only accidental and precarious in as much as the unmoral basis will, to be sure, occasionally produce actions in conformity with the law but more often those contrary to it. The moral law, however, in its purity and genuineness (which is in practice of most importance) can be found only in a pure philosophy. Consequently this (metaphysic) must precede, and without it, no moral philosophy is possible. Even a philosophy which includes these pure principles among the empirical ones is not worthy of the name of a philosophy (for the very difference between a philosophy and ordinary rational knowledge is that it presents as separate disciplines what the other comprehends merely as a confused mixture). Much less can it be called a moral philosophy since by this very confusion it destroys the purity of morals and thus proceeds contrary to its own purpose.

. . .

It is impossible to conceive of anything anywhere in the world or even anywhere out of it that can without qualification be called good, except a Good Will. Reasoning, wit, judgment, or whatever the *talents* of the intellect may be called, or such qualities of *temperament* as courage, determination and constancy of purpose, are doubtless good and desirable in many respects. But they may also be extremely evil and harmful unless the will be good which is to make use of these natural gifts and whose particular quality we therefore designate as *character*. The same is true of the *gifts of fortune*. Power, riches, honor, even health, all comfort and contentment with one's condition which is called *happiness* frequently engender together with courage also an insolence, unless a good will is present which properly directs and thus fits to a general purpose their influence upon the mind and with it the entire principle of activity. Even an impartial sane witness can never take pleasure in the uninterrupted well-being of a person who shows no trace of a pure and good will. Consequently the good will seems to be the indispensable condition even of being worthy of happiness.

Certain qualities are even conducive to this good will itself and yet they have no intrinsic unquestioned value. Rather they still presuppose a good will which detracts from the esteem which we properly have for them and which makes it impossible to consider them absolutely good. Moderation in emotion and passion, self-control and sober consideration are not only in many respects good but they seem even to constitute a part of the *inner* worth of a person. And yet one can hardly call them unreservedly good (however much the ancients may have praised them). For without the principles of a good will they may become very evil indeed. The cold-bloodedness of a villain not only makes him far more dangerous, but also directly makes him seem more despicable to us than he would have seemed without it.

The good will is good not because of what it causes or accomplishes, not because of its usefulness in the attainment of some set purpose, but alone because of the willing, that is to say, of itself. Considered by itself, without any comparison, it is to be valued far more highly than all that might be accomplished through it in favor of some inclination or of the sum of all inclinations. Even though by some special disfavor of fortune or because of the meager provision of a stepmotherly nature this will were entirely lacking in ability to carry out its intentions; if with the greatest of efforts nothing were to be accomplished by it, and nothing were to remain except only the good will (not, to be sure, as a pious wish but as an exertion of every means in our power), it would still sparkle like a jewel by itself, like something that has its full value in itself. Its usefulness or fruitfulness can neither add nor detract from its worth. This would be, as it were, merely the setting to enable an easier handling of it in ordinary intercourse or to draw to it the attention of those who are not yet sufficiently expert in the knowledge of it, but not to recommend it to experts or to determine its worth.

There seems to be something so surprising in the idea of the absolute value of the mere will with no regard for its utility that, though even ordinary reason thoroughly agrees with it, we still must suspect that perhaps merely an extravagant fancy is at the basis of this assertion, and that we are interpreting wrongly the purpose of nature in making reason the ruler of our will. Therefore we will examine this idea from this point of view.

In the natural endowment of an organized being, that is, a being suitably adapted to life, we assume the principle that every organ to be found in it is best fitted and suited to it. If, therefore, in a being which possesses reason and a will the real purpose of nature were its *preservation* and its welfare, in a word, its *happiness,* then nature would have made a bad choice in selecting the reason of this being to carry out its intention. For all actions which such a being must perform to carry out this intention and the entire code of behavior could have been dictated far better and the purpose have been far better maintained by instinct than by reason. If the being was to be endowed also with reason, then the latter should have served only to make observations on the fortunate disposition of the nature of the being, to rejoice in it and be grateful for the beneficent cause of it; but it would not have wanted to entrust its desires to the weak and deceptive direction of reason and thus awkwardly to interfere with the intentions of nature. In a word, it would have prevented reason from breaking forth into *practical use* and assuming the impertinence to plan with its poor insight the structure of its happiness and the means of its attainment. Nature itself would have undertaken the selection not only of its purposes but also of the means of their attainment and with wise foresight would have entrusted both to instinct.

We do indeed find that the more a cultivated reason concerns itself with the meaning of happiness and the enjoyment of life, the farther away man gets from true satisfaction. Because of this there arises in many and even in those most tried in the use of reason, if only they are honest enough to admit it, a certain degree of *misology,* that is to say, a hatred of reason; because after viewing all the advantages which they derive, perhaps not merely from the discovery of the various arts of ordinary life but even from the sciences (which after all seem to them also a luxury of reason), they still find that they have burdened themselves with more trouble than they have won of happiness. Finally they envy rather than despise the common run of men who are more nearly directed by the mere natural instincts and allow their reason to have little influence upon their conduct. In so far one must admit that the judgment of those, who belittle and even rate below zero the boastful glorification of the advantages which reason is supposed to give us in regard to the happiness and satisfaction of life, is in no sense peevish or lacking in gratitude to the kindness of providence. On the contrary, secretly there lies at the basis of this judgment the idea of another and much worthier purpose of the existence of reason, for which, rather than for the sake of happiness, it is really intended, and to which as a supreme condition the private intentions of man must for the most part yield.

However, reason is not sufficiently adapted to guide the will with certainty in respect to its objects and the satisfaction of all our needs which it in part even multiplies and for which purpose the inborn natural instincts would have served far better. Nevertheless reason has been allotted to us as a practical faculty, that is to say, a faculty which is meant to influence the *will.* Therefore, if we are to assume that nature in the distribution of its capacities has everywhere proceeded with expediency, the real destination of reason cannot be to serve as a means to other ends but to produce *a will good in itself,* for which reason is absolutely indispensable. Thus this will, though not the sole and entire good, must nevertheless be the highest good and a condition of every other, even of all desire for happiness. Therefore it is quite in accordance with the wisdom of nature when we realize that the cultivation of reason, demanded by the foremost and unconditional purpose, in various ways restricts, in this life at least, the attainment of the second and generally conditioned purpose, namely our happiness. Yes, it may even reduce its value to below nothing without injury to nature's purpose. For reason, which recognizes its highest office to be the establishing of a good will, in the attainment of this purpose is capable only of its own peculiar satisfaction which arises from the fulfillment of its purpose, even though it meets with many an obstruction raised by the inclinations.

Now, in order to develop the idea of a good will to be esteemed for no other reason than for itself, just as sound common sense already contains it and it therefore needs less to be taught than clarified, and which is foremost in the evaluation of all our actions and the condition of everything else, we will take the concept of DUTY. Duty includes the notion of a good will with certain subjective restrictions and hindrances. However, far from hiding and obscuring it, these rather serve to bring it out by contrast and make it shine forth all the brighter.

I shall pass over all those actions which are at once recognized as being contrary to duty however useful they may be in one or another respect. There can be no question whether or not they have arisen from duty since they plainly contradict the latter. I shall also omit those actions which really conform to duty but to which men have *no* immediate *inclination* because they are impelled to them by some other inclination. For in such actions it is easy to distinguish whether the dutiful action has been performed *out of duty* or for some selfish reason. It is much more difficult to observe the distinction where an action conforms to duty and the subject besides has an immediate inclination for it. For example, it is indeed a matter of duty that a merchant should not take advantage of an inexperienced customer and where business is flourishing no merchant will do so, but he will rather maintain a fixed common price for all. One is therefore served *honestly*. But that is not nearly reason enough to believe that the merchant has been acting out of duty or principles of honesty. It was his advantage to act so. It cannot be assumed in this case that he has besides a direct inclination for his customers which impels him out of love, as it were, to give none of them the advantage in price over the other. Consequently his action arose neither from duty nor from an immediate inclination, but merely out of some selfish purpose.

On the other hand, it is a duty to preserve one's life and besides everyone has an immediate inclination to do so. But the frequently anxious care which most men take of it has no intrinsic value and their maxim no moral content. They indeed preserve their life *dutifully,* but not *out of duty.* However, when adversities and hopeless grief have wholly destroyed the desire for living; when the unfortunate person, stout of soul and angered by his fate rather than dejected or despondent, nevertheless loves his life not because of inclination or fear, but as a matter of duty, then his maxim has a moral content.

It is a duty to help others wherever possible, and there is many a sympathetic soul that, without a trace of vanity or self-interest, takes delight in making others happy and is able to rejoice in the contentment of others, in so far as he has helped produce it. But I maintain that, however dutiful and amiable such an action may be, in this case it still has no moral value, but goes hand in hand with other inclinations as, for example, the inclination toward honor which, when it by chance coincides with what is in fact for the common good and in accordance with duty, and therefore honorable, deserves praise but not a high esteem. For the maxim lacks the moral content, namely, that such actions be done *from duty* and not from inclination.

Let us assume, however, that the mind of such a philanthropist is be-clouded by a private grief which destroys all his interest in the fate of others; that he still has the ability to alleviate the suffering of others, but that the strange need does not move him because he is sufficiently occupied with his own. If now, when there is no inclination to urge him to it, he nevertheless rouses himself from this deadly indifference and performs the act without any inclination, solely out of duty, then the action for the very first time has genuine moral value. Let us assume further still that nature has allotted very little power of sympathy to a certain person, he is cold by temperament and indifferent to the suffering of others, perhaps because he himself possesses the special gift of patience and the power of endurance in respect to his own suffering and presupposes or even demands the same in others. While such a person, who certainly is not its poorest product, has not been fashioned by nature into a philanthropist, will he not still find within himself a source which will afford him a far higher value than that of a friendly temperament can be? Assuredly! This is the very point at which that value of character begins to show which is moral and incomparably highest, namely, to do good, not from inclination, but from duty.

To safeguard one's happiness is a duty, at least indirectly; for discontent with one's condition amidst the press of worries and unsatisfied wants may easily become a great *temptation to the transgression of duties*. But, even without having regard for duty, all men already possess of themselves the strongest and deepest inclination to happiness, because in this very idea all inclinations unite. On the other hand, the prescription for happiness is often such that it greatly detracts from certain inclinations and thus makes it impossible for man to make a definite and certain concept of the satisfaction of all inclinations under the name of happiness. Therefore it is not hard to understand how a single inclination, because of what it promises and the time in which its gratification may be attained, is able to prove more powerful than such a fluctuating idea. For example, a gouty person may choose to enjoy what pleases his palate and suffer greatly because he calculates that, in this instance at least, he has not deprived himself of the enjoyment of the moment for the sake of the, perhaps groundless, expectation of the benefits that are said to lie in health. But also in this case, even though a general inclination to happiness did not determine his will and he did not consider health so necessary, at least for himself, there is still the law, here as in all other cases, namely the law to further his happiness not from inclination, but from duty. And that law alone will give his conduct its real moral worth.

That undoubtedly is the true interpretation of the Scriptures, where we are commanded to love our neighbor, even our enemy. For love from inclination cannot be commanded; but to do good out of duty, even though no inclination at all impels toward it, yes, even when a very natural and uncontrollable disinclination opposes it, is a *practical* and not a *pathological* love. Such a love lies in the will and not in some propensity of affection, in the principles of action and not in tender sympathy. And such love alone can be commanded.

The second proposition is this: An action from duty does *not* have its moral worth *in the purpose* which is to be attained by it, but in the maxim according to which it has been formed. It therefore does not depend upon the actuality of the object of the action, but only on the *principle of voli- tion* according to which the action has taken place, irrespective of all ob- jects of desire. From what has been said above it is clear that, whatever the purpose of our actions, and whatever their effects as ends and drives of the will, these can afford the actions no absolute and moral value. In what then can this value be if it does not lie in the will or in relation to the expected effect? It can be nowhere except *in the principle of the will*, irrespective of the purposes that the action is to realize. For the will stands at the cross- roads, as it were, between its *a priori* principle, which is formal, and its *a posteriori* drive, which is material. Since it must be determined by some- thing, it follows that it must be determined by the formal principle of general volition, whenever an action is done from duty and consequently every material principle has been withdrawn from it.

The third proposition, a consequence of the two preceding, I would formulate thus: *Duty is the necessity of an action out of respect for the law*. For the object as the effect of my intended action I may indeed have an inclination, *but never respect,* for the very reason that it is merely an effect and not the activity of a will. Just so, I can have no respect for any inclination whatever, whether it be my own or another's. At most I may approve of my own and on occasion even have a fondness for another's, that is, consider it favorable to my interests. Only that can be an object of my respect, and hence a command, which has the relation of a basic princi- ple to my will, but never that of an effect; which, instead of serving, rather outweighs my inclination or at least excludes it entirely from consideration in the making of a choice. Since then an action from duty must eliminate entirely the influence of the inclinations and thus every object of the will, there is nothing left to determine the will, except objectively the *law* and subjectively pure respect for this practical law, that is to say, the maxim [1] to obey such a law, even at the expense of all my inclinations.

The moral worth of an action then does not lie in the effect which is expected of it, and consequently in no principle of an action which must borrow its motive from the expected effect. For all these effects (the com- fort of one's condition or even the promotion of the happiness of others) could have been brought about by other causes and did not need the will of a rational being, in which alone, however, the highest and unconditioned good can be found. Therefore the supreme good which we call moral can consist only in *the conception of the law* in itself, *which indeed is possible*

---

[1] Maxim is the subjective principle of volition; the objective principle (that is, that which would also serve subjectively for all rational beings as a practical principle if reason had full power over the faculty of desire) is the practical law. [I.K.]

only in a rational being, in so far as this conception, and not the hoped-for effect, determines his will. This good, however, is already present in the person himself who acts in accordance with it, and it does not need to wait upon the effect to put in its appearance.[2]

But of what sort can this law possibly be, the conception of which, even without regard for the effect expected from it, must determine the will, in order that the latter may without qualification be called purely and simply good? Since I have deprived the will of every stimulus which it might receive from the results of a law, so there is nothing left to serve as principle for the will except the universal lawfulness of actions in general. That is to say, I am never to act otherwise than *so that I could at the same time will that my maxim should become a universal law.* Here the pure lawfulness in general, without the basis of any law whatever which is directed upon definite actions, is that which serves and must serve as principle for the will, unless duty everywhere is to be an empty delusion and a chimerical notion. Ordinary human reason in its practical judgment fully agrees with this and always has this suggested principle in view.

Take this question, for example. If I am sorely pressed, may I make a promise with the intention not to keep it? I readily distinguish between the two principal meanings of this question, whether it is clever or else a matter of duty to make a false promise. The first undoubtedly may quite often be the case. To be sure, I realize that it is not enough to want to extricate myself from a momentary embarrassment by means of this subterfuge, but that I ought to consider whether from this lie there might not arise later much greater difficulties than those from which I am at present freeing myself. Since the results of my assumed *cleverness* cannot easily be foreseen, I ought to consider whether the loss of confidence in me might not constitute

---

[2] I might be accused of taking refuge in some obscure feeling with the use of the word *respect,* instead of clarifying the question by means of a concept of reason. However, although respect is a feeling, still it is not a feeling which has been *received* through some influence, but one which a concept of reason has *produced of itself.* Consequently it is specifically distinct from all feelings of the former kind which can be traced to inclination or fear. What I recognize immediately as a law for me I acknowledge with respect, which merely means the consciousness of the submission of my will to a law, without the intervention of other influences upon my mind. The direct determination of the will by the law and the consciousness of it, we call *respect.* Therefore respect is considered to be the *effect* of the law upon the subject and not the *cause.* Respect is really the conception of a value which lessens my love of self. It is therefore something which is looked upon as an object neither of inclination nor of fear, though it has something analogous to both. The *object* of the respect, therefore, is solely the *law,* the law which we impose upon *ourselves* and yet consider necessary in itself. As a law we are subject to it without reference to our self-love, and thus it is analogous to fear; since we ourselves impose it upon ourselves it is certainly the result of our will, and thus it is analogous to inclination. All respect for a person is really nothing but a respect for the law (of righteousness, etc.) of which the person is an example. Because we consider the expansion of our talents a duty we look upon a person of talents as a sort of an *example of the law* (to become like him by practice), and that constitutes our respect. All so-called moral *interest* consists purely and simply in the *respect* for the law. [I.K.]

a far greater harm than all the evil I am trying to avoid at present; whether I would not be acting *more prudently* if I proceeded according to a universal law and developed the habit of never making a promise except with the intention to keep it. However I soon realize that the basis of such a maxim is after all fear of the consequences of my action. Certainly it is a very different thing to be truthful from duty than because of fear of disadvantageous results. In the first case the very conception of the action in itself contains a law for me to follow, in the other case I must first look about to see what consequences might be connected with it for me. For if I deviate from the principle of duty then it is most certainly evil; if, however, I act against my maxim of cleverness I may at some time greatly profit by this faithlessness, even though it be safer for the present to adhere to it. However, in order to take the shortest and yet surest way toward an answer to this problem, whether or not a deceitful promise is in accordance with duty, I ask myself: Would I indeed be satisfied to have my maxim (to extricate myself from an embarrassing situation by a false promise) considered a universal law? Would I be able to say to myself: Everybody has the right to make a false promise if he finds himself in a difficulty from which he can escape in no other way? In that manner I soon realize that I may will the lie, but never a universal law to lie. For according to such a law there really would be no promise at all, because it would be vain to make a pretense of my will in respect to my future actions to those who have no faith in my pretensions or who, if they were rash enough to do so, would repay me in my own coin. Therefore my maxim would destroy itself as soon as it got to be a universal law.

Therefore I have need of no far-reaching perspicacity to know what to do in order that my volition may be morally good. Inexperienced in understanding the course of the world, incapable of being prepared for all that happens in it, I merely ask myself: Can you will that your maxim becomes a universal law? If not, then it is unsound; and indeed not because of a disadvantage arising from it for you or for others, but because it is not suited as a principle for a possible universal code of law. But reason forces upon me an immediate respect for this code, even though I do not yet *comprehend* upon what it is based (that is a matter for investigation by philosophers). But I at least understand this much: that it is an appreciation of that value which far outweighs all the worth of that which is esteemed by inclination; that the necessity of my action out of *pure* respect for the practical law is what constitutes duty and that, to duty, every other motive must yield because it is the condition of a will good *in itself,* than which there is no greater value.

. . .

Each thing in nature works according to laws. Only a rational being has the faculty to act *according to the conception* of laws, that is according to principles, in other words has a will. Since the deduction of actions from laws requires *reason* the will is nothing but practical reason. If reason invariably determines the will then the actions which such a being recognizes as objectively necessary are subjectively necessary as well, that is to say, the will is the faculty to choose *that only* which reason, independent of inclination, recognizes as practically necessary, that is, good. But if reason of itself alone does not sufficiently determine the will, if the latter is dependent also on subjective conditions (certain impulses) which do not always correspond with the objective conditions; in a word, if the will is not *in itself* in full accord with reason (as is actually the case with men) then the actions which objectively are recognized as necessary are subjectively contingent, and the determination of such a will according to objective laws is *obligation*. By this we mean, the relation of the objective laws to a will which is not good throughout is conceived as the determination of the will of a rational being by principles of reason which, however, this will does not by virtue of its nature necessarily follow.

The conception of an objective principle in so far as it is obligatory for the will, is called a command (of reason), and the formula of the command is called an IMPERATIVE.

All imperatives are expressed by a "Thou Shalt" and thereby indicate the relation of an objective law of reason to a will which is not by virtue of its subjective constitution necessarily determined by it (an obligation). These imperatives say that something would be good to do or to omit, but they say it to a will which does not always do a thing merely because it is presented to it as being good to do. That, however, is practically good which determines the will by means of the conceptions of reason, accordingly not from subjective causes, but from objective ones, that is to say on principles which are valid for every rational being as such. It is distinguished from the *pleasant* as that which influences the will only by means of sensations from merely subjective causes which apply only to the feeling of this or that person, and not as principles of reason valid for everyone.[3]

A completely good will would therefore likewise be subject to objective laws (of the good), but it could not for that reason be conceived as *obliged* to good actions, because of itself according to its subjective constitution it can be determined only by the conception of the good. Therefore no imperatives hold for the *Divine Will* or in general for a *holy* will; the "Thou

---

[3] The dependence of the desire on sensations is called inclination and this accordingly always indicates a *want*. But the dependence of a will which may be determined by chance on principles of reason is called an *interest*. The latter therefore arises only with a dependent will which is not of itself at all times in accord with reason. Within the Divine Will an interest is inconceivable. But also the human will can *take an interest in* something without therefore *acting out of interest*. The former denotes *practical* interest in an action, the latter *pathological* interest in the object of the action. The first shows merely the dependence of the will on principles of reason as such, the second on principles of reason in behalf of inclination, inasmuch as reason merely supplies the practical rules by which the wants of inclination may be met. In the first case the actions themselves interest me, in the second the object of the action (inasmuch as it is pleasant to me). In the first section we have seen that in an action done from duty the interest to be regarded must not be in the object, but in the action itself and in its principle of reason (the law). [I.K.]

Shalt" is out of place here, because already the "*I Will*" is necessarily of itself in harmony with the law. Therefore imperatives are merely formulæ to express the relation of objective laws of volition in general to the subjective imperfection of the will of this or that rational being, for example of the human will.

Now all *imperatives* command either *hypothetically* or *categorically*. The former represents the practical necessity of a possible action as a means to arrive at something else that is willed (or may be willed). The categorical imperative would then be that which represented an action as objectively necessary of itself without relation to another end.

Since every practical law represents a possible action as good and consequently as necessary for a subject who can be determined practically by reason, therefore all imperatives are formulæ for actions which are necessary according to the principle of a will that in some manner or other is good. Now, if the action is meant to be good merely as a means to *something else,* then the imperative is *hypothetical;* but if it is represented as good of itself and thus necessary as a principle of a will which is of itself in accord with reason, then it is *categorical.*

The imperative then tells me which of my possible actions would be good, and presents the practical rule in relation to a will which, however, does not at once perform an act because it is good, partly because the subject does not always know that it is good, partly, even though it knows it, because its maxims may still be opposed to the objective principles of practical reason.

The hypothetical imperative accordingly tells only that an action is good for this or that possible or actual purpose. In the first case it is a PROBLEMATIC principle, in the second case an ASSERTORIAL practical principle. The categorical imperative, which declares that the action is of itself objectively necessary without relation to any purpose and therefore also without any other end than itself, has the nature of a (practical) APODICTIC principle.

That which is possible only by virtue of some rational being may also be conceived as a possible purpose of some will; and therefore the principles of action are indeed infinitely numerous in so far as they are considered necessary for the realization of a possible purpose. All sciences have a practical part consisting of problems stating the possibility of some purpose, and of imperatives that direct how to realize the purpose. The latter may therefore be called in general imperatives of SKILL. Whether the end is reasonable and good is of no concern here at all; but only what must be done to attain it. The prescription given by a physician in order to effect the thorough cure of his patient, and that prepared by a poisoner to bring about certain death, are both of equal value in so far as each serves to realize its purpose perfectly. Because it is unknown what purposes life may later present to youth, parents seek above all to have their children learn *a great many things* and encourage the development of *skill* in the use of the means to *all sorts* of ends, of none of which they are able to determine that it will really become in the future a purpose for the child, though it possibly may. This concern is so great that parents commonly neglect because of it to form and set aright in their children the judgments on the value of the things that may be chosen as ends.

There is nevertheless *one* end that may be assumed as being present in all rational beings (in so far as they are dependent beings and imperatives apply to them) and therefore one purpose of which they not only are *capable,* but of which it may safely be assumed that each and every one must by a natural necessity *possess* it. This purpose is *happiness.* The hypothetical imperative, which represents the practical necessity of an action as means to the advancement of happiness, is ASSERTORIAL. This must be explained as necessary not only to an uncertain and merely possible purpose, but also to a purpose that can be assumed in each person with certainty and *a priori,* because it is part of his being. Now skill in the choice of the means to one's own greatest well-being may be called *prudence,*[4] in the narrowest sense of the word. Therefore the imperative which refers to the choice of the means to one's own happiness, the precept of prudence, is still hypothetical; the action is not commanded absolutely, but only as a means to another purpose.

Finally, there is an imperative which commands a certain conduct directly and which is not based on the condition of attaining any other purpose by it. This imperative is CATEGORICAL. It has nothing to do with the matter of the action or with that which results from it, but with the form and the principle from which it itself proceeds; and its essential good consists of the state of mind irrespective of what may result from it. This imperative may be called the IMPERATIVE OF MORALITY.

In accordance with these three kinds of principles volition is clearly differentiated also by the *dissimilarity* of the will. To make these differences clear it would seem best to describe them in their order as existing either as *rules* of skills, or *counsels* of prudence, or *commands* (*laws*) of morality. For the law alone involves an unconditional and, moreover, objective and, therefore, universally valid necessity; and commands are laws that must be obeyed, that is, must be followed even against the inclinations. Counsels, to be sure, also involve necessity, but this can be valid only under the subjective contingent, whether this or that person considers this or that part of his happiness. The categorical imperative, however, is limited by no condition and may with complete propriety be called a command as being absolutely, though practically, necessary. The first impera-

---

[4] The word *prudence* is taken in two senses. In the one it may be called wordly prudence, in the other private prudence. The first is the skill of a person to influence others so as to use them for his own purposes. The second is the ability to see how to unite all these purposes for one's own lasting benefit. The latter is really the one to which even the value of the former is traced; and when a person is prudent in the first sense, but not in the second, we might better say of him that he is clever and cunning, but, on the whole, imprudent. [I.K.]

tives may also be called *technical* (belonging to art), the second *pragmatic* [5] (to welfare), the third *moral* (belonging to free conduct generally, that is, to *morals*).

.   .   .

We shall then have to investigate wholly *a priori* the possibility of a *categorical* imperative, since we do not have the advantage in the case of this imperative that its actuality is given in experience and that therefore the possibility of its being is not necessary to establish it but merely to explain it. To begin with we must understand, however, that the categorical imperative alone has the form of a practical *law,* while all the other imperatives may indeed be called *principles of* the will, but not laws. For whatever is necessary to do merely to attain some intention or other may be considered as in itself contingent and we can always free ourselves from the precept by giving up the intention; while, on the other hand, the absolute command leaves the will no choice to go contrary to it, and therefore it alone carries with it that necessity which we require in a law.

In the second place, the difficulty of understanding the possibility of this categorical imperative or law of morality is indeed very great. It is an *a priori* synthetical practical proposition.[6] And inasmuch as it is so difficult to understand the possibility of a proposition of this kind in speculative knowledge it easily follows that the difficulty will be no less in practical knowledge.

In attacking this problem we shall investigate first whether perhaps the mere concept of a categorical imperative will not supply also the formula which contains the proposition that alone can be a categorical imperative. To comprehend how such an absolute command is possible, even when we know its formula, will require further special and difficult study which we shall reserve for the last section.

When I conceive a *hypothetical* imperative in general I do not know what it will contain until the condition is supplied. But when I conceive a *categorical* imperative I know at once what it contains. For, since besides the law the imperative contains only the maxim [7] to accord with this law,

---

[5] It seems to me that this is the most accurate determination of the real meaning of the word *pragmatic.* For those *sanctions* are called pragmatic which do not really proceed fom the rights of the states as necessary laws, but from the provision for the general welfare. A *history* is pragmatic when it makes men *prudent,* that is, when it teaches the world how to foster its advantage better than in the past, or at least as well. [I.K.]

[6] I connect the act with the will without implying the condition of any inclination, but *a priori* and consequently necessarily (though only objectively, that is under the idea of a reason which would have full power over all objective motives). This is consequently a practical proposition which does not deduce the willing of an action analytically from another already presupposed (for we have no such perfect will); but rather connects it immediately with the concept of a rational being, as something not contained in it. [I.K.]

[7] A *maxim* is the subjective principle to act and must be distinguished from the *objective principle,* the practical law. The former contains the practical rule which reason determines according to the conditions of the subject (often its ignorance or

the law however contains no condition which limits it; therefore nothing remains but the universality of the law in general with which the maxim of action shall conform, and this conformity alone the imperative really represents as necessary.

Consequently there is only one categorical imperative and it is this: *Act only on that maxim which will enable you at the same time to will that it be a universal law.*

Now if all imperatives of duty can be deduced from this single imperative as from their principle, then, although we here refrain from stating whether what one calls duty may be an empty notion, we shall at least be able to indicate what we understand by it and what the concept means.

Because the universality of the law according to which effects are produced constitutes what we really mean by *nature* in the most general sense (according to form), that is, the existence of things in so far as it is determined by universal laws, the universal imperative of duty may read thus: *Act as if the maxim of your action by your will were to become a* UNI-VERSAL LAW OF NATURE.

We will now enumerate a few duties dividing them in the accustomed manner into duties to ourselves, and to others, and into perfect and imperfect duties.[8]

A person who is wearied with life because of a series of misfortunes that has reduced him to despair still possesses sufficient reason to be able to ask himself, whether it may not be contrary to his duty to himself to take his life. Now he asks himself, whether the maxim of his action could possibly be a universal law of nature. But this maxim reads: Out of love of self I make it my principle to shorten my life if its continuation threatens more evil than it promises comfort. But he will still ask, whether his principle of self-love is capable of being a universal law of nature. Then he will soon see that a nature, whose law it would be to destroy life by the very feeling which is meant to stimulate the promotion of life, would contradict itself and therefore not persist as nature. Accordingly the maxim cannot possibly function as a universal law of nature, and it consequently completely refutes the supreme principle of all duty.

Another person is in need and finds it necessary to borrow money. He knows very well that he will not be able to repay it, but he also realizes that he will not receive a loan unless he promises solemnly to pay at a definite time. He has a desire to make this promise, but he still has enough con-

---

its inclinations), and it is therefore the principle by which the subject *acts*. On the other hand, the law is the objective principle valid for every rational being, and the principle by which it *shall* act, that is, an imperative. [I.K.]

[8] It must be noted that I am reserving altogether the classification of duties for a future *metaphysic of ethics*, and that the present division is merely casual (in order to arrange my examples). I also mean by a perfect duty one that does not permit an exception in favor of inclination, and in this I include not only external but also inner perfect duties. This is contrary to the accepted school-use of the word, but I have no intention of justifying it here because it is indifferent to my purpose whether it is permitted or not. [I.K.]

science to ask himself whether it is not improper and contrary to duty to relieve distress in this manner. If he should nevertheless decide to do so, then the maxim of his action would read thus: When I think that I am in need of money I will borrow and promise to repay, even though I know that I will never do so. Now this principle of my love of self or advantage may perhaps well agree with my whole future well-being; the next question, however, is, whether it is right. Thereby I change the interpretation of self-love into a universal law and arrange my question thus: How would things be if my maxim were a universal law? Then I see at once that it could never count as a universal law of nature and still agree with itself, but must necessarily contradict itself. For the universality of a law, according to which anyone who believed himself in distress could promise anything he pleased with no intention of keeping it, would make promises themselves and any purpose they may have impossible; since nobody would believe that a promise had been made, but everybody would ridicule such statements as vain pretenses.

A third finds that he possesses a gift which with some cultivation could make a useful man of him in all sorts of respects. But he is in comfortable circumstances and prefers to indulge in pleasure rather than trouble himself with the expansion and improvement of his fortunate natural faculties. But he still questions, whether his maxim of neglect of his natural gifts, besides agreeing with his inclination to diversions, also agrees with what is called duty. Then he sees that according to such a universal law a nature could still go on persisting although man, like the South Sea islander, should let his talents rest and his life were intent only on idleness, diversions, propagation, in a word, pleasure; but he cannot possibly *will* this to be a universal law of nature or be given to us as such by a natural instinct. For as a rational being he necessarily wants all his faculties to develop because they after all are given to him and serve him for all sorts of possible purposes.

Again a *fourth,* who is well off while he sees others struggling with great difficulties (which he could well alleviate), thinks: What concern is it of mine? May each man be as happy as the heavens decree or he can make himself to be; I shall deprive him of nothing and not even envy him. But neither do I care to contribute to his welfare nor offer him help in his distress. Now if such an attitude were to be a universal law of nature the human race could subsist very well, to be sure, and doubtless better than when everybody chatters of sympathy and good will, even endeavors occasionally to exert it, but also takes every chance to deceive and to plunder or otherwise to violate the rights of man. But although it is possible that a universal law of nature could exist by that maxim, it is still impossible to *will* that such a principle count as a law of nature generally. For by deciding for such a law a will would run counter to itself, inasmuch as many an occasion might arise where a person of such will might need the love and sympathy of others and where he would deprive himself of all hope of the desired assistance because of such a natural law arisen from his own will.

These are then a few of the duties, actual or at least accepted as such by us, whose derivation from the single principle which we have described is at once clear. The canon of the moral judgment of actions generally is this: One must be *able to will* that the maxim of an action be a universal law. Some actions are so constituted that their maxim cannot even be *conceived* as a universal law of nature, not to mention that one might *will* that it *ought* to be such. In others this inner impossiblity cannot be discovered, but it nevertheless is impossible to *will* that their maxim be elevated to the universality of a law of nature because such a will would contradict itself. Plainly the first kind of maxim runs counter to the more strict or immediate (inflexible) duty, the second to the less immediate (meritorious) duty. Thus all duties, judged by their kind of obligation (and not by the object of the action) are shown by these examples to be completely dependent on the one principle.

If we now examine ourselves at each transgression of a duty we find that we do not really will that our maxim be a universal law; for that would be impossible. We rather will that the opposite generally persist as a law. We merely take the liberty to make an *exception* in our own favor or, just for this one time, in favor of our inclination. Consequently, if we considered everything from one and the same point of view, namely that of reason, then we would discover the contradiction in our own volition that a certain principle objectively is necessary as a universal law and, at the same time, subjectively should not be generally valid, but admit of exceptions. But since we at one time look upon our action from a point of view wholly in accord with reason and then examine the same action from a point of view affected by our inclination, there is really no contradiction at all, but rather a resistance of the inclination to the precept of reason (*antagonismus*) whereby the universality of the principle (*universalitas*) is changed into a mere generality (*generalitas*) by which the practical principle of reason is to meet the maxim halfway. Although this cannot be justified in our own impartial judgment, it nevertheless proves that we really acknowledge the validity of the categorical imperative, and (with all respect for it) merely allow ourselves a few exceptions that seem insignificant and forced upon us by circumstances.

We have thus established at least this much, that if duty is a concept which is to have significance and real legislative force for our actions, this can be expressed only in categorical imperatives but never in hypothetical ones. Also, and this is a great deal, we have presented clearly and determined practically the content of the categorical imperative which must contain the principle of all duty (if such a thing exists at all). But we have not yet reached the point of proving *a priori* that there actually is such an imperative, that there is a practical law which commands absolutely of itself and without any impulsions whatever, and that the observance of this law is duty.

In our approach upon this it is of extreme importance that we should guard against any attempt to deduce the actuality of this principle from the *particular attribute of human nature*. For duty is meant to be the practical unconditional necessity of action. It must therefore be valid for all rational beings (to whom an imperative can apply at all), and *for this reason only* be a law for the human will also. On the other hand, what is deduced from the particular disposition of man's nature; from certain feelings and proclivities; even, where possible, from a particular tendency which might be peculiar to human reason and not necessarily hold for the will of every rational being; all this may supply us with a maxim but not with a law. It may be a subjective principle according to which we have a propensity and inclination to act, but not an objective one by which we are *obliged* to act even though our propensities, inclinations and natural dispositions were opposed to it. In fact the sublimity and inner dignity of the command contained in a duty is the more evident, the less reasons exist for it and the more against it; and this circumstance will not in the least weaken the obligation of the law or subtract from its validity.

Here then we indeed see philosophy confined to an awkward standpoint which is meant to be firmly fixed and yet is neither dependent upon nor supported by anything in heaven or on earth. Here it should prove its purity as containing its laws within itself, and not as the herald of laws prompted by an implanted sense or some tutelary nature or other. For such laws, though they may be better than nothing at all, can never afford principles which nature dictates and which must have their source and also their categorical authority wholly *a priori,* according to which nothing should be expected from man's inclination, but everything from the supremacy of the law; or else man must be condemned to self-contempt and inner abhorrence.

Then all empirical trimmings of the principle of morality are not only unsuited to it but even highly detrimental to the purity of morals. For the real and pricelessly precious value of an absolutely good will consists in this, that the principle of action be free of all influences of contingent motives which experience alone can supply. One cannot warn too much or too often against the carelessness or indeed mean sentiment which searches for the principle among empirical motives and laws; for human reason when it tires likes to rest on this pillow and in the dreams of sweet delusions (though they lead us to embrace a cloud instead of Juno), and it substitutes for morality a bastard patched together from limbs of quite another parentage, which looks like anything one may please, but not like virtue [9] to anyone who has once beheld her in her true form.

The question then is this: Is it a necessary law for *all human beings* that they judge their actions at all times according to maxims of which they

---

[9] To behold *virtue* in its true form is merely to contemplate morality stripped of all admixture of the sensual and of all false adornment of reward or self-love. How much she will then obscure all the other things that seem attractive to the inclination everybody can easily realize by the slightest use of reason, provided it has not been wholly spoiled for abstractions. [I.K.]

themselves can will that they should serve as universal laws? If there is such a law, then it must be connected (wholly *a priori*) with the very concept of the will of a rational being. But to discover this connection one must, however much one may dislike it, take a further step into metaphysic, but into a domain of it which is distinct from speculative philosophy, namely into the metaphysic of ethics. In a practical philosophy, where we are not concerned with ascertaining the grounds for what *happens,* but the laws of what *ought to happen,* even though it never does happen, that is with objective practical laws, there it is not necessary to undertake investigations why this pleases or displeases, how the pleasure of mere sensations is different from taste and whether the latter differs from a general satisfaction of reason; on what the feeling of pleasure or displeasure rests, and how from it desires and inclinations arise and from these again maxims under the coöperation of reason. For all this belongs to an empirical psychology which would comprise the second part of physics considered as a *philosophy of nature* in so far as it is based on empirical laws. Here, however, we are concerned with objective practical laws and consequently with the relation of a will to itself in so far as it determines itself by reason only. Thus everything that has reference to the empirical is necessarily excluded because if *reason of itself alone* determines conduct (the possibility of which we are now about to examine), it must necessarily do this *a priori.*

The will then is conceived as a faculty of determining oneself to action *in accordance with the conception of certain laws.* Such a faculty can be found in rational beings only. That which serves the will as the objective ground of its self-determination is the *end,* and if this is given by reason alone it must be valid equally for all rational beings. What, on the other hand, contains merely the ground for the possibility of the action, the effect of which is the end, is called *means.* The subjective ground of desiring is the *impulsion,* the objective ground of volition is the *motive;* hence the distinction between subjective ends based on impulsions and objective ends dependent on motives valid for all rational beings. Practical principles are *formal* when they disregard all subjective ends; but they are *material* when they are based on subjective ends and consequently on impulses. The ends which a rational being selects arbitrarily as *effects* of his action (material ends) are throughout relative only; for their value lies wholly in their relation to a specifically constituted desire of the subject, and this value can therefore afford no principles universal for all rational beings and valid and necessary for every volition, that is to say, no practical laws. Hence these relative ends are the basis of hypothetical imperatives only.

Assuming, however, that there is something, the *existence of which of itself* has an absolute value which, *as end in itself,* could be the basis of definite laws; then the basis of a possible categorical imperative or practical law would lie in it and in it alone.

Now I say: Man and every rational being anywhere *exists* as end in itself, *not merely as means* for the arbitrary use by this or that will; but in all his actions, whether they are directed upon himself or upon other rational beings, he must at all times be looked upon as an *end*. All objects of the inclinations have merely a conditional value. For if the inclinations and the needs based upon them did not exist, then their object would have no value. But the inclinations themselves as source of the needs are so far from having an absolute value that makes them desirable that, on the contrary, it must be the universal wish of every rational being to be wholly free of them. Consequently the value of all objects *to be acquired* by our actions is always conditional. The creatures, the existence of which depends perhaps not on our will but on nature's, if they are non-rational, have merely a relative value as means and therefore are called *things*. On the other hand, rational beings are called *persons* because their very nature distinguishes them as ends in themselves, that is as something that must not be employed as mere means and which consequently limits arbitrary action to this extent (and is an object of respect). Therefore these are not mere subjective ends the existence of which possesses a value *for us* as effects of our actions, but *objective ends,* that is to say, things whose existence is an end in itself, and moreover an end that cannot be replaced by any other end for which they would serve as means *only,* because that would make it impossible to find anything of *absolute value* anywhere. But if all value were conditional and consequently contingent, then nowhere could there be found a supreme practical principle of reason.

If then there is to be a supreme practical principle and in respect to the human will a categorical imperative, then it must be one which, when we conceive what is necessarily an end for everybody because it is the *end in itself,* must constitute an *objective* principle of the will and therefore be able to serve as universal practical law. The basis of this principle is: *Rational nature exists as end in itself.* Man necessarily conceives his own being in this way, and therefore it is thus far a *subjective* principle of human actions. But every other rational being conceives his existence in the same way and on rational grounds identical with my own;[10] therefore it is at the same time an *objective principle* from which as the supreme practical basis all laws of the will must be capable of being deduced. The practical imperative will then read as follows: *Act so that in your own person as well as in the person of every other you are treating mankind also as an end, never merely as a means.* Let us see whether this can be put into practice.

We shall illustrate this by means of our previous examples.

Firstly according to the concept of the necessary duty to oneself. The person who is contemplating suicide will ask himself, whether his act can coexist together with the idea of mankind *as end in itself.* If he destroys himself in order to escape from a burdensome situation he uses a person merely as a *means* to maintain a tolerable condition up to the end of his

---

[10] This statement I here set up as a postulate. The argument for it will be found in the last section. [I.K.]

life. However, man is not a thing and therefore not something that may be used as means only, but in all his actions he must always be considered as end in itself. Consequently I can make no disposition of the man in my own person to mutilate, destroy or kill him. (The more detailed definition of this principle which would avoid all misunderstanding I must omit here, as for example, the question of the amputation of limbs to preserve life, exposing one's life to danger in order to maintain it, etc. This belongs to ethics proper.)

Secondly in regard to the necessary or bounden duty to others. The person who intends to make a lying promise to others must realize at once that he is about to use some other person as mere means, without the latter at the same time containing the end in himself. For the person whom I am about to use for my purposes by such a promise cannot possibly agree with my conduct toward him, and thus himself contain the end of this action. This conflict with the principle of other men becomes more obvious when examples of attacks upon the freedom and property of others are employed. Then it becomes clear that such a transgressor against the rights of man intends to use the person of others as means without considering that these others as rational beings must always be esteemed also as ends, that is to say as such who must also be able to contain in themselves the end of the very same action.[11]

Thirdly in respect to the contingent (meritorious) duties to oneself, it is not enough that the action should not be in conflict with the humanity in one's person as end in itself, it must also harmonize with it. Now there are in mankind faculties for greater perfection which belong to the end which nature possesses in view of the humanity in us as subjects. To neglect these might perhaps be consistent with the *preservation* of mankind as end in itself, but could not agree with its *advancement*.

Fourthly in regard to the meritorious duties toward others, the natural end which all men possess is their own happiness. Mankind would indeed be able to persist if no one contributed to another's happiness and did not intentionally deprive the latter's happiness of anything. However, it is only a negative and not a positive agreement with *mankind as end in itself* when each person does not also seek to advance the end of others as far as he is able. For the ends of the subject, which is an end in itself, must as far as possible be *my* ends also if the conception of happiness is to be *fully* effective with me.

The principle that humanity and every rational nature generally is an

---

[11] It is wrong to believe that the trivial "Golden Rule": *quod tibi non vis fieri,* etc., can serve here as a rule or principle. For this rule, with various limitations to be sure, is merely deduced from what is described above. It cannot be a universal law, for it does not contain the basis of duties toward oneself; nor of the duties out of love for others; nor finally of the bounden duties to others (for many a person would gladly agree that others should not help him, if only he could be relieved of doing good to them). On this basis the criminal might argue against the judges who punished him, and so forth. [I.K.]

end in itself (which is the supreme limiting condition of the freedom of the action of every single person) is not derived from experience, firstly, because of its universality, inasmuch as it applies to all rational beings and no experience is sufficient to determine anything about it; secondly, because with it mankind is not conceived as an end of men (subjectively), that is as a thing which one actually makes an end of and for oneself, but as an objective end which, whatever ends we may have, is meant to constitute as a law the supreme limiting condition of all subjective ends. It must therefore arise from pure reason. The basis moreover of all practical legislation lies (according to the first principle) *objectively in the rule* and the form of universality which enables it to be a law (perhaps a law of nature), but *subjectively* it lies in the end. The subject of all ends, however, (according to the second principle) is each rational being as end in himself. From this follows the third practical principle of the will as supreme condition of its agreement with the universal practical reason: the idea of *the will of every rational being as a universally legislative* will.

In accord with this principle all maxims are rejected that are inconsistent with the universal legislation of the will itself. Thus the will is not simply subjected to the law, but subjected in such way that it must be looked upon also *as giving itself the law,* and for that reason really subject to the law (of which it can regard itself the author).

In the presentation which we have made of imperatives thus far, in the general lawfulness of actions similar to a *system of natural laws,* or in the general *prerogative* of rational beings *as ends in themselves,* these imperatives, for the very reason that they were taken as categorical, excluded from their high claim to authority every admixture of any interest whatever as impulsions to action. However, they were merely *assumed* to be categorical because this assumption was necessary to explain the concept of duty. But that there are practical propositions that command categorically could not be proved of itself, nor can it be done in this section. However, we might have done one thing, namely shown that the denial of all interest in volition from duty indicates in the imperative itself, by some distinction which it contains, the specific character that differentiates the categorical from the hypothetical imperative. This is done in the present third formula of the principle, in the idea of the will of every rational being as a *universally legislative will.*

Although a will *which is subject to laws* may be bound to the law by means of some interest, a will which is itself a supreme lawgiver cannot possibly as such be dependent on some interest. For such a dependent will would itself need some other law to restrict the interest of its self-love to the condition that it must be valid as universal law.

The *principle* then that every human will is a will which *gives universal laws in all its maxims* [12] would, granted that it exists at all, be very well

---

[12] I may be excused from elucidating this principle by examples, for the examples that were used to elucidate the categorical imperative and its formula may be used here as well. [I.K.]

adapted to be the categorical imperative because it *is based on no interest* by virtue of the very idea of universal legislation, and thus among all possible imperatives it alone can be unconditional. Or better still, let us convert the proposition. If there is a categorical imperative (a law for the will of every rational being), then it can only command that everything be done from the maxim of a will that could also have itself as universal lawgiver as its object. For then alone the practical principle and the imperative which it obeys are unconditional because they simply cannot be based on any interest.

Now as we look back upon all attempts that have been made in the past to discover the principle of morality, we can see why they had to fail. They saw man bound by his duties to laws, but it never occurred to anyone to see that man is subject *only to his own* and yet to *universal legislation,* and that he is obligated to act only in accordance with his own will which, however, in view of the end of nature is a universally legislating will. For when man was thought of as subject to a law (whatever it may be), some interest as impulse or coercion had to be implied because it did not arise as a law from *his* will, but this will was by rule obliged by something else to act in a certain way. But because of this necessary consequence all the labor to find a supreme basis of duty was irretrievably lost. For the result was never duty, but the necessity of the action from a certain interest. This may have been a private interest or a remote one. The imperative, however, always had to prove to be conditional and could not possibly serve as moral law. I shall therefore speak of the principle of the AUTONOMY of the will in contrast with every other which I shall reckon as HETERONOMY.

. . .

QUESTIONS FOR STUDY AND DISCUSSION

1. What does it mean to say that the moral law is pure and not empirical?
2. What is the ultimate criterion of good according to Kant?
3. To what extent must an action be done *out of duty* in order to be moral?
4. Why is the moral obligation called a *categorical imperative* in Kant's moral philosophy?
5. State two formulations of the categorical imperative and show how they can become concrete norms of action.

Johann Gottlieb Fichte

JOHANN GOTTLIEB FICHTE, the first of the great German idealists, was born at Rammenau in Upper Lusatia in 1762. After studying at the Universities of Jena and Leipzig, he worked as a private tutor in Zurich and Leipzig. He made an intensive study of Kantian philosophy, and, although he always considered himself a Kantian, his idealist conclusions separated him more and more from his master. Fichte received his first public recognition for *Critique of All Revelation* (1792), a work that was at first mistakenly attributed to Kant. From 1794 to 1799 he was professor of Philosophy at the University of Jena, and while there he wrote his major works on science and ethics. When charges of atheism forced him to leave Jena, he went to Berlin where, over the next nine years, he wrote many of his popular works, including *The Vocation of Man* (1800) and *Addresses to the German Nation* (1807–08), the latter considered the Magna Charta of German nationalism. From 1810 to 1812 he served as rector and first professor of Philosophy at the newly founded University of Berlin. During the War of Liberation against the French he contracted typhoid fever and died in 1814.

The Vocation of Man

FAITH

I

That voice within my soul in which I believe, and on account of which I believe everything I do believe, does not command me merely to act in general. . . . This voice of my conscience announces to me precisely what I ought to do, and what leave undone, in every particular situation of life; it accompanies me, if I will but listen to it with attention, through all the events of my life, and never refuses me its teaching when I am called upon to act. It justifies immediate conviction, and irresistibly compels my assent to its behests; it is impossible for me to contend against it.

To listen to it, to obey it honestly and unreservedly, without fear or

From pp. 93–135 of *The Vocation of Man* by Johann Gottlieb Fichte, edited by Roderick M. Chisholm. Copyright © 1956 by The Liberal Arts Press, Inc. Reprinted by permission of the Liberal Arts Press Division of The Bobbs-Merrill Company, Inc.

equivocation: this is my true vocation, the whole end and purpose of my existence. My life ceases to be an empty play without truth or significance. There is something that must absolutely be done for its own sake alone; that which conscience demands of me in this particular situation of life it is mine to do. For this only am I here: to know it, I have understanding; to perform it, I have power.

Through this edict of conscience alone, truth and reality are introduced into my conceptions. I cannot refuse them my attention and my obedience without thereby surrendering the very purposes of my existence.

Hence I cannot withhold my belief from the reality which they announce, without at the same time renouncing my vocation. It is absolutely true, without further proof or confirmation—nay, it is the first truth and the foundation of all other truth and certainty—that this voice must be obeyed. And, therefore, everything becomes to me true and certain whose truth and certainty is presupposed in the possibility of such obedience.

There appear before me in space certain phenomena to which I transfer the idea of myself; I conceive of them as beings like myself. Speculation, when carried out to its last results, has indeed taught me, or would teach me, that these supposed rational beings external to me are but the products of my own presentative power; that, according to certain laws of my thought, I am compelled to represent out of myself my conception of myself; and that, according to the same laws, I can transfer this conception only to certain definite objects. But the voice of my conscience thus speaks: "Whatever these beings may be in and for themselves, you shall act toward them as self-existent, free, substantive beings, wholly independent of yourself. Assume it, as already known, that they can give a purpose to their own being, wholly by themselves and quite independently of you; never interrupt the accomplishment of this purpose, but rather further it to the utmost of your power. Honor their freedom, take up their purposes with love as if they were your own." Thus I ought to act; by this course of action all my thought *ought* to be guided; and it will necessarily be so guided if I have resolved to obey the voice of my conscience. Hence I shall always regard these beings as in possession of an existence for themselves wholly independent of mine, as capable of forming and carrying out their own purposes; from this point of view, I shall never be able to conceive of them otherwise, and my previous speculations regarding them shall vanish like an empty dream. I *think* of them as beings like myself, I have said; but, strictly speaking, it is not by mere thought that they are first presented to me as such. It is by the voice of my conscience, by the command: "Here set a limit to your freedom; here recognize and honor purposes which are not your own." This it is which is first translated into the thought, "Here, certainly and truly, are beings like myself, free and independent." To view them otherwise, I must in action renounce, and in speculation disregard, the voice of my own conscience.

Other phenomena present themselves before me which I do not regard as beings like myself, but as things irrational. Speculation finds no difficulty in showing how the conception of such things is developed solely from my own presentative faculty and its necessary modes of activity. But I apprehend these things, also, through want, desire, and enjoyment. Not by the mental conception, but by hunger, thirst, and their satisfaction does anything become for me food and drink. I am necessitated to believe in the reality of that which threatens my sensuous existence, or in that which alone is able to maintain it. Conscience enters the field in order that it may at once sanctify and restrain this natural impulse. "You shall maintain, exercise, and strengthen yourself and your physical powers, for they have been taken account of in the plans of reason. But you can maintain them only by legitimate use, conformable to their nature. There are also, besides you, many other beings like yourself whose powers have been counted upon like your own, and can be maintained only in the same way as your own. Concede to them the same privilege that has been allowed to you. Respect what belongs to them as their possession—use what belongs to you legitimately as your own." Thus ought I to act—according to this course of action must I think. I am compelled to regard these things as standing under their own natural laws—independent of, though perceivable by, me—and, therefore, to ascribe to them an independent existence. I am compelled to believe in such laws; the task of investigating them is set before me, and that empty speculation vanishes like a mist when the genial sun appears.

In short, there is for me absolutely no such thing as an existence which has no relation to myself, and which I contemplate merely for the sake of contemplating it; whatever has an existence for me has it only through its relation to my own being. But there is, in the highest sense, only one relation to me possible, all others are but subordinate forms of this: my vocation to moral activity. My world is the object and sphere of my duties, and absolutely nothing more; there is no other world for me, and no other qualities of my world; my whole united capacity, all finite capacity, is insufficient to comprehend any other. Whatever possesses an existence for me can bring its existence and reality into contact with me only through this relation, and only through this relation do I comprehend it; for any other existence than this I have no organ whatever.

To the question, whether, in fact, such a world exists as that which I represent to myself, I can give no answer more fundamental, or evident, than this: I have, most certainly and truly, these determinate duties which announce themselves to me as duties toward certain objects, to be fulfilled by means of certain materials—duties which I cannot otherwise conceive of, and cannot otherwise fulfill, than within such a world as I represent to myself. Even to one who had never meditated on his own moral vocation, if there could be such a one, or who, if he had given it some general consideration, had never had any intention of fulfilling at any definite time in the future—even for him, his sensuous world, and his belief in its reality, arises in no other manner than from his ideas of a moral world. If he does not apprehend it by the thought of his duties, he certainly does so by the demand for his rights. What he may never require of himself, he certainly exacts from others in their conduct toward him—that they should treat him with propriety, consideration, and respect, not as an irrational thing, but as a free and independent being. And thus, by supposing in them an ability to comply with his own demands, he is compelled also to regard them as themselves considerate, free, and independent of the dominion of mere natural power. Even should he never propose to himself any other purpose in his use and enjoyment of surrounding objects but simply that of enjoying them, he at least demands this enjoyment as a right in the possession of which he claims to be left undisturbed by others; and thus he apprehends even the irrational world of sense by means of a moral idea. These claims of respect for his rationality, independence, and preservation, no one can resign who possesses a conscious existence; and with these claims, at least, there is united in his soul earnestness, renunciation of doubt, and faith in a reality, even if they be not associated with the recognition of a moral law within him. Take the man who denies his own moral vocation, as well as your existence and the existence of a material world, except as a mere futile speculation—approach him practically, apply his own principles to life and act as if either he had no existence at all or were merely a portion of rude matter; he will soon lay aside his scornful indifference, indignantly complain of you; earnestly call your attention to your conduct toward him, maintain that you should not and must not so act, and thus prove to you, by deeds, that you are assuredly capable of acting upon him; that *he is,* and that *you are,* that there is a *medium through which you can influence him,* and that you, at least, have duties to perform toward him.

Our consciousness of a reality external to ourselves is thus not rooted in the operation of supposed external objects, which indeed exist for us, and we for them, only in so far as we already know of them; nor is it an empty vision evoked by our own imagination and thought, the products of which must, like itself, be mere empty pictures; it is rather the necessary faith in our own freedom and power, in our own real activity, and in the definite laws of human action, which lies at the root of all our consciousness of a reality external to ourselves—a consciousness which is itself but faith, since it is founded on another faith, of which however it is a necessary consequence. We are compelled to believe that we act, and that we ought to act in a certain manner. We are compelled to assume a certain sphere for this action: this sphere is the real, actually present world, such as we find it—and the world is absolutely nothing more than this sphere, and cannot in any way extend beyond it. From this necessity of action proceeds the consciousness of the actual world and not the reverse way; the consciousness of the actual world is derived from the necessity of action. We act not because we know, but we know because we are called upon to act: the practical reason is the root of all reason. The laws of action for rational beings are *immediately certain*; their world is certain only through the fact that they are certain. We cannot deny these laws without plunging the world, and ourselves with it, into absolute annihilation; we raise ourselves from this abyss and maintain ourselves above it, solely by our moral activity.

II

There is something which I am called upon to do, simply in order that it may be done; something to avoid doing, solely that it may be left undone. But can I act without having an end in view beyond the action itself, without directing my intention toward something which can become possible by means of my action, and only by means of it? Can I will without having something which I will? No; this would be contradictory to the very nature of my mind. To every action there is united in my thought, immediately and by the laws of thought itself, a condition of future things, to which my action is related as cause to effect. But this purpose or end of my action must not be proposed to me for its own sake through some necessity, say of Nature, and my course of action then determined according to this end; I must not have an end assigned to me, and then inquire how I must act in order to attain this end; my action must not be dependent on the end: I must act in a certain manner simply because I ought so to act—this is the first point. That a result will follow from this course of action is proclaimed by the voice within me. This result necessarily becomes an end to me, since I am bound to perform the action that brings it, and it alone, to pass. I will that something shall come to pass, because I must act so that it may come to pass. I am hungry not because food is before me, but a thing becomes food for me because I am hungry; similarly, I act as I do not because a certain end is to be attained, but the end becomes an end to me because I am bound to act in the manner by which it may be attained. I do not first view the point toward which I am to draw my line, and then, by its position, determine the direction of my line and the angle it shall make; rather I draw my line absolutely in a right angle, and thereby the points are determined through which my line must pass. The end does not determine the commandment; on the contrary, the immediately given purport of the commandment determines the end.

I say it is the commandment to act that of itself assigns an end to my action—the same inward power that compels me to think that I ought to act thus compels me also to believe that from my action some result will arise; it opens to my spiritual vision a prospect into another world, which is indeed a world, a condition, and not an action, but another and better world than that which is present to the physical eye. It constrains me to aspire after this better world, to embrace it with every power, to long for its realization, to live only in it, and in it alone find satisfaction. The commandment is my guarantee for the certain attainment of this end. The same resolution by which I devote my whole thought and life to the fulfillment of this law, and determine to see nothing beyond it, brings with it the indestructible conviction that the promise it implies is likewise true and certain, and renders it impossible for me even to conceive the possibility of the opposite. As I live in obedience to it, so do I live also in the contemplation of its end—in that better world which it promises to me.

Even in the mere consideration of the world as it is, apart from this law, there arises within me the wish, the desire—no, not the mere desire, but the absolute demand—for a better world. I cast a glance on the present relations of men toward each other and toward Nature: on the feebleness of their powers, on the strength of their desires and passions. A voice within me proclaims with irresistible conviction: "It is impossible that it can remain thus; it must become other and better."

I cannot think of the present state of humanity as that in which it is destined to remain; I am unable to conceive of this as its complete and final vocation. Then, indeed, were all a dream and a delusion; and it would not be worth the trouble to have lived and played out this ever-repeated game which tends to nothing and signifies nothing. Only in so far as I can regard this condition as the means toward a better, as the transition point to a higher and more perfect, condition has it any value in my eyes. I can support it, esteem it, and joyfully perform my part in it, not for its own sake, but for the sake of that better world for which it prepares the way. My soul can accept no place in the present, nor rest in it even for a moment; my whole being flows onward, incessantly and irresistibly, toward that future and better state of things.

Shall I eat and drink only that I may be hungry and thirsty, and eat and drink again, till the grave which is open beneath my feet shall swallow me up and I myself become the food of worms? Shall I beget beings like myself, that they too may eat and drink and die, and leave behind them beings like themselves to do over again the same things that I have done? To what purpose this ever-revolving circle, this ceaseless and unvarying round, in which all things appear only to pass away, and pass away only that they may reappear as they were before—this monster continually devouring itself that it may again bring itself forth, and bringing itself forth only that it may again devour itself?

This can never be the vocation of my being, or of all being. There must be something which exists because it has come into existence, and endures and, having once become such as it is, cannot come anew. This abiding existence must be produced amid the vicissitudes of the transitory and perishable, maintain itself there, and be borne onward, pure and inviolate, upon the waves of time.

Our species still laboriously extorts the means of its subsistence and preservation from an opposing Nature. The larger portion of mankind is still condemned through life to severe toil in order to supply nourishment for itself and for the smaller portion which thinks for it; immortal spirits are compelled to fix their whole thoughts and endeavors on the earth that brings forth their food. It still frequently happens that, when the laborer has completed his toil and has promised himself in return a lasting endurance for himself and for his work, a hostile element will destroy in a moment that which it has cost him years of patient forethought and industry to accomplish, and the assiduous and careful man is undeservedly made the prey of hunger and misery; often do floods, storms, volcanoes desolate whole countries, and works which bear the impress of a rational soul are mingled with their authors in the wild chaos of destruction and death. Disease sweeps into an untimely grave men in the pride of their strength and children whose existence has yet borne no fruit; pestilence stalks through blooming lands, leaves the few who escape its ravages like lonely orphans bereaved of the accustomed support of their fellows, and does all that it can do to give back to the wilderness regions which the labor of man has reclaimed from thence as a possession to himself. Thus it is now, but thus it cannot remain forever. No work that bears the stamp of Reason, and has been undertaken to extend her power, can ever be wholly lost in the onward progress of the ages. The sacrifices which the irregular violence of Nature extorts from Reason must at last exhaust, satiate, and appease that violence. The same power which has burst out into lawless fury cannot again commit like excesses; it cannot be destined to renew its ravages; by its own outbreak its energies must henceforth and forever be exhausted. All those outbreaks of unregulated power before which human strength vanishes into nothing, those desolating hurricanes, those earthquakes, those volcanoes can be nothing but the last struggles of the rude mass against the law of regular, progressive, living, and systematic activity to which it is compelled to submit in opposition to its own undirected impulses—nothing but the last shivering strokes by which the perfect formation of our globe has yet to be accomplished. The resistance must gradually become weaker and at length be worn out, since, in the regulated process of things, there can be nothing to renew its strength; that formation must at length be achieved and our destined dwelling place be made complete. Nature must gradually be resolved into a condition in which her regular action may be calculated and safely relied upon, and her power bear a fixed and definite relation to that which is destined to govern it—that of man. In so far as this relation already exists and the cultivation of Nature has attained a firm footing, the works of man, by their mere existence and by an influence altogether beyond the original intent of their authors, shall again react upon Nature and become to her a new vivifying principle. Cultivation shall quicken and ameliorate the sluggish and baleful atmosphere of primeval forests, deserts, and marshes; more regular and varied cultivation shall diffuse throughout the air new impulses to life and fertility; and the sun shall pour his animating rays into an atmosphere breathed by healthful, industrious, and civilized nations. Science, first called into existence by the pressure of necessity, shall afterwards calmly and deliberately investigate the unchangeable laws of Nature, review its powers at large, and learn to calculate their possible manifestations; and, while closely following the footsteps of Nature in the living and actual world, form for itself in thought a new ideal one. Every discovery that Reason has extorted from Nature shall be maintained throughout the ages and become the ground of new knowledge for the common possession of our species. Thus shall Nature ever become more and more intelligible and transparent, even in her most secret depths; human power, enlightened and armed by human invention, shall rule over her without difficulty, and the conquest, once made, shall be peacefully maintained. This dominion of man over Nature shall gradually be extended until, at length, no further expenditure of mechanical labor shall be necessary than what the human body requires for its development, cultivation, and health; and this labor shall cease to be a burden; for a reasonable being is not destined to be a bearer of burdens.

But it is not Nature, it is Freedom itself, by which the greatest and most terrible disorders incident to our race are produced; man is the cruelest enemy of man. Lawless hordes of savages still wander over vast wildernesses—they meet, and the victor devours his foe at the triumphal feast; or where culture has at length united these wild hordes under some social bond, they attack each other, as nations, with the power which law and union have given them. Defying toil and privation, their armies traverse peaceful plains and forests; they meet each other, and the sight of their brethren is the signal for slaughter. Equipped with the mightiest inventions of the human intellect, hostile fleets plow their way through the ocean; through storm and tempest man rushes to meet his fellow men upon the lonely, inhospitable sea; they meet, and defy the fury of the elements that they may destroy each other with their own hands. Even in the interior of states, where men seem to be united in equality under the law, it is still for the most part only force and fraud which rule under that venerable name; and here the warfare is so much the more shameful that it is not openly declared to be war, and the party attacked is even deprived of the privilege of defending itself against unjust oppression. Combinations of the few rejoice aloud in the ignorance, the folly, the vice, and the misery in which the greater number of their fellow men are sunk, avowedly seek to retain them in this state of degradation, and even to plunge them deeper in it in order to perpetuate their slavery—nay, would destroy anyone who should venture to enlighten or improve them. No attempt at amelioration can anywhere be made without rousing up from slumber a host of selfish interests to war against it, and uniting even the most varied and opposite in a common hostility. The good cause is ever the weaker, for it is simple and can be loved only for itself. Evil attracts each individual by the promise which is most seductive to him; and its adherents, always at war among themselves, so soon as the good makes its appearance, conclude a truce that they may unite the whole powers of their wickedness against it. Scarcely, indeed, is such an opposition needed, for even the good themselves are but too often divided by misunderstanding, error, distrust, and secret self-love, and that so much the more violently, the more earnestly each strives to propagate that which he deems to be the best; and thus internal discord dissipates a power which, even when united, could scarcely hold the balance with evil. One blames the other for rushing onward with stormy impetuosity to his object, without waiting until the way shall have been prepared. He in turn is then blamed that, through hesitation and cowardice, he accomplishes nothing, but allows all things to remain as they are, contrary to his better conviction, because for him the hour of action never arrives. Only the Omniscient can determine whether either of the parties in the dispute is in the right. Everyone regards that undertaking the necessity of which is most apparent to him, and for the prosecution of which he has acquired the greatest skill, as most important and needful—as the point from which all improvement must proceed. Each man requires all good men to unite their efforts with his, and to subject themselves to him for the accomplishment of his particular purpose, holding it to be treason to the good cause if they hold back; while they on the other hand make the same demands upon him and accuse him of similar treason for a similar refusal. Thus do all good intentions among men appear to be lost in vain disputations, which leave behind them no trace of their existence, while in the meantime the world goes on as well, or as ill, as it can without human effort—by the blind mechanism of Nature—and so will go on forever.

And so go on forever? No! unless the whole existence of humanity is to be an idle game, without significance and without end. It cannot be intended that those savage tribes should always remain savage; no race can be born with all the capacities of perfect humanity and yet be destined never to develop these capacities, never to become more than that which a sagacious animal by its own proper nature might become. Those savages must be destined to be the progenitors of more powerful, cultivated, and virtuous generations; otherwise it is impossible to conceive of a purpose in their existence, or even of the possibility of their existence in a world ordered and arranged by reason. Savage races may become civilized, for this has already occurred; the most cultivated nations of modern times are the descendants of savages. Whether civilization is a direct and natural development of human society, or whether it is invariably brought about through instruction and outside example, with superhuman guidance as the primary source of all human culture—in whatever way nations which once were savage have emerged into civilization, those who are yet uncivilized will gradually attain it. They must, no doubt, at first pass through the same dangers and corruptions of a merely sensuous civilization by which the civilized nations are still oppressed, but they will thereby be brought into union with the great whole of humanity and be made capable of taking part in its further progress.

It is the vocation of our species to unite itself into one single body, all the parts of which shall be thoroughly known to each other, and all possessed of similar culture. Nature and even the passions and vices of men have from the beginning tended toward this end; a great part of the way toward it is already passed, and we may surely calculate that this end, which is the condition of all further progress, will in time be attained. Let us not ask of history if man, on the whole, has yet become purely moral! To a more extended, comprehensive, and powerful freedom he has certainly attained; but hitherto it has been an almost necessary result of his position that this choice has been applied chiefly to evil purposes. Neither let us ask whether the aesthetic and intellectual culture of the ancient world, concentrated on a few points, may not have excelled in degree that of modern times! It might happen that we should receive a humiliating answer, and that in this respect the human race has not advanced, but rather seemed to retrograde, in its riper years. But let us ask of history at what period the existing culture has been most widely diffused and distributed among the greatest number of individuals, and we shall doubtless find that, from the beginning of history down to our own day, the few landmarks of civilization have extended themselves abroad from their center, that one individual after another, and one nation after another, has been embraced within their circle, and that this wider outspread of culture is proceeding under our own eyes. And this is the first point to be attained in the endless path on which humanity must advance. Until this shall have been attained, until the existing culture of every age shall have been diffused over the whole inhabited globe and our species become capable of the most unlimited intercommunication with itself, one nation or one continent must pause on the great common path of progress and wait for the advance of the others; and each must bring as an offering to the universal commonwealth, for the sake of which alone it exists, its ages of apparent immobility or retrogression. When that first point shall have been attained, when every useful discovery made at one end of the earth shall be at once made known and communicated to all the rest, then, without further interruption, without halt or regress, with united strength and equal step, humanity shall move onward to a higher culture of which we can at present form no conception.

Within those singular associations, thrown together by unreasoning accident, which we call States—after they have subsisted for a time in peace: when the resistance excited by yet new oppression has been lulled to sleep and the fermentation of contending forces appeased, abuse, by its continuance and by general sufferance, assumes a sort of established form; and the ruling classes, in the uncontested enjoyment of their extorted privileges, have nothing more to do but to extend them further and to give to this extension also the same established form. Urged by their insatiable desires, they will continue from generation to generation their efforts to acquire wider and yet wider privileges, and never say, "It is enough!" At last oppression shall reach its limit and become wholly insupportable, and despair give back to the oppressed that power which their courage, extinguished by centuries of tyranny, could not procure for them. They will then no longer endure any among them who cannot be satisfied to stand and to abide on an equality with others. In order to protect themselves against internal violence or new oppression, all will take on themselves the same obligations. Their deliberations, in which, whatever a man may decide, he decides for himself, and not for one subject to him and whose sufferings will never affect him and in whose fate he takes no concern—deliberations, according to which no one can hope that it shall be he who is to *practice* a permitted injustice, but everyone must fear that he may have to *suffer* it—deliberations that alone deserve the name of legislation, which is something wholly different from the ordinances of combined lords to the countless herds of their slaves—these deliberations will necessarily be guided by justice, and will lay the foundation of a true state, in which each individual, from a regard for his own security, will be irresistibly compelled to respect the security of every other without exception; since, under the supposed legislation, every injury which he should attempt to do another would not fall upon its object but would infallibly recoil upon himself.

By the establishment of this only true state, this firm foundation of internal peace, the possibility of foreign war, at least with other true states, is cut off. In a true state, injury to a citizen of a neighboring state will be forbidden as strictly, and prevented as carefully, as injury to a citizen of its own, and it will call forth the same compensation and punishment. The state will so act for its own sake—to prevent the thought of injustice, plunder, and violence entering the minds of its own citizens, and to leave them no possibility of gain except by means of industry and diligence within their legitimate sphere of activity. This law concerning the security of neighbors is necessarily a law in every state that is not a robber state; and by its operation the possibility of any just complaint of one state against another, and consequently every case of self-defense among nations, is entirely prevented. There are no necessary, permanent, and immediate relations of states, as such, with each other, which should be productive of strife; there are, as a rule, only relations of the individual citizens of one state to the individual citizens of another. A state can be injured only in the person of one of its citizens, but such injury will be immediately compensated, and the aggrieved state satisfied. Between states such as these, there is no rank which can be insulted, no ambition which can be offended. No officer of one state is authorized to intermeddle in the internal affairs of another, nor is there any temptation for him to do so, since he could not derive the slightest personal advantage from any such influence. That a whole nation should determine, for the sake of plunder, to make war on a neighboring country is impossible; for in a state where all are equal, the plunder could not become the booty of a few, but must be equally divided amongst all, and the share of no one individual could ever recompense him for the trouble of the war. Only where the advantage falls to the few oppressors, and the injury, the toil, the expense to the countless herd of slaves, is a war of spoliation possible and conceivable. States such as these do not need to fear war from states like themselves. War is to be feared only from savages or barbarians whose lack of skill to enrich themselves by industry impels them to plunder, or from enslaved nations driven by their masters to a war from which they themselves will reap no advantage. In relation to the first of these dangers, every civilized state already has superior strength because of the arts of civilization; against the latter danger, the common advantage of all demands that they should strengthen themselves by union. No free state can reasonably suffer in its vicinity associations governed by rulers whose interests would be promoted by the subjugation of adjacent nations, and whose very existence is therefore a constant source of danger to their neighbors. A regard for their own security compels all free states to transform all around them into free states like themselves, and thus, for the sake of their own welfare, to extend the empire of culture over barbarism, of freedom over slavery. Soon will the nations civilized or enfranchised by them find themselves placed in the same relation toward others still enthralled by barbarism or slavery in which the earlier free nations formerly stood toward them, and be compelled to do the same things for these which were formerly done for themselves; and thus, of necessity, by reason of the existence of some few really free states will the empire of civilization, freedom, and with it universal peace, gradually embrace the whole world.

Thus, from the establishment of a just internal organization and of peace between individuals, there will necessarily result integrity in the external relations of nations toward each other, and universal peace among them. But the establishment of this just internal organization, and the emancipation of the first nation that shall be truly free, arises as a necessary consequence from the ever-growing oppression exercised by the ruling classes toward their subjects, which gradually becomes insupportable—a progress which may be safely left to the passions and the blindness of those classes, even although warned of the result.

In this sole true state, there will be no temptation to evil—not even the possibility of resolving upon an evil deed with any reasonable hope of benefit. The strongest possible inducements will be offered to every man to make virtue the sole object of his life.

There is no man who loves evil because it is evil; it is only the advantages and enjoyments expected from it—and which, in the present condition of humanity, do actually, in most cases, result from it—that are loved. So long as this condition shall continue, so long as a premium shall be set upon vice, a fundamental improvement of mankind, as a whole, can scarcely be hoped for. But in a civil society constituted as it ought to be, as reason requires it to be, as the thinker may easily describe it to himself although he may nowhere find it actually existing at the present day, but as it must necessarily exist in the first nation that shall really acquire true freedom—in such a state of society evil will present no advantages, but rather the most certain disadvantages; and self-love itself will restrain the excess of self-love when it would run out into injustice. By the unerring administration of such a state every fraud or oppression practiced upon others, all self-aggrandizement at their expense, will be rendered vain, and all labor so applied fruitless; moreover, such attempts would even recoil upon their author and assuredly bring home to himself the evil which he would cause to others. He will be punished for every injury he inflicts, whether in his own land or outside of his own land, no matter where in the whole world it may be. But it is not to be expected, even of a bad man, that he would decide upon evil merely for the sake of such a decision if he had no power to carry it into effect and if nothing could arise from it but infamy to himself. The use of liberty for evil purposes is thus destroyed; man must resolve either to renounce his freedom altogether, and patiently to become a mere passive wheel in the great machine of the universe, or else to employ it for good. In soil thus prepared good will easily prosper. When men shall no longer be divided by selfish purposes, nor their powers exhausted in struggles with each other, nothing will remain for them but to direct their united strength against the one common enemy which still remains unsubdued—resisting, uncultivated Nature. No longer estranged from each other by private ends, they will necessarily combine for this common object; and thus there arises a body everywhere animated by the same spirit and the same love. Every misfortune to the individual, since it can no longer be a gain to any other individual, is a misfortune to the whole and to each undividual member of the whole; and is felt with the same pain, and remedied with the same activity, by every member; every step in advance made by one man is a step in advance made by the whole race. Here, where the petty, narrow self of mere individual personality is lost in the more comprehensive unity of the social constitution, each man truly loves every other as himself—as a member of this greater *self* which now claims all his love, and of which he himself is no more than a member, capable of participating only in a common gain or in a common loss. The strife of evil against good is here abolished, for here no evil can intrude. The strife of the good among themselves for the sake of good disappears now that they find it easy to love good for its own sake alone and not because they are its authors; now that it has become all-important to them that the truth should really be discovered, that the useful action should be done—no matter who may be the one who accomplishes it. Here each individual is at all times ready to join his strength to that of others, to make it subordinate to that of others; and whoever is acknowledged by all as most capable of accomplishing the greatest amount of good will be supported by all, and his success rejoiced in by all.

This is the purpose of earthly life, which Reason sets before us, and for the infallible attainment of which she is our pledge and security. It is not a goal which is given to us only that we may strive after it for the mere purpose of exercising our powers on something great, the real existence of which we may perhaps be compelled to abandon to doubt—it shall, it must be realized; there must be a time in which it shall be accomplished, as surely as there is a sensible world and a species of reasonable beings existent in time with respect to which nothing earnest and rational is conceivable besides this purpose, and whose existence becomes intelligible only through this purpose. Unless all human life be metamorphosed into a mere theatrical display for the gratification of some malignant spirit, who has implanted in poor humanity this inextinguishable longing for the imperishable only to amuse himself with its ceaseless pursuit of that which it can never overtake, with its ever-repeated efforts to embrace that which still eludes its grasp, with its restless hurrying on in an ever-recurring circle—only to mock its earnest aspirations with an empty, insipid farce; unless the wise man, seeing through this mockery, and feeling an irrepressible disgust at continuing to play his part in it, is to cast life indignantly from him and make the moment of his awakening to reason also that of his physical death—unless these things are so, this purpose most assuredly must be attained. Yes! it is attainable *in life,* and *through life,* for Reason commands me to live: it is attainable, for *I am.*

.　　.　　.

III

My will is mine, and it is the only thing that is wholly mine and entirely dependent on myself; and through it I have already become a citizen of the realm of freedom and of pure spiritual activity. What determination of my will—of the only thing by which I am raised from earth into this region—is best adapted to the order of the spiritual world is proclaimed to me at every moment by my conscience, the bond that constantly unites me to the spiritual world; it depends solely on myself to give my activity the appointed direction. Thus I cultivate myself for this world, labor in it and for it, in cultivating one of its members; in it, and only in it, I pursue my purpose according to a settled plan, without doubt or hesitation, certain of the result, since here no foreign power stands opposed to my free will. That in the world of sense my will, truly so called, also becomes an action is but the law of this sensuous world. I did not send forth the act as I did the will; only the latter was wholly and purely my work—it was all that proceeded forth from me. It was not even necessary that there should be another particular act on my part to unite the deed to the will; the deed unites itself to it according to the law of that second world with which I am connected through my will, and in which this will is likewise an original force, as it is in the first. When I regard my will, determined according to the dictates of conscience, as a fact and an efficient cause in the world of sense, I am indeed compelled to refer it to that earthly purpose of humanity as a means to the accomplishment of an end. But I do not first survey the plan of the world and from this knowledge calculate what I have to do; rather the specific action which conscience directly enjoins me to do reveals itself to me at once as the only means by which, in my position, I can contribute to the attainment of that end. Even if it should afterwards appear as if this end had not been promoted—nay, if it should even seem to have been hindered—by my action, yet I can never regret it, nor perplex myself about it, so surely as I have truly obeyed my conscience in performing this act. Whatever consequences it may have in this world, in the other world there can nothing but good result from it. And even in this world, should my action appear to have failed of its purpose, my conscience *for that very reason* commands me to repeat it in a manner by which it may more effectually reach its end; or, should the action seem to have hindered that purpose, my conscience *for that very reason* commands me to make good the detriment and annihilate the untoward result. I will as I *ought,* and the new deed follows. It may happen that the consequences of this new action, in the world of sense, may appear to me not more beneficial than those of the first; but with respect to the other world I retain the same calm assurance as before; and in the present it is again my bounden duty to make good my previous failure by new action. And thus should it appear that, during my whole earthly life, I have not advanced the good cause a single hair's breadth in this world, yet I dare not cease my efforts: after every unsuccessful attempt I must still believe that the next will be successful. But in the spiritual world no step is ever lost. In short, I pursue the earthly purpose not for its own sake alone or as a final aim, but only because my true final aim, obedience to the law of conscience, does not present itself to me in this world in any other shape than as the advancement of this end. I may not cease to pursue it unless I were to deny the law of duty, or unless that law were to manifest itself to me, in this life, in some other shape than as a commandment to promote this purpose in my own place; I shall actually cease to pursue it in another life in which that commandment shall have set before me some other purpose wholly incomprehensible to me here. In this life, I must *will* to promote it, because I must obey; whether it be *actually* promoted by the deed that follows my will thus fittingly directed is not my concern: I am responsible only for the *will* (which indeed in the world of sense can have to do only with the earthly purpose), but not for the result. Previous to the actual deed I can never resign this purpose; the deed, when it is completed, I may resign and repeat it or improve it. Thus do I live and labor, even here, in my most essential nature and in my nearest purposes, only for the other world; and my activity for it is the only thing of which I am completely certain. In the world of sense I labor only for the sake of the other, and only because I cannot work for the other without at least *willing* to work for the world of sense.

     .   .   .

This, then, is my whole sublime vocation, my true nature. I am a member of two orders: the one purely spiritual, in which I rule by my will alone; the other sensuous, in which I operate by my deed. The sole end of reason is pure activity, absolutely by itself alone, having no need of any instrument outside of itself—independent of everything which is not reason, absolutely unconditioned. The will is the living principle of reason—is itself reason, when purely and simply apprehended. That reason is active by itself alone—this means that pure will, merely as such, lives and rules. It is only the Infinite Reason that lives immediately and wholly in this purely spiritual order. The finite reason—which does not of itself constitute the world of reason, but is only one of its many members—lives necessarily at the same time in a sensuous order; that is to say, in one which presents to it an end other than the pure activity of reason: a material goal to be promoted by instruments and powers which indeed stand under the immediate dominion of the will, but whose activity is also conditioned by their own natural laws. Yet, as surely as reason is reason, the will must operate absolutely by itself and independently of the natural laws by which the material action is determined; and hence the sensuous life of every finite being points toward a higher life, into which the will, by itself alone, may open the way, and of which it may acquire possession—a possession which indeed we are again constrained to conceive of sensuously as a state, and not as a mere will.

These two orders—the purely spiritual and the sensuous, the latter consisting possibly of an innumerable series of particular lives—have existed for me since the first moment of the development of an active reason within me, and still continue parallel to each other. The latter order is only a phenomenon for myself, and for those with whom I am associated in this life; the former alone gives it significance, purpose, and value. I *am* immortal, imperishable, eternal, as soon as I form the resolution to obey the laws of reason; I do not need to *become* so. The supersensual world is no future world; it is now present; it can at no point of finite existence be more present than at another; not more present after an existence of myriads of lives than at this moment. My sensuous existence may, in the future, assume other forms, but these will be just as little the true life as is its present form. By that resolution I lay hold on eternity, and cast off this earthly life and all other forms of sensuous life which may yet lie before me, and place myself far above them. I become the sole source of my own being and its phenomena, and, henceforth, unconditioned by anything without me, I have life in myself. My will, directed by no foreign agency in the order of the supersensual world but by myself alone, is this source of true life, and of eternity.

But it is my will alone which is this source of true life and of eternity: only by recognizing this will as the true seat of moral goodness, and by actually raising it thereto, do I obtain the assurance and the possession of that supersensual world.

Without regard to any conceivable or visible object, without inquiry as to whether my will may be followed by any result other than the mere volition, I must will in accordance with the moral law. My will stands alone, apart from all that is not itself, and is its own world merely by itself and for itself; not only as being itself an absolutely *first,* primary and original, power, before which there is no preceding influence by which it may be governed, but also as being followed by no conceivable or comprehensible *second* step in the series, by which its activity may be brought under the dominion of a foreign law. If there were to proceed from it any second result, and from this again a third result, and so on, in any conceivable sensuous world distinct from the spiritual world, then its strength would be broken by the resistance of the independent elements which such a world would set in motion; the mode of its activity would no longer exactly correspond to the purpose expressed in the volition; and the will would be no longer free, but be in so far limited by the laws of its heterogeneous sphere of action. And thus must I actually regard the will in the present sensuous world, the only world known to me. I am indeed compelled to believe, and consequently to act as if I thought, that by my mere volition my tongue, my hand, or my foot may be set in motion; but how a mere aspiration, an impress of intelligence upon itself, such as will is, can be the principle of motion to a heavy material mass—this I not only find impossible to conceive, but the mere assertion is, before the tribunal of the understanding, a palpable absurdity. Here the movement of matter, even in myself, can be explained only by the internal forces of matter itself.

Such a view of my will as I have taken, however, is not attained merely through the conviction that the will is the highest active principle for this world—which it certainly might be, without having freedom in itself, by the mere energy of the system of the universe, such as we must conceive of the formative power in Nature. The will rejects absolutely all earthly purposes, all purposes lying outside itself, and recognizes itself, for its own sake, as its own ultimate end. By such a view of my will I am at once directed to a supersensual order of things in which the will, by itself alone and without any instrument lying outside of itself, becomes an efficient cause in a sphere which, like itself, is purely spiritual, and is thoroughly accessible to it. That moral volition is demanded of us absolutely for its own sake alone —a truth which I discover only as a fact in my inward consciousness, and to the knowledge of which I cannot attain in any other way: this was the first step of my thought. That this demand is reasonable, and the source and standard of all else that is reasonable; that it is not modeled upon any other thing whatever, but that all other things must, on the contrary, model themselves upon it, and be dependent upon it—a conviction which, again, I cannot arrive at from without, but can attain only by inward experience, by means of the unhesitating and immovable assent which I freely accord to this demand—this was the second step of my thought. And from these two terms I have attained to faith in a supersensual Eternal World. If I abandon the former, the latter falls to the ground. If it were true—as many say it is, assuming it without further proof as self-evident and extolling it as the highest summit of human wisdom—that all human virtue must have before it a certain definite external object, and that it must first be assured of the possibility of attaining this object, before it can act and before it can become virtue; and if, conseqently, reason by no means contained within itself the principle and the standard of its own activity, but were forced to receive this standard from without through contemplation of an external world—if this were true, then the ultimate end of our existence might be accomplished here below: human nature might be completely developed and exhausted by our earthly vocation, and we should have no rational ground for raising our thoughts above the present life.

. . .

IV

My lawful will, merely as such, in and through itself, shall certainly and invariably produce consequences; every determination of my will in accordance with duty, although no action should follow it, shall operate in another, to me incomprehensible, world in which nothing but this moral determination of the will shall possess efficient activity. What is it that is assumed in this conception?

Obviously a *law*—a rule absolutely without exception, according to which a will determined by duty must have consequences; just as in the material world which surrounds me I assume a law according to which this ball when thrown by my hand with this particular force, in this particular direction, necessarily moves in such a direction with a certain degree of velocity—perhaps strikes another ball with a certain amount of force, which in its turn moves on with a certain velocity, and so on. As here, in the mere direction and motion of my hand, I already recognize and apprehend all the consequent directions and movements with the same certainty as if they were already present before me, even so do I embrace by means of my virtuous will a series of necessary and inevitable consequences in the spiritual world as if they were already present before me; but I cannot define them as I do those in the material world. I know only that they must be, but not *how* they shall be; and even in knowing this I conceive of a *law* of the spiritual world in which my pure will is one of the moving forces, as my hand is one of the moving forces of the material world. My own firm confidence in these results and the conceptions of this *law* of a spiritual world are one and the same; they are not two thoughts, one of which arises by means of the other, but they are entirely the same thought, just as the confidence with which I calculate on a certain motion in a material body and the conception of a mechanical law of nature on which that motion depends are one and the same. The conception of a *law* expresses nothing more than the firm, immovable confidence of reason in a principle, and the absolute impossibility of admitting its opposite.

I assume such a law of a spiritual world—not given by my will nor by the will of any finite being, nor by the will of all finite beings taken together, but a law to which my will, and the will of all finite beings, is subject. Neither I, nor any finite and therefore sensuous being, can conceive how a mere will can have consequences, nor what may be the true nature of those consequences; for herein consists the essential character of our finite nature—that we are unable to conceive this, that, having indeed our will as such wholly within our power, we are yet compelled by our sensuous nature to regard the consequences of that will as sensuous states. How, then, can I or any finite being whatever propose as object, and thereby give reality to, something we can neither imagine nor conceive? I cannot say that, in the material world, my hand, or any other body which belongs to that world and is subject to the universal law of gravity, brings this law into operation; these bodies themselves stand under this law and are able to set another body in motion only in accordance with this law, and only in so far as that body, by virtue of this law, partakes of the universal moving power of Nature. Just as little can a finite will give a law to the supersensual world which no finite spirit can embrace; but all finite wills stand under the law of that world and can produce results therein only inasmuch as that law already exists, and inasmuch as they themselves, in accordance with the form of that law which is applicable to finite wills, bring themselves under its conditions and within the sphere of its activity by moral obedience—by moral obedience, I say, the only tie which unites them to that higher world, the only nerve that descends from it to them, and the only organ through which they can react upon it. As the universal power of attraction embraces all bodies and holds them together in themselves and with each other, and the movement of each separate body is possible only on the supposition of this power, so does that supersensual law unite, hold together, and embrace all finite reasonable beings. My will, and the will of all finite beings, may be regarded from a double point of view: partly as a mere *volition,* an internal act directed upon itself alone, and in so far the will is complete in itself, concluded in this act of volition; and partly as something beyond this, a *fact.* It assumes the latter form to me as soon as I regard it as completed, but it must also become so beyond me; in the *world of sense,* as the moving principle, for instance, of my hand, from the movement of which again other movements follow; in the *supersensual world,* as the principle of a series of spiritual consequences of which I have no conception. In the former point of view, as a mere act of volition, it stands wholly within my own power; its assumption of the latter character, that of an active first principle, depends not upon me, but on a law to which I myself am subject—on the law of nature in the world of sense, on a supersensual law in the world of pure thought.

What, then, is this law of the spiritual world which I conceive? This idea now stands before me in fixed and perfect shape; I cannot and dare not add anything whatever to it; I have only to express and interpret it distinctly. It is obviously not such as I may suppose the principle of my own, or any other possible sensuous world, to be—a fixed, inert existence, altogether different from a mere will, something from which by the encounter of a will an internal power may be evolved. For—and this is the substance of my belief—my will, absolutely by itself, and without the intervention of any instrument that might weaken its expression, shall act in a perfectly congenial sphere; reason shall act upon reason, spirit upon spirit, in a sphere to which nevertheless my will does not give the law of life, activity, and progress, but which has that law in itself; my will shall act, therefore, upon self-active reason. But self-active reason is will. The law of the super-sensual world must, therefore, be a *will*—a will which operates purely as will, by itself and absolutely, without any instrument or sensible material of its activity; which is at the same time both act and product; with whom to "will" is to do, to command is to execute; in which, therefore, the instinctive demand of reason for absolute freedom and independence is realized; a will which in itself is law, determined by no fancy or caprice, through no previous reflection, hesitation, or doubt, but eternal, unchangeable, on which we may securely and infallibly rely as the physical man relies with certainty on the laws of his world; a will in which the moral will of finite beings, and this alone, has sure and unfailing results; since for all else it is unavailing and for it all else is as nothing.

That sublime will thus pursues no solitary path withdrawn from the other parts of the world of reason. There is a spiritual bond between Him and all finite rational beings; and He himself is this spiritual bond of the rational universe. Let me will, purely and decidedly, my duty; and He wills that, in the spiritual world at least, my will shall prosper. Every moral resolution of a finite being goes up before Him, and—to speak after the manner of mortals—moves and determines Him, not in consequence of a momentary satisfaction, but in accordance with the eternal law of His being. With surprising clearness does this thought, which hitherto was veiled in obscurity, now reveal itself to my soul—the thought that my will, merely as such and through itself, shall have results. It has results because it is immediately and infallibly perceived by another will to which it is related, which is its own accomplishment and the only living principle of the spiritual world; *in Him* it has its first results, and *through Him* it acquires an influence on the whole spiritual world, which throughout is but a product of that Infinite Will.

Thus do I approach—the mortal must speak in his own language—thus do I approach that Infinite Will; and the voice of conscience in my soul, which teaches me in every situation of life what I have there to do, is the channel through which again His influence descends upon me. That voice, made audible by my environment and translated into my language, is the oracle of the Eternal World which announces to me how I am to perform my part in the order of the spiritual universe, or in the Infinite Will who is Himself that order. I cannot, indeed, survey or comprehend that spiritual order, and I need not do so; I am but a link in its chain and can no more judge of the whole than a single tone of music can judge of the entire harmony of which it forms a part. But what I myself ought to be in this harmony of spirits I must know, for it is only I myself who can make me so—and this is immediately revealed to me by a voice whose tones descend upon me from that other world. Thus do I stand connected with the One who alone has existence, and thus do I participate in His being. There is nothing real, lasting, imperishable in me, save these two elements: the voice of conscience, and my free obedience. By the first, the spiritual world bows down to me and embraces me as one of its members; by the second, I raise myself into this world, apprehend it, and react upon it. That Infinite Will is the mediator between it and me; for He Himself is the original source of both it and me. This is the one True and Imperishable for which my soul yearns even from its inmost depths; all else is mere appearance, ever vanishing, and ever returning in a new semblance.

QUESTIONS FOR STUDY AND DISCUSSION

1. How does man's belief in the existence of an external world follow from his consciousness of freedom?
2. Explain Fichte's statement: "The commandment to act of itself assigns an end to my action."
3. How does Fichte think that a perpetual peace among men is to be realized?
4. In what sense does the effect of a volition always equal the intention of the agent?
5. What does Fichte understand by "the law of the supersensual world"?

G. W. F. Hegel

GEORG WILHELM FRIEDRICH HEGEL, the giant of nineteenth-century philosophy, was born in Stuttgart in 1770. He studied theology at the
University of Tübingen and served as a private tutor before joining the
faculty of the University of Jena in 1805. Subsequently he served as
editor of the *Kritische Journal der Philosophie,* rector of the Gymna-
sium at Nuremberg, and professor at the University of Heidelberg. In
1818 he went to the University of Berlin, where he occupied the chair of
Philosophy until his death in 1831. As professor at Berlin he had enormous influence through both his lectures and his writings. Hegel's first
major publication was the monumental *Phenomenology of Mind*
(1807). Among his other important works are *Science of Logic* (1812–
16), *Encyclopaedia of the Philosophical Sciences* (1817), and *Philosophy
of Right* (1821).

The Spirit of Christianity

THE MORAL TEACHING OF JESUS: THE SERMON ON THE MOUNT
CONTRASTED WITH THE MOSAIC LAW AND WITH KANT'S ETHICS

(261) Jesus appeared shortly before the last crisis produced by the fermentation of the multiplex elements in the Jewish fate. In this time of inner
fermentation, while these varied elements were developing until they became concentrated into a whole and until sheer oppositions and open war
[with Rome] were the result, several partial outbreaks preceded the final
act. Men of commoner soul, though of strong passions, comprehended the
fate of the Jewish people only partially; hence they were not calm enough
either to let its waves carry them along passively and unconsciously and so
just to swim with the tide or, alternatively, to await the further development necessary before a stronger power could be associated with their
efforts. The result was that they outran the fermentation of the whole and
fell without honor and without achievement.

Jesus did not fight merely against one part of the Jewish fate; to have

From pp. 205–24 of *The Spirit of Christianity,* in *On Christianity: Early Theological
Writings* by G. W. F. Hegel, translated by T. M. Knox. Copyright 1948 by the University of Chicago. Reprinted with the permission of Harper & Row, Publishers. The
numbers in parentheses refer to the pages in the original German edition, *Hegels
theologische Jugendschriften,* edited by Hermann Nohl (Tubingen, 1907).

done so would have implied that he was himself in the toils of another part, and he was not; he set himself against the whole. Thus he was himself raised above it and tried to raise his people above it too. But enmities like those he sought to transcend can be overcome only by valor; they cannot be reconciled by love. Even *his* sublime effort to overcome the whole of the Jewish fate must therefore have failed with his people, and he was bound to become its victim himself. Since Jesus had aligned himself with no aspect of the Jewish fate at all, his religion was bound to find a great reception not among his own people (for it was too much entangled in its fate) but in the rest of the world, among men who no longer had to defend or uphold any share of the fate in question.

Rights which a man sacrifices if he freely recognizes and establishes powers over himself, regulations which, in the spirit of Jesus, we might recognize as grounded in the living modification of human nature [i.e., in an individual human being] were simply commands for the Jews and positive throughout. The order in which the various kinds of Jewish laws (laws about worship, moral laws, and civil laws) are followed here is for them, therefore, (262) a strange and manufactured order, since religious, moral, and civil laws were all equally positive in Jewish eyes, and distinctions between these types are first introduced for the Jews as a result of the manner of Jesus' reaction to them.

Over against commands which required a bare service of the Lord, a direct slavery, an obedience without joy, without pleaure or love, i.e., the commands in connection with the service of God, Jesus set their precise opposite, a human urge and so a human need. Religious practice is the most holy, the most beautiful, of all things; it is our endeavor to unify the discords necessitated by our development and our attempt to exhibit the unification in the *ideal* as fully *existent,* as no longer opposed to reality, and thus to express and confirm it in a deed. It follows that, if that spirit of beauty be lacking in religious actions, they are the most empty of all; they are the most senseless bondage, demanding a consciousness of one's annihilation, or deeds in which man expresses his nullity, his passivity. The satisfaction of the commonest human want rises superior to actions like these, because there lies directly in such a want the sensing or the preserving of a human being, no matter how empty his being may be.

. . .

His disciples gave offense to the Jews by plucking ears of corn on the Sabbath. The hunger which was their motive could find no great satisfaction in these ears of corn; reverence for the Sabbath might well have postponed this trifling satisfaction for all the time necessary for going to a place where they could get cooked food. Jesus contrasted David with the Pharisees who censured this unlawful action, but David had seized the shewbread in extreme need. Jesus also adduced the desecration of the Sabbath by priestly duties; but, since these were lawful, they were no desecration. On the one hand, he magnifies the transgression by the very remark that, while the priests desecrate the Sabbath in the temple merely, here is a greater than the temple, i.e., nature is holier than the temple; and, on the other hand, his general drift is to lift nature, which for the Jews is godless and unholy, above that single restricted building, made by Jewish hands, which was in their view the only part of the world related to God. In plain terms, however, he contrasts the sanctification of a time [the seventh day] with men and declares that the former is inferior to a trivial satisfaction of a human need.

On the same day Jesus healed a withered hand. The Jews' own behavior in connection with a sheep in danger proved to them, like David's misuse of the sacred bread, or the functions of priests on the Sabbath, that even in their own eyes the holiness of the day did not count as absolute, that (264) they themselves knew something higher than the observance of this command. But even here the example which he brings before the Jews is an example of need, and need cancels guilt. The animal which falls into the pit demands instant aid; but whether the man lacked the use of his hand or not until sunset was entirely a matter of indifference. The action of Jesus expressed his whim to perform the action a few hours earlier and the primacy of such a whim over a command issued by the highest authority.

Against the custom of washing the hands before eating bread Jesus puts [Matthew xv. 2] the whole subjectivity of man; and above bondage to a command, above the purity or impurity of an object, he puts purity or impurity of heart. He made undetermined subjectivity, character, a totally different sphere, one which was to have nothing in common with the punctilious following of objective commands.

. . .

We might have expected Jesus to work . . . against the positivity of moral commands, against sheer legality, and to show that, although the legal is a universal whose entire obligatoriness lies in its universality, still, even if every ought, every command, declares itself as something alien, nevertheless as concept (universality) it is something subjective, and, as subjective, as a product of a human power (i.e., of reason as the capacity for universality), it loses its objectivity, its positivity, its heteronomy, and the thing commanded is revealed as grounded in an autonomy of the human will. By this line of argument, however, positivity is only partially removed; and between the Shaman of the Tungus, (266) the European prelate who rules church and state, the Voguls, and the Puritans, on the one hand, and the man who listens to his own command of duty, on the other, the difference is not that the former make themselves slaves, while the latter is free, but that the former have their lord outside themselves, while the latter carries his lord in himself, yet at the same time is his own slave.[1] For the particular—impulses, inclinations, pathological love,

---

[1] Kant held that the only actions which had moral worth were those done "from duty," and Hegel interpreted him as meaning that morality required us to follow the moral law of duty even to the thwarting of all our inclinations. Since the

sensuous experience, or whatever else it is called—the universal is necessarily and always something alien and objective. There remains a residuum
of indestructible positivity which finally shocks us because the content
which the universal command of duty acquires, a specific duty, contains the
contradiction of being restricted and universal at the same time and makes
the most stubborn claims for its one-sidedness, i.e., on the strength of possessing universality of form. Woe to the human relations which are not unquestionably found in the concept of duty; for this concept (since it is not
merely the empty thought of universality but is to manifest itself in an action) excludes or dominates all other relations.

One who wished to restore man's humanity in its entirety could not
possibly have taken a course like this, because it simply tacks on to man's
distraction of mind an obdurate conceit. To act in the spirit of the laws
could not have meant for him "to act out of respect for duty and to contradict inclinations," for both "parts of the spirit" (no other words can describe this distraction of soul), just by being thus divergent, would have
been not in the spirit of the laws but against that spirit, one part because it
was something exclusive and so self-restricted, the other because it was
something suppressed.[2]

This spirit of Jesus, a spirit raised above morality,[3] is visible, directly
attacking laws, in the Sermon on the Mount, which is an attempt, elaborated in numerous examples, to strip the laws of legality, of their legal
form. The Sermon does not teach reverence for the laws; on the contrary, it
exhibits that which fulfils the law but annuls it as law and so is something
higher than obedience to law and makes law superfluous. Since the commands of duty presuppose a cleavage [between reason and inclination]

---

moral law is, in Kant's view, the law of man's own reason, to follow it is to be free.
A man's will may be determined by impulses and other purely natural factors, and
in that event he is not free but the slave of his passions; he is still a slave if it is
determined by the "positive" commands of an external authority, i.e., by commands
posited or laid down by fiat and not deducible from the rational will itself; but
alternatively the will may be self-determining, i.e., obedient to the moral law
issued by the rational will itself. If was from this point of view that in his *Religion
Within the Bounds of Reason Alone* (iv. 2. § 3) Kant said that between the Shaman
and the European prelate, between the Voguls and the Puritans, there was a great
difference in manner, but none in principle; all alike they were obeying positive
authorities, external commands, and not the law of their own reason. Hegel retorts
that the man whose inclinations are in bondage to reason is also a slave, though a
slave of himself; from the point of view of human needs and passions, a man is
asked by Kant to obey commands which are just as external and positive (so far
as these needs are concerned) as the commands of a positive religion. For Kant,
man remains a duality; reason tries to thwart desire, but the two are never syn-
thesized. Hegel attempts to show that a unification of the personality is possible
through love and religion. (The Tungus and the Voguls are Siberian tribes.) For
"pathological love" see *Kant's Theory of Ethics,* trans. T. K. Abbott (London,
1923), p. 176. [T.M.K.]
[2] The two parts are (1) reason, which excludes inclination, and (2) inclination,
suppressed by reason. [T.M.K.]
[3] Morality interpreted, as in the view ascribed by Hegel to Kant, as the domination
of inclination by reason [T.M.K.]

and since the domination of the concept declares itself in a "thou shalt," that which is raised above this cleavage is by contrast an "is," a modification of life, a modification which is exclusive and therefore restricted only if looked at in reference to the object, since the exclusiveness is given only through the restrictedness of the object and only concerns the object.[4] When Jesus expresses in terms of commands what he sets against and above the laws (think not that I [267] wish to destroy the law; let your word be; I tell you not to resist, etc.; love God and your neighbor), this turn of phrase is a command in a sense quite different from that of the "shalt" of a moral imperative. It is only the sequel to the fact that, when life is conceived in thought or given expression, it acquires a *form* alien to it, a conceptual form, while, on the other hand, the moral imperative is, as a universal, in *essence* a concept. And if in this way life appears in the form of something due to reflection, something said to men, then this type of expression (a type inappropriate to life): "Love God above everything and thy neighbor as thyself" was quite wrongly regarded by Kant as a "command requiring respect for a law which commands love." And it is on this confusion of the utterly accidental kind of phraseology expressive of life with the moral imperative (which depends on the opposition between concept and reality) that there rests Kant's profound reduction of what he calls a "command" (love God first of all and thy neighbor as thyself) to his moral imperative. And his remark that "love," or, to take the meaning which he thinks must be given to this love, *"liking* to perform all duties," "cannot be commanded" falls to the ground by its own weight, because in love all thought of duties vanishes. And so also even the honor which he bestows in another way on that expression of Jesus by regarding it as an ideal of holiness unattainable by any creature, is squandered to no purpose; for such an "ideal," in which duties are represented as willingly done, is self-contradictory, since duties require an opposition, and an action that we like to do requires none. And he can suffer this unresolved contradiction in his ideal because he declares that rational creatures (a remarkable juxtaposition of words) can fall but cannot attain that ideal.

Jesus begins the Sermon on the Mount [Matthew v. 2–16] with a species of paradox in which his whole soul forthwith and unambiguously declares to the multitude of expectant listeners that they have to expect from him something wholly strange, a different genius, a different world. There are cries in which he enthusiastically deviates directly from the common estimate of virtue, enthusiastically proclaims a new law and light, a

---

[4] Hegel seems to be thinking here of a precept such as "Love thy neighbor." Love he regards as a "modification of life" (i.e., life expressing itself in a specific mode) and so as an attitude in which the lover's whole self is at one; the lover's reason and inclination are in harmony. The restricted form of the precept (love thy *neighbor*) is a restriction which concerns not the lover but the object of his love; and the restriction is added to the precept (which otherwise would consist of the word "love" only) simply because the object of love is necessarily a restricted object. [T.M.K.]

new region of life whose relation to the world could only be to be hated and persecuted by it. In this Kingdom of Heaven [Matthew v. 17–20], however, what he discovers to them is not that laws disappear but that they must be kept through a righteousness of a new kind, in which there is more than is in the righteousness of the sons of duty and which is more complete because it supplements the deficiency in the laws [or "fulfils" them].

(268) This supplement he goes on to exhibit in several laws. This expanded content we may call an inclination so to act as the laws may command, i.e., a unification of inclination with the law whereby the latter loses its form as law. This correspondence with inclination is the πλήρωμα [fulfilment] of the law; i.e., it is an "is," which, to use an old expression, is the "complement of possibility," since possibility is the object as something thought, as a universal, while "is" is the synthesis of subject and object, in which subject and object have lost their opposition. Similarly, the inclination [to act as the laws may command], a virtue, is a synthesis in which the law (which, because it is universal, Kant always calls something "objective") loses its universality and the subject its particularity; both lose their opposition, while in the Kantian conception of virtue this opposition remains, and the universal becomes the master and the particular the mastered. The correspondence of inclination with law is such that law and inclination are no longer different; and the expression "correspondence of inclination with the law" is therefore wholly unsatisfactory because it implies that law and inclination are still particulars, still opposites. Moreover, the expression might easily be understood to mean that a support of the moral disposition, of reverence for the law, of the will's determinacy by the law, was forthcoming from the inclination which was other than the law, and since the things in correspondence with one another would on this view be different, their correspondence would be only fortuitous, only the unity of strangers, a unity in thought only. In the "fulfilment" of both the laws and duty, their concomitant, however, the moral disposition, etc., ceases to be the universal, opposed to inclination, and inclination ceases to be particular, opposed to the law, and therefore this correspondence of law and inclination is life and, as the relation of differents to one another, love; i.e., it is an "is" which expressed as (α) concept, as law, is of necessity congruent with law, i.e., with itself, or as (β) reality, as inclination opposed to the concept, is likewise congruent with itself, with inclination.[5]

The command "Thou shalt not kill" [Matthew v. 21–22] is a maxim (269) which is recognized as valid for the will of every rational being and

---

[5] In a canceled passage (Nohl, p. 268, note) Hegel wrote here: "A command can express no more than an ought or a shall, because it is a universal, but it does not express an 'is'; and this at once makes plain its deficiency. Against such commands Jesus set virtue, i.e., a loving disposition, which makes the content of the command superfluous and destroys its form as a command, because that form implies an opposition between a commander and something resisting the command." The loving disposition is said to be congruent with both law and inclination because it is the synthesis of these. [T.M.K.]

which can be valid as a principle of a universal legislation. Against such a command Jesus sets the higher genius of reconcilability (a modification of love) which not only does not act counter to this law but makes it wholly superfluous; it has in itself a so much richer, more living, fulness that so poor a thing as a law is nothing for it at all. In reconcilability the law loses its form, the concept is displaced by life; but what reconcilability thereby loses in respect of the universality which grips all particulars together in the concept is only a seeming loss and a genuine infinite gain on account of the wealth of living relations with the individuals (perhaps few) with whom it comes into connection. It excludes not a reality but only thoughts and possibilities, while the form of the command and this wealth of possibility in the universality of the concept is itself a rending of life; and the content of the command is so indigent that it permits any transgression except the one it forbids. For reconcilability, on the other hand, even anger is a crime and amounts to the quick reaction of feeling to an oppression, the uprush of the desire to oppress in turn, which is a kind of blind justice and so presupposes equality, though the equality of enemies. *Per contra,* the spirit of reconcilability, having no inimical disposition of its own, struggles to annul the enmity of the other. If love is the standard of judgment, then by that standard calling one's brother a scoundrel is a crime, a greater crime than anger. Yet a scoundrel in the isolation in which he puts himself by setting himself, a man, over against other men in enmity, and by striving to persist in this disorder, is still of some worth, he still counts since he is hated, and a great scoundrel may be admired. Therefore, it is still more alien to love to call the other a fool, for this annuls not only all relation with the speaker but also all equality, all community of essence. The man called a fool is represented as completely subjugated and is designated a nonentity.[6]

Love, on the other hand [Matthew v. 23–24], comes before the altar conscious of a separation, (270) but it leaves its gift there, is reconciled with its brother, and then and then only approaches the one God in purity and singleness of heart. It does not leave the judge to apportion its rights; it reconciles itself to its enemy with no regard to right whatever.

Similarly [Matthew v. 27–32], over against *dutiful* fidelity in marriage and the *right* to divorce a wife, Jesus sets *love*. Love precludes the lust not forbidden by that duty and, except in one eventuality, cancels this leave to divorce, a leave contradictory to that duty. Hence, on the one hand, the sanctity of love is the completion (the $\pi\lambda\eta\rho\omega\mu\alpha$ [fulfilment]) of the law against divorce, and this sanctity alone makes a man capable of checking

---

[6] Philological exegesis for the most part supports the sense in which "Raca" is taken here; but the chief difficulty is created by the moral sense of the interpreters who find "fool" a softer expression than "scoundrel," and judge both words not by the spirit in which they are uttered but by the impression they make. Thus the man called a fool feels himself made *sui juris,* and if he is as sharp as the other, turns round and calls him a fool. [Hegel takes "Raca" to mean "scoundrel." But modern scholars say that it is a softer expression than "fool" and means "silly fellow." T.M.K.]

any one of his many aspects which may wish to make itself the whole or rear its head against the whole; only the feeling for the whole, love, can stand in the way of the diremption of the man's essence. On the other hand, love cancels the leave to divorce; and in face of love, so long as it lasts, or even when it ceases, there can be no talk of leave or rights. To cease loving a wife who still loves compels love to sin, to be untrue to itself; and a transfer of its passion to another is only a perversion of it, to be atoned for with a bad conscience. To be sure, in this event it cannot evade its fate, and the marriage is inwardly sundered; but the support which the husband draws from a law and a right and through which he brings justice and propriety onto his side means adding to the outrage on his wife's love a contemptible harshness. But in the eventuality which Jesus made an exception (i.e., when the wife has bestowed her love on another) the husband may not continue a slave to her. Moses had to give laws and rights about marriage to the Jews "because of the hardness of their hearts," but in the beginning it was not so.

In a statement about reality the subject and the object are thought of as severed; in a statement about futurity, in a promise, the declaration of a will and the deed are themselves still wholly severed, and [in both cases] the truth, i.e., the firm connection of the separate elements, is the important thing. In a sworn statement, the idea of either a past deed or a future one is linked to something divine, and the connection of word and deed, their linkage, an "is," is represented and figured in a Being. (271) Since the truth of the event sworn to cannot itself be made visible, truth itself, God, is put in its place, and (a) is in this way given to the other to whom the oath is sworn and produces conviction in him, while (b) the opposite of the truth is excluded, when the decision to swear is taken, by the reaction of this Being on the heart of the man on oath. There is no knowing why there is supposed to be any superstition in this. When the Jews swore by heaven, by the earth, by Jerusalem, or by the hair of their head, and committed their oath to God, put it in the hands of the Lord, they linked the reality of what they asserted to an object;[7] they equated both realities and put the connection of this object with what was asserted, the equivalence of the two, into the power of an external authority. God is made the authority over the word, and this connection of object and assertion ought to be grounded in man himself. The deed asserted and the object by which the oath was taken are so interconnected with each other that, if one is canceled, the other is denied too, is represented as canceled. If, then, the act promised or the fact asserted is not performed or not a fact, then the object by which the man swore, heaven, earth, etc., is *eo ipso* denied too; and in this event the Lord of the object must vindicate it, God must be the avenger of his own. This linking of a promised deed to something objective Jesus gainsays [Matthew v. 33–37]. He does not assert the duty of keep-

---

[7] I.e., the earth, Jerusalem, etc. This is one reality. The fact asserted is the other. God is the power external to both. [T.M.K.]

ing the oath; he declares that the oath is altogether superfluous, for neither heaven nor earth nor Jerusalem nor the hair of the head is the spirit of man which alone conjoins his word with an action. Jesus declares that these things are a stranger's property and that the certainty of a deed may not be linked to anything strange, put into the hands of a stranger; on the contrary, the connection of word and action must be a living one and rest on the man himself.

An eye for an eye, a tooth for a tooth, say the laws [Matthew v. 38–42]. Retribution and its equivalence with crime are the sacred principles of all justice, the principles on which any political order must rest. But Jesus makes a general demand on his hearers to surrender their rights, to lift themselves above the whole sphere of justice or injustice by love, for in love there vanish not only rights but also the feeling of inequality and the hatred of enemies which this feeling's imperative demand for equality implies.

The laws and duties of which Jesus had spoken up to this point were on the whole civil, and he did not complete them by confirming them as laws and duties while requiring pure reverence for them as the motive for their observance; on the contrary, he expressed contempt for them. The completion he gave them is a spirit which has no consciousness of rights and duties, although its actions, when (272) judged by laws and moral imperatives, are found to be in accordance with these. Farther on [Matthew vi. 1–4] he speaks of a purely moral duty, the virtue of charity. Jesus condemns in it, as in prayer and fasting, the intrusion of something alien, resulting in the impurity of the action: Do it not in order to be seen of men; let the aim behind the action, i.e., the action as thought of, before it is done, be like the completed action. Apart from banishing this hypocrisy which blends with the thought of the action the other aspect (being seen of men) which is not in the action, Jesus seems here to banish even the consciousness of the action as a duty fulfilled. "Let not the left hand know what the right hand doeth" cannot refer to making the action known to others but is the contrary of "being seen by others," and if, then, it is to have meaning, it must denote one's own reflection on one's dutifulness. Whether in an action of mine I am the sole onlooker or whether I think that others too are onlookers, whether I enjoy only my own consciousness or whether I also enjoy the applause of others, makes no great difference. For when the applause of others at a victory won by duty, by the universal over the particular, is known to me, what has happened is, as it were, that universal and particular are not merely thought but seen, the universal in the ideas of the others, the particular in them as themselves real entities. Moreover, the private consciousness of duty fulfilled is not different in kind from honor but is different from it only in so far as, when honor is given, universality is recognized as not merely ideally but also as really valid. The consciousness of having performed his duty enables the individual to claim universality for himself; he intuits himself as universal, as raised above himself *qua* particular and above the whole sphere of particularity, i.e., above the mass of individuals. For as the concept of universality is applied to the individual, so also the concept of particularity acquires this bearing on individuals and they set themselves, as particulars, over against the individual who recognizes his universality by performing his duty; and this self-consciousness of his is as foreign to the action as men's applause.

Of this conviction of self-righteousness and the consequent disparagement of others (which both stand in necessary connection on account of the necessary opposition of particular to universal), Jesus also speaks in the parable in Luke xviii. 9 ff. The Pharisee thanks God (and is too modest to recognize it as the strength of his own will) that he is not as many other men who are extortioners, unjust, adulterers, or even as this publican beside him; (273) he fasts as the rule prescribes and pays his tithes conscientiously as a righteous man should. Against this consciousness of righteousness (which is never said not to be genuine) Jesus sets the downcast eyes, which do not venture to lift themselves to heaven, of the publican who smites his breast and says: God be merciful to me a sinner. The consciousness of the Pharisee (a consciousness of duty done), like the consciousness of the young man (the consciousness of having truly observed all the laws —Matthew xix. 20), this good conscience, is a hypocrisy because (*a*) even if it be bound up with the intention of the action, it is a reflection on itself and on the action, is something impure not belonging to the action; and (*b*) if it is an idea of the agent's self as a moral man, as in the case of the Pharisee and the young man, it is an idea whose content is made up of the virtues, i.e., of restricted things whose sphere is given, whose matter is limited, and which therefore are one and all incomplete, while the good conscience, the consciousness of having done one's duty, hypocritically claims to be the whole.

In this same spirit Jesus speaks [Matthew vi. 5–18] of praying and fasting. Both are either wholly objective, through and through commanded duties, or else are merely based on some need. They cannot be represented as moral duties [8] because they presuppose no opposition capable of unification in a concept. In both of them Jesus censures the show which a man makes in the eyes of others by their practice, and in the particular case of prayer he also condemns the numerous repetitions which give it the look of a duty and its performance. Jesus judges fasting (Matthew ix. 15 [: Can the children of the bride-chamber mourn so long as the bridegroom is with them? But the days will come when the bridegroom shall be taken from them, and then shall they fast]) by reference to the feeling which lies at its heart, to the need which impels us to it. As well as rejecting impurity of heart in prayer, Jesus prescribes a way to pray. Consideration of the true aspects of prayer is not relevant here.

About the command which follows [Matthew vi. 19–34] to cast aside care for one's life and to despise riches, as also about Matthew xix. 23:

---

[8] I.e., duties as they are conceived in what Hegel takes to be Kant's ethics. [T.M.K.]

"How hard it is for a rich man to enter the Kingdom of Heaven," there is nothing to be said; it is a litany pardonable only in sermons and rhymes, for such a command is without truth for us. The fate of property has become too powerful for us to tolerate reflections on it, to find its abolition thinkable. But this at least is to be noticed, that the possession of riches, with all the rights as well as all the cares connected with it, brings into human life definitive details whose restrictedness prescribes limits to the virtues, imposes conditions on them, and makes them dependent on circumstances. Within these limitations, there is room for duties and virtues, but they allow of no whole, of no complete life, (274) because if life is bound up with objects, it is conditioned by something outside itself, since in that event something is tacked on to life as its own which yet cannot be its property.[9] Wealth at once betrays its opposition to love, to the whole, because it is a right caught in a context of multiple rights, and this means that both its immediately appropriate virtue, honesty, and also the other virtues possible within its sphere, are of necessity linked with exclusion, and every act of virtue is in itself one of a pair of opposites.[10] A syncretism, a service of two masters, is unthinkable because the indeterminate and the determinate cannot retain their form and still be bound together. Jesus had to exhibit not simply the "fulfilment" of duties but also the object of these principles, the essence of the sphere of duties, in order to destroy the domain opposed to love.[11]

The point of view from which Jesus attacks riches is brought forward by Luke (xii. 13) in a context which clarifies it. A man had asked Jesus to intercede with his brother about the division of their inheritance. To refuse a petition for such an intercession will be judged to be merely the behavior of an egoist. In his answer to the petitioner, Jesus seems to have directly alleged only his incompetence to grant it. But there is more in the spirit of the reply than that he has no right to make the division, because he turns at once to his disciples with a warning against covetousness and adds a parable of a rich man whom God startled with the words: "Thou fool, this night thy soul shall be required of thee; whose then shall be what thou hast acquired? So is it with him who amasses treasure for himself and is not rich towards God." So Jesus alleges rights only to the profane inquirer; from his disciples he demands elevation above the sphere of rights, justice, equity, the friendly services men can perform in this sphere, above the whole sphere of property.

---

[9] Hegel conceives of life as a spiritual bond with spiritual properties. If the living being owns things, then they are tacked on to him, but they cannot be a property of his soul. [T.M.K.]

[10] The meaning seems to be that to act in accordance with one right is to exclude and perhaps to transgress other rights. [T.M.K.]

[11] I.e., the justification of what Jesus says about property lies for Hegel in the fact that he teaches that morality is essentially a matter of the inner life, and the danger is that legal rights with the externality and the specific details they entail may encroach upon that life or be taken as a substitute for it. [T.M.K.]

To conscience, the consciousness of one's own dutifulness or undutiful-
ness, there corresponds the application of the laws to others in judgment.
"Judge not," says Jesus [Matthew vii. 1–5], "that ye be not judged; for
with what judgment ye judge, ye shall be judged." This subsumption of
others under a concept manifested in the law may be called a weakness on
the ground that the judge is not strong enough to bear up against them altogether but divides them; he cannot hold out against their independence;
he takes them not as they are but (275) as they ought to be; and by this
judgment he has subjected them to himself in thought, since the concept,
the universality, is his. But with this judging he has recognized a law and
subjected himself to its bondage, has set up for himself also a criterion of
judgment; and with the loving disposition which leads him to remove the
mote from his brother's eye he has himself fallen under the realm of
love.[12]

What follows [Matthew vii. 6–29] does not, like the earlier part, oppose to the laws a realm which is higher than they; it rather exhibits certain
expressions of life in its beautiful free region as the unification of men in
asking, giving, and receiving. The whole Sermon ends with the attempt to
display the picture of man entirely outside the sphere in which it had been
sketched earlier, where we had a picture of man in opposition to determinate prescriptions, with the result that purity of life appeared there rather
in its modifications, in particular virtues, as reconciliation, marital fidelity,
honesty, etc. The picture of man could of course be so displayed only in
inadequate parables.

In contrast to this extinction of law and duty in love, which Jesus sig-
nalizes as the highest morality, there is the manner of John the Baptist, of
which Luke (iii) has preserved some examples. "If you still hope to escape
from the fate of the wrath to come," he says to the Jews, "it matters not
that you have Abraham for your father, for the axe is even now laid to the
root of the trees." And when the Jews then asked him what they were to
do, he replied: "He that hath two coats or hath food to spare, let him give
to him that hath none." He warned the publicans not to exact more than
was appointed them, the soldiers not to maim any man, not to pillage anything, but to live on their pay. It is also known of him (Matthew xiv. 4)
that he launched forth into reproaches on the relations between Herod and

---

[12] The meaning perhaps is that by judging people we try to get the better of them
in *thought*. E.g., envy may bring a consciousness of inferiority, and this may be
transferred into its opposite by dividing (*teilen*) the person envied (i.e., by ab-
stracting his position from his character) and then judging (*urteilen*) his character.
We envy the man as he *is*, and we judge him by a concept, a thought, by our
conception of what he ought to be, or by our conception of the laws by which he
ought to abide. In this way we get the better of him, not in reality, but in thought,
because the standard of judgment lies in our thinking. But this process recoils on
us. We must be judged by the same standard. Further, if I love another enough to
wish to remedy his defects, I must become wholly animated by love and so heal
my own faults by lifting myself onto the plane of love instead of law and judgment. [T.M.K.]

his brother's wife, a reproof which cost him his head. His fate was completed because of a specific reproof, just as his teaching (see the above examples) exhorts to specific virtues and shows that their great spirit, their all-pervasive soul, had not entered his consciousness. He felt this himself too and proclaimed another who with his fan in his hand would purge the threshing floor. John hoped and believed that his successor would substitute for his baptism of water a baptism with fire and the spirit.

Ethics: The Science of What Is
Rather than What Ought to Be

Since philosophy is the exploration of the rational, it is for that very reason the apprehension of the present and the actual, not the erection of a beyond, supposed to exist, God knows where, or rather which exists, and we can perfectly well say where, namely in the error of a one-sided, empty, ratiocination. In the course of this book, I have remarked that even Plato's *Republic,* which passes proverbially as an empty ideal, is in essence nothing but an interpretation of the nature of Greek ethical life. Plato was conscious that there was breaking into that life in his own time a deeper principle which could appear in it directly only as a longing still unsatisfied, and so only as something corruptive. To combat it, he needs must have sought aid from that very longing itself. But this aid had to come from on High and all that Plato could do was to seek it in the first place in a particular external form of that same Greek ethical life. By that means he thought to master this corruptive invader, and thereby he did fatal injury to the deeper impulse which underlay it, namely free infinite personality. Still, his genius is proved by the fact that the principle on which the distinctive character of his Idea of the state turns is precisely the pivot on which the impending world revolution turned at that time.

What is rational is actual and what is actual is rational. On this conviction the plain man like the philosopher takes his stand, and from it philosophy starts in its study of the universe of mind as well as the universe of nature. If reflection, feeling, or whatever form subjective consciousness may take, looks upon the present as something vacuous and looks beyond it with the eyes of superior wisdom, it finds itself in a vacuum, and because it is actual only in the present, it is itself mere vacuity. If on the other hand the Idea passes for "only an Idea," for something represented in an opinion, philosophy rejects such a view and shows that nothing is actual except the

From pp. 10–13 of G. W. F. Hegel, the Preface to *Philosophy of Right,* translated by T. M. Knox. Copyright 1942 by Clarendon Press, Oxford. Reprinted by permission of Clarendon Press, Oxford.

Idea. Once that is granted, the great thing is to apprehend in the show of the temporal and transient the substance which is immanent and the eternal which is present. For since rationality (which is synonymous with the Idea) enters upon external existence simultaneously with its actualization, it emerges with an infinite wealth of forms, shapes, and appearances. Around its heart it throws a motley covering with which consciousness is at home to begin with, a covering which the concept has first to penetrate before it can find the inward pulse and feel it still beating in the outward appearances. But the infinite variety of circumstance which is developed in this externality by the light of the essence glinting in it—this endless material and its organization—this is not the subject matter of philosophy. To touch this at all would be to meddle with things to which philosophy is unsuited; on such topics it may save itself the trouble of giving good advice. Plato might have omitted his recommendation to nurses to keep on the move with infants and to rock them continually in their arms. And Fichte too need not have carried what has been called the "construction" of his passport regulations to such a pitch of perfection as to require suspects not merely to sign their passports but to have their likenesses painted on them. Along such tracks all trace of philosophy is lost, and such supererudition it can the more readily disclaim since its attitude to this infinite multitude of topics should of course be most liberal. In adopting this attitude, philosophic science shows itself to be poles apart from the hatred with which the folly of superior wisdom regards a vast number of affairs and institutions, a hatred in which pettiness takes the greatest delight because only by venting it does it attain a feeling of its self-hood.

This book, then, containing as it does the science of the state, is to be nothing other than the endeavour to apprehend and portray the state as something inherently rational. As a work of philosophy, it must be poles apart from an attempt to construct a state as it ought to be. The instruction which it may contain cannot consist in teaching the state what it ought to be; it can only show how the state, the ethical universe, is to be understood. . . .

To comprehend what is, this is the task of philosophy, because what is, is reason. Whatever happens, every individual is a child of his time; so philosophy too is its own time apprehended in thoughts. It is just as absurd to fancy that a philosophy can transcend its contemporary world as it is to fancy that an individual can overleap his own age, jump over Rhodes. If his theory really goes beyond the world as it is and builds an ideal one as it ought to be, that world exists indeed, but only in his opinions, an unsubstantial element where anything you please may, in fancy, be built.

With hardly an alteration, the proverb . . . would run:

Here is the rose, dance thou here.

What lies between reason as self-conscious mind and reason as an actual world before our eyes, what separates the former from the latter and prevents it from finding satisfaction in the latter, is the fetter of some abstraction or other which has not been liberated [and so transformed] into the concept. To recognize reason as the rose in the cross of the present and thereby to enjoy the present, this is the rational insight which reconciles us to the actual, the reconciliation which philosophy affords to those in whom there has once arisen an inner voice bidding them to comprehend, not only to dwell in what is substantive while still retaining subjective freedom, but also to possess subjective freedom while standing not in anything particular and accidental but in what exists absolutely.

It is this too which constitutes the more concrete meaning of what was described above rather abstractly as the unity of form and content; for form in its most concrete signification is reason as speculative knowing, and content is reason as the substantial essence of actuality, whether ethical or natural. The known identity of these two is the philosophical Idea. It is a sheer obstinacy, the obstinacy which does honour to mankind, to refuse to recognize in conviction anything not ratified by thought. This obstinacy is the characteristic of our epoch, besides being the principle peculiar to Protestantism. What Luther initiated as faith in feeling and in the witness of the spirit, is precisely what spirit, since become more mature, has striven to apprehend in the concept in order to free and so to find itself in the world as it exists to-day. The saying has become famous that "a half-philosophy leads away from God"—and it is the same half-philosophy that locates knowledge in an "approximation" to truth—"while true philosophy leads to God"; and the same is true of philosophy and the state. Just as reason is not content with an approximation which, as something "neither cold nor hot," it will "spue out of its mouth," so it is just as little content with the cold despair which submits to the view that in this earthly life things are truly bad or at best only tolerable, though here they cannot be improved and that this is the only reflection which can keep us at peace with the world: There is less chill in the peace with the world which knowledge supplies.

One word more about giving instruction as to what the world ought to be. Philosophy in any case always comes on the scene too late to give it. As the thought of the world, it appears only when actuality is already there cut and dried after its process of formation has been completed. The teaching of the concept, which is also history's inescapable lesson, is that it is only when actuality is mature that the ideal first appears over against the real and that the ideal apprehends this same real world in its substance and builds it up for itself into the shape of an intellectual realm. When philosophy paints its grey in grey, then has a shape of life grown old. By philosophy's grey in grey it cannot be rejuvenated but only understood. The owl of Minerva spreads its wings only with the falling of the dusk.

· · ·

QUESTIONS FOR STUDY AND DISCUSSION

1. What is the difference between Kant's morality and the ethics of the Gospel according to Hegel's *Spirit of Christianity?*
2. What unites and what distinguishes the juridical and the moral order in the *Philosophy of Right?*
3. In what does the *good* consist in Hegel's ethics?
4. To what extent can the civil society (i.e., the economic community) be said to be an *ethical* institution?
5. Why according to Hegel is the State a necessity for one who wants to lead an ethical life?

Karl Marx

KARL MARX was born in Trier, Prussia, in 1818. The son of a jurist, he studied law, philosophy, and history at the Universities of Bonn and Berlin and received his doctorate in philosophy from the University of Jena in 1842. He served as editor of the radical, short-lived newspaper, *Rheinische Zeitung.* After its suppression he went to Paris, where he met Friedrich Engels. Together they published the famous *Communist Manifesto* in 1847, which set forth the basic tenets of Marxism. Having been expelled from Paris, Brussels, and Cologne as a dangerous revolutionary, Marx went into exile in London in 1850 and remained there until his death in 1883. A prolific writer and founder and leader of the International Workingman's Association, Marx is best known as the author of *Capital,* the first volume of which was published in 1867.

The Alienation of Man

We shall begin from a *contemporary* economic fact. The worker becomes poorer the more wealth he produces and the more his production increases in power and extent. The worker becomes an ever cheaper commodity the more goods he creates. The *devaluation* of the human world increases in direct relation with the *increase in value* of the world of things. Labor does not only create goods; it also produces itself and the worker as a *commodity,* and indeed in the same proportion as it produces goods.

This fact simply implies that the object produced by labor, its product, now stands opposed to it as an *alien being,* as a *power independent* of the producer. The product of labor is labor which has been embodied in an object and turned into a physical thing; this product is an *objectification* of labor. The performance of work is at the same time its objectification. The performance of work appears in the sphere of political economy as a *vitiation* of the worker, objectification as a *loss* and as *servitude to the object,* and appropriation as *alienation.*

So much does the performance of work appear as vitiation that the worker is vitiated to the point of starvation. So much does objectification appear as loss of the object that the worker is deprived of the most essen-

From pp. 95–103 of Karl Marx, *The Economic and Philosophical Manuscripts,* translated by T. B. Bottomore, in Erich Fromm, *Marx's Concept of Man.* © 1961 by Frederick Ungar Publishing Company, Inc. Reprinted by permission of Erich Fromm.

tial things not only of life but also of work. Labor itself becomes an object which he can acquire only by the greatest effort and with unpredictable interruptions. So much does the appropriation of the object appear as alienation that the more objects the worker produces the fewer he can possess and the more he falls under the domination of his product, of capital.

All these consequences follow from the fact that the worker is related to the *product of his labor* as to an *alien* object. For it is clear on this presupposition that the more the worker expends himself in work the more powerful becomes the world of objects which he creates in face of himself, the poorer he becomes in his inner life, and the less he belongs to himself. It is just the same as in religion. The more of himself man attributes to God the less he has left in himself. The worker puts his life into the object, and his life then belongs no longer to himself but to the object. The greater his activity, therefore, the less he possesses. What is embodied in the product of his labor is no longer his own. The greater this product is, therefore, the more he is diminished. The *alienation* of the worker in his product means not only that his labor becomes an object, assumes an *external* existence, but that it exists independently, *outside himself,* and alien to him, and that it stands opposed to him as an autonomous power. The life which he has given to the object sets itself against him as an alien and hostile force.

[XXIII] [1] Let us now examine more closely the phenomenon of *objectification,* the worker's production and the *alienation* and *loss* of the object it produces, which is involved in it. The worker can create nothing without *nature,* without the *sensuous external world.* The latter is the material in which his labor is realized, in which it is active, out of which and through which it produces things.

But just as nature affords the *means of existence* of labor in the sense that labor cannot *live* without objects upon which it can be exercised, so also it provides the *means of existence* in a narrower sense; namely the means of physical existence for the *worker* himself. Thus, the more the worker *appropriates* the external world of sensuous nature by his labor the more he deprives himself of *means of existence,* in two respects: first, that the sensuous external world becomes progressively less an object belonging to his labor or a means of existence of his labor, and secondly, that it becomes progressively less a means of existence in the direct sense, a means for the physical subsistence of the worker.

In both respects, therefore, the worker becomes a slave of the object; first, in that he receives an *object of work,* i.e., receives *work,* and secondly that he receives *means of subsistence.* Thus the object enables him to exist, first as a *worker* and secondly, as a *physical subject.* The culmination of this enslavement is that he can only maintain himself as a *physical subject*

---

[1] The bracketed roman numerals indicate the original pagination of Marx's manuscripts. [L.D.]

so far as he is a *worker,* and that it is only as a *physical subject* that he is a worker.

(The alienation of the worker in his object is expressed as follows in the laws of political economy: the more the worker produces the less he has to consume; the more value he creates the more worthless he becomes; the more refined his product the more crude and misshapen the worker; the more civilized the product the more barbarous the worker; the more powerful the work the more feeble the worker; the more the work manifests intelligence the more the worker declines in intelligence and becomes a slave of nature.)

Political economy conceals the alienation in the nature of labor insofar as it does not examine the direct relationship between the worker (work) and production. Labor certainly produces marvels for the rich but it produces privation for the worker. It produces palaces, but hovels for the worker. It produces beauty, but deformity for the worker. It replaces labor by machinery, but it casts some of the workers back into a barbarous kind of work and turns the others into machines. It produces intelligence, but also stupidity and cretinism for the workers.

The direct relationship of labor to its products is the relationship of the worker to the objects of his production. The relationship of property owners to the objects of production and to production itself is merely a *consequence* of this first relationship and confirms it. We shall consider this second aspect later.

Thus, when we ask what is the important relationship of labor, we are concerned with the relationship of the *worker* to production.

So far we have considered the alienation of the worker only from one aspect; namely, *his relationship with the products of his labor.* However, alienation appears not only in the result, but also in the *process,* of *production,* within *productive activity* itself. How could the worker stand in an alien relationship to the product of his activity if he did not alienate himself in the act of production itself? The product is indeed only the *résumé* of activity, of production. Consequently, if the product of labor is alienation, production itself must be active alienation—the alienation of activity and the activity of alienation. The alienation of the object of labor merely summarizes the alienation in the work activity itself.

What constitutes the alienation of labor? First, that the work is *external* to the worker, that it is not part of his nature; and that, consequently, he does not fulfill himself in his work but denies himself, has a feeling of misery rather than well being, does not develop freely his mental and physical energies but is physically exhausted and mentally debased. The worker therefore feels himself at home only during his leisure time, whereas at work he feels homeless. His work is not voluntary but imposed, *forced labor.* It is not the satisfaction of a need, but only a *means* for satisfying other needs. Its alien character is clearly shown by the fact that as soon as there is no physical or other compulsion it is avoided like the plague. External labor, labor in which man alienates himself, is a labor of self-sacrifice, of mortification. Finally, the external character of work for the worker is shown by the fact that it is not his own work but work for someone else, that in work he does not belong to himself but to another person.

Just as in religion the spontaneous activity of human fantasy, of the human brain and heart, reacts independently as an alien activity of gods or devils upon the individual, so the activity of the worker is not his own spontaneous activity. It is another's activity and a loss of his own spontaneity.

We arrive at the result that man (the worker) feels himself to be freely active only in his animal functions—eating, drinking and procreating, or at most also in his dwelling and in personal adornment—while in his human functions he is reduced to an animal. The animal becomes human and the human becomes animal.

Eating, drinking and procreating are of course also genuine human functions. But abstractly considered, apart from the environment of other human activities, and turned into final and sole ends, they are animal functions.

We have now considered the act of alienation of practical human activity, labor, from two aspects: (1) the relationship of the worker to the *product of labor* as an alien object which dominates him. This relationship is at the same time the relationship to the sensuous external world, to natural objects, as an alien and hostile world; (2) the relationship of labor to the *act of production* within *labor*. This is the relationship of the worker to his own activity as something alien and not belonging to him, activity as suffering (passivity), strength as powerlessness, creation as emasculation, the *personal* physical and mental energy of the worker, his personal life (for what is life but activity?) as an activity which is directed against himself, independent of him and not belonging to him. This is *self-alienation* as against the above-mentioned alienation of the *thing*.

[xxiv] We have now to infer a third characteristic of *alienated labor* from the two we have considered.

Man is a species-being [2] not only in the sense that he makes the community (his own as well as those of other things) his object both practically and theoretically, but also (and this is simply another expression for the same thing) in the sense that he treats himself as the present, living species, as a *universal* and consequently free being.

Species-life, for man as for animals, has its physical basis in the fact that man (like animals) lives from inorganic nature, and since man is more

---

[2] The term "species-being" is taken from Feuerbach's *Das Wesen des Christentums* (*The Essence of Christianity*). Feuerbach used the notion in making a distinction between consciousness in man and in animals. Man is conscious not merely of himself as an individual but of the human species or "human essence." [T.B.B.]

universal than an animal so the range of inorganic nature from which he lives is more universal. Plants, animals, minerals, air, light, etc. constitute, from the theoretical aspect, a part of human consciousness as objects of natural science and art; they are man's spiritual inorganic nature, his intellectual means of life, which he must first prepare for enjoyment and perpetuation. So also, from the practical aspect they form a part of human life and activity. In practice man lives only from these natural products, whether in the form of food, heating, clothing, housing, etc. The universality of man appears in practice in the universality which makes the whole of nature into his inorganic body: (1) as a direct means of life; and equally (2) as the material object and instrument of his life activity. Nature is the *inorganic body* of man; that is to say, nature excluding the human body itself. To say that man *lives* from nature means that nature is his *body* with which he must remain in a continuous interchange in order not to die. The statement that the physical and mental life of man, and nature, are interdependent means simply that nature is interdependent with itself, for man is a part of nature.

Since alienated labor: (1) alienates nature from man; and (2) alienates man from himself, from his own active function, his life activity; so it alienates him from the species. It makes *species-life* into a means of individual life. In the first place it alienates species-life and individual life, and secondly, it turns the latter, as an abstraction, into the purpose of the former, also in its abstract and alienated form.

For labor, *life activity, productive life,* now appear to man only as *means* for the satisfaction of a need, the need to maintain his physical existence. Productive life is, however, species-life. It is life creating life. In the type of life activity resides the whole character of a species, its species-character; and free, conscious activity is the species-character of human beings. Life itself appears only as a *means of life.*

The animal is one with its life activity. It does not distinguish the activity from itself. It is *its activity.* But man makes his life activity itself an object of his will and consciousness. He has a conscious life activity. It is not a determination with which he is completely identified. Conscious life activity distinguishes man from the life activity of animals. Only for this reason is he a species-being. Or rather, he is only a self-conscious being, i.e. his own life is an object for him, because he is a species-being. Only for this reason is his activity free activity. Alienated labor reverses the relationship, in that man because he is a self-conscious being makes his life activity, his *being,* only a means for his *existence.*

The practical construction of an *objective world,* the *manipulation* of inorganic nature, is the confirmation of man as a conscious species-being, i.e. a being who treats the species as his own being or himself as a species-being. Of course, animals also produce. They construct nests, dwellings, as in the case of bees, beavers, ants, etc. But they only produce what is strictly necessary for themselves or their young. They produce only in a single direction, while man produces universally. They produce only under the compulsion of direct physical need, while man produces when he is free from physical need and only truly produces in freedom from such need. Animals produce only themselves, while man reproduces the whole of nature. The products of animal production belong directly to their physical bodies, while man is free in face of his product. Animals construct only in accordance with the standards and needs of the species to which they belong, while man knows how to produce in accordance with the standards of every species and knows how to apply the appropriate standard to the object. Thus man constructs also in accordance with the laws of beauty.

It is just in his work upon the objective world that man really proves himself as a *species-being*. This production is his active species life. By means of it nature appears as *his* work and his reality. The object of labor is, therefore, the *objectification of man's species-life;* for he no longer reproduces himself merely intellectually, as in consciousness, but actively and in a real sense, and he sees his own reflection in a world which he has constructed. While, therefore, alienated labor takes away the object of production from man, it also takes away his *species-life,* his real objectivity as a species-being, and changes his advantage over animals into a disadvantage in so far as his inorganic body, nature, is taken from him.

Just as alienated labor transforms free and self-directed activity into a means, so it transforms the species-life of man into a means of physical existence.

Consciousness, which man has from his species, is transformed through alienation so that species-life becomes only a means for him.

(3) Thus alienated labor turns the *species-life of man,* and also nature as his mental species-property, into an *alien* being and into a *means* for his *individual existence.* It alienates from man his own body, external nature, his mental life and his *human* life.

(4) A direct consequence of the alienation of man from the product of his labor, from his life activity and from his species-life is that *man* is *alienated* from other *men.* When man confronts himself he also confronts *other* men. What is true of man's relationship to his work, to the product of his work and to himself, is also true of his relationship to other men, to their labor and to the objects of their labor.

In general, the statement that man is alienated from his species-life means that each man is alienated from others, and that each of the others is likewise alienated from human life.

Human alienation, and above all the relation of man to himself, is first realized and expressed in the relationship between each man and other men. Thus in the relationship of alienated labor every man regards other men according to the standards and relationships in which he finds himself placed as a worker.

. . .

DIVISION OF LABOUR

Division of labour and private property are . . . identical expressions: in the one the same thing is affirmed with reference to activity as is affirmed in the other with reference to the product of the activity.

Further, the division of labour implies the contradiction between the interest of the separate individual or the individual family and the communal interest of all individuals who have intercourse with one another. And indeed, this communal interest does not exist merely in the imagination, as "the general good," but first of all in reality, as the mutual interdependence of the individuals among whom the labour is divided. And finally, the division of labour offers us the first example of how, as long as man remains in natural society, that is as long as a cleavage exists between the particular and the common interest, as long therefore as activity is not voluntarily, but naturally, divided, man's own deed becomes an alien power opposed to him, which enslaves him instead of being controlled by him. For as soon as labour is distributed, each man has a particular, exclusive sphere of activity, which is forced upon him and from which he cannot escape. He is a hunter, a fisherman, a shepherd, or a critical critic, and must remain so if he does not want to lose his means of livelihood; while in communist society, where nobody has one exclusive sphere of activity but each can become accomplished in any branch he wishes, society regulates the general production and thus makes it possible for me to do one thing to-day and another to-morrow, to hunt in the morning, fish in the afternoon, rear cattle in the evening, criticize after dinner, just as I have a mind, without ever becoming hunter, fisherman, shepherd or critic.

This crystallization of social activity, this consolidation of what we ourselves produce into an objective power above us, growing out of our control, thwarting our expectations, bringing to naught our calculations, is one of the chief factors in historical development up till now. And out of this very contradiction between the interest of the individual and that of the community the latter takes an independent form as the *State*, divorced from the real interests of individual and community, and at the same time as an illusory communal life, always based, however, on the real ties existing in every family and tribal conglomeration (such as flesh and blood, language, division of labour on a larger scale, and other interests) and especially, as we shall enlarge upon later, on the classes, already determined by the division of labour, which in every such mass of men separate out, and of which one dominates all the others. It follows from this that all struggles within the State, the struggle between democracy, aristocracy and monarchy, the struggle for the franchise, etc., etc., are merely the illusory forms

From pp. 22–25 of Karl Marx and Friedrich Engels, *The German Ideology*, translated by R. Pascal. © 1960 by International Publishers Co., Inc. By permission of International Publishers Co., Inc.

in which the real struggles of the different classes are fought out among one another. . . .

Further, it follows that every class which is struggling for mastery, even when its domination, as is the case with the proletariat, postulates the abolition of the old form of society in its entirety and of mastery itself, must first conquer for itself political power in order to represent its interest in turn as the general interest, a step to which in the first moment it is forced. Just because individuals seek *only* their particular interest, i.e. that not coinciding with their communal interest (for the "general good" is the illusory form of communal life), the latter will be imposed on them as an interest "alien" to them, and "independent" of them, as in its turn a particular, peculiar "general interest"; or they must meet face to face in this antagonism, as in democracy. On the other hand too, the *practical* struggle of these particular interests, which constantly *really* run counter to the communal and illusory communal interests, make *practical* intervention and control necessary through the illusory "general-interest" in the form of the State. The social power, i.e. the multiplied productive force, which arises through the cooperation of different individuals as it is determined within the division of labour, appears to these individuals, since their co-operation is not voluntary but natural, not as their own united power but as an alien force existing outside them, of the origin and end of which they are ignorant, which they thus cannot control, which on the contrary passes through a peculiar series of phases and stages independent of the will and the action of man, nay even being the prime governor of these.

This "estrangement" (to use a term which will be comprehensible to the philosophers) can, of course, only be abolished given two *practical* premises. For it to become an "intolerable" power, i.e. a power against which men make a revolution, it must necessarily have rendered the great mass of humanity "propertyless," and produced, at the same time, the contradiction of an existing world of wealth and culture, both of which conditions presuppose a great increase in productive power, a high degree of its development. And, on the other hand, this development of productive forces (which itself implies the actual empirical existence of men in their *world-historical,* instead of local, being) is absolutely necessary as a practical premise: firstly, for the reason that without it only *want* is made general, and with want the struggle for necessities and all the old filthy business would necessarily be reproduced; and secondly, because only with this universal development of productive forces is a *universal* intercourse between men established, which produces in all nations simultaneously the phenomenon of the "propertyless" mass (universal competition), makes each nation dependent on the revolutions of the others, and finally has put *world-historical,* empirically universal individuals in place of local ones.

The Liberation of Man

Just as private property is only the sensuous expression of the fact that man is at the same time an objective fact for himself and becomes an alien and non-human object for himself; just as his manifestation of life is also his alienation of life and his self-realization a loss of reality, the emergence of an alien reality; so the positive supersession of private property, i.e., the sensuous appropriation of the human essence and of human life, of objective man and of human creations, by and for man, should not be taken only in the sense of immediate, exclusive enjoyment, or only in the sense of possession or having. Man appropriates his manifold being in an all-inclusive way, and thus as a whole man. All his human relations to the world—seeing, hearing, smelling, tasting, touching, thinking, observing, feeling, desiring, acting, loving—in short all the organs of his individuality, like the organs which are directly communal in form, are in their objective action (their action in relation to the object) the appropriation of this object, the appropriation of human reality. The way in which they react to the object is the confirmation of *human reality*.[1] It is human effectiveness and human *suffering*, for suffering humanly considered is an enjoyment of the self for man.

Private property has made us so stupid and partial that an object is only *ours* when we have it, when it exists for us as capital or when it is directly eaten, drunk, worn, inhabited, etc., in short, *utilized* in some way; although private property itself only conceives these various forms of possession as *means of life,* and the life for which they serve as means is the life of *private property*—labor and creation of capital.

Thus *all* the physical and intellectual senses have been replaced by the simple alienation of *all* these senses; the sense of *having.* The human being had to be reduced to this absolute poverty in order to be able to give birth to all his inner wealth. . . .

The supersession of private property is therefore the complete *emancipation* of all the human qualities and senses. It is this emancipation because these qualities and senses have become *human,* from the subjective as well as the objective point of view. The eye has become a *human* eye when its *object* has become a *human,* social object, created by man and destined for him. The senses have therefore become directly theoreticians in practice. They relate themselves to the thing for the sake of the thing,

---

[1] It is therefore just as varied as the determinations of human nature and activities are diverse. [K.M.]

From pp. 131–35 of Karl Marx, *The Economic and Philosophical Manuscripts,* translated by T. B. Bottomore, in Erich Fromm, *Marx's Concept of Man.* © 1961 by Frederick Ungar Publishing Company, Inc. Reprinted by permission of Erich Fromm.

but the thing itself is an *objective human* relation to itself and to man, and vice versa.[2] Need and enjoyment have thus lost their *egoistic* character, and nature has lost its mere *utility* by the fact that its utilization has become *human* utilization.

Similarly, the senses and minds of other men have become my *own* appropriation. Thus besides these direct organs, *social* organs are constituted, in the form of society; for example, activity in direct association with others has become an organ for the manifestation of life and a mode of appropriation of *human* life.

It is evident that the human eye appreciates things in a different way from the crude, non-human eye, the human *ear* differently from the crude ear. As we have seen, it is only when the object becomes a *human* object, or objective *humanity,* that man does not become lost in it. This is only possible when the object becomes a *social* object, and when he himself becomes a social being and society becomes a being for him in this object.

On the one hand, it is only when objective reality everywhere becomes for man in society the reality of human faculties, human reality, and thus the reality of his own faculties, that all *objects* become for him the *objectification of himself.* The objects then confirm and realize his individuality, they are *his own* objects, i.e., man himself becomes the object. *The manner in which* these objects become his own depends upon the *nature of the object* and the nature of the corresponding faculty; for it is precisely the *determinate character* of this relation which constitutes the specific *real* mode of affirmation. The object is not the same for the *eye* as for the *ear,* for the ear as for the eye. The *distinctive character* of each faculty is precisely its *characteristic* essence and thus also the characteristic mode of its objectification, of its *objectively real,* living *being.* It is therefore not only in thought, [VIII] but through *all* the senses that man is affirmed in the objective world.

Let us next consider the subjective aspect. Man's musical sense is only awakened by music. The most beautiful music has no meaning for the non-musical ear, is not an object for it, because my object can only be the confirmation of one of my own faculties. It can only be so for me in so far as my faculty exists for itself as a subjective capacity, because the meaning of an object for me extends only as far as the sense extends (only makes sense for an appropriate sense). For this reason, the *senses* of social man are *different* from those of non-social man. It is only through the objectively deployed wealth of the human being that the wealth of subjective *human* sensibility (a musical ear, an eye which is sensitive to the beauty of form, in short, senses which are capable of human satisfaction and which confirm themselves as human faculties) is cultivated or created. For it is not only the five senses, but also the so-called spiritual senses, the practical senses (desiring, loving, etc.), in brief, human sensibility and the human character

---

[2] In practice I can only relate myself in a human way to a thing when the thing is related in a human way to man. [K.M.]

of the senses, which can only come into being through the existence of *its* object, through humanized nature. The cultivation of the five senses is the work of all previous history. Sense which is subservient to crude needs has only a restricted meaning. For a starving man the human form of food does not exist, but only its abstract character as food. It could just as well exist in the most crude form, and it is impossible to say in what way this feeding-activity would differ from that of animals. The needy man, burdened with cares, has no appreciation of the most beautiful spectacle. The dealer in minerals sees only their commercial value, not their beauty or their particular characteristics; he has no mineralogical sense. Thus, the objectification of the human essence, both theoretically and practically, is necessary in order to *humanize* man's *senses,* and also to create the *human senses* corresponding to all the wealth of human and natural being.

Just as society at its beginnings finds, through the development of *private property* with its wealth and poverty (both intellectual and material), the materials necessary for this *cultural development, so* the fully constituted society produces man in all the plenitude of his being, the wealthy man endowed with all the senses, as an enduring reality. It is only in a social context that subjectivism and objectivism, spirtualism and materialism, activity and passivity, cease to be antinomies and thus cease to exist as such antinomies. The resolution of the *theoretical* contradictions is possible *only* through *practical* means, only through the practical energy of man. Their resolution is not by any means, therefore, only a problem of knowledge, but is a *real* problem of life which philosophy was unable to solve precisely because it saw there a purely theoretical problem.

.   .   .

THE COMMUNAL RELATIONSHIP

The contradiction between the productive forces and the form of intercourse, which, as we saw, has occurred several times in past history, without however endangering its basis, necessarily on each occasion burst out in a revolution, taking on at the same time various subsidiary forms, such as all-embracing collisions, collisions of various classes, contradiction of consciousness, battle of ideas, etc., political conflict, etc. From a narrow point of view one may isolate one of these subsidiary forms and consider it as the basis of these revolutions; and this is all the more easy as the individuals who started the revolutions made illusions about their own activity according to their degree of culture and the stage of historical development.

The transformation, through the division of labour, of personal powers (relationships) into material powers, cannot be dispelled by dismissing the general idea of it from one's mind, but only by the action of individuals in again subjecting these material powers to themselves and abolishing the

From pp. 74–78 of Karl Marx and Friedrich Engels, *The German Ideology,* translated by R. Pascal. © 1960 by International Publishers Co., Inc. By permission of International Publishers Co., Inc.

division of labour. This is not possible without the community. Only in community with others has each individual the means of cultivating his gifts in all directions; only in the community, therefore, is personal freedom possible. In the previous substitutes for the community, in the State, etc., personal freedom has existed only for the individuals who developed within the relationships of the ruling class, and only in so far as they were individuals of this class. The illusory community, in which individuals have up till now combined, always took on an independent existence in relation to them, and was at the same time, since it was the combination of one class over against another, not only a completely illusory community, but a new fetter as well. In the real community the individuals obtain their freedom in and through their association.

It follows from all we have been saying up till now that the communal relationship into which the individuals of a class entered, and which was determined by their common interests over against a third party, was always a community to which these individuals belonged only as average individuals, only in so far as they lived within the conditions of existence of their class—a relationship in which they participated not as individuals but as members of a class. With the community of revolutionary proletarians on the other hand, who take their conditions of existence and those of all members of society under their control, it is just the reverse; it is as individuals that the individuals participate in it. It is just this combination of individuals (assuming the advanced stage of modern productive forces, of course) which puts the conditions of the free development and movement of individuals under their control—conditions which were previously abandoned to chance and had won an independent existence over against the separate individuals just because of their separation as individuals, and because their combination had been determined by the division of labour, and through their separation had become a bond alien to them. Combination up till now (by no means an arbitrary one, such as is expounded for example in the *Contrat Social,* but a necessary one) was permitted only upon these conditions, within which the individuals were at the mercy of chance (compare, e.g. the formation of the North American State and the South American republics). This right to the undisturbed enjoyment, upon certain conditions, of fortuity and chance has up till now been called personal freedom: but these conditions are, of course, only the productive forces and forms of intercourse at any particular time.

If from a philosophical point of view one considers this evolution of individuals in the common conditions of existence of estates and classes, which followed on one another, and in the accompanying general conceptions forced upon them, it is certainly very easy to imagine that in these individuals the species, or "man," has evolved, or that they evolved "man"—and in this way one can give history some hard clouts on the ear. One can conceive these various estates and classes to be specific terms of the general expression, subordinate varieties of the species, or evolutionary phases of "man."

This subsuming of individuals under definite classes cannot be abolished until a class has taken shape, which has no longer any particular class interest to assert against the ruling class.

Individuals have always built on themselves, but naturally on themselves within their given historical conditions and relationships, not on the "pure" individual in the sense of the ideologists. But in the course of historical evolution, and precisely through the inevitable fact that within the division of labour social relationships take on an independent existence, there appears a division within the life of each individual, in so far as it is personal and in so far as it is determined by some branch of labour and the conditions pertaining to it. (We do not mean it to be understood from this that, for example, the rentier, the capitalist, etc., cease to be persons; but their personality is conditioned and determined by quite definite class relationships, and the division appears only in their opposition to another class and, for themselves, only when they go bankrupt.)

In the estate (and even more in the tribe) this is as yet concealed: for instance a nobleman always remains a nobleman, a commoner always a commoner, apart from his other relationships, a quality inseparable from his individuality. The division between the personal and the class individual, the accidental nature of the conditions of life for the individual, appears only with the emergence of class, which is itself a product of the bourgeoisie. This accidental character is only engendered and developed by competition and the struggle of individuals among themselves. Thus, in imagination, individuals seem freer under the dominance of the bourgeoisie than before, because their conditions of life seem accidental; in reality, of course, they are less free, because they are more subjected to the violence of things. The difference from the estate comes out particularly in the antagonism between the bourgeoisie and the proletariat. When the estate of the urban burghers, the corporations, etc., emerged in opposition to the landed nobility, their condition of existence—movable property and craft labour, which had already existed latently before their separation from the feudal ties—appeared as something positive, which was asserted against feudal landed property, and therefore in its own way at first took on a feudal form. Certainly the refugee serfs treated their previous servitude as something accidental to their personality. But here they only were doing what every class that is freeing itself from a fetter does; and they did not free themselves as a class but separately. Moreover, they did not rise above the system of estates, but only formed a new estate, retaining their previous mode of labour even in their new situation, and developing it further by freeing it from its earlier fetters, which no longer corresponded to the development already attained.

For the proletarians, on the other hand, the condition of their existence, labour, and with it all the conditions of existence governing modern society, have become something accidental, something over which they, as separate individuals, have no control, and over which no *social* organization can give them control. The contradiction between the individuality of each separate proletarian and labour, the condition of life forced upon him, becomes evident to him himself, for he is sacrificed from youth upwards and, within his own class, has no chance of arriving at the conditions which would place him in the other class. Thus, while the refugee serfs only wished to be free to develop and assert those conditions of existence which were already there, and hence, in the end, only arrived at free labour, the proletarians, if they are to assert themselves as individuals, will have to abolish the very condition of their existence hitherto (which has, moreover, been that of all society up to the present), namely, labour. Thus they find themselves directly opposed to the form in which, hitherto, individuals have given themselves collective expression, that is, the State. In order, therefore, to assert themselves as individuals, they must overthrow the State.

QUESTIONS FOR STUDY AND DISCUSSION

1. How does Marx's theory of alienation differ from Hegel's?
2. Describe the triple alienation of man in capitalist society.
3. What are the causes of the social revolution according to Marx?
4. What is the function of the proletariat in the foundation of a classless society?

Friedrich Engels

FRIEDRICH ENGELS was born in Barmen, Prussia, in 1820. The son of a
wealthy textile manufacturer, Engels was himself a successful busi-
nessman, but the plight of the working class converted him to socialism. In 1842 he took a position in his father's factory near Man-
chester, England, and three years later wrote *The Condition of the
Working Class in England,* a book that attracted wide attention. In
1844 he met Karl Marx in Paris and a close and lifelong friendship
began. From 1845 to 1850 he was active in Germany, France, and
Belgium organizing revolutionary movements and collaborating with
Marx on several works, the most important of which was the *Communist Manifesto* (1847). In 1850 he returned to England, where he
remained until his death in 1895. Among his best-known writings are
Anti-Dühring (1878), *Ludwig Feuerbach* (1888), *Socialism: Utopian
and Scientific* (1892), and *The Origin of the Family* (1884). Considered the most authoritative expositor of Marx's writings, Engels edited
volumes II and III of *Capital* (1885, 1895) after Marx's death.

Are There Eternal Moral Truths?

The moral world "just as much as the world of knowledge in general," has
"its permanent principles and simple elements." The moral principles stand
"above history and above the present differences in national characteristics. . . . The special truths out of which, in the course of evolution, the
more complete moral consciousness and, so to speak, conscience are built
up, in so far as their ultimate basis is understood, may claim a validity and
range similar to the concepts and applications of mathematics. *Pure truths
are absolutely immutable* . . . so that it is altogether a stupidity to think
that the validity of knowledge is something that can be affected by time and
changes in reality." Hence the certitude of exact knowledge and the
adequacy of more common cognition leave no room, when we reflect, for
doubting the absolute validity of the principles of knowledge. "Even
persistent doubt is itself a diseased condition of weakness and only the expression of *sterile confusion,* which sometimes seeks to maintain the ap-

From pp. 95–111, 116–21, and 125–29 of Friedrich Engels, *Anti-Dühring.* Copyright
1939 by International Publishers Co., Inc. By permission of International Publishers
Co., Inc.

pearance of something stable in the systematic consciousness of its *nothingness*. In the sphere of morals, the denial of general principles clutches at the geographical and historical variety of customs and principles, and if one concedes the inevitable necessity of moral wickedness and evil, it believes that it has then all the more got beyond the recognition of the real validity and actual efficacy of concordant moral instincts. This *mordant scepticism,* which is not only directed against particular false doctrines but against mankind's capacity to develop conscious morality, resolves itself ultimately into a real Nothing, in fact into something that is worse than mere nihilism. . . . It flatters itself that it can easily dominate within its *confused chaos* of dissolved moral ideas and open the gates to unprincipled caprice. But it makes a gross error in this: for mere reference even to the inevitable fate of the mind when it is concerned with error and truth suffices to show by this analogy alone that the natural law of fallibility does not necessarily exclude the attainment of accuracy."

Up to now we have calmly put up with all these pompous phrases of Herr Dühring's about final and ultimate truths, the sovereignty of thought, absolute certainty of knowledge, and so forth, because it is only at the point which we have now reached that the matter can be brought to a head. Up to this point it has been enough to enquire how far the separate assertions of the philosophy of reality had "sovereign validity" and "unconditional claim to truth"; now we come to the question whether any, and if so which, products of human knowledge ever can have sovereign validity, and an unconditional claim to truth. When I say "of *human* knowledge" I do not use the phrase with the intention of insulting the inhabitants of other celestial bodies, whom I have not had the pleasure of knowing, but only for the reason that animals also have knowledge, though it is in no way sovereign. To a dog his master is divine, though this master may be the biggest scoundrel on earth.

Is human thought sovereign? Before we can answer yes or no we must first enquire: what is human thought? Is it the thought of the individual human being? No. But it exists only as the individual thought of many billions of past, present and future men. If then, I say that the total thought of all these human beings, including future ones, which is embraced in my idea, is *sovereign,* able to know the world as it exists, if only mankind lasts long enough and in so far as no limits are imposed on its knowledge by its perceptive organs or the objects to be known, then I am saying something which is pretty banal and, in addition, pretty barren. For the most valuable result from it would be that it should make us extremely distrustful of our present knowledge, inasmuch as in all probability we are but little beyond the beginning of human history, and the generations which will put *us* right are likely to be far more numerous than those whose knowledge we—often enough with a considerable degree of contempt—are in a position to correct.

Herr Dühring himself declares that consciousness, and therefore also thought and knowledge, of necessity can only become manifest in a number of individual beings. We can only ascribe sovereignty to the thought of each of these individuals in so far as we are not aware of any power which would be able to impose any idea forcibly on him, when he is of sound mind and wide awake. But as for the sovereign validity of the knowledge in each individual's mind, we all know that there can be no talk of such a thing, and that all previous experience shows that without exception such knowledge always contains much more that is capable of being improved upon than that which cannot be improved upon or is correct.

In other words, the sovereignty of thought is realised in a number of extremely unsovereignly-thinking human beings; the knowledge which has an unconditional claim to truth is realised in a number of relative errors; neither the one nor the other can be fully realised except through an endless eternity of human existence.

Here once again we find the same contradiction as we found above, between the character of human thought, necessarily conceived as absolute, and its reality in individual human beings with their extremely limited thought. This is a contradiction which can only be solved in the infinite progression, or what is for us, at least from a practical standpoint, the endless succession, of generations of mankind. In this sense human thought is just as much sovereign as not sovereign, and its capacity for knowledge just as much unlimited as limited. It is sovereign and unlimited in its disposition, its vocation, its possibilities and its historical goal; it is not sovereign and it is limited in its individual expression and in its realisation at each particular moment.

It is just the same with eternal truths. If mankind ever reached the stage at which it could only work with eternal truths, with conclusions of thought which possess sovereign validity and an unconditional claim to truth, it would then have reached the point where the infinity of the intellectual world both in its actuality and in its potentiality had been exhausted, and this would mean that the famous miracle of the infinite series which has been counted would have been performed.

But in spite of all this, are there any truths which are so securely based that any doubt of them seems to us to amount to insanity? That twice two makes four, that the three angles of a triangle are equal to two right angles, that Paris is in France, that a man who gets no food dies of hunger, and so forth? Are there then nevertheless *eternal* truths, final and ultimate truths?

Certainly there are. We can divide the whole realm of knowledge in the traditional way into three great departments. The first includes all sciences which are concerned with inanimate Nature and are to a greater or less degree susceptible of mathematical treatment: mathematics, astronomy, mechanics, physics, chemistry. If it gives anyone any pleasure to use mighty words for very simple things, it can be asserted that *certain* results obtained by these sciences are eternal truths, final and ultimate truths; for which reason these sciences are also known as the *exact* sciences. But very far from all their results have this validity. With the introduction of variable magnitudes and the extension of their variability to the infinitely small and infinitely large, mathematics, in other respects so strictly moral, fell from grace; it ate of the tree of knowledge, which opened up to it a career of most colossal achievements, but at the same time a path of error. The virgin state of absolute validity and irrefutable certainty of everything mathematical was gone forever; mathematics entered the realm of controversy, and we have reached the point where most people differentiate and integrate not because they understand what they are doing but from pure faith, because up to now it has always come out right. Things are even worse with astronomy and mechanics, and in physics and chemistry we are surrounded by hypotheses as by a swarm of bees. And it must of necessity be so. In physics we are dealing with the motion of molecules, in chemistry with the formation of molecules out of atoms, and if the interference of light waves is not a myth, we have absolutely no prospect of ever seeing these interesting objects with our own eyes. As time goes on, final and ultimate truths become remarkably rare in this field.

We are even worse off for them in geology, which by its nature is concerned chiefly with events which took place not only in our absence but in the absence of any human being whatever. The winning of final and absolute truths in this field is therefore a very troublesome business, and the crop is extremely meagre.

The second department of science is the one which covers the investigation of living organisms. In this field there is such a multitude of reciprocal relations and causalities that not only does the solution of each question give rise to a host of other questions, but each separate problem can usually only be solved piecemeal, through a series of investigations which often requires centuries to complete; and even then the need for a systematic presentation of the interrelations makes it necessary again and again to surround the final and ultimate truths with a luxuriant growth of hypotheses. What a long series of intermediaries from Galen to Malpighi was necessary for correctly establishing such a simple matter as the circulation of the blood in mammals, how slight is our knowledge of the origin of blood corpuscles, and how numerous are the missing links even today, for example, in our attempts to bring the symptoms of a disease into some rational relationship with its causes! And often enough discoveries, such as that of the cell, are made which compel us to revise completely all formerly established final and ultimate truths in the realm of biology, and to put whole piles of them on the scrap heap once and for all. Anyone who wants to establish really pure and immutable truths in this science will therefore have to be content with such platitudes as: all men are mortal, all female mammals have mammary glands, and the like; he will not even be able to assert that the higher mammals digest with their stomach and intestines and not with their heads, for the nervous activity which is centralised in the head is indispensable to digestion.

But eternal truths are in an even worse plight in the third, the historical group of sciences. The subjects investigated by these in their historical sequence and in their present forms are the conditions of human life, social relationships, forms of law and the state, with their ideal superstructure of philosophy, religion, art, etc. In organic nature we are at least dealing with a succession of phenomena which, so far as our immediate observation is concerned, recur with fair regularity between very wide limits. Organic species have on the whole remained unchanged since the time of Aristotle. In social history, however, the repetition of conditions is the exception and not the rule, once we pass beyond the primitive stage of man, the so-called Stone Age; and when such repetitions occur, they never arise under exactly similar conditions—as for example the existence of an original common ownership of the land among all civilised peoples, and the way in which this came to an end. In the realm of human history our knowledge is therefore even more backward than in the realm of biology. Furthermore, when by way of exception the inner connection between the social and political forms of existence in an epoch come to be recognised, this as a rule only occurs when these forms are already out of date and are nearing extinction. Therefore, knowledge is here essentially relative, inasmuch as it is limited to the perception of relationships and consequences of certain social and state forms which exist only at a particular epoch and among particular people and are of their very nature transitory. Anyone therefore who sets out on this field to hunt down final and ultimate truths, truths which are pure and absolutely immutable, will bring home but little, apart from platitudes and commonplaces of the sorriest kind—for example, that generally speaking man cannot live except by labour; that up to the present mankind for the most part has been divided into rulers and ruled; that Napoleon died on May 5, 1821, and so on.

Now it is a remarkable thing that it is precisely in this sphere that we most frequently encounter truths which claim to be eternal, final and ultimate and all the rest of it. That twice two make four, that birds have beaks, and similar statements, are proclaimed as eternal truths only by those who aim at deducing, from the existence of eternal truths in general, the conclusion that there are also eternal truths in the sphere of human history—eternal morality, eternal justice, and so on—which claim a validity and scope equal to those of the truths and deductions of mathematics. And then we can confidently rely on this same friend of humanity to take the first opportunity to assure us that all previous fabricators of eternal truths have been to a greater or lesser degree asses and charlatans, that they have all fallen into error and made mistakes; but that *their* error and *their* fallibility has been in accordance with natural law, and prove the existence of truth and accuracy *in his case;* and that he, the prophet who has now arisen, has in his bag, all ready made, final and ultimate truth, eternal morality and eternal justice. This has all happened so many hundreds and thousands of times that we can only feel astonished that there should still be people credulous enough to believe this, not of others, but of themselves. Nevertheless we have here before us at least another such prophet, who also, quite in the accustomed way, flies into highly moral indignation when other people deny that any individual whatsoever is in a position to hand out to us the final and ultimate truth. Such a denial, or indeed mere doubt of it, is weakness, sterile confusion, nothingness, mordant criticism, worse than pure nihilism, incoherent chaos and other such pleasantries. As with all prophets, instead of critical and scientific examination and judgment we get moral condemnation out of hand.

We might have made mention above of the sciences which investigate the laws of human thought, i.e., logic and dialectics. In these, however, we do not fare any better as regards eternal truths. Herr Dühring declares that dialectics proper is pure nonsense, and the many books which have been and in the future will be written on logic provide abundant proof that also in this science final and ultimate truths are much more sparsely sown than is commonly believed.

For that matter, there is absolutely no need to be alarmed at the fact that the stage of knowledge which we have now reached is as little final as all that have preceded it. It already embraces a vast mass of facts and requires very great specialisation of study on the part of anyone who wants to become an expert in any particular science. But a man who applies the measure of pure, immutable, final and ultimate truth to knowledge which, by the very nature of its object, must either remain relative for long successions of generations and be completed only step by step, or which, as in cosmogony, geology and the history of man, must always remain defective and incomplete because of the faultiness of the historical material—such a man only proves thereby his own ignorance and perversity, even if the real background to his pretensions is not, as it is in this case, his claim to personal infallibility. Truth and error, like all concepts which are expressed in polar opposites, have absolute validity only in an extremely limited field, as we have just seen, and as even Herr Dühring would realise if he had any acquaintance with the first elements of dialectics, which deal precisely with the inadequacy of all polar opposites. As soon as we apply the antithesis between truth and error outside of that narrow field which has been referred to above it becomes relative and therefore unserviceable for exact scientific modes of expression; and if we attempt to apply it as absolutely valid outside that field we then really find ourselves beaten: both poles of the antithesis become transformed into their opposites, truth becomes error and error truth. Let us take as an example the well-known Boyle's law, by which, if the temperature remains constant, the volume of gases varies inversely with the pressure to which they are subjected. Regnault found that this law did not hold good in certain cases. Had he been a philosopher of reality he would have had to say: Boyle's law is mutable, and is therefore not a pure truth, therefore it is not a truth at all, therefore it is an error. But had he done this he would have committed an error far greater than the one that was contained in Boyle's law; his grain of truth would have been lost sight of in a sandhill of error; he would have distorted his originally correct conclusion into an error compared with which Boyle's law, along with the little particle of error that clings to it, would have seemed like truth. But Regnault, being a man of science, did not indulge in such childishness, but continued his investigations and discovered that Boyle's law is in general only approximately correct, and in particular loses its validity in the case of gases which can be liquefied by pressure, as soon as the pressure approaches the point at which liquefaction begins. Boyle's law therefore was proved to be correct only within definite limits. But is it absolutely and finally true even within those limits? No physicist would assert that this was so. He would say that it holds good within certain limits of pressure and temperature and for certain gases; and even within these more restricted limits he would not exclude the possibility of a still narrower limitation or altered formulation as the result of future investigations. This is how things stand with final and ultimate truths in physics for example. Really scientific works therefore as a rule avoid such dogmatic and moral expressions as error and truth, while these expressions meet us everywhere in works such as the philosophy of reality, in which empty phrase-mongering attempts to impose on us as the sovereign result of sovereign thought.

But, a naïve reader may ask, where has Herr Dühring expressly stated that the content of his philosophy of reality is final and even ultimate truth? Where? Well, for example, in the dithyramb on his system, . . . a part of which we cited in Chapter II. Or when he says, in the passage quoted above: Moral truths, in so far as their ultimate basis is understood, claim the same validity as mathematical truths. And does not Herr Dühring assert that, from his really critical standpoint and by means of those researches of his which go to the roots of things, he has forced his way through to these ultimate foundations, to the basic schemata, and has thus bestowed final and ultimate validity on moral truths? Or, if Herr Dühring does not advance this claim either for himself or for his age, if he only meant to say that some day in the dark and nebulous future it will be possible to establish final and ultimate truths, if therefore he meant to say much the same, only in a more confused way, as those he charges with "mordant scepticism" and "barren confusion"—then, in that case, what is all the noise about, and what is Herr Dühring driving at?

If we have not made much progress with truth and error, we can make even less with good and bad. This antithesis belongs exclusively to the domain of morals, that is, a domain belonging to the history of mankind, and it is precisely in this field that final and ultimate truths are most sparsely sown. The conceptions of good and bad have varied so much from nation to nation and from age to age that they have often been in direct contradiction to each other. But all the same, someone may object, good is not bad and bad is not good; if good is confused with bad there is an end to all morality, and everyone can do and leave undone whatever he cares. This is also, stripped of all oracular phrases, Herr Dühring's opinion. But the matter cannot be so simply disposed of. If it was such an easy business there would certainly be no dispute at all over good and bad; everyone would know what was good and what was bad. But how do things stand today? What morality is preached to us today? There is first Christian-feudal morality, inherited from past periods of faith; and this again has two main subdivisions, Catholic and Protestant moralities, each of which in turn has no lack of further subdivisions from the Jesuit-Catholic and Orthodox-Protestant to loose "advanced" moralities. Alongside of these we find the modern bourgeois morality and with it too the proletarian morality of the future, so that in the most advanced European countries alone the past, present and future provide three great groups of moral theories which are in force simultaneously and alongside of one another. Which is then the true one? Not one of them, in the sense of having absolute validity; but certainly that morality which contains the maximum of durable elements is the one which, in the present, represents the overthrow of the present, represents the future: that is, the proletarian.

But when we see that the three classes of modern society, the feudal aristocracy, the bourgeoisie and the proletariat, each have their special morality, we can only draw the conclusion, that men, consciously or unconsciously, derive their moral ideas in the last resort from the practical relations on which their class position is based—from the economic relations in which they carry on production and exchange.

But nevertheless there is much that is common to the three moral theories mentioned above—is this not at least a portion of a morality which is externally fixed? These moral theories represent three different stages of the same historical development, and have therefore a common historical background, and for that reason alone they necessarily have much in common. Even more. In similar or approximately similar stages of economic development moral theories must of necessity be more or less in agreement. From the moment when private property in movable objects developed, in all societies in which this private property existed there must be this moral law in common: Thou shalt not steal. Does this law thereby become an eternal moral law? By no means. In a society in which the motive for stealing has been done away with, in which therefore at the very most only lunatics would ever steal, how the teacher of morals would be laughed at who tried solemnly to proclaim the eternal truth: Thou shalt not steal!

We therefore reject every attempt to impose on us any moral dogma whatsoever as an eternal, ultimate and forever immutable moral law on the pretext that the moral world too has its permanent principles which transcend history and the differences between nations. We maintain on the contrary that all former moral theories are the product, in the last analysis, of the economic stage which society had reached at that particular epoch.

And as society has hitherto moved in class antagonisms, morality was always a class morality; it has either justified the domination and the interests of the ruling class, or, as soon as the oppressed class has become powerful enough, it has represented the revolt against this domination and the future interests of the oppressed. That in this process there has on the whole been progress in morality, as in all other branches of human knowledge, cannot be doubted. But we have not yet passed beyond class morality. A really human morality which transcends class antagonisms and their legacies in thought becomes possible only at a stage of society which has not only overcome class contradictions but has even forgotten them in practical life. And now it is possible to appreciate the presumption shown by Herr Dühring in advancing his claim, from the midst of the old class society and on the eve of a social revolution, to impose on the future classless society an eternal morality which is independent of time and changes in reality. Even assuming—what we do not know up to now—that he understands the structure of the society of the future at least in its main outlines.

Finally, one more revelation which is "absolutely original" but for that reason no less "going to the roots of things." With regard to the origin of evil, we have "the fact that the *type of the cat* with the guile associated with it is found in animal form, and the similar fact that a similar type of character is found also in human beings. . . . There is therefore nothing mysterious about evil, unless someone wants to scent out something mysterious in the existence of that *cat* or of any animal of prey." Evil is—the cat. The devil therefore has no horns or cloven hoof, but claws and green eyes. And Goethe committed an unpardonable error in presenting Mephistopheles as a black dog instead of the said cat. Evil is the cat! That is morality, not only for all worlds, but also—of no use to anyone!

. . .

We have already had more than one occasion to make ourselves acquainted with Herr Dühring's method. It consists in analysing each group of objects of knowledge into what is claimed to be their simplest elements, applying to these elements similarly simple and what are claimed to be self-evident axioms, and then continuing to operate with the aid of the results so obtained. Even a problem in the sphere of social life "must be decided axiomatically, in accordance with particular simple basic forms, just as if we were dealing with the simple . . . basic forms of mathematics." And thus the application of the mathematical method to history, morals and law is to give also in these fields mathematical certainty of the truth of the results obtained, to give them the character of pure, immutable truths.

This is only another form of the old favourite ideological method, also known as the *a priori* method, which consists in arriving at the properties of an object deductively, from the concept of the object, instead of learning them from the object itself. First the concept of the object is formed from the object; then the spit is turned round, and the object is measured by its image, the concept of it. The object is then made to conform to the concept, not the concept to the object. With Herr Dühring the simplest elements, the most ultimate abstractions which he can reach, do service for the concept, which does not alter the case, for these simplest elements are at best of a purely conceptual nature. The philosophy of reality is revealed here again, therefore, as pure ideology, the deduction of reality not from itself but from its mental image.

And when such an ideologist proceeds to construct morality and law from the concept or the so-called simplest elements of "society" instead of from the real social relations of the people round him, what material is then available for this construction? The material is clearly of two kinds: first, the meagre residue of real content which may possibly survive in those abstractions from which he starts and, secondly, the content which our ideologist once more introduces into it from his own consciousness. And what does he find in his consciousness? For the most part, moral and juridical notions which are a more or less accurate expression (positive or negative, approving or attacking) of the social and political relations amid which he lives; perhaps also ideas drawn from the literature on the subject; and finally, it may be, some additional idiosyncrasies. Our ideologist may turn and twist as he likes, but the historical reality which he cast out at the door comes in again at the window, and while he thinks he is framing a doctrine of morals and law for all times and for all worlds, he is in fact only making an image of the conservative or revolutionary tendencies of his time—an image which is distorted because it has been torn from its real basis and, like a reflection in a concave mirror, is standing on its head.

Herr Dühring thus analyses society into its simplest elements, and accordingly discovers that the simplest society consists of at least *two* people. With these two people he then proceeds to operate axiomatically. And so the basic moral axiom spontaneously presents itself: "Two human wills are as such *entirely equal* to each other, and in the first place the one can demand positively nothing of the other." And with this "the basic form of moral justice is characterised," and also that of juridical equity, for "we need only the completely simple and elementary relation of *two persons* for the development of the fundamental concepts of law."

That two people or two human wills are as such *entirely* equal in relation to each other is not only not an axiom but is even a great exaggeration. In the first place, two people, even as such, may be unequal in sex, and this simple fact leads us on at once to the fact that the simplest elements of society—if we enter into this childishness for a moment—are not two people, but a man and a woman, who found a *family,* the simplest and first form of association for the purpose of production. But this cannot in any way suit Herr Dühring. For on the one hand the two founders of society must be made as equal as possible; and secondly even Herr Dühring could not succeed in deducing from the primitive family the moral and juridical equality of man and woman. Of two alternatives, one: either the Dühringian social molecule, by the multiplication of which the whole of society is to be built up, is from the first doomed to disaster, because the two men can never by themselves bring a child into the world; or we must conceive them as two heads of families. And in this case the whole simple basic scheme is turned into its opposite: instead of the equality of men it proves at most the equality of heads of families, and as the wives are not considered, it further proves that they are subordinate.

. . . It would be superfluous to follow Herr Dühring further in his piecemeal destruction of the equality which he set up so axiomatically, of his general human sovereignty and so on; to observe how indeed he manages to set up society with his two men, but in order to create the state he requires a third because—to put the matter briefly—without this third person no majority decisions can be arrived at, and without these, and so also without the rule of the majority over the minority, no state can exist; and then how he gradually steers into calmer waters where he constructs his socialitarian state of the future, where one fine morning we shall have the honour to look him up. We have sufficiently observed that the entire equality of the two wills only exists so long as these two wills *will nothing;* that as soon as they cease to be human wills as such, and are transformed into real, individual wills, into the wills of two real men, equality comes to an end; that childishness, madness, so-called bestiality, what is supposed to be superstition, alleged prejudice and assumed incapacity on the one hand, and fancied humanity and knowledge of truth and science on the other hand—that therefore every difference in the quality of the two wills and in that of the intelligence associated with them—justifies an inequality of treatment which may go as far as subjection. What more can we ask, when Herr Dühring has so deep-rootedly, from the foundation up, laid his own edifice of equality in ruins?

But even though we have finished with Herr Dühring's puerile and superficial treatment of the idea of equality, this does not mean that we have yet finished with the idea itself, which especially thanks to Rousseau played a theoretical, and during and since the Great Revolution a practical political role, and even today still plays an important agitational role in the socialist movement of almost every country. The establishment of its scientific content will also determine its value for proletarian agitation.

The idea that all men, as men, have something in common, and that they are therefore equal so far as these common characteristics go, is of course primeval. But the modern demand for equality is something entirely different from that; this consists rather in deducing from those common characteristics of humanity, from that equality of men as men, a claim to equal political or social status for all human beings, or at least for all citizens of a state or all members of a society. Before the original conception of relative equality could lead to the conclusion that men should have equal rights in the state and in society, before this conclusion could appear to be something even natural and self-evident, however, thousands of years had to pass and did pass. In the oldest primitive communities equality of rights existed at most for members of the community; women, slaves and strangers were excluded from this equality as a matter of course. Among the Greeks and Romans the inequalities of men were of greater importance than any form of equality. It would necessarily have seemed idiotic to the ancients that Greeks and barbarians, freemen and slaves, citizens and dependents, Roman citizens and Roman subjects (to use a comprehensive term) should have a claim to equal political status. Under the Roman Empire all these distinctions gradually disappeared, except the distinction between freemen and slaves, and in this way there arose, for the freemen at least, that equality as between private individuals on the basis of which Roman law developed—the completest elaboration of law based on private property which we know. But so long as the distinction between freemen and slaves existed, there could be no talk of drawing legal conclusions from the fact of general equality *as men;* and we saw this again quite recently, in the slave-owning states of the North American Union.

Christianity knew only *one* point in which all men were equal: that all were equally born in original sin—which corresponded perfectly with its character as the religion of the slaves and the oppressed. Apart from this it recognised, at most, the equality of the elect, which however was only stressed at the very beginning. The traces of common ownership which are also found in the early stages of the new religion can be ascribed to the solidarity of a proscribed sect rather than to real equalitarian ideas. Within a very short time the establishment of the distinction between priests and laymen put an end even to this tendency to Christian equality. The overrunning of Western Europe by the Germans abolished for centuries all ideas of equality, through the gradual building up of a complicated social and political hierarchy such as had never before existed. But at the same time the invasion drew Western and Central Europe into the course of historical development, created for the first time a compact cultural area, and within this area also for the first time a system of predominantly national states exerting mutual influence on each other and mutually holding each other in check. Thereby it prepared the ground on which alone the question of the equal status of men, of the rights of man, could at a later period be raised.

The feudal Middle Ages also developed in its womb the class which was destined in the future course of its evolution to be the standard-bearer of the modern demand for equality: the bourgeoisie. Itself in its origin one of the "estates" of the feudal order, the bourgeoisie developed the predominantly handicraft industry and the exchange of products within feudal society to a relatively high level, when at the end of the fifteenth century the great maritime discoveries opened to it a new and more comprehensive career. Trade beyond the confines of Europe, which had previously been carried on only between Italy and the Levant, was now extended to America and India, and soon surpassed in importance both the mutual exchange between the various European countries and the internal trade within each separate country. American gold and silver flooded Europe and forced its way like a disintegrating element into every fissure, hole and pore of feudal society. Handicraft industry could no longer satisfy the rising demand; in the leading industries of the most advanced countries it was replaced by manufacture.

But this mighty revolution in the economic conditions of life in society was not followed immediately by any corresponding change in its political structure. The state order remained feudal, while society became more and more bourgeois. Trade on a large scale, that is to say, international and, even more, world trade, requires free owners of commodities who are unrestricted in their movements and have equal rights as traders to exchange their commodities on the basis of laws that are equal for them all, at least in each separate place. The transition from handicraft to manufacture presupposes the existence of a number of free workers—free on the one hand from the fetters of the guild and on the other from the means whereby they could themselves utilise their labour power: workers who can contract with their employers for the hire of their labour power, and as parties to the contract have rights equal with his. And finally the equality and equal status of all human labour, because and in so far as it is *human* labour, found its unconscious but clearest expression in the law of value of modern bourgeois economics, according to which the value of a commodity is measured by the socially necessary labour embodied in it.[1] But where economic relations required freedom and equality of rights, the political system opposed them at every step with guild restrictions and special privileges. Local privileges, differential duties, exceptional laws of all kinds affected in trading not only foreigners or people living in the colonies, but often enough also whole categories of the nationals of each country; the privileges of the guilds everywhere and ever anew formed barriers to the path of development of manufacture. Nowhere was the path open and the chances equal for the bourgeois competitors—and yet this was the first and ever more pressing need.

The demand for liberation from feudal fetters and the establishment of equality of rights by the abolition of feudal inequalities was bound soon to assume wider dimensions from the moment when the economic advance of society first placed it on the order of the day. If it was raised in the interests of industry and trade, it was also necessary to demand the same equality of rights for the great mass of the peasantry who, in every degree of bondage from total serfdom upwards, were compelled to give the greater part of their labour time to their feudal lord without payment and in addition to render innumerable other dues to him and to the state. On the other hand,

---

[1] This tracing of the origin of the modern ideas of equality to the economic conditions of bourgeois society was first developed by Marx in *Capital*. [F.E.]

it was impossible to avoid the demand for the abolition also of feudal privileges, the freedom from taxation of the nobility, the political privileges of the various feudal estates. And as people were no longer living in a world empire such as the Roman Empire had been, but in a system of independent states dealing with each other on an equal footing and at approximately the same degree of bourgeois development, it was a matter of course that the demand for equality should assume a general character reaching out beyond the individual state, that freedom and equality should be proclaimed as *human rights*. And it is significant of the specifically bourgeois character of these human rights that the American Constitution, the first to recognise the rights of man, in the same breath confirmed the slavery of the coloured races in America: class privileges were proscribed, race privileges sanctified.

As is well known, however, from the moment when, like a butterfly from the chrysalis, the bourgeoisie arose out of the burghers of the feudal period, when this "estate" of the Middle Ages developed into a class of modern society, it was always and inevitably accompanied by its shadow, the proletariat. And in the same way the bourgeois demand for equality was accompanied by the proletarian demand for equality. From the moment when the bourgeois demand for the abolition of class *privileges* was put forward, alongside of it appeared the proletarian demand for the abolition of the *classes themselves*—at first in religious form, basing itself on primitive Christianity, and later drawing support from the bourgeois equalitarian theories themselves. The proletarians took the bourgeoisie at their word: equality must not be merely apparent, must not apply merely to the sphere of the state, but must also be real, must be extended to the social and economic sphere. And especially since the time when the French bourgeoisie, from the Great Revolution on, brought bourgeois equality to the forefront, the French proletariat has answered it blow for blow with the demand for social and economic equality, and equality has become the battle-cry particularly of the French proletariat.

The demand for equality in the mouth of the proletariat has therefore a double meaning. It is either—as was especially the case at the very start, for example in the peasants' war—the spontaneous reaction against the crying social inequalities, against the contrast of rich and poor, the feudal lords and their serfs, surfeit and starvation; as such it is the simple expression of the revolutionary instinct, and finds its justification in that, and indeed only in that. Or, on the other hand, the proletarian demand for equality has arisen as the reaction against the bourgeois demand for equality, drawing more or less correct and more far-reaching demands from this bourgeois demand, and serving as an agitational means in order to rouse the workers against the capitalists on the basis of the capitalists' own assertions; and in this case it stands and falls with bourgeois equality itself. In both cases the real content of the proletarian demand for equality is the demand for the *abolition of classes*. Any demand for equality which goes beyond that, of necessity passes into absurdity. We have given examples of this, and shall find enough additional ones later when we come to Herr Dühring's phantasies of the future.

The idea of equality, therefore, both in its bourgeois and in its proletarian form, is itself a historical product, the creation of which required definite historical conditions which in turn themselves presuppose a long previous historical development. It is therefore anything but an eternal truth. And if today it is taken for granted by the general public—in one sense or another—if, as Marx says, it "already possesses the fixity of a popular prejudice," this is not the consequence of its axiomatic truth, but the result of the general diffusion and the continued appropriateness of the ideas of the eighteenth century. If therefore Herr Dühring is able without more ado to make his famous two men conduct their economic relations on the basis of equality, this is because it seems quite natural to popular prejudice. And in fact Herr Dühring calls his philosophy *natural* because it is derived from things which seem to him quite natural. But why they seem to him quite natural—is a question which he does not ask.

· · ·

Hegel was the first to state correctly the relation between freedom and necessity. To him, freedom is the appreciation of necessity. "Necessity is *blind* only *in so far as it is not understood.*" Freedom does not consist in the dream of independence of natural laws, but in the knowledge of these laws, and in the possibility this gives of systematically making them work towards definite ends. This holds good in relation both to the laws of external nature and to those which govern the bodily and mental existence of men themselves—two classes of laws which we can separate from each other at most only in thought but not in reality. Freedom of the will therefore means nothing but the capacity to make decisions with real knowledge of the subject. Therefore the *freer* a man's judgment is in relation to a definite question, with so much the greater *necessity* is the content of this judgment determined; while the uncertainty, founded on ignorance, which seems to make an arbitrary choice among many different and conflicting possible decisions, shows by this precisely that it is not free, that it is controlled by the very object it should itself control. Freedom therefore consists in the control over ourselves and over external nature which is founded on knowledge of natural necessity; it is therefore necessarily a product of historical development. The first men who separated themselves from the animal kingdom were in all essentials as unfree as the animals themselves, but each step forward in civilisation was a step towards freedom. On the threshold of human history stands the discovery that mechanical motion can be transformed into heat: the production of fire by friction; at the close of the development so far gone through stands the discovery that heat can be transformed into mechanical motion: the steam engine. And, in spite of the gigantic and liberating revolution in the social world which the steam engine is carrying through—and which is not yet half completed—it is beyond question that the generation of fire by friction was of even greater effectiveness for the liberation of mankind. For the generation of fire by friction gave man for the first time control over one of the forces of Nature, and thereby separated him for ever from the animal kingdom. The steam engine will never bring about such a mighty leap forward in human development, however important it may seem in our eyes as representing all those powerful productive forces dependent on it—forces which alone make possible a state of society in which there are no longer class distinctions or anxiety over the means of subsistence for the individual, and in which for the first time there can be talk of real human freedom and of an existence in harmony with the established laws of Nature. But how young the whole of human history still is, and how ridiculous it would be to attempt to ascribe any absolute validity to our present views, is evident from the simple fact that all past history can be characterised as the history of the epoch from the practical discovery of the transformation of mechanical motion into heat up to that of the transformation of heat into mechanical motion.

QUESTIONS FOR STUDY AND DISCUSSION

1. Are there any eternal truths according to Engels?
2. Under what science does Engels classify moral systems?
3. How will the morality of the communist society differ from all past moralities?
4. To what extent is the equality of men a relative and historically conditioned concept for Engels?
5. How can man be both free and determined?

TOPICS FOR DISCUSSION AND TERM PAPERS

A.

1. What is the basic difference between Kant's approach to ethics and Hegel's?
2. Describe the idealist tendencies in Fichte's ethics as stated in *The Vocation of Man*.
3. What does Hegel consider to be the basic moral message of the Gospel in *The Spirit of Christianity?*
4. On what basis does Hegel consider the State to be the highest realization of ethics?
5. Describe the essential distinction between morality and ethics in Hegel's *Philosophy of Right*.
6. To what extent can one speak of a "Marxist ethics"?
7. To what extent is Marx's social philosophy Hegelian?
8. Compare Engels' position on morality in *Anti-Dühring* with Marx's position in one of his early writings.

B.

1. Aristotle considered his analysis of the virtues as an essential component of his moral system. What virtues are basic in the perspectives of Kierkegaard, Marcel, Hegel, and Kant?
2. Consider Hegel's demand that man identify himself with the universal and Marcel's insistence that the moral person must be sensitive to the particular concrete situation and suspicious of the abstract. Are both views possible?
3. Are there any points of similarity between the idealistic ethics of Hegel and the naturalistic ethics of Dewey? For instance, does the theme of evolutionary development appear essential to both these philosophers?
4. Compare Kant's theory of obligation with that of Aristotle. Would it be true to say that Kant is a voluntarist in ethics whereas Aristotle is an intellectualist?
5. Compare Fichte's observations about man's struggle for freedom being dependent on man's mastery over nature with the existentialist's demand that freedom is a creative act of man himself. Do recent developments such as automation make Fichte's hopes seem nearer to realization? Would Fichte agree with Aristotle that leisure and contemplation are essential to full human living?

RECOMMENDED READINGS

Primary Sources

Fichte, Johann Gottlieb. *Addresses to the German Nation.* Trans. by R. F. Jones and G. H. Turnbull. Chicago: Open Court Publishing Co., 1922. Fichte's most popular work; it became the philosophical basis of German nationalism.
————. *The Vocation of Man.* Ed. and with Introd. by Roderick M. Chisholm. New York: Liberal Arts Press, 1956.

Hegel, G. W. F. *On Christianity: Early Theological Writings*. Trans. by T. M. Knox and with Introd. by Richard Kroner. New York: Harper & Row, 1961. Hegel's early theological writings are easier than his mature works. Kroner's Introduction gives an excellent description of Hegel's intellectual development.

―――. *Philosophy of Right*. Trans. and with notes by T. M. Knox. Oxford: Clarendon Press, 1942. See especially Part II, "Morality," and Part III, "Ethics." This work is too difficult for most undergraduate students. In our Introduction we used and paraphrased as much of the important parts as possible. Selections from the *Philosophy of Right* may also be found in *The Philosophy of Hegel*. Ed. and with Introd. by Carl J. Friedrich. New York: Random House, 1954. Pp. 221–329.

Kant, Immanuel. *The Fundamental Principles of the Metaphysic of Ethics*. Trans. and with Introd. by Otto Manthey-Zorn. New York: Appleton-Century-Crofts, 1938. This exposition of Kant's ethical theory is easier than the more comprehensive *Critique of Practical Reason, and Other Writings in Moral Philosophy*. Trans., ed., and with Introd. by Lewis White Beck. New York: Liberal Arts Press, 1956.

Marx, Karl. *Karl Marx: Early Writings*. Trans. and ed. by T. B. Bottomore. Foreword by Erich Fromm. New York: McGraw-Hill, 1964. This collection contains some of the most important writings of the young Marx: *On the Jewish Question, Contribution to the Critique of Hegel's Philosophy of Right*, and *The Economic and Philosophical Manuscripts*.

―――, and Friedrich Engels. *Basic Writings on Politics and Philosophy*. Ed. by Lewis Feuer. New York: Doubleday & Co., 1959. Contains *Socialism: Utopian and Scientific, Ludwig Feuerbach, Communist Manifesto, Theses on Feuerbach*, and excerpts from *Capital* and from the important historical works of Marx.

―――. *The German Ideology*. Parts I and III. Trans., ed., and with Introd. by R. Pascal. New York: International Publishers, 1960. Part I, pp. 3–78, is very important for a correct understanding of the Marxist view on history, culture, and ethics.

Commentaries

Adamson, R. *Fichte*. Edinburgh: Blackwood & Sons, 1881. No better introduction has yet replaced this clear, accurate, and sympathetic work.

Collins, James. *History of Modern European Philosophy*. Milwaukee: Bruce Publishing Co., 1961. Pp. 515–34. The best history of philosophy available to the American student.

Copleston, Frederick. *A History of Philosophy*. New York: Doubleday & Co., 1964. See VI, Part II, "Kant," pp. 101–40.

Dupré, Louis. *The Philosophical Foundations of Marxism*. New York: Harcourt, Brace & World, 1966. A direct introduction to Marx's own texts, this analytic commentary familiarizes the reader with Marx's technical language and method of thinking. Chapters 1–2 contain a historical introduction to Hegel's social philosophy and a detailed discussion of the *Philosophy of Right*.

Hook, Sidney. *From Hegel to Marx: Studies in the Intellectual Development of Karl Marx*. Ann Arbor, Mich.: University of Michigan Press, 1962. A classic on the historical and philosophical factors that contributed to the formation of Marx's thought.

Marcuse, Herbert. *Reason and Revolution: Hegel and the Rise of Social Theory,* 2nd ed. New York: Humanities Press, 1955. Part I deals with Hegel's philosophy.

Paton, H. J. *The Categorical Imperative: A Study in Kant's Moral Philosophy.* Chicago: University of Chicago Press, 1948.

Royce, Josiah. *Spirit of Modern Philosophy.* New York: George Braziller, 1955. Lecture 5, "Fichte." A well-written and comprehensive account of the basic theses of Fichte's philosophy by an admirer who was a great philosopher in his own right.

Stace, W. T. *The Philosophy of Hegel: A Systematic Exposition.* New York: Dover Publications, 1955. The commentary on Hegel's *Philosophy of Right,* pp. 374–442, is especially valuable to students. The book remains an indispensable aid.

Tucker, Robert C. *Philosophy and Myth in Karl Marx.* Cambridge, Eng., Cambridge University Press, 1961. A brilliant and well-written synthesis of Marx's thought. The ideal introduction to the study of Marxism.

PART THREE

AMERICAN
NATURALISTIC
THOUGHT:

James
Dewey
Edel
Hook
Romanell
Dennes

EDITED BY

Jude P. Dougherty

BELLARMINE COLLEGE

AMERICAN
NATURALISTIC
THOUGHT:
James
Dewey
Edel
Hook
Romanell
Dennes

Introduction

The Naturalistic Temperament

Naturalism as a philosophical term is admittedly vague. In the history of Western thought the word has had many different meanings; in America it has been used to designate a number of different systems. According to current usage, naturalism could generally be defined as a philosophical position that affirms that nature is the whole of reality; that man has his origin, growth, and decay in nature; and that nature is self-explanatory—nature being defined as that which is amenable to scientific investigation.

Most of the proponents of naturalism present it as a tendency, an outlook, or a frame of mind, rather than as a system. Two basic theses underlie all naturalistic investigation. The first affirms that whatever happens in nature is dependent in some fundamental way upon the organization of bodies located in space and time; the second insists that the "scientific method" is the only means of obtaining reliable knowledge.[1] Naturalists, on the whole, are found to be rather ambiguous in stating the nature of

---

[1] Cf. Ernest Nagel, "Naturalism Reconsidered," *Proceedings and Addresses of the American Philosophical Association,* XXVII (Yellow Springs, Ohio: Antioch Press, 1955), 8; Sidney Hook, "Naturalism and Democracy," in *Naturalism and the Human Spirit,* ed. by Yervant H. Krikorian (New York: Columbia University Press, 1944), p. 45.

scientific method, but most would admit of its analogical predication. In a broad sense, scientific method is regarded as nothing more than the use of "critical intelligence." Hence the disciplines of sociology and economics, as well as history in some of its phases, are regarded by the naturalist as genuinely scientific.

Epistemologically, the naturalist must be considered a realist, in the sense that he holds that the objects of knowledge are extra-mental and exist as they are perceived to be, although nominalistic and Kantian tendencies can at times be discerned in some naturalists. Metaphysically, the naturalist presents himself as antidualistic, objecting to the distinctions between the natural and the supernatural, between man and nature, mind and body, and appearance and reality. He will accept the designation "materialist" if he is allowed to distinguish between reductive materialism and his own.[2] Reductive materialism, as the naturalist defines it, reduces mental events immediately to the physical, while nonreductive materialism affirms merely that every mental event is contingent upon the organization of certain physical events. The naturalist is careful to avoid suggesting that an idea is nothing but "a potential or tentative muscular response," or that pain is nothing but "the passing of an electric current through a nerve fiber." But he does assert that the relation between the occurrence of ideas or pains and the occurrence of physiological manifestations is a contingent or causal one. The naturalist denies the existence of God, immortality, separated souls, spirits, and cosmic purpose "for the same generic reasons that he denies the existence of fairies, elves, leprechauns, and an invisible satellite revolving between earth and moon." [3] There is no evidence for any of them.

As to his teaching on man, the naturalist grants that man is unique among animals in ability and accomplishment but denies that he has a special place in nature. Between man and his animal ancestors there is only a difference of degree, not of kind. Consciousness, like any other phenomenon, can be described empirically, at least in its effects, and accounted for in terms of matter and organization of matter. Presupposed by the naturalist is a theory of biological evolution that declares that nature in its evolutionary process regularly gives rise to operations and functions on newer and higher levels. Consciousness and thought are regarded as two such higher levels of operation. They have their sole cause in the organism in which they appear. Admittedly, thought and consciousness are distinct from any previous products of an evolving nature, but the factors from which they arise are no different, except for their particular organization, from the factors from which physical, chemical, and biological processes arise.[4]

---

[2] John Dewey, Hook, and Nagel, "Are Naturalists Materialists?" *Journal of Philosophy,* XLII (Sept. 13, 1945), 515–30.
[3] Hook, "Naturalism in Democracy," in Krikorian, p. 45.
[4] Dewey, Hook, and Nagel, pp. 516 ff.; Nagel, *Sovereign Reason* (Glencoe, Ill.: The Free Press, 1954), p. 56.

By temperament the naturalist is oriented toward the practical. He agrees with the pragmatist that knowledge, if it is to be considered meaningful, must have practical consequences. But while Charles Sanders Peirce and William James would be reluctant to identify pragmatism with any one method, the naturalist regards experimental science as the method of intelligence par excellence, a method combining perfectly theory and practice, knowing and doing. This identification is particularly evident in the instrumentalism of John Dewey.

Historical Development

As a philosophical attitude, naturalism is not indigenous to America. Its European roots are evident in British empiricism and in the positivism and sociologism of August Comte (1798–1857) and Ernest Mach (1836–1916). Although naturalism appeared relatively late on the American scene, only in America has the term "naturalism" been used to designate a particular set of philosophical views. It arose as an alternative to the idealism dominant in American thought during the last quarter of the nineteenth century and influential during the first two decades of the present century. By the nineteen thirties, naturalism had clearly replaced idealism as the predominant trend in American philosophical thinking.

The first major expression of the naturalistic temper in the United States was found in George Santayana, *Life of Reason* (5 vols., 1905–06). Other systematic expressions subsequently appeared in Roy Wood Sellars, *Evolutionary Naturalism* (1921); Frederick Woodbridge, *Nature and Mind* (1937); and James B. Pratt, *Naturalism* (1939). Early contributions which also must be mentioned were those of Morris R. Cohen, *Reason and Nature* (1931); C. I. Lewis, *Mind and the World Order* (1929); and William P. Montague, *The Way of Things* (1940).

Of American naturalists, however, John Dewey (1859–1952) is the most important, not only because of his significant contribution to the doctrinal development of naturalism but also because through him naturalism came to exert a strong influence on public education and consequently on the American mind generally. The history of American naturalism is strikingly reflected in Dewey's own intellectual development as he moved from an early defense of idealism, confident that the new discoveries in biology and psychology could be incorporated into an idealistic framework, to an outright naturalism, presented as the only outlook that could be compatible with the modern scientific world view. The mature naturalism of Dewey is apparent not only in his later works, such as *Experience and Nature* (1925) and *The Quest for Certainty* (1929), but also in the writings of his disciples, particularly in the articles of many of his co-contributors to the platform volumes, *American Philosophy Today and Tomorrow* and *Natu-*

ralism and the Human Spirit.[5] Many of the contributors to these two volumes subsequently developed themes first presented there. Although American naturalism in the 1960s is not to be solely identified with the authors in these symposia, it is evident that they well represent this tendency in American thought. Of the contributors to these volumes, five, in addition to Dewey, may be selected as important representatives of the naturalistic interest and temperament: Sidney Hook, Abraham Edel, Ernest Nagel, John Herman Randall, Jr., and William R. Dennes. Other naturalists who are not included in the two platform volumes but whose contributions to naturalistic ethics will be considered here are Patrick Romanell, Paul Edwards, Paul W. Kurtz, and Robert G. Olson. Although Nagel and Randall have contributed much to the literature of American naturalism, they have not been directly concerned with the advancement of naturalistic ethics.[6] Nagel is primarily interested in the logic of science where he has done much to refine the naturalistic notion of science. Randall is known primarily as a historian of philosophy. As a naturalist he is interested in certain classical metaphysical and epistemological problems such as the problem of substance and the problem of universals.

Theory of Values

What can naturalism offer in the way of practical direction to the political, social, and religious leaders of our time? As the naturalist sees it, before he can make any specific proposals, he must first deal with several fundamental questions: What are values? Do values belong to things, or does man endow things with value? Is it possible to arrive at a scientific treatment of values? What criteria can be established to determine moral action? As a result of being confronted with these and other questions, the naturalist has labored not so much in creating an ethics in the traditional sense as in clearing up preliminary problems and suggesting paths and criteria by

---

[5] These volumes are representative of current American naturalism because they make a conscious attempt to define naturalism and to develop some of its themes. In *American Philosophy Today and Tomorrow,* ed. by Horace M. Kallen and Sidney Hook (New York: Lee Furman, 1935), Irwin Edman and Hook define the naturalistic temper, Ernest Nagel wrestles with several epistemological problems from a naturalistic point of view, and John Herman Randall, Jr., contributes an essay entitled "Historical Naturalism." In *Naturalism and the Human Spirit,* Hook, Nagel, and Randall are joined by Krikorian, John Dewey, Abraham Edel, Sterling P. Lamprecht, Eliseo Vivas, Herbert W. Schneider, George Boas, Edward W. Strong, Thelma Z. Lavine, William R. Dennes, Harry Todd Costello, and Harold A. Larrabee in the development of a broad naturalistic philosophy. Hardly any area of philosophy is neglected.

[6] Cf. Nagel, *The Structure of Science* (New York: Harcourt, Brace & World, 1961) and Randall, *Nature and Historical Experience* (New York: Columbia University Press, 1958).

which an ethics may be developed. What has emerged from his endeavors may loosely be called his "theory of values."

Although the naturalist has been concerned with both ethical and artistic values, what he offers as his theory of values has been developed with the ethical uppermost in mind. His offering is modest, he confesses. He doesn't pretend to have the last word. He avoids seeming dogmatic. What he sets forth is more in the nature of a program than a fixed code, more a guide for the establishment of criteria by which life may be directed than a set of formalized rules.[7] Dewey's answer to the problem of whether man endows things with value or finds them valuable apart from himself is widely accepted. According to Dewey, value is not something that exists independently of man, but it is the name we give to whatever men prize, hold dear, or desire.[8] Man's interests create values and reason organizes them. Thought does not initially create values nor is it needed to discover values, yet it has a role to play in reconstructing and perpetuating values.

For this analysis of the "valuable" or the "good," Dewey is obviously indebted to William James (1842–1910). Although James is not to be considered a naturalist, many themes suggested by him are woven into Dewey's mature philosophy and have been further developed by subsequent naturalists. James's essay "The Moral Philosopher and the Moral Life," included in the selections, was highly suggestive to Dewey insofar as it defines the good in terms of a satisfactory resolution of tensions. From James, Dewey also learned to regard intelligence as simply another mode of behavior in which the living thing interacts with its environment. Intelligence, as James conceived it, is the evolutionary outgrowth of more primitive efforts on the part of the organism to cope with its surroundings. This concept of intelligence forms the basis of Dewey's instrumentalism.

Unfortunately James never published a systematic exposition of his views on ethics. This is not to say that he did not possess a theory of values, but to present the ethics of pragmatism as found in James would largely be by way of construction or implication. Dewey's ethical theory is commonly regarded as a logical development of at least one aspect of James's pragmatism. Dewey's ethics is frequently referred to as "pragmatic" or as a "pragmatic naturalism." The principal difference between their ethical outlooks is that James manifested a greater respect for religion and religiously derived values than did Dewey and his disciples. James did not care where a truth came from or how it originated. If a belief is shown to work when it is applied to a concrete problem, it is to be considered true. Hence James regarded as true many beliefs that had been derived from religious witness. In the saint of Christian tradition, James discovered the apex of moral perfection. Dewey and his disciples, by virtue of a tendency to identify science with empiriometric technique, have not only ruled out

---

[7] See Nagel, *Sovereign Reason*, p. 56.
[8] *Theory of Valuation* (Chicago: University of Chicago Press, 1939), pp. 33–34.

religion as a source of reliable knowledge, but have tended to look upon it as an impediment to the development of a sound code of values.

In developing his ethics, Dewey placed considerable emphasis upon what he called the "value judgment," which is a type of a reflection. Value judgments occur because of a conflict between disparate factors within our experience. They are citations of what seems necessary to make experience more satisfactory, discoveries of what under the circumstances one ought to do if he is to resolve a situation successfully. For Dewey, experience is largely nonintellectual, embracing most of the content of man's life including his loves and hates, his eating and sleeping, his illness and health, and his love for fine arts, sport, and companionship. Experience becomes thinking, or thought, only when incompatibilities between the various elements within experience demand more than mere appreciation for their successful resolution. Thinking comes into play when some situation demands adjustment; the value judgment is one example of such thinking.

It is a point of emphasis with Dewey that the judgment does not discover value outside of experience, but "reconstructs experience to make it more valuable." Thought dips again and again into unthinking experience to discover, preserve, and deepen the values in the creation of which it is instrumental. Values are, therefore, considered immanent in human experience, not secluded in some transcendental or conceptual realm accessible to common men only through priestly or philosophic intermediaries.

Although values are not to be considered apart from the human context in which they arise, this does not mean that they are wholly subjective.[9] The very use of the verb "evaluate" carries with it the implication of an existential relationship between subject and object. According to Dewey, every event or object has some immediate qualities attached to it—good or bad, enjoyable or unenjoyable. Of these immediate qualities little can be said; they are simply enjoyed or they are not. The real value or good is the result of an evaluation or judgment in terms of conditions or consequences. The properties and relationships that entitle an object to be worthy of pursuit are extraneous to the qualities that make it an immediate good. Here the value judgment comes into play to distinguish between what immediately gratifies and what is truly valuable. If the valuable were identified simply as that which gives immediate pleasure, we would be obliged to regard as valuable many acts that, though they may result in immediate gratification, are harmful in the long run. Recognizing this, Dewey distinguished between "what is desired" and "what is desirable." According to Dewey, every person, to the degree to which he is capable of learning from experience, makes this distinction.

John Herman Randall, Jr. (b. 1899), who is perhaps the most ontologically minded of the naturalists under study here, develops this theme in *Nature and Historical Experience,* where he attempts to define the precise

---

[9] Cf. Dewey, *The Quest for Certainty* (New York: Minton, Balch & Co., 1929), Ch. 10; *Reconstruction in Philosophy,* 2nd ed. rev. (Boston: Beacon Press, 1948), Ch. 6.

reality of value. Agreeing with Dewey that to evaluate is to determine "how best" to do something, he finds that value is best understood as a quality of substance, namely, the power of substance to get itself sought. Value is simply an aspect of substance considered as intelligible, for understanding and evaluating are identical processes. Randall asserts that the full intelligibility of any situation or substance depends upon a knowledge of its end or purpose. But according to his analysis, the most we can hope for is partial intelligibility, since it is impossible to discover any ultimate end or purpose. Values are thus relative because the most we can determine is "how best" we can do something under a particular set of circumstances. What is best absolutely is beyond our knowledge. We cannot determine what is best in the ultimate context, because the ultimate context itself is beyond discovery. In a word, since there are no fixed ends, there are no fixed values.

Randall and Dewey agree that values are relative to the specific situation in which they obtain. Moral ends or goods exist only when something has to be done.[10] The good of a situation is determined on the basis of the defect to be rectified. Consequently, each situation gives rise to its own good; and what is expedient at one moment may not be expedient at another. There are no fixed absolutes as the supernaturalist would suppose. The imposition of fixed ends is simply a sign of an emotional grappling for certainty where certainty is impossible.

If, as the naturalist insists, it is impossible to determine fixed codes or unchanging values and if values differ from situation to situation, are not values wholly personal? Can the moralist justify his concern for common ethics? Are there certain general canons of morality that pertain universally? Dewey had no doubt that certain general evaluative propositions "which describe and define certain things as good, fit, or proper" could be made. But these could be attained only with difficulty. The difficulty involved brings us to the important question of procedure.

Establishing Moral Norms

To the naturalist, there are two generic ways of establishing moral norms: the religious approach, "ultimately based on absolute intuitions," and the experimental approach, "which regards the test of consequences as decisive." As far as he is concerned, there is little doubt as to which is better. As Sidney Hook (b. 1902) writes, "The evidence drawn from the fruits and consequences of the way in which ideals function in experience is far more warranted than the evidence for theological and metaphysical assumptions."[11] Furthermore, the achievements of genuine knowledge about

---

[10] Dewey, *Experience and Nature* (La Salle, Ill.: Open Court Publishing Co., 1925), pp. 91–92, 396–97.
[11] *Education for Modern Man,* 2nd ed. (New York: Alfred A. Knopf, 1963), p. 14.

nature—in medicine, biology, psychology, and history—have been largely won by a bitter struggle against the obstacles set in the path of scientific enquiry by the proponents of the religious approach.

Inadequacy of a Religious Approach

Where it is granted that certain codes of behavior advanced by religious bodies are valuable and laudable, it is also affirmed that these are true or good only insofar as they conform to academic standards. William R. Dennes (b. 1897) advises that if we reject his definition of "the valuable" and "the right," and if we are inclined to define "the right" simply as what God commands, then we are faced with the problem of determining which of the various commands offered to us by the various religions have divine authority and origin. If one has reason for obeying the commands of religious bodies, it can only be that their expression has seemed to him to be true and righteous in terms of naturalistic norms of truth and right. It is Dennes' contention that

> Religious experience and theological doctrine add nothing to the meaning or truth of any statement or to the validity of any rule of conduct—add nothing which is not finally traceable to, and which does not owe its meaning and probability to, observations and loves and preferences which remain what they are whether or not they are referred to, or taken as evidence of deity.[12]

Robert G. Olson (b. 1924) goes further perhaps than most naturalists would be willing to go when he asserts in *The Morality of Self-Interest* that "traditional religious views are on the whole inimical to the practice of morality." [13] According to Olson, claims are made by the theist that religion encourages virtuous behavior, that the image of God as a loving father tends to heighten consciousness of the brotherhood of men, thereby encouraging concern for the general human well-being. "But is there the slightest shred of evidence," Olson asks, "for the view that theism has ever had a sufficiently strong hold on the human imagination to have appreciably affected the behavior of any group of human beings?" [14] The evidence seems to be to the contrary. "The impetus for large-scale social reform has usually come from dominantly secular groups, such as the utilitarians, the Marxists, and the pragmatists." Furthermore, religion can be a drain on social energies. Insofar as religion envisages human society in such fashion that earthly miseries are given a recognized and honorable place, religion endows suffering with value and thereby weakens man's concern to diminish it.

---

[12] "A Skepticism Based on an Analysis of Meaning," in *Philosophers Speak of God,* ed. by Charles Hartshorne and William L. Reese (Chicago: Chicago University Press, 1953), p. 489.
[13] (New York: Harcourt, Brace & World, 1965), p. 158.
[14] *Ibid.,* p. 160.

Toward a Scientific Ethics

Of the two generic ways of establishing moral norms, the scientific and the theological, the naturalist leaves no doubt as to which he prefers. Sidney Hook states the naturalistic position clearly when he writes: "Since human values acquire their quality of value by being related to human desire, only the use of scientific intelligence can help us discover the difference between reliable and unreliable values." [15] Having declared his confidence in scientific intelligence, the naturalist must now show the precise manner in which science may be employed in ethics.

One obvious way is through a reliance upon its conclusions. It is evident that any ethical theory must be in tune with the facts of nature, both human and nonhuman. Since desires and feelings are the raw materials of reality, the facts that will have the greatest bearing on ethics will be those provided by psychology, which studies these basic instincts. Biological, sociological, and anthropological data will also be relevant. In constructing its ethical theory, naturalism will draw upon all these sciences,[16] but the relationship of ethics to them will still have to be defined.

In the past, ethics has sometimes been made a department of, or subsumed by, one of the several sciences that have man as their object. One observer of naturalistic ethics, Rollo Handy, in an article entitled "The Naturalistic 'Reduction' of Ethics to Science," concludes that although ethics relies heavily on the data of science, and even defines its concepts in the language of science, it is still able to maintain its autonomy.[17] Yet, if Paul W. Kurtz (b. 1925) is to be accepted as a spokesman for naturalism, ethics must become so closely allied with the behavioral sciences it draws upon that it will no longer be possible to distinguish between it and those sciences. Kurtz writes: "The chief question for the science of value is the question 'What is life?': value will then be defined in terms of it. Thus the definition of value is equivalent to the definition of man." [18] It is Kurtz's thesis that ethics should attempt no more than to render understandable "the nature of human life and the laws by which it continues." It cannot have anything to do with practical application. "It is about time," he con-

---

[15] "On the Battlefield of Philosophy," *Partisan Review*, XVI (1949), 262.

[16] Abraham Edel, "Some Trends in American Naturalistic Ethics," in *Philosophic Thought in France and the United States,* ed. by M. Farber (Buffalo: University of Buffalo Press, 1950), pp. 604–09.

[17] Handy writes: "Obviously many naturalists do want to make ethics amenable to a scientific approach, and one way this can be done is to define ethical concepts so that they have the same kind of descriptive meaning scientific concepts have. Ethical propositions are then cognitively meaningful and in theory either true or false, and ethical terms are definable. In this sense ethics becomes scientific, yet it may retain a type of autonomy. To maintain that there is an intimate connection between the data of the sciences and ethics and that ethical propositions are descriptive, is not to make ethics part of either one or several sciences." (*Journal of Philosophy,* LIII [Dec. 20, 1956], 832.)

[18] "Naturalistic Ethics and the Open Question," *Journal of Philosophy,* LII (March 3, 1955), 127–28.

tinues, "that philosophers cease requiring of other philosophers absolute standards to solve practical problems." Kurtz, in effect, ushers ethics out the door, even in the accepted naturalistic sense, without making it clear to what he wishes to append the old label. In view of the task he has established for it, ethics is practically indistinguishable from the behavioral sciences. To study value is to study behavior. In his own words:

> Thus the explanatory science of man, and not necessarily the criticism of the actual moral problems of practice, is the direct problem of the science and philosophy of value. The principles of behavior become the principles of value, without any ultimate ego-centric connotations.

If Kurtz is representative of its general attitude, naturalism will be deprived of anything that approaches an ethics in the traditional sense of the term.

Methodological Difficulties

Although all naturalists would answer the question "Is a scientific treatment of morality possible?" in the affirmative, not all would use the term "scientific" in a univocal sense when describing, for example, the methods of physics, biology, and ethics. Granted that moral science can make use of certain data supplied by the physical sciences, there is still the question to be faced: "Is its own method 'scientific'?"

The problem of method reaches its most lucid discussion in a work by Patrick Romanell (b. 1912), significantly entitled *Toward a Critical Naturalism*. Romanell, who calls himself a "critical naturalist," is highly sceptical of Dewey's analysis of method in ethics. He contends that Dewey, by insisting on an "identity of method" equally applicable to the physical and moral, rendered void that which is distinctive about moral experience. Romanell considers Dewey's insistence on an identity of method, though not of subject matter, unfounded, because in the last analysis it plunges Dewey into the error he hoped to avoid, namely, that of the crude materialist who confuses an identity of method with an identity of subject matter. To Dewey's critic there is no real difference between the methodological reductionism of instrumentalism and the so-called ontological reductionism of materialism. The former is but a sophistical version of the latter, for they both reduce ethical data to "physical fact."

Romanell also contends that Dewey's ethics rests upon the assumption that there is only one type of scientific method. From that premise it follows that there is an identity of logical procedure in the physical and moral sciences. But Romanell raises the question: Can the method of ethics be identical with the experimental procedure in use elsewhere?

> If it can, then Dewey has made a tremendous contribution to logical theory; but if it cannot, his whole case for a reconstruction of traditional morality on the model of the experimental sciences

breaks down for the simple reason that it rests on a false premise, that of methodological reductionism.[19]

Put another way: Is it possible to verify a normative hypothesis by the same procedure employed in verifying an existential hypothesis? By way of illustration, Romanell takes what is for him a moral proposition, "Women should have the right to vote," and sets it beside another proposition, this time from the field of chemistry, "All acids turn blue litmus red." He then asks whether these propositions are verifiable in the same way. Krikorian has answered: "In theory the problem of verification in ethics should be no different from the same problem in any other field." [20] And in this opinion Randall seems to concur, for he writes, "scientific inquiry is itself precisely a process of evaluation, of 'how best' to do something." [21] It is Romanell's thesis, however, that there is a difference in theory as well as in practice.

> There are several reasons why ethics, no matter how scientific in intent, cannot have its problems settled by the experimental method as we have come to understand that method. The first and most obvious reason is that the experimental method is only good for questions of fact, that is, for determining *what-is-so,* and hence not good for ethics proper, which deals with questions of norms or *what-ought-to-be-so.* Descriptive ethics is not normative ethics. For we can only observe in the experimental sense objects whose logical status is ideal or normative.[22]

Romanell does not deny Dewey's view that human beings naturally institute values, but he points out that observation does not, and cannot, confirm which of the ends and relationships human beings naturally cherish and which of the values they normally institute are desirable in the long run. Observation alone cannot settle such a normative issue. Romanell thus indicts much of what is presented as naturalistic ethics.[23]

---

[19] Patrick Romanell, *Toward a Critical Naturalism* (New York: Macmillan Co., 1958), p. 42. Although Dewey may or may not be guilty as charged, the attitude attributed to him by Romanell is not common to all naturalists. Ernest Nagel writes: "Few if any contemporary naturalists identify scientific method with overt experimental activity, or fail to recognize (and in varying degrees analyze) the function in scientific inquiry of such so-called 'non-experimental' factors as the interpretation of data in terms of theoretical conceptions, the construction of symbolic symbols, or the derivation of consequences from postulated premises." ("On the Method of *Verstehen* as the Sole Method of Philosophy," *Journal of Philosophy,* L [Feb. 26, 1953], 155.)

[20] Krikorian, p. 79.

[21] Randall, p. 180.

[22] Romanell, pp. 43–44.

[23] Romanell writes: "Like Spinoza of old, Dewey and his disciples seem to confuse ethics with social psychology or anthropology. The pity is that the Deweyites think they are writing 'naturalistic morals,' when all they are really doing is writing some sort of naturalistic sociology. I say this, not because I do not respect naturalistic *sociology,* but because naturalistic *sociology* is not the same thing as naturalistic *morals.* So to put it bluntly, it is high time that we naturalists called a spade a spade. The naturalist's respect for all the sciences implies the relative autonomy of each of them as well as their interrelationships." (*Ibid.,* p. 44.)

A second reason why experimental method cannot be applied to the problems of ethics, says Romanell, is that ethical postulates do not lend themselves to factual observations. It may be observed that all acids turn blue litmus red, but it cannot be observed that all women should have the right to vote. A single exception to the first proposition would render the chemical generalization invalid. But by contrast the latter is not, and cannot be, invalidated by the sheer fact that in some places women do not actually have the right to vote. In short, whereas an "existential" hypothesis is necessarily invalidated by being found contrary to fact, a moral hypothesis is not invalidated by being violated. Though observation or experiment ultimately determines the truth or falsity of an existential hypothesis, observation does not necessarily determine the truth or falsity of a moral hypothesis. How, then, can a moral hypothesis be justified? How can we prove that all women *should* vote from the fact that some of them do? How can we prove that they *should* even if they all in fact did? Romanell confesses:

> I do not know what to call this curious problem arising in the logic of normative science, where a proposition undergoes a change from the imperative to the indicative mood, so to speak, but the problem of imperatives is not the traditional problem of induction, which deals with the different question of how we can argue within the same (indicative) mood from some members of a class to all.[24]

Emotive Naturalism

It might be noted parenthetically that in the face of criticism of this kind some naturalists have given up and have fallen back upon a kind of "ethical agnosticism," or "emotive naturalism." The emotive naturalist is one who has given up trying to determine values empirically and who takes the position that ethical sentences have meaning, but that this meaning is emotive rather than cognitive. As the emotivist sees it, one's ethical utterances express one's attitude in much the same way as one's tone of voice may express irritation or annoyance. Thus moral judgments are not to be reasoned about or appraised as valid or invalid.

E. D. Klemke is one such naturalist. According to Klemke, what man ought to do is theoretically indeterminable. But man must nevertheless act. His only reason for acting is his enthusiasm for a particular good.

> I cannot know the answer to what is good, etc. But in existence I am forced to act. I cannot be totally a rational being and nothing else. I must behave as well as think. Since further reflection will not reveal which of the alternatives before me is the right one, I must choose one upon the basis of my interest and passion.[25]

---

[24] *Ibid.*, pp. 46–47.

[25] "Vivas on 'Naturalism' and 'Axiological Realism,'" *Review of Metaphysics*, XII (Dec., 1958), 310 ff.

Another example of emotive naturalism is found in William R. Dennes' *Some Dilemmas of Naturalism*. Dennes admits that value judgments cannot be made into scientific hypotheses to be confirmed and modified like any others, but must be determined in an entirely different way. By definition, says Dennes, a moral choice is one that makes "an appreciable difference to the patterns of social living and the kinds of persons in our world." [26] Many factors tend to influence moral judgments, for example, the authority of an elite or of a church. But most of the time our expression of approval or disapproval conforms to what society has approved or disapproved. In making moral judgments we depend upon custom, but custom is not sacrosanct, for sometimes the individual must evaluate the goals of the community. The question remains: Why do we call certain patterns of living good and others not?

One reason, Dennes explains, is that certain patterns focus on values that are mutually corroborative, values that are not exclusive or divisive. For example, knowledge, friendship, work, and a lively imagination contribute to health, and health in its turn makes these things possible. These goods require certain other subsidiary goods. No one can grow in knowledge without cooperating with others. Cooperation in its turn demands its conditions. Thus goods are chosen because they make possible other goods that we desire, or complement those that we possess.

Consequences are also relevant to moral decisions, Dennes points out. The difficulty is to decide which consequences, which patterns of civilization and human personality ought to be preferred. Here science can be of great help in telling us the results of certain patterns of activity—what kinds of persons, what kinds of societies, and what kinds of total community one choice rather than another is likely to develop. But as to which society is to be preferred, no answer is forthcoming from science. There is only moral commitment.

In the last analysis, says Dennes, moral commitment is blind. It is noncognitive. Moral judgments are simply expressions of approval by which we commit ourselves to the alternative whose consequences we prefer. Knowledge that a pattern of living satisfies basic human needs and develops a minimum of hostile aggression is probable knowledge of fact and is morally neutral. Until the factor of love, approval, or condemnation supervenes, we still have no moral judgment of the goodness of a civilization or the rightness of the moral choices. Hence moral judgments are of themselves neither true nor false, nor are they final or immune to modification. If love has to do with ends, reason has to do with means. Once we approve of certain goals, reason can supply the means.

For Dennes this is the dilemma of naturalistic ethics. Selection of ends is based on approval, but approval itself needs to be justified. Why we ap-

---

[26] (New York: Columbia University Press, 1960), Chs. 4 and 5.

prove of certain goals may in a large measure be the result of parental, religious, and social factors, but our acceptance of these in turn is based on
approval. Unable to work his way out of this dilemma, Dennes suggests
that we abandon the discussion as to whether value stems from knowledge
or desire and concentrate on solutions to problems here and now confronting us in the social and political order.

Dennes admits that he is discouraged by the position to which his naturalism leads him. Concluding that values cannot be determined experimentally, Dennes is forced to fall back upon custom or inclination as a
guide in determining what is morally best. Yet, he concedes, custom or inclination is not a sure guide. The whole point of the naturalist's concern
with morals is to get away from subjectivism.

Paul Edwards (b. 1923), in *The Logic of Moral Discourse* (1955), has
attempted to avoid the emotivist position by fusing the emotive and objective naturalistic points of view. Edwards adopts the emotivist view that
moral judgments express attitudes, chiefly of approval or disapproval, but
he affirms that they are at the same time assertions about the objects of
these attitudes. Moral judgments possess objective meaning. They can be
true or false. Moral disputes and conflicts are capable of resolution by discovering the truths that bear on conflicting claims. "They are capable of
settlement, that is to say, by an appeal to *facts,* whether these facts move
the disputants or not. In this respect they resemble scientific disputes." [27]
Edwards' position is close to that of John Dewey. The chief difference between them is that Edwards exempts what he calls "fundamental moral
judgments" from his assertion that all moral judgments have a descriptive
meaning as well as an emotive one, and therefore in principle can be confirmed or disconfirmed. (Fundamental moral judgments for Edwards are
statements such as: "Stealing is just wrong," "It is wrong to convict an innocent man," and "It is better to be kind than cruel.") Dewey would probably hold that whenever such moral views are introduced in relation to a
concrete problem, they have referents that may or may not sustain their
claim to validity.

Theory of Compossibility

Returning to Romanell, we find that he has one further point of criticism
before he offers his theory of "compossibility" as the ethics of a mature
naturalism. It is his understanding that "strictly speaking, the only thing a
naturalistic ethics is committed to in principle is what is implicit in its initial presupposition regarding the continuity of facts and moral values." [28]

---

[27] (Glencoe, Ill., The Free Press, 1955), p. 179.
[28] Romanell, p. 71.

Yet historically naturalism has gone beyond this. Naturalistic moralists have identified themselves at times with the ethics of evolution and at times with the ethics of utilitarianism.[29] The latter identification seems preferable, for, by and large, it is the ethics of common sense.

Most naturalists, observes Romanell, are agreed in accepting as a criterion for a moral code its capacity for satisfying human wants. Things are not desirable because they are valuable and good, but because they are desired. This means that good and evil, being dependent upon man's likes and dislikes, are relative to the changing tastes of individuals. Clearly naturalistic ethics has its parentage in Benedict Spinoza (1632–77) and in the British utilitarians. To Romanell this is not an unmixed blessing. Utilitarian ethics, while psychologically sound, is nevertheless unsound logically. It is true, he notes, that we judge a thing to be good on account of the fact that we strive for, wish, seek, or desire it. But because we consider a thing to be good on account of desire does not prove that it is good. It only proves that good springs from desire and not that desire arises from good. "If things were deemed automatically desirable or good on the mere ground of our desiring them, ethics would be completely pointless as a discipline."[30] Furthermore, "If ethics is to serve as a general guide to mankind, it should encourage us above all to desire things *on their merits,* that is, for the reason that on deliberation we find they are valuable or good either in themselves or in their bearing on our weal and woe."

Romanell believes that the strength of utilitarianism as a theory of ethics lies precisely in its psychology. Though it is true that nothing is desirable or good in itself except insofar as it is desired by us, it does not follow that all good is subjective. "The argument of the utilitarian moralist, that dependence upon desire implies subjectivity of good, is as fallacious in logic as it is plausible in psychology."[31] But this does not imply that the "ethical absolutist" is right. That human history points to a relativity of moral standards is abundantly clear from studies in anthropology.[32] Nevertheless, in spite of a certain "ethical relativity" disclosed by history, values are not completely arbitrary. A distinction can profitably be made between ethics proper and "ethology": one is normative, the other descriptive. Ethology can never pass normative judgments; history can never disclose what "ought" to be.

Although utilitarianism is compatible with naturalism, as a theory of morals it is incomplete, and it cannot constitute the ethics of a mature

---

[29] It is Romanell's opinion that "contemporary naturalism owes much of its vitality in ethical theory to the influence of British utilitarianism and its inheritor, American pragmatism." (*Ibid.*)

[30] *Ibid.,* p. 74.

[31] *Ibid.,* p. 75.

[32] That the history of moral philosophy is part of the data with which the moral philosopher works has been pointed out by a number of philosophers, notably Richard L. Barber in an essay, "The Special Significance of the History of Moral Philosophy," in *Studies in Ethics: Tulane Studies in Philosophy,* VI (New Orleans: Tulane University Press, 1957), 17–23.

naturalism. Utilitarian naturalism errs by omission. True, it sees man as part and parcel of nature, but it does not see that man is more than a seeker of happiness, or more than an animal bent on satisfying his needs and desires. The quest for happiness is undoubtedly a part of life, but it is not the whole of life.

> Man is not only a producer and consumer of happiness, he is also a maker and keeper of obligations. Man's sense of obligation demanding heed is as much (if not more) the source of morality as his needs demanding satisfaction.[33]

This being so, there are two distinct sides to moral life which any adequate theory of ethics must take into account: the "eudaemonistic side," which has to do with the pursuit of happiness, and the "juristic side," which is concerned with the often distasteful but necessary discharge of duties and responsibilities. In a word, "It is foolish for utilitarians to try to reduce man's concern for justice to the pursuit of happiness." Though a utilitarian ethics can account for the eudaemonistic side, it cannot adequately account for the juristic. It cannot be ignored that life involves many things which have to be done regardless of whether we desire them or whether they bring happiness. According to Romanell,

> The utilitarian version of naturalistic ethics, constituting as it does the dominant view of ethical naturalism, does not measure up to a mature form of naturalistic ethics because, when all is said and done, it looks at the moral life exclusively in terms of the pursuit of happiness, or its equivalent. Now, the worst consequence of such a limited outlook in ethical theory is that it is forced in the end to compensate for its initial narrowness and to see so much connection between justice and happiness that its advocates are apt to harbor an optimistic illusion about the inevitable harmony of these two species of moral value, thereby missing the tragic element in human life.

It is Romanell's plea that naturalism do justice to both aspects of moral life.

> The outcome of such an undertaking, which would amount essentially to a reconciliation of Immanuel Kant and John Stuart Mill, could be named "the double-aspect theory of ethics." In contrast to the "happiness-ethics" of Utilitarianism, the guiding principle of the double-aspect is not maximum harmonization of human desires or maximum attainment of happiness, but maximum harmonization of a life of happiness and a life of duty, or, to adapt a Leibnizian term to the present context, maximum attainment of "compossible" ends.[34]

---

[33] Romanell, pp. 77–78.
[34] *Ibid.*, p. 79.

Hence, according to Romanell's proposed "harmony theory" of ethics, the test for determining the correctness of any theory of conduct is not simply its utility, but its compossibility, its consequences for the harmonious blending of happiness and duty. The test of compossibility is as pragmatic as the test for utility, but unlike the latter, it is concerned not simply with happiness but with duty and the compatibility of the two. As such, it is a much more complex, a much more inclusive, test of consequences than the utilitarian.

Conclusion

Admittedly, naturalistic ethics is incomplete. Not only Romanell's analysis gives evidence of this, but other naturalists have pointed it out as well. Romanell's theory of compossibility has not settled, but merely postponed, the fundamental question, "Whence the source of duty or obligation?" Abraham Edel (b. 1908), after tracing the developments in naturalistic ethics over the past half-century, suggests that if it is to accomplish its goals,

> Naturalistic ethics would do well to take present-day fundamental global needs—peace, increased world productivity, concrete freedom for the submerged masses of the world—and use them as actual bases for the selection of theoretical ethical formulations. And if to this it adds constant attentiveness to the results of the sciences as well as logical refinement, the resulting theory may well remain metaphysically relative or arbitrary, but its selection over its opposite will be as arbitrary as the choice of health over sickness, realistic appraisal over neurotic anxiety, life over death.[35]

With this appeal, Edel ends his treatise.

Naturalism has answered some of the questions put to it. It knows that values are not something found ready-made in nature. Values are man-made, and because man changes, values will likewise change. Just as there are no fixed ends in nature, so there are no fixed values. But though values are relative, they are not completely arbitrary. The valuable is not identified with that which gives immediate gratification but with that which proves most satisfactory in the long run. What is beneficial is determined experimentally—by pragmatic tests. The most important realm to which the naturalist's theory of value is applicable is the moral. An action is moral if it affects the fundamental pattern of one's life. Since values are relative, a blanket rule cannot legislate morality for all times and for all circumstances. Religion, having failed to provide man with an adequate moral code, must make way for science. Although there is some debate as to what constitutes scientific method in ethics, there is no doubt that some

---

[35] Farber, p. 610.

kind of scientific procedure is applicable. Some naturalists use the term "scientific" in a univocal sense when speaking of the methods of physics and ethics; others recognize a difference in method.

Concern with methodology has preoccupied the naturalist to the extent that it has distracted him from the systematic development of a genuine normative science. In the eyes of many of its critics, naturalism to date has not produced an ethics but a meta-ethics, an epistemology, just the opposite of what Dewey thought necessary to accomplish the social reconstruction which he so earnestly desired.

Naturalism, in spite of its inability to resolve successfully the epistemological problem of how values ought to be determined, has not been silent regarding the major social, political, and educational issues of our time. Naturalists such as Dewey, Hook, and Edel have contributed numerous essays of a directive sort, stating and defending naturalistic aims for society. Hardly any major issue has escaped their attention. Comment has focused on topics as diverse as the nature of the Communist threat, academic freedom, capital punishment, sterilization of the unfit, prayer in the school, and federal aid to parochial schools. While naturalists may differ among themselves regarding particular goals, there is nevertheless a consensus regarding the fundamental aims of individual and social action. Naturalists are of one mind in promoting the maximum freedom of the individual in relation to the state and other organizations. They unanimously affirm that democracy is the surest political instrument for providing the individual with the fullest scope for personal development. Equality of opportunity in education and employment are also common naturalistic goals. The concluding lines of Dewey's "Reconstruction in Moral Conceptions," which follows in the readings, summarize the thrust of naturalistic ethics.

> Government, business, art, religion, all social institutions have a meaning, a purpose. That purpose is to set free and develop the capacities of human individuals without respect to race, sex, class or economic status. And this is all one with saying that the test of their value is the extent to which they educate every individual into the full stature of his possibility. Democracy has many meanings, but if it has a moral meaning, it is found in resolving that the supreme test of all political institutions and industrial arrangements shall be the contribution they make to the all-round growth of every member of society.[36]

That these same goals may flow from other and opposing moral philosophies does not discredit the naturalist, but suggests that their adequate defense and epistemological grounding are challenging areas for the philosopher.

---

[36] Dewey, *Reconstruction in Philosophy,* p. 186.

Glossary

DESIRABLE:

As used by Dewey, that which is desired in the long run after relative values are taken into consideration; opposed to what is desired. (See *What-is-desired.*)

DETERMINISM:

Broadly defined as the philosophical position that affirms that no event occurs without a sufficient reason. Psychological determinism maintains that every act of man is the product of antecedent conditions.

END-IN-VIEW:

A goal as envisaged by man; opposed to an end existing in nature apart from man. Naturalism recognizes no ends in nature.

GOOD:

A name we give to whatever we seek or desire. Interest creates goods; they are not discovered as something existing in themselves apart from human desire.

INDETERMINISM:

The philosophical position which holds that at least some events are not predetermined by antecedent causes.

INSTRUMENTALISM:

The name Dewey gave to his philosophy, signifying his conviction that intelligence is an instrument in the service of practical rather than contemplative ends. According to Dewey, theory and practice and knowing and doing are ideally fused into an instrument par excellence in modern experimental science.

META-ETHICS:

A theory of value; an epistemological enquiry into the basis of normative science; opposed to an ethics proper, which offers specific guides.

NATURALISM:

The philosophical position that maintains that nature is the whole of reality, that man has his origin, growth, and decay within nature, and that nature is self-explanatory. Naturalism affirms that whatever happens in nature is dependent in some fundamental way upon the organization of bodies located in space and time.

NATURE:

That which is amenable to scientific investigation. According to the naturalist, nature is coextensive with bodies located in space and time and their discernable effects.

NORMATIVE:

Asserted of propositions that contain the word "ought," or its equivalent.

PRAGMATISM:

The philosophical outlook that maintains that ideas are to be judged in the light of their consequences. The true is the useful in the realm of thought, the good in the realm of action.

SCIENCE:

Narrowly identified with physicomathematical method; more broadly defined as any employment of "critical intelligence"; by some naturalists as "causal explanation."

TELEOLOGICAL:

Purposive; refers to order or design in nature. The naturalist denies that there is evidence that nature is a product of an intelligent designer. The naturalist therefore rules out an attempt at teleological explanation.

UTILITARIANISM:

The ethical position derived from Jeremy Bentham and John Stuart Mill. In Bentham's formulation the supreme criterion of morality is the principle of "the greatest happiness for the greatest number." Bentham measured happiness in terms of duration and intensity of pleasure, whereas Mill recognized qualitative differences between pleasures. Mill also recognized that men act not only for pleasure but from motives of duty as well.

WHAT-IS-DESIRED:

The immediately gratifying, that which is desired before reflection; opposed to the desirable in the long run. (See *Desirable*.)

William James

The Moral Philosopher and the Moral Life

The main purpose of this paper is to show that there is no such thing possible as an ethical philosophy dogmatically made up in advance. We all help to determine the content of ethical philosophy so far as we contribute to the race's moral life. In other words, there can be no final truth in ethics any more than in physics, until the last man has had his experience and said his say. In the one case as in the other, however, the hypotheses which we now make while waiting, and the acts to which they prompt us, are among the indispensable conditions which determine what that "say" shall be.

First of all, what is the position of him who seeks an ethical philosophy? To begin with, he must be distinguished from all those who are satisfied to be ethical sceptics. He *will* not be a sceptic; therefore so far from ethical scepticism being one possible fruit of ethical philosophizing, it can only be regarded as that residual alternative to all philosophy which from the outset menaces every would-be philosopher who may give up the quest discouraged, and renounce his original aim. That aim is to find an account of the moral relations that obtain among things, which will weave them into the unity of a stable system, and make of the world what one may call a genuine universe from the ethical point of view. So far as the world re-

From pp. 184–215 of William James, *The Will to Believe, and Other Essays in Popular Philosophy.* Copyright 1897 by William James.

sists reduction to the form of unity, so far as ethical propositions seem unstable, so far does the philosopher fail of his ideal. The subject-matter of his study is the ideals he finds existing in the world; the purpose which guides him is this ideal of his own, of getting them into a certain form. This ideal is thus a factor in ethical philosophy whose legitimate presence must never be overlooked; it is a positive contribution which the philosopher himself necessarily makes to the problem. But it is his only positive contribution. At the outset of his inquiry he ought to have no other ideals. Were he interested peculiarly in the triumph of any one kind of good, he would *pro tanto* cease to be a judicial investigator, and become an advocate for some limited element of the case.

There are three questions in ethics which must be kept apart. Let them be called respectively the *psychological* question, the *metaphysical* question, and the *casuistic* question. The psychological question asks after the historical *origin* of our moral ideas and judgments; the metaphysical question asks what the very *meaning* of the words "good," "ill," and "obligation" are; the casuistic question asks what is the *measure* of the various goods and ills which men recognize, so that the philosopher may settle the true order of human obligations.

I

The psychological question is for most disputants the only question. When your ordinary doctor of divinity has proved to his own satisfaction that an altogether unique faculty called "conscience" must be postulated to tell us what is right and what is wrong; or when your popular-science enthusiast has proclaimed that "apriorism" is an exploded superstition, and that our moral judgments have gradually resulted from the teaching of the environment, each of these persons thinks that ethics is settled and nothing more is to be said. The familiar pair of names, Intuitionist and Evolutionist, so commonly used now to connote all possible differences in ethical opinion, really refer to the psychological question alone. The discussion of this question hinges so much upon particular details that it is impossible to enter upon it at all within the limits of this paper. I will therefore only express dogmatically my own belief, which is this,—that the Benthams, the Mills, and the Bains have done a lasting service in taking so many of our human ideals and showing how they must have arisen from the association with acts of simple bodily pleasures and reliefs from pain. Association with many remote pleasures will unquestionably make a thing significant of goodness in our minds; and the more vaguely the goodness is conceived of, the more mysterious will its source appear to be. But it is surely impossible to explain all our sentiments and preferences in this simple way. The more minutely psychology studies human nature, the more clearly it finds there traces of secondary affections, relating the impressions of the environment with one another and with our impulses in quite different ways from those mere associations of coexistence and succession which are practically all that pure empiricism can admit. Take the love of drunkenness; take bashfulness, the terror of high places, the tendency to sea-sickness, to faint at the sight of blood, the susceptibility to musical sounds; take the emotion of the comical, the passion for poetry, for mathematics, or for metaphysics, —no one of these things can be wholly explained by either association or utility. They go with other things that can be so explained, no doubt; and some of them are prophetic of future utilities; since there is nothing in us for which some use may not be found. But their origin is in incidental complications to our cerebral structure, a structure whose original features arose with no reference to the perception of such discords and harmonies as these.

Well, a vast number of our moral perceptions also are certainly of this secondary and brain-born kind. They deal with directly felt fitnesses between things, and often fly in the teeth of all the prepossessions of habit and presumptions of utility. The moment you get beyond the coarser and more commonplace moral maxims, the Decalogues and Poor Richard's Almanacs, you fall into schemes and positions which to the eye of commonsense are fantastic and over-strained. The sense for abstract justice which some persons have is as excentric a variation, from the natural-history point of view, as is the passion for music or for the higher philosophical consistencies which consumes the soul of others. The feeling of the inward dignity of certain spiritual attitudes, as peace, serenity, simplicity, veracity; and of the essential vulgarity of others, as querulousness, anxiety, egoistic fussiness, etc.,—are quite inexplicable except by an innate preference of the more ideal attitude for its own pure sake. The nobler thing tastes better, and that is all that we can say. "Experience" of consequences may truly teach us what things are wicked, but what have consequences to do with what is mean and vulgar? If a man has shot his wife's paramour, by reason of what subtile repugnancy in things is it that we are so disgusted when we hear that the wife and the husband have made it up and are living comfortably together again? Or if the hypothesis were offered us of a world in which Messrs. Fourier's and Bellamy's and Morris's utopias should all be outdone, and millions kept permanently happy on the one simple condition that a certain lost soul on the far-off edge of things should lead a life of lonely torture, what except a specific and independent sort of emotion can it be which would make us immediately feel, even though an impulse arose within us to clutch at the happiness so offered, how hideous a thing would be its enjoyment when deliberately accepted as the fruit of such a bargain? To what, once more, but subtile brain-born feelings of discord can be due all these recent protests against the entire race-tradition of retributive justice?—I refer to Tolstoï with his ideas of non-resistance, to Mr. Bellamy with his substitution of oblivion for repentance (in his novel of Dr. Heidenhain's Process), to M. Guyau with his radical condemnation of the punitive ideal. All these subtleties of the moral sensibility go as much beyond what can be ciphered out from the "laws of association" as the delicacies of sentiment possible between a pair of young lovers go beyond such precepts of the "etiquette to be observed during engagement" as are printed in manuals of social form.

No! Purely inward forces are certainly at work here. All the higher, more penetrating ideals are revolutionary. They present themselves far less in the guise of effects of past experience than in that of probable causes of future experience, factors to which the environment and the lessons it has so far taught us must learn to bend.

This is all I can say of the psychological question now. In the last chapter of a recent work [1] I have sought to prove in a general way the existence, in our thought, of relations which do not merely repeat the couplings of experience. Our ideals have certainly many sources. They are not all explicable as signifying corporeal pleasures to be gained, and pains to be escaped. And for having so constantly perceived this psychological fact, we must applaud the intuitionist school. Whether or not such applause must be extended to that school's other characteristics will appear as we take up the following questions.

The next one in order is the metaphysical question, of what we mean by the words "obligation," "good," and "ill."

II

First of all, it appears that such words can have no application or relevancy in a world in which no sentient life exists. Imagine an absolutely material world, containing only physical and chemical facts, and existing from eternity without a God, without even an interested spectator: would there be any sense in saying of that world that one of its states is better than another? Or if there were two such worlds possible, would there be any rhyme or reason in calling one good and the other bad,—good or bad positively, I mean, and apart from the fact that one might relate itself better than the other to the philosopher's private interests? But we must leave these private interests out of the account, for the philosopher is a mental fact, and we are asking whether goods and evils and obligations exist in physical facts *per se*. Surely there is no *status* for good and evil to exist in, in a purely insentient world. How can one physical fact, considered simply as a physical fact, be "better" than another? Betterness is not a physical relation. In its mere material capacity, a thing can no more be good or bad than it can be pleasant or painful. Good for what? Good for the production of another physical fact, do you say? But what in a purely physical universe demands the production of that other fact? Physical facts simply *are* or are *not*; and neither when present or absent, can they be supposed to make demands. If they do, they can only do so by having desires; and then they have ceased to be purely physical facts, and have become facts of con-

---

[1] *The Principles of Psychology*, New York, H. Holt & Co. 1890. [w.j.]

scious sensibility. Goodness, badness, and obligation must be *realized* somewhere in order really to exist; and the first step in ethical philosophy is to see that no merely inorganic "nature of things" can realize them. Neither moral relations nor the moral law can swing *in vacuo*. Their only habitat can be a mind which feels them; and no world composed of merely physical facts can possibly be a world to which ethical propositions apply.

The moment one sentient being, however, is made a part of the universe, there is a chance for goods and evils really to exist. Moral relations now have their *status,* in that being's consciousness. So far as he feels anything to be good, he *makes* it good. It *is* good, for him; and being good for him, is absolutely good, for he is the sole creator of values in that universe, and outside of his opinion things have no moral character at all.

In such a universe as that it would of course be absurd to raise the question of whether the solitary thinker's judgments of good and ill are true or not. Truth supposes a standard outside of the thinker to which he must conform; but here the thinker is a sort of divinity, subject to no higher judge. Let us call the supposed universe which he inhabits a *moral solitude.* In such a moral solitude it is clear that there can be no outward obligation, and that the only trouble the god-like thinker is liable to have will be over the consistency of his own several ideals with one another. Some of these will no doubt be more pungent and appealing than the rest, their goodness will have a profounder, more penetrating taste; they will return to haunt him with more obstinate regrets if violated. So the thinker will have to order his life with them as its chief determinants, or else remain inwardly discordant and unhappy. Into whatever equilibrium he may settle, though, and however he may straighten out his system, it will be a right system; for beyond the facts of his own subjectivity there is nothing moral in the world.

If now we introduce a second thinker with his likes and dislikes into the universe, the ethical situation becomes much more complex, and several possibilities are immediately seen to obtain.

One of these is that the thinkers may ignore each other's attitude about good and evil altogether; and each continue to indulge his own preferences, indifferent to what the other may feel or do. In such a case we have a world with twice as much of the ethical quality in it as our moral solitude, only it is without ethical unity. The same object is good or bad there, according as you measure it by the view which this one or that one of the thinkers takes. Nor can you find any possible ground in such a world for saying that one thinker's opinion is more correct than the other's, or that either has the truer moral sense. Such a world, in short, is not a moral universe but a moral dualism. Not only is there no single point of view within it from which the values of things can be unequivocally judged, but there is not even a demand for such a point of view, since the two thinkers are supposed to be indifferent to each other's thoughts and acts. Multiply the thinkers into a pluralism, and we find realized for us in the ethical sphere something like that world which the antique sceptics conceived of,—in which individual minds are the measures of all things, and in which no one "objective" truth, but only a multitude of "subjective" opinions, can be found.

But this is the kind of world with which the philosopher, so long as he holds to the hope of a philosophy, will not put up. Among the various ideals represented, there must be, he thinks, some which have the more truth or authority; and to these the others *ought* to yield, so that system and subordinaton may reign. Here in the word "ought" the notion of *obligation* comes emphatically into view, and the next thing in order must be to make its meaning clear.

Since the outcome of the discussion so far has been to show us that nothing can be good or right except so far as some consciousness feels it to be good or thinks it to be right, we perceive on the very threshold that the real superiority and authority which are postulated by the philosopher to reside in some of the opinions, and the really inferior character which he supposes must belong to others, cannot be explained by any abstract moral "nature of things" existing antecedently to the concrete thinkers themselves with their ideals. Like the positive attributes good and bad, the comparative ones better and worse must be *realized* in order to be real. If one ideal judgment be objectively better than another, that betterness must be made flesh by being lodged concretely in some one's actual perception. It cannot float in the atmosphere, for it is not a sort of meteorological phenomenon, like the aurora borealis or the zodiacal light. Its *esse* is *percipi*, like the *esse* of the ideals themselves between which it obtains. The philosopher, therefore, who seeks to know which ideal ought to have supreme weight and which one ought to be subordinated, must trace the *ought* itself to the *de facto* constitution of some existing consciousness, behind which, as one of the data of the universe, he as a purely ethical philosopher is unable to go. This consciousness must make the one ideal right by feeling it to be right, the other wrong by feeling it to be wrong. But now what particular consciousness in the universe *can* enjoy this prerogative of obliging others to conform to a rule which it lays down?

If one of the thinkers were obviously divine, while all the rest were human, there would probably be no practical dispute about the matter. The divine thought would be the model, to which the others should conform. But still the theoretic question would remain, What is the ground of the obligation, even here?

In our first essays at answering this question, there is an inevitable tendency to slip into an assumption which ordinary men follow when they are disputing with one another about questions of good and bad. They imagine an abstract moral order in which the objective truth resides; and each tries to prove that this pre-existing order is more accurately reflected in his own ideas than in those of his adversary. It is because one disputant is backed by this overarching abstract order that we think the other should submit. Even so, when it is a question no longer of two finite thinkers, but of God and ourselves,—we follow our usual habit, and imagine a sort of *de jure* relation, which antedates and overarches the mere facts, and would make it right that we should conform our thoughts to God's thoughts, even though he made no claim to that effect, and though we preferred *de facto* to go on thinking for ourselves.

But the moment we take a steady look at the question, *we see not only that without a claim actually made by some concrete person there can be no obligation, but that there is some obligation wherever there is a claim.* Claim and obligation are, in fact, coextensive terms; they cover each other exactly. Our ordinary attitude of regarding ourselves as subject to an overarching system of moral relations, true "in themselves," is therefore either an out-and-out superstition, or else it must be treated as a merely provisional abstraction from that real Thinker in whose actual demand upon us to think as he does our obligation must be ultimately based. In a theistic-ethical philosophy that thinker in question is, of course, the Deity to whom the existence of the universe is due.

I know well how hard it is for those who are accustomed to what I have called the superstitious view, to realize that every *de facto* claim creates in so far forth an obligation. We inveterately think that something which we call the "validity" of the claim is what gives to it its obligatory character, and that this validity is something outside of the claim's mere existence as a matter of fact. It rains down upon the claim, we think, from some sublime dimension of being, which the moral law inhabits, much as upon the steel of the compass-needle the influence of the Pole rains down from out of the starry heavens. But again, how can such an inorganic abstract character of imperativeness, additional to the imperativeness which is in the concrete claim itself, *exist?* Take any demand, however slight, which any creature, however weak, may make. Ought it not, for its own sole sake, to be satisfied? If not, prove why not. The only possible kind of proof you could adduce would be the exhibition of another creature who should make a demand that ran the other way. The only possible reason there can be why any phenomenon ought to exist is that such a phenomenon actually is desired. Any desire is imperative to the extent of its amount; it *makes* itself valid by the fact that it exists at all. Some desires, truly enough, are small desires; they are put forward by insignificant persons, and we customarily make light of the obligations which they bring. But the fact that such personal demands as these impose small obligations does not keep the largest obligations from being personal demands.

If we must talk impersonally, to be sure we can say that "the universe" requires, exacts, or makes obligatory such or such an action, whenever it expresses itself through the desires of such or such a creature. But it is better not to talk about the universe in this personified way, unless we believe in a universal or divine consciousness which actually exists. If there be such a consciousness, then its demands carry the most of obligation simply because they are the greatest in amount. But it is even then not *abstractly* right that we should respect them. It is only *concretely* right,—or right after the fact, and by virtue of the fact, that they are actually made. Suppose we do not respect them, as seems largely to be the case in this queer world. That ought not to be, we say; that is wrong. But in what way is this fact of wrongness made more acceptable or intelligible when we imagine it to consist rather in the laceration of an *à priori* ideal order than in the disappointment of a living personal God? Do we, perhaps, think that we cover God and protect him and make his impotence over us less ultimate, when we back him up with this *à priori* blanket from which he may draw some warmth of further appeal? But the only force of appeal to *us,* which either a living God or an abstract ideal order can wield, is found in the "everlasting ruby vaults" of our own human hearts, as they happen to beat responsive and not irresponsive to the claim. So far as they do feel it when made by a living consciousness, it is life answering to life. A claim thus livingly acknowledged is acknowledged with a solidity and fulness which no thought of an "ideal" backing can render more complete; while if, on the other hand, the heart's response is withheld, the stubborn phenomenon is there of an impotence in the claims which the universe embodies, which no talk about an eternal nature of things can gloze over or dispel. An ineffective *à priori* order is as impotent a thing as an ineffective God; and in the eye of philosophy, it is as hard a thing to explain.

We may now consider that what we distinguished as the metaphysical question in ethical philosophy is sufficiently answered, and that we have learned what the words "good," "bad," and "obligation" severally mean. They mean no absolute natures, independent of personal support. They are objects of feeling and desire, which have no foothold or anchorage in Being, apart from the existence of actually living minds.

Wherever such minds exist, with judgments of good and ill, and demands upon one another, there is an ethical world in its essential features. Were all other things, gods and men and starry heavens, blotted out from this universe, and were there left but one rock with two loving souls upon it, that rock would have as thoroughly moral a constitution as any possible world which the eternities and immensities could harbor. It would be a tragic constitution, because the rock's inhabitants would die. But while they lived, there would be real good things and real bad things in the universe; there would be obligations, claims, and expectations; obediences, refusals, and disappointments; compunctions and longings for harmony to come again, and inward peace of conscience when it was restored; there would, in short, be a moral life, whose active energy would have no limit but the intensity of interest in each other with which the hero and heroine might be endowed.

We, on this terrestrial globe, so far as the visible facts go, are just like the inhabitants of such a rock. Whether a God exist, or whether no God exist, in yon blue heaven above us bent, we form at any rate an ethical republic here below. And the first reflection which this leads to is that ethics have as genuine and real a foothold in a universe where the highest consciousness is human, as in a universe where there is a God as well. "The religion of humanity" affords a basis for ethics as well as theism does. Whether the purely human system can gratify the philosopher's demand as well as the other is a different question, which we ourselves must answer ere we close.

III

The last fundamental question in Ethics was, it will be remembered, the *casuistic* question. Here we are, in a world where the existence of a divine thinker has been and perhaps always will be doubted by some of the lookers-on, and where, in spite of the presence of a large number of ideals in which human beings agree, there are a mass of others about which no general consensus obtains. It is hardly necessary to present a literary picture of this, for the facts are too well known. The wars of the flesh and the spirit in each man, the concupiscences of different individuals pursuing the same unshareable material or social prizes, the ideals which contrast so according to races, circumstances, temperaments, philosophical beliefs, etc.,—all form a maze of apparently inextricable confusion with no obvious Ariadne's thread to lead one out. Yet the philosopher, just because he is a philosopher, adds his own peculiar ideal to the confusion (with which if he were willing to be a sceptic he would be passably content), and insists that over all these individual opinions, there is a *system of truth* which he can discover if he only takes sufficient pains.

We stand ourselves at present in the place of that philosopher, and must not fail to realize all the features that the situation comports. In the first place we will not be sceptics; we hold to it that there is a truth to be ascertained. But in the second place we have just gained the insight that that truth cannot be a self-proclaiming set of laws, or an abstract "moral reason," but can only exist in act, or in the shape of an opinion held by some thinker really to be found. There is, however, no visible thinker invested with authority. Shall we then simply proclaim our own ideals as the lawgiving ones? No; for if we are true philosophers we must throw our own spontaneous ideals, even the dearest, impartially in with that total mass of ideals which are fairly to be judged. But how then can we as philosophers ever find a test; how avoid complete moral scepticism on the one hand, and on the other escape bringing a wayward personal standard of our own along with us, on which we simply pin our faith?

The dilemma is a hard one, nor does it grow a bit more easy as we revolve it in our minds. The entire undertaking of the philosopher obliges him to seek an impartial test. That test, however, must be incarnated in the demand of some actually existent person; and how can he pick out the person save by an act in which his own sympathies and prepossessions are implied?

One method indeed presents itself, and has as a matter of history been taken by the more serious ethical schools. If the heap of things demanded proved on inspection less chaotic than at first they seemed, if they furnished their own relative test and measure, then the casuistic problem would be solved. If it were found that all goods *quâ* goods contained a common essence, then the amount of this essence involved in any one good would show its rank in the scale of goodness, and order could be quickly made; for this essence would be *the* good upon which all thinkers were agreed, the relatively objective and universal good that the philosopher seeks. Even his own private ideals would be measured by their share of it, and find their rightful place among the rest.

Various essences of good have thus been found and proposed as bases of the ethical system. Thus, to be a mean between two extremes; to be recognized by a special intuitive faculty; to make the agent happy for the moment; to make others as well as him happy in the long run; to add to his perfection or dignity; to harm no one; to follow from reason or flow from universal law; to be in accordance with the will of God; to promote the survival of the human species on this planet,—are so many tests, each of which has been maintained by somebody to constitute the essence of all good things or actions so far as they are good.

No one of the measures that have been actually proposed has, however, given general satisfaction. Some are obviously not universally present in all cases,—*e. g.*, the character of harming no one, or that of following a universal law; for the best course is often cruel; and many acts are reckoned good on the sole condition that they be exceptions, and serve not as examples of a universal law. Other characters, such as following the will of God, are unascertainable and vague. Others again, like survival, are quite indeterminate in their consequences, and leave us in the lurch where we most need their help: a philosopher of the Sioux Nation, for example, will be certain to use the survival-criterion in a very different way from ourselves. The best, on the whole, of these marks and measures of goodness seems to be the capacity to bring happiness. But in order not to break down fatally, this test must be taken to cover innumerable acts and impulses that never *aim* at happiness; so that, after all, in seeking for a universal principle we inevitably are carried onward to the *most* universal principle,—that *the essence of good is simply to satisfy demand.* The demand may be for anything under the sun. There is really no more ground for supposing that all our demands can be accounted for by one universal underlying kind of motive than there is ground for supposing that all physical phenomena are cases of a single law. The elementary forces in ethics are probably as plural as those of physics are. The various ideals have no common character apart from the fact that they are ideals. No single abstract principle can be so used as to yield to the philosopher anything like a scientifically accurate and genuinely useful casuistic scale.

A look at another peculiarity of the ethical universe, as we find it, will still further show us the philosopher's perplexities. As a purely theoretic problem, namely, the casuistic question would hardly ever come up at all. If the ethical philosopher were only asking after the best *imaginable* system of goods he would indeed have an easy task; for all demands as such are *primâ facie* respectable, and the best simply imaginary world would be one in which *every* demand was gratified as soon as made. Such a world would, however, have to have a physical constitution entirely different from that of the one which we inhabit. It would need not only a space, but a time, "of *n*-dimensions," to include all the acts and experiences incompatible with one another here below, which would then go on in conjunction,—such as spending our money, yet growing rich; taking our holiday, yet getting ahead with our work; shooting and fishing, yet doing no hurt to the beasts; gaining no end of experience, yet keeping our youthful freshness of heart; and the like. There can be no question that such a system of things, however brought about, would be the absolutely ideal system; and that if a philosopher could create universes *à priori,* and provide all the mechanical conditions, that is the sort of universe which he should unhesitatingly create.

But this world of ours is made on an entirely different pattern, and the casuistic question here is most tragically practical. The actually possible in this world is vastly narrower than all that is demanded; and there is always a *pinch* between the ideal and the actual which can only be got through by leaving part of the ideal behind. There is hardly a good which we can imagine except as competing for the possession of the same bit of space and time with some other imagined good. Every end of desire that presents itself appears exclusive of some other end of desire. Shall a man drink and smoke, *or* keep his nerves in condition?—he cannot do both. Shall he follow his fancy for Amelia, *or* for Henrietta?—both cannot be the choice of his heart. Shall he have the dear old Republican party, *or* a spirit of unsophistication in public affairs?—he cannot have both, etc. So that the ethical philosopher's demand for the right scale of subordination in ideals is the fruit of an altogether practical need. Some part of the ideal must be butchered, and he needs to know which part. It is a tragic situation, and no mere speculative conundrum, with which he has to deal.

Now we are blinded to the real difficulty of the philosopher's task by the fact that we are born into a society whose ideals are largely ordered already. If we follow the ideal which is conventionally highest, the others which we butcher either die and do not return to haunt us; or if they come back and accuse us of murder, every one applauds us for turning to them a deaf ear. In other words, our environment encourages us not to be philosophers but partisans. The philosopher, however, cannot, so long as he clings to his own ideal of objectivity, rule out any ideal from being heard. He is confident, and rightly confident, that the simple taking counsel of his own intuitive preferences would be certain to end in a mutilation of the fulness of the truth. The poet Heine is said to have written "Bunsen" in the place of *"Gott"* in his copy of that author's work entitled "God in History," so as to make it read *"Bunsen in der Geschichte."* Now, with no disrespect to the good and learned Baron, is it not safe to say that any single philosopher, however wide his sympathies, must be just such a *Bunsen in der Geschichte* of the moral world, so soon as he attempts to put his own ideas of order into that howling mob of desires, each struggling to get breathing-room for the ideal to which it clings? The very best of men must not only be insensible, but be ludicrously and peculiarly insensible, to many goods. As a militant, fighting free-handed that the goods to which he *is* sensible may not be submerged and lost from out of life, the philosopher, like every other human being, is in a natural position. But think of Zeno and of Epicurus, think of Calvin and of Paley, think of Kant and Schopenhauer, of Herbert Spencer and John Henry Newman, no longer as one-sided champions of special ideals, but as schoolmasters deciding what all must think,—and what more grotesque topic could a satirist wish for on which to exercise his pen? The fabled attempt of Mrs. Partington to arrest the rising tide of the North Atlantic with her broom was a reasonable spectacle compared with their effort to substitute the content of their clean-shaven systems for that exuberant mass of goods with which all human nature is in travail, and groaning to bring to the light of day. Think, furthermore, of such individual moralists, no longer as mere schoolmasters, but as pontiffs armed with the temporal power, and having authority in every concrete case of conflict to order which good shall be butchered and which shall be suffered to survive,—and the notion really turns one pale. All one's slumbering revolutionary instincts waken at the thought of any single moralist wielding such powers of life and death. Better chaos forever than an order based on any closet-philosopher's rule, even though he were the most enlightened possible member of his tribe. No! if the philosopher is to keep his judicial position, he must never become one of the parties to the fray.

What can he do, then, it will now be asked, except to fall back on scepticism and give up the notion of being a philosopher at all?

But do we not already see a perfectly definite path of escape which is open to him just because he is a philosopher, and not the champion of one particular ideal? Since everything which is demanded is by that fact a good, must not the guiding principle for ethical philosophy (since all demands conjointly cannot be satisfied in this poor world) be simply to satisfy at all times *as many demands as we can?* That act must be the best act, accordingly, which makes for the *best whole,* in the sense of awakening the least sum of dissatisfactions. In the casuistic scale, therefore, those ideals must be written highest which *prevail at the least cost,* or by whose realization the least possible number of other ideals are destroyed. Since victory and defeat there must be, the victory to be philosophically prayed for is that of the more inclusive side,—of the side which even in the hour of triumph will to some degree do justice to the ideals in which the vanquished party's interests lay. The course of history is nothing but the story of men's struggles from generation to generation to find the more and more inclusive order. *Invent some manner* of realizing your own ideals which will also satisfy the alien demands,—that and that only is the path of peace! Following this path, society has shaken itself into one sort of relative equilibrium after another by a series of social discoveries quite analogous to those of science. Polyandry and polygamy and slavery, private warfare and liberty to kill, judicial torture and arbitrary royal power have slowly succumbed to actually aroused complaints; and though some one's ideals are unquestionably the worse off for each improvement, yet a vastly greater total number of them find shelter in our civilized society than in the older savage ways. So far then, and up to date, the casuistic scale is made for the philosopher already far better than he can ever make it for himself. An experiment of the most searching kind has proved that the laws and usages of the land are what yield the maximum of satisfaction to the thinkers taken all together. The presumption in cases of conflict must always be in favor of the conventionally recognized good. The philosopher must be a conservative, and in the construction of his casuistic scale must put the things most in accordance with the customs of the community on top.

And yet if he be a true philosopher he must see that there is nothing final in any actually given equilibrium of human ideals, but that, as our present laws and customs have fought and conquered other past ones, so they will in their turn be overthrown by any newly discovered order which will hush up the complaints that they still give rise to, without producing others louder still. "Rules are made for man, not man for rules,"—that one sentence is enough to immortalize Green's *Prolegomena to Ethics*. And although a man always risks much when he breaks away from established rules and strives to realize a larger ideal whole than they permit, yet the philosopher must allow that it is at all times open to any one to make the experiment, provided he fear not to stake his life and character upon the throw. The pinch is always here. Pent in under every system of moral rules are innumerable persons whom it weighs upon, and goods which it represses; and these are always rumbling and grumbling in the background, and ready for any issue by which they may get free. See the abuses which the institution of private property covers, so that even to-day it is shamelessly asserted among us that one of the prime functions of the national government is to help the adroiter citizens to grow rich. See the unnamed and unnamable sorrows which the tyranny, on the whole so beneficent, of the marriage-institution brings to so many, both of the married and the unwed. See the wholesale loss of opportunity under our *régime* of so-called equality and industrialism, with the drummer and the counter-jumper in the saddle, for so many faculties and graces which could flourish in the feudal world. See our kindliness for the humble and the outcast, how it wars with that stern weeding-out which until now has been the condition of every perfection in the breed. See everywhere the struggle and the squeeze; and everlastingly the problem how to make them less. The anarchists, nihilists, and free-lovers; the free-silverites, socialists, and single-tax men; the free-traders and civil-service reformers; the prohibitionists and anti-vivisectionists; the radical Darwinians with their idea of the suppression of the weak, —these and all the conservative sentiments of society arrayed against them, are simply deciding through actual experiment by what sort of conduct the maximum amount of good can be gained and kept in this world. These experiments are to be judged, not *à priori,* but by actual finding, after the fact of their making, how much more outcry or how much appeasement comes about. What closet-solutions can possibly anticipate the result of trials made on such a scale? Or what can any superficial theorist's judgment be worth, in a world where every one of hundreds of ideals has its special champion already provided in the shape of some genius expressly born to feel it, and to fight to death in its behalf? The pure philosopher can only follow the windings of the spectacle, confident that the line of least resistance will always be towards the richer and the more inclusive arrangement, and that by one tack after another some approach to the kingdom of heaven is incessantly made.

IV

All this amounts to saying that, so far as the casuistic question goes, ethical science is just like physical science, and instead of being deducible all at once from abstract principles, must simply bide its time, and be ready to revise its conclusions from day to day. The presumption of course, in both sciences, always is that the vulgarly accepted opinions are true, and the right casuistic order that which public opinion believes in; and surely it would be folly quite as great, in most of us, to strike out independently and to aim at originality in ethics as in physics. Every now and then, however, some one is born with the right to be original, and his revolutionary thought or action may bear prosperous fruit. He may replace old "laws of nature" by better ones; he may, by breaking old moral rules in a certain place, bring in a total condition of things more ideal than would have followed had the rules been kept.

On the whole, then, we must conclude that no philosophy of ethics is possible in the old-fashioned absolute sense of the term. Everywhere the ethical philosopher must wait on facts. The thinkers who create the ideals come he knows not whence, their sensibilities are evolved he knows not how; and the question as to which of two conflicting ideals will give the best universe then and there, can be answered by him only through the aid of the experience of other men. I said some time ago, in treating of the "first" question, that the intuitional moralists deserve credit for keeping most clearly to the psychological facts. They do much to spoil this merit on the whole, however, by mixing with it that dogmatic temper which, by absolute distinctions and unconditional "thou shalt nots," changes a growing, elastic, and continuous life into a superstitious system of relics and dead bones. In point of fact, there are no absolute evils, and there are no non-moral goods; and the *highest* ethical life—however few may be called to bear its burdens—consists at all times in the breaking of rules which have grown too narrow for the actual case. There is but one unconditional commandment, which is that we should seek incessantly, with fear and trembling, so to vote and to act as to bring about the very largest total universe of good which we can see. Abstract rules indeed can help; but they help the less in proportion as our intuitions are more piercing, and our vocation is the stronger for the moral life. For every real dilemma is in literal strictness a unique situation; and the exact combination of ideals realized and ideals disappointed which each decision creates is always a universe without a precedent, and for which no adequate previous rule exists. The philosopher, then, *quâ* philosopher, is no better able to determine the best universe in the concrete emergency than other men. He sees, indeed, somewhat better than most men what the question always is,—not a question of this good or that good simply taken, but of the two total universes with which these goods respectively belong. He knows that he must vote always for the richer universe, for the good which seems most organizable, most fit to enter into complex combinations, most apt to be a member of a more inclusive whole. But which particular universe this is he cannot know for certain in advance; he only knows that if he makes a bad mistake the cries of the wounded will soon inform him of the fact. In all this the philosopher is just like the rest of us non-philosophers, so far as we are just and sympathetic instinctively, and so far as we are open to the voice of complaint. His function is in fact indistinguishable from that of the best kind of statesman at the present day. His books upon ethics, therefore, so far as they truly touch the moral life, must more and more ally themselves with a literature which is confessedly tentative and suggestive rather than dogmatic,—I mean with novels and dramas of the deeper sort, with sermons, with books on statecraft and philanthropy and social and economical reform. Treated in this way ethical treatises may be voluminous and luminous as well; but they never can be *final,* except in their abstractest and vaguest features; and they must more and more abandon the old-fashioned, clear-cut, and would-be "scientific" form.

V

The chief of all the reasons why concrete ethics cannot be final is that they have to wait on metaphysical and theological beliefs. I said some time back that real ethical relations existed in a purely human world. They would exist even in what we called a moral solitude if the thinker had various ideals which took hold of him in turn. His self of one day would make demands on his self of another; and some of the demands might be urgent and tyrannical, while others were gentle and easily put aside. We call the tyrannical demands *imperatives*. If we ignore these we do not hear the last of it. The good which we have wounded returns to plague us with interminable crops of consequential damages, compunctions, and regrets. Obligation can thus exist inside a single thinker's consciousness; and perfect peace can abide with him only so far as he lives according to some sort of a casuistic scale which keeps his more imperative goods on top. It is the nature of these goods to be cruel to their rivals. Nothing shall avail when weighed in the balance against them. They call out all the mercilessness in our disposition, and do not easily forgive us if we are so soft-hearted as to shrink from sacrifice in their behalf.

The deepest difference, practically, in the moral life of man is the difference between the easy-going and the strenuous mood. When in the easy-going mood the shrinking from present ill is our ruling consideration. The strenuous mood, on the contrary, makes us quite indifferent to present ill, if only the greater ideal be attained. The capacity for the strenuous mood probably lies slumbering in every man, but it has more difficulty in some than in others in waking up. It needs the wilder passions to arouse it, the big fears, loves, and indignations; or else the deeply penetrating appeal of some one of the higher fidelities, like justice, truth, or freedom. Strong relief is a necessity of its vision; and a world where all the mountains are brought down and all the valleys are exalted is no congenial place for its habitation. This is why in a solitary thinker this mood might slumber on forever without waking. His various ideals, known to him to be mere preferences of his own, are too nearly of the same denominational value: he can play fast or loose with them at will. This too is why, in a merely human world without a God, the appeal to our moral energy falls short of its maximal stimulating power. Life, to be sure, is even in such a world a genuinely ethical symphony; but it is played in the compass of a couple of poor octaves, and the infinite scale of values fails to open up. Many of us, indeed, —like Sir James Stephen in those eloquent "Essays by a Barrister," —would openly laugh at the very idea of the strenuous mood being awakened in us by those claims of remote posterity which constitute the last appeal of the religion of humanity. We do not love these men of the future keenly enough; and we love them perhaps the less the more we hear of their evolutionized perfection, their high average longevity and education, their freedom from war and crime, their relative immunity from pain and zymotic disease, and all their other negative superiorities. This is all too finite, we say; we see too well the vacuum beyond. It lacks the note of infinitude and mystery, and may all be dealt with in the don't-care mood. No need of agonizing ourselves or making others agonize for these good creatures just at present.

When, however, we believe that a God is there, and that he is one of the claimants, the infinite perspective opens out. The scale of the symphony is incalculably prolonged. The more imperative ideals now begin to speak with an altogether new objectivity and significance, and to utter the penetrating, shattering, tragically challenging note of appeal. They ring out like the call of Victor Hugo's alpine eagle, *"qui parle au précipice et que le gouffre entend,"* [2] and the strenuous mood awakens at the sound. It saith among the trumpets, ha, ha! it smelleth the battle afar off, the thunder of the captains and the shouting. Its blood is up; and cruelty to the lesser claims, so far from being a deterrent element, does but add to the stern joy with which it leaps to answer to the greater. All through history, in the periodical conflicts of puritanism with the don't-care temper, we see the antagonisms of the strenuous and genial moods, and the contrast between the ethics of infinite and mysterious obligation from on high, and those of prudence and the satisfaction of merely finite need.

The capacity of the strenuous mood lies so deep down among our natural human possibilities that even if there were no metaphysical or traditional grounds for believing in a God, men would postulate one simply as a pretext for living hard, and getting out of the game of existence its keenest possibilities of zest. Our attitude towards concrete evils is entirely different in a world where we believe there are none but finite demanders, from what it is in one where we joyously face tragedy for an infinite demander's sake. Every sort of energy and endurance, of courage and capacity for handling life's evils, is set free in those who have religious faith. For this reason the strenuous type of character will on the battle-field of human history always outwear the easy-going type, and religion will drive irreligion to the wall.

It would seem, too,—and this is my final conclusion,—that the stable and systematic moral universe for which the ethical philosopher asks is fully possible only in a world where there is a divine thinker with all-enveloping demands. If such a thinker existed, his way of subordinating the demands to one another would be the finally valid casuistic scale; his claims would be the most appealing; his ideal universe would be the most inclusive realizable whole. If he now exist, then actualized in his thought already must be that ethical philosophy which we seek as the pattern which our own must evermore approach.[3] In the interests of our own ideal of systematically unified moral truth, therefore, we, as would-be philosophers, must postulate a divine thinker, and pray for the victory of the religious cause. Meanwhile, exactly what the thought of the infinite thinker may be is hidden from us even were we sure of his existence; so that our postulation of him after all serves only to let loose in us the strenuous mood. But this is what it does in all men, even those who have no interest in philosophy. The ethical philosopher, therefore, whenever he ventures to say which

---

[2] *Qui parle au précipice et que le gouffre entend:* who speaks to the precipice and is heard by the abyss. [J.P.D.]

[3] All this is set forth with great freshness and force in the work of my colleague, Professor Josiah Royce: "The Religious Aspect of Philosophy." Boston, 1885. [W.J.]

course of action is the best, is on no essentially different level from the common man. "See, I have set before thee this day life and good, and death and evil; therefore, choose life that thou and thy seed may live," —when this challenge comes to us, it is simply our total character and personal genius that are on trial; and if we invoke any so-called philosophy, our choice and use of that also are but revelations of our personal aptitude or incapacity for moral life. From this unsparing practical ordeal no professor's lectures and no array of books can save us. The solving word, for the learned and the unlearned man alike, lies in the last resort in the dumb willingness and unwillingness of their interior characters, and nowhere else. It is not in heaven, neither is it beyond the sea; but the word is very nigh unto thee, in thy mouth and in thy heart, that thou mayest do it.

QUESTIONS FOR STUDY AND DISCUSSION

1. Why does James maintain that there can be no final truth in ethics?
2. How are personal moral values attained and how are they to be judged?
3. Are values wholly subjective?
4. What do we mean when we call an object "good"?
5. What is the source of moral obligation according to James?
6. Is the ability to produce happiness the sole criterion of value?
7. Is James satisfied with the utilitarian formula, "the greatest good of the greatest number"?
8. State as clearly as possible the nature of the old-fashioned, absolute ethics against which James is rebelling. Who are some of the philosophers identified with that outlook?
9. How does belief in God affect one's ethical outlook?

John Dewey

JOHN DEWEY was born in Burlington, Vermont, in 1859. He was graduated from the University of Vermont in 1879, and received his doctorate from the Johns Hopkins University in 1884. The next twenty years
he spent in the Midwest, teaching at the Universities of Michigan, Min-
nesota, and Chicago. Philosophically, these were his formative years;
they record his gradual intellectual development from an early defense
of idealism to an opposing naturalism. From 1904 to 1930 he taught at
Columbia University and remained as professor emeritus until 1939.
He died in 1952. One of America's most distinguished and controversial
philosophers, Dewey was a prolific writer. His most important works
include *Democracy and Education* (1916), *Reconstruction in Philosophy*
(1920), *Experience and Nature* (1925), and *The Quest for Certainty*
(1929).

Reconstruction in Moral Conceptions

The impact of the alteration in methods of scientific thinking upon moral
ideas is, in general, obvious. Goods, ends are multiplied. Rules are softened
into principles, and principles are modified into methods of understanding.
Ethical theory began among the Greeks as an attempt to find a regulation
for the conduct of life which should have a rational basis and purpose instead of being derived from custom. But reason as a substitute for custom
was under the obligation of supplying objects and laws as fixed as those of
custom had been. Ethical theory ever since has been singularly hypnotized
by the notion that its business is to discover some final end or good or
some ultimate and supreme law. This is the common element among the
diversity of theories. Some have held that the end is loyalty or obedience to
a higher power or authority; and they have variously found this higher
principle in Divine Will, the will of the secular ruler, the maintenance of
institutions in which the purpose of superiors is embodied, and the rational
consciousness of duty. But they have differed from one another because
there was one point in which they were agreed: a single and final source of
law. Others have asserted that it is impossible to locate morality in con-

formity to law-giving power, and that it must be sought in ends that are goods. And some have sought the good in self-realization, some in holiness, some in happiness, some in the greatest possible aggregate of pleasures. And yet these schools have agreed in the assumption that there is a single, fixed and final good. They have been able to dispute with one another only because of their common premise.

The question arises whether the way out of the confusion and conflict is not to go to the root of the matter by questioning this common element. Is not the belief in the single, final and ultimate (whether conceived as good or as authoritative law) an intellectual product of that feudal organization which is disappearing historically and of that belief in a bounded, ordered cosmos, wherein rest is higher than motion, which has disappeared from natural science? It has been repeatedly suggested that the present limit of intellectual reconstruction lies in the fact that it has not as yet been seriously applied in the moral and social disciplines. Would not this further application demand precisely that we advance to a belief in a plurality of changing, moving, individualized goods and ends, and to a belief that principles, criteria, laws are intellectual instruments for analyzing individual or unique situations?

The blunt assertion that every moral situation is a unique situation having its own irreplaceable good may seem not merely blunt but preposterous. For the established tradition teaches that it is precisely the irregularity of special cases which makes necessary the guidance of conduct by universals, and that the essence of the virtuous disposition is willingness to subordinate every particular case to adjudication by a fixed principle. It would then follow the submission of a generic end and law to determination by the concrete situation entails complete confusion and unrestrained licentiousness. Let us, however, follow the pragmatic rule, and in order to discover the meaning of the idea ask for its consequences. Then it surprisingly turns out that the primary significance of the unique and morally ultimate character of the concrete situation is to transfer the weight and burden of morality to intelligence. It does not destroy responsibility; it only locates it. A moral situation is one in which judgment and choice are required antecedently to overt action. The practical meaning of the situation—that is to say the action needed to satisfy it—is not self-evident. It has to be searched for. There are conflicting desires and alternative apparent goods. What is needed is to find the right course of action, the right good. Hence, inquiry is exacted: observation of the detailed makeup of the situation; analysis into its diverse factors; clarification of what is obscure; discounting of the more insistent and vivid traits; tracing the consequences of the various modes of action that suggest themselves; regarding the decision reached as hypothetical and tentative until the anticipated or supposed consequences which led to its adoption have been squared with actual consequences. This inquiry is intelligence. Our moral failures go back to some weakness of disposition, some absence of sympathy, some one-sided bias that makes us perform the judgment of the concrete case carelessly or perversely. Wide sympathy, keen sensitiveness, persistence in the face of the disagreeable, balance of interests enabling us to undertake the work of analysis and decision intelligently are the distinctively moral traits—the virtues or moral excellencies.

It is worth noting once more that the underlying issue is, after all, only the same as that which has been already threshed out in physical inquiry. There too it long seemed as if rational assurance and demonstration could be attained only if we began with universal conceptions and subsumed particular cases under them. The men who initiated the methods of inquiry that are now everywhere adopted were denounced in their day (and sincerely) as subverters of truth and foes of science. If they have won in the end, it is because, as has already been pointed out, the method of universals confirmed prejudices and sanctioned ideas that had gained currency irrespective of evidence for them; while placing the initial and final weight upon the individual case, stimulated painstaking inquiry into facts and examination of principles. In the end, loss of eternal truths was more than compensated for in the accession of quotidian facts. The loss of the system of superior and fixed definitions and kinds was more than made up for by the growing system of hypotheses and laws used in classifying facts. After all, then, we are only pleading for the adoption in moral reflection of the logic that has been proved to make for security, stringency and fertility in passing judgments upon physical phenomena. And the reason is the same. The old method in spite of its nominal and esthetic worship of reason discouraged reason, because it hindered the operation of scrupulous and unremitting inquiry.

More definitely, the transfer of the burden of the moral life from following rules or pursuing fixed ends over to the detection of the ills that need remedy in a special case and the formation of plans and methods for dealing with them, eliminates the causes which have kept moral theory controversial, and which have also kept it remote from helpful contact with the exigencies of practice. The theory of fixed ends inevitably leads thought into the bog of disputes that cannot be settled. If there is one *summum bonum,* one supreme end, what is it? To consider this problem is to place ourselves in the midst of controversies that are as acute now as they were two thousand years ago. Suppose we take a seemingly more empirical view, and say that while there is not a single end, there also are not as many as there are specific situations that require amelioration; but there are a number of such natural goods as health, wealth, honor or good name, friendship, esthetic appreciation, learning and such moral goods as justice, temperance, benevolence, etc. What or who is to decide the right of way when these ends conflicts with one another, as they are sure to do? Shall we resort to the method that once brought such disrepute upon the whole business of ethics: Casuistry? Or shall we have recourse to what Bentham well called the *ipse dixit* method: the arbitrary preference of this or that person for this or that end? Or shall we be forced to arrange them all in an order of degrees from the highest good down to the least precious? Again we find ourselves in the middle of unreconciled disputes with no indication of the way out.

Meantime, the special moral perplexities where the aid of intelligence is required go unenlightened. We cannot seek or attain health, wealth, learning, justice or kindness in general. Action is always specific, concrete, individualized, unique. And consequently judgments as to acts to be performed must be similarly specific. To say that a man seeks health or justice is only to say that he seeks to live healthily or justly. These things, like truth, are adverbial. They are modifiers of action in special cases. How to live healthily or justly is a matter which differs with every person. It varies with his past experience, his opportunities, his temperamental and acquired weaknesses and abilities. Not man in general but a particular man suffering from some particular disability aims to live healthily, and consequently health cannot mean for him exactly what it means for any other mortal. Healthy living is not something to be attained by itself apart from other ways of living. A man needs to be healthy *in* his life, not apart from it, and what does life mean except the aggregate of his pursuits and activities? A man who aims at health as a distinct end becomes a valetudinarian, or a fanatic, or a mechanical performer of exercises, or an athlete so one-sided that his pursuit of bodily development injures his heart. When the endeavor to realize a so-called end does not temper and color all other activities, life is portioned out into strips and fractions. Certain acts and times are devoted to getting health, others to cultivating religion, others to seeking learning, to being a good citizen, a devotee of fine art and so on. This is the only logical alternative to subordinating all aims to the accomplishment of one alone—fanaticism. This is out of fashion at present, but who can say how much of distraction and dissipation in life, and how much of its hard and narrow rigidity is the outcome of men's failure to realize that each situation has its own unique end and that the whole personality should be concerned with it? Surely, once more, what a man needs is to live healthily, and this result so affects all the activities of his life that it cannot be set up as a separate and independent good.

Nevertheless the general notions of health, disease, justice, artistic culture are of great importance: Not, however, because this or that case may be brought exhaustively under a single head and its specific traits shut out, but because generalized science provides a man as physician and artist and citizen, with questions to ask, investigations to make, and enables him to understand the meaning of what he sees. Just in the degree in which a physician is an artist in his work he uses his science, no matter how extensive and accurate, to furnish him with tools of inquiry into the individual case, and with methods of forecasting a method of dealing with it. Just in the degree in which, no matter how great his learning, he subordinates the individual case to some classification of diseases and some generic rule of treatment, he sinks to the level of the routine mechanic. His intelligence and his action become rigid, dogmatic, instead of free and flexible.

Moral goods and ends exist only when something has to be done. The fact that something has to be done proves that there are deficiencies, evils in the existent situation. This ill is just the specific ill that it is. It never is an exact duplicate of anything else. Consequently the good of the situation has to be discovered, projected and attained on the basis of the exact defect and trouble to be rectified. It cannot intelligently be injected into the situation from without. Yet it is the part of wisdom to compare different cases, to gather together the ills from which humanity suffers, and to generalize the corresponding goods into classes. Health, wealth, industry, temperance, amiability, courtesy, learning, esthetic capacity, initiative, courage, patience, enterprise, thoroughness and a multitude of other generalized ends are acknowledged as goods. But the *value* of this systematization is intellectual or analytic. Classifications *suggest* possible traits to be on the lookout for in studying a particular case; they suggest methods of action to be tried in removing the inferred causes of ill. They are tools of insight; their value is in promoting an individualized response in the individual situation.

Morals is not a catalogue of acts nor a set of rules to be applied like drugstore prescriptions or cook-book recipes. The need in morals is for specific methods of inquiry and of contrivance: Methods of inquiry to locate difficulties and evils; methods of contrivance to form plans to be used as working hypotheses in dealing with them. And the pragmatic import of the logic of individualized situations, each having its own irreplaceable good and principle, is to transfer the attention of theory from preoccupation with general conceptions to the problem of developing effective methods of inquiry.

Two ethical consequences of great moment should be remarked. The belief in fixed values has bred a division of ends into intrinsic and instrumental, of those that are really worth while in themselves and those that are of importance only as means to intrinsic goods. Indeed, it is often thought to be the very beginning of wisdom, of moral discrimination, to make this distinction. Dialectically, the distinction is interesting and seems harmless. But carried into practice it has an import that is tragic. Historically, it has been the source and justification of a hard and fast difference between ideal goods on one side and material goods on the other. At present those who would be liberal conceive intrinsic goods as esthetic in nature rather than as exclusively religious or as intellectually contemplative. But the effect is the same. So-called intrinsic goods, whether religious or esthetic, are divorced from those interests of daily life which because of their constancy and urgency form the preoccupation of the great mass. Aristotle used this distinction to declare that slaves and the working class though they are necessary *for* the state—the commonweal—are not constituents *of* it. That which is regarded as *merely* instrumental must approach drudgery;

it cannot command either intellectual, artistic or moral attention and respect. Anything becomes *unworthy* whenever it is thought of as intrinsically lacking worth. So men of "ideal" interests have chosen for the most part the way of neglect and escape. The urgency and pressure of "lower" ends have been covered up by polite conventions. Or, they have been relegated to a baser class of mortals in order that the few might be free to attend to the goods that are really or intrinsically worth while. This withdrawal, in the name of higher ends, has left, for mankind at large and especially for energetic "practical" people the lower activities in complete command.

No one can possibly estimate how much of the obnoxious materialism and brutality of our economic life is due to the fact that economic ends have been regarded as *merely* instrumental. When they are recognized to be as intrinsic and final in their place as any others, then it will be seen that they are capable of idealization, and that if life is to be worth while, they must acquire ideal and intrinsic value. Esthetic, religious and other "ideal" ends are now thin and meagre or else idle and luxurious because of the separation from "instrumental" or economic ends. Only in connection with the latter can they be woven into the texture of daily life and made substantial and pervasive. The vanity and irresponsibility of values that are merely final and not also in turn means to the enrichment of other occupations of life ought to be obvious. But now the doctrine of "higher" ends gives aid, comfort and support to every socially isolated and socially irresponsible scholar, specialist, esthete and religionist. It protects the vanity and irresponsibility of his calling from observation by others and by himself. The moral deficiency of the calling is transformed into a cause of admiration and gratulation.

The other generic change lies in doing away once for all with the traditional distinction between moral goods, like the virtues, and natural goods like health, economic security, art, science and the like. The point of view under discussion is not the only one which has deplored this rigid distinction and endeavored to abolish it. Some schools have even gone so far as to regard moral excellencies, qualities of character as of value only because they promote natural goods. But the experimental logic when carried into morals makes every quality that is judged to be good according as it contributes to amelioration of existing ills. And in so doing, it enforces the moral meaning of natural science. When all is said and done in criticism of present social deficiencies, one may well wonder whether the root difficulty does not lie in the separation of natural and moral science. When physics, chemistry, biology, medicine, contribute to the detection of concrete human woes and to the development of plans for remedying them and relieving the human estate, they become moral; they become part of the apparatus of moral inquiry or science. The latter then loses its peculiar flavor of the didactic and pedantic, its ultra-moralistic and hortatory tone. It loses its thinness and shrillness as well as its vagueness. It gains agencies that are efficacious. But the gain is not confined to the side of moral science. Natural science loses its divorce from humanity; it becomes itself humanistic in quality. It is something to be pursued not in a technical and specialized way for what is called truth for its own sake, but with the sense of its social bearing, its intellectual indispensableness. It is technical only in the sense that it provides the technique of social and moral engineering.

When the consciousness of science is fully impregnated with the consciousness of human value, the greatest dualism which now weighs humanity down, the split between the material, the mechanical, the scientific and the moral and ideal will be destroyed. Human forces that now waver because of this division will be unified and reinforced. As long as ends are not thought of as individualized according to specific needs and opportunities, the mind will be content with abstractions, and the adequate stimulus to the moral or social use of natural science and historical data will be lacking. But when attention is concentrated upon the diversified concretes, recourse to all intellectual materials needed to clear up the special cases will be imperative. At the same time that morals are made to focus in intelligence, things intellectual are moralized. The vexatious and wasteful conflict between naturalism and humanism is terminated.

These general considerations may be amplified. First: Inquiry, discovery take the same place in morals that they have come to occupy in sciences of nature. Validation, demonstration become experimental, a matter of consequences. Reason, always an honorific term in ethics, becomes actualized in the methods by which the needs and conditions, the obstacles and resources, of situations are scrutinized in detail, and intelligent plans of improvement are worked out. Remote and abstract generalities promote jumping at conclusions, "anticipations of nature." Bad consequences are then deplored as due to natural perversity and untoward fate. But shifting the issue to analysis of a specific situation makes inquiry obligatory and alert observation of consequences imperative. No past decision nor old principle can ever be wholly relied upon to justify a course of action. No amount of pains taken in forming a purpose in a definite case is final; the consequences of its adoption must be carefully noted, and a purpose held only as a working hypothesis until results confirm its rightness. Mistakes are no longer either mere unavoidable accidents to be mourned or moral sins to be expiated and forgiven. They are lessons in wrong methods of using intelligence and instructions as to a better course in the future. They are indications of the need of revision, development, readjustment. Ends grow, standards of judgment are improved. Man is under just as much obligation to develop his most advanced standards and ideals as to use conscientiously those which he already possesses. Moral life is protected from falling into formalism and rigid repetition. It is rendered flexible, vital, growing.

In the second place, every case where moral action is required becomes of equal moral importance and urgency with every other. If the need and deficiencies of a specific situation indicate improvement of health as the end and good, then for that situation health is the ultimate and supreme good. It is no means to something else. It is a final and intrinsic value. The same thing is true of improvement of economic status, of making a living, of attending to business and family demands—all of the things which under the sanction of fixed ends have been rendered of secondary and merely instrumental value, and so relatively base and unimportant. Anything that in a given situation is an end and good at all is of equal worth, rank and dignity with every other good of any other situation, and deserves the same intelligent attention.

We note thirdly the effect in destroying the roots of Phariseeism. We are so accustomed to thinking of this as deliberate hypocrisy that we overlook its intellectual premises. The conception which looks for the end of action within the circumstances of the actual situation will not have the same measure of judgment for all cases. When one factor of the situation is a person of trained mind and large resources, more will be expected than with a person of backward mind and uncultured experience. The absurdity of applying the same standard of moral judgment to savage peoples that is used with civilized will be apparent. No individual or group will be judged by whether they come up to or fall short of some fixed result, but by the direction in which they are moving. The bad man is the man who no matter how good he *has* been is beginning to deteriorate, to grow less good. The good man is the man who no matter how morally unworthy he *has* been is moving to become better. Such a conception makes one severe in judging himself and humane in judging others. It excludes that arrogance which always accompanies judgment based on degree of approximation to fixed ends.

In the fourth place, the process of growth, of improvement and progress, rather than the static outcome and result, becomes the significant thing. Not health as an end fixed once and for all, but the needed improvement in health—a continual process—is the end and good. The end is no longer a terminus or limit to be reached. It is the active process of transforming the existent situation. Not perfection as a final goal, but the ever-enduring process of perfecting, maturing, refining is the aim of living. Honesty, industry, temperance, justice, like health, wealth and learning, are not goods to be possessed as they would be if they expressed fixed ends to be attained. They are directions of change in the quality of experience. Growth itself is the only moral "end."

Although the bearing of this idea upon the problem of evil and the controversy between optimism and pessimism is too vast to be here discussed, it may be worth while to touch upon it superficially. The problem of evil ceases to be a theological and metaphysical one, and is perceived to be the practical problem of reducing, alleviating, as far as may be removing, the evils of life. Philosophy is no longer under obligation to find ingenious methods for proving that evils are only apparent, not real, or to elaborate schemes for explaining them away or, worse yet, for justifying them. It assumes another obligation:—That of contributing in however humble a way to methods that will assist us in discovering the causes of humanity's ills. Pessimism is a paralyzing doctrine. In declaring that the world is evil wholesale, it makes futile all efforts to discover the remediable causes of specific evils and thereby destroys at the root every attempt to make the world better and happier. Wholesale optimism, which has been the consequence of the attempt to explain evil away, is, however, equally an incubus.

After all, the optimism that says that the world is already the best possible of all worlds might be regarded as the most cynical of pessimisms. If this is the best possible, what would a world which was fundamentally bad be like? Meliorism is the belief that the specific conditions which exist at one moment, be they comparatively bad or comparatively good, in any event may be bettered. It encourages intelligence to study the positive means of good and the obstructions to their realization, and to put forth endeavor for the improvement of conditions. It arouses confidence and a reasonable hopefulness as optimism does not. For the latter in declaring that good is already realized in ultimate reality tends to make us gloss over the evils that concretely exist. It becomes too readily the creed of those who live at ease, in comfort, of those who have been successful in obtaining this world's rewards. Too readily optimism makes the men who hold it callous and blind to the sufferings of the less fortunate, or ready to find the cause of troubles of others in their personal viciousness. It thus cooperates with pessimism, in spite of the extreme nominal differences between the two, in benumbing sympathetic insight and intelligent effort in reform. It beckons men away from the world of relativity and change into the calm of the absolute and eternal.

The import of many of these changes in moral attitude focuses in the idea of happiness. Happiness has often been made the object of the moralists' contempt. Yet the most ascetic moralist has usually restored the idea of happiness under some other name, such as bliss. Goodness without happiness, valor and virtue without satisfaction, ends without conscious enjoyment—these things are as intolerable practically as they are self-contradictory in conception. Happiness is not, however, a bare possession; it is not a fixed attainment. Such a happiness is either the unworthy selfishness which moralists have so bitterly condemned, or it is, even if labelled bliss, an insipid tedium, a millennium of ease in relief from all struggle and labor. It could satisfy only the most delicate of molly-coddles. Happiness is found only in success; but success means succeeding, getting forward, moving in advance. It is an active process, not a passive outcome. Accordingly it includes the overcoming of obstacles, the elimination of sources of defect and ill. Esthetic sensitiveness and enjoyment are a large constituent in any worthy happiness. But the esthetic appreciation which is totally separated from renewal of spirit, from re-creation of mind and purification of emotion is a weak and sickly thing, destined to speedy death from starvation.

That the renewal and re-creation come unconsciously not by set intention but makes them the more genuine.

Upon the whole, utilitarianism has marked the best in the transition from the classic theory of ends and goods to that which is now possible. It had definite merits. It insisted upon getting away from vague generalities, and down to the specific and concrete. It subordinated law to human achievement instead of subordinating humanity to external law. It taught that institutions are made for man and not man for institutions; it actively promoted all issues of reform. It made moral good natural, humane, in touch with the natural goods of life. It opposed unearthly and other worldly morality. Above all, it acclimatized in human imagination the idea of social welfare as a supreme test. But it was still profoundly affected in fundamental points by old ways of thinking. It never questioned the idea of a fixed, final and supreme end. It only questioned the current notions as to the nature of this end; and then inserted pleasure and the greatest possible aggregate of pleasures in the position of the fixed end.

Such a point of view treats concrete activities and specific interests not as worth while in themselves, or as constituents of happiness, but as mere external means to getting pleasures. The upholders of the old tradition could therefore easily accuse utilitarianism of making not only virtue but art, poetry, religion and the state into mere servile means of attaining sensuous enjoyments. Since pleasure was an outcome, a result valuable on its own account independently of the active processes that achieve it, happiness was a thing to be possessed and held onto. The acquisitive instincts of man were exaggerated at the expense of the creative. Production was of importance not because of the intrinsic worth of invention and reshaping the world, but because its external results feed pleasure. Like every theory that sets up fixed and final aims, in making the end passive and possessive, it made all active operations *mere* tools. Labor was an unavoidable evil to be minimized. Security in possession was the chief thing practically. Material comfort and ease were magnified in contrast with the pains and risk of experimental creation.

These deficiencies, under certain conceivable conditions, might have remained merely theoretical. But the disposition of the times and the interests of those who propagated the utilitarian ideas, endowed them with power for social harm. In spite of the power of the new ideas in attacking old social abuses, there were elements in the teaching which operated or protected to sanction new social abuses. The reforming zeal was shown in criticism of the evils inherited from the class system of feudalism, evils economic, legal and political. But the new economic order of capitalism that was superseding feudalism brought its own social evils with it, and some of these ills utilitarianism tended to cover up or defend. The emphasis upon acquisition and possession of enjoyments took on an untoward color in connection with the contemporary enormous desire for wealth and the enjoyments it makes possible.

If utilitarianism did not actively promote the new economic materialism, it had no means of combating it. Its general spirit of subordinating productive activity to the bare product was indirectly favorable to the cause of an unadorned commercialism. In spite of its interest in a thoroughly social aim, utilitarianism fostered a new class interest, that of the capitalistic property-owning interests, provided only property was obtained through free competition and not by governmental favor. The stress that Bentham put on security tended to consecrate the legal institution of private property provided only certain legal abuses in connection with its acquisition and transfer were abolished. *Beati possidentes*—provided possessions had been obtained in accord with the rules of the competitive game —without, that is, extraneous favors from government. Thus utilitarianism gave intellectual confirmation to all those tendencies which make "business" not a means of social service and an opportunity for personal growth in creative power but a way of accumulating the means of private enjoyments. Utilitarian ethics thus afford a remarkable example of the need of philosophic reconstruction which these lectures have been presenting. Up to a certain point, it reflected the meaning of modern thought and aspirations. But it was still tied down by fundamental ideas of that very order which it thought it had completely left behind: The idea of a fixed and single end lying beyond the diversity of human needs and acts rendered utilitarianism incapable of being an adequate representative of the modern spirit. It has to be reconstructed through emancipation from its inherited elements.

If a few words are added upon the topic of education, it is only for the sake of suggesting that the educative process is all one with the moral process, since the latter is a continuous passage of experience from worse to better. Education has been traditionally thought of as preparation: as learning, acquiring certain things because they will later be useful. The end is remote, and education is getting ready, is a preliminary to something more important to happen later on. Childhood is only a preparation for adult life, and adult life for another life. Always the future, not the present, has been the significant thing in education: Acquisition of knowledge and skill for future use and enjoyment; formation of habits required later in life in business, good citizenship and pursuit of science. Education is thought of also as something needed by some human beings merely because of their dependence upon others. We are born ignorant, unversed, unskilled, immature, and consequently in a state of social dependence. Instruction, training, moral discipline are processes by which the mature, the adult, gradually raise the helpless to the point where they can look out for themselves. The business of childhood is to grow into the independence of adulthood by means of the guidance of those who have already attained it. Thus the process of education as the main business of life ends when the young have arrived at emancipation from social dependence.

These two ideas, generally assumed but rarely explicitly reasoned out, contravene the conception that growing, or the continuous reconstruction of experience, is the only end. If at whatever period we choose to take a person, he is still in process of growth, then education is not, save as a by-product, a preparation for something coming later. Getting from the present the degree and kind of growth there is in it is education. This is a constant function, independent of age. The best thing that can be said about any special process of education, like that of the formal school period, is that it renders its subject capable of further education: more sensitive to conditions of growth and more able to take advantage of them. Acquisition of skill, possession of knowledge, attainment of culture are not ends: they are marks of growth and means to its continuing.

The contrast usually assumed between the period of education as one of social dependence and of maturity as one of social independence does harm. We repeat over and over that man is a social animal, and then confine the significance of this statement to the sphere in which sociality usually seems least evident, politics. The heart of the sociality of man is in education. The idea of education as preparation and of adulthood as a fixed limit of growth are two sides of the same obnoxious untruth. If the moral business of the adult as well as the young is a growing and developing experience, then the instruction that comes from social dependencies and interdependencies are as important for the adult as for the child. Moral independence for the adult means arrest of growth, isolation means induration. We exaggerate the intellectual dependence of childhood so that children are too much kept in leading strings, and then we exaggerate the independence of adult life from intimacy of contacts and communication with others. When the identity of the moral process with the processes of specific growth is realized, the more conscious and formal education of childhood will be seen to be the most economical and efficient means of social advance and reorganization, and it will also be evident that the test of all the institutions of adult life is their effect in furthering continued education. Government, business, art, religion, all social institutions have a meaning, a purpose. That purpose is to set free and to develop the capacities of human individuals without respect to race, sex, class or economical status. And this is all one with saying that the test of their value is the extent to which they educate every individual into the full stature of his possibility. Democracy has many meanings, but if it has a moral meaning, it is found in resolving that the supreme test of all political institutions and industrial arrangements shall be the contribution they make to the all-around growth of every member of society.

QUESTIONS FOR STUDY AND DISCUSSION

1. Are there any fixed ends in nature?
2. How do moral goods and ends arise?
3. Are there any ethical universals?

4. Does man endow things with value or find them valuable apart from himself?
5. What is Dewey's reaction to utilitarianism?
6. Is Dewey's instrumentalism the same as utilitarianism?
7. What is the relationship of ethics to education?

The Construction of Good

We saw at the outset of our discussion that insecurity generates the quest for certainty. Consequences issue from every experience, and they are the source of our interest in what is present. Absence of arts of regulation diverted the search for security into irrelevant modes of practice, into rite and cult; thought was devoted to discovery of omens rather than of signs of what is to occur. Gradually there was differentiation of two realms, one higher, consisting of the powers which determine human destiny in all important affairs. With this religion was concerned. The other consisted of the prosaic matters in which man relied upon his own skill and his matter-of-fact insight. Philosophy inherited the idea of this division. Meanwhile in Greece many of the arts had attained a state of development which raised them above a merely routine state; there were intimations of measure, order and regularity in materials dealt with which give intimations of underlying rationality. Because of the growth of mathematics, there arose also the ideal of a purely rational knowledge, intrinsically solid and worthy and the means by which the intimations of rationality within changing phenomena could be comprehended within science. For the intellectual class the stay and consolation, the warrant of certainty, provided by religion was henceforth found in intellectual demonstration of the reality of the objects of an ideal realm.

With the expansion of Christianity, ethico-religious traits came to dominate the purely rational ones. The ultimate authoritative standards for regulation of the dispositions and purposes of the human will were fused with those which satisfied the demands for necessary and universal truth. The authority of ultimate Being was, moreover, represented on earth by the Church; that which in its nature transcended intellect was made known by a revelation of which the Church was the interpreter and guardian. The system endured for centuries. While it endured, it provided an integration of belief and conduct for the western world. Unity of thought and practice extended down to every detail of the management of life; efficacy of its operation did not depend upon thought. It was guaranteed by the most powerful and authoritative of all social institutions.

Its seemingly solid foundation was, however, undermined by the conclusions of modern science. They effected, both in themselves and even more in the new interests and activities they generated, a breach between what man is concerned with here and now and the faith concerning ultimate reality which, in determining his ultimate and eternal destiny, had previously given regulation to his present life. The problem of restoring integration and coöperation between man's beliefs about the world in which he lives and his beliefs about the values and purposes that should direct his conduct is the deepest problem of modern life. It is the problem of any philosophy that is not isolated from that life.

The attention which has been given to the fact that in its experimental procedure science has surrendered the separation between knowing and doing has its source in the fact that there is now provided within a limited, specialized and technical field the possibility and earnest, as far as theory is concerned, of effecting the needed integration in the wider field of collective human experience. Philosophy is called upon to be the theory of the practice, through ideas sufficiently definite to be operative in experimental endeavor, by which the integration may be made secure in actual experience. Its central problem is the relation that exists between the beliefs about the nature of things due to natural science to beliefs about values— using that word to designate whatever is taken to have rightful authority in the direction of conduct. A philosophy which should take up this problem is struck first of all by the fact that beliefs about values are pretty much in the position in which beliefs about nature were before the scientific revolution. There is either a basic distrust of the capacity of experience to develop its own regulative standards, and an appeal to what philosophers call eternal values, in order to ensure regulation of belief and action; or there is acceptance of enjoyments actually experienced irrespective of the method or operation by which they are brought into existence. Complete bifurcation between rationalistic method and an empirical method has its final and most deeply human significance in the ways in which good and bad are thought of and acted for and upon.

As far as technical philosophy reflects this situation, there is division of theories of values into two kinds. On the one hand, goods and evils, in every region of life, as they are concretely experienced, are regarded as characteristic of an inferior order of Being—intrinsically inferior. Just because they are things of human experience, their worth must be estimated by reference to standards and ideals derived from ultimate reality. Their defects and perversion are attributed to the same fact; they are to be corrected and controlled through adoption of methods of conduct derived from loyalty to the requirements of Supreme Being. This philosophic formulation gets actuality and force from the fact that it is a rendering of the beliefs of men in general as far as they have come under the influence of institutional religion. Just as rational conceptions were once superimposed upon observed and temporal phenomena, so eternal values are superimposed upon experienced goods. In one case as in the other, the alternative is supposed to be confusion and lawlessness. Philosophers suppose these eternal values are known by reason; the mass of persons that they are divinely revealed.

Nevertheless, with the expansion of secular interests, temporal values have enormously multiplied; they absorb more and more attention and energy. The sense of transcendent values has become enfeebled; instead of permeating all things in life, it is more and more restricted to special times and acts. The authority of the Church to declare and impose divine will and purpose has narrowed. Whatever men say and profess, their tendency in the presence of actual evils is to resort to natural and empirical means to remedy them. But in formal belief, the old doctrine of the inherently disturbed and unworthy character of the goods and standards of ordinary experience persists. This divergence between what men do and what they nominally profess is closely connected with the confusions and conflicts of modern thought.

It is not meant to assert that no attempts have been made to replace the older theory regarding the authority of immutable and transcendent values by conceptions more congruous with the practices of daily life. The contrary is the case. The utilitarian theory, to take one instance, has had great power. The idealistic school is the only one in contemporary philosophies, with the exception of one form of neo-realism, that makes much of the notion of a reality which is all one with ultimate moral and religious values. But this school is also the one most concerned with the conservation of "spiritual" life. Equally significant is the fact that empirical theories retain the notion that thought and judgment are concerned with values that are experienced independently of them. For these theories, emotional satisfactions occupy the same place that sensations hold in traditional empiricism. Values are constituted by liking and enjoyment; to be enjoyed and to be a value are two names for one and the same fact. Since science has extruded values from its objects, these empirical theories do everything possible to emphasize their purely subjective character of value. A psychological theory of desire and liking is supposed to cover the whole ground of the theory of values; in it, immediate feeling is the counterpart of immediate sensation.

I shall not object to this empirical theory as far as it connects the theory of values with concrete experiences of desire and satisfaction. The idea that there is such a connection is the only way known to me by which the pallid remoteness of the rationalistic theory, and the only too glaring presence of the institutional theory of transcendental values can be escaped. The objection is that the theory in question holds down value to objects *antecedently* enjoyed, apart from reference to the method by which they come into existence; it takes enjoyments which are casual because unregulated by intelligent operations to be values in and of themselves. Operational thinking needs to be applied to the judgment of values just as it has now finally been applied in conceptions of physical objects. Experimental empiricism in the field of ideas of good and bad is demanded to meet the conditions of the present situation.

The scientific revolution came about when material of direct and uncontrolled experience was taken as problematic; as supplying material to be transformed by reflective operations into known objects. The contrast between experienced and known objects was found to be a temporal one; namely, one between empirical subject-matters which were had or "given" prior to the acts of experimental variation and redisposition and those which succeeded these acts and issued from them. The notion of an act whether of sense or thought which supplied a valid measure of thought in immediate knowledge was discredited. Consequences of operations became the important thing. The suggestion almost imperatively follows that escape from the defects of transcendental absolutism is not to be had by setting up as values enjoyments that happen anyhow, but in defining value by enjoyments which are the consequences of intelligent action. Without the intervention of thought, enjoyments are not values but problematic goods, becoming values when they re-issue in a changed form from intelligent behavior. The fundamental trouble with the current empirical theory of values is that it merely formulates and justifies the socially prevailing habit of regarding enjoyments as they are actually experienced as values in and of themselves. It completely side-steps the question of regulation of these enjoyments. This issue involves nothing less than the problem of the directed reconstruction of economic, political and religious institutions.

There was seemingly a paradox involved in the notion that if we turned our backs upon the immediately perceived qualities of things, we should be enabled to form valid conceptions of objects, and that these conceptions could be used to bring about a more secure and more significant experience of them. But the method terminated in disclosing the connections or interactions upon which perceived objects, viewed as events, depend. Formal analogy suggests that we regard our direct and original experience of things liked and enjoyed as only *possibilities* of values to be achieved; that enjoyment becomes a value when we discover the relations upon which its presence depends. Such a causal and operational definition gives only a conception of a value, not a value itself. But the utilization of the conception in action results in an object having secure and significant value.

The formal statement may be given concrete content by pointing to the difference between the enjoyed and the enjoyable, the desired and the desirable, the satis*fying* and the satis*factory*. To say that something is enjoyed is to make a statement about a fact, something already in existence; it is not to judge the value of that fact. There is no difference between such a proposition and one which says that something is sweet or sour, red or black. It is just correct or incorrect and that is the end of the matter. But to call an object a value is to assert that it satisfies or fulfills certain conditions. Function and status in meeting conditions is a different matter from bare existence. The fact that something is desired only raises the *question* of its desirability; it does not settle it. Only a child in the degree of his immaturity thinks to settle the question of desirability by reiterated proclamation: "I want it, I want it, I want it." What is objected to in the current empirical theory of values is not connection of them with desire and enjoyment but failure to distinguish between enjoyments of radically different sorts. There are many common expressions in which the difference of the two kinds is clearly recognized. Take for example the difference between the ideas of "satisfying" and "satisfactory." To say that something satisfies is to report something as an isolated finality. To assert that it is satis*factory* is to define it in its connections and interactions. The fact that it pleases or is immediately congenial poses a problem to judgment. How shall the satisfaction be rated? Is it a value or is it not? Is it something to be prized and cherished, *to be* enjoyed? Not stern moralists alone but everyday experience informs us that finding satisfaction in a thing may be a warning, a summons to be on the lookout for consequences. To declare something satis*factory* is to assert that it meets specifiable conditions. It is, in effect, a judgment that the thing "will do." It involves a prediction; it contemplates a future in which the thing will continue to serve; it *will* do. It asserts a consequence the thing will actively institute; it will *do*. That it is satisfying is the content of a proposition of fact; that it is satisfactory is a judgment, an estimate, an appraisal. It denotes an attitude *to be* taken, that of striving to perpetuate and to make secure.

It is worth notice that besides the instances given, there are many other recognitions in ordinary speech of the distinction. The endings "able," "worthy" and "ful" are cases in point. Noted and notable, noteworthy; remarked and remarkable; advised and advisable; wondered at and wonderful; pleasing and beautiful; loved and lovable; blamed and blameable, blameworthy; objected to and objectionable; esteemed and estimable; admired and admirable; shamed and shameful; honored and honorable; approved and approvable, worthy of approbation, etc. The multiplication of words adds nothing to the force of the distinction. But it aids in conveying a sense of the fundamental character of the distinction; of the difference between mere report of an already existent fact and judgment as to the importance and need of bringing a fact into existence; or, if it is already there, of sustaining it in existence. The latter is a genuine practical judgment, and marks the only type of judgment that has to do with the direction of action. Whether or no we reserve the term "value" for the latter (as seems to me proper) is a minor matter; that the distinction be acknowledged as the key to understanding the relation of values to the direction of conduct is the important thing.

This element of direction by an idea of value applies to science as well as anywhere else. For in every scientific undertaking, there is passed a constant succession of estimates; such as "it is worth treating these facts as data or evidence; it is advisable to try this experiment; to make that observation; to entertain such and such a hypothesis; to perform this calculation," etc.

The word "taste" has perhaps got too completely associated with arbitrary liking to express the nature of judgments of value. But if the word be used in the sense of an appreciation at once cultivated and active, one may say that the formation of taste is the chief matter wherever values enter in, whether intellectual, esthetic or moral. Relatively immediate judgments, which we call tact or to which we give the name of intuition, do not precede reflective inquiry, but are the funded products of much thoughtful experience. Expertness of taste is at once the result and the reward of constant exercise of thinking. Instead of there being no disputing about tastes, they are the one thing worth disputing about, if by "dispute" is signified discussion involving reflective inquiry. Taste, if we use the word in its best sense, is the outcome of experience brought cumulatively to bear on the intelligent appreciation of the real worth of likings and enjoyments. There is nothing in which a person so completely reveals himself as in the things which he judges enjoyable and desirable. Such judgments are the sole alternative to the domination of belief by impulse, chance, blind habit and self-interest. The formation of a cultivated and effectively operative good judgment or taste with respect to what is esthetically admirable, intellectually acceptable and morally approvable is the supreme task set to human beings by the incidents of experience.

Propositions about what is or has been liked are of instrumental value in reaching judgments of value, in as far as the conditions and consequences of the thing liked are thought about. In themselves they make no claims; they put forth no demand upon subsequent attitudes and acts; they profess no authority to direct. If one likes a thing he likes it; that *is* a point about which there can be no dispute:—although it is not so easy to state just *what* is liked as is frequently assumed. A judgment about what is *to be* desired and enjoyed is, on the other hand, a claim on future action; it possesses *de jure* and not merely *de facto* quality. It is a matter of frequent experience that likings and enjoyments are of all kinds, and that many are such as reflective judgments condemn. By way of self-justification and "rationalization," an enjoyment creates a tendency to assert that the thing enjoyed is a value. This assertion of validity adds authority to the fact. It is a decision that the object has a right to exist and hence a claim upon action to further its existence.

The analogy between the status of the theory of values and the theory of ideas about natural objects before the rise of experimental inquiry may be carried further. The sensationalistic theory of the origin and test of thought evoked, by way of reaction, the transcendental theory of *a priori* ideas. For it failed utterly to account for objective connection, order and regularity in objects observed. Similarly, any doctrine that identifies the mere fact of being liked with the value of the object liked so fails to give direction to conduct when direction is needed that it automatically calls forth the assertion that there are values eternally in Being that are the standards of all judgments and the obligatory ends of all action. Without the introduction of operational thinking, we oscillate between a theory that, in order to save the objectivity of judgments of values, isolates them from experience and nature, and a theory that, in order to save their concrete and human significance, reduces them to mere statements about our own feelings.

Not even the most devoted adherents of the notion that enjoyment and value are equivalent facts would venture to assert that because we have once liked a thing we should go on liking it; they are compelled to introduce the idea that *some* tastes are to be cultivated. Logically, there is no ground for introducing the idea of cultivation; liking is liking, and one is as good as another. If enjoyments *are* values, the judgment of value cannot regulate the form which liking takes; it cannot regulate its own conditions. Desire and purpose, and hence action, are left without guidance, although the question of regulation of their formation is the supreme problem of practical life. Values (to sum up) may be connected inherently with liking, and yet not with *every* liking but only with those that judgment has approved, after examination of the relation upon which the object liked depends. A casual liking is one that happens without knowledge of how it occurs nor to what effect. The difference between it and one which is sought because of a judgment that it is worth having and is to be striven for, makes just the difference between enjoyments which are accidental and enjoyments that have value and hence a claim upon our attitude and conduct.

In any case, the alternative rationalistic theory does not afford the guidance for the sake of which eternal and immutable norms are appealed to. The scientist finds no help in determining the probable truth of some proposed theory by comparing it with a standard of absolute truth and immutable being. He has to rely upon definite operations undertaken under definite conditions—upon method. We can hardly imagine an architect getting aid in the construction of a building from an ideal at large, though we can understand his framing an ideal on the basis of knowledge of actual conditions and needs. Nor does the ideal of perfect beauty in antecedent Being give direction to a painter in producing a particular work of art. In morals, absolute perfection does not seem to be more than a generalized hypostatization of the recognition that there is a good to be sought, an obligation to be met—both being concrete matters. Nor is the defect in this respect merely negative. An examination of history would reveal, I am confident, that these general and remote schemes of value actually obtain a content definite enough and near enough to concrete situations as to afford guidance in action only by consecrating some institution or dogma already having social currency. Concreteness is gained, but it is by protecting from inquiry some accepted standard which perhaps is outworn and in need of criticism.

When theories of values do not afford intellectual assistance in framing ideas and beliefs about values that are adequate to direct action, the gap must be filled by other means. If intelligent method is lacking, prejudice, the pressure of immediate circumstance, self-interest and class-interest, traditional customs, institutions of accidental historic origin, are *not* lacking, and they tend to take the place of intelligence. Thus we are led to our main position: *Judgments about values are judgments about the conditions and the results of experienced objects; judgments about that which should regulate the formation of our desires, affections and enjoyments.* For whatever decides their formation will determine the main course of our conduct, personal and social.

If it sounds strange to hear that we should frame our judgments as to what has value by considering the connections in existence of what we like and enjoy, the reply is not far to seek. As long as we do not engage in this inquiry enjoyments (values if we choose to apply that term) are casual; they are given by "nature," not constructed by art. Like natural objects in their qualitative existence, they at most only supply material for elaboration in rational discourse. A *feeling* of good or excellence is as far removed from goodness in fact as a feeling that objects are intellectually thus and so is removed from their being actually so. To recognize that the truth of natural objects can be reached only by the greatest care in selecting and arranging directed operations, and then to suppose that values can be truly determined by the mere fact of liking seems to leave us in an incredible position. All the serious perplexities of life come back to the genuine difficulty of forming a judgment as to the values of the situation; they come back to a conflict of goods. Only dogmatism can suppose that serious moral conflict is between something clearly bad and something known to be good, and that uncertainty lies wholly in the will of the one choosing. Most conflicts of importance are conflicts between things which are or have been satisfying, not between good and evil. And to suppose that we can make a hierarchial table of values at large once for all, a kind of catalogue in which they are arranged in an order of ascending or descending worth, is to indulge in a gloss on our inability to frame intelligent judgments in the concrete. Or else it is to dignify customary choice and prejudice by a title of honor.

The alternative to definition, classification and systematization of satisfactions just as they happen to occur is judgment of them by means of the relations under which they occur. If we know the conditions under which the act of liking, of desire and enjoyment, takes place, we are in a position to know what are the consequences of that act. The difference between the desired and the desirable, admired and the admirable, becomes effective at just this point. Consider the difference between the proposition "That thing has been eaten," and the judgment "That thing is edible." The former statement involves no knowledge of any relation except the one stated; while we are able to judge of the edibility of anything only when we have a knowledge of its interactions with other things sufficient to enable us to foresee its probable effects when it is taken into the organism and produces effects there.

To assume that anything can be known in isolation from its connection with other things is to identify knowing with merely having some object before perception or in feeling, and is thus to lose the key to the traits that distinguish an object as known. It is futile, even silly, to suppose that some quality that is directly present constitutes the whole of the thing presenting the quality. It does not do so when the quality is that of being hot or fluid or heavy, and it does not when the quality is that of giving pleasure, or being enjoyed. Such qualities are, once more, effects, ends in the sense of closing termini of processes involving causal connections. They are something to be investigated, challenges to inquiry and judgment. The more connections and interactions we ascertain, the more we *know* the object in question. Thinking is search for these connections. Heat experienced as a consequence of directed operations has a meaning quite different from the heat that is casually experienced without knowledge of how it came about. The same is true of enjoyments. Enjoyments that issue from conduct directed by insight into relations have a meaning and a validity due to the way in which they are experienced. Such enjoyments are not repented of; they generate no after-taste of bitterness. Even in the midst of direct enjoyment, there is a sense of validity, of authorization, which intensifies the enjoyment. There is solicitude for perpetuation of the *object* having value which is radically different from mere anxiety to perpetuate the *feeling* of enjoyment.

Such statements as we have been making are, therefore, far from implying that there are values apart from things actually enjoyed as good. To find a thing enjoy*able* is, so to say, a *plus* enjoyment. We saw that it was foolish to treat the scientific object as a rival to or substitute for the perceived object, since the former is intermediate between uncertain and settled situations and those experienced under conditions of greater control. In the same way, judgment of the value of an object to be experienced is instrumental to appreciation of it when it is realized. But the notion that every object that happens to satisfy has an equal claim with every other to be a value is like supposing that every object of perception has the same cognitive force as every other. There is no knowledge without perception; but objects perceived are *known* only when they are determined as consequences of connective operations. There is no value except where there is satisfaction, but there have to be certain conditions fulfilled to transform a satisfaction into a value.

The time will come when it will be found passing strange that we of this age should take such pains to control by every means at command the formation of ideas of physical things, even those most remote from human concern, and yet are content with haphazard beliefs about the qualities of objects that regulate our deepest interests; that we are scrupulous as to methods of forming ideas of natural objects, and either dogmatic or else driven by immediate conditions in framing those about values. There is, by implication, if not explicitly, a prevalent notion that values are already well known and that all which is lacking is the will to cultivate them in the order of their worth. In fact the most profound lack is not the will to act upon goods already known but the will to know what they are.

It is not a dream that it is possible to exercise some degree of regulation of the occurrence of enjoyments which are of value. Realization of the possibility is exemplified, for example, in the technologies and arts of industrial life—that is, up to a definite limit. Men desired heat, light, and speed of transit and of communication beyond what nature provides of itself. These things have been attained not by lauding the enjoyment of these things and preaching their desirability, but by study of the conditions of their manifestation. Knowledge of relations having been obtained, ability to produce followed, and enjoyment ensued as a matter of course. It is, however, an old story that enjoyment of these things as goods is no warrant of their bringing only good in their train. As Plato was given to pointing out, the physician knows how to heal and the orator to persuade, but the ulterior knowledge of whether it is better for a man to be healed or to be persuaded to the orator's opinion remains unsettled. Here there appears the split between what are traditionally and conventionally called the values of the baser arts and the higher values of the truly personal and humane arts.

With respect to the former, there is no assumption that they can be had and enjoyed without definite operative knowledge. With respect to them it is also clear that the degree in which we value them is measurable by the pains taken to control the conditions of their occurrence. With respect to the latter, it is assumed that no one who is honest can be in doubt what they are; that by revelation, or conscience, or the instruction of others, or immediate feeling, they are clear beyond question. And instead of action in their behalf being taken to be a measure of the extent to which things *are* values to us, it is assumed that the difficulty is to persuade men to act upon what they already know to be good. Knowledge of conditions and consequences is regarded as wholly indifferent to judging what is of serious value, though it is useful in a prudential way in trying to actualize it. In consequence, the existence of values that are by common consent of a secondary and technical sort are under a fair degree of control, while those denominated supreme and imperative are subject to all the winds of impulse, custom and arbitrary authority.

This distinction between higher and lower types of value is itself something to be looked into. Why should there be a sharp division made between some goods as physical and material and others as ideal and "spiritual"? The question touches the whole dualism of the material and the ideal at its root. To denominate anything "matter" or "material" is not in truth to disparage it. It is, if the designation is correctly applied, a way of indicating that the thing in question is a condition or means of the existence of something else. And disparagement of effective means is practically synonymous with disregard of the things that are termed, in eulogistic fashion, ideal and spiritual. For the latter terms if they have any concrete application at all signify something which is a desirable consummation of conditions, a cherished fulfillment of means. The sharp separation between material and ideal good thus deprives the latter of the underpinning of effective support while it opens the way for treating things which should be employed as means as ends in themselves. For since men cannot after all live without some measure of possession of such matters as health and wealth, the latter things will be viewed as values and ends in isolation unless they are treated as integral constituents of the goods that are deemed supreme and final.

The relations that determine the occurrence of what human beings experience, especially when social connections are taken into account, are indefinitely wider and more complex than those that determine the events termed physical; the latter are the outcome of definite selective operations. This is the reason why we know something about remote objects like the stars better than we know significantly characteristic things about own own bodies and minds. We forget the infinite number of things we do not know about the stars, or rather that what we call a star is itself the product of the elimination, enforced and deliberate, of most of the traits that belong to an actual existence. The amount of knowledge we possess about stars would not seem very great or very important if it were carried over to human beings and exhausted our knowledge of them. It is inevitable that genuine knowledge of man and society should lag far behind physical knowledge.

But this difference is not a ground for making a sharp division between the two, nor does it account for the fact that we make so little use of the experimental method of forming our ideas and beliefs about the concerns of man in his characteristic social relations. For this separation religions and philosophies must admit some responsibility. They have erected a distinction between a narrower scope of relations and a wider and fuller one into a difference of kind, naming one kind material, and the other mental and moral. They have charged themselves gratuitously with the office of diffusing belief in the necessity of the division, and with instilling contempt for the material as something inferior in kind in its intrinsic nature and worth. Formal philosophies undergo evaporation of their technical solid contents; in a thinner and more viable form they find their way into the minds of those who know nothing of their original forms. When these diffuse and, so to say, airy emanations re-crystallize in the popular mind they form a hard deposit of opinion that alters slowly and with great difficulty.

What difference would it actually make in the arts of conduct, personal and social, if the experimental theory were adopted not as a mere theory, but as a part of the working equipment of habitual attitudes on the part of everyone? It would be impossible, even were time given, to answer the question in adequate detail, just as men could not foretell in advance the consequences for knowledge of adopting the experimental method. It is the nature of the method that it has to be tried. But there are generic lines of difference which, within the limits of time at disposal, may be sketched.

Change from forming ideas and judgments of value on the basis of conformity to antecedent objects, to constructing enjoyable objects directed by knowledge of consequences, is a change from looking to the past to looking to the future. I do not for a moment suppose that the experiences of the past, personal and social, are of no importance. For without them we should not be able to frame any ideas whatever of the conditions under which objects are enjoyed nor any estimate of the consequences of esteeming and liking them. But past experiences are significant in giving us intellectual instrumentalities of judging just these points. They are tools, not finalities. Reflection upon what we have liked and have enjoyed is a necessity. But it tells us nothing about the *value* of these things until enjoyments are themselves reflectively controlled, or, until, as they are recalled, we form the best judgment possible about what led us to like this sort of thing and what has issued from the fact that we liked it.

We are not, then, to get away from enjoyments experienced in the past and from recall of them, but from the notion that they are the arbiters of things to be further enjoyed. At present, the arbiter is found in the past, although there are many ways of interpreting what in the past is authoritative. Nominally, the most influential conception doubtless is that of a revelation once had or a perfect life once lived. Reliance upon precedent, upon institutions created in the past, especially in law, upon rules of morals that have come to us through unexamined customs, upon uncriticized tradition, are other forms of dependence. It is not for a moment suggested that we can get away from customs and established institutions. A mere break would doubtless result simply in chaos. But there is no danger of such a break. Mankind is too inertly conservative both by constitution and by education to give the idea of this danger actuality. What there is genuine danger of is that the force of new conditions will produce disruption externally and mechanically: this is an ever present danger. The prospect is increased, not mitigated, by that conservatism which insists upon the adequacy of old standards to meet new conditions. What is needed is intelligent examination of the consequences that are actually effected by inherited institutions and customs, in order that there may be intelligent consideration of the ways in which they are to be intentionally modified in behalf of generation of different consequences.

This is the significant meaning of transfer of experimental method from the technical field of physical experience to the wider field of human life. We trust the method in forming our beliefs about things not directly connected with human life. In effect, we distrust it in moral, political and economic affairs. In the fine arts, there are many signs of a change. In the past, such a change has often been an omen and precursor of changes in other human attitudes. But, generally speaking, the idea of actively adopting ex-

perimental method in social affairs, in the matters deemed of most enduring and ultimate worth, strikes most persons as a surrender of all standards
and regulative authority. But in principle, experimental method does not
signify random and aimless action; it implies direction by ideas and knowledge. The question at issue is a practical one. Are there in existence the
ideas and the knowledge that permit experimental method to be effectively
used in social interests and affairs?

Where will regulation come from if we surrender familiar and traditionally prized values as our directive standards? Very largely from the
findings of the natural sciences. For one of the effects of the separation
drawn between knowledge and action is to deprive scientific knowledge of
its proper service as a guide of conduct—except once more in those technological fields which have been degraded to an inferior rank. Of course, the
complexity of the conditions upon which objects of human and liberal
value depend is a great obstacle, and it would be too optimistic to say that
we have as yet enough knowledge of the scientific type to enable us to regulate our judgments of value very extensively. But we have more knowledge
than we try to put to use, and until we try more systematically we shall not
know what are the important gaps in our sciences judged from the point of
view of their moral and humane use.

For moralists usually draw a sharp line between the field of the natural
sciences and the conduct that is regarded as moral. But a moral that frames
its judgments of value on the basis of consequences must depend in a most
intimate manner upon the conclusions of science. For the knowledge of the
relations between changes which enable us to connect things as antecedents
and consequences *is* science. The narrow scope which moralists often give
to morals, their isolation of some conduct as virtuous and vicious from
other large ranges of conduct, those having to do with health and vigor,
business, education, with all the affairs in which desires and affection are
implicated, is perpetuated by this habit of exclusion of the subject-matter
of natural science from a rôle in formation of moral standards and ideals.
The same attitude operates in the other direction to keep natural science a
technical specialty, and it works unconsciously to encourage its use exclusively in regions where it can be turned to personal and class advantage, as
in war and trade.

Another great difference to be made by carrying the experimental habit
into all matter of practice is that it cuts the roots of what is often called
subjectivism, but which is better termed egoism. The subjective attitude is
much more widespread than would be inferred from the philosophies which
have that label attached. It is as rampant in realistic philosophies as in any
others, sometimes even more so, although disguised from those who hold
these philosophies under the cover of reverence for and enjoyment of ultimate values. For the implication of placing the standard of thought and
knowledge in antecedent existence is that our thought makes no difference

in what is significantly real. It then affects only our own attitude toward it.

This constant throwing of emphasis back upon a change made in ourselves instead of one made in the world in which we live seems to me the essence of what is objectionable in "subjectivism." Its taint hangs about even Platonic realism with its insistent evangelical dwelling upon the change made within the mind by contemplation of the realm of essence, and its depreciation of action as transient and all but sordid—a concession to the necessities of organic existence. All the theories which put conversion "of the eye of the soul" in the place of a conversion of natural and social objects that modifies goods actually experienced, is a retreat and escape from existence—and this retraction into self is, once more, the heart of subjective egoisms. The typical example is perhaps the other-worldliness found in religions whose chief concern is with the salvation of the personal soul. But other-worldliness is found as well in estheticism and in all seclusion within ivory towers.

It is not in the least implied that change in personal attitudes, in the disposition of the "subject," is not of great importance. Such change, on the contrary, is involved in any attempt to modify the conditions of the environment. But there is a radical difference between a change in the self that is cultivated and valued as an end, and one that is a means to alteration, through action, of objective conditions. The Aristotelian-medieval conviction that highest bliss is found in contemplative possession of ultimate Being presents an ideal attractive to some types of mind; it sets forth a refined sort of enjoyment. It is a doctrine congenial to minds that despair of the effort involved in creation of a better world of daily experience. It is, apart from theological attachments, a doctrine sure to recur when social conditions are so troubled as to make actual endeavor seem hopeless. But the subjectivism so externally marked in modern thought as compared with ancient is either a development of the old doctrine under new conditions or is of merely technical import. The medieval version of the doctrine at least had the active support of a great social institution by means of which man could be brought into the state of mind that prepared him for ultimate enjoyment of eternal Being. It had a certain solidity and depth which is lacking in modern theories that would attain the result by merely emotional or speculative procedures, or by any means not demanding a change in objective existence so as to render objects of value more empirically secure.

The nature in detail of the revolution that would be wrought by carrying into the region of values the principle now embodied in scientific practice cannot be told; to attempt it would violate the fundamental idea that we know only after we have acted and in consequences of the outcome of action. But it would surely effect a transfer of attention and energy from the subjective to the objective. Men would think of themselves as agents not as ends; ends would be found in experienced enjoyment of the fruits of a transforming activity. In as far as the subjectivity of modern thought represents a discovery of the part played by personal responses, organic and acquired, in the causal production of the qualities and values of objects, it marks the possibility of a decisive gain. It puts us in possession of some of the conditions that control the occurrence of experienced objects, and thereby it supplies us with an instrument of regulation. There is something querulous in the sweeping denial that things as experienced, as perceived and enjoyed, in any way depend upon interaction with human selves. The error of doctrines that have exploited the part played by personal and subjective reactions in determining what is perceived and enjoyed lies either in exaggerating this factor of constitution into the sole condition—as happens in subjective idealism—or else in treating it as a finality instead of, as with all knowledge, an instrument in direction of further action.

A third significant change that would issue from carrying over experimental method from physics to man concerns the import of standards, principles, rules. With the transfer, these, and all tenets and creeds about good and goods, would be recognized to be hypotheses. Instead of being rigidly fixed, they would be treated as intellectual instruments to be tested and confirmed—and altered—through consequences effected by acting upon them. They would lose all pretense of finality—the ulterior source of dogmatism. It is both astonishing and depressing that so much of the energy of mankind has gone into fighting for (with weapons of the flesh as well as of the spirit) the truth of creeds, religious, moral and political, as distinct from what has gone into effort to try creeds by putting them to the test of acting upon them. The change would do away with the intolerance and fanaticism that attend the notion that beliefs and judgments are capable of inherent truth and authority; inherent in the sense of being independent of what they lead to when used as directive principles. The transformation does not imply merely that men are responsible for acting upon what they profess to believe; that is an old doctrine. It goes much further. Any belief as such is tentative, hypothetical; it is not just to be acted upon, but is to be *framed* with reference to its office as a guide to action. Consequently, it should be the last thing in the world to be picked up casually and then clung to rigidly. When it is apprehended as a tool and only a tool, an instrumentality of direction, the same scrupulous attention will go to its formation as now goes into the making of instruments of precision in technical fields. Men, instead of being proud of accepting and asserting beliefs and "principles" on the ground of loyalty, will be as ashamed of that procedure as they would now be to confess their assent to a scientific theory out of reverence for Newton or Helmholz or whomever, without regard to evidence.

If one stops to consider the matter, is there not something strange in the fact that men should consider loyalty to "laws," principles, standards, ideals to be an inherent virtue, accounted unto them for righteousness? It is as if they were making up for some secret sense of weakness by rigidity and intensity of insistent attachment. A moral law, like a law in physics, is not something to swear by and stick to at all hazards; it is a formula of the way to respond when specified conditions present themselves. Its soundness and pertinence are tested by what happens when it is acted upon. Its claim or authority rests finally upon the imperativeness of the situation that has to be dealt with, not upon its own intrinsic nature—as any tool achieves dignity in the measure of needs served by it. The idea that adherence to standards external to experienced objects is the only alternative to confusion and lawlessness was once held in science. But knowledge became steadily progressive when it was abandoned, and clews and tests found within concrete acts and objects were employed. The test of consequences is more exacting than that afforded by fixed general rules. In addition, it secures constant development, for when new acts are tried new results are experienced, while the lauded immutability of eternal ideals and norms is in itself a denial of the possibility of development and improvement.

The various modifications that would result from adoption in social and humane subjects of the experimental way of thinking are perhaps summed up in saying that it would place *method and means* upon the level of importance that has, in the past, been imputed exclusively to ends. Means have been regarded as menial, and the useful as the servile. Means have been treated as poor relations to be endured, but not inherently welcome. The very meaning of the word "ideals" is significant of the divorce which has obtained between means and ends. "Ideals" are thought to be remote and inaccessible of attainment; they are too high and fine to be sullied by realization. They serve vaguely to arouse "aspiration," but they do not evoke and direct strivings for embodiment in actual existence. They hover in an indefinite way over the actual scene; they are expiring ghosts of a once significant kingdom of divine reality whose rule penetrated to every detail of life.

It is impossible to form a just estimate of the paralysis of effort that has been produced by indifference to means. Logically, it is truistic that lack of consideration for means signifies that so-called ends are not taken seriously. It is as if one professed devotion to painting pictures conjoined with contempt for canvas, brush and paints; or love of music on condition that no instruments, whether the voice or something external, be used to make sounds. The good workman in the arts is known by his respect for his tools and by his interest in perfecting his technique. The glorification in the arts of ends at the expense of means would be taken to be a sign of complete insincerity or even insanity. Ends separated from means are either sentimental indulgences or if they happen to exist are merely accidental. The ineffectiveness in action of "ideals" is due precisely to the supposition that means and ends are not on exactly the same level with respect to the attention and care they demand.

It is, however, much easier to point out the formal contradiction implied in ideals that are professed without equal regard for the instruments and techniques of their realization, than it is to appreciate the concrete ways in which belief in their separation has found its way into life and borne corrupt and poisonous fruits. The separation marks the form in which the traditional divorce of theory and practice has expressed itself in actual life. It accounts for the relative impotency of arts concerned with enduring human welfare. Sentimental attachment and subjective eulogy take the place of action. For there is no art without tools and instrumental agencies. But it also explains the fact that in actual behavior, energies devoted to matters nominally thought to be inferior, material and sordid, engross attention and interest. After a polite and pious deference has been paid to "ideals," men feel free to devote themselves to matters which are more immediate and pressing.

It is usual to condemn the amount of attention paid by people in general to material ease, comfort, wealth, and success gained by competition, on the ground that they give to mere means the attention that ought to be given to ends, or that they have taken for ends things which in reality are only means. Criticisms of the place which economic interest and action occupy in present life are full of complaints that men allow lower aims to usurp the place that belongs to higher and ideal values. The final source of the trouble is, however, that moral and spiritual "leaders" have propagated the notion that ideal ends may be cultivated in isolation from "material" means, as if means and material were not synonymous. While they condemn men for giving to means the thought and energy that ought to go to ends, the condemnation should go to them. For they have not taught their followers to think of material and economic activities as *really* means. They have been unwilling to frame their conception of the values that should be regulative of human conduct on the basis of the actual conditions and operations by which alone values can be actualized.

Practical needs are imminent; with the mass of mankind they are imperative. Moreover, speaking generally, men are formed to act rather than to theorize. Since the ideal ends are so remotely and accidentally connected with immediate and urgent conditions that need attention, after lip service is given to them, men naturally devote themselves to the latter. If a bird in the hand is worth two in a neighboring bush, an actuality in hand is worth, for the direction of conduct, many ideals that are so remote as to be invisible and inaccessible. Men hoist the banner of the ideal, and then march in the direction that concrete conditions suggest and reward.

Deliberate insincerity and hypocrisy are rare. But the notion that action and sentiment are inherently unified in the constitution of human nature has nothing to justify it. Integration is something to be achieved. Division of attitudes and responses, compartmentalizing of interests, is easily acquired. It goes deep just because the acquisition is unconscious, a matter of habitual adaptation to conditions. Theory separated from concrete doing and making is empty and futile; practice then becomes an immediate seizure of opportunities and enjoyments which conditions afford without the direction which theory—knowledge and ideas—has power to supply. The problem of the relation of theory and practice is not a problem of theory alone; it is that, but it is also the most practical problem of life. For it is the question of how intelligence may inform action, and how action may bear the fruit of increased insight into meaning: a clear view of the values that are worth while and of the means by which they are to be made secure in experienced objects. Construction of ideals in general and their sentimental glorification are easy; the responsibilities both of studious thought and of action are shirked. Persons having the advantage of positions of leisure and who find pleasure in abstract theorizing—a most delightful indulgence to those to whom it appeals—have a large measure of liability for a cultivated diffusion of ideals and aims that are separated from the conditions which are the means of actualization. Then other persons who find themselves in positions of social power and authority readily claim to be the bearers and defenders of ideal ends in church and state. They then use the prestige and authority their representative capacity as guardians of the highest ends confers on them to cover actions taken in behalf of the harshest and narrowest of material ends.

The present state of industrial life seems to give a fair index of the existing separation of means and ends. Isolation of economics from ideal ends, whether of morals or of organized social life, was proclaimed by Aristotle. Certain things, he said, are conditions of a worthy life, personal and social, but are not constituents of it. The economic life of man, concerned with satisfaction of wants, is of this nature. Men have wants and they must be satisfied. But they are only prerequisites of a good life, not intrinsic elements in it. Most philosophers have not been so frank nor perhaps so logical. But upon the whole, economics has been treated as on a lower level than either morals or politics. Yet the life which men, women and children actually lead, the opportunities open to them, the values they are capable of enjoying, their education, their share in all the things of art and science, are mainly determined by economic conditions. Hence we can hardly expect a moral system which ignores economic conditions to be other than remote and empty.

Industrial life is correspondingly brutalized by failure to equate it as the means by which social and cultural values are realized. That the economic life, thus exiled from the pale of higher values, takes revenge by declaring that it is the only social reality, and by means of the doctrine of materialistic determination of institutions and conduct in all fields, denies to deliberate morals and politics any share of causal regulation, is not surprising.

When economists were told that their subject-matter was merely material, they naturally thought they could be "scientific" only by excluding all reference to distinctively human values. Material wants, efforts to satisfy them, even the scientifically regulated technologies highly developed in industrial activity, are then taken to form a complete and closed field. If any reference to social ends and values is introduced it is by way of an external addition, mainly hortatory. That economic life largely determines the conditions under which mankind has access to concrete values may be recognized or it may not be. In either case, the notion that it is the means to be utilized in order to secure significant values as the common and shared possession of mankind is alien and inoperative. To many persons, the idea that the ends professed by morals are impotent save as they are connected with the working machinery of economic life seems like deflowering the purity of moral values and obligations.

The social and moral effects of the separation of theory and practice have been merely hinted at. They are so manifold and so pervasive that an adequate consideration of them would involve nothing less than a survey of the whole field of morals, economics and politics. It cannot be justly stated that these effects are in fact direct consequences of the quest for certainty by thought and knowledge isolated from action. For, as we have seen, this quest was itself a reflex product of actual conditions. But it may be truly asserted that this quest, undertaken in religion and philosophy, has had results which have reinforced the conditions which originally brought it about. Moreover, search for safety and consolation amid the perils of life by means other than intelligent action, by feeling and thought alone, began when actual means of control were lacking, when arts were undeveloped. It had then a relative historic justification that is now lacking. The primary problem for thinking which lays claim to be philosophic in its breadth and depth is to assist in bringing about a reconstruction of all beliefs rooted in a basic separation of knowledge and action; to develop a system of operative ideas congruous with present knowledge and with present facilities of control over natural events and energies.

We have noted more than once how modern philosophy has been absorbed in the problem of effecting an adjustment between the conclusions of natural science and the beliefs and values that have authority in the direction of life. The genuine and poignant issue does not reside where philosophers for the most part have placed it. It does not consist in accommodation to each other of two realms, one physical and the other ideal and spiritual, nor in the reconciliation of the "categories" of theoretical and practical reason. It is found in that isolation of executive means and ideal interests which has grown up under the influence of the separation of theory and practice. For this, by nature, involves the separation of the material and the spiritual. Its solution, therefore, can be found only in action wherein the phenomena of material and economic life are equated with the purposes that command the loyalties of affection and purpose, and in which ends and ideals are framed in terms of the possibilities of actually experienced situations. But while the solution cannot be found in "thought" alone, it can be furthered by thinking which is operative—which frames and defines ideas in terms of what may be done, and which uses the conclusions of science as instrumentalities. William James was well within the bounds of moderation when he said that looking forward instead of backward, looking to what the world and life might become instead of to what they have been, is an alteration in the "seat of authority."

It was incidentally remarked earlier in our discussion that the serious defect in the current empirical philosophy of values, the one which identifies them with things actually enjoyed irrespective of the conditions upon which they depend, is that it formulates and in so far consecrates the conditions of our present social experience. Throughout these chapters, primary attention has perforce been given to the methods and statements of philosophic theories. But these statements are technical and specialized in formulation only. In origin, content and import they are reflections of some condition or some phase of concrete human experience. Just as the theory of the separation of theory and practice has a practical origin and a momentous practical consequence, so the empirical theory that values are identical with whatever men actually enjoy, no matter how or what, formulates an aspect, and an undesirable one, of the present social situation.

For while our discussion has given more attention to the other type of philosophical doctrine, that which holds that regulative and authoritative standards are found in transcendent eternal values, it has not passed in silence over the fact that actually the greater part of the activities of the greater number of human beings is spent in effort to seize upon and hold onto such enjoyments as the actual scene permits. Their energies and their enjoyments are controlled in fact, but they are controlled by external conditions rather than by intelligent judgment and endeavor. If philosophies have any influence over the thoughts and acts of men, it is a serious matter that the most widely held empirical theory should in effect justify this state of things by identifying values with the objects of any interest as such. As long as the only theories of value placed before us for intellectual assent alternate between sending us to a realm of eternal and fixed values and sending us to enjoyments such as actually obtain, the formulation, even as only a theory, of an experimental empiricism which finds values to be identical with goods that are the fruit of intelligently directed activity has its measure of practical significance.

QUESTIONS FOR STUDY AND DISCUSSION

1. What is the difference between a normative and a factual hypothesis?
2. According to Dewey, how do value judgments arise?
3. Is the valuable to be identified with what is desired?
4. How does Dewey propose to avoid subjectivism in ethics?
5. How is experimental procedure to be employed in ethics?
6. Why does Dewey stress the unity of theory and practice?
7. What objection does he have to a God-oriented ethics?

Morality Is Social

Intelligence becomes ours in the degree in which we use it and accept responsibility for consequences. It is not ours originally or by production. "It thinks" is a truer psychological statement than "I think." Thoughts sprout and vegetate; ideas proliferate. They come from deep unconscious sources. "I think" is a statement about voluntary action. Some suggestion surges from the unknown. Our active body of habits appropriates it. The suggestion then becomes an assertion. It no longer merely comes to us. It is accepted and uttered by us. We act upon it and thereby assume, by implication, its consequences. The stuff of belief and proposition is not originated by us. It comes to us from others, by education, tradition and the suggestion of the environment. Our intelligence is bound up, so far as its materials are concerned, with the community life of which we are a part. We know what it communicates to us, and know according to the habits it forms in us. Science is an affair of civilization, not of individual intellect.

So with conscience. When a child acts, those about him re-act. They shower encouragement upon him, visit him with approval, or they bestow frowns and rebuke. What others do to us when we act is as natural a consequence of our action as what the fire does to us when we plunge our hands in it. The social environment may be as artificial as you please. But its action in response to ours is natural not artificial. In language and imagination we rehearse the responses of others just as we dramatically enact other consequences. We foreknow how others will act, and the foreknowledge is the beginning of judgment passed on action. We know *with* them; there is conscience. An assembly is formed within our breast which discusses and appraises proposed and performed acts. The community without becomes a forum and tribunal within, a judgment-seat of charges, assessments and exculpations. Our thoughts of our own actions are saturated with the ideas that others entertain about them, ideas which have been expressed not only in explicit instruction but still more effectively in reaction to our acts.

Liability is the beginning of responsibility. We are held accountable by others for the consequences of our acts. They visit their like and dislike of these consequences upon us. In vain do we claim that these are not ours; that they are products of ignorance not design, or are incidents in the execution of a most laudable scheme. Their authorship is imputed to us. We are disapproved, and disapproval is not an inner state of mind but a most definite act. Others say to us by their deeds we do not care a fig whether you did this deliberately or not. We intend that you *shall* deliberate before you do it again, and that if possible your deliberation shall prevent a repetition of this act we object to. The reference in blame and every unfavorable judgment is prospective, not retrospective. Theories about responsibility may become confused, but in practice no one is stupid enough to try to change the past. Approbation and disapprobation are ways of influencing the formation of habits and aims; that is, of influencing future acts. The individual is *held* accountable for what he *has* done in order that he may be responsive in what he is *going* to do. Gradually persons learn by dramatic imitation to hold themselves accountable, and liability becomes a voluntary deliberate acknowledgment that deeds are our own, that their consequences come from us.

These two facts, that moral judgment and moral responsibility are the work wrought in us by the social environment, signify that all morality is social; not because we *ought* to take into account the effect of our acts upon the welfare of others, but because of facts. Others *do* take account of what we do, and they respond accordingly to our acts. Their responses actually *do* affect the meaning of what we do. The significance thus contributed is as inevitable as is the effect of interaction with the physical environment. In fact as civilization advances the physical environment gets itself more and more humanized, for the meaning of physical energies and events becomes involved with the part they play in human activities. Our conduct *is* socially conditioned whether we perceive the fact or not.

The effect of custom on habit, and of habit upon thought is enough to prove this statement. When we begin to forecast consequences, the consequences that most stand out are those which will proceed from other people. The resistance and the cooperation of others is the central fact in the furtherance or failure of our schemes. Connections with our fellows furnish both the opportunities for action and the instrumentalities by which we take advantage of opportunity. All of the actions of an individual bear the stamp of his community as assuredly as does the language he speaks. Difficulty in reading the stamp is due to variety of impressions in consequence of membership in many groups. This social saturation is, I repeat, a matter of fact, not of what should be, not of what is desirable or undesirable. It does not guarantee the rightness of goodness of an act; there is no excuse for thinking of evil action as individualistic and right action as social. Deliberate unscrupulous pursuit of self-interest is as much conditioned upon social opportunities, training and assistance as is the course of action prompted by a beaming benevolence. The difference lies in the quality and degree of the perception of ties and interdependencies; in the use to which they are put. Consider the form commonly assumed today by self-seeking; namely command of money and economic power. Money is a social institution; property is a legal custom; economic opportunities are dependent upon the state of society; the objects aimed at, the rewards sought for, are what they are because of social admiration, prestige, competition and power. If money-making is morally obnoxious it is because of the way these social facts are handled, not because a money-making man has withdrawn from society into an isolated selfhood or turned his back upon society. His "individualism" is not found in his original nature but in his habits acquired under social influences. It is found in his concrete aims, and these are reflexes of social conditions. Well-grounded moral objection to a mode of conduct rests upon the kind of social connections that figure, not upon lack of social aim. A man may attempt to utilize social relationships for his own advantage in an inequitable way; he may intentionally or unconsciously try to make them feed one of his own appetites. Then he is denounced as egoistic. But both his course of action and the disapproval he is subject to are facts *within* society. They are social phenomena. He pursues his unjust advantage as a social asset.

Explicit recognition of this fact is a prerequisite of improvement in moral education and of an intelligent understanding of the chief ideas or "categories" of morals. Morals is as much a matter of interaction of a person with his social environment as walking is an interaction of legs with a physical environment. The character of walking depends upon the strength and competency of legs. But it also depends upon whether a man is walking in a bog or on a paved street, upon whether there is a safeguarded path set aside or whether he has to walk amid dangerous vehicles. If the standard of morals is low it is because the education given by the interaction of the individual with his social environment is defective. Of what avail is it to preach unassuming simplicity and contentment of life when communal admiration goes to the man who "succeeds"—who makes himself conspicuous and envied because of command of money and other forms of power? If a child gets on by peevishness or intrigue, then others are his accomplices who assist in the habits which are built up. The notion that an abstract ready-made conscience exists in individuals and that it is only necessary to make an occasional appeal to it and to indulge in occasional crude rebukes and punishments, is associated with the causes of lack of definitive and orderly moral advance. For it is associated with lack of attention to social forces.

There is a peculiar inconsistency in the current idea that morals *ought* to be social. The introduction of the moral "ought" into the idea contains an implicit assertion that morals depend upon something apart from social relations. Morals *are* social. The question of ought, should be, is a question of better and worse *in* social affairs. The extent to which the weight of theories has been thrown against the perception of the place of social ties and connections in moral activity is a fair measure of the extent to which social forces work blindly and develop an accidental morality. The chief obstacle for example to recognizing the truth of a proposition frequently set forth in these pages to the effect that all conduct is potential, if not actual, matter of moral judgment is the habit of identifying moral judgment with praise and blame. So great is the influence of this habit that it is safe to say that every professed moralist when he leaves the pages of theory and faces some actual item of his own or others' behavior, first or "instinctively" thinks of acts as moral or non-moral in the degree in which they are exposed to condemnation or approval. Now this kind of judgment is certainly not one which could profitably be dispensed with. Its influence is much needed. But the tendency to equate it with all moral judgment is largely responsible for the current idea that there is a sharp line between moral conduct and a larger region of non-moral conduct which is a matter of expediency, shrewdness, success or manners.

Moreover this tendency is a chief reason why the social forces effective in shaping actual morality work blindly and unsatisfactorily. Judgment in which the emphasis falls upon blame and approbation has more heat than light. It is more emotional than intellectual. It is guided by custom, personal convenience and resentment rather than by insight into causes and consequences. It makes toward reducing moral instruction, the educative influence of social opinion, to an immediate personal matter, that is to say, to an adjustment of personal likes and dislikes. Fault-finding creates resentment in the one blamed, and approval, complacency, rather than a habit of scrutinizing conduct objectively. It puts those who are sensitive to the judgments of others in a standing defensive attitude, creating an apologetic, self-accusing and self-exculpating habit of mind when what is needed is an impersonal impartial habit of observation. "Moral" persons get so occupied with defending their conduct from real and imagined criticism that they have little time left to see what their acts really amount to, and the habit of self-blame inevitably extends to include others since it is a habit.

Now it is a wholesome thing for any one to be made aware that thoughtless, self-centered action on his part exposes him to the indignation and dislike of others. There is no one who can be safely trusted to be exempt from immediate reactions of criticism, and there are few who do not need to be braced by occasional expressions of approval. But these influences are immensely overdone in comparison with the assistance that might be given by the influence of social judgments which operate without accompaniments of praise and blame; which enable an individual to see for himself what he is doing, and which put him in command of a method of analyzing the obscure and usually unavowed forces which move him to act. We need a permeation of judgments on conduct by the method and materials of a science of human nature. Without such enlightenment even the best-intentioned attempts at the moral guidance and improvement of others often eventuate in tragedies of misunderstanding and division, as is so often seen in the relations of parents and children.

The development therefore of a more adequate science of human nature is a matter of first-rate importance. The present revolt against the notion that psychology is a science of consciousness may well turn out in the future to be the beginning of a definitive turn in thought and action. Historically there are good reasons for the isolation and exaggeration of the conscious phase of human action, an isolation which forgot that "conscious" is an adjective of some acts and which erected the resulting abstraction, "consciousness," into a noun, an existence separate and complete. These reasons are interesting not only to the student of technical philosophy but also to the student of the history of culture and even of politics. They have to do with the attempt to drag realities out of occult essences and hidden forces and get them into the light of day. They were part of the general movement called phenomenalism, and of the growing importance of individual life and private voluntary concerns. But the effect was to isolate the individual from his connections both with his fellows and with nature, and thus to create an artificial human nature, one not capable of being understood and effectively directed on the bais of analytic undertanding. It shut out from view, not to say from scientific examination, the forces which really move human nature. It took a few surface phenomena for the whole story of significant human motive-forces and acts.

As a consequence physical science and its technological applications were highly developed while the science of man, moral science, is backward. I believe that it is not possible to estimate how much of the difficulties of the present world situation are due to the disproportion and unbalance thus introduced into affairs. It would have seemed absurd to say in the seventeenth century that in the end the alteration in methods of physical investigation which was then beginning would prove more important than the religious wars of that century. Yet the wars marked the end of one era; the dawn of physical science the beginning of a new one. And a trained imagination may discover that the nationalistic and economic wars which are the chief outward mark of the present are in the end to be less significant than the development of a science of human nature now inchoate.

It sounds academic to say that substantial bettering of social relations waits upon the growth of a scientific social psychology. For the term suggests something specialized and remote. But the formation of habits of belief, desire and judgment is going on at every instant under the influence of the conditions set by men's contact, intercourse and associations with one another. This is the fundamental fact in social life and in personal character. It is the fact about which traditional human science gives no enlightenment—a fact which this traditional science blurs and virtually denies. The enormous rôle played in popular morals by appeal to the supernatural and quasi-magical is in effect a desperate admission of the futility of our science. Consequently the whole matter of the formation of the predispositions which effectively control human relationships is left to accident, to custom and immediate personal likings, resentments and ambitions. It is a commonplace that modern industry and commerce are conditioned upon a control of physical energies due to proper methods of physical inquiry and analysis. We have no social arts which are comparable because we have so nearly nothing in the way of psychological science. Yet through the development of physical science, and especially of chemistry, biology, physiology, medicine and anthropology we now have the basis for the development of such a science of man. Signs of its coming into existence are present in the movements in clinical, behavioristic and social (in its narrower sense) psychology.

At present we not only have no assured means of forming character except crude devices of blame, praise, exhortation and punishment, but the very meaning of the general notions of moral inquiry is matter of doubt and dispute. The reason is that these notions are discussed in isolation from the concrete facts of the interactions of human beings with one another—an abstraction as fatal as was the old discussion of phlogiston, gravity and vital force apart from concrete correlations of changing events with one another. Take for example such a basic conception as that of Right involving the nature of authority in conduct. There is no need here to rehearse the multitude of contending views which give evidence that discussion of this matter is still in the realm of opinion. We content ourselves with pointing out that this notion is the last resort of the anti-empirical school in morals and that it proves the effect of neglect of social conditions.

In effect its adherents argue as follows: "Let us concede that concrete ideas about right and wrong and particular notions of what is obligatory have grown up within experience. But we cannot admit this about the idea of Right, of Obligation itself. Why does moral authority exist at all? Why is the claim of the Right recognized in conscience even by those who violate it in deed? Our opponents say that such and such a course is wise, expedient, better. But *why* act for the wise, or good, or better? Why not follow our own immediate devices if we are so inclined? There is only one answer: We have a moral nature, a conscience, call it what you will. And this nature responds directly in acknowledgment of the supreme authority of the Right over all claims of inclination and habit. We may not act in accordance with this acknowledgment, but we still know that the authority of the moral law, although not its power, is unquestionable. Men may differ indefinitely according to what their experience has been as to just *what* is Right, what its contents are. But they all spontaneously agree in recognizing the supremacy of the claims of whatever is thought of as Right. Otherwise there would be no such thing as morality, but merely calculations of how to satisfy desire."

Grant the foregoing argument, and all the apparatus of abstract moralism follows in its wake. A remote goal of perfection, ideals that are contrary in a wholesale way to what is actual, a free will of arbitrary choice; all of these conceptions band themselves together with that of a non-empirical authority of Right and a non-empirical conscience which acknowledges it. They constitute its ceremonial or formal train.

Why, indeed, acknowledge the authority of Right? That many persons do not acknowledge it in fact, in action, and that all persons ignore it at times, is assumed by the argument. Just what is the significance of an alleged recognition of a supremacy which is continually denied in fact? How much would be lost if it were dropped out, and we were left face to face with actual facts? If a man lived alone in the world there might be some sense in the question "Why be moral?" were it not for one thing: No such question would then arise. As it is, we live in a world where other persons live too. Our acts affect them. They perceive these effects, and react upon us in consequence. Because they are living beings they make demands upon us for certain things from us. They approve and condemn—not in abstract theory but in what they do to us. The answer to the question "Why not put your hand in the fire?" is the answer of fact. If you do your hand will be burnt. The answer to the question why acknowledge the Right is of the same sort. For Right is only an abstract name for the multitude of concrete demands in action which others impress upon us, and of which we are obliged, if we would live, to take some account. Its authority is the exigency of their demands, the efficacy of their insistencies. There may be good ground for the contention that in theory the idea of the Right is subordinate to that of the good, being a statement of the course proper to attain good. But in fact it signifies the totality of social pressures exercised upon us to induce us to think and desire in certain ways. Hence the Right can in fact become the road to the good only as the elements that compose this unremitting pressure are enlightened, only as social relationships become themselves reasonable.

It will be retorted that all pressure is a non-moral affair partaking of force, not of Right; that Right must be ideal. Thus we are invited to enter again the circle in which the ideal has no force and social actualities no ideal quality. We refuse the invitation because social pressure is involved in our own lives, as much so as the air we breathe and the ground we walk upon. If we had desires, judgments, plans, in short a mind, apart from social connections, then the latter would be external and their action might be regarded as that of a nonmoral force. But we live mentally as physically only *in* and *because* of our environment. Social pressure is but a name for the interactions which are always going on and in which we participate, living so far as we partake and dying so far as we do not. The pressure is not ideal but empiricial, yet empirical here means only actual. It calls attention to the fact that considerations of Right are claims originating not outside of life, but within it. They are "ideal" in precisely the degree in which we intelligently recognize and act upon them, just as colors and canvas become ideal when used in ways that give an added meaning to life.

Accordingly failure to recognize the authority of Right means defect in effective apprehension of the realities of human association, not an arbitrary exercise of free will. This deficiency and perversion in apprehension indicates a defect in education—that is to say, in the operation of actual conditions, in the consequences upon desire and thought of existing interactions and interdependencies. It is false that every person has a consciousness of the supreme authority of Right and then misconceives it or ignores it in action. One has such a sense of the claims of social relationships as those relationships enforce in one's desires and observations. The belief in a separate, ideal or transcendental, practically ineffectual Right is a reflex of the inadequacy with which existing institutions perform their educative office—their office in generating observation of social continuities. It is an endeavor to "rationalize" this defect. Like all rationalizations, it operates to divert attention from the real state of affairs. Thus it helps maintain the conditions which created it, standing in the way of effort to make our institutions more humane and equitable. A theoretical acknowledgment of the supreme authority of Right, of moral law, gets twisted into an effectual substitute for acts which would better the customs which now produce vague, dull, halting and evasive observation of actual social ties. We are not caught in a circle; we traverse a spiral in which social customs generate some consciousness of interdependencies, and this consciousness is embodied in acts which in improving the environment generate new perceptions of social ties, and so on forever. The relationships, the interactions are forever there as fact, but they acquire meaning only in the desires, judgments and purposes they awaken.

We recur to our fundamental propositions. Morals is connected with actualities of existence, not with ideals, ends and obligations independent of concrete actualities. The facts upon which it depends are those which arise out of active connections of human beings with one another, the consequences of their mutually interwined activities in the life of desire, belief, judgment, satisfaction and dissatisfaction. In this sense conduct and hence morals are social: they are not just things which *ought* to be social and which fail to come up to the scratch. But there are enormous differences of better and worse in the quality of what is social. Ideal morals begin with the perception of these differences. Human interaction and ties are there, are operative in any case. But they can be regulated, employed in an orderly way for good only as we know how to observe them. And they cannot be observed aright, they cannot be understood and utilized, when the mind is left to itself to work without the aid of science. For the natural and unaided mind means precisely the habits of belief, thought and desire which have been accidentally generated and confirmed by social institutions or customs. But with all their admixture of accident and reasonableness we have at last reached a point where social conditions create a mind capable of scientific outlook and injury. To foster and develop this spirit is the social obligation of the present because it is its urgent need.

Yet the last word is not with obligation nor with the future. Infinite relationships of man with his fellows and with nature already exist. The ideal means, as we have see, a sense of these encompassing continuities with their infinite reach. This meaning even now attaches to present activities because they are set in a whole to which they belong and which belongs to them. Even in the midst of conflict, struggle and defeat a consciousness is possible of the enduring and comprehending whole.

To be grasped and held this consciousness needs, like every form of consciousness, objects, symbols. In the past men have sought many symbols which no longer serve, especially since men have been idolators worshiping symbols as things. Yet within these symbols which have so often claimed to be realities and which have imposed themselves as dogmas and intolerances, there has rarely been absent some trace of a vital and enduring reality, that of a community of life in which continuities of existence are consummated. Consciousness of the whole has been connected with reverences, affections, and loyalties which are communal. But special ways of expressing the communal sense have been established. They have been limited to a select social group; they have hardened into obligatory rites and been imposed as conditions of salvation. Religion has lost itself in cults, dogmas and myths. Consequently the office of religion as sense of community and one's place in it has been lost. In effect religion has been distorted into a possession—or burden—of a limited part of human nature, of a limited portion of humanity which finds no way to universalize religion except by imposing its own dogmas and ceremonies upon others; of a limited class within a partial group; priests, saints, a church. Thus other gods have been set up before the one God. Religion as a sense of the whole is the most individualized of all things, the most spontaneous, undefinable and varied. For individuality signifies unique connections in the whole. Yet it has been perverted into something uniform and immutable. It has been formulated into fixed and defined beliefs expressed in required acts and ceremonies. Instead of marking the freedom and peace of the individual as a member of an infinite whole, it has been petrified into a slavery of thought and sentiment, an intolerant superiority on the part of the few and an intolerable burden on the part of the many.

Yet every act may carry within itself a consoling and supporting consciousness of the whole to which it belongs and which in some sense belongs to it. With responsibility for the intelligent determination of particular acts may go a joyful emancipation from the burden for responsibility for the whole which sustains them, giving them their final outcome and quality. There is a conceit fostered by perversion of religion which assimilates the universe to our personal desires; but there is also a conceit of carrying the load of the universe from which religion liberates us. Within the flickering inconsequential acts of separate selves dwells a sense of the whole which claims and dignifies them. In its presence we put off mortality and live in the universal. The life of the community in which we live and have our being is the fit symbol of this relationship. The acts in which we express our perception of the ties which bind us to others are its only rites and ceremonies.

QUESTIONS FOR STUDY AND DISCUSSION

1. How is individual conscience formed?
2. What is the relation of science to moral judgment?

3. How is the formation of conscience properly achieved?
4. Why is the claim of Right recognized in conscience even by those who violate it?
5. Does Dewey identify what should be with what in fact is?
6. Can religion supply the values required for moral education?

Abraham Edel

ABRAHAM EDEL was born in Pittsburgh, Pennsylvania, in 1908. He studied
at McGill and Oxford Universities and received his Ph.D. from Columbia
in 1934. He has held Guggenheim (1944–45) and Rockefeller (1952–53)
fellowships and has taught at the City College of New York since 1931.
Edel is the author of *The Theory and Practice of Philosophy* (1946),
Ethical Judgment (1955), and *Method in Ethical Theory* (1963).

Relation of Ethical to Nonethical Systems

In our Western tradition ethical analysis has been far from naturalistic.
The investigation of ethical values has not been considered an empirical
project. The dominant stress has been on insight, introspection, and the immediate apprehension of essences. Results have been framed in the absolutes of conviction rather than the probabilities of science, for scientific
method has been held to be inapplicable to the world of the spirit.

For these reasons present-day naturalism is bound to emphasize the
need for extending empirical or scientific method to the treatment of values. A naturalistic approach involves reanalysis of ethical ideas in terms of
our present logical equipment, designation of the empirical material with
which ethics is concerned, and continual testing of the utility of ethical formulations in terms of this material. Insistence on such testing is part of the
naturalistic stress on the primacy of matter; recognition that ethical formulations may require alteration is a consequence of noting the pervasiveness
of change. Reliance on scientific method, together with an appreciation of
the primacy of matter and the pervasiveness of change, I take to be the
central points of naturalism as a philosophic outlook.

In constructing its ethical theory naturalism today may draw upon two
major sources. One is the results of the sciences, especially the biological,
psychological, and social studies. The other is the history of ethical theory
in which a broad naturalistic current may be traced through portions of
many theoretical writings. Thus we may draw upon the formal analysis of
Aristotle, who built a structure upon the "nature" of man, which he filled

From pp. 65–66 and 89–95 of Abraham Edel, "Naturalism and Ethical Theory," in
Naturalism and the Human Spirit, edited by Yervant H. Krikorian. Copyright © 1944
Columbia University Press. Reprinted by permission of the publisher.

in with biologic material and everyday observations and prejudices. The history of materialism from Democritus through Hobbes and the French materialists to the Marxian school provides a long tradition in which the naturalistic approach achieved maturity. In addition, there is the temporal stress of evolutionary ethical theory and the stubborn empiricism of much of the Utilitarian structure. In American philosophy of our own time Dewey in his various writings and Santayana in his *Life of Reason* have to some extent gathered the strands and produced substantially naturalistic ethical systems.

.   .   .

The logical pattern of the possible relationship between an ethical and a nonethical system is, of course, the same as for any two systems. That is, terms of one and terms of the other system, each independently interpreted, are empirically correlated. If ethical terms are thus correlated with terms in another system, ethical statements might thereafter turn out to be deducible from statements in the nonethical system. We may illustrate by the complete connections which exist in the following somewhat Hobbesian theory. In this, the ethical expression "*x* is good" is taken to be correlated with the psychological expression "A desires *x*." And since feeling is declared to be a kind of interior movement, "A desires *x*" is eventually translated (with the aid of correlation statements) into the language of physics as "the complex of particles, A1, A2, A3 is moving in a certain fashion with regard to *x*." This is therefore correlated with "*x* is good." The remaining terms of ethics being likewise translated, it would then be hoped that the generalizations of ethics could be deduced from physical laws. Thus "self-preservation is good" might be deducible from a physical law that certain movements (into which desire was ultimately translatable) would occur whenever certain other movements (into which self-preservation was resolved) occurred. This complete translation of terms and the complete deducibility of ethical from physical generalizations would constitute an ideally necessary connection—what has traditionally been called the complete "reduction" of ethics to physics.

The direction of such "reduction" is not limited a priori. Thus, even when ethical terms are translated into psychological ones, it is possible for the psychological to be translated into something other than physical terms. This sort of thing has actually happened in some evolutionary theories, where "*x* is good" is equated with the "biological" assertion "*x* has survival value for the group," and the latter is accompanied by the belief that evolution is the deity's special plan to make the universe culminate in man. Hence the ultimate translation of "*x* is good" would be "*x* fulfills the divine plan." But it could equally well have ended in a physical rather than a theological translation.

The traditional problem of "free will" versus "determinism" may itself be translated into the empirical question of the relation of ethics to nonethical systems. On this analysis, free will is equivalent to insistence on the "autonomy" of choice and the ethical system; determinism is equivalent to the belief in (or hope for) discoverable interrelations of ethical and nonethical systems. Complete or universal determinism postulates a complete "reduction"—usually to physical terms and laws.

The fact that ethics has not so been "reduced" is sometimes taken by nonnaturalistic philosophies to be evidence for "emergent qualities," "autonomous domains," or a dualism between the mental field, where ethics belongs, and the physical, where the physical sciences fall. A naturalistic approach is committed neither to such inferences nor to a complete determinism. The failure to discover the interrelations of ethics and nonethical domains has no more significance than the inability to "reduce" psychology to physiology or physiology to physics. For the relation of the sciences is an empirical matter, and there is no a priori reason to believe that complete "reduction" of any domain to another must be either impossible or inevitable. Natural events are rich enough and complex enough so that relatively irreducible phases are possible. Any assertion of ultimate results remains program, not metaphysical fact.

Nevertheless, the development of common experience and scientific knowledge has been sufficient to indicate that the act of choice is not utterly unrelated to other natural events occurring around it. A choice itself is an event in nature, complex indeed, but clearly grounded in the influences of physical, psychological, and social factors. There is no reason why the preconceptions of an idealist or a dualist philosophy should linger to bar the most intensive exploration of its relations. The field of ethics not only may be but is being constantly developed by the progress of all other sciences, especially the psychological and social studies.

Since any attempt to describe the interrelations of ethical and nonethical phenomena is bound to be sketchy or programmatic, I shall limit the discussion to brief comments on the empirical studies from which it seems to me ethics can most profit at present.

The first of these is the careful scrutiny (psychological and phenomenological) of the act of choosing or valuing. Ordinary language bears witness to possible differences within the act itself. There is wholehearted choice and halfhearted choice, and a whole possible scale of intensity. To study it one would have to focus attention on the way in which alternative rules and developed habits function in the act of choice. This might be done both introspectively and by observing the relative frequency of specific types of choice in regulated situations, or by any other device the scientific imagination may formulate. In fact, Aristotle began this study at some length in his ethics, when he distinguished the virtuous man from the continent man and the vicious from the incontinent. The continent and the incontinent have internal struggles in their choice, the former checking evil desires, the latter yielding to them against his better judgment; the virtuous man has no evil desires to fight against, whereas the vicious man takes pleasure in carrying out his evil desires and so has no pain, remorse, or struggle concerning them. In terms of such an investigation ordinary phrases like "strength of character" will find more precise empirical significance.

Again, within the evaluating act, on its reflective level, ordinary language reveals a differentiated series of degrees of approval and disapproval which certainly can be rendered more precise and may or may not be correlated with the previous differentiations in choice. Hartmann, for example, works such a rising scale out of the predicates employed by Aristotle in the *Nicomachean Ethics*. The predicates are: worthy of praise; beautiful; worthy of honor; lovable; admirable; superb. It may well be the case that in scales of this sort different shades of emotion are attached to each predicate. Or perhaps in some instances there is also a differentiation in fields of subject matter. Such analysis will aid in the discovery of any consistent scales which may be implicitly employed and in the development of such scales as may be deemed desirable.

The second study is the discovery (historical and anthropological) of the varieties of values that have actually existed. This involves both description and conceptual refinement. It examines, for instance, the content of jealousy among present-day Eskimos, French, and Americans; and the persons to whom reverence is obligatory in various societies; and how the notion of honor differs in a knight quick to resent insult and a business man scrupulous in paying his debts. Inevitably the problem will arise why in each case differing manifestations are grouped together as exemplifying the same value and whether in fact they should be so grouped. Solutions to this problem will provide empirical meaning to broad values. Sometimes the varying content will be found to have a psychological unity in the fact that there are different ways in which the same deep-seated impulse is expressed, as in the sexual drive. Sometimes the unity will lie in the fact that there are different ways of meeting a common social need, as in avoiding in-group conflict. Often the unity lies in the production of a similar effect; for example, the common ideal of justice may express merely the widespread desire for the removal of suffering at the hands of others. Often the common element will turn out to be merely analogy, as when desire for prestige is treated as a form of acquisitiveness. In such cases the result may be the substitution of several motives for a single notion. This general study may also provide empirical criteria for the affirmation of identical elements in cultural diversity. For the student of ethics it will likewise suggest tentative patterns which may be applied with alterations to meet problems within another culture. In short, the task is not merely fact-gathering, to be performed by handmaiden sciences, but it entails philosophical analysis throughout.

The third study (involving all the sciences, from biology and physiology to economics, social psychology, and history) is the search for causal elements or necessary conditions of men's choice. The holding of a particular value or pattern of values by an individual or group is not simply a brute fact; it calls for causal explanation. Several factors point toward the possibility of success in such a study. There is the common core of conscious education of taste or preference in ourselves and others. There is a growing recognition that values are not innate traits or elements of character stamped in men by nature, but products in the growing child and still malleable adult of tremendous cultural and social pressures. Our insight into the force of tradition, the pervasive influence of economic factors, and the critical role of existent attitudes has grown tremendously. We thus realize that the fashioning of values is a task carried on in a society whether knowingly or in ignorance of what we are in effect doing. The observation around us of mass transformations in fundamental values has directed attention to the study of change. The large-scale investigation of causality in choice may perhaps be best carried out by examining historically what changes in values go along with other social changes and tracing more minutely their relations.

The naturalistic tradition in philosophy has constantly pointed to the need for causal examination of values and the relation of ethical to nonethical phenomena. It has sought the aid of the prevailing sciences and in turn mapped programs for them. As the sciences grew, naturalism had concomitant phases. It interpreted values on a physical analogy as special movements of the particles or internal movements. Nineteenth-century naturalism was to a great extent biological, under Darwin's influence. Marxian materialism was an exception, and it marked the beginning of a fuller naturalism, which recognized the causal role of social factors.

The study of conditioning elements of men's values and the broad discovery that they lie to a great extent somewhere in the domain of human activity have revealed the possibility of the redirection of values. In spite of the shuddering of some poets and some philosophers, mankind at large would probably welcome a discovery that the milk of human kindness could be injected into the blood stream by means of a gland extract or even, as some novelistic psychology would have it, that men could shift their character-values with their climate. Although the problem is tremendously more complicated than these simple dreams, there is no reason to oppose the causal study of values on the ground of a special human spontaneity called "freedom of the will." There is plenty of room for spontaneity in human affairs, but it is an empirical phenomenon that falls within the context of men who are striving to achieve their values, to redirect some and preserve others. It is not an explanation of their doings. The mere assumption of freedom tends to make men leave the direction of change of values to chance. Freedom, in a naturalistic ethics, is to be found in the widest understanding that may be attained of the conditions and causes of choice, so that choice may be a function of knowledge.

What we have spoken of as the redirection of values is not, however, an appeal from the ethical to the nonethical. It is carried on within a set of values and involves altering some to preserve or enhance or achieve others. It occurs in social groups, as in our personal lives, when a conflict of values drives us to seek consistency by shifting some goals to make room for others, when we discover fresh goals emerging and estimate the interplay of means and ends. Redirection of values is not the mere occurrence of this process, but its conscious occurrence.

The stress of a naturalistic ethics emerges most clearly in the analysis of the redirection of social values. A naturalistic ethics does not consider the problem to be purely a matter of the individual's purification of his heart, whether on the principles of a specific theology or in some moral rearmament. It does not appeal to an unknown good to justify the evil that exists or to men's patience and resignation to enable them to endure. It does not urge that men's wickedness is a ground for their misfortunes. It does not turn ends into autonomous internal values restricted to consciousness and disregard means as mere technicalities. It does not commit itself to eternal values irrespective of their specific content and social consequences. On the contrary, it insists on the continuous testing of goals in the light of their social functioning, on the deep roots of values in the practices and institutions of a society, on the necessity of altering institutions and social forms as part of the process of achieving and redirecting values, on the need for a comprehensive view of the way in which values fit together, what causal props they have, what are to be the consequences of various means. In short, the naturalistic moral philosopher, estimating the values of his group or society, cannot stop short of fashioning a whole conception of good men functioning well in a good society.

QUESTIONS FOR STUDY AND DISCUSSION

1. Can ethical expressions be reduced to physical facts?
2. Can ethical deductions be deduced from physical laws?
3. Is Edel a strict determinist?
4. How do biological, psychological, and social studies bear upon ethics?
5. How can ordinary-language analysis aid the moral philosopher?
6. What is the distinction between individual and social ethics, and how are the two related?

Sidney Hook

SIDNEY HOOK was born in Brooklyn in 1902 and received his first philosophical training under Morris R. Cohen at the City College of New York. After his graduation in 1923 he taught in the New York public school system and also attended graduate school at Columbia, studying under Dewey, Frederick Woodbridge, and William P. Montague. He received his doctorate in 1927 and then joined the faculty of New York University, where, since 1947, he has been chairman of the division of philosophy and psychology. A popular lecturer, Hook has also written extensively on social and political questions. His works include: *John Dewey: An Intellectual Portrait* (1939); *Reason, Social Myths, and Democracy* (1940); *Education for Modern Man* (1950); *The Quest for Being* (1961); and *The Paradoxes of Freedom* (1963).

Moral Freedom in a Determined World

In the last year of the Weimar Republic, when ordinary criminals were sometimes more philosophical than the judges of Hitler's Third Reich subsequently proved to be, a strange case was tried before the tribunal of Hannover. The evidence showed that one Waldemar Debbler had been guilty of burglary, and the prosecutor proposed two years of penal servitude. Whereupon the prisoner rose and said:

"Gentlemen, you see in me the victim of an unwavering destiny. So-called freedom of decision does not exist. Every human action in this world is determined. The causes are given by the circumstances and the results inevitable. By my inclinations of character, for which I am not responsible, since they were born in me, by my upbringing, my experiences, I was predetermined to become what I am. If you, gentlemen, had a heredity similar to mine and had been subjected to the same influence as I, you would also have committed the burglary in this particular situation. With this theory I am in good company. I refer you to Spinoza and Leibniz. Even St. Augustine and, later, Calvin attributed all human actions to the immutable decree of destiny. As I have only done what I had to do, you have no moral right to punish me, and I therefore plead for my acquittal."

From pp. 26–48 of Sidney Hook, *The Quest for Being, and Other Studies in Naturalism and Humanism.* © 1961 by St. Martin's Press, Inc. Reprinted by permission of the publisher.

To which peroration the court answered:

"We have followed the prisoner's reasoning with attention. Whatever happens is the necessary and immutable sequel of preceding causes which, once given, could not be other than it is. Consequently the prisoner, by reason of his character and experience, was destined to commit the burglary. On the other hand, destiny also decrees that the court, as a result of the submitted testimony, must judge the prisoner guilty of burglary. The causes—the deed, the law, the nature of the judge—being given, the sentence of guilty and punishment follows as a natural consequence."

When asked whether he accepted the sentence, the prisoner declared: "Destiny demands that I appeal." To which the judge replied: "That may be. However, destiny will see to it that your appeal is rejected."

This story, for whose authenticity with respect to exact detail I will not vouch, confuses the concept of determinism with that of fatalism. It confuses an event whose occurrence depends upon, or is caused by, what the individual in this particular situation desires and does, with an event whose occurrence does not depend upon any event antecedent to it, and which would occur no matter what the antecedent event was. It confuses conditional necessity with unconditional necessity, what is *predetermined* with what is predictable with reference to certain laws and initial data. It further fails to distinguish clearly between the concept of punishment and the concept of moral responsibility. Nonetheless, in its appeal to a double standard of judgment it illustrates a defect which appears in the writings of more sophisticated philosophers who have returned to the theme of determinism and moral responsibility in recent years.

Those philosophers who have thought that progress in philosophy consists in part in showing that the traditional problems of philosophy are either pseudo-problems, or a confusing mixture of psychology, logic, and sociology, have been rudely awakened from their complacency by a revival of interest in the question of free will, determinism, and responsibility. It had been widely assumed that the whole problem of whether the *will* is free had been replaced, in consequence of the writings of Hobbes, Locke, Hume, Mill, and the modern naturalists and positivists, by the problem of the *conditions* under which men's actions are free. The general solution had been that *men* are free when their actions are determined by their own will, and not by the will of others, or by factors which lead us to say that their actions were involuntary. To the extent that conditions exist which prevent a man from acting as he wishes (*e.g.,* ignorance, physical incapacity, constraint used upon his body and mind) he is unfree. This view accepts the postulate of determinism as valid, regardless of whether a man's action is free or coerced—in one case his action is determined by his own volition, in the other not. The fact that my volition, say, to undergo an operation, is caused by a complex of factors, among which the existence of sickness or disease, or the belief in the existence of sickness or disease, is normally a necessary condition, does not make my action less free. After all, it would be absurd to suggest that my action in undergoing an operation would be free only if there were no cause or reason to undergo it. If one insisted on undergoing an operation when one knew there was no cause for the operation, one would normally be regarded as insane. That there would be a cause for the decision, for the insistence on the unnecessary operation, would not affect our judgment of it. On this view, the distinction between free and unfree acts, sane or insane acts, lies in the specific character of the causes at work, not in the presence or absence of causes.

What has been until recently considered a commonplace is now in several quarters described and repudiated as a wild paradox. That an action can be characterized as both "determined" and "free," or "determined" and "responsible," is denied from two different points of view. The first view accepts determinism, indeed insists on it, because of the findings of modern medicine and psychotherapy, and then argues the invalidity of judgments of responsibility in any and every case. The second accepts the validity of the principle of responsibility, but denies the validity of the postulate of determinism or of its universal applicability.

Those who believe that one cannot legitimately square the doctrine of determinism with the acceptance of responsibility argue generally as follows: an individual is neither responsible nor blamable for his actions unless he could have acted differently from the way he did. Given the sum total of conditions which preceded his action, the latter is in principle always predictable or determined, and therefore unavoidable. But if an action is unavoidable, then no one can be held morally responsible for it.

The usual retort to this is to point out that an act is determined, among other things, by a wish or desire or volition for which we shall use the generic term "choice." Consequently it is sometimes true to say that if an individual had chosen differently, he would have acted differently. To which the rejoinder comes that this is merely an evasion. If every event is in principle predictable and therefore determined, then the choice itself, given all the antecedent conditions, is unavoidable. An individual cannot be held morally responsible for his choice if it could not have been other than it was. And even if it were true that his choice now was a consequence of an earlier choice, which *if* it had been different *would* have led to different present choice and action, that earlier choice *could not* have been different, given its antecedent conditions, and so on for any other choice in the series. And since the choice could not have been different, we cannot blame the person choosing since he is not morally responsible. He is "a victim of circumstances."

There is a certain ambiguity in the writings of those who, accepting the principle of determinism, criticize the attribution of moral responsibility to individuals or the judgment of blameworthiness on their actions. Sometimes their criticism has an air of high moral concern. They imply that under certain circumstances, which they often spell out in advance, individuals are being improperly considered responsible. They inveigh against the injustice of improperly blaming those who, because their desires and choices are determined, are the victims not the agents of misfortune. This plea is sometimes forensically very effective, as the legal career of Clarence Darrow shows. Defending the accused in the Leopold-Loeb murder case, which is now enjoying a revival in popular concern, he said in his closing address to the jury, after quoting Housman's poem, the soliloquy of a boy about to be hanged, "I do not know what it was that made these boys do this mad act, but I know there is a reason for it. I know they did not beget themselves. I know that any one of an infinite number of causes reaching back to the beginning might be working out in these boys' minds, whom you are asked to hang in malice and in hatred and injustice, because someone in the past has sinned against them."

One does not, of course, look for precision in an *ex parte* plea. To a determinist, what difference does it make whether human beings are begotten by others, whether they reproduce by fission or by spontaneous generation in test tubes? In any case the process is determined. Of course we did not choose to be born. But suppose we did choose to be born: would that make us more responsible? The choice to be born would not be any less determined. And if the argument is that in a determined world, where our choices are bound to be what they are, it is unfair to blame anybody for any action to which that choice leads, how would we be better off, *i.e.,* more responsible, if we chose to be born? And if it is unjust to tax anyone with sinning who is not responsible for his being born, is it any more legitimate to speak of his being sinned against? If children cannot sin against parents, neither can parents sin against children.

Darrow's inconsistencies are less surprising than the fact that some sophisticated philosophers have adopted pretty much the same position. They fortify it with complex and subtle elaborations of the findings of psychoanalysis as these bear upon the motives and compulsive behavior of men. Yet the logic of their argument makes all the evidence of psychoanalysis irrelevant to the question of blame and responsibility. For if every psychoanalytical theory were discarded as false, the life of mind would still be determined if one accepts the postulate of universal determinism. The piling up of the data which exhibit the specific mechanism of determination adds only a rhetorical force to the position. Further, it is one thing to imply that the concept of moral responsibility is empty, that although in fact no individuals are morally responsible, there are conditions or circumstances under which they could be legitimately held responsible; it is quite another thing to hold that the concept of moral responsibility is completely *vacuous,* that no matter what the specific conditions are under which men choose to act, it would still be inappropriate to hold them morally responsible or blame them. And it is this view, *i.e.,* that moral responsibility is a vacuous or unintelligible expression, which seems to me to be entailed by those who urge Darrow's position, for they never seem able to indicate the rule or conditions for its proper use. If one cannot indicate any possible situation on a deterministic view under which actions can be blamed, the term "blame" is cognitively meaningless.

Nonetheless, the paradox of the position is that those who hold it, blame us for blaming others. Just as the burglar in our story makes an appeal whose sense depends upon there being alternatives, that is upon the possibility of making or not making that specific appeal, so some philosophers find us blameworthy for not acting on the recognition that in a determined world in which no one chooses to be born, no one can be held at fault.

I think it will be pretty generally admitted that whether a person could or could not have acted differently (or have chosen to act differently), it is a fact that we do blame him for an action which is evil, if it is apparent that he is the cause of it. Whether we *should* blame him for the action is a question which we cannot decide without reflection, *i.e.*, cannot decide until we discover whether what is apparently so, is actually so. "We should think in each case before we should blame" is a maxim universally agreed upon by all writers in this age-old discussion But if "should blame" is an unintelligible expression, then so is "should think." If anyone interposes and objects that the belief that a person could not have acted (or chosen) differently under the circumstances entails the view that it is impermissible "to blame" or "to hold responsible," then by the same logic the belief that a person could not have thought differently entails the view that it is impermissible to say that "he should" or "he should not have" thought as he did. A philosopher who took that alleged entailment seriously would not only have to abandon the expressions "should have blamed" and "should not have blamed"—and restrict himself to asking whether "we *will*" or "we *will not*" blame—(an entirely different kind of question from the one which provoked the discussion originally)—he would have to forswear the use of "should" and "should not" in every other normative context.

This is not, as we shall see, merely a dialectical or debating point. It cuts the nerve of the argument of those who believe, like Darrow, that their position necessarily makes for greater humanity and kindliness. As a matter of fact, such a position often makes for sentimentality—the refusal to blame or punish where blame and punishment may prevent actions which are undesirable. It often leads to pity for the criminal as a victim, not of a special set of particular circumstances which might have made it harder for him than for others to refrain from committing a crime, but as a victim of any circumstance in general (referred to as heredity and environment or the sway of the law of causality). This is sometimes carried to the point where there is not sufficient pity or compassion left for the criminal's victims, not only for his past victims but his future ones and the victims of others whose action the criminal may inspire. To blame and to punish, of course, are two distinct things logically (except when blame is considered a form of punishment), but psychologically there is a great reluctance to punish if one believes blame is absent. Darrow argued on the abstract *a priori* grounds of universal determinism that all men were blameless, and with his dramatic pleas often won acquittals, not on the specific evidence, but despite it. Yet surely, if needless pain and curelty are evils, then punishment which prevents or deters actions likely to result in much greater pain and cruelty than it imposes on the guilty, is obviously the lesser evil. Without being a saint, one can forgive the pain a criminal causes to oneself; but not even a saint can claim that this therefore justifies him in forgiving the criminal the pain he causes others.

In passing I should like to comment on some peripheral points, confusion about which seems to have encouraged the view that belief in the incompatibility of determinism and moral responsibility is a mark of enlightenment. The first is that if one holds human beings blameless, one will necessarily treat them more humanely and eliminate capital punishment. But actually the issue of capital punishment has nothing to do with the question of determinism and responsibility. The valid argument against capital punishment is that its abolition makes the rectification of occasional injustice possible. But such an argument presupposes precisely what Darrow and those who think like him deny, *i.e.,* that it is blameworthy to punish an innocent man. And as for the humanitarian aspect of the situation, although Darrow won the Leopold-Loeb case with a plea for imprisonment of the criminals rather than their execution, the judge in announcing sentence declared: "Life imprisonment, at the moment, strikes the public imagination less forcibly than would death by hanging; but to the offenders, particularly of the type they are, the prolonged suffering of years of confinement may well be the severest form of retribution and expiation."

It may be argued that nonetheless there is a psychological if not logical connection between the view that determinism strictly entails the absence of moral responsibility and the abandonment of retributive punishment. This can be challenged on many grounds. From Augustine to Calvin and their latter-day followers, the torment of eternal damnation is assigned and approved independently of moral responsibility. It is not related of the oft-cited Puritan who piously observed to his son when they saw a man being led to the gallows: "There but for the grace of God go I," that he opposed retributive punishment. Nor could the determinist of this kind say that he morally *should* repudiate retributive punishment since he cannot help believing it. On the other hand, if it is retributive punishment which is the target of the analysis, there is no necessary logical connection between a belief in moral responsibility and approval of retributive punishment. Certainly those determinists who assign responsibility to actions only when there is reason to believe that blame or punishment will modify future conduct are hardly likely to defend retributive punishment which is directed exclusively to the past.

Although the concept of moral responsibility in a deterministic system is neither empty nor vacuous, it is far from having a clear meaning in ordinary usage and experience. Before discussing it further I wish to comment briefly upon the position of those who accept the validity of the concept of moral responsibility, but believe they must therefore contest the belief in the postulate of determinism. Now it may be granted straightaway that we cannot prove that all events have sufficient causes, such that given these causes the events must occur. This is a postulate which we accept because of its fruitfulness in enabling us to predict and control our experience. Nor is it necessary to assume on the basis of this postulate that we can predict in principle the occurrence or emergence of all qualities of events. What is absolutely novel in experience cannot be derived either deductively or inductively from the qualities of the initial conditions or given data from which, together with general laws, we predict future events. Nonetheless we know enough about human behavior under everyday as well as laboratory conditions to make a reasonable induction that, given certain antecedent conditions, certain choices will be made (or even more strongly, certain choices are unavoidable). That we cannot always infallibly predict how people will choose is no more a decisive consideration against the belief that with more knowledge we can increase the accuracy of our predictions of human choices, than the fact that we cannot always infallibly predict the behavior of things is a decisive consideration against reliance upon the laws of physics. Now those who hold that the belief in moral responsibility entails an acceptance of indeterminism do not believe that *nothing* in the world is determined. They admit that some events, including some choices, are determined. And of the choices they believe undetermined, they are prepared to grant that certain *necessary* conditions of their occurrence exist. They deny that these undetermined choices follow from any set of *sufficient* conditions.

The difficulty with this view, as I see it, is that the distinction between determined and allegedly undetermined choices does not always correspond with the attributions we make or refuse to make of moral responsibility. It is sometimes said that in human relations the prediction that an individual will choose a certain course of conduct, if publicly made, has a consequence which may affect his choice. Suppose I predict that you will refuse to give alms to the beggar. You therefore set out to disprove my statement. Knowing this will be your reaction, I make a fresh prediction that you will give alms because I say you won't. Realizing I am now counting on your being shamed into giving alms, you truculently may refuse to do so. And no matter what further prediction I make, that prediction will have an effect which presumably I cannot rely on. Therefore, concludes

Maurice Cranston, from whom I borrow the illustration, "that is why I say predictions made to you about you are impossible." Karl Popper and D. M. MacKay have argued in a similar vein that "any proffered description of your choice would automatically be self-invalidating." The law of determinism even for macroscopic phenomena breaks down.

I do not believe such predictions are impossible, but let us grant the point for the sake of the argument. Now consider two situations. In the first I make a successful prediction about you but not to you, concerning your behavior or choice at the sight of a beggar in great distress. Here the choice or action is determined. In the second, I make an unsuccessful prediction to you about you, in relation to the beggar. Here your choice is allegedly undetermined. But now would anyone seriously maintain that you were not morally responsible for the action which I successfully predicted, but you were morally responsible for the action which I failed to predict because it was unpredictable? Unless other factors are introduced, it seems to me that you would hold yourself, and be held by others, equally responsible for your action with respect to the beggar in distress, quite independently of the success of the prediction, independently of whether I made the prediction *to* you or *about* you to someone else. The predictability or unpredictability of the choice seems irrelevant to the question of its moral responsibility. And all this aside from the fact that it is highly disputable whether predictions made to you about you are in principle unconfirmable. All of us have seen human beings cleverly and unscrupulously manipulated by individuals who make predictions of their behavior to their face and shrewdly calculate the reactions to the predictions. A man who dares another to jump knowing that the person dared hardly ever resists a dare and that the leap in question is very hazardous, may be guilty of murder.

The great difficulty with the indeterminist view in most forms is the suggestion it carries that choices and actions, if not determined, are capricious. Caprice and responsibility are more difficult to reconcile than determinism and responsibility, for it seems easier to repudiate a choice or action which does not follow from one's character, or history, or nature, or self, than an act which does follow. Consequently, the more thoughtful indeterminists are those who do not deny the operation of determining forces or tendencies altogether, but insist upon a certain kind of determination which manifests itself in addition to, or over and above, the factors extrinsic to the particular siutation in which the choosing individual finds himself. For example, they believe that the free action is not the habitual action, not the coerced action, not the instinctive or impulsive action, but the action which is determined by reflection. And as we shall see, there is a sense in which ordinarily we do characterize an action as responsible, depending upon whether it was intended, and if intended, upon the character and extent of the reflection which preceded it. But so long as "reasons" are not disembodied entities but express reflective choices of men in nature, there is nothing here at which a determinist need boggle. On the contrary, he may define the locus of moral freedom and responsibility in the capacity of the human creature, using his insight and foresight, to modify his preferences and control his inclinations whenever they conflict or lead to "actions involving others."

Not only indeterminists who recognize moral responsibility, but some determinists who regard it as an empty concept, write as if a person would be responsible if he could "ultimately and completely shape or choose his own character." Surely the notion of ultimately and completely shaping or choosing one's own character is more difficult to grasp than any it would illumine. Since every decision to shape or choose one's character, to be responsibly attributed to oneself, must be one's own, and therefore is already an indication of the kind of person one is, the notion that one can ultimately and completely shape or choose one's character seems to be unintelligible. C. A. Campbell [1] in a stimulating article distinguishes between a choice which is the expression of a formed character, and therefore determined, and a choice of a self. But aside from the difficulty of separating self from character, it is hard to understand why we should be more willing to accept responsibility or blame for the decision of a raw or pure self that has no history, than to accept responsibility or blame for the choices of our formed characters.

We return now to consider some of the difficulties which the determinist faces who attributes blame or responsibility to himself or others. If all actions are in principle predictable or unavoidable, how can he blame the actor? If every judgment of "ought" or "should" implies a "can" or "could," and if of every act we can say (once given its antecedent conditions) that it cannot or could not have been avoided, why blame, why praise, why, indeed, in a determined universe, pass any moral judgment whatsoever, whether it be on a petty sneak-thief or on a Hitler or Stalin?

I shall try to show that the difficulty lies uniquely in the use of the concept of blame, not of praise, and not of moral judgment *per se*. The difficulty in the concept of blame is that ordinary usage is itself confusing, that the confusion requires a reconstruction of our use in such a way as to bring out more consistently and systematically the pragmatic character of judgments of blame. I do not believe that if we guide ourselves by ordinary usage we can make ends meet, because in this instance ordinary usage is vague and inconsistent.

First of all, although it may be difficult to square the belief that all choices are determined with judgments of blame and responsibility, I do not see that there is any difficulty in squaring the belief that all choices are determined with the moral judgment that these choices, and the actions to

---

[1] See C. A. Campbell, "Is Free Will a Pseudo-Problem?" (*Mind*, 1951). Campbell was professor of Logic and Rhetoric at the University of Glasgow from 1938 to 1961. He is the author of *Scepticism and Construction* (1931), *Defense of Free Will* (1938), and *On Selfhood and Godhood* (1957). The last volume is based on the Gifford Lectures he delivered at the University of St. Andrews, 1953–55. [J.P.D.]

which they lead, are good or bad. Pain is evil, and an intentional action which imposes unnecessary pain, or a desire to impose unnecessary pain, is wicked. After all, we blame persons only for those acts of omission or commission which we condemn. If such actions were not initially or ante-cedently judged good or bad, we could not blame anybody for failing to do the one, or failing to prevent the other. No matter whether an action is de-termined or undetermined, accidental or intentional, I can still pronounce it good or bad. We may not blame the child whose actions cause the house to burn, or the maniac who kills those who minister to his wants; but we can and do deplore and condemn these actions as bad. And I believe that this is legitimate from the standpoint of any analysis of the meaning of "good" or "bad" which philosophers have offered, except the Kantian analysis. So, too, although there are difficulties about feelings of "remorse" similar to those about judgments of blame, I can only feel remorse about something I regret, and the qualities of the action I regret are what they are, independently of whether the action is determined or not.

It is sometimes said that if it is unwarranted to pass judgments of blame on actions that are predictable or unavoidable, it is also unwar-ranted to pass judgments of praise. I am not so sure of this, because of the broader semantic range of judgments of praise. When we praise a person for his or her beauty, talent, intelligence, charm, personality, warmth, etc., etc., we do not have in mind at all whether or not the person could help being or doing that which evokes our praise. Formally, we can always praise a person for not committing an act that we would blame, and in this sense the logic of the judgments is symmetrical. But aside from such cases, and some others in which praise seems to be justified because an individual might have acted differently, *e.g.,* in which he fights against odds instead of running away, there is an indefinitely large number of situations in which we unembarrassedly praise, regardless of whether the person can help being as he is or acting as he does. And when judgments of praise do not have this character, they may plausibly be regarded as having the social function of inducing individuals to do what we regard as desirable and to forgo doing the undesirable. But if it is possible to carry out such an analy-sis without difficulty for judgments of praise, is it possible to do so for judgments of blame and attributions of moral responsibility?

The facts of responsibility must be distinguished from their justifica-tion. By facts of responsibility I mean that in every society there are social relations or institutional arrangements which are regarded as binding on human behavior, for violations of which human beings are called to ac-count. When individuals are called to account, this involves the possibility that sanctions may be applied. These facts of responsibility are an anthro-pological datum—varied and multiform. In some cultures children are held responsible for their parents; in others, parents for children. Leaving aside questions of legal responsibility, or rather legal liability, which are often only matters of social convenience and rules of the road, the justification of responsibility is a moral question. Should a child be held personally responsible for the sins of its father, not only for the Biblical three generations, but even for one? Should a parent ever be held responsible for the misdeeds of his children? Now those who hold that determinism is incompatible with reasoned judgments of blame presumably do not mean to deny the existence of the facts of responsibility. They simply contest the justification of the facts—not the justification of any specific fact of responsibility, but the possibility of any justification whatsoever on the determinist view. If this were true, then, since social life is impossible without recognition of some kind of responsibility in behavior, the whole basis of social life would appear utterly unintelligible, or if justified, only by some extrinsic consideration that had no moral relevance. But, as our illustration shows, there are obviously good reasons why in general we regard it as more justifiable to blame parents up to a point for the misdeeds of their children than to blame children for the misdeeds of their parents. First, we know there is some causal connection between the training or absence of training which parents give their children and the children's behavior outside the home, a causal connection which is not reversible; second, and more important, we blame parents for their children rather than children for their parents, primarily because in this way we can get more desirable conduct on the part of both parents and children. We influence the future by our judgments of blame and, to the extent that they are not merely judgments of spontaneous admiration or excellence, by our judgments of praise as well.

There are some obvious difficulties with this interpretation of judgments of blame. For example, as C. A. Campbell observes, we can influence the future behavior of infants and animals by punishment, but we certainly do not blame them when we are reflective. On the other hand, we do not seem to be able to influence the future behavior of the hardened criminal, but we certainly do blame him. Further, how explain remorse, as distinct from regret, for actions committed long ago?

Because the behavior of children and animals is modifiable by appropriate reward and deprivation, we punish them, even though we may hesitate to use the term to identify what we do. We do not "blame" them, however, even when we find it necessary to punish, because blame is directed to volitions, or, if we do not believe in volition, to intentions. If children's actions reveal intentions or if we suspect, as we sometimes do, that animals have intentions, we count upon the sting of our blame to prod them to different behavior. Otherwise there is no point in blaming. But, it is objected, this only tells us whether our blame is effective rather than deserved. The blame is "deserved" if the action we wish to correct is bad, and the worse the action the more deserved—provided the blame has point in the first place When we distribute blame—as when we say "I blame you more than I do him"—it is because we believe that the intentions (or volitions) of the one had a greater role in the commission of the act, or could have a greater role in preventing similar actions in the future, than the intention of the other. We must be able to answer the question; what is the use of blaming any individual? before we can properly distribute blame among individuals. I can see no earthly use of blaming an individual save directly or indirectly to prevent the undesirable act from being repeated in the future. This is the justification for blame in a determined world.

Another element enters into the picture. The more rational an individual is, the more susceptible he is to understanding and giving reasons, the more blameworthy we hold him—not because the intelligent man's choice is less determined than that of the stupid man but because the choice, which is determined among other things by insight into reasons, is generally more informed, more persistent, and more decisive in redetermining the stream of events. We blame children more as they approach the age of rationality, not because they come into possession of a soul, not because they become more subject to causal laws, but because the growth of intelligence enhances the subtlety, range, and effectiveness of their choice. And if animals could think or respond to reasons, we would blame them, too, because we could build up within them a sense of blame, shame, and responsibility. A sense of blame, shame, and responsibility has a sound therapeutic use in the moral education of men.

Why, then, do we blame the hardened criminal for his actions, when the continued life of crime makes blame and punishment almost as inefficacious in his case—so it is said—as in the case of an alcoholic, a dope addict, or a kleptomaniac? I believe here that most people in blaming a hardened offender are blaming him for the entire series of his actions and not only for his latest action; what revolts them is the cumulative series of evil things done; and they make the mistake of running these evils together, as if it were one great evil which one great blame or punishment might effectively forestall in the future, if not for the offender in question then for others. If, however, one were to isolate the latest dereliction of the hardened offender, and show that no blame or punishment one can devise is more likely to modify his conduct than blame or punishment can prevent an alcoholic addict from drinking or a kleptomaniac from stealing or a pyromaniac from arson, then I believe blame of the hardened criminal would be pointless. We would tend to regard him as criminally insane, confine him without blaming him.

It is sometimes said that we can legitimately blame only when the person blamed has failed to do his duty or live up to an obligation, and that wherever a person has a duty, wherever we say he "ought" to do something, then he in fact "could have" done so. As I have already indicated, I am not at all sure that our actual usage of terms like "blame," "duty," or "ought" in life and law bears this out. In some contexts "ought" clearly does not entail or even imply "can." "A, the contestant in a quiz, ought to have answered x instead of y to question z" is perfectly intelligible and leaves completely open the question whether he could or could not answer question z, or even see question z. Even in strictly moral situations, when I say "Since he was on guard duty, he ought not to have fallen asleep," I am not sure that I am implying necessarily that this particular soldier could have stayed awake, although I am undoubtedly referring to the general capacities of soldiers. But it is undoubtedly true that the evidence that this particular soldier had not slept for seventy-two hours and was assigned to guard duty by mistake, or that he suffered from sleeping sickness, leads to the judgment that he is not as blameworthy as a sentry who had had normal sleep and enjoyed perfect health. That the actions of both sentries, given the antecedent conditions, were determined or predictable, although in one case it was easier than in the other, seems irrelevant. Yet in one case we say that the sentry could not help falling asleep, and in the second we say he could help it. This produces the appearance of paradox. But if one is challenged to explain the judgment, he would probably say that no matter how hard the first sentry tried, it would not have helped him stay awake, whereas if the second sentry had tried, thoroughly rested and throughly healthy as he was, he could have remained awake. The distinction between what one can and what one cannot help doing is perfectly intelligible to a determinist, even though in concrete situations it may be difficult to determine which is which. Normally we do not go beyond that distinction. To the question: could he help trying? we normally reply in the affirmative, and expect the burden of proof to rest upon the person who claims that the second sentry could not help not trying because say (a) either he had been doped or (b) hypnotized. In both cases we are prepared to make allowances or excuses for anything which seems to be an external constraint upon choice or volition. But merely because an action is caused, it is not therefore excused.

Our ordinary common-sense judgments are here rather faltering, because the criteria of what is an external constraint as distinct from an internal constraint, and the distinction between an internal constraint which has originally been set up by an outside agency and one which develops naturally within the system, are vague. The progress of science affects our moral judgment of wrongdoers by uncovering the *specific* factors which tend to make the *wrongdoing* uncontrollable by the volition or decision of the agent involved. If one believes that alcoholism is a disease which operates independently of what one wishes or of how one tries, one will judge differently from the way one will if alcoholism is regarded merely as a bad habit. In law as in common sense, the individual is expected to take responsibility for what is self-determined, for one's character or the kind of person one is, even though no one is completely self-determined. If A develops a fateful passion for B, given A's character, then although there may seem to be a tragic inevitability about the course of the affair, we normally do not expect A to duck responsibility by claiming that he could not help being born, or could not help having the character he has. However, if A, as in Tristan and Isolde, is the victim of a love potion administered by others, we are likely to feel and judge quite differently; for in that case it is not A's choice, but someone else's choice, which coerces his own. The cause was of a compelling kind. I venture to suggest that in all these cases the difference in our response does not depend upon our belief that in one class of situations the individuals are free to choose and in another they are not, but on the belief that, where responsibility and blame are appropriate, the uncompelled choice had some determining influence on the action, and that *our* judgments of responsibility and blame will have some influence upon the future choice of actions of the person judged, as well as on the actions of all other persons contemplating similar measures.

I believe that considerations of this character are acted upon in many different fields of experience, and that where we excuse human beings from responsibility, it is not because of a belief in determinism generally, but only because specific investigation reveals specific causes which are interpreted as of a "compelling" nature. Here is a person who is suffering from a very violent skin eruption accompanied by general malaise. Inquiry reveals that he is allergic to every variety of sea food. Now if he continues to eat sea food, we properly regard him as responsible for his plight. If he continues to bemoan his condition, we are inclined to think of him as a self-indulgent whiner who either does not know what he wants or wants to eat his eels but with impunity. However, if on the basis of independent evidence, we are convinced that he really wants to get rid of his allergy and its effects, then we suspect that perhaps some hidden hunger for iodine or some other element plentiful in sea food compels him despite himself to persist in his food habits. We no longer blame him. His craving for iodine is like the thirst of a diabetic. But if iodine in some other form is available, we expect him to take it. If he refuses, we revise our judgment once again. Given the antecedent conditions, the choice, of course, was unavoidable. But wherever it is possible to alter these conditions by informed action, *that* particular choice can no longer be regarded as unavoidable.

The law, when enlightened, offers perhaps the best illustrations of the relevant distinctions, especially in considering cases of those suspected of insanity. The McNaughton Rules, which until recently guided judges in Anglo-American countries, have been severely criticized for being too narrow in their conception of what constitutes responsibility in adults charged with crime. As far as they go, however, they recognize the distinction between a voluntary and an involuntary act. They exonerate a person of diseased mind from responsibility. Where the death sentence obtains, this means that the person of diseased mind cannot be executed. But these Rules conceive of mental disease primarily as "a defect of reason." A person of diseased mind is one who does not know what he is doing, or who did not know that what he was doing was against the law. Although humane at the time they were formulated, the McNaughton Rules no longer reflect what we know today, or believe we know, about mental disease. According to these Rules, the "Mad Bomber of New York," whose actions showed that he knew very well what he was doing and that what he was doing was against the law, would have to be declared sane although he fervently believed that what he was doing—planting bombs in public places—was an appropriate way of getting even with the Consolidated Edison Company. Anyone found insane under the McNaughton Rules certainly could not have his behavior influenced by blame or punishment, since he does not know what he is doing and whether it is legal or not. Today insanity is considered a disabling emotional disorder; even if the unfortunate person has sufficient wit to know that he is violating the law, he may still be so emotionally disturbed as to be "beyond influence" by any threat of blame or punishment. Because an "emotional disorder" is a vaguer and more comprehensive term than knowledge or a defect of knowledge, it is more difficult to apply, particularly when individuals plead temporary insanity or uncontrollable impulse. But in all cases the rough-and-ready test is whether blame and punishment would tend to influence future behavior in similar situations.

This also explains why in the absence of a case history of emotional disorder we are, or should be, rightly suspicious of pleas that at the time a crime was committed the individual did not have sufficient power to prevent himself from committing it. "Temporarily insane" sounds like insanity made to order. Nonetheless, both in law and morals we do recognize situations in which, as the Scottish phrase goes, a person is guilty but with diminished responsibility. This may range from actions of self-defense to actions provoked by gross infidelity. It may be argued, however, that in many of these situations of "diminished responsibility," in which the subject is unquestionably sane, a severe sentence may have the effect of increasing responsibility.

One of the obvious absurdities of the view that judgments of blame and responsibility cannot be squared with an acceptance of thoroughgoing determinism is that it wipes out or ignores the relevance of distinctions between the sane and insane, and undercuts the basis of rational legal and moral judgment with respect to intentional and unintentional actions. It suggests that the difference between the criminal and non-criminal is *merely* a matter of accidental power, that the difference between the sane and insane, the responsible and irresponsible, is only a question of majority and minority. It even goes so far as to call all moral terms into dispute. In the words of Clarence Darrow, "I do not believe that there is any sort of distinction between the moral condition in and out of jail. One is just as good as the other. The people here [in jail] can no more help being here than the people outside can avoid being outside. I do not believe that people are in jail because they deserve to be. They are in jail simply because they cannot avoid it, on account of circumstances which are entirely beyond their control and for which they are in no way responsible." To analyze this seems as cruel as dissecting a butterfly, except that its contradictions and sentimentalities have been incorporated in the attitudes of many social workers. But all we need ask is what sense the word "deserve" has on Darrow's view. If no action can *possibly* merit deserved punishment, on what ground can any punishment be justifiably considered "undeserved"? Once more we ask: if the people in jail can no more help being there than the people outside of jail can help being outside, how can those outside help jailing those on the inside? And, if they can't help it, why condemn them?

The belief that because men are determined they cannot be morally responsible is a mistaken one. Not only is it a mistaken belief, it is a mischievous one. For far from diminishing the amount of needless suffering and cruelty in the world, it is quite certain to increase it. It justifies the infamous dictum of Smerdyakov in *The Brothers Karamazov:* "All things are permissible," if only one can get away with them. One of the commonest experiences of teachers, if not parents, is to observe young men and women whose belief that they can't help doing what they are doing, or failing to do, is often an excuse for not doing as well as they can do, or at the very least better than they are at present doing. When we have, as we often do, independent evidence that they are capable of doing better, is it so absurd to hold them at least partly responsible for not doing better? Do we not know from our own experience that our belief that we are responsible, or that we will be held responsible, enables us to do things which had previously seemed beyond our power?

I do not think that the theories of psychoanalysis contradict the belief that moral responsibility is a valid concept of psychological experience. If they did it would be only additional evidence of their unempirical character. At any rate some psychoanalysts agree with Franz Alexander,[2] who writes: "The fundamental principle, however, no matter what practical disposition is made [of the criminal delinquent] is that every person must be held responsible for the consequences of his acts." He concludes that this sense of moral responsibility is not only indispensable to society, but to individual growth. "A person reared according to the principle of responsibility will eventually internalize this feeling of responsibility towards others as a responsibility towards himself as well."

I must confess, however, that I find psychoanalytic literature full of inconsistencies on the subject, most of them present in Freud. For example,

---

[2] Franz Alexander was born in Hungary in 1891. He has taught psychiatry at the Universities of Budapest, Berlin, Chicago, Illinois, and Southern California, and is known for his pioneering research in the field of psychosomatic medicine. His approach to psychiatry is psychoanalytic in origin: He maintains that the repression of hostile impulses together with anxiety constitute the core of neurotic problems. He considers the central feature of psychoanalytic therapy to be the creation of an emotional atmosphere conducive to undoing the traumatic effects of early family influences. He is the author of more than one hundred and fifty published works in psychiatry and psychosomatic medicine. [J.P.D.]

Freud's answer to the question: "Should a person be held responsible for his dreams, which are the products of unconscious forces over which he has no conscious control?" was, "Who else but the dreamer should be responsible for his dreams?" This seems to me a clear equivocation. The question speaks of *moral* responsibility. Freud replies in terms of causal attribution. Certainly if in a sleepwalking dream an individual did something hurtful or mischievous, no reasonable person would hold him morally or legally responsible.

What often passes as irremediable evil in the world, or the inevitable ills and suffering to which the flesh is heir, is a consequence of our failure to act in time. We are responsible, whether we admit it or not, for what it is in our power to do; and most of the time we can't be sure what is in our power to do until we attempt it. If only we are free to try, we don't have to claim also to be free to try to try, or look for an ultimate footing in some prime metaphysical indeterminate to commit ourselves responsibly. Proximate freedom is enough. And although what we are now is determined by what we were, what we will be is still determined also by what we do now. Human effort can within limits re-determine the direction of events even though it cannot determine the conditions which make human effort possible. It is time enough to reconcile oneself to what is unalterable, or to disaster, after we have done our best to overcome them.

There are some people—even some philosophers—who, observing the human scene, declare themselves unable to give an intelligible meaning to judgments of human responsibility. They say: "It's all a matter of luck." This is no more sensible than saying, "Nothing is a matter of luck," even if "luck" has an intelligible meaning in a determined world. It is true that we did not choose to be born. But from this it only follows that we should not blame or punish anyone merely for being born, whether he is black or white, male or female. It is also true that we choose, most of us adults who are sound of limb and mind, to keep on living. And if we do, we bear a contributory responsibility for remaining in the world. The Stoics, who so lamentably confused physics and ethics, were right in pointing out that most of us are free to leave "life's smoky chamber." It is not true that everything which happens to us is like "being struck down by a dread disease." The treatment and cure of disease, to use an illustration that can serve as a moral paradigm of the whole human situation, would never have begun unless we believed that some things which were did not have to be; that they could be different; and that *we* could make them different. And what we can make different, we are responsible for.

With respect to judgments of blame and responsibility, the pragmatic theory stresses not the multiplication of such judgments, but only their use as means of individual help and social protection. It eschews the automatic judgment of blame and responsibility, in order to devote itself to the difficult task of discriminating in the light of all the relevant scientific evidence what it is reasonable or unreasonable to expect from a human being in the situation in which he finds himself. It also expresses a certain human ideal of man as a contributing maker or creator of his own destiny, rather than as a passive creature of fate. Sickness, accident, or incapacity aside, we feel lessened as human beings if our actions are always excused or explained away on the ground that, despite appearances, we are really not responsible for them. For whoever treats us this way is treating us like an object or an infant, or like someone out of his mind. Our dignity as rational human beings sometimes leads us to protest when an overzealous friend seeks to extenuate our conduct on the ground that we are not really responsible, that we are either too stupid to know, or too lost in illusion, really to intend to do what we actually have done. There are times when this unfortunately is only too true. But there are also times when we burst out and declare that we really are responsible, that we know what we are doing and are prepared to take the consequences. As bad as the priggishness of the self-righteous is the whine of the self-pitying. To the extent that the priggishness and the whine follow from mistaken beliefs about blame and responsibility, they are both avoidable. In the end, but only in the end, our character is our fate. But until the end, it is a developing pattern on which we work with whatever courage and intelligence we have. To that extent we make our character.

QUESTIONS FOR STUDY AND DISCUSSION

1. Can one reconcile the doctrine of determinism with the acceptance of moral responsibility?
2. Does belief in moral responsibility entail an acceptance of indeterminism?
3. Describe Hook's pragmatic theory of blame and responsibility?
4. Does Hook settle the question of freedom vs. determinism?
5. Is Hook a determinist?
6. For practical purposes, is Hook's resolution of the problem a satisfactory one?

Patrick Romanell

PATRICK ROMANELL was born in Mola di Bari, Italy, in 1912. Educated
in the United States, he studied at Brooklyn College and then pursued
graduate studies at Columbia University, receiving his doctorate in 1937.
A Carnegie Fellow, Romanell has taught at Brooklyn College, the
National University of Mexico, Wells College, and the University of
Texas. Since 1962 he has been associated with the University of Okla-
homa. Although a naturalist, Romanell is highly critical of Dewey and
some of his disciples. His principal work is *Toward a Critical Naturalism*
(1958).

Naturalistic Ethics Reconsidered

The most vital question that has been discussed at considerable length in
recent American thought is the possibility of arriving at a scientific treatment of morality. An examination of the current literature on the subject
discloses that the appeal for an extension of scientific method to the field of
morals is popular not only among many of our academic philosophers, but
also among some of our professional scientists, especially the biologists.

In a terrifying age of atomic bombs, it is somewhat heartening to be
assured from various quarters that more and more scientists are becoming
increasingly aware of the ethical implications of their work and of the
pressing need for solving the concrete problems that beset this bewildered
world of ours. One of the most perceptive of these scientists is my friend
Chauncey D. Leake of Ohio State. Dr. Leake is convinced that it is possible to approach moral problems in a scientific manner, and urges philosophers to cooperate with scientists in the realization of this possibility.
However, before such a cooperative endeavor can be actually effected, it is
necessary for philosophers and scientists to reach a common ground; and I
submit that no common ground can be reached between them unless they
first face squarely the theoretical obstacles which stand in the way of arriving at an intelligent solution of our moral problems. This essay is addressed
to the task of pointing out briefly what some of those obstacles are, with
the hope of paving the way to more fruitful discussions on the logic of
ethics in the future.

From pp. 39–47 of Patrick Romanell, *Toward a Critical Naturalism*. © 1958 by The
Macmillan Company. Reprinted by permission of the author.

A word of explanation is in order before proceeding any further. The following critique of the current argument for a scientific ethics is not written from a Kantian or transcendentalist standpoint. Being a philosophical naturalist myself, I sympathize with any wholehearted faith in the possibility of a scientific approach to ethics. In fact, a naturalistic moralist could not be such without that faith. But every philosophical faith needs a rational foundation; and what that particular philosophical faith called "naturalism" needs, at bottom, is respect for the conclusions of *all* the sciences. Now one of the fundamental conclusions of the sciences themselves which we ought to respect, may well turn out to be that ethical science differs *in method* from physical science. So the point at issue here is not whether or not moral science is possible, but whether the current case for a scientific ethics stands up under the fire of naturalistic criticism itself.

Over fifty years ago John Dewey, the dean of American philosophers, wrote an essay which may be viewed in retrospect as a primary source of inspiration to all those of us who believe in the possibility of ethical science. The essay is entitled "Logical Conditions of a Scientific Treatment of Morality," and is published in *Problems of Men* (1946). In the Prefatory Note to the book, the author makes it clear that this specific essay is important "as an anticipation of the direction" of his thought. In it he declares that his "point of view expressly disclaims any effort to reduce the statement of matters of conduct to forms comparable with those of physical science. But it also expressly proclaims *an identity of logical procedure in the two cases.*"

In other words, to restate Dewey's position, first negatively, the essay takes a firm stand against the materialistic and transcendental schools of philosophy on the ground that both of them deny the logical principle of identity of method. On the one hand, transcendentalism denies it by making a "radical disparity" between physical and ethical judgments. On the other hand, materialism denies the same principle by confusing identity of method with "identity of subject-matter." Curiously enough, the author criticizes materialism for wiping out moral experience in reducing it to physical terms, but he does not seem to realize that the logic of his own point of view, despite its good intentions, in reducing ethical to physical method, also wipes out in the end what is distinctively moral about our experience. For, in the last analysis, what is the real difference between the *methodological* reductionism of instrumentalism and the *ontological* reductionism of materialism? The former, after all, is it not but a sophisticated version of the latter?

Whether it is or not, let us rest content at the moment with a restatement of Dewey's argument for a scientific ethics in positive terms. The simplest way of putting it is that, since the logical procedure in ethics may be identical with the logical procedure in the physical sciences, it follows that a scientific ethics is possible. This is the basic argument in the current case for a scientific ethics. It is a very popular argument shared by a large number of thinkers in the contemporary world who have directly or indirectly come under Dewey's influence.

Historically considered, instrumentalism may be regarded as the most persistent, if not consistent, attempt since the British empirical tradition to introduce the experimental method of the physical sciences into moral matters. Even a cursory reading of Dewey's *Reconstruction in Philosophy* (1920), perhaps his most militant book, will bear this out. Like every good pragmatist, John Dewey was essentially a moralist at heart, and saw all philosophical problems in that context. This moralistic strain (depuritanized) lies behind his technical reasons for dismissing so many traditional problems of philosophy as irrelevant to its task of social and moral reconstruction via the unprejudiced use of scientific methods.

Viewed logically, Dewey's great effort to bridge the gap between the physical sciences and ethics rests on the dubious assumption that there is only *one type* of scientific method (or methods). Given that premise, of course, it follows that there must be "an identity of logical procedure in the two cases," the two cases being the existential (not in the "existentialist" sense in vogue at present) and the normative sciences. But can the method of ethics really be identical with experimental procedure in use elsewhere? If it can, then Dewey has made a tremendous contribution to logical theory; but if it can not, his whole case for a reconstruction of traditional morality on the model of the experimental sciences breaks down for the simple reason that it rests on a false premise, that of methodological reductionism.

In order to determine whether there is a possible identity of method in physical and ethical inquiry, another preliminary matter must be taken up, namely, the essence of scientific method itself. The question is highly important because, ironically enough, there is so much Baconian confusion of tongues as to its nature in this age of ours, which boasts of being so scientific. To put it in the briefest terms possible, scientific method is the continuous commitment to base conclusions upon *evidence*. Thus scientific methods, properly speaking, are modes of *verifying* or (falsifying) claims to truth, not ways of discovering it; they are means of *testing* the validity of alternative hypotheses in a given field of investigation. In short, the proper business of scientific method is with the search for reliable *criteria* of truth.

It is time now to restate the crucial question of this essay in the light of the foregoing analysis of scientific method: Is it possible to verify a normative hypothesis by the same procedure employed in verifying an existential hypothesis? To illustrate, is the moral proposition, "All women should have the right to vote," verifiable in the same way as the chemical proposition, "All acids turn blue litmus red"? One of Dewey's disciples answers confidently: *"In theory* the problem of verification in ethics should be no different from the same problem in any other field." And Dewey himself is just as confident when he asserts in his *Logic* that only "practical difficulties" stand in the way of applying the scientific method to social phenomena.

However, to appreciate the *theoretical* difficulties of a normative inquiry like ethics, the subject-matter of which is inherently, not accidentally, complex (the naive assumption that there are no theoretical difficulties interferes with the very cause of removing the "practical difficulties" themselves), we must come more seriously to grips with the difference *in theory* between the problem of verification in ethics and the same problem in the experimental sciences.

Quite apart from the traditional debate between empiricists and rationalists as to what constitutes the *initial* phase of scientific inquiry, contemporary thinkers of diverse schools substantially agree as to what constitutes its *terminal* phase, to wit, recourse whenever possible to experimentation or observation of the facts under controlled conditions. (Incidentally, even a thoroughgoing rationalist like Morris R. Cohen admitted that physics differs from mathematics in that it deals with questions of fact and, as a consequence, its procedure must be empirical at least at the end, if not at the beginning, of any given investigation of nature it undertakes.) Without such experimental observation of the relevant facts, no theory, however elegant in mathematical form, can be said to be ever verified. Everybody knows, of course, about the revolutionary effect of the experimental method in the modern world. But are problems of ethics amenable to such a method of testing? There's the question!

There are several reasons why ethics, no matter how scientific in intent, cannot have its problems settled by the experimental method as we have come to understand that method. The first and most obvious reason is that the experimental method is only good for questions of fact, that is, for determining *what-is-so,* and hence no good for ethics proper, which deals with questions of norms or *what-ought-to-be-so.* (Descriptive ethics is *not* normative ethics.) For we can only observe in the experimental sense objects whose logical status is factual or existential, not those whose logical status is ideal or normative.

To this "radical disparity" between the existential and the normative, Dewey would reply, again confidently, as follows: "If there is anything confirmed by observation it is that human beings naturally cherish ends and relationships, that, in short, they naturally institute values. Having desires and having to guide their conduct by aims and purposes, nothing else is possible." True enough, naturally. But what *observation* does not, and can not, confirm is *which* of the ends and relationships human beings naturally cherish and *which* of the values they naturally institute are *desirable.* Observation alone cannot settle such a normative issue. Like Spinoza of old, Dewey and his disciples seem to confuse ethics with social psychology or anthropology. The pity is that the Deweyites think they are writing "naturalistic morals," when all they are really doing is writing some sort of naturalistic sociology. I say this, not because I do not respect naturalistic *sociology*, but because naturalistic *sociology* is not the same thing as naturalistic *morals*. So, to put it bluntly, it is high time that we naturalists called a spade a spade. The naturalist's respect for *all* the sciences implies the relative *autonomy* of each of them as well as their interrelationships.

The second reason why the experimental method can not be applied to the problem of ethics is a corollary of the first. In the existential sciences the final determiner of the fate of any hypothesis or theory is factual observation. (Pure mathematics is a formal, not an existential, science.) To return to our previous examples, if the chemist were to find by experimentation a single exception to the proposition, "All acids turn blue litmus red," the chemical generalization would no longer be valid as a universal proposition. However, in contrast, the moral proposition, "All women *should* have the right to vote," is not, and can not be, invalidated by the sheer fact that in such and such places women do not actually have the right to vote. We could always argue like good feminists that they should, even if they do not, enjoy that right. Thus as mistakes in reasoning cannot invalidate the principles of logic, so misdeeds in conduct cannot invalidate the principles of ethics.

Moreoever, suppose for the sake of the argument we change the proposition to: "All women *have* the right to vote." Obviously the new proposition, falling as it does within the area of political science, is false *according to observation,* that is, because it does not hold in fact. Finally, in order to see the bearing of the conclusions of the existential sciences on ethics, suppose our original proposition is changed once more to: "All individuals should have the right to vote *at age fifteen.*" Here psychology, for one thing, would seriously question the validity of this moral generalization on the ground that intelligence tests show that individuals require a certain degree of maturity in order to vote.

Let us draw the implications of the foregoing statements. (1) Whereas an existential hypothesis is necessarily invalidated by being found contrary to fact, a moral hypothesis is not invalidated by being violated. (2) Observation (or experiment) ultimately determines the truth or falsity of an existential hypothesis. (3) Observation does not necessarily determine the *truth* of a moral hypothesis, but may determine its *falsity.* (4) Whence it follows that the existential sciences can determine which human ideals (or possibilities) *cannot* be, but not those which *can.* (5) While concrete observations in the existential sciences serve as tests of the validity of the hypotheses proposed, in the field of ethics, on the other hand, it is the hypotheses themselves which act as standards for measuring the value of our concrete moral experiences. Thus what makes the Golden Rule, for instance, a valid principle of morals is not that it can be used to explain what the facts of our moral life happen to be, but rather that it can be used to understand what those facts would be if we lived up to its standard of conduct. All of which shows that the validity of a moral hypothesis depends on its *intrinsic* value as a measure of our actual conduct. In contrast, an existential hypothesis, like gravitation, is dependent on something *extrinsic* to it, namely, factual observation, not only for its original derivation but also for its final validation.

The third reason for questioning the applicability of the experimental method to moral problems has to do with a special difficulty inherent in Dewey's particular interpretation of that method along pragmatic lines. According to his interpretation, all principles and policies are to be treated for methodological purposes as "working hypotheses." But, as the critics of pragmatism have charged time and time again, such a pragmatic test of truth is hopelessly ambiguous unless qualified. The doctrine that an hypothesis is true if it works well may mean either of two things at least: (1) works in fact, that is empirically, or (2) works in the utilitarian sense, that is, brings happiness. Both meanings of "working well" are found in instrumentalism. (Incidentally, Dewey was more careful than William James in keeping the two meanings distinct.)

Now, if we take the pragmatic test of truth in its first or empirical sense, we are faced with the difficulty that no moral hypothesis can be justified. How can an ideal of life, which a moral hypothesis describes and prescribes, be justified by a mere empirical study of the relevant facts? For it should be obvious that it is logically impossible to infer a conclusion containing an *ought* (expressed through the ideal itself) from premises that are, by definition, limited to what *is*. In other words, to cite our old example again, we can not prove that all women *should* vote from the fact that some women *do*, e.g., in the U.S.A., Sweden, Finland, Italy. (We could not even prove that they *should* even if they all *did* in fact.) I do not know exactly what to call this curious problem arising in the logic of a normative science, where a proposition undergoes a change from the *indicative* to the *imperative* mood, so to speak, but the problem of imperatives is not the traditional problem of induction, which deals with the different question of how we can argue within the same (indicative) mood from *some* members of a class to *all*.

Turning next to the pragmatic test of truth in its second or utilitarian sense, a new difficulty presents itself. For the utilitarian answer that any doctrine which brings happiness to those who believe in it is true, is itself not determined by evidence in its favor, but by the faith of its believers. Now, whatever cognitive significance faith may have in religion, it certainly does not constitute evidence in science, ethical or otherwise. To select the most crucial example at the present moment, how can the "cold war" between democracy and communism be settled pragmatically, if each side is convinced as much as the other that its point of view works well and, thus, is true? This does not mean, to be sure, that democracy cannot be justified as the most promising of the moral hypotheses for society to live by, but what it does mean is that its justification cannot be done on pragmatic grounds *alone*. In short, even if the utilitarian test is applied to questions of morals, the fact remains that the fundamental issue itself, namely, *which* of the alternative programs of action will bring the greatest good to the greatest number, is left unresolved.

In the light of the foregoing theoretical considerations, I must come to the sad conclusion that John Dewey has not established his case for a science of ethics and that, therefore, the problem as to the logical conditions of a scientific treatment of morality still needs the kind of thing he always insisted upon, to wit, "reconstruction in philosophy."

QUESTIONS FOR STUDY AND DISCUSSION

1. What are some of the obstacles to a scientific approach to ethics?
2. How does method in ethical science differ from method in physical science?
3. What is Romanell's objection to Dewey's instrumentalism?
4. What is the essence of scientific method according to Romanell?
5. Is it possible to verify a normative hypothesis by the same procedure employed in verifying a factual hypothesis?
6. Give two reasons why the experimental method cannot be applied to the problems of ethics?
7. Why does Romanell reject the pragmatic test of truth?

Toward a Theory of Compossibility

No matter how satisfactory naturalism may be as a working philosophy to the scientist in his pursuit of knowledge, we can never expect its tenets to be convincing to mankind as a whole unless they can provide a general guide to the difficult art of living. Thus a crucial test for any type of naturalistic philosophy is its implications for morals. What guiding principle of ethics is compatible with a naturalistic conception of the world, and, at the same time, is consistent with a naturalistic method of approach? It is plain that to determine the ethics of naturalism we must first state at least summarily what is intended by philosophic naturalism itself. However, in view of the great variety of naturalistic systems of thought, the most telling way of arriving at what naturalism is *for* is to see what it is *against*.

The most characteristic thing about philosophic naturalism is its relentless opposition to all sorts of "bifurcation" which are rampant in the field of philosophy. In the first place, naturalism is opposed by definition to all metaphysical doctrines (for example, Cartesian dualism) that separate

From pp. 69–81 of Patrick Romanell, *Toward a Critical Naturalism.* © 1958 by The Macmillan Company. Reprinted by permission of the author.

man from the rest of nature. And in the second place, it is opposed by conviction to all methodological doctrines (for example, Bergsonian intuitionism) that separate the study of the humanities from the study of the sciences. Positively stated, all forms of naturalistic philosophy substitute the postulate of "continuity" for the postulate of "discontinuity." In other words, naturalistic philosophies hold that man is in fact an integral part of nature and that scientific method is in theory applicable to any field of inquiry. Of course, where naturalistic philosophers differ is in their ideas on man as a natural being and in their ideas on science as a method, as well as in their concepts of nature itself.

The major split within the naturalistic school of thought from the time of the ancient Greeks has been between the reductionist variety of naturalism (which goes under the traditional name of "materialism" and which gets its inspiration directly or indirectly from Democritus) and the antireductionist variety (which in turn gets its inspiration ultimately from Aristotle). But although this split is manifest throughout the whole history of Western philosophy, it should be added to complete the picture that since the turn of the century there have been some definite signs, particularly in the United States, pointing to the maturity of the naturalistic tradition along antireductionist lines. Future historians will in all probability look at dogmatic materialism as an exaggeration of the naturalistic tradition in philosophy—a tradition which has enjoyed the greatest continuity in Western thought.

In any case, whatever intellectual historians in the future may have to say on the subject and despite all the specific metaphysical and methodological differences between the type of naturalist who is reductionist in mentality and the type who is not, one general implication of the naturalistic position for ethical theory should be perfectly clear from the outset. If a naturalistic philosophy signifies "antibifurcationism" in theory of nature and theory of logic, it evidently signifies the same thing in theory of ethics. That is, a naturalistic philosophy is against any system of ethics (for example, Kantian rigorism) which separates moral values from facts and separates the study of the former from the study of the latter. Or, in positive terms, the naturalistic postulate of continuity in metaphysics (the continuity of nature and man) and in methodology (the continuity of the sciences and the humanities) implies the continuity of facts and moral values in ethics.

Strictly speaking, the only thing a naturalistic ethics is committed to in principle is what is implicit in its initial presupposition regarding the continuity of facts and moral values. However, historically speaking, naturalistic moralists have gone beyond this general commitment to the presupposition of continuity and have attempted to identify the ethics of naturalism —to give some examples from the history of the subject—with "the ethics of Hercules," the ethics of Happiness, the ethics of Evolution. Of all the naturalistic attempts at grafting a moral upon a natural philosophy, apparently the least objectionable has been the one which makes the ethics of naturalism synonymous with the ethics of happiness, the old classical name of which is "eudaemonism" and the modern British expression of which is "utilitarianism." Accordingly, for purposes of identification, it would be advisable to use some convenient label, such as "utilitarian naturalism," to denote the predominant form of naturalistic ethics in Western thought.

There are two principal reasons why the great majority of naturalists in philosophy are utilitarians in ethics. One is that the ethics of happiness is the ethics of common sense. Here at least the old naturalists and the new are on the side of the common man, if not on the side of the angels. The other reason for the close alliance, particularly in the last hundred years or so, between naturalism and utilitarianism has to do with the fact that the explicit objective of the British utilitarian movement, to treat ethics as a *science,* fitted in beautifully with the implicit faith of the whole naturalistic tradition in the possibility of a science of ethics. In fact, contemporary naturalism owes much of its vitality in ethical theory to the influence of British utilitarianism and its inheritor, American pragmatism. Unfortunately, however, along with the healthy element which contemporary naturalism inherited from the utilitarians and the pragmatists—their anti-authoritarian and down-to-earth attitude in matters of morals—there came also with that inheritance an element which has proven not to be so healthy for the development of a thoroughgoing naturalistic ethics. I have in mind the positivistic or purely inductive conception of scientific method underlying the entire movement of British utilitarianism.

Getting away from the historical ties between British utilitarianism and contemporary naturalism, it is obvious that, given the philosophical naturalist's complete respect for scientific findings, any ethical theory which purports to be naturalistic must meet at least one prerequisite: it must not be out of tune with the facts of nature, human and nonhuman. Desires and feelings of obligation being the raw materials of morality, the facts which have the greatest bearing on ethics belong to the field of the behavioral sciences, especially psychology. Now doubtless the reason why there has been and continues to be so much disputing in moral philosophy is that psychology is not an exact science in the sense that, say, mathematical physics is, and, considering its very complexity, probably never will be. (Incidentally, the psychologists themselves are the first to admit this.) Yet, we must learn how to get along with our problems in science, as elsewhere, and make the best of an imperfect situation. We certainly can't wait till psychology becomes a full-fledged science to settle the social and moral problems confronting us. Besides, the best antidote to a sense of defeat in matters of theory is a sense of history, not to speak of a sense of humor.

Proceeding then without further apologies, let us examine a classic statement of ethical naturalism which is accepted by most philosophical naturalists today and, for that matter, even by some philosophical idealists. Back in "the century of genius" (the seventeenth), when what we now call psychology was still a highly speculative affair, Spinoza observed in his masterpiece "that we neither strive for, wish, seek, nor desire anything *because* we think it to be good, but, on the contrary, we adjudge a thing to be good *because* we strive for, wish, seek, or desire it." In other words, according to Spinoza, things are not desired because they are valuable or good, but they are valuable or good because they are desired. All of which means that good and evil, being dependent upon man's likes and dislikes, are relative to the changing tastes of individuals; and, since not only is one man's food another man's poison, but a man's food at one time may be his own poison at another, it follows that good and evil are purely subjective. Thus, in the last analysis, the sole test for judging the correctness of any moral code lies in its capacity to satisfy human wants, the satisfaction of which makes for the good or happy life. This is precisely the standard of "utility" advocated subsequently in systematic fashion by British utilitarianism. Therefore, we may conclude that Spinoza is a Utilitarian *ante litteram,* and that in him and his consistent followers ethical naturalism and utilitarianism coincide.

Is the utilitarian version of naturalistic ethics, first, *sound,* and secondly, does it constitute the ethics of a *mature* naturalism? We take up each of these two closely related questions in order.

A utilitarian conception of naturalistic ethics is, on the whole, psychologically sound but unsound logically. This dual judgment on our part can be easily substantiated by showing how the argument for ethical relativity in Spinoza's famous passage from the *Ethics* rests on the ambiguity of the word "because" which appears there in two different senses. One sense of "because" is the conjunction itself, the other is the prepositional "because of." Now, the first "because" in the text quoted is being used as the conjunction proper, meaning "for the reason that," which is "cause" in the old logical or formal sense of Aristotle's. On the other hand, the second "because" is being used prepositionally as "because of," meaning "on account of," which is "cause" proper in the modern scientific sense, corresponding to Aristotle's "efficient cause." (The psychological term "motive," the equivalent of "because," suffers from exactly the same ambiguity.)

To restate Spinoza's text in terms of the two meanings of "because," he is really arguing "that we neither strive for, wish, seek, nor desire anything *for the reason that* we think it to be good, but, on the contrary, we adjudge a thing to be good *on account of* the fact that we strive for, wish, seek, or desire it." Now, the argument as restated is psychologically true, because to think otherwise would be to put the cart before the horse. But, because we consider a thing to be good *on account* of desire does not prove that it *is* good *for that reason.* All that it proves, to borrow the words of a present-day utilitarian who quotes Spinoza's text with full approval, is that *"in the last analysis* good springs from desire and not desire from good." For, just as the origin of our ideas from experience does not determine their final *validity,* so the origin of our ideals from desire does not determine their final *value*. To believe that their origin *does* is to commit the genetic fallacy.

To select the most serious illustration on the international scene at the present time, communism as a way of life or a way of administration is not proven to be good in the *moral* sense by the fact that millions of people all over the world prefer it to the democratic way. (The same argument would apply with equal force conversely, of course.) If things were deemed automatically desirable or good on the mere ground of our desiring them, ethics would be completely pointless as a discipline, except perhaps as a sheer exercise in either sentimentalism on the one hand or in cynicism on the other. If ethics is to serve as a general guide to mankind, it should encourage us above all to desire things *on their merits*, that is, for the reason that on deliberation we find they are valuable or good either in themselves or in their bearing on our weal and woe. That this is no easy task is no excuse for defeatism, either of the sentimental or cynical variety. In any event, isn't it the height of irony that, of all people, an arch-rationalist like Spinoza, who sets out to write an "Ethics from the Standpoint of the Geometer," should actually come out with an "Ethics from the Standpoint of the Behaviorist"?

In contrast to the usual position taken by contemporary thinkers, I have said quite deliberately that the strength of utilitarianism as a theory of ethics lies precisely in its psychology. To be sure, in saying this, I am not unaware of the objections which have been brought by naturalistic philosophers, let alone others, against the hedonistic psychology underlying the whole utilitarian movement, nor am I unaware of the difficulties encountered by John Stuart Mill in particular, who during the Victorian Age tried so desperately to justify Bentham's "greatest happiness principle" by means of that psychology. Nevertheless, whether psychological hedonism is adequate or not as a general explanation of human motivation is, in the main, a matter of finesse in psychological theory. The question is doubtless important to psychology but not so important to ethics. A hedonistic psychology in its original setting may have been hopelessly naive in thinking that man is such a sophisticated animal and, accordingly, may well be outmoded from a contemporary vantage point, but its theory of human desires (if not taken literally) is at bottom physiologically correct. Men may like some things (e.g., friends) and dislike others (e.g., foes), rather than seek pleasures *per se* or avoid pains *per se,* but after all they still like and dislike. In short, a hedonistic psychology is good as far as it goes, and the fundamental trouble with ethical hedonism is not really its *psychology* of ethics—which could be and has been modified anyway—but its *logic* of ethics.

A hedonistic ethic suffers from the general defect inherent in any relativistic or subjectivistic type of ethical theory, egoistic or altruistic, beyond conscience or not. That defect is not so easy to recognize because the main contention of relativistic ethics, that dependence upon desire implies subjectivity of good, rests on an assumption which is really a truism in psychology: nothing is *desirable* or good in itself except insofar as it is *desired* by us. This assumption is just as plausible as its counterpart in theory of knowledge: nothing is *believable* or true in itself except insofar as it is *believed* by us. But, just as it would be illogical in epistemology to draw the conclusion that all truth is subjective from the psychological assumption of the relativity of beliefs, so it would be illogical in ethics to draw the conclusion that all good is subjective from the psychological assumption of the relativity of values. Therefore, the argument of the utilitarian moralist, that dependence upon desire implies subjectivity of good, is as fallacious in logic as it is plausible in psychology.

To make use again of our previous illustration, we can no more infer the subjectivity of good from the historical fact that some people like communism and some don't, than we can infer the subjectivity of truth from the historical fact that the ancients believed the motion of the blood to be one thing and the moderns believe it to be another. In short, it is a *non sequitur* in logic to argue from a psychological truism which nobody would deny, to repeat, that nothing is desirable or good in itself except insofar as it is desired by us, to the ethical conclusion that something is desirable or good simply on the ground that it is desired by us, individually or collectively. Ironically, the fallacy here in arguing that the relativity of values implies their subjectivity is not an instance of the fallacy of *false* premise but an instance of the fallacy of *true* premise, namely, relativity of desire implies relativity of value. In sum, if the relativist's argument for epistemological subjectivism is not valid, neither is his argument for ethical subjectivism. This does not imply that the ethical absolutist is right. All it implies is that there is something wrong with the logic of his opponent, the ethical relativist.

That human history points to a relativity of moral standards is abundantly evident from studies in anthropology, but this empirical fact in itself is no proof of ethical subjectivism. Those philosophers and social scientists who are so impressed with the phenomenon of "ethical relativity" should be more careful about jumping at normative conclusions in ethical theory from descriptive statements concerning moral codes accepted or rejected by this or that society. They should bear always in mind that there is a significant difference between ethics proper and "ethology" (to exploit for our purposes a term of the American sociologist William Graham Sumner). Failure to make such distinction is ultimately responsible for the fallacy in ethical theory which recent critics have called "the naturalistic fallacy," after G. E. Moore, but whose more appropriate name would be "the positivistic fallacy." So much, then, for our answer to the first question as to the soundness of a naturalistic ethics of the utilitarian variety.

We turn next to the other of our two questions: Does utilitarianism constitute the ethics of a *mature* naturalism? In order to see the import of this second question, suppose we grant the point (which is questionable), that there is nothing wrong with the *logic* of utilitarianism. There still remains, however, the possibility that there may be something wrong with its *ethics*. This is, of course, the familiar stand taken by antinaturalists in general and antiutilitarians in particular, especially since the monumental contribution to ethics made by Kant in the eighteenth century. On the other hand, what would be novel here, if anything, is a position taken against utilitarian naturalism *from a fuller naturalistic standpoint itself*. This is precisely the thesis I submit for consideration. I shall argue that what is wrong with utilitarianism is its *incompleteness* as a theory of ethics and, hence, its inadequacy to fulfill the requirements of a thoroughgoing naturalistic ethics. In a word, utilitarian naturalism commits an error of omission. What does its horizon omit from the human scene?

The central difficulty with a utilitarian version of naturalistic ethics is that it sees man as part and parcel of nature all right, but does not see that man is more than a seeker of happiness, or more than an animal bent on satisfying his desires or needs. The quest for happiness is undoubtedly *part* of life, but it is not the *whole* of life. Actually, then, the incompleteness of a utilitarian version of naturalistic ethics stems from its incomplete view of man himself. That is, the root of the trouble goes back to an accidental shortcoming within that particular version, not to a necessary shortcoming within naturalistic ethics as such. In other words, utlitarian naturalism goes only halfway in its *ethics* of man because it goes only halfway in its *metaphysics* of man. What Whitehead had to say about mechanists in biology applies equally well to utilitarians in ethics: "Some of the major disasters of mankind have been produced by the narrowness of men with a good methodology."

Man is not only a producer and consumer of happiness, he is also a maker and keeper of obligations. Man's sense of obligation demanding heed is as much (if not more) the source of morality as his needs demanding satisfaction. This being so, there are two distinct sides to the moral life which any adequate theory of ethics must take into account. For lack of better terminology, we shall call those two sides "the eudaemonistic" and "the juristic." The eudaemonistic side of moral life has to do, to be sure, with the pursuit of happiness, but the juristic side has to do with something quite different and, though often distasteful, quite necessary just the same, to wit, the discharge of duties and responsibilities. Now, there is no doubt in my mind that a psychologically and logically polished theory of utilitarian ethics can account for the eudaemonistic or soft side of morality, but I am extremely dubious as to whether it can do so for the juristic or tough side. The converse, I think, is the case with the opposite theory of ethics derived from Kant. Each of these two rival theories of ethics is exceedingly artificial, suffering from the "defects of its qualities." The Kantian view *obliges* us to look for happiness in the next world, the Utilitarian *obliges* us to do likewise in this one. But all this is ridiculous, not to say an utter confusion of the moral categories. We can oblige a person to be *just,* but we can't oblige him to be *happy.* Life involves many things which have to be done, regardless of whether we desire them or whether they bring happiness, such as having a policeman on the beat and a fireman on the run, and, though we are entitled to make *virtues* out of necessities if we like, it is silly to make *goods* or objects of happiness out of them. My friend Herbert Schneider of Columbia, a reformed utilitarian, is perfectly right when he admits with the utmost candor, in a recent article, that it is foolish for utilitarians to try to reduce man's concern for justice to the pursuit of happiness. In fine, since the two aspects of moral life are not actually reducible to each other, they must not be treated in theory as if they were in fact.

In the light of all the foregoing considerations, my answer to the question under examination should be clear. The utilitarian version of naturalistic ethics, constituting as it does the dominant view of ethical naturalism, does *not* measure up to a mature form of naturalistic ethics because, when all is said and done, it looks at the moral life exclusively in terms of the pursuit of happiness, or its equivalent. Now, the worst consequence of such a limited outlook in ethical theory is that it is forced in the end to compensate for its initial narrowness and to see so much connection between justice and happiness that its advocates are apt to harbor an optimistic illusion about the inevitable harmony of these two species of moral value, thereby missing the *tragic* element in human life.

That this element is inescapable, is clearly evident not only from our daily conflicts of goods to pursue and daily conflicts of obligations to discharge, but also from the primary conflict that may readily arise in human life, which is that of having to choose between a pattern of action devoted to the pursuit of happiness and one devoted to the performance of duty. Granting that the quest for happiness and the call of duty are interrelated and that at times they are at harmony with each other, it must also be granted that at times they are not. It will get us nowhere to soft-pedal the conflicts of loyalties in human experience, since like the poor they are always with us in one form or another, in the life of drama as in the drama of life. Needless to say, the so-called "cold war" makes this only too plain at the moment on an international scale.

To pinpoint the whole plea of this essay for a fuller version of naturalistic ethics, an ethical system to be consistent with a mature or sober naturalism must do justice to *both* aspects of moral life—the juristic as well as the eudaemonistic—be they in harmony or not. The outcome of such an undertaking, which would amount essentially to a reconciliation of Immanuel Kant and John Stuart Mill, could be named "the *double-aspect* theory of ethics." In contrast to the "happiness-ethics" of utilitarianism, the guiding principle of the double-aspect theory is not maximum harmonization of human desires or maximum attainment of happiness, but maximum harmonization of a life of happiness *and* a life of duty, or, to adapt a Leibnizian term to the present context, maximum attainment of "compossible" ends. Hence, according to the proposed harmony theory of ethics, the test for determining the correctness of any code of conduct is not simply its "utility," that is, its consequences for happiness, but its "compossibility," that is, its consequences for the harmonization of happiness and duty.

But, it may be quickly noted, isn't this latter test itself just a new name for the old utilitarian way of thinking, that the determining factor in moral action is the usefulness of its *consequences?* To which my reply would be: Consequences *for what?* For happiness *alone?* What about consequences for *duty?* If the charge is made that the suggested "compossibility" test of morality is just as pragmatic as the "utility" test in that it, too, appeals to consequences, I shall not quarrel, as long as it is acknowledged to be a much more complex test of consequences than the utilitarian. And if it is further charged that the difference between the two tests is only one of degree of complexity, again I shall not quarrel, as long as it is conceded that such difference in degree may make all the difference between an adequate and an inadequate view of naturalistic ethics. In brief, the pragmatic test of consequences which fits the requirement of a double-aspect theory of ethics must be more inclusive than the conventional one of avowed utilitarians, who at heart consider the consequences of actions only as they affect human happiness or unhappiness, as if nothing else really mattered in life.

In closing, let me say that this bare outline of an attempt at a possible synthesis of the Kantian and Utilitarian systems of ethics *in naturalistic terms* calls for greater elaboration, obviously. But even with all its bareness as it stands, it may prove to be valuable in one or two respects. For one thing, the emphasis the double-aspect version of naturalistic ethics places on the conflicting possibilities of action (the tragic element in life) may throw some light on what might otherwise be a big mystery for psychiatry, namely, the high percentage of the mentally ill inside and outside of our hospitals today. We could say many trite things about human life and its difficulties, but what we say about it does not change its problematic nature. Here at least the existentialists are on the right track. And finally, I like to think of my suggestion of a double-aspect theory of ethics as a sort of counterpart in moral philosophy of Spinoza's double-aspect theory of metaphysics. Whether this is merely a fond illusion on my part, the important thing as I see it is that the urgent task of naturalistic philosophy in the years to come is to show that its moral insights, when properly understood and fully developed, *can* help mankind find a reasonable way to live under any and all circumstances, favorable or not. For who in the long run is better equipped philosophically than the thoroughgoing critical naturalist to teach men in an Atomic Age what tremendous possibilities for good or ill are latent in human nature and culture?

QUESTIONS FOR STUDY AND DISCUSSION

1. What is the relation of ethical naturalism to British utilitarianism?
2. What are Romanell's objections to utilitarian ethics?
3. Is the pursuit of justice basically a dimension of the pursuit of happiness?
4. How does Kant differ from Mill regarding the attainment of happiness?
5. How does Romanell propose to harmonize the Kantian and utilitarian systems of ethics?
6. Is Romanell's test for compossibility any less pragmatic than Dewey's instrumentalism?

William R. Dennes

WILLIAM R. DENNES is Mills Professor of Intellectual and Moral Philosophy
at the University of California, Berkeley. Born in Healdsburg, California,
in 1898, he holds degrees from the University of California, Oxford
University, and New York University. From 1948 to 1955 he was Dean
of the Graduate Division at Berkeley and taught previously at Yale,
Harvard, and Stanford Universities. He is the author of *Civilization and
Values* (1945), *Conflict* (1946), *Meaning and Interpretation* (1950), and
Some Dilemmas of Naturalism (1960).

Reason and Moral Imperatives

How shall we best interpret the meaning of moral imperatives? Let us consider the following as examples: Be fair; We *ought* to carry out whatever
we promise; It is every man's *duty,* as C. I. Lewis [1] has argued, to take into
account as much relevant knowledge as he can when he decides on a course
of action; We *must* not make exceptions in our own favor in applying
moral rules; and so on.

Perhaps nothing is plainer than that no single sort of standard interpretation will be adequate for all of these. Each of them, and many other instances of moral imperatives, will require different detailed explications,
and also different detailed justifications. So whatever we may say generally
about the factors relevant to the interpretation and the justification of
moral judgments, even if it should be relatively satisfactory, will need a
great deal of concrete specification in every actual application, or illustration, of it. A man asks himself in specific predicaments what he ought to
do; he asks others (including perhaps the wisest and most expert people he
knows) what he ought to do; he asks what his fellow men ought to do, or

---

[1] C. I. Lewis was born in Stoneham, Massachusetts, in 1883. He taught philosophy at
Harvard University from 1920 to 1953, and is noted for his contributions to mathematical logic, epistemology, and ethical theory. A pragmatist and naturalist indebted
to Peirce, James, and Dewey, he is the author of *Mind and World Order* (1929),
Symbolic Logic (1932), and *Analysis of Knowledge and Valuation* (1946). [J.P.D.]

---

be induced to do. The answer he seeks from himself or others is an answer that expresses a moral imperative, in that it states that he and others ought to do this or that.

It has been characteristic of the greater part of recent naturalistic thinking to conceive of human beings, as we are acquainted with them and as we have evidence of their earlier history, as gregarious animals who have come to be what they now are in the course of millions of years of biological development in a changing natural environment. There is nothing in such thinking that does—there is nothing in it that logically could—entail any slightest denial or reduction of any of the differences found (or responsibly inferred) between men and other animals. And certainly among the most striking of those differences are man's use of language and of tools; the range of his curiosity and his efforts and achievements towards satisfying his curiosity; and the extent of his concern about what he ought to do.

It is by and through the use of *language,* and so far as we can imagine only so, that man has been able to extend the scope of his curiosity—to frame hypotheses, to formulate their relations to one another and to what confirms them, and to record and communicate all these and his hopes, fears, and expectations, his lookings-before-and-after—and it is also largely by and through the use of language that all of these procedures have influenced the behavior and the attitudes of human beings in their social relations.

In some ways continuous with symbols, in other ways distinguishable from them, tools have enabled man to extend the confirmation of his beliefs, to develop new beliefs and new sorts of beliefs to confirm, and also to construct new sorts of tools, and by all of these procedures to modify his own activities and the physical structures around him so that he may, for example, still read and write when he is old, may more frequently survive heat, cold, pestilence, and the threat of famine, and may ever more rapidly and easily communicate with his fellows and move among them. But perhaps the greatest difference between men and other animals (surely the greatest difference in respect to its influence, direct and indirect, upon man's joys and sorrows) is the extent to which human beings have developed *conscience*—the interest in and concern about what we ought to do.

Now a philosophical naturalist, like anybody else, may accept the results of biological and anthropological studies and conclude that curiosity and its instruments and its expressions, and responsibility for some sorts of cooperative behavior (for doing what is right), have probably reached the development they have among human beings because they were conducive to the survival and to the multiplication of those individuals, but more especially of those herds in which some individuals' genes were especially favorable to such developments. But whatever account of the historical sources of conscience any philosopher may accept as plausible, his main concern is likely to be to understand what he and others are doing when they utter, and when they accept, moral imperatives—and not merely accept them *de facto,* but accept them (and even dedicate their lives to fulfilling them) *as justified.*

Now when a man says seriously that he and all men ought to be fair in dealings with one another, that all ought to carry out whatever they promise, that it is every man's duty to avoid inflicting needless pain, is it plausible or true to say that he is merely expressing his casual liking for fairness and reliability in conduct and his occurrent dislike of cruelty? I know of no serious philosopher who holds or has held such a view, although it is a favorite pastime to make merry over the silliness of naturalists (like Prall or Stevenson) as if this were their opinion. Indeed, unless animals like us reacted *differentially*—and not only to what is sweet and bitter, bright and dark, hot and cold, but also to objects and to patterns of activity (whatever their immediate qualities or feel may be) that do or do not satisfy deep-seated drives such as those called hunger, thirst, sex, elimination, nurturance, succorance, affiliation, exploratory drives, and so on—unless animals like us reacted differentially and affectively to such objects and patterns of activity, nothing that we would want to call a value question, or a moral question, would arise. It is a brute fact that men do react thus differentially and are not indifferent as, so far as we know, water is indifferent to being boiled or frozen or broken down into its constituents. In the course of our relatively long infancy we appear to develop differential reactions, positive and negative motor-affective attitudes, to a much greater array of kinds of objects and activities than do other sorts of organisms, even though some of the others do react differentially to differences which we are unable to notice except with the aid of elaborate artificial mechanisms. Such differential reactions may produce interjections of delight or dismay; but so far as I can see it is when they come into conflict, and only when they come into conflict, either in our own experience or in what we can make out as the behavior and experience of others, that the question "What *ought* to be done?" can intelligibly arise. I believe the phrase "moral question," or even "genuine moral question," is justified in order to mark a difference—where there is and can be no sharp division—between such questions as those requiring, say, a nonmoral choice between beef and mutton from a restaurant menu, if we have no reason to believe (although a Buddhist might believe, and for him it would be a moral choice) that the choice will make an appreciable difference to the patterns of social living and the kinds of persons in our world, and other choices where there are grounds for believing that they may make appreciable differences in such respects, or where in fact, even apart from adequate grounds, the choices are regarded by our neighbors or, to speak somewhat metaphorically, by our society, as likely to make such differences.

It is not merely or mainly when actions or attitudes triggered by basic drives like hunger and succorance conflict with one another that we ask such moral questions. Much more characteristically, it is when the patterns of living and acting to which we have become habituated, supported by affiliative and other needs, collide with the manifestations of some basic drive like hunger or sex, or confront some total threat to their continuance as from hostile men or nations, or still more, when we consider conflicting alternative sorts of realization, or of alteration, to which the habitual patterns may themselves be susceptible, that we have on our hands genuine moral questions. And not only moral questions, but the further philosophical questions "How can we satisfactorily answer the moral questions?" "How can one acceptably determine what ought to be done?"

A naturalist is likely to answer these philosophical questions by suggesting that the first thing to do is to try to understand the conflict as thoroughly as possible in the time that may be at one's disposal—to make out the content of the socially accepted rules or the habitual action-patterns that are in collision with specific desires, or with external threats, or with other actual, imagined, or proposed patterns of activity. The second thing to do (and the first and second, of course, go on concurrently and influence one another) is to learn as much as one can in the time at one's disposal about the probable consequences that would follow from one or other compromise or resolution of the conflicting factors.

The dilemma that here faces the naturalist is this. Are such steps as those just mentioned precisely the kind of work carried out by the descriptive psychological and social sciences? If so, will theoretical conclusions as to the truth or probability of statements about the consequences of one choice or another constitute an answer to our question—constitute a cognitive determination of what would be right to do, and what would be wrong? Can an assertion about matter of fact after all entail an "ought-statement"? What, in other words, is the bearing of activities called reason on the interpretation and the justification of moral imperatives?

If we should be willing to accept, for all their interweaving, the distinctions discussed [elsewhere] between "Reason I" as the developing and confirming of scientific hypotheses which, so far as they are general, can at best be probable; "Reason II" as logic and mathematics which develop necessary truths as determined by the meanings, or the definitions, of terms that are the ingredients of statements, or the names of statements, but entail and exclude no synthetic beliefs about matters of fact; "Reason III" as elucidation of the meanings of puzzling notions and of the differences, for example, between material science and logic; and "Reason IV" as reasonableness, that is, among other things, the *disposition* to respect science and logic, to develop our tastes and make our moral decisions in the light of the fullest knowledge of relevant factors available to us, to sympathize and cooperate with our fellows in the advancement of such acitvities as, and the spread of such attitudes as, constitute Reason I, II, III, and IV—if we are willing to accept these distinct sorts of activity as all included in what "reason" means, then reason has everything to do with the understanding and the justification of moral imperatives. But we have always to remind ourselves that what I have labeled Reason IV is not an instance of reasoning at all if we choose to confine that name to the work of science and logic and mathematics. It is rather what Hume called it, the disposition to form opinions "after a calm and profound reflection," and to hold them with the degree of "doubt, and caution, and modesty, which in all kinds of scrutiny and decision, ought forever to accompany a just reasoner"—all this is a manifestation of attitudes and preferences and really a matter of feeling, even when the objects of preference are the acitivities I have labeled Reason I, II, and III, that is, science, logic, and philosophical analysis. It is reason in sense IV that Hume, and after him men like Perry and Prall and Stevenson, thought to be the factor in all moral judgments that sets them off from neutral judgments of fact. And it is for this reason that naturalistic philosophers have insisted that moral judgments are not themselves susceptible of truth or falsity or probability, although their cognitive ingredients (as developed by Reason I and II, with any aid available from Reason III) certainly are.

Now we could very easily *say* that reason as logic and as philosophical analysis, or as sharpened attention to ordinary English usage, establishes that it is not only an obligation, but quite necessary, that promises be kept so far as that is in the power of him who makes a promise. And how could reason do this? By arguing that a promise is not really a promise, but some kind of lie or deception; or that the word "promise," as against the phrase "pretended promise," is not actually used of a commitment if it is not kept so far as that is within the power of him who makes the promise. Otherwise he didn't really promise. But such analyses, although they may usefully sharpen our attention, do not help us very much with serious questions. Should I keep a promise, should I tell the truth, when I discover that consequences I abhor would follow—a thug's finding his innocent projected victim, to use a familiar example from casuistry?

But if consequences are relevant to a moral decision, how do we go about reaching probable judgments about them—and upon which of the unlimited sectors of possible consequences should we concentrate our attention? And in just what way do the results bear on the establishment or the justification of a moral judgment? Have any of us any better answer than to say: by showing us the kind of civilization, and the kind of persons, to the development of which we may reasonably expect some some moral choices to be conducive. But what can knowledge do towards establishing which patterns of civilization and of human personality ought to be preferred?

For eighty years and more, anthropologists and sociologists and a good many psychologists were busy destroying the fictions about fixed and original human nature, and in doing so they taught us unforgettable lessons about the variety of institutions, of ways of life, of economic, jural, and moral systems that men have actually developed. But in the past twenty years evidence has accumulated of the manifestation of similar basic drives or needs in the most diverse cultures. These drives or needs of men are here called basic, not only in the sense that they are exhibited in all the human groups we know about, but also in the sense that although all of them may be very variously expressed, thwarting any of them—unless a powerful and non-destructive compensation can be found—leads to paralysis of function and often to the death of the organism concerned. More than this, psychologists have developed progressively confirmed, but still only approximate, hypotheses about the average chronology of the manifestations of various needs, about their conflicts, about the factors that produce conflicts and deviations from normal chronology, about derivative second-order and third-order interests that develop as new phases of basic needs, or as offering substitutes for their satisfaction. And they have learned a good deal, not only about the ways in which basal needs conflict, but also about the ways in which derivative interests conflict—seriously, and often destructively—with basal interests: destructively not merely in the sense of diminishing the satisfaction of those interests, but also in the sense of destroying the health, and even the life of the organisms that may be involved.

If we rely on notions about basic needs in explaining human conduct, we do well to take seriously the lessons that were driven home a generation ago by critics (such as John Dewey) of *simpliste* psychologies of instinct. And of course we must recognize that the doctrine is much less clearly defined and much less adequately confirmed than many of the principles of current physical and biological science appear to be. It is always quite possible that factors other than supposed needs, their interrelations, conditioning, and stimulation may actually be what is operating to produce the specific sorts of human behavior we may be desirous of explaining. But it is also always quite possible that factors other than the fine-scale particles (or the quanta of energy) upon which our physics now relies (and how these have multiplied through the past twenty years!) may actually operate to produce the observable changes in mechanical systems which we try to explain. The difference between the reliability of theories of particles in physics and theories of drives (or needs) in psychology and the social sciences is a difference of degree but not of logical kind.

Now, explicit interests and preferences, so far as we have any knowledge of the matter at all, appear to be resultants (and symptoms) of the operations, the conflicts, and the various patterns of integration of basal needs. It is not surprising, therefore, that any man, whether he be a naturalist philosopher or not, should, on examining his own and other men's interests and preferences, come to approve those which facilitate the satisfaction and integration of the basal needs that generated them. But it is not logically necessary that a naturalist—or any other man—should advance to this attitude of approval and preference. The question is this: when it becomes clear that alternatives lead to physiological and psychological disease, to war, to untimely breakdown, and to death, *is there any better reason* that can be found (or imagined) to justify a man in taking as his norm for evaluating civilizations the degree to which they, with their patterns of living, their arts and sciences, enable men—and are likely to enable men—to understand and to satisfy more fully, more generally, and more reliably, their basic needs? Such needs include many besides those for air, food, drink, elimination, sexual expression. We know man only as we find him, and we have found him nowhere, and in no epoch, in which he has not manifested cravings to explore, to understand, to affiliate, to cooperate, to be loyal, to play, to imagine, to sing, to dance, to produce and enjoy various rhythms, as well as cravings for air, food, drink, rest, shelter, sex, child nurturance and tendance, sleep, and pain avoidance. The needs for knowledge, beauty, and cooperation are thus as basal as those for air, food, and sex. And not only in the sense of being as widespread. They are as basal in the further sense that extreme frustration of them leads to the derangement and even the death of the organism. To be sure, if you frustrate totally a man's need for food or for air, his activities are very quickly deranged, and soon thereafter terminate. If you frustrate his needs for affiliation (as our own culture does in so many ways) and for understanding, you get, after a longer period, such results as love strangled by aggressions which, in the mistreatment of children, in wars, and in other cruel ways, lead to death (a slower and in some respects more agonizing death) just as surely as does asphyxiation or starvation.

The tentative conclusions of our psychologists for the most part confirm and extend, rather than radically alter, the opinions generally held in our time by men of common sense, of average literacy, and of good will. Can we conceive of any better grounds to stand on? Is the notion of satisfaction of basal needs the best normative conception to employ in evaluating civilizations? And would the adoption of this norm transform the task of moral intelligence into the objective and scientific one of determining the facts and the probabilities with respect to the satisfaction of those needs, in various patterns of group living, and the relevance of moral choices to the maintenance and development of such patterns? What are the main objections to this normative concept?

One objection springs to mind immediately. If all we know about men's needs and interests is what we observe (or infer) to be, or to have been, men's actual behavior (molar and molecular), then *whatever* men do, *whatever* patterns of civilization they develop will all equally be outgrowths, expressions, and satisfactions of their needs, and all equally good; for what is not in this sense *needed* just does not come into being in human history. Therefore, it is urged again, we need norms and criteria that are independent of the facts of human behavior in order to evaluate those facts significantly.

This criticism is an example of the sort of partial insight for which there ought to be a name, as there is a name for half-truths. The criticism rightly recognizes that no naturalist evaluations are final or are immune to modification. But it falsely infers from this fact a principle very dubious even with respect to its meaning: the principle that, if we are to criticize and modify naturalistic evaluations, then there must be a higher and more authoritative type of evaluation than the naturalistic from the vantage ground of which we can carry out our criticisms and our modifications of them. So far as I can make out, attempts to specify what the higher type is have not succeeded in demarcating it, seriously and recognizably, from the expression of preferences. The critics are indeed quite right in pointing out that the judgment "It is good that hunger should be satisfied" is not the same thing as—and does not mean—the occurrence of a need for food, or the satisfaction (by eating) of such a need. The judgment is much more likely to be (a) the verbal symbolization of our having, and recognizing, many, many needs and interests besides the need for food; and (b) the symbolization of the conviction that if the need for food is not satisfied, all (or most of) these other needs will, in various ways and to various degrees, be frustrated; and (c) the expression of disapproval of such frustrations.

Many have answered that it is not by its bearing upon the satisfaction of other needs that we evaluate the satisfaction of a specific need, but by its contribution to the realization of ideals like those of truth and justice, or to the achievement of an integrated personality, which is no mere organization of needs and satisfactions, but a metaphysical or moral presupposition of their significance, on a level higher than theirs and with a justification which does not depend upon them, *their* justification, on the contrary, depending upon it.

Can we answer here that the genesis of an ideal is irrelevant to its content and its validity? That at some stage in the natural history of thought an event of discernment occurs (having a content which is no part of natural history, and an authority which does not depend upon any spatial or temporal events), and that what supervenes, in this act of discernment, is insight into objective excellence?

If we do say these things, would there be any serious grounds for anybody else to accept, or to comply with, what we thus report as our insight, except whatever empirical evidence there might be that such compliance would probably open the way to a fuller realization of the values he in fact cherishes, or to a fuller satisfaction of human needs generally?

Actually, the evaluation of patterns of human culture in terms of the satisfaction of basic needs does not oblige us to say either that all patterns are equally good, since all satisfy some needs, or that, if some are really better than others, it must be because they approach some other norm than the satisfaction of needs. Where what satisfies some needs nevertheless leads to conflict, frustration, and the judgment that all is not well, is it not because other needs are blocked by it, and it is these others that are speaking out in our criticisms?

It is, of course, well known that different patterns of civilized living develop, satisfy, and frustrate different interests and needs, and that men have managed to survive in the various patterns of group living for longer or shorter periods. Not only have they survived! The influential and articulate participants in each pattern have tended to be happy, and have celebrated theirs as the best of civilizations. For obviously, or even truistically, it is persons who are well adjusted to a given social order that rise to eminence in it. The badly adjusted drop into relative insignificance, or migrate, or even die, unless by an exceedingly aggressive drive to otherthrow and transform it they succeed in altering the social order to one that better fits their pattern of personality. Of those who survive and thrive, each quite sincerely finds the pattern of his own group life admirable. It is such facts as these that have prompted so many critical minds, from the ancient Sophists to Aldous Huxley (of the day before yesterday, not today) to veer away from every doctrine of native human needs, to develop the myth that man's nature is infinitely plastic, and to adopt a historical and cultural relativism according to which the most we could ever say is that some patterns of living nourish some interests and others—others!

Now such conclusions are intolerable to a serious intelligence. That is why we all sympathize with the motives and efforts of the thinkers, ancient and modern, who have sought by various metaphysics of authoritative norms to do two things: (1) to escape such relativism as is illustrated by the statement that all we can meaningfully say, when we evaluate National Socialist policies of the 1930's and 1940's in Germany, is that to the Nazis many aspects of our ways of living were offensive, whereas to most of us many of theirs were; and (2) to defend the conviction that the higher values, such as those of science and the fine arts, are those in relation to which the satisfaction of biological needs is to be justified, and not vice versa. The rendering of values as functions of human needs is thus plagued by the *reductio ad absurdum:* whatever anyone says that human needs require for their satisfaction, anyone else can totally dismiss, simply by saying that he has needs which require its elimination or even its reversal. But the metaphysics of objective norms—developed in the course of a quest for a kind of certainty—do not seem to have answered this *reductio* effectively. On the other hand, empirical studies of human behavior in various patterns of civilization, while they give us no authority to say, "You are absolutely wrong irrespective of relations to human needs," to the man who might claim (as did Gabriele d'Annunzio) [2] that his very special and distinguished needs ought to take precedence over the needs of the many, of the vulgar, or over the basal needs of all mankind, nevertheless do give us grounds for saying that (a) unless he can integrate with the needs and interests of others the special needs which he seeks to satisfy, he will not be able to satisfy them at all fully or securely, any more than a poet writing in a tongue known only to himself could achieve the expression which he craves; and (b) the frustration of the basal needs of others leads to re-

---

[2] Gabriele d'Annunzio (1863–1938): Italian author and patriot, whose works include poetry, short stories, dramatic pieces, and novels. [J.P.D.]

sentments, aggression, breakdowns in health, war—from the results of which, if they are widespread in the world, no man can escape.

Let us turn our attention to the second major objective of many of the non-naturalistic metaphysics of value. That objective has been to establish that the higher values, mediated by reflection and symbolization—such values as those of science and art—are those in terms of which the satisfaction of biological needs is to be justified, and not vice versa.

Would that civilization be desirable in which mathematics, music, jurisprudence, painting were brought by an elite to what experts might call exceptionally high development, but in which most of the population were not only ignorant, but also ill-nourished, overworked, and sexually starved or degraded? On the other hand, would a civilization be desirable in which all the participants were perfectly comfortable, their "biological needs" satisfied, but their imaginations unstirred and unexpressed in song and poetry and plastic art, their curiosity not developed into what we should call serious and extensive science? Are the "higher civilized activities" best regarded (1) as instumental to, or (2) as quite independent of, or (3) as inimical to, or (4) as the justifying ends of, the activities by which men satisfy their "simpler" biological needs? Dewey's view on this issue was so enlightening that, familiar as it is, we cannot recall it too often. He held that all four of these positions are theoretically unsatisfactory and also actually dangerous both to the so-called "ideal interests" and to the satisfaction of simpler biological needs. In order to be effective *in their own terms,* he argued, the highly civilized activities must be firmly rooted in men's basal needs, and must deal in large part—directly or indirectly—with the concrete tensions and conflicts which develop in the struggle to satisfy those needs. Art and science that cut themselves off from such roots become trivial, however technically expert their development may be. But the arts and sciences, when thus healthily rooted, are not merely instrumental to the enlightenment and the satisfaction of pre-existent basal needs; they also generate new interests—interests especially precious to many men. But these new interests can never, without disastrous consequences, be taken as eliminating (and replacing) the basal needs, their conflicts, and the problems thus engendered, which were in all cases their foundations, and also the ladders of their ascent.

The four alternative views just formulated may sound like merely dialectical variations upon the possible relations between ideal interests and the commoner human needs. But they are much more than that. They are tragically serious alternatives—and every one of them is misleading. What are usually called the higher civilized activities—cooperation in the development and dissemination of the sciences, fine arts, criticism, philosophy—all depend upon (and some of them are largely constituted by) a marked development of activities of symbolizing. It is by means of these that human beings emancipate themselves from the tyranny of the present and the local, share the experience of other ages and of other nations, preserve and interpret their own observations, consider possibilities unbounded in range, predict the future and guide themselves in shaping it. We do not see things clearly if our eyes are pressed smack up against them. The effectiveness of symbolization depends in part upon the distance introduced, by general notions and by rules of procedure, between us and the concrete events and objects we want to understand. The magnificent convenience of some mathematical constructs, when used in science and in technology, illustrates this point; and, except for the satisfaction of a kind of aesthetic curiosity, I suppose that such convenience is the serious justification of mathematics as a theoretical discipline. By means of it, forces can be reckoned, of magnitudes so immense or so minute (and above all so complex in structure) that the measuring, remembering, or imagining of them as concrete individual factors would be too much for our powers. On occasions when we are tempted to say—in contradiction to Saint Paul—that knowledge is good in itself apart from our appreciation of it or our use of it, that truth is an *absolute* value, I think we are usually meaning, by the truth thus praised, true or probable beliefs about matters we judge to be important: knowledge used, or usable, to produce effects we approve.

It would be hard to exaggerate the importance of cognitive factors in serious efforts to determine what we ought to do. When the questions that face us are questions about national policies, about improving our schools, about what may appear to be conflicts among our personal commitments and responsibilities and desires, we find quite generally an almost overwhelming need (1) to get clearer about the *meanings* of the sentences that describe our predicaments (and this involves distinguishing as well as we can hopes and fears, which are factual occurrences of one kind, from beliefs about the states of affairs that may be the objects of hopes and fears); and (2) as the meanings are made clearer, to explore the evidence for and against the truth or probability, not only of the beliefs just mentioned, but also of a very wide range of beliefs about the consequences of these states of affairs and also about the consequences of various steps that might be taken to alter them. Thus, in developing and controlling serious moral judgments, we need to avail ourselves of the results of any philosophical work that yields satisfactory conceptions of meaning, of evidence, of truth and probability. And we shall make the best use of such results in the course of actually appropriating, and wherever we can in developing further, knowledge that is not in itself evaluative but neutral—knowledge of the probable effects upon men's lives and work of each of several moral decisions we might make, or might judge that we ought to make. But it will be noticed that such statements as I have just uttered are full of phrases like "best use of," "ought," and the like.

Reasonable people are likely to agree that if we are to develop and to use completer knowledge of the consequences of various patterns of activity, it is important that investigation go on vigorously in a kind of middle area. To be sure, notions articulate or inarticulate and generally pretty vague, of what is important as logical structure in explanatory systems and as to what is important as knowledge bearing on areas of human conflicts and needs, guide and ought to guide inquiry. But within such very tenuous guidance, we like to say that intelligence should range *freely*—that only if we knew in advance the answers to all our questions could we prescribe in advance any rigid guide lines to inquiry. If a love of Greek poetry leads a man to thorough linguistic studies we may rejoice, but if these should lead him into a total preoccupation with listing and relisting the frequencies of occurrence of an enclitic, we are likely to regret that outcome. It is the old story of a man's energies shifting from productive work to the miser's preoccupation with accumulating more and more of what may, in some economic structures, have been the necessary condition of his doing productive work. Some years ago when I asked a zoologist who wanted a great deal of money to enlarge a collection of California quail how comprehensive such a collection ought to be, he answered: *"Ideally* it should contain absolutely all individuals of the species, for as long as one is left out I cannot be sure that that very one might not justify the most significant alterations of accepted theories." In order to understand living birds as fully as possible, none should be left alive for all should have been dissected in laboratories or preserved in museums!

Now we don't have much trouble in dealing with such extremes, although we know that we can never quite rule out the possibility that the grammarian's preoccupation with his enclitic or the zoologist's hankering for more and more specimens to examine may turn out to be the condition of interpretations or discoveries of the greatest theoretic interest or practical importance. Intellectuals may split hairs, but it is some of them who also split atoms. Lately some humanists, horrified by the threats to man's existence which scientific discoveries have made it possible to mount, have urged that scientific research be restricted by government to areas not susceptible of such dangerous applications. Scientists have hastened to reply that the highest values of intellectual curiosity and intellectual integrity require that no limits be put upon inquiry, as if in some sense knowing more were absolutely better than knowing less. Is a reasonable view importantly different from both of these? Should we say that knowledge as such never determines what use will be made of it, and cannot therefore be blamed for what we may wish to call evil applications of it; that none of us really wants to identify knowledge with value, with the highest good; for none of us, in saying that knowledge is good means by that statement merely that knowledge is knowledge. Knowledge may as such satisfy a set of needs lumped together as curiosity, and its pursuit and its achievements may delight many of us and to some degree most of us. Nothing but scientific knowledge itself—not our hopes and fears or other attitudes—can support serious predictions either of the dire consequences or of the happier consequences that may be the result of some of its applications. There is some hope that scientific investigation may succeed in explaining the factors that influence men towards making destructive, and the factors that influence them towards making humane, uses of scientific knowledge. But in saying all this it is clear that we are saying that knowledge itself is just knowledge, that some men delight intensely in developing it, and perhaps all appreciate it to some degree; but that there is no sense at all in pretending that it is as such good, or the highest good, and that there is no certainty whatever that by something that we might call an unforeseen accident (if any of us should survive long enough to call it by that or any other name), some operation involved in the course of sincere attempts to advance knowledge, might not sweep mankind off the face of the earth. If such an unforeseen occurrence swept mosquitoes off the face of the earth, or if deliberate steps eradicated the virus of poliomyelitis, or if deliberate steps killed all the California quail but taught us, say, how to free men from the wonderful complexities of the arthritides, most of us (but not, I suppose, the mosquitoes) would rejoice—unless, of course, the general ecology were such that, being put out of balance by the eradication of one plague, it allowed something worse to develop. But if it swept mankind off the face of the earth? Even that Tolstoy was willing to face when he urged that human beings give up the carnal affections—the world would be a fairer place without such degenerates as sexual lust had made of us, and God had shown that he could create whatever creatures (including men) he wanted without the stain which Tolstoy, in his old age, felt was so ruinous to mankind. In other words, if a man is willing to accept the consequences, there are no consequences that theoretic knowledge could present to him which would as such prove the wrongness of a moral judgment.

If we say that knowledge is not in itself good (any more than a sharp knife is in itself good—a sharp knife that lends itself equally to murder, to sculpture, or to healing surgery), we are not thereby denying that we appreciate knowledge and some of its uses. But we are saying that knowledge is only one fairly vaguely defined set of activities among others that satisfy human needs, and unless we also mean that we approve the satisfaction of human needs, our statement is no more a value judgment than is the statement that water quenches fire. The truth of a belief about fission of uranium or plutonium may satisfy our curiosity, but beyond that it is every bit as compatible with our using it to make our planet wholly uninhabitable as it is with a very limited use of it to produce power in regions of the earth where power is needed to give a humane amplitude to life.

One of the hardest lessons we have to learn is that we can make sense (and indeed we must make sense, for probably we have no alternative) of approving a great number of kinds of activity, cognitive and other, without pretending to be able to specify their just proportion in relation to one another. It is not unreasonable to condemn eccentric pedantry—from counting grains of sand to counting and recounting the occurrences of enclitics or types of match folders—although we have had too much experience of what had been denounced as aberration coming to be recognized as illuminating insight not to realize the fallibility of our judgments in these areas. It is not unreasonable to condemn extravagant flourishes in music or painting or poetry or women's clothes, but we must always admit while we do so that what may now appear excessively rococo might be developed into what we should appreciate as beautiful adornment. Who can say, for example, just what combination of firmness, permissiveness, detachment, and love makes the good father, but who will deny that some combination of these qualities, if sensitive to varying circumstances, does?

To construe value judgments as expressions of approval does not (as logically it could not) prevent us from approving and from energetically supporting kinds of activity that satisfy basic human needs in ways that produce the least destructive conflicts; does not prevent us (indeed requires us if we are in earnest) from undertaking the most thorough and systematic investigations of the needs and interests of men in relation to their cosmic setting and of the probable results of various patterns of responding to such needs; does not prevent us (indeed, we can never safely take moral holidays) from using the rhetoric of duty and obligation to express and to invite others to share our best-informed and deepest-felt commitments, provided that we recognize all the while that our needs and interests may themselves change with cognitive enlightenment and with the functioning of the very structures that may have been developed to express them. Does naturalism—does intelligence—face the dilemma of establishing what are called absolute or objective norms of value or, if it fails at that, deliquescing not only in cultural relativism, but in moral chaos? I have left until last the hardest lesson—which I certainly have not fully learned myself. If we interpret the notions of meaning and truth as we have suggested, and if we find ourselves constrained to interpret value judgments as differing from cognitive judgments in that they are expressions of delight, of approval, of commendation, of love—then how can we distinguish *reasonable* moral judgments, reasonable duties, from capricious preferences and whims?

Who, except perhaps a writer of advertising copy, would pretend that there is one precise balance of specific size, specific color, specific tartness, specific sweetness, specific firmness with tenderness of texture, specific thinness and easy detachability of rind, specific resistance to decay (keeping qualities), specific digestibility, and so on, that constitutes the *right* conception of a perfect orange? But who would deny that some combination of degrees (not infinitely variable) of a fair number or of all of these characteristics is what is usually meant in the United States by "a top quality orange"? Who (again, except our obsessed advertiser) would pretend to specify *just* the combination of power, quiet operation, size, shape, weight, firmness of springing, quickness and smoothness of braking deceleration, etc., etc., that constitutes the right conception of a perfect automobile? But who would deny that within a range of combinations in which none of these characteristics may vary without limits, lie the kinds of vehicles we mean by the phrase "good motor cars"? An orange too tough for any average man to chew, an automobile with too little power to propel its weight up a steep hill, these are not good whatever other characteristics they may have.

Who will pretend, within our economic structure or any other, to determine precisely what the just wage is—the just access to goods and services, to education and medical care, and so on (since all of these must in all situations be something less than unlimited); the just participation of each (or of any) man? Yet who will deny—certainly no one needs feel that the situation described requires him to deny—the importance of taking pains to make that participation more and more just: that is, more and more such as will be conducive to the realization and dissemination of the values he prizes? And who will deny that anyone who seriously considers many possible combinations of characteristics of oranges or of automobiles, and in the light of learning a lot about their relations offers the judgment that "such and such is the best orange" or "such and such is the best car" may induce people to appreciate, or may divert people from appreciating, more than they had previously done the sort of thing he thus describes and praises. And who will deny that serious studies of the probable consequences of various patterns of participation of members of a community in using the goods and services available in the community, and in determining the policies that should guide such use, may not only help us to find ways to realize what we may very much desiderate, but may also lead us to devote ourselves to values of which we were hitherto unaware?

Interpreting moral judgments is of course a much more serious and complicated business than interpreting evaluations of oranges and of motor cars. Is it more serious because it aims to deal with patterns of men's living and acting in communities, patterns to which the uses of oranges and motor cars and, as Plato thought, all other human actions, are subordinate? And more complicated because there are no limits to the knowledge that may be relevant to the judgment? And is it still the case that such judgments, for all the cognitive factors implied by them or relevant to them, are essentially expressions of delight or of commendation or the like, which we would not want to call true, false, or probable any more than we would use such adjectives of locutions like "please open the window" or "God help us"?

The risks that accompany our activities of symbolizing are in general quite as great as the advantages; for by means of symbols we can take account of other symbols, as well as of nonsymbolic experiences and actions. That is, in some respects, a very useful job to do. But since symbols are generally so much better behaved—so much easier to get hold of and manage—than are the sorts of processes originally symbolized, it is very easy for us to transfer our whole interest to the symbolizing devices, which may thus become substitutes for—instead of instruments for use in the explanation of—the concrete processes which we need to understand and to control. An interest in symbolic structures is innocent enough and may yield most helpful insights. But to treat symbolic structures as substitutes for what they symbolize always leads to mischief, and sometimes to dreadful mischief. Even if we maintain a reference outside of symbols for our symbolizing, there is always the further danger that, where our thinking achieves extensive symbolic distance from its referents, we shall become insensitive to the human importance (as serving or not serving basal needs) of the concrete processes thought about.

Could generals and their scientific and technical staffs carry on wars if they were constantly as vividly aware of the sufferings of thousands or millions of human beings—wounded soldiers, drowning sailors, starved, diseased, and radiation-mutilated civilians—as when those generals may encounter, let us say, the broken bodies of their own sons? But the principles of strategy are *another* matter. By virtue of them, generals can consider dispassionately steps that may lead to the consequences I have mentioned. If a country has been doing a good (and that means an improving) job of civilized living, and is invaded or threatened by a destructive aggressor, its members may well rejoice that symbolization, in the forms of science, engineering, and strategic theory, enables their generals to plan maximum programs of destruction that may deter their enemy, as those same military leaders could not do if the individual agony of every probable victim were vividly before their imagination. But if no leaders on any side were able to substitute symbolization—scientific, technological, strategic, along with talk of historical destiny, dialectical necessity, and national glory—for thinking directly about the hideous actions, the sufferings, and the destruction of individual persons, it might well be that *none* could plan and carry out a war.

It is not at all my purpose to deal in horror, but only to bring home the dangerous as well as the extremely useful ways which our symbols have of cloaking from us the concrete actual effects of many of our most important actions, and the concrete actual referents of many of our most ingenious theories. And it is not in juvenile or inept theorizing, but precisely in our most highly developed thought, that we are most in danger of being cut off by our instruments of explanation from the very things that we are, or ought to be, trying to think about. The fact that a society's leaders and their influential advisers—and to a lesser extent all the rest of us—deal in highly theoretical and symbolically mediated considerations of strategy, and of relations of political, economic, and military forces, is all too likely to prevent us from conceiving adequately the concrete individual experiences involved, so that we can judge whether the balance of satisfaction over frustration of human needs justifies the decisions we take and the policies that we may be willing to support at the cost of innumerable lives.

But this is a familiar story. People have learned the grammars of foreign languages in order to understand the science, literature, history, philosophy, expressed in them. But comparative grammar may easily come to monopolize a man's attention to the point where it stands in the way of his understanding anything else. The same comments apply, *mutatis mutandis,* to symbolizing in art, ritual, government, philosophy, metaphysics. All these have been developed by organisms who are unusual (a) in the complexity of their needs and the sensitivity of their reactions, and (b) in the long period of their infantile dependence upon adults—parents or others—which some students conclude engenders the emotional ambivalence of love and resentment towards those who so long support—but also control—us, and also towards the institutions that later serve as parent substitutes. In what we call civilized communities, economic dependence upon parents, and consequent control by them, commonly continues long after the young are psychologically and physiologically fit for—and in need of—a larger measure of autonomy. Our very long infancy and adolescence, it is held, induce a strong feeling of insecurity when finally we do emerge from the guidance and control of our elders. So far, in what we know of human history, the most effective remedy for this insecurity may have been the sense of solidarity nourished by life in some tribal cultures—in some fairly small societies. In the last few millennia the civilizing activities, particularly the scientific, have broken down, for the intelligent, such tribal solidarity. But these civilizing activities have yielded, in the form of reliable knowledge of the immense impersonal world, a partial substitute for what they have destroyed, and, through the arts, they have rendered some parts of the surface of the world more immediately satisfying. They are capable of developing programs of cooperative work for the better housing, better health, better education of mankind, which might be complete and magnificent substitutes for tribal solidarity. But where civilized, symbol-mediated activities cut us off from what they began by symbolizing—still more, where they become barriers to the satisfaction of basal needs, barriers either as substitutes, as compensations, as escapes, as rationalizing denials of the existence of the needs, or as means of unduly strengthening taboos and restraints which may, in proper measure, have been indispensable to the development of civilized activities—there civilized activities contribute to making us more anxious, more insecure, more estranged from one another, more aggressive, more violently destructive, not only than are some primitive tribes, but than is compatible with physiological and psychological health. And a good example of a highly civilized activity which seems to imperil human values may be the second-order symbolizing activity which constitutes those theories that defend the higher civilized activities as ends in themselves.

A. L. Kroeber has recently written:

> That needs exist and that they underlie, and precondition, culture is indubitable. It is obvious that culture cannot be explained or derived from needs except very partially. Hunger has to be satisfied; but how it is satisfied by human beings can never be derived from their being hungry, nor from their specific bodily construction. Over-

whelmingly, the how can be understood only with reference to the remainder of the culture adhered to, present and past; modified somewhat . . . by interaction with the opportunities afforded by natural environment. Moreover, large segments of culture begin to operate, to come into being, only after the primal needs have been satisfied, have had their tensions reduced or alleviated.

I think Kroeber is right. Knowledge that a pattern of living satisfies basic human needs and develops a minimum of hostile aggression, is probable knowledge of fact and is morally neutral. Until the factor of love, of approval, of commendation supervenes we have still no judgment of the goodness of a civilization or of the rightness of the moral choices that may tend to support it or to damage it.

But what about the priority of the factor of "oughtness"? What about the notion that approval is not only groundless but indeed meaningless unless we have first (and independently) recognized that the state of affairs we come to approve *ought* to be brought into existence, or *ought* to be conserved? Such "oughtness" may very well be experienced as a kind of echo of the voices of parents or teachers or other authority figures. And rather generally, what they induce us to feel ought-to-be, conforms very exactly with what is customarily done and approved in the society we share with them. The results of psychological and psychoanalytic, as well as of sociological and anthropological investigations of the phenomena of conscience, incomplete as they are, are hardly to be ignored by any of us, and least of all by those who would make the recognition of "oughtness" essential to value judgments generally or to moral judgments in particular. Sometimes what one means by judging that something ought to be, or ought to be done (and indeed, whether one likes it or not, as in the case of some very dangerous, difficult, and exhausting chore) is that one believes (1) that failure to do it will damage and diminish the cooperation of people in such activities as realize or serve the values one prizes, or that tend to satisfy with a minimum of incidental hostility and destructiveness, the basic needs of human beings, or will threaten the general maintenance of moral rules and the solidarity of the society; and (2) that its being (or its being done) will in some degree serve to realize such values.

But is there any way to make out which of these senses of "ought," or any other sense of "ought," is such that when an instance of it is experienced it *ought* to determine our moral judgments? On the whole, the man whose conscience mirrors rigidly the influence of the authority figures of his infancy and youth, or reflects rigidly the customary approvals of his community, and is not sensitive to the bearing of many sorts of new situations and of possibilities probably not dreamed of in the past that shaped him, would seem to be in large part an enemy of the living activities by which, in changing situations, the needs of men may be harmoniously satisfied. On the other hand, a man who is so widely aware of the ranges of possibility which make up what Emily Dickinson called that "richer house than prose," and who recognizes that the knowledge which could be relevant to a choice cannot be limited in advance—since we do not know what knowledge might not prove relevant—can easily be paralyzed, unable to make any choice or to act at all. Some persons and some human cultures have tended to the one extreme of positive choice and positive action in rigid conformity to folkways or authoritarian commands interpreted as conscience, others to the other extreme of a meditation on possibilities and an unquenchable thirst for knowledge which could lead to the indefinite postponement of moral decision and of moral action. Can we, by constructing a philosophy or any other sort of theoretical structure, establish that one or other of these extremes or any precisely demarcated middle course is intrinsically right?

Some of us may judge that the most admirable use of language is its use by a man well-habituated to its established forms, conscious of the echoes of great poetry and great theoretical insights as well as the echoes of everyday use associated with much of its structure, and yet able to use the language with some freshness and originality; but we may be quite unable to draw boundary lines to demarcate these ingredients of his thought and speech. Analogously, many of us would judge him to be the morally responsible and morally admirable man who, conscious and appreciative of the customary approvals and commitments of his society and of the necessity that there be *some* rules, is also sensitive to the respects in which these commitments may hinder the free play of intelligence in developing the artistic expression, the sciences, and the practical policies that may, in new situations or in old, be required if the basic needs of men are not to be unnecessarily thwarted, and consequent destructive hostilities produced. But the basic philosophical question remains. Can we interpret satisfactorily the judgment that expresses moral approval of some particular blending of conformity and innovation—the judgment that says of any particular instance of rigid conformity, of extravagant openmindedness, or of a blending of these, that it ought to be approved or enacted—can we interpret such a judgment satisfactorily except as expressing, along with whatever beliefs may be suggested or implied, preference for the instance in question and for its probable consequences over what we are able in the time at our disposal to understand as alternatives?

Those philosophers, like the late David Prall, who have stressed immediate liking as the essential factor in evaluation, have not only insisted that one needs to be clearly and sharply aware of what it is that one is liking, and that one will probably, though by no means necessarily, achieve more of such awareness as one learns more of the genesis and context of what one is liking, but have also taken much more pains, it seems to me, to explore and to set forth the structure and qualities and context of what they thus like than did their critics, some of whom argued that cognitive factors are and should be decisive in value judgments. They took more pains; and I submit that a comparison of their accounts, say, of the aesthetic objects and of the ways of life that they approved and recommended will often show that they were more successful in such explorations than were their critics. Read Prall and Bosanquet for example, on a similar moral issue, or on the same or a similar poem or musical composition, and their works will in these respects speak for themselves. There is always a risk of identifying dullness and slowness of wit with moral seriousness when we are tempted to say that in a wise and good man's immediate likings, for which he may not formulate reasons, less knowledge is operating than in the case of another who tells himself or tells us a great deal about the causes, consequences, and context of what he approves.

The rhetoric of large views is all about us. But it is not often that we have either the time or the knowledge to consider moral decisions effectively in the light of large views. So far as we ever do approach such considerations, can we do anything more or other than ask ourselves in the end: what kinds of persons, what kinds of societies, what kinds of total human community, is one choice or another the more likely to develop or to hinder developing? And so far as we know, or can find—by the ordinary reasoning of science, of theoretical explanation, and not by any special kind of reason called moral reasoning—probable answers to these questions, what can our moral judgment express beyond such probable scientific knowledge except our sincere choice and our genuine affective commitment to one kind of life and one kind of world, and to all that is likely to nourish them?

QUESTIONS FOR STUDY AND DISCUSSION

1. In Dennes' view, what are the basic problems confronting naturalistic ethics?
2. Are moral affirmations nothing more than an expression of approval?
3. For Dennes, what role can science play in the establishment of moral norms?
4. Is knowledge of consequences the only factor required for moral judgment?
5. Why can't the desirable be identified with what in fact is desired?
6. What function can linguistic analysis perform in ethics?
7. On what basis is Dennes able to distinguish between reasonable moral judgments and capricious preferences and whims?
8. How are the larger aims and goals of life to be chosen? Does Dennes provide a satisfactory answer to this question?

TOPICS FOR DISCUSSION AND TERM PAPERS

A.

1. What are the basic features of the naturalistic outlook in philosophy?
2. How does a naturalistic outlook affect one's theory of values?
3. What are the basic points of agreement and difference between James's pragmatism, Dewey's instrumentalism, and Romanell's theory of compossibility?
4. How does the naturalist propose to establish ethics as a science?
5. What problems confront the naturalist in his attempt to make ethics scientific?
6. Why does the naturalist reject religion as a source of reliable values?
7. Does naturalism successfully resolve the difficulties encountered in utilitarian ethics?
8. Does the employment of data gained from biology, psychology, and sociology make ethics scientific?
9. How can one successfully move from *what is* to *what ought to be?*
10. What are the strong and weak points of naturalistic ethics? Has naturalistic ethics moved significantly beyond Mill's utilitarianism?

B.

1. Does naturalism recognize any ethical universals? Compare the Socratic and naturalistic attitudes toward moral norms.
2. What is the basic reason for the naturalist's dissatisfaction with the classical-Christian tradition in ethics?
3. Regarding the origin, nature, and end of man, Marxism and naturalism seem to be in basic agreement. How does one account, then, for difference in ethical outlook?
4. Does naturalistic ethics differ in any important respects from the situation ethics of contemporary existentialism?
5. Compare Hook's soft determinism with Sartre's account of freedom.
6. Is an emotive ethics the logical outcome of the naturalistic approach to morality?

RECOMMENDED READINGS

Primary Sources

Dennes, William R. *Some Dilemmas of Naturalism.* New York: Columbia University Press, 1960. Based on the Woodbridge Lectures that Dennes gave at Columbia University in 1958. The author separates several strands of naturalistic thought and shows how they have led to certain basic dilemmas. The work contains Dennes' essay "Reason and Moral Imperatives."

Dewey, John. *Democracy and Education.* New York: Macmillan Co., 1916. One of Dewey's most influential books, relating his value theory to education in a democratic society.

Dewey, John. *Experience and Nature.* La Salle, Ill.: Open Court Publishing Co., 1925. Presents Dewey's theory of nature, man, and values.

————. *Human Nature and Conduct.* New York: Henry Holt and Co., 1922. Subtitled "An Introduction to Social Psychology," this book investigates the role of habit, impulse, and intelligence in the determination of human conduct.

————. *The Quest for Certainty.* New York; Minton, Balch & Co., 1929. A study of the relation of knowledge and action that attempts to define philosophy and establish the role it must play in relation to science and social needs. Chapter 10, "The Construction of the Good," is important for an understanding of Dewey's ethical theory.

————, Sidney Hook, and Ernest Nagel. "Are Naturalists Materialists?" *Journal of Philosophy,* XLII (Sept. 13, 1945), 515–30.

Edel, Abraham. *The Use of Science in Ethics.* Glencoe, Ill.: The Free Press, 1955. A naturalistic approach to the foundations of ethical theory. See especially the chapters on the relevance of biological, psychological, sociological, and historical data to ethics.

————. "Vivas and the Dragons of Naturalism," *Review of Metaphysics,* V (March, 1952), 405–16.

Hook, Sidney. *Education for Modern Man,* 2nd ed. New York: Alfred A. Knopf, 1963. A general theory of education that presents Hook's views on the aims of education and their relation to the democratic social order.

————. "Is Physical Realism Sufficient?" *Journal of Philosophy,* XLI (Sept. 28, 1944), 544–51.

————. *John Dewey: An Intellectual Portrait.* New York: John Day Co., 1939. A faithful and readable summary of Dewey's general philosophy, which can be profitably used for an introduction to the thought of Dewey.

————. *Political Power and Personal Freedom.* New York: Collier Books, 1962. Critical studies in democracy, communism, and civil rights that relate Hook's value theory to some pressing contemporary problems.

————. *The Quest for Being, and Other Studies in Naturalism and Humanism.* New York: St. Martin's Press, 1961. This collection of essays includes the following that are addressed to ethical topics: "Philosophy and Human Conduct," "The Ethical Theory of John Dewey," "Moral Freedom in a Determined World," and "Nature and the Human Spirit."

Romanell, Patrick. *Toward a Critical Naturalism.* New York: Macmillan Co., 1958. Three of the six chapters of this book deal with naturalistic ethics. Although Randall is critical of Dewey's approach to ethics, he remains a naturalist.

Commentaries

Adams, E. M. *Ethical Naturalism and the Modern World View.* Chapel Hill, N.C.: University of North Carolina Press, 1960. Adams examines three streams of naturalistic ethics—classical, emotive, and logical. Although he begins his study convinced that some form of naturalism can be made tenable, he becomes convinced that the basic program itself, and not merely certain ways of carrying it out, is indefensible.

Bernstein, Richard. "Dewey's Naturalism," *Review of Metaphysics,* XII (Dec., 1959), 340–53.

Bertocci, Peter A. "The Logic of Naturalistic Arguments Against Theistic Hypotheses," *Philosophical Review*, LVI (Jan., 1947), 82–87.

Bouwsma, O. K. "Naturalism," *Journal of Philosophy*, XLV (Jan. 1, 1948), 12–22.

Collins, James. *Three Paths in Philosophy*. Chicago: Henry Regnery Co., 1962. See Ch. 8, "How Dewey Became a Naturalist," for an account of the genesis of Dewey's thought from an early idealism to an outright naturalism. Chapter 9, "Humanistic Naturalism in Marx and Dewey," contains an evaluation of Dewey's contribution to philosophy.

Davenport, M. M. "Self-Determination and the Conflict Between Naturalism and Non-naturalism," *Journal of Philosophy*, LVI (June 16, 1959), 633–44.

Ferm, Vergilius. "Christianity: A Naturalistic Viewpoint," *Crozer Quarterly*, VIII (1940), 192–204.

Handy, Rollo. "The Naturalistic 'Reduction' of Ethics to Science," *Journal of Philosophy*, LIII (Dec. 20, 1956), 829–35.

Klausner, Neal W. "Naturalism: Self-conscious and Self-critical," *Review of Metaphysics*, XV (June, 1962), 480–93.

Krikorian, Yervant H., ed. *Naturalism and the Human Spirit*. New York: Columbia University Press, 1944. A platform volume for American naturalism. See especially the essays by Dewey, Randall, Nagel, Hook, Dennes, and Schneider. In subsequent writings many of these authors develop themes presented tentatively within this volume.

Kurtz, Paul W. "Decision Making and Ethical Naturalism," *Journal of Philosophy*, LVIII (Oct. 26, 1961), 693–94.

———. "Naturalistic Ethics and the Open Question," *Journal of Philosophy*, LII (March 3, 1955), 113–28.

Murphy, Arthur E. "John Dewey and American Liberalism," *Journal of Philosophy*, LVII (June 23, 1960), 420–36.

Nagel, Ernest. "Naturalism Reconsidered," *Proceedings and Addresses of the American Philosophical Association*, XXVII. Yellow Springs, Ohio: Antioch Press, 1955.

———. *The Structure of Science*. New York: Harcourt, Brace & World, 1961. Clarifies the meaning of the term "science" within the naturalistic context. Shows the precise sense in which scientific method is applicable in the area of biological, historical, and social studies.

Olson, Robert G. *The Morality of Self-Interest*. New York: Harcourt, Brace & World, 1965. Olson argues that the individual is most likely to contribute to social betterment by rationally pursuing his own long-range interest. He also maintains that prevailing religious views, far from being conducive to moral uprightness, in fact seriously undermine the practice of morality.

Randall, John Herman, Jr. *Nature and Historical Experience*. New York: Columbia University Press, 1958. Although this volume is not specifically concerned with ethical problems, it contains a number of significant essays on nature, mind, and history as an instrument of understanding by one of the foremost American naturalists.

Schilpp, Paul A. *The Philosophy of John Dewey*, 2nd ed. New York: Tudor Publishing Co., 1951. Contains a complete bibliography of Dewey's works, plus a 45-page biography of Dewey written by his daughters from material that he furnished.

Sheldon, W. H. "Critique of Naturalism," *Journal of Philosophy,* XLII (May 10, 1945), 253–70.

Suits, Bernard. "Naturalism: Half-hearted or Broken-backed," *Journal of Philosophy,* LVIII (March 30, 1961), 169–79.

Werkmeister, William H. *A History of Philosophical Ideas in America.* New York: Ronald Press Co., 1949. Locates the pragmatism of James and the instrumentalism of Dewey within the general context of American philosophy.

PART FOUR

Introduction
___

Historical Setting

The Meaning of Ethical Terms and Statements

Moore: Intuitionism

Schlick: Naturalism

Ayer, Stevenson, Toulmin: Emotivism

The Responsibility Issue

Nowell-Smith: The Conditions of Responsibility

Readings
___

MOORE: *What Is Meant by "Good"?*

SCHLICK: *What Is the Meaning of "Moral"?*
Are There Absolute Values?
When Is a Man Responsible?

AYER: *An Emotive Interpretation of Ethical Language*

STEVENSON: *The Nature of Ethical Disagreement*

TOULMIN: *A Critique of A. J. Ayer*

NOWELL-SMITH: *The Meaning of "Could Have Acted Otherwise"*
*The Relation of Responsibility to "Could Have
Acted Otherwise"*

ANALYTIC-POSITIVIST THOUGHT:

Moore
Schlick
Ayer
Stevenson
Toulmin
Nowell-Smith

EDITED BY

Frank Ellis

ST. MARY'S COLLEGE, CALIFORNIA

ANALYTIC-POSITIVIST THOUGHT:
Moore
Schlick
Ayer
Stevenson
Toulmin
Nowell-Smith

Introduction

Historical Setting

Analytic philosophy has a long and distinguished ancestry, going back as far as Plato's analysis of piety in the dialogue *Euthyphro*. The name "analytic philosophy," however, refers to a distinctively twentieth-century philosophical trend, which today is followed widely in the United States and Britain, and much less widely on the Continent. This trend differs from its ancestry in the following way: whereas earlier philosophers regarded analysis as but a preliminary step in the achievement of other, higher goals, analytic philosophers tend to regard analysis as the chief, if not the sole, task of properly conducted philosophical investigation.

Analysis, as that process is understood by analytic philosophers, is essentially an attempt to achieve conceptual and methodological clarity. This meaning, which may be taken as a working definition of analytic philosophy, has several implications. For one thing, analysts—with the notable exception of George Edward Moore (1873–1958), an elder statesman of analytic philosophy—are not metaphysicians, and their reactions to metaphysics range from mild suspicion to militant hostility. The former arises from the belief that metaphysicians traditionally have employed concepts without clarifying their meanings and have attempted to establish truths without sufficiently considering the validity of the methods used. Militant hostility arises from the belief that whatever the metaphysicians are trying to talk about is beyond the realm of the knowable and, consequently, cannot be meaningful. At the same time, while analysts generally esteem the positive sciences, they are not themselves scientists; that is, they do not see their task as that of either discovering facts or establishing any truths about the empirical order. Nor do they profess to offer a philosophy of life, as the philosophers represented in the other parts of this book do. Instead, analysts are concerned with clarifying the meanings and interrelations of concepts and statements used in ordinary life and/or in the positive sciences and with clarifying the methods that are appropriate to the discovery of truth.

This search by analytic philosophy for conceptual and methodological clarity was in large part inaugurated at the turn of the twentieth century by G. E. Moore and Bertrand Russell (b. 1872) as a protest against Hegelian philosophy and, in particular, against the British Hegelian F. H. Bradley (1846–1924), who was at the time the dominant philosophical figure in England. Hegelianism, in its desire to achieve a total system of philosophy and to see reality as a unified whole, has never been unwilling to sacrifice clarity and exactness for the sake of system and unity; in its manifestation in Britain, it developed a language almost incomprehensible to the uninitiated and turned ordinary nouns into names—Reality, Mind, the Absolute —that were supposed to designate a shadowy, yet supremely real, Something Else lying behind the ordinary and familiar. Although Moore and Russell, as students at Cambridge University in 1894, were enthusiastic admirers of Bradley, they both eventually came to feel, each in his own way, that clarity of meaning was a more important task for philosophy than totality of system.

Another major figure in analytic philosophy was Ludwig Wittgenstein (1889–1951), who succeeded Moore in 1937 as professor of Philosophy at Cambridge, and thereafter sought and influenced others to seek ways of eliminating philosophical puzzles and paradoxes through a scrupulously careful use of language. Earlier in his life Wittgenstein influenced the analytic movement in another way; he provided in an extraordinary book called *Tractatus Logico-Philosophicus* (1921) some of the seeds that were later developed by the members of the Vienna Circle into logical positivism. The Vienna Circle, a philosophically oriented group that evolved in 1923 out of a series of seminars led by Moritz Schlick (1882–1936), was chiefly interested in the foundations of logic, mathematics, and the positive sciences. Out of these discussions grew an international philosophical movement—logical positivism—characterized by an extremely critical, almost contemptuous, attitude toward metaphysics, a strong admiration for logic and the positive sciences, and a stringent methodological requirement called the verifiability principle. According to this principle (which is still not definitely formulated by the positivists), any statement that purports to assert something about reality but that cannot be verified by empirical observation is meaningless. Not all analysts are logical positivists, but analytic philosophy since the late 1920s has been strongly influenced by positivist thought.

The Meaning of Ethical Terms and Statements

The literature of analytic philosophy, unlike the literature of other traditions represented in this book, does not offer a normative ethics—that is, an ethics that develops, usually on metaphysical or psychological bases, a conception of what is good and what is evil and a set of *norms* according to which men ought to act. With two exceptions—Moore's speculations about an ideal state of things and the means for achieving it and Russell's public declarations on politics—analytic philosophers have not seen fit to explore questions about what the good life consists in or what we are obligated to do or not do. For them, the task of ethics is to clarify the meanings, presuppositions, and interrelations of the terms and statements with which people discuss ethical matters and to clarify the logic by which people reason about such matters.

The chief terms that analysts have nominated as candidates for this clarifying process are "good," "bad," "right," "wrong," and "ought." Determining the implications of these ethical terms, together with the statements in which they occur, has become the major problem because such terms are disturbingly ambiguous, at least as they are ordinarily used, and because the way in which one understands all other terms relevant to morality is affected by the way in which one understands these. Since some of the principles that analysts employ in clarifying ethical terms are structured in accordance with earlier philosophical doctrines, it will be helpful, before proceeding further into the nature of this clarification, to survey briefly the historical background.

Humean and Kantian Distinctions

The eighteenth-century British philosopher David Hume developed important premises which the analysts have used as the basis for discussing ethical terms and statements. Hume made a sharp distinction between what he called "relations of ideas" and what he called "matters of fact," two classes that were taken by him to exhaust the realm of the knowable. A statement expressing relations of ideas, as in mathematics or logic, is regarded as either necessarily true (the square of the hypotenuse is equal to the sum of the squares of the other two sides) or as contradictory (a triangle is four sided); and discovering the truth or falsity of such a statement requires only the operation of thought, without dependence upon experience. Statements expressing matters of fact are likewise either true or false; but, because they deal with existing states of affairs rather than with logical or mathematical relations, their truth or falsity can be determined only by experience. The implications of this distinction, as Hume saw them, are summarized in the final paragraph of *An Enquiry Concerning Human Understanding* (1748):

> When we run over libraries, persuaded of these principles, what havoc must we make? If we take in our hand any volume—of divinity or school metaphysics, for instance—let us ask, *Does it contain any abstract reasoning concerning quantity or number?* No. *Does it contain any experimental reasoning concerning matter of fact and existence?* No. Commit it then to the flames, for it can contain nothing but sophistry and illusion.

Hume's sharp contrast between abstract reason and experience inevitably led him to the conclusion that unless a statement conforms to one of the two acceptable models—that is, unless it expresses either a necessary, purely ideal relation of ideas discoverable by the operation of thought alone or a matter of fact discoverable by experience—then the statement simply does not have any meaning.

Hume's distinction between statements expressing relations of ideas and statements expressing matters of fact was taken over by Immanuel Kant (1724–1804), who, after introducing some modifications, renamed the two kinds of statements "analytic" and "synthetic," the names by which they have been discussed ever since. An analytic statement is one in which the meaning of the predicate term is already contained in (and hence can be *analyzed* out of) the meaning of the subject term, as in, for example, the statement "All bachelors are unmarried." A synthetic statement, on the other hand, is one in which the meaning of the predicate term adds something to, and is therefore not already contained in, the meaning of the subject term: "A freely falling body traverses a distance whose length is proportional to the square of the time elapsed." The logic of the distinction then works out the following way: Synthetic statements are the only ones that add to our knowledge about the way things actually are, since in them alone does the predicate give us new information about the subject. At the same time, however, such statements are discoverable or verifiable only by experience and are therefore regarded as the province of the various positive sciences. Hence the only genuine knowledge about the way things actually are is the kind of knowledge that is, or could be, provided by the positive sciences. And, similarly, the only legitimate questions about the way things actually are are questions that might be investigated by these same sciences.

Discussion among analytic ethicians has been concerned to a great extent with the implications that the analytic/synthetic distinction has for the status of ethical terms and statements.[1] Clearly, such statements cannot be understood according to the analytic model. The statement "Promise-breaking is bad" is not, and does not pretend to be, an attempt to spell out

---

[1] The similarity of the names "analytic statement" and "analytic ethics" does not imply anything noteworthy at this point.

the logical implications of the meaning of the term "promise-breaking." Hence if such statements can be understood at all they will have to be handled according to the synthetic model, which requires that they be viewed as basically similar to the type of statements found in the positive sciences and, correspondingly, capable of being empirically verified. And this requirement can be met only if ethical statements are somehow statements about facts, about the way things actually are.

Precisely at this point, however, a major problem arises—one that has been constantly discussed in analytic circles—as to whether statements about values (what ought to be) are really reducible to statements about facts (what is). Here again the analysts point to Hume as having first clearly stated the issue.

> In every system of morality which I have hitherto met with, I have always remarked, that the author proceeds for some time in the ordinary way of reasoning, and establishes the being of a God, or makes observations concerning human affairs; when of a sudden I am surprised to find, that instead of the usual copulations of propositions, *is,* and *is not,* I meet with no proposition that is not connected with an *ought,* or an *ought not.* This change is imperceptible; but is, however, of the last consequence. For as this *ought,* or *ought not,* expresses some new relation or affirmation, it is necessary that it should be observed and explained; and at the same time that a reason should be given, for what seems altogether inconceivable, how this new relation can be a deduction from others, which are entirely different from it.[2]

What Hume is saying is that previous ethical systems really deal with two entirely different sets of statements—one set about facts and one about values. On the one side, they propose factual statements about God, human nature, and the structure of society. On the other side, they make ethical statements about what is good and bad and how one ought to conduct oneself. In addition, they portray the first set as premises and the second set as conclusions following logically from these premises. But such reasoning must be invalid because ethical terms appear in the conclusions and not in the premises.

Against the background of this problem, analysts are troubled by the danger that if ethical statements have a special "ethical" character about them, in virtue of which they are in some way sharply distinct from nonethical statements, then attempts to reduce the former to the latter might mask the difference between them, and thereby create a distorted picture of the meaning that ethical statements really have. If, for example, the statement "X is morally good" can, without losing any of its ethical character, be reduced to a presumably nonethical statement such as "X is pleasurable" or "X contributes to the harmony of society" or "X is commanded by

---

[2] David Hume, *A Treatise of Human Nature* (Garden City, N.Y.: Doubleday & Co., 1961), Book III, Part I, Sect. 1, p. 423.

the law"—statements that are, at least in principle, verifiable by observation—then it can be understood according to the ordinary synthetic model and should cause no great difficulties. But if, on the other hand, the ethical character is lost in such reductions, which would imply that there is an irreducible difference between ethical and nonethical statements, then ethical statements will have to be given some unique kind of status—but what kind?

According to the way in which they resolve such problems about the meaning of ethical terms and statements, analytic ethical theories are customarily divided into three types: intuitionism (sometimes called "nonnaturalism"), naturalism, and various forms of emotivism. Intuitionism (represented in the selection by Moore in the readings) treats ethical terms and statements as meaningful and as totally or partially irreducible to nonethical counterparts. Naturalism (represented in the selections by Schlick) also treats ethical terms and statements as meaningful, but only insofar as they are reducible to what is nonethical. Emotivism (represented in the selections by A. J. Ayer and Charles Stevenson and criticized in the selection by Stephen Toulmin) treats ethical terms and statements as meaningless.

Moore: Intuitionism

G. E. Moore's major contribution to the literature of ethics is *Principia Ethica* (1903). The object of the book, Moore explained in the Preface, is to provide a prolegomena (borrowing a famous title from Kant) to any future ethics that can possibly pretend to be scientific. This implies that Moore's primary concern was to discover and explain what it is that we are doing when we reason about ethical questions and what the fundamental principles are that govern such reasoning. The first requisite to this discovery and explanation is to become extraordinarily clear about the meaning of these questions; Moore attributed the philosophical disputes plaguing the history of ethics precisely to the attempt by philosophers to answer questions without first discovering the meaning of the questions that they desire to answer.

Moore found that moral philosophers have traditionally confused two kinds of questions and as a result have failed to give adequate answers to either kind. Kept carefully distinct by Moore, these questions are about *intrinsic value* and *right action*. From an insight into the difference between the two and an understanding of what each means, it becomes clear what kinds of *evidence* are relevant as arguments for or against particular answers to either. There are, then, three general questions with which *Principia Ethica* deals: What is intrinsically good? What kinds of actions ought we to perform? What is the nature of the evidence by which any ethical statement can be proved or disproved? Although Moore did offer a positive doctrine to answer the first two questions (a doctrine largely neglected by subsequent ethicians), the major part of the critical analysis in the book is given over to clarifying the *meaning* of the two questions and to defining the kinds of evidence relevant to answering each.

Current interest in Moore centers chiefly on the way in which he handled the first question. He found that questions about intrinsic value are likely to be confused with questions about right conduct, but he regarded as far more important the fact that two kinds of questions about intrinsic value itself are virtually always confused with each other. The question "What is intrinsically good?" is really two different questions: "What things are good in themselves?" and "How is 'good' to be defined?" In view of the fact that Moore regarded the second of these two questions as the most fundamental question of ethics, his answer, on first reading at least, is somewhat disappointing. For he answered that "good" cannot be defined. It cannot be defined by example because, although it is possible to point to good things, it is not possible to point to goodness itself. It cannot be defined in the more important sense of analyzing a complex whole into its components because, Moore insisted, goodness is a simple and therefore unanalyzable property of things. Hence, while all other ethical terms can be defined by the notion of good, that notion itself is primitive and irreducible, and must be regarded as an indefinable given for ethical thought.

Such statements as "good is the same as pleasurable" or "good is the same as that which is desired" would be examples of what Moore called "the naturalistic fallacy," by which he meant the attempt to reduce the unique and indefinable property goodness to some other, "natural" property of things. Moore's argument is simple: about anything that is pleasant or desired or happiness-producing, it is always possible to ask if it is really good. The very possibility of such a question shows that the term "good" cannot *mean* the same as "pleasant" or "desired" or "happiness-producing" and, consequently, that to reduce *it* to one of *them* is to destroy its meaning.

It is noteworthy that there are some synonyms for the term "good" to which Moore did not object. He often used "desirable" (in the sense of what *ought* to be desired, not simply what *is* desired) and "valuable" in place of "good." "Desirable," "valuable," and "good" are interchanged in this way because Moore regarded them as ethical terms, whereas he saw "pleasurable," "desired," and "happiness-producing" as nonethical, designating natural properties of things. This contrast, however, creates the further requirement of producing a criterion by which to distinguish the ethical realm from the nonethical or natural, a requirement that Moore did not meet satisfactorily and that has been a persistently recurring problem for subsequent analysts.

In any case, Moore maintained a sharp contrast between the ethical order and the natural order, hence between ethics and psychology, and ultimately between the ought to be and the is. The other alternative—namely, that the moral order is based upon the natural order, that ethics is based upon psychology, and that what ought to be is ultimately reducible to what is—was worked out by Moritz Schlick on the Continent. The British wing of the analytic movement, however, tended to retain a sharp distinction between ethical and nonethical terms and, correspondingly, to concern itself with working out the implications of this contrast, particularly those that bear on the way in which ethical terms themselves are to be understood.

Schlick: Naturalism

Like Moore, Moritz Schlick in his *Problems of Ethics* (1930) presented a conception of ethics according to which ethical questions concern the meaning of "good." But unlike Moore, Schlick maintained that questions about the meaning of "good" could be reduced to—and when properly understood were nothing other than—questions about nature, particularly human nature: Why do people hold the principles that they hold? What do people desire? What is the relationship between their desires and their activities?

In formulating his conception of ethics, Schlick had only two alternatives. One was to assume that ethical terms and statements are reducible to purely empirical statements about desire, pleasure, and, if different from pleasure, happiness; that, correspondingly, ethics deals with objects about which empirically verifiable assertions can be made and is therefore reducible to some positive science, probably psychology; and that, finally, there is no really sharp distinction between value and fact, between morality and nature, between ought to be and is. In short, this first alternative was to attempt the very thing that Moore had called the naturalistic fallacy. The other alternative was to regard ethical statements as meaningless; according to the requirements of the Vienna Circle, if ethical statements could not be "naturalistically" reduced to statements capable of being empirically tested, then they were without meaning. The Vienna Circle did not dispute the view that ethical statements, if meaningful, would have to be analyzed and treated in a manner similar to that employed by Schlick, but most of the other members strongly suspected that such statements were simply not meaningful. It is not surprising that, with the exception of Schlick, the Vienna Circle was not greatly interested in ethics.

Normative Ethics and Explanatory Ethics

The analysis in *Problems of Ethics* centers around a distinction between what Schlick called "normative ethics" (a term that he used in an unusual sense) and "explanatory ethics." Normative ethics determines the content of the concept "good," either by a formal definition or—what to Schlick amounted to the same thing—by specifying the exact conditions under which the word "good" is commonly predicated of actions. All actions commonly thought to be good can be grouped together; whatever elements they have in common will, when coherently organized, make up the content of the concept "good." Schlick further explained that elements common to a specific type of good activity can be expressed as a *norm:* a given kind of activity must have such and such characteristics in order to be called "good." Various norms, so derived from the examination of various kinds of activity recognized as good, can *themselves* be grouped into kinds on the basis of similarities that *they* exhibit and thus be subsumed under (justified by) more general norms. Optimally, one would reach a most general norm—perhaps the Golden Rule—that would include all other norms as special cases and that would apply to any instance of human conduct.

It is exactly at this point, however, that the normative aspect of ethics must give way to the explanatory aspect. Although it is perfectly legitimate to say that a given action ought to be valued because it falls under a particular norm and to say, further, that the particular norm itself ought to be valued because it is an instance of a more general norm and, ultimately, of the highest norm, it is clear that the question of why the highest norm *ought to be* valued cannot be answered in the same way—if, indeed, the question is meaningful at all. Schlick insisted that in regard to the ultimate norm it is legitimate to ask not why *ought* it to be valued but why it *is* valued.

> The *determination* of the contents of the concepts of good and evil is made by the use of moral principles and a system of norms, and affords a relative justification of the lower moral rules by the higher; scientific *knowledge* of the good, on the other hand, does not concern norms, but refers to the cause, concerns not the justification but the explanation of moral judgments. The theory of norms asks, *"What* does actually serve as the standard of conduct?" Explanatory ethics, however, asks, *"Why* does it serve as the standard of conduct?" [3]

The hierarchy of norms by which men make valuations (and which is described by normative ethics) cannot be justified by any principle beyond the hierarchy itself. In fact, it cannot be justified at all, if by "justified" is meant shown to conform to what ought to be.

Nevertheless, valuations and norms can be explained, and to develop such an explanation is the chief task of ethics. To explain means to reduce to causes, and in this case the causes are to be found in human nature, particularly human desire. Schlick's goal was the discovery of the motives that lead men to distinguish between good and evil and to govern their conduct by a pattern of norms. Accordingly, the major problem of ethics concerns the causal explanation of moral behavior: Why do men act morally? The consequence is that ethics has to be viewed as—and, according to Schlick, should be viewed as—a part of psychology.

---

[3] Moritz Schlick, *Problems of Ethics,* trans. by David Rynin (New York: Dover Publications, 1939), p. 25.

Values: Objective Versus Subjective

Two of the selections from *Problems of Ethics* ("What Is the Meaning of 'Moral'?" and "Are There Absolute Values?") represent the core of Schlick's position concerning the meaning of the term "good" and the motives that lead men to distinguish between good and evil and to govern their conduct by a pattern of norms. His twofold thesis, in brief, is as follows: first, that the term "good," when applied in a morally significant sense to behavior, is *applied* only to such behavior as promises the social group an increase in happiness; second, that the term "good," when so applied, simply *means* promising an increase in happiness for the social group. In the development of this thesis, Schlick carefully distinguished between what he called "objective (or absolute) values" and what he called "the subjective interpretation of values." Because in the literature of modern ethics and in everyday discussions about ethical problems the term "objective values" is taken to suggest values that are grounded and rational, and the term "subjective values" to suggest values that are in some sense arbitrary and irrational, it is possible for a reader to work through the selections without becoming clearly aware that such meanings do not apply to Schlick's understanding of the distinction.

The term "objective value," as Schlick used it, corresponds to the conception that value, or goodness, is independent of, and hence can be understood apart from, a relationship to anything else. In this way, value is understood, as it was by Moore, not relationally but "absolutely" or "objectively." By those who understand value in this way, it is usually held that what has value ought to be desired; it is sometimes held that what has value actually is desired, either because it has value or for some other reason; it is always held that being an object of desire, and therefore being related to desire, is not what constitutes being valuable.

On the other hand, a "subjective value," according to Schlick's interpretation, cannot be understood apart from desire. From this point of view, being desired and having value form an inseparable unity such that the essential mark of the valuable is that it is desired. It should be clear that Schlick's premises required him to reject the absolute interpretation of value and to adopt the subjective interpretation, for then values could be regarded as facts, ethical statements about what is good and what is bad could be given an empirical ground in the phenomena of human desires, and ethical inquiry could be directed not to the realm of what ought to be desired but to the realm of what is desired. It is also true that in keeping value and desire together, Schlick chose a position that—despite important differences on other points—is similar to traditional ethical theory as represented, for example, by Aristotle and Aquinas. Neither one considered the valuable, or (to use their language) the good, as intelligible apart from desire, and both included some idea of desire in their definition of the good. Indeed, the notion that there is a gap between value and desire did not become a major doctrine in Western philosophical literature until the eighteenth century, when Kant made the notion the basis of an impressive and extraordinarily influential ethical system and thereby prepared the modern world for its acceptance. Accordingly, while much of the argument in *Problems of Ethics* (particularly in the sections "What Is the Meaning of 'Moral'?" and "Are There Absolute Values?") constitutes a criticism of Moore, Schlick's chief target, as he made clear, is Kant.

Ayer, Stevenson, Toulmin: Emotivism

The intuitionists represented by Moore and the naturalists by Schlick agree that ethical terms and the statements in which they occur are meaningful. Another group of analytic ethicians, usually referred to as emotivists, does not accept this view. The members of this group agree with Schlick that ethical terms and statements are meaningful only if they can be reduced to nonethical counterparts. But they also agree with Moore's claim that to make such a reduction is to commit the naturalistic fallacy. Consequently they take the position that such ethical terms as "good," "bad," "right," "wrong," or "ought" do not describe anything, that ethical statements do not (at least insofar as they embody ethical terms) assert anything and are in that sense meaningless, and that ethics as a normative discipline is an illusion.

A. J. Ayer (b. 1910), Charles L. Stevenson (b. 1908), and—by way of criticism—Stephen Toulmin (b. 1922) explore various aspects of this position. Ayer finds that the language of ordinary ethical systems consists of four kinds of statements: (1) definitions of ethical terms along with allied statements investigating the legitimacy of such definitions, (2) descriptions of "moral experience" and of the causes of "moral experience" (a term left rather vague by Ayer), (3) exhortations to moral virtue, and (4) ethical statements themselves. The last two kinds of statements are found upon analysis to be cognitively meaningless, although they serve to evoke the emotions of others and to express our own. Statements of the second type belong to the existing sciences of psychology or sociology and hence have no proper place in ethics. Unlike Schlick, Ayer keeps a sharp separation between ethics and psychology. Finally, statements of the first type are the proper business of ethical inquiry, and such inquiry, as Ayer finds, turns out to consist in saying that ethical concepts are pseudoconcepts.

Stevenson's form of the emotive theory is somewhat more developed than that of Ayer, as Ayer himself has said, although Stevenson admits that he is in sympathy with Ayer's views. In the essay presented in the readings, Stevenson proposes to extend the limits of ethical inquiry sufficiently to make room for an examination of the way in which emotive expressions figure in disagreements about ethical matters. He agrees with Ayer that people cannot argue directly about their attitudes toward what is valuable, for while two attitudes can *conflict* with each other they cannot *contradict* one another. But while Ayer is satisfied that attitudes about value are ultimately irrational and therefore disagreements in attitude ultimately irresolvable, Stevenson is prepared to conjecture over the assumption that one's basic attitudes about value might result from one's beliefs about fact; and, since people can reason about and therefore resolve disagreements in their beliefs, the assumption would imply that reason can, at least in principle, resolve all disagreements in attitude. For Stevenson, however, the assumption remains purely conjectural.

The selection from Toulmin is largely a critique of Ayer's position, which Toulmin designates as "imperative" rather than "emotive," the term used by Ayer. The central problem of the book from which the selection is taken is to answer the question "What is the place of reason in ethics?"— implying, in opposition to Ayer and in a lesser degree to Stevenson, that reason definitely does have a place in ethical matters. Toulmin, along with other contemporary British and American analysts such as Stuart Hampshire, Peter Frederick Strawson, R. M. Hare, P. H. Nowell-Smith, H. D. Aiken, A. I. Melden, Paul Edwards, and John Rawls, represents an attempt to get beyond the treatment given to ethical language by Ayer and Stevenson. These several writers tend to view ethical statements as different from and irreducible to nonethical ones but nevertheless as inherently rational and supportable by factual reasons.

The implications of these recent tendencies have not yet been satisfactorily worked out by analysts, nor have the implications of Stevenson's conjecture that attitudes about value might ultimately be governed by beliefs about fact. But such implications would be far-reaching, for if beliefs about fact do finally govern attitudes about value, then the gaps between fact and value, knowledge and morality, and empirical disciplines and ethics would all tend to close. It might turn out that what classical moral theorists called "the true" and "the good" have something to do with one another after all.

The Responsibility Issue

Although analytic ethicians have been primarily interested in problems concerning the meaning of value terms, they have also developed an impressive literature dealing with other kinds of problems relevant to ethics. Of these, the most widely discussed in recent years is a group of problems centering around the meanings and interrelations of responsibility, voluntariness and freedom, causality and determination, praise and blame, and reward and punishment. The discussion can be best appreciated when seen against its historical background, which, again, is found largely in the thought of Hume, but also, more remotely, in Greek ethical speculation, for Hume's own approach to the responsibility issue was heavily influenced by considerations arising out of the thought of Plato and Aristotle.

Historical Background: Greek Philosophy and Hume

One of Plato's most famous views is that no one ever knowingly does what is evil. Basing his position upon the two premises that doing evil actions inevitably entails being unhappy and that no one desires to be unhappy, Plato concluded that no one desires to do evil, that a man who does evil does so in the erroneous belief that what he is doing is good (that is, it will bring him happiness), and that such a man acts in ignorance of the ramifications of what he is doing. This was all taken to mean that in doing what is evil a man is not doing what he really wants to do, a conclusion that Plato expressed by saying all evil actions are involuntary. Why then should anyone ever be punished? Plato's answer, perfectly consistent, was that since a man who does evil things is corrupted by ignorance about what is good and bad, punishment is a kind of healing directed toward his improvement. On these premises ignorance, far from excusing, is precisely what makes punishment appropriate.

Aristotle differed from Plato in several ways. For one thing Aristotle thought that evil actions can be voluntary as well as involuntary—by voluntary he meant that which is within a man's power to do or not to do. Moreover, although he agreed with Plato that a man doing an evil action is in some sense ignorant, he thought that ignorance about what is good and bad is itself voluntary. Further, he thought that a man should be punished only for a voluntary evil action. The reason for punishing such a man is not simply that he has done something bad but, more important, that it was within his power to act otherwise.

It was this latter point—the notion that one "could have acted otherwise"—that fascinated Hume. He treated the point, however, in terms somewhat different from those used by Aristotle, for the ethical problem of the distinction between voluntary and involuntary had, by the time Hume took it over, become amalgamated with seventeenth- and eighteenth-century controversies about necessity of nature versus freedom of will. In brief, one view was that everything in nature is part of a unified order of causal agents necessarily producing their proper effects. Consequently, nothing can be other than what it is or act other than the way it does. This position came to be called "determinism" (a word that, regrettably, is charged with what Ayer would call emotive content). The other view was that, while determinism might be adequate as an account of nature, it is not adequate as an account of properly human activity. For, it was held, such activity is chosen by the will, and although the will might be influenced by such factors as one's character, motives, desires, and surrounding circumstances, it is nevertheless not determined by anything. It is free. In these controversies, freedom was opposed to necessity, the notion "acted freely" was lined up with the notion "could have acted otherwise," and free activity in the sense defined was held by its defenders to be the only activity for which one is responsible.

Out of this background Hume developed his own position, which consisted of two essential theses. He maintained that there is no such thing as freedom (in the sense defined), and he also maintained, somewhat startlingly, that freedom would destroy responsibility. The first thesis rests upon an analysis of causality. Hume attempted to show that the very essence of causality involves necessity and that, consequently, if an effect follows from a cause at all, it follows necessarily. Therefore, to say that human actions are free rather than necessary is to imply that such actions (insofar as they are free) have no cause at all, hence that they are chance events, and that they are absolutely unaccountable not only to spectators but even to the agent acting—implications which, because Hume had no trouble in discrediting them, exploded that conception of freedom.

The more interesting thesis in Hume's position is the second, namely, that freedom (so defined) and responsibility are incompatible with one another. Since free activity precisely as free cannot be regarded as resulting from the agent's character, it follows that the freedom hypothesis postulates a gap between one's character and one's free activity. In that case, however, a man's evil actions, no matter how wicked *they* might be, could not imply that *he* is wicked—there would be no necessary connection, precisely because of which *he* would not be responsible for what *they* are.

Hume's manner of stating the problem has largely defined the issue as it is understood by almost all recent American and British ethicians doing work in the area of responsibility. His speculation about the nature and universality of the cause-effect sequence is ignored, but his provocative proposal that freedom and responsibility are incompatible has brought about an unprecedented interest in understanding what responsibility really implies. Apart from Hume, it has been very widely believed in the history of philosophy that determinism and morality are incompatible, but it has become clear today that there is a vantage point from which the incompatibility disappears. Treated in the third selection by Schlick and in both selections by Nowell-Smith, the major questions raised from this vantage point concern the meaning of responsibility, the meaning of freedom and of the notion that one "could have acted otherwise," and the meaning of and grounds for blaming, praising, excusing, and punishing. Nowell-Smith's treatment is a particularly good introduction to present-day discussion of the issue, and it will be helpful here to examine his major points.

Nowell-Smith: The Conditions of Responsibility

The selections by P. H. Nowell-Smith (b. 1914) offer an attempt to clarify the conditions under which a man who has broken a moral rule is held responsible. Since it appears evident that we hold such a man responsible (and thus blame and perhaps punish him) only insofar as we believe that in breaking the rule he could have acted otherwise, the major points are to determine what we mean by the notion that one "could have acted otherwise" and to discover why we think that notion is relevant to holding him responsible.

According to Nowell-Smith there is no dispute about the meaning of "could have" phrases when they are used in referring to nonmoral situations. So used, they clearly mean "would have . . . if." Thus, to say that Jones *could have* passed the examination is to say that he *would have* passed it *if* he had had more time to study, or *if* he had gotten up on time, or *if* he had felt better, or—in general—*if* some conditions had prevailed which in fact did not prevail.

The disputed question is whether this meaning is appropriate to cases involving moral responsibility. A negative answer is given by what Nowell-Smith calls the "libertarian view" (which as he explains it is similar to the free-will theory previously described). In this view a man can be held responsible for having broken a moral rule only if he could have acted otherwise *given* the conditions that actually prevailed. It is not essentially relevant whether the conditions in question are external circumstances or traits of his own character. In either case, his action, insofar as it necessarily results from such conditions, is causally determined; therefore it is not free; therefore he is not responsible for it and cannot be blamed or punished. The libertarian view of responsibility requires a self that is free in the sense of being able to rise above external circumstances and its own character as well, that in its truly free activity is not determined by these conditions, and that in this sense "could have acted otherwise."

On the other hand, the determinist view that Nowell-Smith adopts is that "could have" phrases can be construed the same way in moral as in nonmoral cases. To say about the rule-breaker that he is responsible because he could have acted otherwise is simply to say that if certain conditions had been different he would have acted differently. What is puzzling about this view is how we can hold the rule-breaker responsible while at the same time portraying his ability to have acted otherwise as dependent upon certain if's that did not occur. According to the ordinary usage of moral language we would be inclined to say that, insofar as the necessary if's did in fact not occur, the rule-breaker could not have acted otherwise and, consequently, is not responsible and cannot be blamed. Since the libertarian view regards this puzzle as the major objection to any determinist account of responsibility, the adequacy of Nowell-Smith's position rests heavily upon his ability to develop an acceptable solution to the puzzle.

The first step of his solution is to distinguish between cases in which "could not have acted otherwise" excuses and cases in which it does not. When the reason for a man's having broken a moral rule is that external circumstances prevented him from keeping it, we do not hold him responsible. But when the reason is a moral defect of his character, we do. Accordingly, the explanation "I could not have kept my promise because I am the sort of person who takes promises lightly," does not excuse. This distinction narrows the puzzle but does not eliminate it. For now the question is to understand how we can hold a rule breaker responsible—blaming and punishing him—if his ability to have acted otherwise depended upon a state of character which he in fact does not have. The second step of Nowell-Smith's solution is to answer this question by developing a reformative theory of punishment. We hold such people responsible precisely because they have moral defects, which we hope to correct through punishment.

The final step of the solution is to determine a criterion for distinguishing between moral defects and nonmoral defects. This is an essential step, for, in Nowell-Smith's account, "could not have acted otherwise" is allowed to excuse the rule-breaker in all cases except the case in which the inability to have acted otherwise is rooted in a moral defect. Only for this kind of defect do we punish a man. And it is precisely in the notion of punishment that Nowell-Smith finds the essence of moral defect. His analysis reaches the conclusion that a moral defect is simply any defect that can be corrected by punishment. It is not merely a fact about the world that moral defects can be corrected by punishment; "moral defect" *means* a defect that can be corrected by punishment.

The solution to the puzzle, then, works out the following way. It is a given fact that some defects can be corrected by punishment and some cannot. The former we call moral defects, the latter nonmoral. We punish a man whose moral defects have led him to break rules because we wish to correct his defects. But we do not punish him for having nonmoral defects because they (by definition) cannot be corrected by punishment.

Nowell-Smith's solution to the puzzle, however, is not entirely satisfactory, for there is at least one remaining difficulty to which he does not sufficiently attend. He offers a good deal of analysis about the purpose of punishment, but he offers very little about what punishment consists in and, particularly, about the marks by which we might distinguish punishment from other correctional procedures that are ordinarily thought to be different from punishment. His claim that physical weakness and anemia are nonmoral defects because they cannot be corrected by punishment does not rule out the fact that such defects can be corrected by *something*—let us call it "healing." The difficulty is to distinguish between punishment and healing. We cannot use for this purpose the distinction between moral and nonmoral defects because, in Nowell-Smith's account, making *that* distinction presupposes that we know what punishment is and how it differs from healing. A second possibility would be to employ an independent criterion, but Nowell-Smith fails to offer such a criterion. The only other possibility would be to say that, when seen from the right point of view, punishment and healing are somehow the same thing. That alternative, however, would require considerable revision not only of Nowell-Smith's conception of the responsibility issue but also of the way most of us ordinarily use the language of morality.

Glossary

ANALYTIC STATEMENT:

A statement in which the meaning of the predicate term is included in or (if the statement is false) excluded from the meaning of the subject term. The truth or falsity of such statements is discoverable by the rules of logic or the rules of language. For example, "All bachelors are unmarried." When the relation between two or more items—terms or statements—is discoverable in this way, they are said to be analytically, or necessarily, connected. (See *Synthetic Statement.*)

INTUITIONISM:

The doctrine that ethical terms and statements, while meaningful, cannot validly be reduced to or understood in terms of nonethical counterparts and that, correspondingly, values cannot, in the last analysis, be determined by empirical facts.

NATURALISM:

In ethics, the doctrine that ethical terms and statements are meaningful insofar as they can be reduced to and understood in terms of nonethical counterparts and that, correspondingly, all values are derived from, or *are*, empirical facts.

NATURALISTIC FALLACY:

The attempt to reduce ethical terms and statements to nonethical counterparts. The term, coined by Moore, is generally used by those thinkers who regard such an attempt as unsound. Clearly, naturalists do not think that the naturalistic fallacy is really a fallacy.

NORMATIVE:

Describes doctrines (and the terms and statements occurring therein) about what is good and bad and about what ought and ought not to be done. The word is generally distinguished from "descriptive" and tends to be used in contexts in which a sharp distinction is made between value and fact.

SUBJECTIVE AND OBJECTIVE:

In the field of modern ethics, "subjective" and "objective" are not exact words, and the descriptive content that they do have is often clouded by honorific and pejorative usage. Generally, "subjective" is used to describe doctrines according to which value, or goodness, has no meaning apart from people's desires, tastes, interests, and feelings. "Objective" is used to describe doctrines according to which the essence of value, or goodness, is entirely independent of and therefore understandable without reference to people's desires and tastes. These minimal meanings are augmented in various ways by different authors.

SYNTHETIC STATEMENT:

A statement in which the meaning of the predicate term adds something to and is therefore not already contained in the meaning of the subject term. The truth or falsity of such statements is discoverable only by experience. When the relation between two or more items—terms or statements—is discoverable only by experience, they are said to be synthetically, or contingently, connected. Many philosophers reject the analytic/synthetic distinction on the ground that it involves an untenable contrast between necessity and contingency and between reason and experience. (See *Analytic Statement.*)

George Edward Moore

GEORGE EDWARD MOORE was born in London in 1873. One of the most influential twentieth-century philosophers, he was associated with Cambridge University during most of his adult life. Entering in 1892 with the intention of studying classics and with the modest aspiration of becoming a teacher "to the Sixth Form of some public school," he was persuaded by Bertrand Russell, then a student at Cambridge himself, to study philosophy instead. He finally left Cambridge in 1939, upon retirement from active teaching. In 1940, Moore was visiting professor at Smith College in the United States, and he remained in the United States for several years thereafter, teaching at Princeton and Columbia Universities and at Mills College. From 1921 to 1947 he was the editor of the philosophical journal *Mind*. He then returned to Cambridge, where he died in 1958. Several of his works contain writings relevant to ethics, such as *Principia Ethica* (1903), *Ethics* (1912), and *Philosophical Studies* (1922).

What Is Meant by "Good"?

PRELIMINARY CONSPECTUS

SECTION

1. In order to define Ethics, we must discover what is both common and peculiar to all undoubted ethical judgments;
2. but this is not that they are concerned with human conduct, but that they are concerned with a certain predicate "good," and its converse "bad," which may be applied both to conduct and to other things.
3. The subjects of the judgments of a scientific Ethics are not, like those of some studies, "particular things";
4. but it includes all *universal* judgments which assert the relation of "goodness" to any subject, and hence includes Casuistry.
5. It must, however, enquire not only what things are universally related to goodness, but also, what this predicate, to which they are related, is:
6. and the answer to this question is that it is indefinable
7. or simple: for if by definition be meant the analysis of an object of thought, only complex objects can be defined;
8. and of the three senses in which "definition" can be used, this is the most important.

From pp. 1–21 of George Edward Moore, *Principia Ethica*. © 1959 by Cambridge University Press. Reprinted by permission of the publisher.

9. What is thus indefinable is not "the good," or the whole of that which always possesses the predicate "good," but this predicate itself.
10. "Good," then, denotes one unique simple object of thought among innumerable others; but this object has very commonly been identified with some other—a fallacy which may be called "the naturalistic fallacy"
11. and which reduces what is used as a fundamental principle of Ethics either to a tautology or to a statement about the meaning of a word.
12. The nature of this fallacy is easily recognised;
13. and if it were avoided, it would be plain that the only alternatives to the admission that "good" is indefinable, are either that it is complex or that there is no notion at all peculiar to Ethics—alternatives which can only be refuted by an appeal to inspection, but which can be so refuted.
14. The "naturalistic fallacy" illustrated by Bentham; and the importance of avoiding it pointed out.

THE SUBJECT-MATTER OF ETHICS

1. It is very early to point out some among our every-day judgments, with the truth of which Ethics is undoubtedly concerned. Whenever we say, "So and so is a good man," or "That fellow is a villain"; whenever we ask, "What ought I to do?" or "Is it wrong for me to do like this?"; whenever we hazard such remarks as "Temperance is a virtue and drunkenness a vice"—it is undoubtedly the business of Ethics to discuss such questions and such statements; to argue what is the true answer when we ask what it is right to do, and to give reasons for thinking that our statements about the character of persons or the morality of actions are true or false. In the vast majority of cases, where we make statements involving any of the terms "virtue," "vice," "duty," "right," "ought," "good," "bad," we are making ethical judgments; and if we wish to discuss their truth, we shall be discussing a point of Ethics.

So much as this is not disputed; but it falls very far short of defining the province of Ethics. That province may indeed be defined as the whole truth about that which is at the same time common to all such judgments and peculiar to them. But we have still to ask the question: What is it that is thus common and peculiar? And this is a question to which very different answers have been given by ethical philosophers of acknowledged reputation, and none of them, perhaps, completely satisfactory.

2. If we take such examples as those given above, we shall not be far wrong in saying that they are all of them concerned with the question of "conduct"—with the question, what, in the conduct of us, human beings, is good, and what is bad, what is right, and what is wrong. For when we say that a man is good, we commonly mean that he acts rightly; when we say that drunkenness is a vice, we commonly mean that to get drunk is a wrong or wicked action. And this discussion of human conduct is, in fact, that with which the name "Ethics" is most intimately associated. It is so associated by derivation; and conduct is undoubtedly by far the commonest and most generally interesting object of ethical judgments.

Accordingly, we find that many ethical philosophers are disposed to accept as an adequate definition of "Ethics" the statement that it deals with the question what is good or bad in human conduct. They hold that its enquiries are properly confined to "conduct" or to "practice"; they hold that the name "practical philosophy" covers all the matter with which it has to do. Now, without discussing the proper meaning of the word (for verbal questions are properly left to the writers of dictionaries and other persons interested in literature; philosophy, as we shall see, has no concern with them), I may say that I intend to use "Ethics" to cover more than this—a usage, for which there is, I think, quite sufficient authority. I am using it to cover an enquiry for which, at all events, there is no other word: the general enquiry into what is good.

Ethics is undoubtedly concerned with the question what good conduct is; but, being concerned with this, it obviously does not start at the beginning, unless it is prepared to tell us what is good as well as what is conduct. For "good conduct" is a complex notion: all conduct is not good; for some is certainly bad and some may be indifferent. And on the other hand, other things, beside conduct, may be good; and if they are so, then, "good" denotes some property, that is common to them and conduct; and if we examine good conduct alone of all good things, then we shall be in danger of mistaking for this property, some property which is not shared by those other things: and thus we shall have made a mistake about Ethics even in this limited sense; for we shall not know what good conduct really is. This is a mistake which many writers have actually made, from limiting their enquiry to conduct. And hence I shall try to avoid it by considering first what is good in general; hoping, that if we can arrive at any certainty about this, it will be much easier to settle the question of good conduct: for we all know pretty well what "conduct" is. This, then, is our first question: What is good? and What is bad? and to the discussion of this question (or these questions) I give the name of Ethics, since that science must, at all events, include it.

3. But this is a question which may have many meanings. If, for example, each of us were to say "I am doing good now" or "I had a good dinner yesterday," these statements would each of them be some sort of answer to our question, although perhaps a false one. So, too, when A asks B what school he ought to send his son to, B's answer will certainly be an ethical judgment. And similarly all distribution of praise or blame to any personage or thing that has existed, now exists, or will exist, does give some answer to the question "What is good?" In all such cases some particular thing is judged to be good or bad: the question "What?" is answered by "This." But this is not the sense in which a scientific Ethics asks the question. Not one, of all the many million answers of this kind, which must be true, can form a part of an ethical system; although that science must contain reasons and principles sufficient for deciding on the truth of all of them. There are far too many persons, things and events in the world, past,

present, or to come, for a discussion of their individual merits to be embraced in any science. Ethics, therefore, does not deal at all with facts of this nature, facts that are unique, individual, absolutely particular; facts with which such studies as history, geography, astronomy, are compelled, in part at least, to deal. And, for this reason, it is not the business of the ethical philosopher to give personal advice or exhortation.

4. But there is another meaning which may be given to the question "What is good?" "Books are good" would be an answer to it, though an answer obviously false; for some books are very bad indeed. And ethical judgments of this kind do indeed belong to Ethics; though I shall not deal with many of them. Such is the judgment "Pleasure is good"—a judgment, of which Ethics should discuss the truth, although it is not nearly as important as that other judgment, with which we shall be much occupied presently—"Pleasure *alone* is good." It is judgments of this sort, which are made in such books on Ethics as contain a list of "virtues"—in Aristotle's "Ethics" for example. But it is judgments of precisely the same kind, which form the substance of what is commonly supposed to be a study different from Ethics, and one much less respectable—the study of Casuistry. We may be told that Casuistry differs from Ethics, in that it is much more detailed and particular, Ethics much more general. But it is most important to notice that Casuistry does not deal with anything that is absolutely particular—particular in the only sense in which a perfectly precise line can be drawn between it and what is general. It is not particular in the sense just noticed, the sense in which this book is a particular book, and A's friend's advice particular advice. Casuistry may indeed be *more* particular and Ethics *more* general; but that means that they differ only in degree and not in kind. And this is universally true of "particular" and "general," when used in this common, but inaccurate, sense. So far as Ethics allows itself to give lists of virtues or even to name constituents of the Ideal, it is indistinguishable from Casuistry. Both alike deal with what is general, in the sense in which physics and chemistry deal with what is general. Just as chemistry aims at discovering what are the properties of oxygen, *wherever it occurs,* and not only of this or that particular specimen of oxygen; so Casuistry aims at discovering what actions are good, *whenever they occur.* In this respect Ethics and Casuistry alike are to be classed with such sciences as physics, chemistry and physiology, in their absolute distinction from those of which history and geography are instances. And it is to be noted that, owing to their detailed nature, casuistical investigations are actually nearer to physics and to chemistry than are the investigations usually assigned to Ethics. For just as physics cannot rest content with the discovery that light is propagated by waves of ether, but must go on to discover the particular nature of the ether-waves corresponding to each several colour; so Casuistry, not content with the general law that charity is a virtue must attempt to discover the relative merits of every different form of charity. Casuistry forms, therefore, part of the ideal of ethical science:

Ethics cannot be complete without it. The defects of Casuistry are not defects of principle; no objection can be taken to its aim and object. It has failed only because it is far too difficult a subject to be treated adequately in our present state of knowledge. The casuist has been unable to distinguish, in the cases which he treats, those elements upon which their value depends. Hence he often thinks two cases to be alike in respect of value, when in reality they are alike only in some other respect. It is to mistakes of this kind that the pernicious influence of such investigations has been due. For Casuistry is the goal of ethical investigation. It cannot be safely attempted at the beginning of our studies, but only at the end.

5. But our question "What is good?" may have still another meaning. We may, in the third place, mean to ask, not what thing or things are good, but how "good" is to be defined. This is an enquiry which belongs only to Ethics, not to Casuistry; and this is the enquiry which will occupy us first.

It is an enquiry to which most special attention should be directed; since this question, how "good" is to be defined, is the most fundamental question in all Ethics. That which is meant by "good" is, in fact, except its converse "bad," the *only* simple object of thought which is peculiar to Ethics. Its definition is, therefore, the most essential point in the definition of Ethics; and moreover a mistake with regard to it entails a far larger number of erroneous ethical judgments than any other. Unless this first question be fully understood, and its true answer clearly recognised, the rest of Ethics is as good as useless from the point of view of systematic knowledge. True ethical judgments, of the two kinds last dealt with, may indeed be made by those who do not know the answer to this question as well as by those who do; and it goes without saying that the two classes of people may lead equally good lives. But it is extremely unlikely that the *most general* ethical judgments will be equally valid, in the absence of a true answer to this question: I shall presently try to shew that the gravest errors have been largely due to beliefs in a false answer. And, in any case, it is impossible that, till the answer to this question be known, any one should know *what is the evidence* for any ethical judgment whatsoever. But the main object of Ethics, as a systematic science, is to give correct *reasons* for thinking that this or that is good; and, unless this question be answered, such reasons cannot be given. Even, therefore, apart from the fact that a false answer leads to false conclusions, the present enquiry is a most necessary and important part of the science of Ethics.

6. What, then, is good? How is good to be defined? Now, it may be thought that this is a verbal question. A definition does indeed often mean the expressing of one word's meaning in other words. But this is not the sort of definition I am asking for. Such a definition can never be of ultimate importance in any study except lexicography. If I wanted that kind of definition I should have to consider in the first place how people generally used the word "good"; but my business is not with its proper usage, as established by custom. I should, indeed, be foolish, if I tried to use it for some-

thing which it did not usually denote: if, for instance, I were to announce that, whenever I used the word "good," I must be understood to be thinking of that object which is usually denoted by the word "table." I shall, therefore, use the word in the sense in which I think it is ordinarily used; but at the same time I am not anxious to discuss whether I am right in thinking that it is so used. My business is solely with that object or idea, which I hold, rightly or wrongly, that the word is generally used to stand for. What I want to discover is the nature of that object or idea, and about this I am extremely anxious to arrive at an agreement.

But, if we understand the question in this sense, my answer to it may seem a very disappointing one. If I am asked "What is good?" my answer is that good is good, and that is the end of the matter. Or if I am asked "How is good to be defined?" my answer is that it cannot be defined, and that is all I have to say about it. But disappointing as these answers may appear, they are of the very last importance. To readers who are familiar with philosophic terminology, I can express their importance by saying that they amount to this: That propositions about the good are all of them synthetic and never analytic; and that is plainly no trivial matter. And the same thing may be expressed more popularly, by saying that, if I am right, then nobody can foist upon us such an axiom as that "Pleasure is the only good" or that "The good is the desired" on the pretence that this is "the very meaning of the word."

7. Let us, then, consider this position. My point is that "good" is a simple notion, just as "yellow" is a simple notion; that, just as you cannot, by any manner of means, explain to any one who does not already know it, what yellow is, so you cannot explain what good is. Definitions of the kind that I was asking for, definitions which describe the real nature of the object or notion denoted by a word, and which do not merely tell us what the word is used to mean, are only possible when the object or notion in question is something complex. You can give a definition of a horse, because a horse has many different properties and qualities, all of which you can enumerate. But when you have enumerated them all, when you have reduced a horse to his simplest terms, then you can no longer define those terms. They are simply something which you think of or perceive, and to any one who cannot think of or perceive them, you can never, by any definition, make their nature known. It may perhaps be objected to this that we are able to describe to others, objects which they have never seen or thought of. We can, for instance, make a man understand what a chimaera is, although he has never heard of one or seen one. You can tell him that it is an animal with a lioness's head and body, with a goat's head growing from the middle of its back, and with a snake in place of a tail. But here the object which you are describing is a complex object; it is entirely composed of parts, with which we are all perfectly familiar—a snake, a goat, a lioness; and we know, too, the manner in which those parts are to be put together, because we know what is meant by the middle of a lioness's back,

and where her tail is wont to grow. And so it is with all objects, not previously known, which we are able to define: they are all complex; all composed of parts, which may themselves, in the first instance, be capable of similar definition, but which must in the end be reducible to simplest parts, which can no longer be defined. But yellow and good, we say, are not complex: they are notions of that simple kind, out of which definitions are composed and with which the power of further defining ceases.

8. When we say, as Webster says, "The definition of horse is 'A hoofed quadruped of the genus Equus,'" we may, in fact, mean three different things. (1) We may mean merely: "When I say 'horse,' you are to understand that I am talking about a hoofed quadruped of the genus Equus." This might be called the arbitrary verbal definition: and I do not mean that good is indefinable in that sense. (2) We may mean, as Webster ought to mean: "When most English people say 'horse,' they mean a hoofed quadruped of the genus Equus." This may be called the verbal definition proper, and I do not say that good is indefinable in this sense either; for it is certainly possible to discover how people use a word: otherwise, we could never have known that "good" may be translated by *"gut"* in German and by *"bon"* in French. But (3) we may, when we define horse, mean something much more important. We may mean that a certain object, which we all of us know, is composed in a certain manner: that it has four legs, a head, a heart, a liver, etc., etc., all of them arranged in definite relations to one another. It is in this sense that I deny good to be definable. I say that it is not composed of any parts, which we can substitute for it in our minds when we are thinking of it. We might think just as clearly and correctly about a horse, if we thought of all its parts and their arrangement instead of thinking of the whole: we could, I say, think how a horse differed from a donkey just as well, just as truly, in this way, as now we do, only not so easily; but there is nothing whatsoever which we could so substitute for good; and that is what I mean, when I say that good is indefinable.

9. But I am afraid I have still not removed the chief difficulty which may prevent acceptance of the proposition that good is indefinable. I do not mean to say that *the* good, that which is good, is thus indefinable; if I did think so, I should not be writing on Ethics, for my main object is to help towards discovering that definition. It is just because I think there will be less risk of error in our search for a definition of "the good," that I am now insisting that *good* is indefinable. I must try to explain the difference between these two. I suppose it may be granted that "good" is an adjective. Well "the good," "that which is good," must therefore be the substantive to which the adjective "good" will apply: it must be the whole of that to which the adjective will apply, and the adjective must *always* truly apply to it. But if it is that to which the adjective will apply, it must be something different from that adjective itself; and the whole of that something different, whatever it is, will be our definition of *the* good. Now it may be that this something will have other adjectives, beside "good," that will apply to

it. It may be full of pleasure, for example; it may be intelligent: and if these two adjectives are really part of its definition, then it will certainly be true, that pleasure and intelligence are good. And many people appear to think that, if we say "Pleasure and intelligence are good," or if we say "Only pleasure and intelligence are good," we are defining "good." Well, I cannot deny that propositions of this nature may sometimes be called definitions; I do not know well enough how the word is generally used to decide upon this point. I only wish it to be understood that that is not what I mean when I say there is no possible definition of good, and that I shall not mean this if I use the word again. I do most fully believe that some true proposition of the form "Intelligence is good and intelligence alone is good" can be found; if none could be found, our definition of *the* good would be impossible. As it is, I believe *the* good to be definable; and yet I still say that good itself is indefinable.

10. "Good," then, if we mean by it that quality which we assert to belong to a thing, when we say that the thing is good, is incapable of any definition, in the most important sense of that word. The most important sense of "definition" is that in which a definition states what are the parts which invariably compose a certain whole; and in this sense "good" has no definition because it is simple and has no parts. It is one of those innumerable objects of thought which are themselves incapable of definition, because they are the ultimate terms by reference to which whatever *is* capable of definition must be defined. That there must be an indefinite number of such terms is obvious, on reflection; since we cannot define anything except by an analysis, which, when carried as far as it will go, refers us to something, which is simply different from anything else, and which by that ultimate difference explains the peculiarity of the whole which we are defining: for every whole contains some parts which are common to other wholes also. There is, therefore, no intrinsic difficulty in the contention that "good" denotes a simple and indefinable quality. There are many other instances of such qualities.

Consider yellow, for example. We may try to define it, by describing its physical equivalent; we may state what kind of light-vibrations must stimulate the normal eye, in order that we may perceive it. But a moment's reflection is sufficient to shew that those light-vibrations are not themselves what we mean by yellow. *They* are not what we perceive. Indeed we should never have been able to discover their existence, unless we had first been struck by the patent difference of quality between the different colours. The most we can be entitled to say of those vibrations is that they are what corresponds in space to the yellow which we actually perceive.

Yet a mistake of this simple kind has commonly been made about "good." It may be true that all things which are good are *also* something else, just as it is true that all things which are yellow produce a certain kind of vibration in the light. And it is a fact, that Ethics aims at discovering what are those other properties belonging to all things which are good. But far too many philosophers have thought that when they named those other properties they were actually defining good; that these properties, in fact, were simply not "other," but absolutely and entirely the same with goodness. This view I propose to call the "naturalistic fallacy" and of it I shall now endeavour to dispose.

11. Let us consider what it is such philosophers say. And first it is to be noticed that they do not agree among themselves. They not only say that they are right as to what good is, but they endeavour to prove that other people who say that it is something else, are wrong. One, for instance, will affirm that good is pleasure, another, perhaps, that good is that which is desired; and each of these will argue eagerly to prove that the other is wrong. But how is that possible? One of them says that good is nothing but the object of desire, and at the same time tries to prove that it is not pleasure. But from his first assertion, that good just means the object of desire, one of two things must follow as regards his proof:

(1) He may be trying to prove that the object of desire is not pleasure. But, if this be all, where is his Ethics? The position he is maintaining is merely a psychological one. Desire is something which occurs in our minds, and pleasure is something else which so occurs; and our would-be ethical philosopher is merely holding that the latter is not the object of the former. But what has that to do with the question in dispute? His opponent held the ethical proposition that pleasure was the good, and although he should prove a million times over the psychological proposition that pleasure is not the object of desire, he is no nearer proving his opponent to be wrong. The position is like this. One man says a triangle is a circle: another replies "A triangle is a straight line, and I will prove to you that I am right: *for*" (this is the only argument) "a straight line is not a circle." "That is quite true," the other may reply; "but nevertheless a triangle is a circle, and you have said nothing whatever to prove the contrary. What is proved is that one of us is wrong, for we agree that a triangle cannot be both a straight line and a circle: but which is wrong, there can be no earthly means of proving, since you define triangle as straight line and I define it as circle." —Well, that is one alternative which any naturalistic Ethics has to face; if good is *defined* as something else, it is then impossible either to prove that any other definition is wrong or even to deny such definition.

(2) The other alternative will scarcely be more welcome. It is that the discussion is after all a verbal one. When A says "Good means pleasant" and B says "Good means desired," they may merely wish to assert that most people have used the word for what is pleasant and for what is desired respectively. And this is quite an interesting subject for discussion: only it is not a whit more an ethical discussion than the last was. Nor do I think that any exponent of naturalistic Ethics would be willing to allow that this was all he meant. They are all so anxious to persuade us that what they call the good is what we really ought to do. "Do, pray, act so, because the word 'good' is generally used to denote actions of this nature": such,

on this view, would be the substance of their teaching. And in so far as they tell us how we ought to act, their teaching is truly ethical, as they mean it to be. But how perfectly absurd is the reason they would give for it! "You are to do this, because most people use a certain word to denote conduct such as this." "You are to say the thing which is not, because most people call it lying." That is an argument just as good!—My dear sirs, what we want to know from you as ethical teachers, is not how people use a word; it is not even, what kind of actions they approve, which the use of this word "good" may certainly imply: what we want to know is simply what *is* good. We may indeed agree that what most people do think good, is actually so; we shall at all events be glad to know their opinions: but when we say their opinions about what *is* good, we do mean what we say; we do not care whether they call that thing which they mean "horse" or "table" or "chair," "*gut*" or "*bon*" or "*agathos*"; we want to know what it is that they so call. When they say "Pleasure is good," we cannot believe that they merely mean "Pleasure is pleasure" and nothing more than that.

12. Suppose a man says "I am pleased"; and suppose that is not a lie or a mistake but the truth. Well, if it is true, what does that mean? It means that his mind, a certain definite mind, distinguished by certain definite marks from all others, has at this moment a certain definite feeling called pleasure. "Pleased" *means* nothing but having pleasure, and though we may be more pleased or less pleased, and even, we may admit for the present, have one or another kind of pleasure; yet in so far as it is pleasure we have, whether there be more or less of it, and whether it be of one kind or another, what we have is one definite thing, absolutely indefinable, some one thing that is the same in all the various degrees and in all the various kinds of it that there may be. We may be able to say how it is related to other things: that, for example, it is in the mind, that it causes desire, that we are conscious of it, etc., etc. We can, I say, describe its relations to other things, but define it we can *not*. And if anybody tried to define pleasure for us as being any other natural object; if anybody were to say, for instance, that pleasure *means* the sensation of red, and were to proceed to deduce from that that pleasure is a colour, we should be entitled to laugh at him and to distrust his future statements about pleasure. Well, that would be the same fallacy which I have called the naturalistic fallacy. That "pleased" does not mean "having the sensation of red," or anything else whatever, does not prevent us from understanding what it does mean. It is enough for us to know that "pleased" does mean "having the sensation of pleasure," and though pleasure is absolutely indefinable, though pleasure is pleasure and nothing else whatever, yet we feel no difficulty in saying that we are pleased. The reason is, of course, that when I say "I am pleased," I do *not* mean that "I" am the same thing as "having pleasure." And similarly no difficulty need be found in my saying that "pleasure is good" and yet not meaning that "pleasure" is the same thing as "good," that pleasure *means* good, and that good *means* pleasure. If I were to imagine that when

I said "I am pleased," I meant that I was exactly the same thing as "pleased," I should not indeed call that a naturalistic fallacy, although it would be the same fallacy as I have called naturalistic with reference to Ethics. The reason of this is obvious enough. When a man confuses two natural objects with one another, defining the one by the other, if for instance, he confuses himself, who is one natural object, with "pleased" or with "pleasure" which are others, then there is no reason to call the fallacy naturalistic. But if he confuses "good," which is not in the same sense a natural object, with any natural object whatever, then there is a reason for calling that a naturalistic fallacy; its being made with regard to "good" marks it as something quite specific, and this specific mistake deserves a name because it is so common. As for the reasons why good is not to be considered a natural object, they may be reserved for discussion in another place. But, for the present, it is sufficient to notice this: Even if it were a natural object, that would not alter the nature of the fallacy nor diminish its importance one whit. All that I have said about it would remain quite equally true: only the name which I have called it would not be so appropriate as I think it is. And I do not care about the name: what I do care about is the fallacy. It does not matter what we call it, provided we recognise it when we meet with it. It is to be met with in almost every book on Ethics; and yet it is not recognised: and that is why it is necessary to multiply illustrations of it, and convenient to give it a name. It is a very simple fallacy indeed. When we say that an orange is yellow, we do not think our statement binds us to hold that "orange" means nothing else than "yellow," or that nothing can be yellow but an orange. Supposing the orange is also sweet! Does that bind us to say that "sweet" is exactly the same thing as "yellow," that "sweet" must be defined as "yellow"? And supposing it be recognised that "yellow" just means "yellow" and nothing else whatever, does that make it any more difficult to hold that oranges are yellow? Most certainly it does not: on the contrary, it would be absolutely meaningless to say that oranges were yellow, unless yellow did in the end mean just "yellow" and nothing else whatever—unless it was absolutely indefinable. We should not get any very clear notion about things, which are yellow—we should not get very far with our science, if we were bound to hold that everything which was yellow, *meant* exactly the same thing as yellow. We should find we had to hold that an orange was exactly the same thing as a stool, a piece of paper, a lemon, anything you like. We could prove any number of absurdities; but should we be the nearer to the truth? Why, then, should it be different with "good"? Why, if good is good and indefinable, should I be held to deny that pleasure is good? Is there any difficulty in holding both to be true at once? On the contrary, there is no meaning in saying that pleasure is good, unless good is something different from pleasure. It is absolutely useless, so far as Ethics is concerned, to prove, as Mr. Spencer tries to do, that increase of pleasure coincides with increase of life, unless good *means* something different from either life or pleasure. He might just as well try to prove that an orange is yellow by shewing that it always is wrapped up in paper.

13. In fact, if it is not the case that "good" denotes something simple and indefinable, only two alternatives are possible: either it is a complex, a given whole, about the correct analysis of which there may be disagreement; or else it means nothing at all, and there is no such subject as Ethics. In general, however, ethical philosophers have attempted to define good, without recognising what such an attempt must mean. They actually use arguments which involve one or both of the absurdities considered in § 11. We are, therefore, justified in concluding that the attempt to define good is chiefly due to want of clearness as to the possible nature of definition. There are, in fact, only two serious alternatives to be considered, in order to establish the conclusion that "good" does denote a simple and indefinable notion. It might possibly denote a complex, as "horse" does; or it might have no meaning at all. Neither of these possibilities has, however, been clearly conceived and seriously maintained, as such, by those who presume to define good; and both may be dismissed by a simple appeal to facts.

(1) The hypothesis that disagreement about the meaning of good is disagreement with regard to the correct analysis of a given whole, may be most plainly seen to be incorrect by consideration of the fact that, whatever definition be offered, it may be always asked, with significance, of the complex so defined, whether it is itself good. To take, for instance, one of the more plausible, because one of the more complicated, of such proposed definitions, it may easily be thought, at first sight, that to be good may mean to be that which we desire to desire. Thus if we apply this definition to a particular instance and say "When we think that A is good, we are thinking that A is one of the things which we desire to desire," our proposition may seem quite plausible. But, if we carry the investigation further, and ask ourselves "Is it good to desire to desire A?" it is apparent, on a little reflection, that this question is itself as intelligible, as the original question "Is A good?"—that we are, in fact, now asking for exactly the same information about the desire to desire A, for which we formerly asked with regard to A itself. But it is also apparent that the meaning of this second question cannot be correctly analysed into "Is the desire to desire A one of the things which we desire to desire?": we have not before our minds anything so complicated as the question "Do we desire to desire to desire to desire A?" Moreover any one can easily convince himself by inspection that the predicate of this proposition—"good"—is positively different from the notion of "desiring to desire" which enters into its subject: "That we should desire to desire A is good" is *not* merely equivalent to "That A should be good is good." It may indeed be true that what we desire to desire is always also good; perhaps, even the converse may be

true: but it is very doubtful whether this is the case, and the mere fact that we understand very well what is meant by doubting it, shews clearly that we have two different notions before our minds.

(2) And the same consideration is sufficient to dismiss the hypothesis that "good" has no meaning whatsoever. It is very natural to make the mistake of supposing that what is universally true is of such a nature that its negation would be self-contradictory: the importance which has been assigned to analytic propositions in the history of philosophy shews how easy such a mistake is. And thus it is very easy to conclude that what seems to be a universal ethical principle is in fact an identical proposition; that, if, for example, whatever is called "good" seems to be pleasant, the proposition "Pleasure is the good" does not assert a connection between two different notions, but involves only one, that of pleasure, which is easily recognised as a distinct entity. But whoever will attentively consider with himself what is actually before his mind when he asks the question "Is pleasure (or whatever it may be) after all good?" can easily satisfy himself that he is not merely wondering whether pleasure is pleasant. And if he will try this experiment with each suggested definition in succession, he may become expert enough to recognise that in every case he has before his mind a unique object, with regard to the connection of which with any other object, a distinct question may be asked. Every one does in fact understand the question "Is this good?" When he thinks of it, his state of mind is different from what it would be, were he asked "Is this pleasant, or desired, or approved?" It has a distinct meaning for him, even though he may not recognise in what respect it is distinct. Whenever he thinks of "intrinsic value," or "intrinsic worth," or says that a thing "ought to exist," he has before his mind the unique object—the unique property of things—which I mean by "good." Everybody is constantly aware of this notion, although he may never become aware at all that it is different from other notions of which he is also aware. But, for correct ethical reasoning, it is extremely important that he should become aware of this fact; and, as soon as the nature of the problem is clearly understood, there should be little difficulty in advancing so far in analysis.

14. "Good," then, is indefinable; and yet, so far as I know, there is only one ethical writer, Prof. Henry Sidgwick, who has clearly recognised and stated this fact.[1] We shall see, indeed, how far many of the most reputed ethical systems fall short of drawing the conclusions which follow from such a recognition. At present I will only quote one instance, which will serve to illustrate the meaning and importance of this principle that "good" is indefinable, or, as Prof. Sidgwick says, an "unanalysable notion." It is an instance to which Prof. Sidgwick himself refers in a note on the passage, in which he argues that "ought" is unanalysable.

---

[1] Henry Sidgwick (1838–1900): a British writer on ethics and the history of ethics. What Moore says here about Sidgwick is based on the latter's book, *Methods of Ethics*. [F.E.]

"Bentham," says Sidgwick, "explains that his fundamental principle 'states the greatest happiness of all those whose interest is in question as being the right and proper end of human action' "; and yet "his language in other passages of the same chapter would seem to imply" that he *means* by the word "right" "conducive to the general happiness." Prof. Sidgwick sees that, if you take these two statements together, you get the absurd result that "greatest happiness is the end of human action, which is conducive to the general happiness"; and so absurd does it seem to him to call this result, as Bentham calls it, "the fundamental principle of a moral system," that he suggests that Bentham cannot have meant it. Yet Prof. Sidgwick himself states elsewhere that Psychological Hedonism is "not seldom confounded with Egoistic Hedonism"; and that confusion, as we shall see, rests chiefly on that same fallacy, the naturalistic fallacy, which is implied in Bentham's statements. Prof. Sidgwick admits therefore that this fallacy is sometimes committed, absurd as it is; and I am inclined to think that Bentham may really have been one of those who committed it. Mill, as we shall see, certainly did commit it. In any case, whether Bentham committed it or not, his doctrine, as above quoted, will serve as a very good illustration of this fallacy, and of the importance of the contrary proposition that good is indefinable.

Let us consider this doctrine. Bentham seems to imply, so Prof. Sidgwick says, that the word "right" *means* "conducive to general happiness." Now this, by itself, need not necessarily involve the naturalistic fallacy. For the word "right" is very commonly appropriated to actions which lead to the attainment of what is good; which are regarded as *means* to the ideal and not as ends-in-themselves. This use of "right," as denoting what is good as a means, whether or not it be also good as an end, is indeed the use to which I shall confine the word. Had Bentham been using "right" in this sense, it might be perfectly consistent for him to *define* right as "conducive to the general happiness," *provided only* (and notice this proviso) he had already proved, or laid down as an axiom, that general happiness was *the* good, or (what is equivalent to this) that general happiness alone was good. For in that case he would have already defined *the* good as general happiness (a position perfectly consistent, as we have seen, with the contention that "good" is indefinable), and, since right was to be defined as "conducive to *the* good," it would actually *mean* "conducive to general happiness." But this method of escape from the charge of having committed the naturalistic fallacy has been closed by Bentham himself. For his fundamental principle is, we see, that the greatest happiness of all concerned is the *right* and proper *end* of human action. He applies the word "right," therefore, to the end, as such, not only to the means which are conducive to it; and, that being so, right can no longer be defined as "conducive to the general happiness," without involving the fallacy in question. For now it is obvious that the definition of right as conducive to general happiness can be used by him in support of the fundamental principle that general happiness is the right end; instead of being itself derived from that principle. If right, by definition, means conducive to general happiness, then it is obvious that general happiness is the right end. It is not necessary now first to prove or assert that general happiness is the right end, before right is defined as conducive to general happiness—a perfectly valid procedure; but on the contrary the definition of right as conducive to general happiness proves general happiness to be the right end—a perfectly invalid procedure, since in this case the statement that "general happiness is the right end of human action" is not an ethical principle at all, but either, as we have seen, a proposition about the meaning of words, or else a proposition about the *nature* of general happiness, not about its rightness or goodness.

Now, I do not wish the importance I assign to this fallacy to be misunderstood. The discovery of it does not at all refute Bentham's contention that greatest happiness is the proper end of human action, if that be understood as an ethical proposition, as he undoubtedly intended it. That principle may be true all the same; we shall consider whether it is so in succeeding chapters. Bentham might have maintained it, as Prof. Sidgwick does, even if the fallacy had been pointed out to him. What I am maintaining is that the *reasons* which he actually gives for his ethical proposition are fallacious ones so far as they consist in a definition of right. What I suggest is that he did not perceive them to be fallacious; that, if he had done so, he would have been led to seek for other reasons in support of his Utilitarianism; and that, had he sought for other reasons, he *might* have found none which he thought to be sufficient. In that case he would have changed his whole system—a most important consequence. It is undoubtedly also possible that he would have thought other reasons to be sufficient, and in that case his ethical system, in its main results, would still have stood. But, even in this latter case, his use of the fallacy would be a serious objection to him as an ethical philosopher. For it is the business of Ethics, I must insist, not only to obtain true results, but also to find valid reasons for them. The direct object of Ethics is knowledge and not practice; and any one who uses the naturalistic fallacy has certainly not fulfilled this first object, however correct his practical principles may be.

My objections to Naturalism are then, in the first place, that it offers no reason at all, far less any valid reason, for any ethical principle whatever; and in this it already fails to satisfy the requirements of Ethics, as a scientific study. But in the second place I contend that, though it gives a reason for no ethical principle, it is a *cause* of the acceptance of false principles—it deludes the mind into accepting ethical principles, which are false; and in this it is contrary to every aim of Ethics. It is easy to see that if we start with a definition of right conduct as conduct conducive to general happiness; then, knowing that right conduct is universally conduct conducive to the good, we very easily arrive at the result that the good is general happiness. If, on the other hand, we once recognise that we must start our Ethics without a definition, we shall be much more apt to look about us, before we adopt any ethical principle whatever; and the more we look about us, the less likely are we to adopt a false one. It may be replied to this: Yes, but we shall look about us just as much, before we settle on our definition, and are therefore just as likely to be right. But I will try to shew that this is not the case. If we start with the conviction that a definition of good can be found, we start with the conviction that good *can mean* nothing else than some one property of things; and our only business will then be to discover what that property is. But if we recognise that, so far as the meaning of good goes, anything whatever may be good, we start with a much more open mind. Moreover, apart from the fact that, when we think we have a definition, we cannot logically defend our ethical principles in any way whatever, we shall also be much less apt to defend them well, even if illogically. For we shall start with the conviction that good must mean so and so, and shall therefore be inclined either to misunderstand our opponent's arguments or to cut them short with the reply, "This is not an open question: the very meaning of the word decides it; no one can think otherwise except through confusion."

QUESTIONS FOR STUDY AND DISCUSSION

1. What does Moore mean by "good" and "the good"? How are these two related?
2. Why, according to Moore, is "good" indefinable?
3. Why does he say that no statements about the good are analytic?
4. Explain and give examples of what Moore calls the "naturalistic fallacy."
5. Does Moore's argument, assuming it to be satisfactory, rule out the claim that the only good is pleasure? Why or why not?

Moritz Schlick

MORITZ SCHLICK, born in Berlin in 1882, is best known for his contributions to the development of logical positivism and for his leadership of the Vienna Circle, a philosophically oriented group that he inaugurated shortly after he arrived in 1922 at the University of Vienna as professor of Philosophy. In 1929 and 1932 he was a visiting professor in California. He returned to Vienna and was murdered in 1936 at the age of fifty-four by a demented student who shot him as he was entering the University. Although the Austrian press in some of the obituaries was hostile to Schlick, hinting that logical positivists deserved to be killed, one of his associates described him as a "kindly, truly great and noble man [whose death] was bitterly lamented by his many friends." Only three of Schlick's books have been translated into English: *Space and Time in Contemporary Physics* (1920), *Problems of Ethics* (published in Vienna in 1930; translated, 1939), and *Philosophy of Nature* (1949).

What Is the Meaning of "Moral"?

THE MORALITY OF DEMAND AND THE MORALITY OF DESIRE

The single example of a moral value-judgment which has thus far concerned us was the moral condemnation of egoism. We have taken this concept in the sense in which it implies moral disapprobation, and have determined its meaning more exactly. Our discussion was begun at this point purposely, because for our currently prevailing morality the criticism of selfishness is typical.

It is characteristic of this morality that all of its most important demands end in the repression of personal desires in favor of the desires of fellow men. These demands require *considerateness,* reject egoism, and appear to range themselves against the self, in favor of the other person. (According to Fichte all immorality has its basis in "selfishness.") Our morality is essentially a morality of *renunciation.* Among religions it is Christianity and Buddhism in particular whose moral precepts are of this character. In the Mosaic decalogue, likewise, curbing of the self is the chief postulate, and this finds its external expression in the negative form of most

From pp. 79–99 of *Problems of Ethics* by Moritz Schlick, translated by David Rynin. Copyright 1939 by David Rynin. Published by Dover Publications, Inc., and reprinted through permission of the publisher.

of the commandments: "Thou shalt not—," "thou shalt not—." The positive commandments (the third and fourth) demand consideration for the desires of God and parents. It is a morality of obedience. In Christianity the emphasis is on positive altruistic behavior, as opposed to selfishness: "Thou shalt love thy neighbor."

The constant theme of this morality is consideration of others; in its precepts, too, our fellow men and society speak and express their desires and needs; they tell us how it is desired that we should act. Hence the *demand* character of this system, which Kant held to be the essence of morality. The morality of ancient classical times, the Socratic, Stoic, and Epicurean, is quite different. Its fundamental question is not, "What is demanded of me?" but, "How must I live to be happy?" It has its source in the desires of the individual, of the agent himself, and thus bears the character not of demand but of *desire*. We could ascribe autonomy to it, in opposition to the heteronomy of the morality of demand, if another meaning did not usually lay claim to this expression. The ancient classical ethics is not an ethics of self-limitation, but of self-realization, not of renunciation, but of affirmation. The subjugation of selfishness is so little characteristic of it that, subsequently, objections were often made against its egoistic tendencies. But these objections are unjust, for condemnation of egoism and consideration for others and society (for example, the state) are present in it with all desirable distinctness, although usually not in the form of an original, ultimate obligation, but as a derivative demand.

In general it should be noted that judgments of particular acts in different moral systems deviate very little from each other. Base acts (at least within one's own society) are everywhere detested, and magnanimity everywhere praised; only the spirit or state of mind from which the valuation proceeds seems different, that is, the valuation appears to be justified differently.

The search which we begin here for the meaning of the word "moral" would constitute, according to the considerations of Chapter I, a general preparatory task of ethics; and the systematic arrangements of all the cases of its use, in different times among different people, circles, and circumstances, would lead to a system of norms (or to several) upon which the causal explanation of ethics would have to base itself. But we renounce from the outset any attempt to develop such a system; we have passed at once to its peak, where the most general formulation of the concept of "moral good" is to be found. We do this because we desire to deal with the most general ethical problems, and not to concern ourselves with special moral valuations. This shortened procedure is possible because the transition from the lower to the higher levels of the system is, in practice, always necessary and constantly made; so that we may presuppose the greater part of the task to be done, even though the results do not lie before us carefully formulated. Thus we see how little the theory of norms, to which this formulation belongs, contributes to actual ethical knowledge.

An essential difference between the morality of demand and the morality of desire, between the ethics of self-limitation and that of self-assertion, is not hard to find: at bottom there lies a different concept of the *good*. With Socrates the word "good" appears to have a unified meaning; in the Platonic dialogues there is talk of good shoes, a good cobbler, a good citizen, and so forth, without any difference in meaning being apparent. In Chapter I we considered the fact that the word "good" is also used in an extra-moral sense, and suggested that moral good is a species of the universal genus "good," being distinguished from this latter by certain specific differences, but having the most important properties in common with it. Socrates and most of the ancients never doubted this, and considered the common element so exclusively that they failed altogether to inquire into the specific properties of the "moral" good. Aristotle did so and determined the specific difference very nicely when he said, When we call anyone a good cobbler or a good pilot or a good architect, we use the word in an extra-moral sense; but when we call him a good *man,* then we use the word with its moral meaning.

However, the Aristotelian formulation is no more than a hint for us, which we improve and perfect by proposing the following, in order to express the actual meaning of the word:

The word "good" has a moral sense when (1) it refers to human *decisions,* and (2) expresses an approbation by human *society*.

In order to explain the words "approve" and "society" we add that when we say: the decision of an individual is "approved by society," this means: is *desired* by a large majority of those persons with whom the individual comes into contact through word or deed. It is essential to these statements that they be vague.

For the Greeks, originally, "good" meant nothing but what is desired, that is, in our language, what is imagined with pleasure; therefore ancient ethics is for the most part a theory of pleasure, hedonism. Even today "good" means, in the most general sense, the same thing: a thing is good if it is as one desires it. But from this, under the influence of our morality of renunciation, the narrower meaning of the *morally good* has arisen. Good in *this* sense means merely what is desired by human society, something which confronts the individual as an *alien* desire, which may or may not coincide with personal desires. The desires of others are the *demands* which they make of individuals. Hence an ethics which concerns the good in this sense alone is not a theory of pleasure, but of what is obligatory; it is "deontology."

The *ethical theory* of the Greeks was based on desires and not upon demands, for the Greek could not imagine otherwise than that the individual himself must be his own moral lawgiver; moral norms were of course, then, as in every community, also formulated as *commands*. Because of the fact that modern ethics makes central the facts of demand and renunciation, it runs the risk of putting senseless questions and going wholly astray;

on the other hand, its path leads nearer to certain fundamental insights of great importance for the understanding of ethical matters. For, in fact, in the concept of renunciation or in the emphasis upon altruism lies a hint leading toward the most essential point of morality.

MORAL DEMANDS AS EXPRESSIONS
OF THE DESIRES OF SOCIETY

For us it is clear that there must be no insuperable opposition between an ethics as theory of pleasure and as theory of moral obligation; or, as we may put it, between the theory of goods or pleasures and the theory of duty; but the latter will be grounded by and deduced from the former. For, according to our conception, the moral demands or duties go back in the last analysis to the feelings of pleasure and pain of individuals, since they are nothing but the average, prevailing desires of society. It is, of course, comprehensible that in practice the morality of self-realization should arrive also at demands of renunciation, which appear to be necessary means to the end of happiness. Thus the ideals of the wise man and the saint approach one another; performance of duty appears as the condition of self-realization.

If, on the other hand, the precepts of renunciation were something final and absolute, as their exponents would have us believe, and not derivable from any desires, there would be no bridge between happiness and virtue, there would be enmity or complete indifference. If a virtuous person should ever be happy this would be the merest accident, and if he were *always* happy this would be an incomprehensible miracle. A connection between the performance of duty and happiness exists, a reconciliation of the ethics of renunciation with the ethics of joy is possible, the agreement of their valuations in individual practical cases is explicable, only if moral commands themselves rise out of human needs and desires. We affirmed that this is actually the case when we formulated the hypothesis that the moral precepts are nothing but the expressions of the desires of human society; in the moral valuation of definite acts or dispositions as good or bad is mirrored only the measure of joy or sorrow that society expects to receive from those acts or dispositions. Thus we see how very important is the validity of the proposition made at the end of the preceding chapter; let us now devote ourselves to its proof.

In the thesis with whose proof we are concerned there are, strictly, two different assertions to be distinguished: first, that, in fact, whatever is morally approved does promise to increase the joys of human society; and second, that this effect expected by society is really the only reason *why* it is approved. It is clear that these assertions are to be distinguished carefully. It could be that everything called "morally good" by society did in fact serve to benefit society, and vice versa, but that the reason for calling it good and approving it lay elsewhere. The case (of which we convinced ourselves in the discussion of egoism) is as follows: the determination of the complete extensional equality of the concepts "morally good" and "what advances the pleasure of society" leads any unbiased person to believe also in their intensional equality; and special opposing reasons would be necessary to make this belief appear to be unjustified. Without such opposing reasons the inference to the identity of both concepts is simply obvious in terms of the method of empirical knowledge. If, in addition, we should succeed in deducing from psychological laws that behavior which is favorable to the genesis of pleasure in the human community must be approved by it, while what increases sorrow necessarily is subjected to its disapproval (as we have seen in the case of egoism), then no one will be able to upset our conviction that this approbation and disapprobation is nothing but "moral" approbation and disapprobation.

Accordingly, the proof of our thesis would involve two steps: (1) to show that in fact the moral predicate "good" is bestowed only upon such behavior as promises the social group an increase in pleasure, and (2) to refute the reasons which lead many philosophers to believe that, despite the foregoing fact, the predicate "good" *means* something different from promising an increase of happiness or a decrease of sorrow for society. For if these reasons do not hold good the validity of the second assertion is self-evident.

CRITIQUE OF UTILITARIANISM

The first thesis which we have to defend and which asserts that "good" is what tends to further the happiness of society bears a special name in ethics; it is the moral principle of "Utilitarianism." It has this name because it says, roughly, "Good is what is useful (utile) to human society." The formulation of our thesis is perhaps not unessentially different from that which it received in the classical systems of Utilitarianism. These systems say (at least according to their sense): "The good *is* what *brings* the greatest possible happiness to society." We express it more carefully: "In human society, that is *called* good which is *believed* to bring the greatest happiness."

Is it necessary to point out the difference between these formulae? In the first it might seem (and this was actually the opinion of certain champions of the utilitarian principle) that it contains the absolute demand that everyone must set as the final goal of his action the happiness of the greatest number; while the second merely wishes to express, as a fact, the demands which society actually makes of its members.

Whoever advocates a demand must make its content as precise as possible. Hence the Utilitarian who seeks a moral principle cannot be satisfied with the vague statement that good is what furthers the "happiness of human society," but must seek to make this latter concept more exact. The inevitable attempt to attain a more exact determination led Bentham to the famous Utilitarian formula that those acts are morally good which under given circumstances have the "greatest happiness of the greatest number of human beings" (or living creatures in general?) as their consequences. A few words can show the utter inapplicability of this formula. In the first place, the results of every act are simply incalculable, for they stretch on into time indefinitely; and even the resultant events of the near future cannot be predicted, for they depend more or less upon "chance," that is, slightly differing acts can have extraordinarily different effects. In the second place, "the greatest happiness of the greatest number" is a senseless conjunction of words, which can indeed be given a meaning by means of certain conventions, but such a conventional meaning, because of its arbitrariness, will not express the thought which the formula would like to express. Furthermore, Utilitarianism did not attempt to find a meaningful convention, but believed that these words had a clear meaning, presupposing that one can speak of the pleasure of different persons as of something comparable in magnitude. And this is the fundamental mistake. If it has been shown that even the individual feelings of pleasure are not amenable to quantitative comparison, then this holds even more of the vague concept of happiness, which is difficult to construct in any way except as a sort of conjunction or "summation" of feelings of pleasure. The Utilitarian would find himself confronted by such questions as these: "How should I act when the circumstances are such that my conduct can lead either to a certain definite amount of happiness in each of four persons, or double that amount for each of two?" The absurdity of such a question is apparent; but the Utilitarian cannot avoid them; his formula makes sense only if he can tell us exactly what it means to say, "*A* is three-and-a-half times as happy as *B*."

We are in a better situation with respect to this matter than are the followers of Bentham; for we do not wish, as they do, to establish a formula or a command. We do not desire to construct a concept of the "good"—which we should have to define exactly—but we want only a simple determination of what, in human society, is held to be good. Thus we are not required to state of what the highest good consists, and which modes of behavior lead to it; we determine only that men *believe,* on the average, and are in wide agreement, that certain modes of behavior lead to the greatest common good. The reasons for this belief do not at present interest us, and whether they are *good* reasons, whether they are *valid,* we are not required to know by our formulation of the question.

One other important observation is here included: every philosopher, including the Utilitarian, knows of course that no one can predict the results of conduct with complete assurance, that this is always in part an effect of chance. If, despite this, Utilitarianism or any other ethical theory apparently judges the moral value of a decision by its results, this can only be the average or *probable* result. It has always been evident that the *decisions* (the "intentions") alone are the objects of moral judgment. Therefore it is incorrect to distinguish, as is often done, between an "ethics of intention" and an "ethics of result." There has never been an "ethics of result."

THE GOOD APPEARS TO SOCIETY AS THE USEFUL

In order to show that that is considered "morally good" which, *according to the opinion of society,* is to its advantage (pleasure increasing) we must establish that moral valuations of modes of behavior change when the structure of human society changes, and that this change takes place in a manner which is inevitable if the opinion entertained regarding the conditions of the welfare of society is determinative of that valuation. For if it appears that the actual alteration of moral valuations corresponds to changes of certain states of, and opinions in, the community, then we may with certainty assume that these states and views represent the basis upon which the valuations rest.

This is actually the case. Ethnography and history agree in teaching that the diversities in moral precepts, which change from people to people and epoch to epoch, always correspond to diversities in what, under the prevailing circumstances, is favorable to the welfare of the society; or rather to what is so considered. We here point to a single set of facts in which this alteration shows itself especially clearly, namely, the change in moral views correlated with the increase in *size* of the community in which they prevail. In such times and places in which the community of persons (determined by their instinctive drawing together in the common struggle for existence) extends over only a small tribe, a clan, or a family, the moral rules that are recognized demand consideration only for the members of the group itself; with respect to those who stand outside it there is no ethical obligation. Often, indeed, everyone who does not belong to the group is *eo ipso* considered an enemy, an outlaw. It is well known that in primitive tribes under certain circumstances the murder of a member of a neighboring tribe is considered to be as great a moral service as the murder of a member of one's own tribe would be a crime.

And these valuations are not merely proclaimed externally and recognized by the individual because of the application of sanctions, but appear to him as the voice of his own conscience, which commands him with incontrovertible authority and terrible emotional force (for, obviously, the conscience is formed by external suggestion, whose whisperings resound in the mind as through a powerful trumpet). We find a famous example of this in the writings of Darwin, who tells of the dreadful pangs of conscience suffered by an African savage who had neglected to take revenge on a neighboring tribe for injury done him by some sort of magic. A missionary had impressed upon him that it is a great sin to murder a man, and the savage did not dare to carry out the act of vengeance. But the consciousness of his neglected "duty" oppressed him so much that he went about disturbed and upset, rejected food and drink, and could enjoy nothing. In

short, he showed all the signs of an "evil conscience." Finally he could bear
it no longer, stole away secretly, slew a member of the other clan and returned light of heart: he had performed his duty and pacified his conscience by means of the murder. Would anyone wish to deny that the feelings of the savage are "real" pangs of conscience, as these are felt by a
moral civilized man? If so, we can only attribute this to prejudice, for one
will search in vain for the difference. Of course, in general, the European
feels scruples of conscience under different circumstances, namely, after
committing murder, and not when the deed has been omitted; but even this
does not hold without exceptions. For in *war* the great majority of men
consider the destruction of their enemies to be not only not forbidden, but
actually a moral obligation.

The difference between the moral views of the African and a modern
European in this respect is explained by the fact that the group which furnishes the standard for the formation of those views is for the savage the
tribe or clan, but for the civilized man is extended to include a whole nation or state; and further upon the fact that the state of enmity is enduring
for the one, and transitory for the other. And if to a philosopher war between two nations appears quite as immoral as a conflict between two
armed bands of a single nation, this is because for him the human society
which makes the moral laws has extended over the whole world: in his
conscience re-echoes the voice of all humanity.

What appears here in a single example holds universally. The content
of the moral precepts that hold in a community, and that are taken over
completely into the moral consciousness of its members, depends entirely
upon its living conditions, upon its size and strength, its relation to the surrounding world, its civilization, customs, and religious ideas. I forego the
introduction of further evidence, and refer to Westermarck's *Origin and
Development of Moral Ideas,* and to Spencer's *Data of Ethics,* which contain rich material. We see in the dependence of moral valuations upon the
states of human society a sure indication that the content of morality is
actually determined by society. It also seems to be the moral lawgiver concerning whom (according to Chapter I) ethics must inquire. We shall soon
see whether this result is final or requires a more thorough proof.

THE FORMULATION OF MORAL LAWS TAKES PLACE
ACCORDING TO THE UTILITARIAN PRINCIPLE

Closer examination of the content of moral precepts shows that the community anticipates a furtherance of its welfare from their observance. It is
not necessary to prove this in particular cases, since it is generally not disputed. For whatever be one's opinion regarding the nature and origin of
moral rules, it is generally believed that society is benefited if all of its
members obey them. For the confirmation of this we point out that everywhere the laws promulgated by the state (which are not, indeed, identical
with moral laws, but which still should represent their essential minimum)

are thought out with no other purpose in mind than to advance the general welfare. It is inconceivable that any modern lawmaker could give any other justification for the proposal of a law than this utilitarian one (the lawmaker always appears as a utilitarian because he says in justification of his proposals, "They *are* useful to society," not, "Society considers them to be useful"). Whenever legislatures or parliaments discuss a law or precept the discussion centers solely on the question, "Which decision will be *most* useful to society?" No one asks, "Which decision is moral or has the greatest moral value?" It may happen that in debate mention is made of the "honor" of the community or the "holiness" of an institution is stressed, but such arguments are never directed *against* the increase of happiness, but are introduced only when it is silently assumed that the observance of them does not stand in opposition to society's striving for happiness. The lawmakers have thus the unenviable task of deciding what *in fact* will be most advantageous to the welfare of the state or humanity. And they do not despair of the solution of this task only because they can, generally, replace it by an easier one, namely: to hinder what would directly injure society. In so doing they make the (not self-evident) assumption that the avoidance of immediate injury is likewise the path to the greatest general welfare.

What holds of the formulated laws, of legality, also holds for the moral views of society, for the moral code: the conviction prevails that moral behavior furthers the general happiness, indeed that it is the necessary if not the sufficient condition of that happiness. The opposing view has been held occasionally by a few individuals, but that need not surprise us, for there is hardly any possible opinion regarding matters of human importance which has not been expressed by someone. If many philosophers proclaim with great feeling that morality is independent of welfare, by saying that one must always do what is "right," even though one sees clearly that the greatest harm will result, then such a standpoint of *"fiat justitia, pereat mundus"* does indeed partake of the sublime, which is always the attribute of the unconditioned; but no wise guide of a nation's destiny would actually assume the responsibility of acting according to that prescription. And to the blame he would thus receive from the absolutist philosopher would be opposed the praise that a grateful society would bestow upon him for not having sacrificed its well-being in favor of an abstract principle. Society would unquestionably consider his behavior to be morally good. Of course the divergent attitude of the philosopher must also be made intelligible; we must understand how he arrives at his approbations and disapprobations. We shall deal with this question in a moment.

CONCLUSIONS

By means of considerations like the foregoing we arrive at the following results:

(1) The meaning of the word "good" (that is, what is considered as

moral) is determined by the opinion of society, which is the lawgiver formulating moral demands. Since, with respect to a social group, there can only be an *average* or prevailing opinion, one cannot raise an objection to this view based upon the fact that there are deviations from some of the usual norms.

(2) The content of the concept "good" is determined in such a way by society that all and only those modes of behavior are subsumed under it which society believes are advantageous to its welfare and preservation (which is indeed the presupposition of its welfare).

Considering propositions (1) and (2) together we deduce from them, or consider the assertion justified, that:

(3) The moral demands are established by society *only because* the fulfillment of these demands appears to be useful to it.

We can also formulate proposition (3) by saying, "The good is good only because it is considered by society to be useful"; and in the last analysis this means: considered to be conducive to pleasure. Or also thus: the *material* meaning of the word "moral" *exhausts itself* in denoting what, according to the prevailing opinion in society, is advantageous (its *formal* meaning consists in being demanded by society).

It is clear that a logical connection must exist between (1) and (2); for the reason that moral behavior is demanded must somehow or other lie in the nature of morality, and if this nature is completely given by proposition (2) it must contain the grounds of (1). But this connection need not be as direct and simple as proposition (3) would make out. It might be that even though morality were undoubtedly advantageous to the general welfare it would be approved upon *other* grounds. In other words, it might be that the idea of moral behavior did not owe its pleasure-tone to belief in the usefulness of such behavior to society, but that this joy had some other origin, for example, in a "conscience," whose presence expressed itself in certain special feelings and ideas (or actually was composed of them) and whose origin constituted a special problem. We mention for example the metaphysical hypothesis that divine insight furnished man with a conscience in order to implant in him a motive of moral behavior, such behavior as would be (again according to the divine insight) in the last analysis most useful to him. We require no such hypotheses, however, for what they would explain is explained for us by known psychological relationships. As soon, that is, as one feels himself to be a member of society and feels his own good and evil to be bound up with that of others, the idea of a happy community must become a pleasant idea; and this emotional tone extends itself according to known laws to all modes of behavior which he supposes are advantageous to the welfare of society. In other words: a social man *desires* that his environment be happy and unendangered, desires all modes of behavior which are conducive to this, values, approves and commends them, and condemns and persecutes contrary conduct. All these are only different ways of saying the same thing.

Of course the processes whereby the general welfare becomes a pleasant goal are complicated; and one must not, above all, attribute too great a role to rational *insight*. For even if men thought much more and more accurately than they usually do about the consequences of action, such considerations would have but little influence in the realm of feelings. And these processes take place chiefly in this realm, in the absence of subtle thinking. But here we can appeal to a general principle which has otherwise proved to be valid in psychology and biology, namely, that the result of organic, unconscious, or instinctive processes is the same as would have resulted from a rational calculation. This principle is closely connected with that general "purposiveness" of the organic world which is usually called "teleology." If one would trace the development of these psychic processes, one must keep specially in mind that they have their origin in concrete situations, and that such abstract concepts as the "general welfare" are quite useless in the formation of powerful centers of feeling. In what follows we shall have occasion to offer contributions to the psychology of moral valuation, but at present we are satisfied to see at least the path along which the human spirit necessarily arrives at the praise and approbation of "moral" behavior.

With this we have not of course strictly shown that the valuation of morality, which we have deduced, is actually *moral valuation* (that it does not merely constitute the basis of a certain type of value of the moral life, a "utility value," but constitutes the whole of moral valuation); but we shall, according to our program, consider it certain and thus hold our proposition (3) to be true if we also succeed in showing that the most important attempt in ethics to conceive the nature of moral valuation differently cannot be carried out. Our only reasons for considering this attempt at all are historical; apart from them, considered factually, what has been adduced appears to us to contain a sufficient foundation of our thesis, however inexhaustive it may be. But since, especially at present, many philosophical writers represent a very different point of view, we turn to the *critical* considerations, which we proposed as the second stage in the proof of our thesis (p. 472).

QUESTIONS FOR STUDY AND DISCUSSION

1. According to Schlick, what is the difference between a morality of demand and a morality of desire?
2. What assumptions about duty have to be made if duty and happiness are to be reconcilable?
3. How does Schlick's position differ from utilitarianism?
4. What observations does Schlick offer to support his second conclusion?
5. What difficulty causes Schlick to postpone a categorical assertion of his third conclusion?

Are There Absolute Values?

THE THEORY OF OBJECTIVE VALUES

The opinion we have to examine may best be expressed negatively in the assertion that the moral value of a disposition cannot in any way be grounded in feelings of pleasure. Value is something wholly independent of our feelings, something pertaining to valuable objects, in a definite amount and degree, quite independently of the way in which we react emotionally to them, and to whether anyone acknowledges the value or not. Pleasure, to be sure, is a value, but only one among many, and obviously not the highest. Often it is admitted that the valuable produces feelings of pleasure in the observer, but this fact is supposed to have nothing to do with the *essence* of the value, but is, in a sense, accidental. I say "in a sense," for many who hold this view do not wish, I believe, to deny that perhaps the generation of feelings of pleasure in the presence of something valuable is a natural law, and that a causal connection exists between the two. But they say that this is quite unessential, that if it were not so it would make no difference to the value of the valuable thing; this value would exist even if the law of nature read: "The idea of the valuable thing is quite indifferent to all men," or "extremely annoying" or "horrible."

The role played in ethics by this theory of the objectivity of value is too well known to require one to dwell upon it. It proclaims the existence of a system of values, which, like the Platonic ideas, consitutes a realm independent of actuality, and in which is exhibited an essential order of such a nature that the values compose a hierarchy arranged according to higher and lower. And its relation to reality is only established by the moral command, which runs, approximately, "Act so that the events or things produced by your actions are as valuable as possible."

The criticism which we make of this view is extremely simple. Its main lines are prescribed by our philosophical method. We ask *first,* "What does the word value *mean?*" or, which comes to the same thing, "What is the meaning of an assertion which ascribes a certain value to any object?" This question can be answered only by stating the method of determining the truth of a value judgment; that is, one must state exactly under what empirical conditions the proposition "This object is valuable" is true, and under what conditions it is false. If one cannot state these conditions, then the proposition is a meaningless combination of words.

Thus we ask the philosopher, "How do you recognize the value of an object?" And since no one is here to answer (the author writes these lines in deep seclusion on the rocky coast of the Adriatic Sea) we shall search for the usual and possible answers together.

PLEASURE AS THE CRITERION OF OBJECTIVE VALUE

(*a*) In case anyone (I do not know whether there is any such person) should answer that values are in fact to be recognized only in feelings of pleasure which valuable things awaken in us, and that also the rank of the value is disclosed to us only by means of the intensity of the corresponding feeling, and that in addition there is no other criterion of the existence and rank of the value, yet that nevertheless the value does not *consist* in the activity of producing pleasure, but is something else, then we must accuse him of logical nonsense. However, we do it very unwillingly, for factually we do not find anything to dispute regarding the consequences of his theory. The nonsense consists in the fact that with respect to all *verifiable* consequences his view is in complete agreement with our own (that "value" is nothing but a name for the dormant pleasure possibilities of the valuable object), but despite this he asserts that they are different. The proposition that "to be valuable" means something quite different from "to bring pleasure" presupposes that there is some property which belongs only to the valuable, and not to the pleasure-bringing: the assertion becomes senseless if pleasure-producing is the *only* characteristic of the valuable. If we should peacefully grant the existence of "objective" value, this would be nothing but a contentless addition. Everything would remain as if it were essentially subjective, for we would be able to make an assertion about it only because of its pleasure consequences, as is also the case according to our own view.

I add that from the criticized standpoint every feeling of pleasure must be interpreted as the sign of an objective value. If this held only in certain cases, but not in others, we should have to be able to say how the cases differed, and this would require a new criterion and the rejection of the original one, which was simply pleasure. The advocate of objective values requires, then, an empirical criterion of value which cannot be identical with pleasure.

OBJECTIVE CRITERIA OF VALUE?

(*b*) It is natural to want to give an objective criterion for objective values —just as we recognize that an animal is a camel by the fact that it has two humps, concerning whose existence one can convince himself by sense-perception. Sense-perception, whose value as a criterion for objectivity has often been disputed in epistemological considerations, may be unhesitatingly accepted as the judge in our problem, as in all questions of daily life. Hence if value could be seen or touched as can a camel's hump, ethics would have no occasion to discuss its nature. But since this is not so, one seeks some objective fact which shall serve as the sign of values; and thus one asserts, for example, "Whatever furthers the progress of evolution is valuable," or, "Whatever contributes to the creation of spiritual possessions, for example, works of art, and science, is valuable," or similar statements. If I am not mistaken, Wilhelm Wundt in his ethics of objective spiritual products made such an attempt.

We feel at once what is wrong in such attempts. Even if one should succeed in finding a formula which fitted everything generally considered to be valuable, such a formula, it seems to me, would always appear to be circular. Since, for example, what a "spiritual possession" is, what shall pass for an "upward evolution" (as opposed to downward) can only be determined by comparison with some standard. It cannot itself determine the standard. And if, in order to escape the circle, one arbitrarily establishes what should be understood by spiritual possessions, and things of the sort, this determination would be arbitrary; at best one would have produced the definition of a concept, based upon opinion, which one decides to call "value"; but this would not offer a criterion for *that* which we all *mean* when we use the word "value."

A fundamental error lies at the basis of the whole attempt: it consists in seeking value distinctions in the objective facts themselves, without reference to the acts of preference and selection, through which alone value comes into the world.

SUBJECTIVE CRITERIA OF VALUE

(c) Thus there remains no alternative to locating the characteristic of value once more in an immediate datum and to finding the verification of a proposition concerning value in the occurrence of a definite experience. Our own criterion is of this sort: the corresponding experience is simply the feeling of pleasure, with which we dealt at length in Chapter II. According to our opinion the *essence* of value is completely exhausted by it. The opposing theory of absolute value cannot, as was shown in (a), use pleasure as the characteristic of value; it must therefore assert the occurrence of a wholly different experience which indicates the existence of a value. This is, in fact, if I understand them rightly, the opinion of the noteworthy representatives of that theory (of Brentano,[1] and the schools following him). According to them we possess the capacity of determining the existence of a value in much the same way as we are acquainted with the presence of a material object by means of perception. The role here played by sensation is there taken over by a specific experience, which one may call the feeling or experience of value, insight, or what not; without of course contributing anything to a closer description by this naming. In any case, it is always something ultimate, unanalyzable, which must appear when a value judgment is verified, and which one either has or does not have, concerning which therefore there can be no further discussion.

---

[1] Franz Brentano (1838–1917): German philosopher who made influential studies on the nature of knowing and of valuing. [F.E.]

What should we say regarding this theory? In so far as it asserts the existence of a special datum of consciousness, a "value-experience," any disagreement would be senseless, for each person alone can know what he experiences. One could simply accept or reject the theory without any proof. (I personally could not accept it, because I do not succeed in distinguishing between the feeling of pleasure that I have when I hear "Don Juan" or see a noble face or read about the personality of Abraham Lincoln, and an elementary value-experience which, according to that view, must first assure me that what gives me joy is also a *value*.)

But the theory asserts not only the existence or occurrence of a certain datum of consciousness, but asserts further that this informs me of something objective, independent of me, that it guarantees for me the existence of an absolute value. Does this assertion also not require verification? That the criterion is finally found in a datum of consciousness, that is, in the realm of the "subjective," would not in itself be suspicious; for this cannot be avoided, and the example of perception teaches us that "subjective" sensations can lead us to objects whose independence of us, and objectivity, leave for all practical purposes nothing to be desired. And in ethics we are concerned with practical knowledge in the significant sense. But the sensations are able to carry out that performance only because they obey very definite *laws*. The play of perceptions, however colorful it be, exhibits a very definite regularity, which is expressed by the fact that we are able to make verifiable predictions concerning the occurrence of sensations. (Regularity does not indicate something objective, but is itself objectivity.) If something of the sort held of the hypothetical value-feelings, as holds for sensations; if value propositions cohered in a consistent system, as do the propositions about perceptions, *then* value-feelings could guarantee objective values. But that is not the case. The chaos of valuations is proverbial, and there is no hope of putting value theory, ethics and aesthetics, on a level with physics, which would otherwise be easy.

Thus there is no possibility of passing from elementary value-experiences to the justification of objective absolute values. But if one says that the justification lies already contained within the experience itself I can only answer that I cannot imagine how such an assertion would be verified, and that therefore I do not know what it means.

DO VALUE JUDGMENTS HAVE THE VALIDITY
OF LOGICO-MATHEMATICAL PROPOSITIONS?

(*d*) Perhaps many hold the comparison of absolute values to objective material bodies to be improper, because the realm of values seems incomparable to gross physical reality. At least we hardly ever find the analogy to perception drawn.[2] Instead of it, the more often, another, that is, the value-

---

[2] Nevertheless the advocates of absolute values often say that these are *intuitively* known, and their whole outlook is thus called "intuitionism," a term in use in particular among English writers. But intuition signifies something similar to perception. [M.S.]

propositions are compared to the propositions of logic or mathematics, and explained by means of them. Neither deals with "actual" objects, and the validity of both is of the same sort. In the example of logic or mathematics we see best, it is supposed, how it is possible, despite the subjectivity of our experience of evidence, to arrive at what is intrinsically valid, absolute, and existing independently of any assent or any act of thought or feeling. The law of contradiction, and the proposition "Two times two equals four" hold simply, whether anyone thinks and understands them or not. As here with absolute truth, so there with absolute value. The notion of the objectivity of value is usually made plausible in this way (for example, see Nicolai Hartmann, *Ethics* [3]), and generally it remains the *only* way.

But, however misleading the argument is, our comparison with perception and its objects is a thousand times better, even from the standpoint of the absolutist theory. A comparison of any propositions with those of logic (which in this context also include the mathematical) always leads to nonsense; for logic is simply not comparable to anything (I hope I may be forgiven this somewhat paradoxical statement, but the way in which even today the essence of logic is misunderstood demands forthright criticism). This is not the place for me to expand this point; I note briefly only that the propositions of logic and the so-called propositions of mathematics are tautologies, or tautology-like forms, that is, they express nothing whatever (they are merely rules for the transformation of propositions). It is to this alone that they owe their absolute (independent of every experience) truth, which is really only a meaningless limiting case of truth. Thus in logic it is not as, according to the hopes or statements of the absolutists, it should be in value theory: namely, that here, in some sense, there is a realm of nonactual essences, independent of us, but ready to be recognized by us at any time, or, perhaps, in the case of values, to be realized. Logical propositions furnish us with no knowledge whatever, they express no facts, and teach us nothing about what exists in the world, or how anything does or should behave in the world. Thus if the value-propositions were similar to them it would only follow that they too were mere tautologies, in all strictness saying nothing; a consequence that would certainly cause us to wish value-propositions to have as little similarity as possible to those of logic. Judgments about value ought to tell us just what is most important.

Tautological propositions can be formed about anything, and of course, about values. When, for example, I write the proposition: "If the value A is greater than the value B, then the value B is smaller than the value A," I have clearly said in this true proposition nothing at all about values, but have merely shown the equivalence of two different modes of expression. Indeed the proposition is not a proposition of value theory, but belongs to

---

Nicolai Hartmann (1882–1950): a major figure in twentieth-century European philosophy, particularly ethics. In his work *Ethics* (published in 1926, four years before the German edition of Schlick's *Problems of Ethics*), Hartmann regarded moral values as an independent realm. [F.E.]

logic. And so it is always: whenever I come upon a proposition that is true independently of every experience, I am in the realm of logic. Only the propositions of logic, and all of them, have this character. In this lies their peculiarity, which I spoke of before.

Thus also in a comparison with logic and mathematics we fail to find a verifiable meaning in propositions about absolute values.

THE "ABSOLUTE OUGHT"

(e) Here it is necessary to bestow a moment's attention upon Kant's ethics. His concept of *ought* represents exactly what we have hitherto called "value-experience." There was undoubtedly at work in him a motive which presumably also plays a role in the genesis of modern absolutist theories: the desire to elevate ethics entirely above the empirical level. Kant showed correctly that the moral precepts have the character of demands, and that each appears to us as an "ought." But he could not bring himself to leave its empirical meaning to this word, in which alone it is actually used. Everyone knows this meaning: "I ought to do something" never means anything but "Someone wants me to do it." And in fact the desire of another, directed upon me, is described as an ought only when that person is able to add pressure to his desire and thus to reward fulfillment and to punish neglect, or at least to point out the natural consequences of observance or neglect. This is the meaning the word has in daily life; nor does it occur there with any other meaning. We call such a desire a command (imperative); therefore it is of the essence of the imperative to be hypothetical, that is, to presuppose some sanction, a promise or a threat.

According to our own view, developed in the previous chapter, the lawgiver who sanctions the moral commands is human society, which is furnished with the necessary power to command. Thus we may rightly say that morality makes demands on men, that they *ought* to behave in certain ways; because we use the word "ought" here in exactly the determined empirical sense. But, as we said, Kant cannot be satisfied with this. No matter whom he might find to be the source of the ethical command it would always be hypothetical, dependent upon the power and desire of this being, ceasing upon his absence or with a change of his desires. Since Kant, in order to avoid the hypothetical, did not wish to make even God responsible for the moral rules, there remained for him nothing but a leap into the void. He explained that the ought proceeded from *no* "other"; it is an absolute ought, and the ethical command is a categorical, not a conditional, imperative.

But we have seen that a relationship to a power which expresses its desires is *essential* to the concept of the ought, just as essential as the relationship to some conditions (sanctions) is for the concept of the imperative. These characteristics belong to the definition of both concepts as we know them. Thus, for example, the concept "uncle" is defined relative to nephews and nieces; an "absolute uncle" would be nonsense. Since Kant, for his concepts of the ought and of the imperative, expressly repudiates the relation to one who commands, and to sanctions, both terms must have for him a wholly different meaning from that explained by us. It is, of course, the privilege of every author to use words as he pleases, and to give the terms he finds in daily life a new meaning, *if only he defines this meaning exactly* and retains it. But Kant does not give a new definition. He speaks as if the word "ought" is used by him in the usual sense, minus only its relative character. However, this is a *contradiction,* for relativity, the relation to another desiring person, is constitutive of the ought in its usual sense. It is just as if Kant had said, "I wish to use the phrase 'to take a walk' with such a meaning that I can say 'a walk is being taken' without anyone there who takes it." An ought without someone who gives commands is an uncle who is such, not relatively to some nephew or niece, but simply in himself.

In order to rid the Kantian ethics of this nonsense we must use the word "ought" with a meaning which has nothing in common with its original meaning; and therefore the same word should not be used. The role which it plays, apart from that unfortunate explanation in Kant's ethics, is, as has been suggested, that which fell to the "value-experience" in the views considered earlier, with the here unessential difference that it exclusively represents the *moral* values: it is the "moral law in me." (By the "in me" there is apparently given to Kant another opportunity to introduce a lawgiver of the ought, namely the ego itself. However, not the empirical ego—otherwise the ought would simply be the expression of its will—but the super-empirical "practical reason" of the ego, which makes it "autonomous." And in his metaphysics Kant finally also adds the sanctions in the form of other-worldly rewards.) "The practical reason" which lays down the moral law is, however, either an empty word or it reveals itself in some verifiable experience. It could be defined only in terms of such. Accordingly, for Kant the ought is to be defined as the consciousness of moral value. But with this we arrive at the problem of section (*d*), and we may consider the untenability of this view to be established.

Still, it may be asked, might there not perhaps be given with the word "ought" at least some hint regarding the kind of psychological properties the asserted "feeling of value" would have, so that we might know where to seek for such a subtle experience, alleged to be so different from every feeling of pleasure? Is there not, perhaps, in consciousness a demonstrable experience of the "ought" complementary to that of "volition"?

We must answer that volition itself is not an elementary experience, but is resolvable into a series of processes (cf. Chapter II), and therefore one cannot well speak of an elementary experience opposed to it. When the command of another person confronts me under the conditions described on page 484, then definite conscious processes take place in me, which represent just that experience which in everyday life we call "ought." It is complex, yet not so difficult to analyze. The decisive thing is the consciousness of "compulsion," which consists of the fact that a persistent idea is established by the one who commands, and is equipped by means of his sanctions with feeling tones so strong that they affect adversely the pleasure components of all other ideas, and (in the case of obedience) suppress them. The ought stands in opposition to something *desired,* but not to volition; the ought is rather a part of the motivation process, and as such itself belongs to volition, and does not stand in opposition to it. We seek in vain for another immediate experience of the ought.

One more point. The ought, before it can, and in order that it may, occur must also be *willed.* Kant strove in vain to make conceivable [4] how the ought, which with him had the extremely abstract character of a moral "law," could be taken up into volition; and this difficulty seems to me to exist for every absolutist theory. In order that the valuable be actually sought and realized it must arouse our feelings. Why then does anyone oppose the recognition of the essence of value in this excitation of feeling? For one cannot make values comprehensible here below after they have been removed into a [place above the heavens.] The assertion that *moral* values in particular have nothing to do with pleasure and pain is certainly false, for no one can deny that a feeling of *joy* is bound up with the act of moral approbation, and that one always expresses moral blame unwillingly, with pain or anger. Otherwise there is no real disapprobation, but it is only pretended.

THE EMPTINESS OF THE HYPOTHESIS OF ABSOLUTE VALUES

Thus we come to the second argument against objective values, which is quite conclusive, and which frees us from and raises us above the hairsplitting that we, perhaps, began to feel in the line of thought of the first argument. This (beginning on p. 480) simply asked for the *meaning* of socalled absolute value judgments, and concluded that none could be shown, however one tried.

But now let us assume that the desired meaning has been found, so that we are able to determine in some way that there is a hierarchy of objective values wholly independent of our feelings. We now consider "value" to be a property of objects, qualifying them in various forms (for example, beautiful, good, sublime, and so forth) and in different degrees. All these possible properties together form a system, and in each case it is unambiguously determined which of these properties a specific object has, and to what degree; thereby assigning to it a definite position in the system of the value hierarchy.

Good, we say, let it be so! What follows? What have we to do with that? *How does it concern us?*

---

[4] "How a law can be immediately and in itself the determining ground of volition (which is the essence of all morality) is for human reason an insoluble problem." (Kant, *Critique of Practical Reason.*) [M.S.]

The only interest we could take in this realm of values would be a purely scientific interest; that is, it might be of interest to an investigator that the things in the world, in addition to other properties, also have these, and by means of them can be ordered in a certain way; and he might devote much labor to the description of this system. But for life and conduct this arrangement would be no more important than, say, the arrangement of the stars in the order of their magnitudes, or the serial arrangement of objects according to the alphabetical order of their names in the Swahili language.

This is no exaggeration or misrepresentation, but is actually the case. To my question, "What do these objective values mean to me?" the absolutist answers, "They constitute the guiding lines of your conduct! In setting up your goals of action you should prefer the higher to the lower." If I then ask, "Why?" the absolutist simply cannot give any answer. This is the decisive point, that because of his thesis of the independence of values, the absolutist has cut himself off from all possibility of giving any other answer to my question, "What happens if I don't do it?" than "Then you don't do it, that is all!" Should he answer, "In that case you are not a good man," then we should note that this answer is relevant and can influence my action only if I desire, or have reason to desire, to be a "good man," that is, only if it is presupposed that certain feelings are connected with that concept. And just such a presupposition may not be made by the absolutist; he may not say, "You will be more highly respected as a good man, you will lead a happier life, you will have a better conscience, you will be more at peace with yourself," and so forth; for in doing so he appeals to my feelings, as though the value were really binding upon me only because it brought me joy; and this doctrine is expressly repudiated. Even though in every way it were pleasant to me to be a scoundrel, and if I had the cordial respect of others, genuine peace in my soul, and pure inner joy as a result (imagine this in a lively manner, though it is difficult to do so, because the fact is otherwise), if, thus, my life were more agreeable, exalted and happier because of my failure to obey the moral laws, still the absolutist would have to say, "Yet you must obey them, even though you become extremely unhappy." Whether happy or unhappy, pleasant or unpleasant, all this has, for the intuitionist, absolutely nothing to do with moral value—which has been emphasized by no one more sharply than by Kant. But in these philosophers we still always find a hidden appeal to the feelings, even though it consist only in the use of certain honorific terms, like "honorable" itself.

Perhaps the philosopher is even proud that he cannot answer the question, "What do absolute values mean to me? What happens if I pay no attention to them?" Perhaps he even despises our question. If so, we answer his proud silence with the statement that in all seriousness we simply have no concern with such values, to which it makes no difference whether we are concerned with them or not, whose existence has no influence upon our peace of mind, our joy or sorrow, upon all those things that interest us in life. Indeed we *cannot* be concerned with such "values," for (see Chapter II) only those objects can arouse our volition which in some way or other arouse feelings of pleasure or pain in us. They would not be values for us.

Thus we conclude: if there were values which were "absolute" in the sense that they had absolutely nothing to do with our feelings, they would constitute an independent realm which would enter into the world of our volition and action at no point; for it would be as if an impenetrable wall shut them off from us. Life would proceed as if they did not exist; and for ethics they would not exist. But if the values, in addition to and without injuring their absolute existence, also had the property or power of influencing our feelings, then they would enter into our world; but only in so far as they thus affected us. Hence values also exist for ethics only to the extent that they make themselves felt, that is, are relative to us. And if a philosopher says, "Of course, but they *also* have an absolute existence," then we know that these words add nothing new to the verifiable facts, that therefore they are empty, and their assertion meaningless.

QUESTIONS FOR STUDY AND DISCUSSION

1. What does Schlick mean by "objective values"?
2. In what ways is Schlick sympathetic and not sympathetic to the doctrine that pleasure is the criterion of objective value?
3. Why is the attempt to compare value statements with logical propositions entirely unsatisfactory to Schlick?
4. In what sense is "ought to" meaningful for Schlick, and in what sense is it not meaningful?
5. According to Schlick, why is the absolutist unable to offer as a reason for leading a good life that one will thereby be happier?

When Is a Man Responsible?

THE PSEUDO-PROBLEM OF FREEDOM OF THE WILL

With hesitation and reluctance I prepare to add this chapter to the discussion of ethical problems. For in it I must speak of a matter which, even at present, is thought to be a fundamental ethical question, but which got into ethics and has become a much discussed problem only because of a misunderstanding. This is the so-called problem of the freedom of the will.

From pp. 143–58 of *Problems of Ethics* of Moritz Schlick, translated by David Rynin. Copyright 1939 by David Rynin. Published by Dover Publications, Inc., and reprinted through permission of the publisher.

Moreover, this pseudo-problem has long since been settled by the efforts of certain sensible persons; and, above all, the state of affairs just described has been often disclosed—with exceptional clarity by Hume. Hence it is really one of the greatest scandals of philosophy that again and again so much paper and printer's ink is devoted to this matter, to say nothing of the expenditure of thought, which could have been applied to more important problems (assuming that it would have sufficed for these). Thus I should truly be ashamed to write a chapter on "freedom." In the chapter heading, the word "responsible" indicates what concerns ethics, and designates the point at which misunderstanding arises. Therefore the concept of responsibility constitutes our theme, and if in the process of its clarification I also must speak of the concept of freedom I shall, of course, say only what others have already said better; consoling myself with the thought that in this way alone can anything be done to put an end at last to that scandal.

The main task of ethics (of which we convinced ourselves in Chapter I) is to explain moral behavior. To explain means to refer back to laws: every science, including psychology, is possible only in so far as there are such laws to which the events can be referred. Since the assumption that *all* events are subject to universal laws is called the principle of causality, one can also say, "Every science presupposes the principle of causality." Therefore every explanation of human behavior must also assume the validity of causal laws; in this case the existence of psychological laws. (If for example our law of motivation [1] of Chapter II were incorrect, then human conduct would be quite unexplained.) All of our experience strengthens us in the belief that this presupposition is realized, at least to the extent required for all purposes of practical life in intercourse with nature and human beings, and also for the most precise demands of technique. Whether, indeed, the principle of causality holds universally, whether, that is, *determinism* is true, we do not know; no one knows. But we do know that it is impossible to settle the dispute between determinism and indeterminism by mere reflection and speculation, by the consideration of so many reasons for and so many reasons against (which collectively and individually are but pseudo-reasons). Such an attempt becomes especially ridiculous when one considers with what enormous expenditure of experimental and logical skill contemporary physics carefully approaches the question of whether causality can be maintained for the most minute intra-atomic events.

But the dispute concerning "freedom of the will" generally proceeds in such fashion that its advocates attempt to refute, and its opponents to prove, the validity of the causal principle, both using hackneyed arguments, and neither in the least abashed by the magnitude of the undertaking. (I

---

[1] In every case of an act of will the decision is determined in the direction of the most pleasant, or the least unpleasant, motive. [F.E.]

can exclude only Bergson from this criticism, with whom, however, this whole question is not an ethical but a metaphysical problem. His ideas, which in my opinion will not stand epistemological analysis, are of no significance for us.) Others distinguish two realms, in one of which determinism holds, but not in the other. This line of thought (which was unfortunately taken by Kant) is, however, quite the most worthless (though Schopenhauer considered it to be Kant's most profound idea).

Fortunately, it is not necessary to lay claim to a final solution of the causal problem in order to say what is necessary in ethics concerning responsibility; there is required only an analysis of the concept, the careful determination of the meaning which is in fact joined to the words "responsibility" and "freedom" as these are actually used. If men had made clear to themselves the sense of those propositions, which we use in everyday life, that pseudo-argument which lies at the root of the pseudo-problem, and which recurs thousands of times within and outside of philosophical books, would never have arisen.

The argument runs as follows: "If determinism is true, if, that is, all events obey immutable laws, then my will too is always determined, by my innate character and my motives. Hence my decisions are necessary, not free. But if so, then I am not responsible for my acts, for I would be accountable for them only if I could do something about the way my decisions went; but I can do nothing about it, since they proceed with necessity from my character and the motives. And I have made neither, and have no power over them: the motives come from without, and my character is the necessary product of the innate tendencies and the external influences which have been effective during my lifetime. Thus determinism and moral responsibility are incompatible. Moral responsibility presupposes freedom, that is, exemption from causality."

This process of reasoning rests upon a whole series of confusions, just as the links of a chain hang together. We must show these confusions to be such, and thus destroy them.

TWO MEANINGS OF THE WORD "LAW"

It all begins with an erroneous interpretation of the meaning of "law." In practice this is understood as a rule by which the state prescribes certain behavior to its citizens. These rules often contradict the natural desires of the citizens (for if they did not do so, there would be no reason for making them), and are in fact not followed by many of them; while others obey, but under *compulsion*. The state does in fact compel its citizens by imposing certain sanctions (punishments) which serve to bring their desires into harmony with the prescribed laws.

In natural science, on the other hand, the word "law" means something quite different. The natural law is not a *pre*scription as to how something should behave, but a formula, a *de*scription of how something does in fact behave. The two forms of "laws" have only this in common: both tend to be expressed in *formulae*. Otherwise they have absolutely nothing to do with one another, and it is very blameworthy that the same word has been used for two such different things; but even more so that philosophers have allowed themselves to be led into serious errors by this usage. Since natural laws are only descriptions of what happens, there can be in regard to them no talk of "compulsion." The laws of celestial mechanics do not prescribe to the planets how they have to move, as though the planets would actually like to move quite otherwise, and are only forced by these burdensome laws of Kepler to move in orderly paths; no, these laws do not in any way "compel" the planets, but express only what in fact planets actually do.

If we apply this to volition, we are enlightened at once, even before the other confusions are discovered. When we say that a man's will "obeys psychological laws," these are not civic laws, which compel him to make certain decisions, or dictate desires to him, which he would in fact prefer not to have. They are laws of nature, merely expressing which desires he *actually has* under given conditions; they describe the nature of the will in the same manner as the astronomical laws describe the nature of planets. "Compulsion" occurs where man is prevented from realizing his natural desires. How could the rule according to which these natural desires arise itself be considered as "compulsion"?

COMPULSION AND NECESSITY

But this is the second confusion to which the first leads almost inevitably: after conceiving the laws of nature, anthropomorphically, as order imposed *nolens volens* upon the events, one adds to them the concept of "necessity." This word, derived from "need," also comes to us from practice, and is used there in the sense of inescapable compulsion. To apply the word with this meaning to natural laws is of course senseless, for the presupposition of an opposing desire is lacking; and it is then confused with something altogether different, which is actually an attribute of natural laws. That is, universality. It is of the essence of natural laws to be universally valid, for only when we have found a rule which holds of events without exception do we *call* the rule a law of nature. Thus when we say "a natural law holds necessarily" this has but one legitimate meaning: "It holds in *all* cases where it is applicable." It is again very deplorable that the word "necessary" has been applied to natural laws (or, what amounts to the same thing, with reference to causality), for it is quite superfluous, since the expression "universally valid" is available. Universal validity is something altogether different from "compulsion"; these concepts belong to spheres so remote from each other that once insight into the error has been gained one can no longer conceive the possibility of a confusion.

The confusion of two concepts always carries with it the confusion of their contradictory opposites. The opposite of the universal validity of a formula, of the existence of a law, is the nonexistence of a law, indeterminism, acausality; while the opposite of compulsion is what in practice everyone calls "freedom." Here emerges the nonsense, trailing through centuries, that freedom means "exemption from the causal principle," or "not subject to the laws of nature." Hence it is believed necessary to vindicate indeterminism in order to save human freedom.

FREEDOM AND INDETERMINISM

This is quite mistaken. Ethics has, so to speak, no moral interest in the purely theoretical question of "determinism or indeterminism," but only a theoretical interest, namely: in so far as it seeks the laws of conduct, and can find them only to the extent that causality holds. But the question of whether man is morally free (that is, has that freedom which, as we shall show, is the presupposition of moral responsibility) is altogether different from the problem of determinism. Hume was especially clear on this point. He indicated the inadmissible confusion of the concepts of "indeterminism" and "freedom"; but he retained, inappropriately, the word "freedom" for both, calling the one freedom of "the will," the other, genuine kind, "freedom of conduct." He showed that morality is interested only in the latter, and that such freedom, in general, is unquestionably to be attributed to mankind. And this is quite correct. Freedom means the opposite of compulsion; a man is *free* if he does not act under *compulsion,* and he is compelled or unfree when he is hindered from without in the realization of his natural desires. Hence he is unfree when he is locked up, or chained, or when someone forces him at the point of a gun to do what otherwise he would not do. This is quite clear, and everyone will admit that the everyday or legal notion of the lack of freedom is thus correctly interpreted, and that a man will be considered quite free and responsible if no such external compulsion is exerted upon him. There are certain cases which lie between these clearly described ones, as, say, when someone acts under the influence of alcohol or a narcotic. In such cases we consider the man to be more or less unfree, and hold him less accountable, because we rightly view the influence of the drug as "external," even though it is found within the body; it prevents him from making decisions in the manner peculiar to his nature. If he takes the narcotic of his own will, we make him completely responsible for *this* act and transfer a part of the responsibility to the consequences, making, as it were, an average or mean condemnation of the whole. In the case also of a person who is mentally ill we do not consider him free with respect to those acts in which the disease expresses itself, because we view the illness as a disturbing factor which hinders the normal functioning of his natural tendencies. We make not him but his disease responsible.

THE NATURE OF RESPONSIBILITY

But what does this really signify? What do we mean by this concept of responsibility which goes along with that of "freedom," and which plays such an important role in morality? It is easy to attain complete clarity in this matter; we need only carefully determine the manner in which the concept is used. What is the case in practice when we impute "responsibility" to a person? What is our aim in doing this? The judge has to discover who is responsible for a given act in order that he may *punish* him. We are inclined to be less concerned with the inquiry as to who deserves *reward* for an act, and we have no special officials for this; but of course the principle would be the same. But let us stick to punishment in order to make the idea clear. What is punishment, actually? The view still often expressed, that it is a natural *retaliation* for past wrong, ought no longer to be defended in cultivated society; for the opinion that an increase in sorrow can be "made good again" by further sorrow is altogether barbarous. Certainly the origin of punishment may lie in an impulse of retaliation or vengeance; but what is such an impulse except the instinctive desire to destroy the *cause* of the deed to be avenged, by the destruction of or injury to the malefactor? Punishment is concerned only with the institution of causes, of *motives* of conduct, and this alone is its meaning. Punishment is an educative measure, and as such is a means to the formation of motives, which are in part to prevent the wrongdoer from repeating the act (reformation) and in part to prevent others from committing a similar act (intimidation). Analogously, in the case of reward we are concerned with an incentive.

Hence the question regarding responsibility is the question: Who, in a given case, is to be punished? Who is to be considered the true wrongdoer? This problem is not identical with that regarding the original instigator of the act; for the great-grandparents of the man, from whom he inherited his character, might in the end be the cause, or the statesmen who are responsible for his social milieu, and so forth. But the "doer" is the one *upon whom the motive must have acted* in order, with certainty, to have prevented the act (or called it forth, as the case may be). Consideration of remote causes is of no help here, for in the first place their actual contribution cannot be determined, and in the second place they are generally out of reach. Rather, we must find the person in whom the decisive junction of causes lies. The question of who is responsible is the question concerning the *correct point of application of the motive*. And the important thing is that in this its meaning is completely exhausted; behind it there lurks no mysterious connection between transgression and requital, which is merely *indicated* by the described state of affairs. It is a matter only of knowing who is to be punished or rewarded, in order that punishment and reward function as such—be able to achieve their goal.

Thus, all the facts connected with the concepts of responsibility and imputation are at once made intelligible. We do not charge an insane person with responsibility, for the very reason that he offers no unified point for the application of a motive. It would be pointless to try to affect him by means of promises or threats, when his confused soul fails to respond to such influence because its normal mechanism is out of order. We do not try to give him motives, but try to heal him (metaphorically, we make his sickness responsible, and try to remove its causes). When a man is forced by threats to commit certain acts we do not blame him, but the one who held the pistol at his breast. The reason is clear: the act would have been prevented had we been able to restrain the person who threatened him; and this person is the one whom we must influence in order to prevent similar acts in the future.

THE CONSCIOUSNESS OF RESPONSIBILITY

But much more important than the question of when a man is said to be responsible is that of when he *himself* feels responsible. Our whole treatment would be untenable if it gave no explanation of this. It is, then, a welcome confirmation of the view here developed that the subjective feeling of responsibility coincides with the objective judgment. It is a fact of experience that, in general, the person blamed or condemned is conscious of the fact that he was "rightly" taken to account—of course, under the supposition that no error has been made, that the assumed state of affairs actually occurred. What is this consciousness of having been the true doer of the act, the actual instigator? Evidently not merely that it was he who took the steps required for its performance; but there must be added the awareness that he did it "independently," "of his own initiative," or however it be expressed. This feeling is simply the consciousness of *freedom,* which is merely the knowledge of having acted of one's *own* desires. And "one's own desires" are those which have their origin in the regularity of one's character in the given situation, and are not imposed by an external power, as explained above. The absence of the external power expresses itself in the well-known feeling (usually considered characteristic of the consciousness of freedom) *that one could also have acted otherwise.* How this indubitable experience ever came to be an argument in favor of indeterminism is incomprehensible to me. It is of course obvious that I should have acted differently had I *willed* something else; but the feeling never says that I could also have willed something else, even though this is true, if, that is, other motives had been present. And it says even less that under *exactly the same* inner and outer conditions I could also have willed something else. How could such a feeling inform me of anything regarding the purely theoretical question of whether the principle of causality holds or not? Of course, after what has been said on the subject, I do not undertake to demonstrate the principle, but I do deny that from any such fact of consciousness the least follows regarding the principle's validity. This feeling is not the consciousness of the absence of a cause, but of something altogether different, namely, of *freedom,* which consists in the fact that I can act as I desire.

Thus the feeling of responsibility assumes that I acted freely, that my own desires impelled me; and if because of this feeling I willingly suffer blame for my behavior or reproach myself, and thereby admit that I might have acted otherwise, this means that other behavior was compatible with the laws of volition—of course, granted other motives. And I myself desire the existence of such motives and bear the pain (regret and sorrow) caused me by my behavior so that its repetition will be prevented. To blame oneself means just to apply motives of improvement to oneself, which is usually the task of the educator. But if, for example, one does something under the influence of torture, feelings of guilt and regret are absent, for one knows that according to the laws of volition no other behavior was possible—no matter what ideas, because of their feeling tones, might have functioned as motives. The important thing, always, is that the feeling of responsibility means the realization that one's self, one's own psychic processes constitute the point at which motives must be applied in order to govern the acts of one's body.

CAUSALITY AS THE PRESUPPOSITION OF RESPONSIBILITY

We can speak of motives only in a causal context; thus it becomes clear how very much the concept of responsibility rests upon that of causation, that is, upon the regularity of volitional decisions. In fact if we should conceive of a decision as utterly without any cause (this would in all strictness be the indeterministic presupposition) then the act would be entirely a matter of *chance,* for chance is identical with the absence of a cause; there is no other opposite of causality. Could we under such conditions make the agent responsible? Certainly not. Imagine a man, always calm, peaceful and blameless, who suddenly falls upon and begins to beat a stranger. He is held and questioned regarding the motive of his action, to which he answers, in his opinion truthfully, as we assume: "There was no motive for my behavior. Try as I may I can discover no reason. My volition was without any cause—I desired to do so, and there is simply nothing else to be said about it." We should shake our heads and call him insane, because we have to believe that there was a cause, and lacking any other we must assume some mental disturbance as the only cause remaining; but certainly no one would hold him to be responsible. If decisions were causeless there would be no sense in trying to influence men; and we see at once that this is the reason why we could not bring such a man to account, but would always have only a shrug of the shoulders in answer to his behavior. One can easily determine that in practice we make an agent the more responsible the more motives we can find for his conduct. If a man guilty of an atrocity was an enemy of his victim, if previously he had shown violent tendencies, if some special circumstance angered him, then we impose severe punishment upon him; while the fewer the reasons to be found for an offense the less do we condemn the agent, but make "unlucky chance," a momentary aberration, or something of the sort, responsible. We do not find the causes of misconduct in his character, and therefore we do not try to influence it for the better: this and only this is the significance of the fact that we do not put the responsibility upon him. And he too feels this to be so, and says, "I cannot understand how such a thing could have happened to me."

In general we know very well how to discover the causes of conduct in the characters of our fellow men; and how to use this knowledge in the prediction of their future behavior, often with as much certainty as that with which we know that a lion and a rabbit will behave quite differently in the same situation. From all this it is evident that in practice no one thinks of questioning the principle of causality, that, thus, the attitude of the practical man offers no excuse to the metaphysician for confusing freedom from compulsion with the absence of a cause. If one makes clear to himself that a causeless happening is identical with a chance happening, and that, consequently, an indetermined will would destroy all responsibility, then every desire will cease which might be father to an indeterministic thought. No one can prove determinism, but it is certain that we assume its validity in all of our practical life, and that in particular we can apply the concept of responsibility to human conduct only in so far as the causal principle holds of volitional processes.

For a final clarification I bring together again a list of those concepts which tend, in the traditional treatment of the "problem of freedom," to be confused. In the place of the concepts on the left are put, mistakenly, those of the right, and those in the vertical order form a chain, so that sometimes the previous confusion is the cause of that which follows:

Natural Law	Law of State
Determinism (Causality)	Compulsion
(Universal Validity)	(Necessity)
Indeterminism (Chance)	Freedom
(No Cause)	(No Compulsion)

QUESTIONS FOR STUDY AND DISCUSSION

1. How does Schlick distinguish between the correct and the incorrect understanding of the notion that a man's will obeys psychological laws?
2. What are the reasons that lead one into the error of thinking that freedom requires exemption from the laws of nature?
3. What meaning of freedom does Schlick accept?
4. According to Schlick, why is an insane person not held responsible for his actions? What conception of the purpose of punishment is implied by Schlick's answer?
5. What interpretation does Schlick give to the feeling that one could have acted otherwise, and what interpretation does he reject?

A. J. Ayer

ALFRED JULES AYER, born in London in 1910, was educated at Christ Church College, Oxford University, from which he received his B.A. in 1932 and M.A. in 1936. During the Second World War he served with British Military Intelligence, and in 1945 he was an attaché to the British Embassy in Paris. He was appointed Grote Professor of Philosophy at the University of London in 1946, and two years later spent an academic year as visiting professor at New York University. In 1959 he accepted a professorship at Oxford. One of the most lucid exponents of logical positivism, Ayer has written the following books: *Language, Truth, and Logic* (1936), *Foundations of Empirical Knowledge* (1940), *Thinking and Meaning* (1947), *Philosophical Essays* (1954), and *The Problem of Knowledge* (1956).

An Emotive Interpretation of Ethical Language

The ordinary system of ethics, as elaborated in the works of ethical philosophers, is very far from being a homogeneous whole. Not only is it apt to contain pieces of metaphysics, and analyses of non-ethical concepts: its actual ethical contents are themselves of very different kinds. We may divide them, indeed, into four main classes. There are, first of all, propositions which express definitions of ethical terms, or judgements about the legitimacy or possibility of certain definitions. Secondly, there are propositions describing the phenomena of moral experience, and their causes. Thirdly, there are exhortations to moral virtue. And, lastly, there are actual ethical judgements. It is unfortunately the case that the distinction between these four classes, plain as it is, is commonly ignored by ethical philosophers; with the result that it is often very difficult to tell from their works what it is that they are seeking to discover or prove.

In fact, it is easy to see that only the first of our four classes, namely that which comprises the propositions relating to the definitions of ethical terms, can be said to constitute ethical philosophy. The propositions which describe the phenomena of moral experience, and their causes, must be assigned to the science of psychology, or sociology. The exhortations to

From pp. 103–13 of *Language, Truth, and Logic* by Alfred J. Ayer. Published by Dover Publications, Inc., and reprinted through permission of the publisher and of Victor Gollancz Ltd., London.

moral virtue are not propositions at all, but ejaculations or commands which are designed to provoke the reader to action of a certain sort. Accordingly, they do not belong to any branch of philosophy or science. As for the expressions of ethical judgements, we have not yet determined how they should be classified. But inasmuch as they are certainly neither definitions nor comments upon definitions, nor quotations, we may say decisively that they do not belong to ethical philosophy. A strictly philosophical treatise on ethics should therefore make no ethical pronouncements. But it should, by giving an analysis of ethical terms, show what is the category to which all such pronouncements belong. And this is what we are now about to do.

A question which is often discussed by ethical philosophers is whether it is possible to find definitions which would reduce all ethical terms to one or two fundamental terms. But this question, though it undeniably belongs to ethical philosophy, is not relevant to our present enquiry. We are not now concerned to discover which term, within the sphere of ethical terms, is to be taken as fundamental; whether, for example, "good" can be defined in terms of "right" or "right" in terms of "good," or both in terms of "value." What we are interested in is the possibility of reducing the whole sphere of ethical terms to non-ethical terms. We are enquiring whether statements of ethical value can be translated into statements of empirical fact.

That they can be so translated is the contention of those ethical philosophers who are commonly called subjectivists, and of those who are known as utilitarians. For the utilitarian defines the rightness of actions, and the goodness of ends, in terms of the pleasure, or happiness, or satisfaction, to which they give rise; the subjectivist, in terms of the feelings of approval which a certain person, or group of people, has towards them. Each of these types of definition makes moral judgements into a sub-class of psychological or sociological judgements; and for this reason they are very attractive to us. For, if either was correct, it would follow that ethical assertions were not generically different from the factual assertions which are ordinarily contrasted with them; and the account which we have already given of empirical hypotheses would apply to them also.

Nevertheless we shall not adopt either a subjectivist or a utilitarian analysis of ethical terms. We reject the subjectivist view that to call an action right, or a thing good, is to say that it is generally approved of, because it is not self-contradictory to assert that some actions which are generally approved of are not right, or that some things which are generally approved of are not good. And we reject the alternative subjectivist view that a man who asserts that a certain action is right, or that a certain thing is good, is saying that he himself approves of it, on the ground that a man who confessed that he sometimes approved of what was bad or wrong would not be contradicting himself. And a similar argument is fatal to utilitarianism. We cannot agree that to call an action right is to say that of all the actions possible in the circumstances it would cause, or be likely to cause, the greatest happiness, or the greatest balance of pleasure over pain, or the greatest balance of satisfied over unsatisfied desire, because we find that it is not self-contradictory to say that it is sometimes wrong to perform the action which would actually or probably cause the greatest happiness, or the greatest balance of pleasure over pain, or of satisfied over unsatisfied desire. And since it is not self-contradictory to say that some pleasant things are not good, or that some bad things are desired, it cannot be the case that the sentence *"x is good"* is equivalent to *"x is pleasant,"* or to *"x is desired."* And to every other variant of utilitarianism with which I am acquainted the same objection can be made. And therefore we should, I think, conclude that the validity of ethical judgements is not determined by the felicific tendencies of actions, any more than by the nature of people's feelings; but that it must be regarded as "absolute" or "intrinsic," and not empirically calculable.

If we say this, we are not, of course, denying that it is possible to invent a language in which all ethical symbols are definable in non-ethical terms, or even that it is desirable to invent such a language and adopt it in place of our own; what we are denying is that the suggested reduction of ethical to non-ethical statements is consistent with the conventions of our actual language. That is, we reject utilitarianism and subjectivism, not as proposals to replace our existing ethical notions by new ones, but as analyses of our existing ethical notions. Our contention is simply that, in our language, sentences which contain normative ethical symbols are not equivalent to sentences which express psychological propositions, or indeed empirical propositions of any kind.

It is advisable here to make it plain that it is only normative ethical symbols, and not descriptive ethical symbols, that are held by us to be indefinable in factual terms. There is a danger of confusing these two types of symbols, because they are commonly constituted by signs of the same sensible form. Thus a complex sign of the form *"x is wrong"* may constitute a sentence which expresses a moral judgement concerning a certain type of conduct, or it may constitute a sentence which states that a certain type of conduct is repugnant to the moral sense of a particular society. In the latter case, the symbol "wrong" is a descriptive ethical symbol, and the sentence in which it occurs expresses an ordinary sociological proposition; in the former case, the symbol "wrong" is a normative ethical symbol, and the sentence in which it occurs does not, we maintain, express an empirical proposition at all. It is only with normative ethics that we are at present concerned; so that whenever ethical symbols are used in the course of this argument without qualification, they are always to be interpreted as symbols of the normative type.

In admitting that normative ethical concepts are irreducible to empirical concepts, we seem to be leaving the way clear for the "absolutist" view of ethics—that is, the view that statements of value are not controlled by observation, as ordinary empirical propositions are, but only by a mysterious "intellectual intuition." A feature of this theory, which is seldom recognized by its advocates, is that it makes statements of value unverifiable. For it is notorious that what seems intuitively certain to one person may seem doubtful, or even false, to another. So that unless it is possible to provide some criterion by which one may decide between conflicting intuitions, a mere appeal to intuition is worthless as a test of a proposition's validity. But in the case of moral judgements, no such criterion can be given. Some moralists claim to settle the matter by saying that they "know" that their own moral judgements are correct. But such an assertion is of purely psychological interest, and has not the slightest tendency to prove the validity of any moral judgement. For dissentient moralists may equally well "know" that their ethical views are correct. And, as far as subjective certainty goes, there will be nothing to choose between them. When such differences of opinion arise in connection with an ordinary empirical proposition, one may attempt to resolve them by referring to, or actually carrying out, some relevant empirical test. But with regard to ethical statements, there is, on the "absolutist" or "intuitionist" theory, no relevant empirical test. We are therefore justified in saying that on this theory ethical statements are held to be unverifiable. They are, of course, also held to be genuine synthetic propositions.

Considering the use which we have made of the principle that a synthetic proposition is significant only if it is empirically verifiable, it is clear that the acceptance of an "absolutist" theory of ethics would undermine the whole of our main argument. And as we have already rejected the "naturalistic" theories which are commonly supposed to provide the only alternative to "absolutism" in ethics, we seem to have reached a difficult position. We shall meet the difficulty by showing that the correct treatment of ethical statements is afforded by a third theory, which is wholly compatible with our radical empiricism.

We begin by admitting that the fundamental ethical concepts are unanalysable, inasmuch as there is no criterion by which one can test the validity of the judgements in which they occur. So far we are in agreement with the absolutists. But, unlike the absolutists, we are able to give an explanation of this fact about ethical concepts. We say that the reason why they are unanalysable is that they are mere pseudo-concepts. The presence of an ethical symbol in a proposition adds nothing to its factual content. Thus if I say to someone, "You acted wrongly in stealing that money," I am not stating anything more than if I had simply said, "You stole that money." In adding that this action is wrong I am not making any further statement about it. I am simply evincing my moral disapproval of it. It is as if I had said, "You stole that money," in a peculiar tone of horror, or written it with the addition of some special exclamation marks. The tone, or the exclamation marks, adds nothing to the literal meaning of the sentence. It merely serves to show that the expression of it is attended by certain feelings in the speaker.

If now I generalise my previous statement and say, "Stealing money is wrong," I produce a sentence which has no factual meaning—that is, expresses no proposition which can be either true or false. It is as if I had written "Stealing money!!"—where the shape and thickness of the exclamation marks show, by a suitable convention, that a special sort of moral disapproval is the feeling which is being expressed. It is clear that there is nothing said here which can be true or false. Another man may disagree with me about the wrongness of stealing, in the sense that he may not have the same feelings about stealing as I have, and he may quarrel with me on account of my moral sentiments. But he cannot, strictly speaking, contradict me. For in saying that a certain type of action is right or wrong, I am not making any factual statement, not even a statement about my own state of mind. I am merely expressing certain moral sentiments. And the man who is ostensibly contradicting me is merely expressing his moral sentiments. So that there is plainly no sense in asking which of us is in the right. For neither of us is asserting a genuine proposition.

What we have just been saying about the symbol "wrong" applies to all normative ethical symbols. Sometimes they occur in sentences which record ordinary empirical facts besides expressing ethical feeling about those facts: sometimes they occur in sentences which simply express ethical feeling about a certain type of action, or situation, without making any statement of fact. But in every case in which one would commonly be said to be making an ethical judgement, the function of the relevant ethical word is purely "emotive." It is used to express feeling about certain objects, but not to make any assertion about them.

It is worth mentioning that ethical terms do not serve only to express feeling. They are calculated also to arouse feeling, and so to stimulate action. Indeed some of them are used in such a way as to give the sentences in which they occur the effect of commands. Thus the sentence "It is your duty to tell the truth" may be regarded both as the expression of a certain sort of ethical feeling about truthfulness and as the expression of the command "Tell the truth." The sentence "You ought to tell the truth" also involves the command "Tell the truth," but here the tone of the command is less emphatic. In the sentence "It is good to tell the truth" the command has become little more than a suggestion. And thus the "meaning" of the word "good," in its ethical usage, is differentiated from that of the word "duty" or the word "ought." In fact we may define the meaning of the various ethical words in terms both of the different feelings they are ordinarily taken to express, and also the different responses which they are calculated to provoke.

We can now see why it is impossible to find a criterion for determining the validity of ethical judgements. It is not because they have an "absolute" validity which is mysteriously independent of ordinary sense-experience, but because they have no objective validity whatsoever. If a sentence makes no statement at all, there is obviously no sense in asking whether what it says is true or false. And we have seen that sentences which simply express moral judgements do not say anything. They are pure expressions of feeling and as such do not come under the category of truth and falsehood. They are unverifiable for the same reason as a cry of pain or a word of command is unverifiable—because they do not express genuine propositions.

Thus, although our theory of ethics might fairly be said to be radically subjectivist, it differs in a very important respect from the orthodox subjectivist theory. For the orthodox subjectivist does not deny, as we do, that the sentences of a moralizer express genuine propositions. All he denies is that they express propositions of a unique non-empirical character. His own view is that they express propositions about the speaker's feelings. If this were so, ethical judgements clearly would be capable of being true or false. They would be true if the speaker had the relevant feelings, and false if he had not. And this is a matter which is, in principle, empirically verifiable. Furthermore they could be significantly contradicted. For if I say, "Tolerance is a virtue," and someone answers, "You don't approve of it," he would, on the ordinary subjectivist theory, be contradicting me. On our theory, he would not be contradicting me, because, in saying that tolerance was a virtue, I should not be making any statement about my own feelings or about anything else. I should simply be evincing my feelings, which is not at all the same thing as saying that I have them.

The distinction between the expression of feeling and the assertion of feeling is complicated by the fact that the assertion that one has a certain feeling often accompanies the expression of that feeling, and is then, indeed, a factor in the expression of that feeling. Thus I may simultaneously express boredom and say that I am bored, and in that case my utterance of the words, "I am bored," is one of the circumstances which make it true to say that I am expressing or evincing boredom. But I can express boredom without actually saying that I am bored. I can express it by my tone and gestures, while making a statement about something wholly unconnected with it, or by an ejaculation, or without uttering any words at all. So that even if the assertion that one has a certain feeling always involves the expression of that feeling, the expression of a feeling assuredly does not always involve the assertion that one has it. And this is the important point to grasp in considering the distinction between our theory and the ordinary subjectivist theory. For whereas the subjectivist holds that ethical statements actually assert the existence of certain feelings, we hold that ethical statements are expressions and excitants of feeling which do not necessarily involve any assertions.

We have already remarked that the main objection to the ordinary subjectivist theory is that the validity of ethical judgements is not determined by the nature of their author's feelings. And this is an objection which our theory escapes. For it does not imply that the existence of any feelings is a necessary and sufficient condition of the validity of an ethical judgement. It implies, on the contrary, that ethical judgements have no validity.

There is, however, a celebrated argument against subjectivist theories which our theory does not escape. It has been pointed out by Moore that if ethical statements were simply statements about the speaker's feelings, it would be impossible to argue about questions of value. To take a typical example: if a man said that thrift was a virtue, and another replied that it was a vice, they would not, on this theory, be disputing with one another. One would be saying that he approved of thrift, and the other that *he* didn't; and there is no reason why both these statements should not be true. Now Moore held it to be obvious that we do dispute about questions of value, and accordingly concluded that the particular form of subjectivism which he was discussing was false.

It is plain that the conclusion that it is impossible to dispute about questions of value follows from our theory also. For as we hold that such sentences as "Thrift is a virtue" and "Thrift is a vice" do not express propositions at all, we clearly cannot hold that they express incompatible propositions. We must therefore admit that if Moore's argument really refutes the ordinary subjectivist theory, it also refutes ours. But, in fact, we deny that it does refute even the ordinary subjectivist theory. For we hold that one really never does dispute about questions of value.

This may seem, at first sight, to be a very paradoxical assertion. For we certainly do engage in disputes which are ordinarily regarded as disputes about questions of value. But, in all such cases, we find, if we consider the matter closely, that the dispute is not really about a question of value, but about a question of fact. When someone disagrees with us about the moral value of a certain action or type of action, we do admittedly resort to argument in order to win him over to our way of thinking. But we do not attempt to show by our arguments that he has the "wrong" ethical feeling towards a situation whose nature he has correctly apprehended. What we attempt to show is that he is mistaken about the facts of the case. We argue that he has misconceived the agent's motive: or that he has misjudged the effects of the action, or its probable effects in view of the agent's knowledge; or that he has failed to take into account the special circumstances in which the agent was placed. Or else we employ more general arguments about the effects which actions of a certain type tend to produce, or the qualities which are usually manifested in their performance. We do this in the hope that we have only to get our opponent to agree with us about the nature of the empirical facts for him to adopt the same moral attitude towards them as we do. And as the people with whom we argue have generally received the same moral education as ourselves, and live in the same social order, our expectation is usually justified. But if our opponent happens to have undergone a different process of moral "conditioning" from ourselves, so that, even when he acknowledges all the facts, he still disagrees with us about the moral value of the actions under discussion, then we abandon the attempt to convince him by argument. We say that it is impossible to argue with him because he has a distorted or undeveloped moral sense; which signifies merely that he employs a different set of values from our own. We feel that our own system of values is superior, and therefore speak in such derogatory terms of his. But we cannot bring forward any arguments to show that our system is superior. For our judgement that it is so is itself a judgement of value, and accordingly outside the scope of argument. It is because argument fails us when we come to deal with pure questions of value, as distinct from questions of fact, that we finally resort to mere abuse.

In short, we find that argument is possible on moral questions only if some system of values is presupposed. If our opponent concurs with us in expressing moral disapproval of all actions of a given type *t,* then we may get him to condemn a particular action A, by bringing forward arguments to show that A is of type *t.* For the question whether A does or does not belong to that type is a plain question of fact. Given that a man has certain moral principles, we argue that he must, in order to be consistent, react morally to certain things in a certain way. What we do not and cannot argue about is the validity of these moral principles. We merely praise or condemn them in the light of our own feelings.

If anyone doubts the accuracy of this account of moral disputes, let him try to construct even an imaginary argument on a question of value which does not reduce itself to an argument about a question of logic or about an empirical matter of fact. I am confident that he will not succeed in producing a single example. And if that is the case, he must allow that its involving the impossibility of purely ethical arguments is not, as Moore thought, a ground of objection to our theory, but rather a point in favour of it.

Having upheld our theory against the only criticism which appeared to threaten it, we may now use it to define the nature of all ethical enquiries. We find that ethical philosophy consists simply in saying that ethical concepts are pseudo-concepts and therefore unanalysable. The further task of describing the different feelings that the different ethical terms are used to express, and the different reactions that they customarily provoke, is a task for the psychologist. There cannot be such a thing as ethical science, if by ethical science one means the elaboration of a "true" system of morals. For we have seen that, as ethical judgements are mere expressions of feeling, there can be no way of determining the validity of any ethical system, and, indeed, no sense in asking whether any such system is true. All that one may legitimately enquire in this connection is, What are the moral habits of a given person or group of people, and what causes them to have precisely those habits and feelings? And this enquiry falls wholly within the scope of the existing social sciences.

It appears, then, that ethics, as a branch of knowledge, is nothing more than a department of psychology and sociology. And in case anyone thinks that we are overlooking the existence of casuistry, we may remark that casuistry is not a science, but is a purely analytical investigation of the structure of a given moral system. In other words, it is an exercise in formal logic.

When one comes to pursue the psychological enquiries which constitute ethical science, one is immediately enabled to account for the Kantian and hedonistic theories of morals. For one finds that one of the chief causes of moral behaviour is fear, both conscious and unconscious, of a god's displeasure, and fear of the enmity of society. And this, indeed, is the reason why moral precepts present themselves to some people as "categorical" commands. And one finds, also, that the moral code of a society is partly determined by the beliefs of that society concerning the conditions of its own happiness—or, in other words, that a society tends to encourage or discourage a given type of conduct by the use of moral sanctions according as it appears to promote or detract from the contentment of the society as a whole. And this is the reason why altruism is recommended in most moral codes and egotism condemned. It is from the observation of this connection between morality and happiness that hedonistic or eudæmonistic theories of morals ultimately spring, just as the moral theory of Kant is based on the fact, previously explained, that moral precepts have for some people the force of inexorable commands. As each of these theories ignores the fact which lies at the root of the other, both may be criticized as being one-sided; but this is not the main objection to either of them. Their essential defect is that they treat propositions which refer to the causes and attributes of our ethical feelings as if they were definitions of ethical concepts. And thus they fail to recognise that ethical concepts are pseudo-concepts and consequently indefinable.

QUESTIONS FOR STUDY AND DISCUSSION

1. Explain Ayer's criticism of the "subjectivist view" and the "utilitarian view."
2. What is the difference, as Ayer understands it, between a normative ethical symbol and a descriptive ethical symbol? How is this distinction relevant to his interpretation of ethics?
3. How does Ayer's position differ from what he calls the "ordinary subjectivist position"?
4. According to Ayer's analysis, what is really going on when we engage in what are ordinarily termed "disputes about questions of value"?

Charles L. Stevenson

CHARLES L. STEVENSON, born in Cincinnati in 1908, was graduated from Yale University in 1930 and then studied at Cambridge University, where in 1933 he received a second bachelor's degree with specialized work in philosophy. In 1935 he was awarded a Ph.D. from Harvard University, and he has taught at Harvard as well as at Yale University and the University of Michigan. The author of many articles published in British and American journals of philosophy, Stevenson wrote *Ethics and Language* (1944), widely regarded as the best-developed presentation of the emotivist point of view in ethics.

The Nature of Ethical Disagreement

I

When people disagree about the value of something—one saying that it is good or right and another that it is bad or wrong—by what methods of argument or inquiry can their disagreement be resolved? Can it be resolved by the methods of science, or does it require methods of some other kind, or is it open to no rational solution at all?

The question must be clarified before it can be answered. And the word that is particularly in need of clarification, as we shall see, is the word "disagreement."

Let us begin by noting that "disagreement" has two broad senses: In the first sense it refers to what I shall call "disagreement in belief." This occurs when Mr. A believes *p,* when Mr. B believes *not-p,* or something incompatible with *p,* and when neither is content to let the belief of the other remain unchallenged. Thus doctors may disagree in belief about the causes of an illness; and friends may disagree in belief about the exact date on which they last met.

In the second sense the word refers to what I shall call "disagreement in attitude." This occurs when Mr. A has a favorable attitude to something, when Mr. B has an unfavorable or less favorable attitude to it, and when neither is content to let the other's attitude remain unchanged. The term "attitude" is here used in much the same sense that R. B. Perry uses "inter-

From pp. 1–9 of Charles L. Stevenson, *Facts and Values: Studies in Ethical Analysis.* © 1964 by Yale University Press. Reprinted by permission of the author.

est"; it designates any psychological disposition of being *for* or *against* something. Hence love and hate are relatively specific kinds of attitudes, as are approval and disapproval, and so on.

This second sense can be illustrated in this way: Two men are planning to have dinner together. One wants to eat at a restaurant that the other doesn't like. Temporarily, then, the men cannot "agree" on where to dine. Their argument may be trivial, and perhaps only half serious; but in any case it represents a disagreement *in attitude*. The men have divergent preferences and each is trying to redirect the preference of the other—though normally, of course, each is willing to revise his own preference in the light of what the other may say.

Further examples are readily found. Mrs. Smith wishes to cultivate only the four hundred; Mr. Smith is loyal to his old poker-playing friends. They accordingly disagree, in attitude, about whom to invite to their party. The progressive mayor wants modern school buildings and large parks; the older citizens are against these "new-fangled" ways; so they disagree on civic policy. These cases differ from the one about the restaurant only in that the clash of attitudes is more serious and may lead to more vigorous argument.

The difference between the two senses of "disagreement" is essentially this: the first involves an opposition of beliefs, both of which cannot be true, and the second involves an opposition of attitudes, both of which cannot be satisfied.

Let us apply this distinction to a case that will sharpen it. Mr. A believes that most voters will favor a proposed tax and Mr. B disagrees with him. The disagreement concerns attitudes—those of the voters—but note that A and B are *not* disagreeing in attitude. Their disagreement is *in belief about* attitudes. It is simply a special kind of disagreement in belief, differing from disagreement in belief about head colds only with regard to subject matter. It implies not an opposition of the actual attitudes of the speakers but only of their beliefs about certain attitudes. Disagreement *in* attitude, on the other hand, implies that the very attitudes of the speakers are opposed. A and B may have opposed beliefs about attitudes without having opposed attitudes, just as they may have opposed beliefs about head colds without having opposed head colds. Hence we must not, from the fact that an argument is concerned with attitudes, infer that it necessarily involves disagreement *in* attitude.

II

We may now turn more directly to disagreement about values, with particular reference to normative ethics. When people argue about what is good, do they disagree in belief, or do they disagree in attitude? A long tradition of ethical theorists strongly suggest, whether they always intend to or not, that the disagreement is one *in belief*. Naturalistic theorists, for instance, identify an ethical judgment with some sort of scientific statement, and so make normative ethics a branch of science. Now a scientific argument typically exemplifies disagreement in belief, and if an ethical argument is simply a scientific one, then it too exemplifies disagreement in belief. The usual naturalistic theories of ethics that stress attitudes—such as those of Hume, Westermarck, Perry, Richards, and so many others—stress disagreement in belief no less than the rest. They imply, of course, that disagreement about what is good is disagreement *in belief* about attitudes; but we have seen that that is simply one sort of disagreement in belief, and by no means the same as disagreement *in* attitude. Analyses that stress disagreement *in* attitude are extremely rare.

If ethical arguments, as we encounter them in everyday life, involved disagreement in belief exclusively—whether the beliefs were about attitudes or about something else—then I should have no quarrel with the ordinary sort of naturalistic analysis. Normative judgments could be taken as scientific statements and amenable to the usual scientific proof. But a moment's attention will readily show that disagreement in belief has not the exclusive role that theory has so repeatedly ascribed to it. It must be readily granted that ethical arguments usually involve disagreement in belief; but they *also* involve disagreement in attitude. And the conspicuous role of disagreement in attitude is what we usually take, whether we realize it or not, as the distinguishing feature of ethical arguments. For example:

Suppose that the representative of a union urges that the wage level in a given company ought to be higher—that it is only right that the workers receive more pay. The company representative urges in reply that the workers ought to receive no more than they get. Such an argument clearly represents a disagreement in attitude. The union is *for* higher wages; the company is *against* them, and neither is content to let the other's attitude remain unchanged. *In addition* to this disagreement in attitude, of course, the argument may represent no little disagreement in belief. Perhaps the parties disagree about how much the cost of living has risen and how much the workers are suffering under the present wage scale. Or perhaps they disagree about the company's earnings and the extent to which the company could raise wages and still operate at a profit. Like any typical ethical argument, then, this argument involves both disagreement in attitude and disagreement in belief.

It is easy to see, however, that the disagreement in attitude plays a unifying and predominating role in the argument. This is so in two ways:

In the first place, disagreement in attitude determines what beliefs are *relevant* to the argument. Suppose that the company affirms that the wage scale of fifty years ago was far lower than it is now. The union will immediately urge that this contention, even though true, is irrelevant. And it is irrelevant simply because information about the wage level of fifty years ago, maintained under totally different circumstances, is not likely to affect the present attitudes of either party. To be relevant, any belief that is introduced into the argument must be one that is likely to lead one side or the other to have a different attitude, and so reconcile disagreement in attitude. Attitudes are often functions of beliefs. We often change our attitudes to something when we change our beliefs about it; just as a child ceases to *want* to touch a live coal when he comes to *believe* that it will burn him. Thus in the present argument any beliefs that are at all likely to alter attitudes, such as those about the increasing cost of living or the financial state of the company, will be considered by both sides to be relevant to the argument. Agreement in belief on these matters may lead to agreement in attitude toward the wage scale. But beliefs that are likely to alter the attitudes of neither side will be declared irrelevant. They will have no bearing on the disagreement in attitude, with which both parties are primarily concerned.

In the second place, ethical argument usually terminates when disagreement in attitude terminates, even though a certain amount of disagreement in belief remains. Suppose, for instance, that the company and the union continue to disagree in belief about the increasing cost of living, but that the company, even so, ends by favoring the higher wage scale. The union will then be content to end the argument and will cease to press its point about living costs. It may bring up that point again, in some future argument of the same sort, or in urging the righteousness of its victory to the newspaper columnists; but for the moment the fact that the company has agreed in attitude is sufficient to terminate the argument. On the other hand: suppose that both parties agreed on all beliefs that were introduced into the argument, but even so continued to disagree in attitude. In that case neither party would feel that their dispute had been successfully terminated. They might look for other beliefs that could be introduced into the argument. They might use words to play on each other's emotions. They might agree (in attitude) to submit the case to arbitration, both feeling that a decision, even if strongly adverse to one party or the other, would be preferable to a continued impasse. Or, perhaps, they might abandon hope of settling their dispute by any peaceable means.

In many other cases, of course, men discuss ethical topics without having the strong, uncompromising attitudes that the present example has illustrated. They are often as much concerned with redirecting their own attitudes, in the light of greater knowledge, as with redirecting the attitudes of others. And the attitudes involved are often altruistic rather than selfish. Yet the above example will serve, so long as that is understood, to suggest the nature of ethical disagreement. Both disagreement in attitude and disagreement in belief are involved, but the former predominates in that (1) it determines what sort of disagreement in belief is relevantly disputed in a given ethical argument, and (2) it determines by its continued presence or its resolution whether or not the argument has been settled. We may see further how intimately the two sorts of disagreement are related: since attitudes are often functions of beliefs, an agreement in belief may lead people, as a matter of psychological fact, to agree in attitude.

III

Having discussed disagreement, we may turn to the broad question that was first mentioned, namely: By what methods of argument or inquiry may disagreement about matters of value be resolved?

It will be obvious that to whatever extent an argument involves disagreement in belief, it is open to the usual methods of the sciences. If these methods are the *only* rational methods for supporting beliefs—as I believe to be so, but cannot now take time to discuss—then scientific methods are the only rational methods for resolving the disagreement in *belief* that arguments about values may include.

But if science is granted an undisputed sway in reconciling beliefs, it does not thereby acquire, without qualification, an undisputed sway in reconciling attitudes. We have seen that arguments about values include disagreement in attitude, no less than disagreement in belief, and that in certain ways the disagreement in attitude predominates. By what methods shall the latter sort of disagreement be resolved?

The methods of science are still available for that purpose, but only in an indirect way. Initially, these methods have only to do with establishing agreement in belief. If they serve further to establish agreement in attitude, that will be due simply to the psychological fact that altered beliefs may cause altered attitudes. Hence scientific methods are conclusive in ending arguments about values only to the extent that their success in obtaining agreement in belief will in turn lead to agreement in attitude.

In other words: the extent to which scientific methods can bring about agreement on values depends on the extent to which a commonly accepted body of scientific beliefs would cause us to have a commonly accepted set of attitudes.

How much is the development of science likely to achieve, then, with regard to values? To what extent *would* common beliefs lead to common attitudes? It is, perhaps, a pardonable enthusiasm to *hope* that science will do everything—to hope that in some rosy future, when all men know the consequences of their acts, they will all have common aspirations and live peaceably in complete moral accord. But if we speak not from our enthusiastic hopes but from our present knowledge, the answer must be far less exciting. We usually *do not know,* at the beginning of any argument about values, whether an agreement in belief, scientifically established, will lead to an agreement in attitude or not. It is logically possible, at least, that two men should continue to disagree in attitude even though they had all their beliefs in common, and even though neither had made any logical or inductive error, or omitted any relevant evidence. Differences in temperament, or in early training, or in social status, might make the men retain different attitudes even though both were possessed of the complete scientific truth. Whether this logical possibility is an empirical likelihood I shall not presume to say; but it is unquestionably a possibility that must not be left out of account.

To say that science can always settle arguments about value, we have seen, is to make this assumption: Agreement in attitude will always be consequent upon complete agreement in belief, and science can always bring about the latter. Taken as purely heuristic, this assumption has its usefulness. It leads people to discover the discrepancies in their beliefs and to prolong enlightening argument that *may* lead, as a matter of fact, from commonly accepted beliefs to commonly accepted attitudes. It leads people to reconcile their attitudes in a rational, permanent way, rather than by rhapsody or exhortation. But the assumption is *nothing more,* for present knowledge, than a heuristic maxim. It is wholly without any proper foundation of probability. I conclude, therefore, that scientific methods cannot be guaranteed the definite role in the so-called normative sciences that they may have in the natural sciences. Apart from a heuristic assumption to the contrary, it is possible that the growth of scientific knowledge may leave many disputes about values permanently unsolved. Should these disputes persist, there are nonrational methods for dealing with them, of course, such as impassioned, moving oratory. But the purely intellectual methods of science, and, indeed, *all* methods of reasoning, may be insufficient to settle disputes about values even though they may greatly help to do so.

For the same reasons I conclude that normative ethics is not a branch of any science. It deliberately deals with a type of disagreement that science deliberately avoids. Ethics is not psychology, for instance; for although psychologists may, of course, agree or disagree in belief about attitudes, they need not, as psychologists, be concerned with whether they agree or disagree with one another *in* attitude. Insofar as normative ethics draws from the sciences, in order to change attitudes *via* changing people's beliefs, it *draws* from *all* the sciences; but a moralist's peculiar aim—that of *redirecting* attitudes—is a type of activity, rather than knowledge, and falls within no science. Science may study that activity and may help indirectly to forward it; but is not *identical* with that activity.

IV

I can take only a brief space to explain why the ethical terms, such as "good," "wrong," "ought," and so on, are so habitually used to deal with disagreement in attitude. On account of their repeated occurrence in emotional situations they have acquired a strong emotive meaning. This emotive meaning makes them serviceable in initiating changes in a hearer's attitudes. Sheer emotive impact is not likely, under many circumstances, to change attitudes in any permanent way; but it *begins* a process that can then be supported by other means.

There is no occasion for saying that the meaning of ethical terms is *purely* emotive, like that of "alas" or "hurrah." We have seen that ethical *arguments* include many expressions of *belief,* and the rough rules of ordinary language permit us to say that some of these beliefs are expressed by an ethical judgment itself. But the beliefs so expressed are by no means always the same. Ethical terms are notable for their ambiguity, and opponents in an argument may use them in different senses. Sometimes this leads to artificial issues, but it usually does not. So long as one person says "this is good" with emotive praise, and another says "no, it is bad," with emotive condemnation, a disagreement in attitude is manifest. Whether or not the beliefs that these statements express are logically incompatible may not be discovered until later in the argument; but even if they are actually compatible, disagreement in attitude will be preserved by emotive meaning; and this disagreement, so central to ethics, may lead to an argument that is certainly not artificial in its issues so long as it is taken for what it is.

The many theorists who have refused to identify ethical statements with scientific ones have much to be said in their favor. They have seen that ethical judgments mold or alter attitudes, rather than describe them, and they have seen that ethical judgments can be guaranteed no definitive scientific support. But one need not on that account provide ethics with any extramundane, *sui generis subject matter.* The distinguishing features of an ethical judgment can be preserved by a recognition of emotive meaning and disagreement in attitude, rather than by some nonnatural quality—and with far greater intelligibility. If a unique subject matter is *postulated,* as it usually is, to preserve the important distinction between normative ethics and science, it serves no purpose that is not served by the very simple analysis I have here suggested. Unless nonnatural qualities can be defended by positive arguments, rather than as an "only resort" from the acknowledged weakness of ordinary forms of naturalism, they would seem nothing more than the invisible shadows cast by emotive meaning.

QUESTIONS FOR STUDY AND DISCUSSION

1. Explain Stevenson's distinction between disagreement in belief and disagreement in attitude.
2. Why does Stevenson say that in an ethical argument disagreement in attitude is more basic than disagreement in belief?
3. How are the "methods of science" relevant to resolving ethical arguments?
4. What appears to be the most important difference between Ayer and Stevenson?

Stephen Toulmin

STEPHEN TOULMIN, born in London in 1922, was educated at King's College, Cambridge University, where he received his Ph.D. in 1948. A fellow of King's College from 1947 to 1959, he was a lecturer in the Philosophy of Science at Oxford University (1949–1955) and professor of Philosophy at the University of Leeds (1955–1959). In 1960 Toulmin began doing work in the history of ideas for an independent foundation. In addition to *An Examination of the Place of Reason in Ethics* (1950), which has been widely read and quoted during the past several years, he has written *The Philosophy of Science: An Introduction* (1953), *The Uses of Argument* (1958), *Foresight and Understanding* (1961), *The Fabric of the Heavens* (1961), and *The Architecture of Matter* (1962).

A Critique of A. J. Ayer

The last of the three traditional approaches [1] for us to discuss is the "imperative" approach. The starting-point of this approach is the doctrine that, in calling anything good or right, we are only evincing (displaying) our feelings towards it. In saying "You ought not to steal," for example, we are (it is said) doing no more, from the logician's point of view, than if we cried "Stealing!" in a peculiarly horrified tone.

This doctrine has a lot in common with the modified ("attitude") form of subjective theory discussed in the last chapter; much of what was said there in criticism applies again with equal force. I shall show that, in spite of the important resemblances between ethical statements, commands and exhortations, the imperative doctrine fails to lead to an adequate account of ethics, principally because it side-steps the question, "What is a good reason for an ethical judgment?" rather as the theory of attitudes did. The philosopher who adopts the imperative approach has too narrow a view of the uses of reasoning—he assumes too readily that a mathematical

---

[1] Toulmin discussed in previous chapters the other two of "the three traditional approaches." These two are, in Toulmin's terms, the "objective approach," which regards value statements as assertions about properties of objects, and the "subjective approach," which regards value statements as assertions about the speaker's feelings. [F.E.]

or logical proof or a scientific verification can be the only kind of "good reason" for any statement. As a result, he dismisses all evaluative inferences (arguments from facts to values or duties) as rationalisation or rhetoric, and regards our central problem, not merely as trivial, but as nonsense.

In this, his arguments run counter to common sense and common usage, and can be rejected. They do, however, raise our central problem again with the greatest force. Moreover, they make it clear that it is our question, rather than the question, "What *is* goodness?" which is really the central one.

THE RHETORICAL FORCE OF ETHICAL JUDGEMENTS

It may seem odd to have ignored until now a doctrine according to which the very problem I am discussing is nonsense. I have done so (I hope and believe) justifiably.

In the first place, the imperative approach is the youngest and most artless of the three traditional approaches. The objective and subjective doctrines have, in one form or another, been bandied about and criticised for 2000 years and more; their weaknesses have been apparent for almost as long, and their advocates have been used to retire to their second lines of defence. Only ingenuous amateurs still call goodness a "property," in the ordinary sense of the word, or regard ethical sentences as straightforward expressions of the feelings. For professionals, things have become more complicated—it is with the world of "non-natural properties" rather than ordinary "properties," of "attitudes" rather than simple "feelings," that they are concerned.

By contrast, the imperative doctrine is fresh and uncomplicated. It does not call ethical sentences "non-natural commands," but wears its obvious paradox bravely and defiantly. To have disposed, at the start, of the imperative doctrine, and to have passed on later to consider the more hardy objective and subjective doctrines, would have been to shoot the sitting bird first. And, moreover, it would have been impossible, while rejecting the approach, to do justice to its force and importance.

This leads on to the second point. The imperative approach is the youngest of the approaches, by no mere chance, but because it is the result of a reaction against the two older ones. To appreciate its strength, it is necessary to have seen beforehand the weaknesses in the objective and subjective doctrines which it is intended to overcome. No doubt one might dismiss the doctrine out of hand, simply on grounds of factual falsehood—it is just not true that the phrase "ethical reasoning" is self-contradictory, or that to talk of "valid evaluative inferences" is nonsense. In the same way, one might dismiss Russell's conclusion that "all one ever sees is a part of one's own brain" on the grounds that we do as a matter of fact often see chairs and tables and motor-cars and trees, and rarely if ever see parts of our own brains. But to do this and this alone would be perversely commonsensical, for the imperative doctrine is only obliquely directed at preventing people from discussing our central problem, and we can learn a good deal by examining its more immediate aims.

The advocate of the imperative doctrine is determined, from the start, to avoid some of the mistakes in the subjective and objective doctrines. Ethical concepts, as he recognises, correspond neither to processes "in" the object nor to processes "in" or "in the mind of" the speaker: there is no quality and no response which can plausibly be taken as that to which our value-sentences refer. Our philosopher, therefore, condemns the form of words "So-and-so is *X*" ("Meekness is good," "Promise-keeping is morally obligatory") as a misleading one—one which gives a false idea of the part that ethical sentences play in our lives. He insists that it is not possible to find a place for such sentences in that series of statements, of which a clear-sighted man's judgement of shape is near one extreme, and an eccentric's gourmandise near the other—and not merely in fact impossible but wrong-headed, since (for him) the question "Where on this series do ethical sentences come?" has no meaning. In contrast to those sentences of the form "So-and-so is *X*" which give information of some kind, the whole force of ethical statements (according to him) is *rhetorical*. They are, he asserts, disguised imperatives or ejaculations; our least misleading ethical utterances being those like "Good!" the cry of joy, and "Naughty!" the command to desist.

"In saying 'tolerance is a virtue,' " he explains,[2] "I should not be making a statement about my feelings or anything else. I should simply be *evincing* my favourable feelings towards tolerance; a very different thing from saying that I have them, or that there is something about tolerance, some quality which intolerance has not got. Again, if I said to someone, 'You acted wrongly in stealing that money,' I should not be *stating* any more than if I had simply said 'You stole that money,' cried 'Stealing! Oh!' in a peculiar tone of horror, or written it with special exclamation marks."

This doctrine often strikes newcomers as "cynical" or "pessimistic"; philosophers who advocate it seem to the unsympathetic to be "fiddling and playing tricks while the world burns." Their reaction is significant, but to understand the doctrine we must discount this appearance, at any rate until we are in a position to account for it. As matters turn out, it is quite misleading. One soon discovers in practice that advocates of the doctrine are no less cheerful or "idealistic" (in the everyday sense) than others, and that they will happily support the most rigorous of ethical judgements.

The point of the doctrine is logical, not empirical. Just as those who adopt the objective and subjective approaches assimilate ethical concepts to the logical categories of "properties" and "subjective relations" respectively, the supporters of the imperative doctrine assimilate all ethical sen-

---

[2] Cf. Ayer's discussion from *Language, Truth, and Logic*, pp. 500–02 in this section. [F.E.]

tences to the class of interjections—exclamations, ejaculations, commands and so on.

In order to see why they do this, let us consider typical members of the class. To start with, there are those spontaneous reactions, like blushing, smiling, laughing and weeping, which play an important part in our relations with our fellows, and which mean (indicate) so much to those we meet. Next, there are the manner and tone of voice in which we speak, which convey to a hearer nuances difficult to put into writing. With these we may class ejaculations like "Blast!" and "Hurrah!" which, without stating anything, release our feelings of annoyance or jubilation; and those stimuli, by means of which we move others to act—"Gee-up!" and "Whoa!"; "Stop!" and "Stand to attention!" The whole force of each of these is rhetorical; the blush, the manner, the curse, the command, all evince feelings—and so (it is said) do ethical utterances.

Unquestionably, many of the facts to which our philosopher will draw attention in presenting his case are true and important. In practice, moral exhortation is often no more than straight persuasion or intimidation. Ethical remarks are, indeed, made with the intention that hearers should act or reflect on them. Certainly they evince our feelings: what we call "wicked" horrifies us, the "admirable" gratifies us. The schoolboy who, on hearing that he has won his cricket colours or a scholarship, exclaims "That *is* good news!" might equally well cry out "Good!" or "Hurrah!" or "I *am* pleased!" Likewise when, in your childhood, your father said to you, "Naughty! Naughty! You mustn't take all the jam," he was not so much interested in conveying information to you—apart perhaps from information about your chances of the slipper—as he was in stopping you before you finished the pot. All these facts are true and important, and moral philosophers have in the past paid too little attention to them. But more is required in order to establish the literal truth of the imperative doctrine.

THE IMPOSSIBILITY OF DISPUTING ABOUT EXCLAMATIONS

In addition to their rhetorical force, ejaculations and commands have important logical characteristics in common. First (though this must not be put too strongly), none of them can be said to "give information," or to "state" anything. Of course, if they "mean a lot" to our friends, in one sense they do give information, but there is a clear sense in which they cannot be said to. If someone blushes, that is a sign that she is embarrassed, if he shouts it is a sign that he is angry, if he curses that is one too, and if he starts giving orders, you gather he wants things done. But it is "gathering" in each case: you would not say that she had told you she was embarrassed, or that he had told you he was angry, or even that he had told you he wanted you to do anything (although he "told you to do it"). Leaving aside the sense in which such signs do "give you information," there is a common and important sense, which I am using here, in which his utterance does not give you information unless he tells you.

Again, there is no disputing about exclamations in the way in which we dispute about questions of fact, because no two exclamations can be said to be logically incompatible with one another. If Featherstone maximus blushes and says to Smith minor in a reproachful tone, "Beast! You told him I was late for school. Do mind your own business in future," the only subject for dispute is the fact in question; namely, whether or not Smith did tell on Featherstone. The blush, the tone of reproach, the exclamation ("Beast!") and the imperative ("Do mind your own business") are to be distinguished from the fact in question; for, in spite of the considerable part that they play in the total situation, they *state* nothing whatever. To put this in another way: many things bear upon the statement of fact ("I heard you telling him," "He told me you had," "I knew that you must have from the way in which he carried on," etc.), in a way in which they cannot bear upon the other elements in the situation. One can quite properly ask about the "verification" of a statement of fact; but there is no meaning to the "truth" or "falsity" of a blush or an exclamation.

ARE ETHICAL SENTENCES EJACULATIONS?

Our philosopher maintains that what applies to interjections applies equally to ethical sentences. "It is impossible to dispute about questions of value," he says.[3] "When ethical statements appear to be subjects for dispute, or are opposed, the dispute—if it has any meaning at all—is reducible to differences regarding the facts of the case—such as whether anyone really did steal anything." All we can do, he suggests, is to hope that, if we get an opponent to agree with us about the facts of the case, he will adopt the same "moral attitude" towards them as we do. As for the question of good reasons and valid arguments in ethics, he declares bluntly that ethical judgements "have no validity."[4]

The position he takes up is similar to the "theory of attitudes," which we considered in the last chapter,[5] but with two main differences. Although both theories agree that the aim of ethical discourse is to achieve convergent "moral attitudes," they differ in their accounts of these attitudes. The modified subjective theory[6] identifies them as attitudes of approval and disapproval; the imperative theory leaves them unexplained, making no attempt to specify the peculiarities of the "moral" attitudes and "ethical" feelings evinced in the course of ethical discussions.

Again, although they agree in ignoring the question of the validity of evaluative inferences, it is for different reasons. The advocate of the subjective theory does so because he regards the question as *trivial,* the supporter of the imperative doctrine does so because he regards it as *nonsense.* From

---

[3] *Ibid.*, p. 503. [F.E.]
[4] *Ibid.* [F.E.]
[5] Toulmin is referring to Stevenson's theory as presented in Stevenson's major work, *Ethics and Language.* [F.E.]
[6] Again, Stevenson's theory. [F.E.]

their different points of view, however, both succeed in ironing out a distinction which is, in practice, central—the distinction between those ethical arguments we should accept and those we should ignore or reject.

In this lies the principal paradox of the imperative doctrine. We might dismiss it at once, having seen the ridiculous consequences to which, when taken literally, it leads; but this would be a pedantic and disingenuous thing to do. It will be more interesting to examine, with the help of examples, the weaknesses of the approach, and see whether we can account for its origin and for its appearance of cynicism. If we can do this before abandoning it, we shall be better placed to appreciate its value.

THE WEAKNESSES OF THE IMPERATIVE APPROACH

Consider, first, a genuine imperative. If the sergeant-major says to me, "Stand to attention!" I do not stop to argue, but stand to attention at once. And if I ask him for "a good reason for accepting what he says as true," he will put me on a charge, or send me to the Medical Officer for a psychological inspection. In such a case, no questions of truth, falsity or verification arise; and they do not arise, not just because of the threat of the "glass-house," but because they have no meaning in this context.

Now consider a very similar ethical sentence. Suppose that the sergeant-major says to me instead, "You ought to be standing at attention." I shall stand to attention at once in just the same way—and this shows the justice of the imperative doctrine's claims about the rhetorical force of ethical judgements. And once again, if I ask him about "a good reason for agreeing with what he says," he will act as before. Once again, that is to say, no questions of truth, falsity or verification will arise. But there is this important difference between the two cases: if these questions do not arise in this case it will be because of the threat of the "glass-house," and not because it would be nonsense to ask them. If, for example, I had asked the sergeant-major, "How am I to know that I ought?" he could with perfect logic have said, "By consulting King's Regulations and Army Council Instructions, Section so-and-so"; and this would indeed have been to "give a reason."

Is this example a fair one? Or is the issue confused by questions of legal obligation, which can only be called "ethical" as a courtesy matter? Questions of legal obligation, our philosopher may say, are of course open to dispute and verification—that is what the Law Courts are for—but questions of moral obligation are not.

This objection, however, does not get him very far: quite apart from legal considerations, questions of truth, falsity and rational justification (or verification, in a broad sense of the term) do continually arise in ethics. If you tell a child, "You ought to take off your dirty shoes before going into the drawing room," and he asks "Why?," then the answers, "Because your Mama does not like you to dirty the carpet" and "Because it makes unnecessary work," are "reasons"—and pretty good ones, too—while the answer, "Because it's the third Tuesday before Pentecost," seems a poor one.

For that matter, we often talk of "reasons" (some "good," some "bad") for commands, too. Thus, in an undisciplined army, with the threat of a court-martial absent, my response to the sergeant-major's "Stand to attention!" might well be to ask, "Why?"

In the case of commands, however, these reasons can never be "reasons for agreeing to the truth of what has been said." If, when the sergeant-major has bellowed his order, I go up to a private and say to him, "D'you know; the R.S.M. wasn't telling the truth," he may stare at me or laugh, but he will certainly not understand. But if the sergeant-major has only said to him, "You ought to be standing at attention," and I do the same, he will agree, ask for my reasons, or begin to argue with me. He will not regard my statement as strange or unintelligible, for he will be thoroughly familiar with such discussions. That being so, it is quite wrong to call it nonsense.

A major weakness of the imperative doctrine of ethics is, therefore, this: it treats the contingent proposition that questions of truth, falsity and verification often *do not* arise in ethical discourse, as if it were logically identical with the necessary proposition that, over exclamations and commands, such questions *cannot* arise. That is, it treats ethical statements, which approximate in some respects to commands and interjections, as if they were just commands and interjections. And this paradox is inevitable if one is to dismiss all evaluative inferences as beyond the scope of reasoning. If we are to overcome it, we must grant that ethical reasoning is possible, and so that some types of reasoning are "good" and some "bad"—some of the arguments leading to true conclusions "valid" ones, and all which lead to false conclusions "invalid."

THE SOURCES OF THE IMPERATIVE DOCTRINE

The nature of this weakness also helps to explain how the doctrine arises. Despite our ordinary usage, in which "reasons" can be brought for anything from mathematical theorems to curses, the advocate of the imperative doctrine wishes to limit the meaning and scope of "reasoning." For him, "truth," "falsity" and "proof" or "verification" are features of logical, mathematical and factual statements only, and strict proof or factual verification the only kind of good reason which can be said to support any statement.

In view of the debt to Hume which the advocates of both the imperative doctrine and the theory of attitudes themselves acknowledge, it is interesting to remark that he, too, deliberately limited the scope of reasoning in the same way. Recall the famous outburst standing at the end of his *Enquiry Concerning Human Understanding:* [7]

> If we take in our hand any volume; of divinity or school metaphysics, for instance; let us ask, *Does it contain any abstract reasoning*

---

[7] Ed. Selby-Bigge (2nd ed., 1902), p. 165. Ayer quotes this passage with approval (*Language, Truth, and Logic,* p. 54); and Stevenson acknowledges a general debt to Hume in his *Ethics and Language,* VII, 273–76. [S.T.]

concerning quantity or number? No. *Does it contain any experimental reasoning concerning matter of fact and existence?* No. Commit it then to the flames: for it can contain nothing but sophistry and illusion.

For him and them alike, logic, mathematics and experimental science alone are logically respectable: other attempts at reasoning are shams.

To do justice to Hume and his present-day followers: it is, of course, important not to apply to one mode of reasoning criteria of proof or truth appropriate only to another. Thus "$x^2 = 9$" is a bad reason for concluding "$x = 5$," "I have thrown double-six three times running with unbiased dice" is a bad reason for concluding "I shall throw double-six next time," "I know of no-one over 7 ft.. 6 in. in height" is a bad reason for concluding "there is no-one over 7 ft. 6 in. in height" and "Everybody kicks the niggers around" is a bad reason for concluding "It is all right for me to kick the niggers around"; but each is a bad reason of a logically different kind, and it will not do to treat any two of them as logically indistinguishable.

One point which the imperative doctrine fairly emphasises is the difference between arguments from logical, mathematical or factual premises to conclusions of a *similar* logical type, and arguments from factual premises to conclusions of a *different* kind, conclusions about duties or values. It is this distinction which is the strongest point in any refutation of the "naturalistic fallacy" [8]—that is, the idea that the value of any object can be identified with some ordinary property of it. Although factual reasons (R) may be good reasons for an ethical conclusion (E), to assert the conclusion is not just to assert the reasons, or indeed anything of the same logical type as R. It is to declare that one ought to approve of, or pursue, or do something-or-other. It is a wicked man who beats his wife; but to say that he is wicked is not just to say that he beats his wife—or, for that matter, to assert any other fact about him. It is to *condemn* him for it.

The bias in favour of logic, mathematics and science is not confined to the "empiricists." Logicians of all schools have traditionally concerned themselves, first, with deductive logic; next, with the logic of probability—a nice mixture of deduction and induction; and, lastly and more briefly, with inductive logic. The other uses of reasoning have commonly been ignored. In their books, the word "reason" has been used primarily for the facts which support a factual conclusion, and then mainly when the support offered is conclusive.

Even within philosophy, the use has naturally not been constant. In an inductive argument, data about the past and present are taken as "reasons" for a conclusion about the future: in a syllogism, factual or logical premises are "reasons" for a factual or logical conclusion: in a mathematical argument, the axioms and proof are the "reasons" which establish the theorem. When these differences have been forgotten, there has been trou-

---

[8] See Moore's discussion from *Principia Ethica*, pp. 459–60 in this section. [F.E.]

ble: the history of philosophy is littered with the corpses of theories attempting to prove that there is no real difference between the canons of deduction and induction. (And, likewise, the history of philosophical ethics is largely a record of attempts to identify evaluation with some form of inductive or deductive inference.)

All the same, past practice does not justify present neglect. We are all familiar with the idea of "giving reasons" in contexts other than logical, mathematical and factual. The most that can be said for the advocate of the imperative doctrine is that this wider use of "reason" and "valid" is an everyday and colloquial, rather than an esoteric and technical one. But this does not justify him in declaring that ethical judgements have *no* validity: all that it does is to help to explain the logical temptation to which he gives way.

Furthermore, past practice, conditioning present preoccupations, can hardly be the only reason for the plausibility of the imperative doctrine. It would be surprising if no deeper, "paralogistic" source could be found—and I think it can.

Historically, as I pointed out, the imperative approach is a reaction against the objective and subjective approaches. Like so many reactions, it goes a little too far, and in doing so makes the same mistake as its opponents.

"When two people are in ethical disagreement," said the first philosopher, "they contradict one another. If they are to do this, there must be something in the object they are discussing for them to contradict one another about. Therefore, goodness must be a property of the object."

"Nonsense!" replied the second philosopher. "Goodness is no property of the object. All they are doing is expressing divergent reactions to the object: the contradiction is only apparent. It is in their attitudes towards the object, not about any property of it, that they disagree."

"A plague on both your houses!" retorts our third philosopher. "You're both overlooking the rhetorical force of ethical judgements. People who have ethical disagreements are not talking about their own attitudes, and they are not talking about any property of the object either. The truth of the matter is that they are not "talking about" anything, for there isn't anything for them to "talk about"—all they are doing is answering each other back, and bringing pressure to bear on each other to behave differently."

The objective doctrine relies for its plausibility on the premise (usually suppressed) that, if there is to be a contradiction between two people, there must at least be a property of some kind for them to contradict one another about: otherwise the judgement can only be personal, referring to the speaker's psychological state. This premise is tacitly assumed in the argument for the subjective doctrine, too. Now the advocate of the imperative doctrine is under the tyranny of the same idea—that, in order to be logically respectable, to be capable of being regarded as "true" or "false" or of being reasoned about, a sentence must be made up only of concepts *refer-*

ring to something, something either "in the object" or "in the subject." The novelty of his paralogism is that he rejects both alternatives: he recognises that ethical sentences and ethical concepts "refer to" nothing of the kind required and concludes (paradoxically but firmly) that they can only be "pseudo-statements" and "pseudo-concepts."

We, however, have already seen the faultiness of the suppressed premise, and so of any argument depending on it. And, in seeing the nature of the fallacy involved, we have come to realise what it is that people in ethical disagreement really do have to contradict each other about— nothing physically or psychologically "concrete" or "substantial," but something which, for logical purposes, is quite as solid and important— namely, whether or not there is a good reason for reaching one ethical conclusion rather than another.

THE APPARENT CYNICISM OF THE IMPERATIVE DOCTRINE

Can we, as a result of our discussion, understand why it is that people complain, when first presented with this doctrine, of its cynicism and pessimism? I think the reasons are directly connected with the central fallacy of the approach.

The fundamental doctrine of the imperative approach may be put in several forms: "There is no good reason for passing from any set of facts to an ethical judgement," or "There is never any good reason for saying that anything is good or right, or for ascribing to ourselves or others any duty or moral obligation to do anything," or "All that happens, when anyone makes an ethical judgement, is that he bears the facts and the feelings of others in mind, and then exclaims in whatever sense he feels most like." When anyone is first presented with such statements, he is likely to be misled by their form into thinking that they express ordinary matters-of-fact.

The statements, "There is no good reason for passing from any set of facts to an ethical judgement" and "There is never any good reason for saying that anything is good or right," are at first sight very like the statement, "There is no good reason for supposing that he will come before five o'clock." The assertion, "All that happens, when anyone makes an ethical judgement, is that he exclaims in whatever sense he feels most like," immediately brings to mind statements of the form, "All that happens, when anyone pokes a hippopotamus in the ribs, is that it turns over."

If, in consequence, you suppose that the philosopher really is expressing an ordinary matter-of-fact—a natural assumption for a newcomer to the doctrine—what a terrible pessimist you must think him! "Poor, deluded humans," he seems to be saying, "spending their time looking for reasons for ethical judgements! If only they saw what a hopeless task they've taken on! Even looking for a needle in a haystack is a job with more prospect of success than that. And fancy their imagining that anyone making an ethical judgement ever does anything but exclaim! Why, I've watched thousands of them, and I've never *once* seen one who did."

The point of his doctrine is (as we have seen) quite otherwise; his pre-occupation is with logic, rather than with everyday matters-of-fact. If all he were saying were that in only a negligible proportion of cases do people *in fact* arrive at moral decisions on the basis of reason, he could not draw the conclusions he wants to. And this shows why the appearance of pessimism is deceptive.

The imperative doctrine arises out of a confusion between the logical proposition, "There are (can be) no good reasons for ejaculations," and the matter-of-fact proposition, "There are (may be) no good reasons for ethical judgements." The philosopher formulates the differences between factual and ethical statements in the logical proposition, "There are (can be) no good reasons for ethical judgements." The newcomer mistakes this for the matter-of-fact proposition, "There are (in fact) no good reasons for ethical judgements," and concludes that all his moral striving has been in vain. Hence the feeling of pessimism.

And it is not only the newcomer who is misled into behaving as if these were the kind of statements they seem to be: as often as not the philoso-pher begins to as well. Struck by the matter-of-fact appearance of his own remarks, and knowing that such statements are often enough true in spite of being paradoxical (see the "Believe It or Not" feature in the Sunday paper), he starts to treat his theory as really true, and common sense as really mistaken in its firm belief that some reasons *are* good reasons for ethical judgements, and that sometimes people making ethical statements are *not* just exclaiming.

But the only "matter of fact" with which the philosopher can be said to be concerned is whether or no the phrases "ethical reasoning," "an ethical dispute," "a valid evaluative inference," "a sound ethical judgement," "a good reason for doing this rather than that," and the like, are all nonsense. He mistakenly believes that they are, and concludes that we ought not to call the facts, which we bring in support of our ethical judgements, "rea-sons" for the ethical conclusions. He is afraid that, if we do, we shall con-fuse them (as philosophers sometimes have done) with the 'reasons' which, in deductive and inductive arguments, lead us to draw *factual* conclusions. "You ought never to use the word "reasons" for the facts we feel justify us in drawing an ethical conclusion; or say that a man who calls anything good or right is making a 'reasoned' statement—say, rather, that he is 'exclaiming.' "

The feeling of pessimism passes off, when we realise what it is that the philosopher is really asserting: that to ask for "good reasons for ethical judgements" is like asking for "the colour of heat," and not like asking for the moon. When, in addition, we realise that he wants us to *change* the use of our words "reason" and "validity," our natural conservatism will assert itself, and we shall lose the temptation to take his theory too seriously—that is, at its face value. For if, as he recommends, we stop calling the facts which support our ethical conclusions "reasons," we shall have to find another name for them; and if we are to stop talking of the "validity" of evaluative inferences, we shall have to invent another word for that too. The sensible thing to do is to bear in mind the facts to which he has drawn our attention, as an insurance against falling into philosophical errors, and afterwards to go on talking of "reasons" and "validity" in the way in which we always have done.

Our conservatism is justifiable. It is well over two thousand years since philosophers made the first recorded linguistic demands of this kind. About 430 B.C., Anaxagoras of Klazomene, under the impression that the everyday use of the concepts "coming into being" and "passing away" carried with it more in the way of metaphysical implications than it did, complained:

> The Hellenes follow a wrong usage in speaking of "coming into being" and "passing away"; for nothing comes into being or passes away, but there is mingling or separation of things that are. So they would be right to call "coming into being" "mixture" and "passing away" "separation."

As far as I know, nobody took any notice. Even the philosophers soon found something else to dispute about, so that the dangers of metaphysical confusion which Anaxagoras feared abated. Everyone went on using "coming into being" and "passing away" as before, and no harm (again as far as I know) resulted. Need we pay any more attention to the metaphysical scruples of our contemporaries than the Hellenes did to those of Anaxagoras?

CONCLUSION

Sometimes, when we make ethical judgements, we are not just ejaculating. When we say that so-and-so is good, or that I ought to do such-and-such, we do so sometimes for good reasons and sometimes for bad ones. The imperative approach does not help us in the slightest to distinguish the one from the other—in fact, by saying that to talk of reasons in this context is nonsense, it dismisses our question altogether. However, the doctrine is not only false but innocuous, for it draws its own fangs. If, as we must, we will refuse to treat ethical judgements as ejaculations, its advocate can produce no further reasons for his view. By his own account, all he can do is to evince his disapproval of our procedure, and urge us to give it up: it would be inconsistent of him to advance "reasons" at this stage. And if, instead, he retorts, "Very well; but nothing else will get you anywhere," that is a challenge worth accepting, a prediction worth falsifying.

QUESTIONS FOR STUDY AND DISCUSSION

1. According to Toulmin, what lends plausibility to Ayer's claim that ethical sentences can be assimilated into the realm of exclamations, ejaculations, and commands?

2. What is the major weakness that Toulmin finds in the "imperative approach"? Show how his example of giving orders illustrates this weakness.

3. What is the common premise assumed by all three of the doctrines that Toulmin criticizes, and how is each governed by that premise?

4. Using Toulmin's distinction between logical propositions and matter-of-fact propositions, explain why he claims that the proposals of the imperative doctrine appear—but only appear—to be cynical. What does Toulmin think that these proposals really amount to?

P. H. Nowell-Smith

P. H. NOWELL-SMITH, an Englishman born in 1914, was educated at Winchester and New College, Oxford University. In 1937 he studied philosophy at Harvard University under a Commonwealth Fellowship. After service with the British army in the Middle East and in India, he was elected in 1946 a fellow in Philosophy at Trinity College, Oxford. Author of articles on ethics, politics, and the nature of philosophy, and participant in many broadcasts mostly on the philosophy of religion, he is best known in the United States for his *Ethics* (1954).

The Meaning of "Could Have Acted Otherwise"

I

We have now to consider the logic of the language which we use to ascribe responsibility, to award praise and blame, and to justify our moral verdicts. I shall consider five types of moral judgement.

He broke a law or moral rule.	(1)
He could have acted otherwise.	(2)
He deserves censure (or punishment).	(3)
It would be just to censure (or punish) him.	(4)
He is a bad (cruel, mean, dishonest, etc.) man.	(5)

It is clear that all these are logically connected. It is not just a fact about the world that we learn from experience that only bad men deserve blame or that it is only just to blame those who could have acted otherwise. Yet the items cannot all be treated as analytically connected; for we should then find that it was senseless to ask certain questions that obviously do make sense.

For example, the character-words used in (5) are partly descriptive; and it makes sense to ask whether a person who is consistently mean or dishonest deserves blame. To give, as most of us would, an affirmative answer would be to use, not to analyse moral language. It would also be a mistake to say that it must (logically) be unjust to blame someone who could not have acted otherwise, on the ground that this is part of what "unjust" means. For (2) is a theoretical statement, while "unjust" is a G-word contextually implying that no one ought to blame him.[1] Nor does it help to say that we have insight into necessary synthetic connexions between the items on the list; for this is simply to say that we know them to be connected but cannot understand how. The connexions are of the quasi-logical kind that can only be understood by examining the conditions under which the various expressions are used and the purposes of using them.

I shall start by considering the connexions between (1), (3), and (4). The connexion between (3) and (4) seems to be analytic. If a man deserves blame, someone would be justified in blaming him. Not necessarily you; for you may be in no position to cast the first stone or to cast any stone at all.

Now "punishment" is a legal term and, in the case of punishment at least, (3) and (4) logically imply (1). A man can be justly punished only if he has broken a law, and the same applies, although naturally in a looser way, to moral censure. To deserve censure a man must have done something wrong, that is to say broken a moral rule. Now why should this be so? This question has already been partly answered in chapter 16. "Punishment" is a complex idea consisting of the ideas of inflicting pain, on someone who has broken a law, in accordance with a rule laying down the correct punishment. But we have still to ask why we make use of this complex idea at all. Remembering that "just" is a G-word, it is necessary to suppose that anyone who says that Jones deserves punishment must have a pro-attitude towards his being punished. But why should we wish to encourage the infliction of pain on those who have broken a law? The classical utilitarian answer is that it will either reform the criminal or deter potential criminals or both. Now, since laws and moral rules are devices for bringing about ends, we must have a pro-attitude towards reforming those who break them and deterring others. So, if it is a fact that punishment has these effects, this will explain the connexion between the infliction of pain and the breach of a rule.

But this simple theory will not do, if only because potential criminals would be as efficiently deterred by the punishment of an innocent scapegoat who was believed to be guilty as by that of a guilty man; and, whatever the effects might be, this would not be just. And we have also seen in chapter 16 how this simple theory can be amended. For we there saw that,

---

[1] The notion of contextual implication is used by Nowell-Smith and some other writers as an attempt to by-pass the analytic-synthetic dichotomy. Contextual implication is understood as a connection beween two (or more) words or statements such as provides a basis for anyone who knows the normal conventions of language to infer one from the other in the context in which they occur. Thus, if Jones says "X is good," it is contextually implied that Jones approves of X.

G-words are words used in advising, exhorting, and commanding, and hence belong to the language of "you ought." To say to Smith, "X is unjust," contextually implies that, for reasons not explicitly specified, Smith ought to disapprove of X. [F.E.]

although we might have a system of dealing with each situation as it arose, there were great advantages in having legal and moral codes. And it is because we have these codes that neither the punishment of Jones nor an adverse moral verdict on him could (logically) be called "just" unless he has broken a law. Without the code we could still recommend people to inflict pain on Jones to stop him doing what he does, but the peculiar force of "just" could not be carried by any word. And, granted that we have rules, it is clear that the *purpose* of punishment and blame is relevant, not to the question "Should Jones be punished or blamed?" but to the question "Should the sort of thing that Jones did be prohibited by a rule to which a penalty is attached?"

The question "What justifies punishment?" in fact conceals an ambiguity which is largely responsible for the dispute between those who answer it in terms of retribution for crime and those who answer it in terms of deterrence and reform. If we have in mind the judge's problem, the utilitarian answer is clearly inadequate; but if we are thinking about the legislator's problem, it seems very plausible. Each party has tried to extend their answer to cover both cases. But even if we are thinking about the legislator's problem, it would be an over-simplification to say that legislators either do or should decide what laws to have solely by reference to the purpose of having laws. There are two reasons why they do not do so, one bad and one good. The bad reason is that they are still to some extent in the thrall of the philosophical theory of Natural Law, which itself confuses the judge's problem with the legislator's. But there is also a good reason. It is desirable (on grounds of utility) that the law should be consistent and stable and that the penalty laid down for one offence should not be wildly out of line with those laid down for others. Consequently, unless we are to revise the whole legal code every time we make a new law, it is expedient not to consider the proposed law in isolation but to consider it as part of a system that we do not, on this occasion, wish to disturb.

Just as we might, but do not, live in a world in which every case was decided by an omnicompetent judge without reference to any general principle other than that of utility, so we might live in a world in which legislators decided what laws to pass solely by reference to this standard. But there are as good reasons for rejecting this system as there are for rejecting the system of judges not bound by laws. We know too little about the probable effects of any particular penalty and about the repercussions which a new law-*cum*-penalty is likely to have on other parts of the system. Hence even legislators do well to criticize proposed laws not only by reference to the purpose of having laws but by reference to the current system of laws, that is to say "Justice." The connexions between the justice of a punishment and its utility are thus exceedingly complex; but the fact that utilitarians have oversimplified them is a reason, not for abandoning their theory or retreating into the asylum of intuition, but for revising the theory. It cannot be an accident that the punishments we call "just" on the whole tend to reform and deter. And if in a particular case we find that they do not serve these ends, we tend to amend the law. On the Natural Law theory it would only be right to amend a law if we discovered that it conflicted with natural law. How we discover this is in any case a mystery, and it would be most remarkable if the discovery always went hand in hand with the discovery that the law fails to fulfil its purpose.

II

The most difficult and important of the items on our list of moral judgements is "He could have acted otherwise" (2). The facts about its logical connexions with the others are tolerably clear. It is a necessary condition of all except (1), and it is also a necessary condition of (1) if "He broke a law" is taken to imply that he broke it voluntarily. What is not so clear is what (2) means or why it should be a necessary condition of the other items.

A man is not considered blameworthy if he could not have acted otherwise; and, although it is often easy to decide in practice whether he could have acted otherwise or not, it is not clear how we do this or why we should think it necessary to do it. Let us first examine the use of "could have" in some non-moral cases.

"Could have" is a modal phrase, and modal phrases are not normally used to make straight-forward, categorical statements. "It might have rained last Thursday" tells you something about the weather, but not in the way that "It rained last Thursday" does. It is sometimes said that it is used to express the speaker's ignorance of the weather; but what it expresses is not just this but his ignorance of any facts that would strongly tend to rule out the truth of "It rained." It would be a natural thing to say in the middle of an English, but not of a Californian summer. But, whatever it does express, what it does *not* express is a belief in a third alternative alongside "it rained" and "it did not rain." Either it rained or it did not; and "it might have rained" does not represent a third alternative which excludes the other two in the way that these exclude each other.

But these modal phrases are also sometimes used in cases in which they cannot express ignorance since they imply a belief that the event concerned did not occur. It would be disingenuous for a rich man to say "I might have been a rich man"; but he could well say "I might have been a poor man" while knowing himself to be rich. The puzzle here arises from the fact that, if he is rich, he cannot be poor. His actual riches preclude his possible poverty in a way that would seem to imply that we could have no use for "he might have been poor." But this is only puzzling so long as we try to treat these modal expressions in a categorical way.

"Would have" and "might have" are clearly suppressed hypotheticals, incomplete without an "if . . ." or an "if . . . not . . . ." Nobody would say "Jones would have won the championship" unless (a) he believed that Jones did not win and (b) he was prepared to add "if he had entered" or "if he had not sprained his ankle" or some such clause.

It is not so obvious that "could have" sentences also express hypotheticals; indeed in some cases they obviously do not. If a man says "it could have been a Morris, but actually it was an Austin," it would be absurd to ask him under what conditions it could or would have been a Morris. "Could have" is here used to concede that, although I happen to know it was an Austin, your guess that it was a Morris was not a bad one. But "could have" also has a use which is more important for our purpose and in which, as I shall try to show, it is equivalent to "would have . . . if . . . ." It refers to a tendency or capacity. Consider the following examples:

(1) He could have read *Emma* in bed last night, though he actually read *Persuasion;* but he could not have read *Werther* because he does not know German.

(2) He could have played the *Appassionata,* though he actually played the *Moonlight;* but he could not have played the *Hammerklavier,* because it is too difficult for him.

These are both statements, since they could be true or false; and to understand their logic we must see how they would be established or rebutted. Neither could be established or rebutted in the way that "He read *Persuasion*" could, by observing what he actually did; and it is partly for this reason that we do not call them categorical. But, although they could not be directly verified or falsified by observation of what he did, this might be relevant evidence. It would be almost conclusive evidence in the first case, since it would be very odd if a man who actually read *Persuasion* was incapable of reading *Emma*. On the other hand, his having played the *Moonlight* is only weak evidence that he could have played the *Appassionata,* since the latter is more difficult and also because he might never have learnt it.

In each of these cases, in order to establish the "could have" statement we should have to show (a) that he has performed tasks of similar difficulty sufficiently often to preclude the possibility of a fluke, and (b) that nothing prevented him on this occasion. For example we should have to establish that there was a copy of *Emma* in the house.

Statements about capacities, whether of the "can" or of the "could have" kind, contextually imply unspecified conditions under which alone the person might succeed; and "could have" statements can be refuted either by showing that some necessary condition was absent (there was no copy of *Emma*) or by showing that the capacity was absent. The first point could be established directly. How could the second be established? In practice we do this either by appealing to past performances or failures or by asking him to try to do it now. It is clear that neither of these methods could be applied directly to the occasion in question. We know that he did not read *Emma,* and it is nonsense to ask him to try to have read *Emma* last night. And the very fact that evidence for or against "could have" statements must be drawn from occasions other than that to which they refer is enough to show that "he could have acted otherwise" is not a straightforward categorical statement, at least in the type of case we have been considering. Whether it is possible or necessary to interpret it categorically in moral cases is a point which I shall examine in the next section.

It might be argued that the sort of evidence by which "could have" statements are supported or rebutted is never conclusive; and this is true. The argument used is an inductive one, with a special type of conclusion. We might use an ordinary inductive argument to predict his future performance from known past performances or in support of a statement about an unknown past performance. But in this special case we know that he did not do the thing in question, because we know that he did something else; so we put our conclusion in the form "he could have done X."

Whatever the evidence, it is always open to a sceptic to say "I know he has always succeeded (failed) in the past; but he *might* have failed (succeeded) on this occasion." Now this sort of scepticism is not peculiar to "could have" statements; it is one variety of general scepticism about induction. It is *possible* that if I had tried to add 15 and 16 last night (which I did not) I should have failed; but it is also possible that if I tried now I should fail. Our use of "could have" statements, like our use of predictions and generalizations, always ignores such refined scepticism; and it would be absurd to try to base either freedom or responsibility on the logical possibility of such contingencies. In practice we ignore the sceptic unless he can produce reasons for his doubt, unless he can say why he believes that a man who has always succeeded might have failed on just that occasion. If no such reason is forthcoming we always allow inductive evidence which establishes the existence of a general capacity to do something to establish also the statement that the man could have done it on a particular occasion. Nor is this practice due to the fact that (the world being what it is) we are unfortunately unable to find better evidence and must fall back on probabilities. Our practice lies at the heart of the logic of "can" and "could have." For the sceptic is, here as elsewhere, asking for the logically impossible; he is asking us to adopt a criterion for deciding whether a man could have done something on a particular occasion which would make the words "can" and "could have" useless. What would be the result of accepting this suggestion? We should have to say that the only conclusive evidence that a man can do (could have done) X at time *t* is his actually doing (having done) X at time *t*. Thus the evidence that entitles us to say "He could have done X at time *t*" would also entitle us to say "He did X at time *t*," and the "could have" form would be otiose.

Capacities are a sub-class of dispositions. To say that a man "can" do something is not to say that he ever has or will; there may be special reasons why the capacity is never exercised, for example that the occasion for exercising it has never arisen. A man might go through his whole life without ever adding 15 and 16; and we should not have to say that he couldn't do this. Yet a man cannot be said to be able to do something if all the necessary conditions are fulfilled and he has a motive for doing it. It is logically odd to say "Smith can run a mile, has had several opportunities, is passionately fond of running, has no medical or other reasons for not doing so, but never has in fact done so." And, if it is true that this is logically odd, it follows that "can" is equivalent to "will . . . if . . ." and "could have" to "would have . . . if . . . ." To say that Smith could have read *Emma* last night is to say that he would have read it, if there had been a copy, if he had not been struck blind, etc., etc., and if he had wanted to read it more than he wanted to read anything else. Both the "etc." and the last clause are important; we cannot specify all the necessary conditions; and, granted that the conditions were present and that he could have read it, he might still not have read it because he did not want to. But if he did not want to do anything else more than he wanted to read *Emma,* he could not in these conditions be said to have *chosen* to do something else. He might have *done* something else, but not in the important sense of "done" which implies choosing.

III

Liberatarianism. Before considering why "he could have acted otherwise," interpreted in this hypothetical way, is regarded as relevant to ascriptions of responsibility, it is necessary to examine the theory that, although the hypothetical interpretation is correct in most cases, in the special case of moral choice the phrase must be interpreted in a categorical way. It would indeed be remarkable if modal forms which are normally used in a hypothetical way were used categorically in one type of case alone; and I have already suggested that their logic is partly determined by the method that would be used to support or rebut statements which employ them. The thesis that "he could have acted otherwise" is categorical is equivalent to the thesis that it could be verified or falsified by direct observation of the situation to which it refers.

It is essential to notice that the categorical interpretation is supposed to be necessary only in a very small, but very important part of the whole range of human choice. And this too is remarkable; for it implies that the words "free" and "choose" are logically different in moral and in non-moral cases. There is a sense of "free" to which I have already alluded in which it is contrasted with "under compulsion"; and in this sense actions are still free when they are completely determined by the agent's tastes and character. For to say that they are determined in this way is not to say that he is a Pawn in the hands of Fate or a Prisoner in the iron grip of Necessity. It is only to say that anyone who knew his tastes and character well enough could predict what he will do. The fact that we can predict with a high degree of probability how Sir Winston Churchill will vote at the next election does not imply that he does not cast his vote freely. To be "free" in this sense is to be free to do what one wants to do, not to be able to act in spite of one's desires.

According to the theory to be examined most of our voluntary actions are "free" only in this sense which implies no breach in causal continuity. I choose what I choose because my desires are what they are; and they have been moulded by countless influences from my birth or earlier. But, it is said, *moral* choices are free in a quite different sense, and one that is incompatible with their being predictable. This unpredictability is an essential feature in the categorical interpretation of "he could have acted otherwise"; for, if anyone could predict what I am going to do, I should not really be choosing between genuinely open alternatives, although I might think I was.

Professor Campbell [2] puts the contrast in the following way: "Freewill does not operate in those practical situations in which no conflict arises in the agent's mind between what he conceives to be his 'duty' and what he feels to be his 'strongest desire.' It does not operate here because there is just no occasion for it to operate. There is no reason whatever why the agent should here even contemplate choosing any course other than that prescribed by his strongest desire. In all such situations, therefore, he naturally wills in accordance with his strongest desire. But his 'strongest desire' is simply the specific expression of that system of conative and emotive dispositions which we call his 'character.' In all such situations, therefore, whatever may be the case elsewhere, his will is in effect determined by his character as so far formed. . . ."

. . . (On the other hand) "in the situation of moral conflict, I, as agent, have before my mind a course of action, X, which I believe to be my duty; and also a course of action, Y, incompatible with X, which I feel to be that which I most strongly desire. Y is, as it is sometimes expressed, 'in the line of least resistance' for me—the course which I am aware that I should take, if I let my purely desiring nature operate without hindrance. It is the course towards which I am aware that my *character,* as so far formed, naturally inclines me. Now, as actually engaged in this situation, I find that I cannot help believing that I *can* rise to duty and choose X; the 'rising to duty' being affected by what is commonly called 'effort of will.' And I further find, if I ask myself just what it is I am believing when I believe that I 'can' rise to duty, that I cannot help believing that it lies with me, here and now, quite absolutely, which of two genuinely open possibilities I adopt; whether, that is, I make the effort of will and choose X or, on the other hand, let my desiring nature, my character as so far

[2] C. A. Campbell (b. 1897): a British ethician who has criticized both Schlick and Nowell-Smith and whose writings on the responsibility issue are widely read today. [F.E.]

formed, 'have its way,' and choose Y, the course in the line of least re-sistance." [3]

Now it is certainly true that many determinists have paid too little at-tention to the concept of "trying" or "making an effort"; but I think that there are certain difficulties in Professor Campbell's account of moral con-flict and, in particular, in his attempt to construe "I could have acted other-wise" in a categorical way. The first point to which I wish to draw attention is the question of method.

1. Campbell insists that the question whether choice is "free" in a contra-causal sense must be settled by introspection.[4] But is this so? To doubt the findings of his self-examination may seem impertinent; but the doubt is concerned, not with what he finds, but with the propriety of the language he uses to describe what he finds. The universal negative form of statement ("Nothing caused my decision," "No one could have predicted my decision") does not seem to be a proper vehicle for anything that one could be said to *observe* in self-examination. That I know introspectively what it is like to choose may be true; but I cannot be said to know intro-spectively that my choice was contra-causal or unpredictable; and this is the point at issue. He represents "I can rise to duty" as a report of a mental event or, perhaps, a state of mind, not as a statement about a capacity, and "I could have . . ." as a statement about a past state of mind or mental event. But, if this is really so, it is at least surprising that, in this one con-text alone, we use the modal words "can" and "could have" for making categorical reports. The issue between determinists and libertarians is an issue about the way in which expressions such as "choose," "can," and "alternative possibilities" are to be construed; and this is surely an issue which is to be settled not by self-observation but by logical analysis.

There are many other phrases in Campbell's account which give rise to the same doubts about the propriety of the introspective method. The phrase "conative disposition" is embedded in a large and complex mass of psychological theory and its use implies the acceptance of this theory; so that one could hardly be said to know by introspection that one has a conative tendency to do something. And phrases such as "determined," "contra-causal," and even "desiring nature" take us beyond psychology into metaphysics. To say this is not to condemn the phrases; perhaps meta-physics is just what is needed here. But a metaphysician is not a reporter; he is an interpreter of what he "sees"; and it is over the interpretation that the disputes arise.

2. A more obvious difficulty—and it is one of which libertarians are well aware—is that of distinguishing a "free" action from a random event. The essence of Campbell's account is that the action should not be pre-dictable from a knowledge of the agent's character. But, if this is so, can

---

[3] Campbell, "Is 'Free Will' a Pseudo-Problem?" *Mind* (1951), pp. 460–63. [P.H.N.-S.]
[4] *Scepticism and Construction*, p. 131. [P.H.N.-S.]

what he does be called *his* action at all? Is it not rather a *lusus naturae,* an Act of God or a miracle? If a hardened criminal, bent on robbing the poor-box, suddenly and *inexplicably* fails to do so, we should not say that he *chose* to resist or deserves *credit* for resisting the temptation; we should say, if we were religious, that he was the recipient of a sudden outpouring of Divine Grace or, if we were irreligious, that his "action" was due to chance, which is another way of saying that it was inexplicable. In either case we should refuse to use the active voice.

The reply to this criticism is that we must distinguish *In*determinism from *Self*-determinism. Choice is a creative act of the "self" and is not only unconstrained by external forces but also unconstrained by desire or character. But the difficulty here is to construe "self-determinism" in such a way that the "self" can be distinguished from the "character" without lapsing into indeterminism.

If we could construe "self-determined" by analogy with other "self"-compounds, such as self-adjusting, self-regulating, self-propelled, self-centred, self-controlled, and self-governing, there would be no difficulty. Some of these words apply to non-human objects, and they never imply that there is a part of the object called the "self" which adjusts, regulates, or controls the rest, though the object does have a special part without which it would not be self-adjusting, etc. I can point to the self-starter of a car, but not to the self that starts the car; to say that a heating system is "self-regulating" is to say that it maintains a constant temperature without anyone watching the dials and turning the knobs. Coming to the human scene, to say that a state is "self-governing" is to say that its inhabitants make their own laws without foreign intervention; and to say that a man is "self-centred" is to say, not that he is always thinking and talking about something called his "self," but that he is always thinking and talking about *his* dinner, *his* golf-handicap, the virtues of *his* wife, and the prowess of *his* children. In each case there is a subject and an object; but the "self" is neither subject nor object.

But if we construe "self-determined" in this way, it is clear that being self-determined implies only that a man acts freely in the ordinary sense of "freely" which the libertarian rejects as inadequate in the special case of moral choice. There would be no incompatibility between an action's being "self-determined" and its being predictable or characteristic of the agent; for "self-determined" would mean "determined by *his* motives and character," as opposed to "forced on him by circumstances or other people." But the libertarian regards explanation in terms of character as incompatible with genuine freedom and must therefore draw a contrast between "the self" and "the character." But if "self-determined" is to mean "determined by the self," it is necessary to give some account of what the "self" is. And if the question whether an action was determined by the "self" or not is to be relevant to the ascription of responsibility and the justice of adverse verdicts, we must be able to provide some criterion for deciding whether the self which determined the action is the same self that we are proposing to hold responsible or condemn.

Now the problem of Personal Identity is admittedly a difficult one and the danger of desert-island argument is particularly acute here, since Jekyll-and-Hyde cases that a layman would dismiss as flights of fancy have been known to occur. In fact we decide whether the man I met yesterday is the same that I met last year partly by seeing whether he looks the same, partly by observing an identity of characteristic behaviour, and partly by discovering what he can remember. And if we are to avoid the rather crude course of defining "same self" in terms of the spatio-temporal continuity of bodily cells, it seems that we must define it in terms of character and memory. But the libertarian's "self" is neither an empirical object nor displayed in characteristic action.

3. If it is necessary to decide whether or not a man could have acted otherwise before ascribing responsibility, it is necessary that we should have some criterion for deciding this; and on the libertarian theory such a criterion is quite impossible. For, let us suppose that we know a great deal about his character and also that the temptation which he faced seems to be a fairly easy one for such a man to overcome. On the libertarian hypothesis this information will not be sufficient to enable us to conclude that he could have acted otherwise. If he in fact does the wrong thing, there are three alternative conclusions that we might draw. (a) The action was not against his moral principles at all, so that no conflict between "duty" and "inclination" arose. This is what I have called "wickedness"; (b) he knew it was wrong and could have resisted the temptation but did not (moral weakness); (c) he knew it was wrong but the temptation was *too* strong for him; he *could* not overcome it (addiction). Now it is essential to be able to distinguish case (b) from case (c), since (b) is a culpable state while (c) is not. By treating "he could have acted otherwise" in a hypothetical way, the determinist thesis does provide us with a criterion for distinguishing between these cases; but the categorical interpretation cannot provide one, since no one, not even the man himself, could know whether he could have overcome the temptation or not.

4. The libertarian theory involves putting a very special construction on the principle that "ought" implies "can," which it is very doubtful whether it can bear. If we take this principle in a common-sense way it is undoubtedly true. It is no longer my duty to keep a promise, if I literally *cannot* do so. But when we say this we have in mind such possibilities as my being detained by the police or having a railway accident or the death of the promisee; and it is possible to discover empirically whether any of these exonerating conditions obtained. But if "cannot" is construed in such a way that it covers my being too dishonest a person or not making the necessary effort, it is no longer obvious that "ought" implies "can." These reasons for failure, so far from exonerating, are just what make a man culpable.

5. Even if it were possible to discover whether or not a man could have acted otherwise by attending to the actual occasion, as the categorical interpretation insists, why should this be held relevant to the question whether or not he is to blame? I shall try to explain this connexion in the next chapter; but on the libertarian hypothesis it will, I think, be necessary to fall back on insight into a relation of fittingness between freedom and culpability.

IV

The Concept of "Trying." It might be thought that the libertarian could discover a criterion for distinguishing culpable weakness of will from non-culpable addiction in the concept of "trying." For the addict fails, try as he may, while the weak-willed man fails because he does not try hard enough. The concept of "trying" is an important one for ethics since, whatever may be the case in a court of law, the question of moral blameworthiness often turns, not on what the agent did, but on what he tried or did not try to do. Morally we blame people, not for failing to live up to a certain standard, but for not trying hard enough to do so; and this is because, while we do not believe that they could always succeed, we do believe that they could always try. We must now see whether the introduction of this concept helps to save the categorical analysis.

We all know what it *feels* like to make an effort. These feelings are phenomena or occurrences that we experience in the same sort of way that we experience aches, pains, qualms, and twinges. And, if we take the introspective language of the libertarian seriously, it would seem that the question "Did he try?" can be answered only by the man himself and that he answers it by observing whether or not one of these feelings occurred. The logical status of this question will be like that of "Did it hurt?" But on this view an effort is not something that a man *makes;* it is something that *happens* to (or inside) him; and it would be highly unplausible to make the question of his responsibility turn on the occurrence or non-occurrence of such a feeling. If "making an effort" is to be relevant to responsibility, it must be thought of as something which a man can choose to do or not to do. The substitution of the active for the passive voice is an important advance; unfortunately it is fatal to the categorical interpretation of "he could have acted otherwise."

For "trying" is now thought of as something that a man can choose to do or not to do, and the difficulties encountered in construing "he could have acted otherwise" will emerge again in construing "he could have tried to act otherwise." On the libertarian analysis, if a man fails to act rightly, we must say either that his failure is inexplicable or that it was due to circumstances beyond his control—in which cases he is blameless—or that it was due to his not having tried as hard as he could have tried. For what exonerates is not "I tried," but "I tried as hard as I could"; and, in order to distinguish the blameworthy man from the addict who literally couldn't help it because he tried as hard as he could, we must be in a position to answer the question "Could he have tried harder than he did?" But how can we answer this question? *Ex hypothesi* he did not try harder than he did; so that we must say either that his failure to try harder is inexplicable or that it was due to circumstances beyond his control—in which cases he is blameless—or that it was due to his not having tried to try as hard as he could have tried to try.

But this is absurd. In the first place "try to try" is meaningless; and, if this be doubted, we must push the analysis one stage further. In fact he did not try to try harder than he did. But can he be justly blamed for this? Only if he could have tried to try harder. We must say either that his not having tried to try harder is inexplicable or that it was due to circumstances beyond his control—in which cases he is blameless—or that he failed to try to try harder because he did not try to try to try harder . . . and so on.

Libertarians sometimes speak in terms of our failure to make the best use of our stock of "will-energy"; but this usage gives rise to the same infinite regress. If using will-energy is thought of as something that we do not choose to do, but which just happens to us, it would appear to be irrelevant to responsibility; but if it is something that we can choose to do or not to do, we must be able to distinguish the man whose failure to use sufficient will-energy was due to circumstances beyond his control from the man who failed (culpably) to use it because he did not try hard enough to use it. And this involves answering the question "Had he sufficient second-order will-energy to enable him to make more use of his first-order will-energy?"

On these lines there is clearly no way out of the wood. The attempt to discover one is, I think, due to two mistakes. (a) It is noticeable that, on Campbell's analysis, a man's desires and even his character are continually referred to as "it"; desires are thought of as forces which, sometimes successfully and sometimes unsuccessfully, prod a man into doing what he ought not, and his "character as so far formed" is the sum of these forces. Thus I am said to be able to choose whether or not to "let my desiring nature, my character as so far formed, have *its* way." And this is to treat all cases of "doing what I want to do" on the model of the opium-addict, as the actions of a man who is a slave to his desires.

And since Campbell uses "desire" for every motive except the sense of duty, his treatment presupposes that I can choose whether to act from a certain motive or not; and this is not so. If I am both hungry and thirsty I can choose whether to have a meal or a drink; but I cannot choose whether to act from hunger or thirst, unless this strange phrase is used simply as a (very misleading) synonym for "choosing whether to eat or to drink." In the same way, if I have a certain sum of money, I can choose whether to pay a debt or give my aunt a Christmas present. If I choose the former, my motive is conscientiousness; if the latter, it is generosity. And we might, therefore, say that I can choose whether to do the conscientious or the generous thing. But I cannot choose whether to act from conscientiousness or from generosity. What I do will depend on my character; and this "cannot choose" is not a lamentable restriction on my freedom of action. For to say that my choice depends on my character is not to say that my character compels me to do what I do, but to say that the choice was characteristic of me. The creative "self" that sits above the battle of motives and chooses between them seems to be a legacy of the theory that a man is not free when he does what he wants to do, since he is then the victim or slave of his desires; and it is postulated to avoid the unplausible doctrine that all action is involuntary.

(b) Campbell takes as a typical and, by implication, the only case of moral choice to which appraisals are relevant, that of a man who knows what he ought to do but is tempted to do something else. Now this, so far from being the only case, is not even the commonest or most important. For in the great majority of cases of moral difficulty what is difficult is not to decide to do what one knows he ought to do, but to decide what one ought to do. This sort of difficulty arises in three main types of case. (i) A humble and unimaginative person who accepts a customary code of morals without much question may find that two rules conflict; the voice of conscience is in this case ambiguous. (ii) A more self-confident, imaginative, and reflective person may wonder whether he ought, in the case before him, to do what the customary rule enjoins. He knows very well what the rule enjoins; but what prompts him to depart from it is not "part of his desiring nature," but a suspicion that the rule is one that, in this particular case, he ought not to follow. (iii) A man of fixed moral principles (whether or not they are those customarily adopted) may find himself in a radically new situation that is not catered for in his code. What is he to do? It is here, if anywhere, that the idea of an unpredictable "creative" choice seems to make sense. He takes a leap in the dark, but just because it is a leap in the dark I doubt if we should be inclined to blame him if he leapt in what turned out to be the wrong direction.

Men who belong to a generation for whom the questioning of accepted principles has been no mere academic exercise and who have found themselves faced with momentous choices in situations not covered by their traditional rules will be less likely than their fathers perhaps were to suppose that the only sort of moral difficulty is that of resisting temptation.

If, in the first two of these three cases, a man decided that he ought to do something and did it, he might still be held to blame. For reasons given in chapter 17 conscientiousness is so valuable a motive that we should be chary of blaming a man who did what he honestly thought he ought to do, however misguided we thought him. But we should not necessarily excuse him, which we should have to do if all wrong-doing were failure to resist temptation. Integrity is not the only moral virtue, any more than it is the only virtue in an artist; and the belief that it is is one of the more regrettable consequences of the Romantic Movement. We blame people, not only for failing to live up to their moral principles, but also for having bad moral principles; and I shall examine the logic of this type of blame in the next chapter.

Perhaps the most crucial objection to the libertarian thesis lies in the sharp discontinuity which it presupposes between moral and non-moral choice and between moral and non-moral appraisal. It is not enough to admit that we can, within broad limits, predict what a man of known habits, tastes, and interests will do and to insist that our powers of prediction only break down in the small, but important area of moral choice. For it is not the extent of the area open to prediction that is at issue.

It is true that we can, within broad limits, predict what a man will choose from a menu, whether he will make a century to-day, or finish his cross-word puzzle; but we can also predict, again within broad limits only, whether or not he will resist the temptation to run away or to cheat at cards. Our reliance on the integrity of a bank clerk is not different from our reliance on his accuracy. In neither case do we believe that he "must" or "is compelled to" be honest or accurate; and what is paradoxical is not so much the libertarian's defence of moral freedom as his willingness to accept mechanical determinism as an explanation of non-moral action. For the rigid distinction between "formed character" (where determinism reigns) and "creative choice" (which is in principle unpredictable) it would be better to substitute a conception of continual modification of character in both its moral and its non-moral aspects. This not only does justice to the fact that we use both choosing and appraising language in the same way in moral and non-moral contexts, but it is closer to the facts. A man can grow more or less conscientious as time goes on, just as he can become better at tennis or more fond of Mozart.

QUESTIONS FOR STUDY AND DISCUSSION

1. Explain the hypothetical interpretation of "could have acted otherwise."
2. Explain the categorical interpretation.
3. Distinguish between the interpretation of "self-determined" that is required by the libertarian theory of moral choice and the interpretation of "self-determined" that is rejected by the libertarian theory of moral choice.
4. In what way, according to Nowell-Smith, does the introduction of the notion of "trying" reduce the categorical interpretation of "could have acted otherwise" to absurdity?
5. What objection does Nowell-Smith have to referring to one's character as "it"?

The Relation of Responsibility
to "Could Have Acted Otherwise"

I

In the last chapter I tried to show that "could have" sentences in non-moral contexts can be analysed in terms of "would have . . . if . . .";
and we must now see whether the application of this analysis to moral cases is consistent with our ordinary use of moral language.

The first question to be considered is the question what sorts of if-clauses are in fact allowed to excuse a man from blame. Clearly "I could not have kept my promise because I was kidnapped" will exculpate me while "I could not have kept my promise because I am by nature a person who takes promises very lightly" will not. Translated into the hypothetical form, these become respectively "I would have kept my promise if I had not been kidnapped" and "I would have kept my promise if I had been a more conscientious person." Again it is clear that the first exculpates while the second does not. The philosophical difficulties, however, are to decide just why some "would . . . ifs" excuse while others do not and to provide a criterion for distinguishing the exculpating from the non-exculpating cases. Forcible seizure exculpates; but do threats or psychological compulsion? And if, as some suggest, desires are internal forces which operate on the will, do they exculpate in the way in which external forces do? The problem of freewill is puzzling just because it seems impossible, without indulging in sheer dogmatism, to know just where to stop treating desires as "compelling forces."

Now before tackling this difficulty it will be prudent to examine what goes on in a place where questions of responsibility are settled every day and have been settled daily for hundreds of years, namely a court of law. Lawyers have evolved a terminology of remarkable flexibility, refinement, and precision and, although there may be a difference between moral and legal verdicts, it would be strange if the logic of lawyers' talk about responsibility were very different from our ordinary moral talk.

To establish a verdict of "guilty" in a criminal case it is necessary to establish that the accused did that which is forbidden by the law or, in technical language, committed the *actus reus,* and also that he had what is called *mens rea.* This last phrase is sometimes translated "guilty mind" and in many modern textbooks of jurisprudence it is supposed to consist of two elements, (a) foresight of the consequences and (b) voluntariness. But,

From pp. 291–314 of P. H. Nowell-Smith, *Ethics.* Copyright 1954 by Penguin Books, Inc. Reprinted by permission of Penguin Books Ltd., Harmondsworth, Middlesex.

whatever the textbooks may say, in actual practice lawyers never look for a positive ingredient called volition or voluntariness. A man is held to have *mens rea,* and therefore to be guilty, if the *actus reus* is proved, *unless* there are certain specific conditions which preclude a verdict of guilty. "What is meant by the mental element in criminal liability (*mens rea*) is only to be understood by considering certain defences or exceptions, such as Mistake of Fact, Accident, Coercion, Duress, Provocation, Insanity, Infancy." [1] The list of pleas that can be put up to rebut criminal liability is different in different cases; but in the case of any given offence there is a restricted list of definite pleas which will preclude a verdict of guilty.

This is not to say that the burden of proof passes to the defence. In some cases, such as murder, it is necessary for the prosecution to show that certain circumstances were not present which would, if present, defeat the accusation. The essential point is that the concept of a "voluntary action" is a negative, not a positive one. To say that a man acted voluntarily is in effect to say that he did something when he was not in one of the conditions specified in the list of conditions which preclude responsibility. The list of pleas is not exhaustive; we could, if we wished, add to it; and in making moral judgements we do so. For example we sometimes allow the fact that a man acted impulsively to exonerate him morally or at least to mitigate his offence in a case in which the law would not allow this. But it remains true that, in deciding whether an action was voluntary or not, we do not look for a positive ingredient but rather for considerations that would preclude its being voluntary and thereby exonerate the agent. In moral cases the most important types of plea that a man can put forward are (a) that he was the victim of certain sorts of ignorance, and (b) that he was the victim of certain sorts of compulsion.

II

Ignorance. A man may be ignorant of many elements in the situation in which he acts. For example he may not know that it was a policeman who told him to stop, that the stuff he put in the soup was arsenic, that the money he took was not his own. In such cases he would be blamed only if it was thought that he ought to have known or taken the trouble to find out. And his vicious trait of character was not contumacy or callousness or greed or disregard for any moral principle, but carelessness; and carelessness can amount to a vice. Fire-arms are so notoriously dangerous that the excuse "I didn't know it was loaded" will not do. The reason why he is blamed for carelessness and not for the specific vice for which he would have been blamed if he had done any of these things intentionally is that, although he intended to do what he did, he did not intend to break a moral rule. He intended to take the money, but not to steal. His action was not,

---

[1] Professor H. L. A. Hart: *Proceedings of the Aristotelian Society,* 1948–49. Aristotle in effect defines "the voluntary" in the same negative way as what is done not under compulsion and not through ignorance. [P.H.N.-S.]

therefore, a manifestation of the particular vice that the actions of thieves manifest. Ignorance of fact excuses or reduces the seriousness of an offence; but there is one type of ignorance that never excuses; and that is, in legal contexts, ignorance of the law and, in moral contexts, ignorance of right and wrong.

Now why should ignorance of fact excuse while ignorance of rules does not? Why should a man who takes someone else's money, thinking it to be his own, be guiltless of anything (except possibly carelessness), while a man who takes it, knowing it not to be his own but because he sees nothing wrong in taking other people's money, be held guilty and therefore blameworthy? We are not here concerned with the question why some types of action should be stigmatized as "wrong," but solely with the question why ignorance of what is wrong should not be held to exculpate.

The reason is that while the man who thought the money was his own did not intend to act on the maxim "It is permitted to take other people's money," the thief does act on this maxim. If a man does something because he does not think it wrong he cannot plead that he did not choose to do it, and it is for choosing to do what is *in fact* wrong, whether he knows it or not, that a man is blamed. The situation is exactly analogous to that in which some non-moral capacity is concerned. "I would have solved the problem, if I had known all the data" would, if substantiated, allow me to get full marks. But "I would have solved the problem if I had known more mathematics" would not. Since competence at mathematics is not a moral trait of character, men are not blamed for lack of it; but they are given low marks and denied prizes.

III

Compulsion. So long as "compulsion" is used in the literal sense it is not difficult to see why it should be held to exonerate. If a man is compelled to do something, he does not choose to do it and his action is not a manifestation of his moral character or principles. Now, since the purpose of blame and punishment is to change a man's character and principles, neither blame nor punishment is called for in such a case. It would be unjust to punish him since the rules for punishing lay down that a man who acts under compulsion is not to be punished; and the rules lay this down because, with due allowance for superstition and stupidity, we do not have pointless rules. Once more we must be careful to avoid the mistake of saying that the justice of a sentence turns on the question whether the accused is likely to be reformed by it. What is at issue here is not our reason for exonerating this accused, but our reason for making a *general* exception in the case of men whose actions are not expressions of their moral character. Physical compulsion is an obvious case where this is so.

But what if the source of compulsion is within the man himself? It is not an accident that we use "compulsion" in a psychological way and exonerate compulsives. There are two questions that are relevant here. In the first place we ask whether the man could have resisted the "compulsion"; and we decide this in the way that we decide all "could have" questions. We look for evidence of his past behaviour in this, and also in related matters; for the behaviour of the compulsive is usually odd in matters unconnected with his special compulsion; and we compare his case with other known cases. Once the capacity to resist the compulsion is established beyond reasonable doubt we do not allow unsupported sceptical doubts about his capacity to resist it in a particular case to rebut the conclusion that he could have helped it. And we do not allow this because there is no way of establishing or refuting the existence of a capacity except by appeal to general evidence. If the capacity has been established and all the necessary conditions were present, we would not say that, in this case, he was the victim of a compulsion. Indeed a "compulsion" is not something that could be said to operate in a particular case only; for to say that a man has a psychological compulsion is to say something about his behaviour over a long period. A compulsion is more like a chronic disorder than like a cold; and it is still less like a sneeze.

It is also relevant to raise the question whether he had any motive for doing what he did. Part of the difference between a kleptomaniac and a thief lies in the fact that the former has no motive for what he does; and he escapes blame because the point of blame is to strengthen some motives and weaken others. We are sometimes inclined to take the psychologists' talk about compulsions too seriously. We think that a man is excused because he has a "compulsion," as if the compulsion could be pointed to in the way that an external object which pushed him could be pointed to. But compulsions are not objects inside us; and we use the word "compulsion," not because we have isolated and identified the object which caused him to do what he did, but because we want to excuse him in the same sort of way that we excuse someone who is literally pushed; and we want to excuse him for the same sort of reason. We know that it will do no good to punish him.

Desires. A man might plead that he would have acted otherwise if he had not had a strong desire to do what he did; but the desire was so strong that, as things were, he could not have acted otherwise. Would this plea be allowed to exonerate him? In some cases it would; for there are, as we have seen, cases of addiction in which we allow that a man is not to blame since his craving was too strong for him. But in most cases it would be considered frivolous to say "I would have done the right thing if I hadn't wanted to do the wrong thing"; for it is just for this that men are blamed.

To distinguish an overwhelming desire from one that the agent could have resisted is not always easy; but the criterion that we in fact use for making the distinction is not difficult to understand. We know from experience that most men can be trained to curb some desires, but not others; and we assume that what is true in most cases is true in a given case unless special reasons are given for doubting this. Now it might seem that, although this evidence enables us to predict that we shall be able to train the man to curb his desire in future, it sheds no light on the question whether he could have curbed it on the occasion in question. I shall say more about this question of moral training later; here I only wish to point out that we have no criterion for deciding whether a man could have resisted a desire on a given occasion other than general evidence of his capacity and the capacity of others like him. We do not, because we cannot, try to answer this question as if it referred solely to the given occasion; we treat it as a question about a capacity.

Character. Finally a man might plead that he could not help doing what he did because that's the sort of man he is. He would not have done it if he had been more honest or less cowardly or less mean and so on. This sort of plea is paradoxical in the same sort of way that the plea of ignorance of moral rules and the plea that he did it because he wanted to are paradoxical. And all three paradoxes stem from the same source, the uncritical extension of "ought implies can" and of the exculpatory force of "he could not have acted otherwise" to cases which they will not cover. We know that these pleas are not in fact accepted; the puzzle is to see why.

The plea "I could not help it because I am that sort of person" might be backed up by an explanation of how I came to be that sort of person. Just as the discovery of a compelling cause exonerates, so, it might be argued, to reveal the causes of my character being what it is is to show that I could not help being what I am and thus to exonerate me. But this argument is fallacious. In the first place to discover the cause of something is not to prove that it is inevitable. On the contrary the discovery of the cause of a disease is often the first step towards preventing it.

Now it is logically impossible to prevent something happening if we know the cause of it, since it could not have a cause unless it occurred and therefore it was not prevented. So when we talk of preventing diseases or accidents we are not talking about preventing cases which have occurred but about ensuring that there are no future cases. Similarly, if I know how Jones came to be a dishonest man I cannot prevent him from being dishonest now; but it may be possible to prevent others from becoming dishonest and to cure Jones of his dishonesty.

Secondly, the discovery of a cause of something has no necessary bearing on a verdict about that thing. We know that a man has come to be what he is because of three main types of cause, heredity, education, and his own past actions. These three factors are not independent of each other and it is not the business of a philosopher to say exactly what is the effect of each or which is the most important for moral training. The question "Granted that we want people to be better and that we have fairly clear ideas about what 'being better' means, should we try to breed a superior race or pay more attention to education?" is not a philosophical question. But it is the business of a philosopher to show in what ways these "causes" are related to responsibility.

Now these three factors also play a part in situations in which non-moral verdicts are given. Leopold Mozart was a competent musician; his son Wolfgang was given a good musical education and practised his art assiduously. Each of these facts helps to explain how he was able to compose and play so well. There is plenty of evidence that musical ability runs in families and still more of the effect of teaching and practice. But, having learnt these facts, we do not have the slightest tendency to say that, because Mozart's abilities were "due" to heredity, teaching, and practice, his compositions were not "really" his own, or to abate one jot of our admiration. In the same way, however a man came by his moral principles, they are still *his* moral principles and he is praised or blamed for them. The plea that, being what he is he cannot help doing what he does, will no more save the wicked man than it will save the bad pianist or actor who has the rashness to expose his incompetence in public. Nor is he saved by being able to explain how he has come to be what he is.

Hereditary tendencies are not causes and do not compel, although a man may inherit a tendency to some form of psychological compulsion. In general to say that a man has a tendency to do something is to say that he usually does it; and to add that the tendency is hereditary is to say that his father also used to do the same sort of thing; and neither of these facts has any tendency to exculpate.

The belief that heredity or a bad upbringing excuse a man's present character is partly due to the false belief that to explain something is to assign an antecedent cause to it and that, to be voluntary, an action must be uncaused. But there is also a good reason for this belief. In fact we do sometimes allow these factors to exculpate; and if the question of explanation was as irrelevant to the question of responsibility as I have suggested it would be hard to understand why we do this. Why do we tend to deal less harshly with juvenile delinquents who come from bad homes than with those who have had every chance? The question is not one of justice, since it is not a question whether Jones ought to be punished, but whether the law should lay down that people whose bad characters are due to certain causes should be punished. We must therefore ask what is our reason for differentiating between two boys whose characters and actions are the same but who come respectively from bad and good homes. And the reason is that in the first case we have not had a chance to see what kindness and a good education could do, while in the second we know that they have failed. Since punishment involves the infliction of pain and since it is a moral rule that unnecessary pain should not be inflicted, there is a general presumption that people should not be punished if the same end could be achieved without the infliction of pain. This consideration is, of course, irrelevant to the question whether Jones should be punished; but it is highly relevant to the question whether a distinction should be made between those whose characters have come to be what they are because of a bad education and those whose characters are bad in spite of a good one.

But suppose a man should plead that he cannot now help doing what he does because his character was formed by his own earlier actions? This also will not excuse him. The logic of this plea is that he did X because he was, at the time, the sort of man to do X and that he became this sort of man because he did Y and Z in the past. But if he cannot be blamed for doing X now, can he be blamed for having done Y and Z in the past? It would seem that he cannot, for he will exculpate himself in exactly the same way.

Once again the argument presupposes that if his present character can be explained in terms of what happened in the past he necessarily escapes blame. The assumption is that a man's actions form a causal chain in which each necessitates the next. Now, if we suppose that, to be free, an action must be uncaused, either we shall find a genuinely uncaused action at the beginning of the chain or we shall not. If we do not, then no action is culpable; and if we do, then we must suppose that, while most of our actions are caused and therefore blameless, there was in the past some one uncaused action for which alone a man can be held responsible. This theory has in fact been held, although even in the history of philosophy it would be hard to find another so bizarre. The objections to it are clear. In the first place we praise and blame people for what they do now, not for what they might have done as babies; and secondly this hypothetical infantile action could hardly be said to be an action of the agent at all, since it is *ex hypothesi* inexplicable in terms of his character.

The conclusion of the foregoing argument is that "He could not have acted otherwise" does not always exculpate and, in particular, that it does not exculpate if the reason which is adduced to explain just why he could not have acted otherwise is that he was a man of a certain moral character. We have seen that "He could have acted otherwise" is to be construed as "He would have acted otherwise, if . . ." and we have seen which types of "if" are not allowed to exculpate. We must now see why they are not.

IV

What is moral character? The key to the logical relationships between the five types of judgement seems to lie in the judgement of moral character (5).[2] For (2) is thought to be a necessary condition of (1), (3), and (4) only because we exclude those cases of incapacity to act otherwise in which the incapacity lies in the moral character. If it is due to an external force or to a "compulsion" (which we talk of as if it were an external force), or to some non-moral defect, the incapcity to act otherwise is allowed to excuse; but not if it is due to a moral defect. And it is now necessary to provide some criterion for deciding what a moral defect is.

Moral traits of character are tendencies or dispositions to behave in certain ways. How are they to be distinguished from other tendencies? If

---

[2] Cf. p. 526 in the text. [F.E.]

any tendency were to count as "moral" we should have to say that conformity to physical laws was a universal trait of human character and that susceptibility to colds was part of the moral character of a particular man.

The first and most obvious limitation lies in the fact that the names of virtues and vices are not purely descriptive words. They are terms of praise and blame used to express approval and disapproval and to influence the conduct of the person whose character is appraised and also of others. These three functions are tied together in a way that should by now be familiar. Appraising, praising, and blaming are things that men *do* and can only be understood on the assumption that they do them for a purpose and use means adapted to their purpose. The logic of virtue- and vice-words is tailor-made to fit the purposes and conditions of their use.

Men would not employ a special form of speech for changing the character and conduct of others unless they had a pro-attitude towards those changes; so that the first limitation that can be put on "moral character" is that traits of character are tendencies to do things that arouse approval or disapproval. But moral verdicts do not just express the attitudes of the speaker; they are couched in impersonal language and imply accepted standards because the traits of character that a given man wants to strengthen or inhibit in others are usually those that other men also want to strengthen and inhibit. The impersonal language of morals implies a rough community of pro- and con-attitudes. Moreover men would not have adopted the moral language they have unless it was likely to achieve its purpose; and its purpose is achieved because most men dislike disapprobation. The power of moral language is greatly enhanced by the very facts which make impersonal moral language possible. No one likes to be universally condemned and most men are willing to take considerable pains to avoid it.

But this limitation is not enough. There are many things for which men are applauded and condemned which do not count as parts of their moral character. A great musician, mathematician, actor, or athlete is applauded and rewarded for what he does and his ability may be called a "virtue," but not a moral virtue. Conversely, if a man fails to save a life because he cannot swim, we may regret his incapacity and urge him to learn, but his incapacity is not called a vice.

A man may fail to achieve some worthy object because he is physically or intellectually incompetent, too weak or too stupid. But he may also fail because he is too cowardly or too dishonest or has too little regard for the welfare of others. Why do we call the first set of traits "non-moral" and never condemn them, while the second are called "moral" and condemned? It is clear that it will not help to say that we intuit a non-natural relation of fittingness which holds between blameworthiness and dishonesty or meanness but not between blameworthiness and physical weakness or stupidity. For this is only to say that the former traits deserve blame while the latter do not and that we cannot understand why.

To discover why we draw the line in the way that we do we must first ask exactly where we draw it; and all that is necessary for this purpose is to construct two lists, the one of moral traits, the other of non-moral. Cowardice, avarice, cruelty, selfishness, idleness would go into the first list; clumsiness, physical weakness, stupidity, and anaemia into the second. The second list will, of course, contain items of many different sorts, since we are interested, not in the way in which non-moral characteristics differ from each other, but in the distinction between moral and non-moral.

If we construct these lists we shall find that the items in list 1 have two properties in common which the items in list 2 do not have. (a) We believe that if a man's action can be explained by reference to a list 1 characteristic, he could have acted otherwise. And it would appear at first sight that this is the crucial feature which distinguishes moral from non-moral characteristics. Why does a schoolmaster punish a lazy boy but not a stupid one for equally bad work if not because he believes that the lazy boy could have done better while the stupid boy could not? But why does the schoolmaster believe this? In fact he appeals to the evidence of past performance. On the libertarian view this would scarcely be relevant, since the boy might not have been lazy in the past but was lazy at just that moment. And perhaps his momentary laziness was no more under his control than the stupid boy's stupidity? An analysis on these lines could hardly fail to lead to the paradoxical conclusion that no one has any reason whatever for ascribing responsibility. And even if it were possible to answer the question whether he could have acted otherwise, we should be left with the question why this is considered relevant to the propriety of holding him responsible.

Moreover it would be circular to make the phrase "he could have acted otherwise" the distinguishing criterion of moral characteristics; since, as we have seen, it is necessary to make use of the distinction between actions explained by reference to moral, and actions explained by reference to non-moral characteristics in order to elucidate the phrase 'he could have acted otherwise."

(b) There is, however, another element which all the characteristics in list 1 have and those in list 2 do not. It is an empirical fact that list 1 characteristics can be strengthened or weakened by the fear of punishment or of an adverse verdict or the hope of a favourable verdict. And when we remember that the purpose of moral verdicts and of punishment is to strengthen or weaken certain traits of character it is not difficult to see that this feature, so far from being synthetically connected with the notion of a "moral" characteristic, a virtue or a vice, is just what constitutes it. What traits of character can be strengthened or weakened in this way is a matter of empirical fact. Knives can be sharpened, engines decarbonized, fields fertilized, and dogs trained to do tricks. And men also can be trained, within certain limits, to behave in some ways and not in others. Pleasure and pain, reward and punishment are the rudders by which human conduct is steered, the means by which moral character is moulded; and "moral" character is just that set of dispositions that can be moulded by these means. Moral approval and disapproval play the same role. It is not just an accident that they please and hurt and that they are used only in cases in which something is to be gained by pleasing or hurting.

We might therefore say that moral traits of character are just those traits that are known to be amenable to praise or blame; and this would explain why we punish idle boys but not stupid ones, thieves but not kleptomaniacs, the sane but not the insane. This is not to say that amenability to praise and blame is what justifies either of these in a particular case; that, as we have seen, is a question to be decided by reference to the rules. But a breach of a moral rule is only considered to be culpable when it is attributable to the agent's character, his vice or moral weakness; and our theory is intended to explain just what is included in and what excluded from "moral character" and to explain why this distinction should be considered relevant to responsibility.

According to this explanation there is no need to postulate any special insight into necessary connexions between the five moral judgements with which we started; for the whole weight of the analysis is now seen to rest on the proposition that people only do those things which are either objects of a direct pro-attitude (i.e. that they want to do or enjoy doing for their own sake) or are believed to produce results towards which they have pro-attitudes. It is absurd to ask why a man who thinks that praise and blame will alter certain dispositions which he wishes to alter should praise and blame them. For this is a special case of the question "Why do people adopt means that they believe to be the best means of achieving their ends?"; and this is an absurd question in a way in which "Why does a man deserve blame only if he acted voluntarily and has broken a moral rule?" is not.

Nevertheless this way of tracing the connexions between pro-attitudes, moral rules, verdicts on character, and ascriptions of responsibility is obviously too simple and schematic. It is more like an account of the way in which moral language would be used by people who knew all the facts and thoroughly understood what they were doing than like a description of the way in which moral language is actually used. In practice these connexions are much looser than the theory suggests; and there are two reasons for this. In the first place there is the inveterate conservatism of moral language. Even when it is known that a certain type of conduct, for example homosexuality, is not amenable to penal sanctions or moral disapproval, it is difficult to persuade people that it is not morally wrong.

The second reason is more respectable. We are still very ignorant of the empirical facts of human nature, and this ignorance both makes it wise for us to make moral judgements in accordance with a more or less rigid system of rules and also infects the logic of moral language. Our moral verdicts do not, therefore, always imply that the person condemned has in fact done something "bad" or "undesirable" in a non-moral sense. An act of cowardice or dishonesty might, by chance, be attended with the happiest consequences; but it would still be blamed. But this fact does not involve any major modification in the theory that bad traits of character are those which (a) tend to bring about undesirable results in most cases and (b) are alterable by praise and blame. For, in deciding whether a trait of character is vicious or not, we consider its effects in the majority of cases. We do not want to reinforce a tendency to behave in a certain way just because it turns out, on rare occasions, to be beneficial. And, in making a moral judgement, we do not consider the actual consequences of the action concerned. Nor do we even need to consider the consequences that such actions usually have. A man has broken faith or been cowardly or mean; we condemn him forthwith without considering why such actions are condemned. The fact that deceitful, cowardly, and mean actions are, by and large, harmful is relevant, not to the questions: "Has Jones done wrong? Is he a bad man? Does he deserve to be blamed?" but to the question "Why are deceitfulness, cowardice, and meanness called 'vices' and condemned?"

This theory enables us to understand why it is not only moral weakness that is blamed, but also wickedness; and it also enables us to distinguish between moral weakness and addiction in a way that the libertarian theory could not. A wicked character can be improved by moral censure and punishment; and if we really thought that a man was so bad as to be irremediable we should, I think, cease to blame him, though we might impose restraints on him as we would on a mad dog. Moral weakness is considered to be a less culpable state, since the morally weak man has moral principles which are good enough, but fails to live up to them. He is therefore more likely to be improved by encouragement than the wicked man is. What he needs is the confidence which comes from knowing that others are on the side of his principles. But both he and the wicked man differ from the addict or compulsive in that the latter will respond neither to threats nor to encouragement.

V

Moral Principles. Traits of character, then, are dispositions to do things of which a spectator (including the agent himself) approves or disapproves and which can be, if not implanted or wholly eradicated, at least strengthened or weakened by favourable and adverse verdicts. But they are dispositions to *do* things, in the active sense of "do," dispositions to choose certain courses of action. It is not, therefore, an accident that the names of virtues and vices, such as "generosity" and "avarice," are motive-words which necessarily imply a pro-attitude towards doing the things called "generous" or "greedy" for their own sake. And since moral principles are also dispositions to choose, they also must be classed as "pro-attitudes." How do they differ from other pro-attitudes?

(a) In the first place a pro-attitude does not count as a moral principle unless it is a relatively dominant one and concerned with an important matter. However regularly I choose to drink coffee for breakfast no one would call this disposition to choose one of my moral principles. To act on principle is consistently to pursue a policy of doing certain sorts of things for their own sake; and for this reason "acting on principle" must be sharply distinguished from "acting from a sense of duty," although we shall see later that the two are connected. The reason for distinguishing them is that to act from a sense of duty is consistently to pursue a policy of obeying certain rules for the sake of obeying those rules; it is therefore a special case of acting on principle. "Acting on principle" cannot, therefore, be identified with either the "sense of duty" or the "impulses" which, according to some philosophers, are the only types of motive. It is distinguished from "acting on impulse" by regularity and consistency and from "acting from the sense of duty" by the fact that the man who acts on principle does what he does for its own sake.

Now since a moral principle is a disposition to choose, a man cannot be said to have a certain moral principle if he regularly breaks it, and we discover what a man's moral principles are mainly by seeing how he in fact conducts himself. But this is not the only test. A man's moral principles are "dominant" in the sense that he would not allow them to be over-ridden by any pro-attitude other than another moral principle. Thus a man may belong to many organizations and be allowed by the laws of his country to do something that he is not allowed to do by the rules of his trade union, profession, or church. When a conflict of principles or loyalties arises he may wonder what he ought to do; but it is part of the force of the phrase "moral principle" that he cannot (logically) wonder what he ought to do if there is a moral principle on one side and not on the other. If I regard something as immoral, then, however trivial it may be and however great may be the non-moral advantages of doing it, I cannot debate with myself whether I ought to do it; and we discover what our own moral principles are very often by putting just this sort of question to ourselves.

A similar limitation in the use of the phrase "moral principle" comes out in our attitude to compensation. A man will not lightly give up a moral principle; nor will he lightly give up anything else that he regards as valuable. But our attitude towards giving up a moral principle differs from all other cases. If a man has a picture that he values very highly he may reject a low price and be more inclined to part with it if the bid is raised. But if a man refuses a bribe of ten pounds and you offer him a hundred, he might say: "You don't understand; it is not a question of how much; doing that sort of thing is against my moral principles." Indeed he must say this, if it is really a matter of moral principle, unless he can manage to bring the acceptance of the offer under some other moral principle. It is for this reason that Napoleon's dictum that every man has his price sounds so cynical; it implies that no man has any moral principles.

(b) But consistency in action is not the only test of a man's moral principles. Although a man cannot claim that it is against his moral principles to be cowardly or mean if he regularly does cowardly or mean things, he can do such things occasionally and still justify this claim. His claim is justified if he is prepared to condemn his own actions and if he feels remorse. His moral principles are not those on which he always acts, but those which he acknowledges or avows and those about which he feels remorseful when he breaks them. His moral principles are those on which, in his more reflective moments, he honestly says that he would like to act; they are the moral principles of the person he is striving to become. I shall return to this point in the last section of this chapter.

(c) A principle is not usually called a moral one unless the person who adopts it is prepared to apply it universally. If a man says that he does something as a matter of principle, he cannot (logically) make exceptions unless another moral principle is involved. However narrow in scope it may be, a moral principle must be applied to all cases that are alike in all relevant respects. If there are two people of roughly similar character, tastes, and habits, it may well be that a man likes one of them better than the other. If asked why, he may be unable to give a reason; he just happens to like Jones, although he concedes that Smith is just as virtuous, charming, and amusing. And, although there is an oddity about his taste that might interest a psychologist, there is nothing logically odd about it. But he is abusing language if he says that it is a matter of moral principle with him to pay his debts and he pays Jones, while refusing to pay Smith, without being able to give any reason for the discrepancy.

The logical fact that a pro-attitude is not called a "moral principle" unless a man is prepared to universalize it has led some philosophers to suppose that it can be proved that we ought to be impartial. But this is to commit the fallacy of deducing a moral injunction from a feature of moral language. A man who has no principles that he is prepared to apply impartially has no moral principles; but we cannot prove that he ought to have any moral principles by pointing out how the phrase "moral principles" is used.

(d) The fact that a man's moral principles are those which he acknowledges in his more reflective moments throws some light on the connexion between moral principles and rules. A man's moral principles are those on which he thinks he ought to act and the word "ought," like all deontological words, is only used in connexion with rules and therefore in connexion with relatively long-range principles and policies that we avow and adopt in our more reflective moments.

Moreover these deontological words contextually imply a background of general agreement; so that, in deliberating about what to do, we tend to use the language of "ought" only in connexion with principles of action that we know to be generally approved. Now, for reasons given in chapter 14, moral codes never contain injunctions to people to pursue their own pleasure; and most moral rules are concerned with the welfare of others. These pervasive features of moral codes infect the logic of deontological words. It is odd to describe a man as a "conscientious egoist" or to say that pleasure-seeking is his highest moral principle, because people do not in fact use the language of "ought" when they are being deliberately and consistently selfish. And the reason for this is that it is hard to dissociate this word from its moorings in the language of advice, exhortation, and command. Nevertheless, if a man regularly decides that he ought (in the verdict-giving sense of "ought") to do whatever brings him pleasure or profit, his dominant pro-attitude is towards his own pleasure or profit. Whether or not we choose to call selfishness a moral principle with him, depends on the criterion we are using for the phrase "moral principle." If he behaves selfishly without acknowledging his wickedness and without feeling remorse, we could say that selfishness was one of his moral principles; and we hesitate to say this partly because he almost certainly does not address himself in the language of "ought" (in the self-hortatory sense) and partly because we are reluctant to believe that he really is what he makes himself out to be.

VI

Can a man choose to act against his own moral principles or choose to change them? Some moral principles are fundamental in the sense that we can give no reasons for adopting them; they do not follow from any higher principles. And it follows that a man cannot, at the moment of choosing, question the validity of the principle on which he chooses to act. For to do this would be to criticize the principle in the light of a higher principle; and in that case the principle in question is not a fundamental one. A man cannot condemn the principle on which he acts unless he has a con-attitude towards it; and in that case it is not a fundamental pro-attitude.

Now this seems to entail that a man cannot choose to act against his own moral principles, that he cannot choose to do what he knows to be wrong. But this is not so. Self-criticism is possible because, in criticizing my own character or conduct, I apply, not the principles on which I act, but the principles that I acknowledge on those occasions when there is no question of their being manifested or not manifested. I can, for example, think that I ought to be less greedy, vindictive, or sanctimonious than I am, and this implies a con-attitude towards these particular traits in my character. But I cannot (logically) condemn any of these vices in myself while at the same time exercising them. For if I behave vindictively while at the same time condemning myself for doing so, I am a weak-willed but not a vindictive person. If, on the other hand, I deliberately choose to do something vindictive, then I am a vindictive person; and I can still claim that to be vindictive is against my principles only in the sense that, in my more reflective moments, I am prepared to condemn what I did.

The answer to the question whether a man can choose to change his moral principles is partly logical, partly empirical. In the case of principles that are not fundamental there is no logical difficulty, since we adopt these for reasons and both can and should abandon them if we find that the reasons are bad reasons, although it may be in practice difficult to do so. Traditionally a large part of moral philosophy has consisted in the attempt to show that many moral principles are subordinate in this way to one or a few very general principles, such as the Golden Rule or the Greatest Happiness Principle.

But, although there is no logical difficulty in the notion of trying to change a subordinate principle, there must, at any given moment, be some principles that are, here and now, fundamental moral principles for me. If this were not so, we could not talk about *choosing* or *trying* to change a principle, since this implies having a pro-attitude towards making the change. And it is here that the logical difficulty arises.

To try to change a principle implies having a pro-attitude towards making the change, and this implies that the principle is not a fundamental one. But it does not follow from this that there are any moral principles that are unchangeable. The fact that it makes no sense for me to ask whether I ought to act on a certain principle that is for me a fundamental one has often been cited as a proof that there are self-evident principles. For is not to say that it is senseless to question the principles to say that it is self-evident? But this argument confuses the practical impossibility of asking a certain question at a certain time with the logical impossibility of asking it at any time; and it also confuses the role of the advocate with that of the judge.

So long as a man is considering whether or not to act in a certain way, he addresses himself in the split-personality language of "you ought." But sooner or later he must make up his mind; he must decide. No doubt perpetual indecision is logically possible; but in many cases not to decide is to take a momentous decision, since the situation alters and the opportunity for choosing has passed. Moreover the logic of practical language is adopted to the practice of ordinary men, not to that of mental paralytics.

Sooner or later, then, he must proceed to a verdict "This is what I ought to do; this is the principle on which I shall act." And it is logically impossible for him to question this decision only in the sense that, if he questioned it, he would be returning to the standpoint of the advocate and it would not be a decision. It does not follow that at some future time he might not reconsider the decision and wonder whether he had been right. But to question the morality of a decision or principle is to criticize or appraise it in the light of a higher principle. Could this principle be questioned in its turn? Unless it were tautologous (in which case it could not serve as a moral principle at all, since it would be compatible with every course of action), it could be. Self-guaranteeing moral principles are impossible; and the demand for them rests on the failure to notice that "there must always be some moral principle that I cannot now question" does not entail "There must be some moral principle that I cannot ever question." Every sentence must (logically) end with a full stop; but there is no point in any sentence at which a full stop must (logically) be put.

A man can, therefore, question the morality of his own principles and try to change them; but he cannot do so while applying them or if he has no pro-attitude towards making the change. Whether or not he can change them if these logical conditions are satisfied is an empirical question, to which the only answer is: "Sometimes. He may not always succeed; but he can always try." And since no one, not even the man himself, knows the limits of what he can do if he tries, it is a question to which no more precise answer can be given. There are moral principles which it is difficult to imagine any man wanting to change, because it is difficult to imagine what it would be like to adopt the contrary principle or to have a pro-attitude towards adopting it. But we must not confuse the difficulty of imagining something with its logical impossibility.

What sort of principles a man adopts will, in the end, depend on his vision of the Good Life, his conception of the sort of world that he desires, so far as it rests with him, to create. Indeed his moral principles just *are* this conception. The conception can be altered; perhaps he meets someone whose character, conduct, or arguments reveal to him new virtues that he has never even contemplated; or he may do something uncharacteristic and against his principles without choosing to do it and, in doing it, discover how good it is. Moral values, like other values, are sometimes discovered accidentally. But the one thing he cannot do is to *try* to alter his conception of the Good Life; for it is ultimately by reference to this conception that all his choices are made. And the fact that he cannot choose to alter this conception neither shields him from blame nor disqualifies him from admiration.

QUESTIONS FOR STUDY AND DISCUSSION

1. Explain Nowell-Smith's distinction between ignorance that excuses and ignorance that does not excuse.
2. According to Nowell-Smith, what distinguishes a moral characteristic in a person from a nonmoral characteristic?
3. Why is it entirely unsatisfactory to try to make the notion "could have acted otherwise" the distinguishing criterion of moral (as opposed to nonmoral) characteristics?
4. How is Nowell-Smith's theory able to distinguish successfully between moral weakness and addiction? Why, according to Nowell-Smith, is the libertarian theory unable to do so (cf. the preceding selection)?

TOPICS FOR DISCUSSION AND TERM PAPERS

A.

1. Discuss Schlick's major thesis in the light of Moore's position. Are they compatible If so, how? If not, whose position seems to be the better, and why?
2. What do Ayer and Moore have in common? In spite of these similarities, why do they reach widely divergent conclusions?
3. Given his meaning for objective (or absolute) values, Schlick thinks that there is no answer to the question of why such values should mean anything to anyone. Do you agree? If so, are you then logically required to agree with all of Schlick's other major points? If you are not, explain why. If, on the other hand, you do not agree, then what is the answer and how do you support it?
4. Is Ayer's critique of utilitarianism also in effect a critique of Schlick's major thesis? If not, why not? If so, does it satisfactorily undermine Schlick's position?
5. Ayer and Stevenson both see a sharp contrast between fact and value and between belief (or knowledge) and attitude. Schlick, however, does not see such a contrast. Taking the standpoint of Ayer and Stevenson, find the assumptions in Schlick's thought that make him blind. Taking the position of Schlick, find the assumptions in Ayer's and Stevenson's thought that make them see double. Which position do you find more satisfactory, and why?
6. Does Toulmin's criticism of Ayer seem cogent? If you think so, do you believe Ayer would think so? If you think that it is cogent but believe that Ayer would not think so, how do you explain the discrepancy between yourself and Ayer? If, on the other hand, Toulmin's criticism of Ayer does not seem cogent, explain where Toulmin goes wrong.
7. Why is knowing whether one could have acted otherwise relevant in deciding whether one is to be held responsible? Make clear in your answer what you mean by "could have acted otherwise."
8. Should people be excused from (not held responsible and punished for) their misdeeds if their actions are governed by character traits that are themselves inherited or molded by past experiences? If your answer is different from that of Schlick and Nowell-Smith, explain where their accounts go wrong. What considerations are crucial in determining an answer?
9. Schlick and Nowell-Smith both think that the purpose of punishment is to reform the character of the offender and perhaps to deter others from imitating him. Other philosophers, Kant for example, have held that reformation and deterrence are irrelevant and that punishment is justified by the fact that an offender *deserves* to be punished for his offense. Which of these two conceptions appears to be more satisfactory?
10. The distinction between fact and value, which is implied by Ayer's claim that we can argue about questions of fact but not about questions of value, seems to correspond to Nowell-Smith's distinction between ignorance about the facts of the case (which he excuses) and ignorance about what is right and wrong (which he does not excuse). Ayer's further claim, namely, that

since there is no way to show whose system of values is superior we can settle value disputes only by resorting to abuse, would imply that what Nowell-Smith calls punishing a man for doing what is wrong (even though *he* may think it is right) is really abusing him for having a different set of values from our own. Nowell-Smith avoids this consequence only by postulating criteria for recognizing the "right" set of values. What are these criteria? Ayer obviously does not postulate them. Why not? Whose position do you find more satisfactory? Why?

B.

1. Could good exist in a universe devoid of any creatures with tendencies or desires? How would Moore answer this question? How would Schlick answer? Which position is closer to the views of Aristotle and Aquinas? Why?
2. What philosophers (one or more) represented in other chapters of the present volume commit the naturalistic fallacy? How and where? Criticize them from the standpoint of Moore, or, if you think that the naturalistic fallacy is not really a fallacy, criticize Moore from their standpoint.
3. Kant assumes that the paradigmatic case of moral choice is found where there is a conflict between duty and desire. Nowell-Smith explicitly challenges this assumption, and Schlick does so implicitly. Moreover, such an assumption is foreign to the thought of Aristotle and Aquinas. What do the latter four thinkers have in common that prevents them from making Kant's assumption?
4. Is Schlick's and Nowell-Smith's interpretation of "could have acted otherwise" compatible with Aristotle's account of responsibility? If not, explain why. If so, explain how.
5. Does the conception of freedom accepted by Schlick and Nowell-Smith seem to be compatible with Aquinas' conception of voluntary action and free will? If so, are there any important differences between the two conceptions? If, on the other hand, they seem to be incompatible, explain why. Would Schlick and Nowell-Smith be in general agreement with Sidney Hook's conception of moral freedom in a determined world? Are Hook's views closer to those of Aquinas or to those of Schlick and Nowell-Smith?

RECOMMENDED READINGS

Primary Sources

Ammerman, Robert R., ed. *Classics of Analytic Philosophy*. New York: McGraw-Hill, 1965. The most serviceable general anthology of readings in the analytic movement, including Ammerman's own concise, orderly, and informative "short history of analytic philosophy."

Ayer, A. J. *Philosophical Essays*. London: Macmillan Co., 1963. See "Freedom and Necessity," pp. 271–84, for Ayer's position on the responsibility issue, namely, that responsibility and determinism are entirely compatible.

Carnap, Rudolf. *Philosophy and Logical Syntax*. London: Routledge & Kegan Paul, 1935. An early and brief proposal that the meaning of good is emotive rather than cognitive. See Ch. 1, Sect. 4. The text is reprinted by Morton White, ed., in *The Age of Analysis*. New York: The New American Library, 1963. Pp. 216–18.

Ebersole, F. B. "Free Choice and the Demands of Morals," *Mind*, LXI (1952), 234–57. Suggests that determinism and indeterminism are both consistent with morality, and therefore irrelevant to it.

Ewing, A. C., *The Definition of Good*. New York: Macmillan Co., 1947. A comprehensive statement of intuitionism.

Hampshire, Stuart. *Thought and Action*. New York: Viking Press, 1960. An attempt to analyze the ordinary language of ethical discourse for the purpose of discovering and clarifying the principle upon which it is based.

Hare, R. M. *The Language of Morals*. Oxford: Clarendon Press, 1952. Also analyzes the ordinary language of ethical discourse.

Hume, David. *An Enquiry Concerning Human Understanding*. Ed. by Charles W. Hendel. New York: Liberal Arts Press, 1957. See Sects. 2 and 4 for Hume's discussion of the distinction between matters of fact and relations of ideas—a less rigorous treatment than that contained in the *Treatise*. See also Sect. 8 for a discussion of the responsibility issue in ethical matters.

————. *An Enquiry Concerning the Principles of Morals*. Ed. by Charles W. Hendel. New York: Liberal Arts Press, 1957. Contains Hume's ethical writings, which, like those in the *Treatise* and *Enquiry Concerning Human Understanding,* were strongly affected by his distinction between matters of fact and relations of ideas. Informative editorial introductions and bibliographical materials are provided in the two volumes edited by Hendel.

————. *A Treatise of Human Nature*. Garden City, N.Y.: Doubleday & Co., 1961. See Book I, Part I, and Sects. 1 and 2 of Part III, for Hume's rigorous and elaborate examination of the all-important distinction between matters of fact and relations of ideas. His specifically ethical writings are found in Books II and III. For his position on the responsibility issue, see Book II, Part III, Sects. 1 and 2.

Moore, George Edward. *Ethics*. New York: Henry Holt and Co., 1912. Less technical than *Principia Ethica,* this book develops a version of utilitarianism, incorporating the major points of the earlier work.

————. *Philosophical Studies*. London: Routledge & Kegan Paul, 1958. See Moore's essay, "The Nature of Moral Philosophy," pp. 310–39, which offers a discussion of moral obligation and intrinsic goodness.

————. *Principia Ethica*. New York: Cambridge University Press, 1959. Contains an extended criticism of all forms of naturalism in ethics, the relationship of ethics to conduct, and an outline of the ideal state of things.

Nowell-Smith, P. H. *Ethics*. Baltimore: Penguin Books, 1954. A widely read and quoted analysis of the ordinary language of ethical discourse.

Ogden, C. K., and I. A. Richards. *The Meaning of Meaning*, 4th ed. New York: Harcourt, Brace & World, 1936. See p. 125 for a rebuttal of Moore's notion of good as an unanalyzable property and a defense of good as purely emotive in meaning. First published in 1923, this statement appears to have originated the emotive theory of ethics in its present form.

Stevenson, Charles L. *Ethics and Language*. New Haven: Yale University Press, 1960. First published in 1944 and now commonly regarded as the most sophisticated and well-developed presentation of emotivism in ethics, this is a technical, unified, and rather difficult book, best read as a whole.

Stevenson, Charles L. *Facts and Values: Studies in Ethical Analysis*. New Haven: Yale University Press, 1964. Further elaboration of emotivism in ethics.

Toulmin, Stephen. *An Examination of the Place of Reason in Ethics*. London: Cambridge University Press, 1950. An analysis of the ordinary language of ethical discourse, which, like the Hampshire, Hare, and Nowell-Smith books cited above, is widely read and quoted.

Commentaries

Brandt, Richard, ed. *Value and Obligation*. New York: Harcourt, Brace & World, 1961. Contains many useful articles relevant to the study of analytic ethics. See especially Frederick Strawson, "Ethical Intuitionism," and C. A. Campbell, "Is 'Freewill' a Pseudo-Problem?" Campbell's article offers a searching criticism of the way in which Schlick and Nowell-Smith handle the responsibility issue, a criticism which may profitably be compared to the examination that Nowell-Smith makes of Campbell, beginning on p. 533 of his first selection, "The Meaning of 'Could Have Acted Otherwise.' "

Dewey, John. *Theory of Valuation in the International Encyclopaedia of Unified Science*, II, 4. Chicago: University of Chicago Press, 1939. A polemical work directed against the positivistic treatment of ethical judgments. Offers a searching critique of Ayer's position and a particularly worthwhile examination of what Dewey regards as Ayer's arbitrary use of the notion of "ethical feelings."

Hook, Sidney, ed. *Determinism and Freedom in the Age of Modern Science*. New York: Collier Books, 1961. A paperbound anthology offering a fine collection of papers on the responsibility issue, including John Hospers, "What Means This Freedom?" and Paul Edwards, "Hard and Soft Determinism," both of which lean toward determinism and defend the view that responsibility and determinism are incompatible. Also see Richard Taylor, "Determinism and the Theory of Agency," which proposes that determinism and indeterminism are both inconsistent with morality.

Melden, A. I., ed. *Essays in Moral Philosophy*. Seattle: University of Washington Press, 1958. An anthology of recent papers on ethics. Analytic approaches are represented.

Proceedings of the American Catholic Philosophical Association, XXXIV. Washington, D.C., 1960. A number of articles about analytic philosophy from the Thomistic point of view. Including, on ethics, Ronald Lawler, "The Nature of Analytic Ethics"; Ivan Boh, "The Emotive Analysis of Value Judgments"; and James McGlynn, "A Critical Evaluation of Analytic Ethics."

Schilpp, P. A., ed. *The Philosophy of G. E. Moore*, 2nd ed. Evanston, Ill.: Northwestern University Press, 1952. A collection of papers discussing various aspects of Moore's philosophy, including Moore's own "A Reply to My Critics."

Sellars, W. S., and John Hospers, eds. *Readings in Ethical Theory*. New York: Appleton-Century-Crofts, 1952. A large anthology of readings by twentieth-century British and American analytic ethicians. Includes W. K. Frankena, "The Naturalistic Fallacy," a criticism of Moore's position. A sampling of essays representing various versions of intuitionism is provided on pp. 115–249.

Warnock, M. *Ethics Since 1900*. London: Oxford University Press, 1960. A review and critical examination of recent British and American moral philosophy.

White, Morton. "The Analytic and the Synthetic: An Untenable Dualism," in *Semantics and the Philosophy of Language*. Ed. by L. Linsky. Urbana, Ill.: University of Illinois Press, 1952. Offers a reappraisal of the widely accepted analytic-synthetic distinction.

PART FIVE

EXISTENTIALIST AND POST-EXISTENTIALIST THOUGHT.

Kierkegaard

Nietzsche

Sartre

Marcel

Camus

Teilhard
de Chardin

EDITED BY

Wilfrid Desan

GEORGETOWN UNIVERSITY

EXISTENTIALIST AND POST-EXISTENTIALIST THOUGHT:
Kierkegaard
Nietzsche
Sartre
Marcel
Camus
Teilhard de Chardin

Introduction

Historical Perspective

The purpose of this essay is to acquaint the reader with the ethical commitment of existentialism. Although it is one of the most recent developments in Western thought, existentialism has already made a place for itself in the realm of philosophy. It has done so in a way that was at first considered unorthodox—French existentialism, for example, began its life in the cafés of the Parisian boulevards—but the movement has outgrown these earlier stages, and is now taught and studied in most universities.

In their remote origin all existentialist philosophies can be considered to descend from René Descartes' (1596–1650) emphasis upon the importance of the *Subject*. More immediately, existentialism is a reaction against the Hegelian stress upon the *objective* and the systematic. Whatever may be its precise origin—and a clear-cut one is not readily discovered—it is definitely a philosophy centered upon man rather than nature. Moreover, it is a philosophy of the total man, not of his rational aspect alone. The freedom of the individual is of the utmost importance, freedom being not merely the "possibility of choice," but, more importantly, that which in man enables him to be creator of the new. This emphasis has been aptly summarized in the slogan "Existence precedes essence."

If the individual man is sovereign and center for the existentialist, he is so in a very special way. The Subject is shown as the center of a world that he constitutes around himself; man is defined as that entity that by its very presence creates a world. He does not create in a divine way, *ex nihilo,* but once thrown onto this earth (Heidegger's *geworfen*) he "humanizes" or "makes" the brute reality that he confronts. Matter derives its meaning from man: a mountain becomes an obstacle or observatory, a tree poem or tool, a stone weapon or protection. Every man builds his own universe, and there are as many worlds as there are men.

Yet for anyone who starts from the individual man many things remain unresolved. The realm of mystery engulfing man is immense. The theistic existentialist corrects this despair by calling upon God; his atheistic comrade finds no answer and consequently calls this world absurd.

Obviously, some of the ideas propounded by the existential philosophers are not new. St. Augustine stressed the value of the Self, and Pascal revolted against reason as the exclusive source of knowledge. It is with Kierkegaard, however, that we definitely enter into a phase where the Subjective, in reaction against Hegel, becomes of primary importance. We shall therefore start with Kierkegaard and trace in his writings what may be called his moral philosophy, and then study in succession the ethical positions of Nietzsche, Sartre, Marcel, and Camus.

This list is far from complete. Preference has been given to those existentialists who can be said to have some kind of moral philosophy, albeit an unsystematic one. The texts of Kierkegaard, Nietzsche, and Sartre reflect the overwhelming importance of the individual subject, although in vastly diversified ways. While discovering a similar concern in the selections from Marcel and Camus, we will sense that the Subject is being brought under a measure of control. Camus' rebel is a man in revolt, one whose attitude of negation is a manifestation of freedom, but he is no longer alone. As is shown in the extracts from *The Rebel,* the trend is toward a position where the collective gains more respect. Having observed this slowly growing trend towards the collective, we will not be surprised to discover that with Teilhard de Chardin we leave the world of the existential and step into the world of the collective, or what might be called the "post-existential."

Kierkegaard: The First Contemporary Existentialist

Søren Kierkegaard (1813–55) wrote some thirty books during his lifetime, yet he fell into semioblivion until the existential literature of our times forcefully brought him a new renown. Because events in his personal life strongly influenced his writings, a brief biographical sketch is in order. The son of a small industrialist, he grew up amid certain wealth, but wealth or comfort did not mean joy in the household of Mikael Kierkegaard. Born in the dreary moors of Jutland, the father emerges as a melancholy figure.

Profoundly affected by the most depressing aspects of Christianity—his preferred image was the representation of Christ on the cross—he inflicted upon his family a sense of sin and penance. The revelation of a moral flaw in his father profoundly affected the oversensitive young Kierkegaard, for here was sin close at hand. Indeed, sin and penance were to constitute the dominant themes of the future theologian, not so much as the essential, abstract themes of ethical speculation, but rather as the inner dimension of his own self. In a diary Søren Kierkegaard described how he himself went through a moral decline; [1] his own guilt and the guilt of his father created a complex that was to stay with him all his life.

Although he felt the need for love, he was unable to fulfill it. He abandoned his studies for the ministry; he broke his engagement to Regina Olsen and never married. "Like a solitary fir tree, egoistically constricted and towering loftily, I stand without casting a shadow, and only the wood pigeon makes its nest in my branches." [2] Kierkegaard's religion, as we shall see, consists mainly of a deep interiorization of consciousness and a refinement of self-awareness, which in this extreme form contains equal elements of pleasure and torture.

No wonder then that for a man so much imbued with the self and the individual, the Church in its organized structure was to become an encumbrance. A few months before his death he launched his most violent attacks against the Established Lutheran Church of Denmark, even though he loved it and Christianity. Kierkegaard knew that he was destined to stand alone, as an outcast; his God has no existential touch with other people. All this must be kept in mind in order to understand Kierkegaard's ethics.

Kierkegaard's Ethics

For Kierkegaard true ethics is inseparable from a Christian conception of life. The Christian is above all conscious of sin. Christian revelation has created that awareness, and it is precisely in this anguished consciousness that the redemption through Christ reaches us. This salvation, however, does not reach us collectively, but individually. God is present only to me, not to us, for only when I am alone do I fully realize my unworthiness. [3]

Kierkegaard's fascination with the story of Abraham and Isaac is generally credited to the element of the absurd inherent in this drama: Abraham was willing to go against nature in obedience to God, and thus showed an absolute trust and faith. Yet Kierkegaard saw something else in this story, namely, the example of a lonely and extremely individualistic man, standing alone before his God. In *Fear and Trembling* (1843) Kierkegaard made it clear that in the case of Abraham the individual stands above the

---

[1] *Stages on Life's Way*, trans. by Walter Lowrie (Princeton, N.J.: Princeton University Press, 1940), p. 298.
[2] From "Diary I," trans. by Louis Dupré, in *Kierkegaard as Theologian* (New York: Sheed and Ward, 1963), p. 196.
[3] *Ibid.*, p. 83.

universal, and that the willingness to sacrifice Isaac is above the universal law. But what is important is that Abraham was an *exception;* in his case, and in his case only, the ethical was suspended. Kierkegaard, however much an individualist, tolerated no autonomous morality. No one is permitted to take away the law, or the Objective, for only through the Objective of the universal law can the Subjective be saved. One serves one master, and that master is God. Just as the young Kierkegaard unconditionally recognized the authority of his parents, the Christian follows the universal law without protest.

Yet this lover of introspection fell prey once more to his own self when he wrote that ethical concern is above all internal. Although this statement seems innocuous, its meaning is far-reaching, for it stresses the importance of the *intention* more than anything else, forcefully bringing to mind Augustine's emphasis upon interiority: *Deum et animan scire cupio!* . . . *Nihilne plus! Omnino nihil!* Augustine's desire to know God and his own soul, and nothing more, has something in common with Kierkegaard's emphasis upon introspection—they share the same intensity and the same burning conviction of the thorough vanity of all human achievement. At certain times in Kierkegaard's life this feeling was prevalent, yet in a later publication, *Works of Love* (1847), depth of interiority does not eliminate the need for acts of charity, for ethics is life.

Thus we reach the core of Kierkegaardian morality: Ethics is life. Yet this emphasis on deed should not be construed to be in opposition to the interior life that the Christian carries unflaggingly within himself; it is, rather, against the speculation of the philosopher, who from behind his desk dominates the world, or believes he does, but who has no real concern for the suffering of his fellow-men. Ethics is born in the either/or alternative, but once the choice is made, the deed is what matters and speculation is totally accidental. Only the philosopher who practices what he teaches is worth listening to; only the minister who fulfills in real life the advice he gives from the pulpit has any authority. Kierkegaard absolutely rejected the well-known argument of *"opus operatum"* whereby the Catholic Church protects the juridical authority of its priests, whatever their personal conduct may be. Ethics is existential, and only in the existential fulfillment of the commandments does authority assert itself.

Reaction Against Hegel

Kierkegaard reacted most strongly against the philosophy of G. W. F. Hegel (1770–1831).[4] Although we will not analyze here the accuracy of his interpretation of Hegel, it is important to note his specific points of disagreement, each of which was intended to act as a corrective to Hegel's thought. Hegel was a philosopher of the totality, and he believed in the

---

[4] For more detail on this topic, see Jean Wahl, *Etudes Kierkegaardiennes* (Paris: Aubier, 1938).

gradual conquest of Nature by what he called the Idea; this results in the advent of the Spirit or the salvation of the totality. Kierkegaard saw no salvation through some abstract Spirit but vigorously asserted that it is the individual who is saved and saved only through Christ. That such an act of salvation implies a mystery did not bother Kierkegaard because he accepted mystery as a part of the definition of man. He had, after all, grown up in an atmosphere of mystery, where no rationality gave him relief from the awkward relation with his father and no concepts enabled him to fulfill his love for Regina.

In reaction to Hegel, Kierkegaard claimed that reason cannot clarify the real and that there is ample room for the absurd, the element that later becomes so important to the existentialists. In still another contrast, we should mention that Hegel, in his later years, could no longer be called a Christian. In the light of the global evolution of spirit, Christianity became for him merely one link in the gigantic dialectic, while the notion of sin and Christian faith disappeared in the synthesis. On all this Kierkegaard could not have disagreed more.[5]

Of Kierkegaard it can be said that ethics is born with the act of faith; it results from a decisive either/or choice and constitutes the bridge between the individual and Christ. Christianity remains, but the Church itself is not needed for the mediation of grace. If after all this one gathers that the Christian travels a lonely road, one would be truly in the spirit of Kierkegaard. For in his world the Church Militant has only individuals, and any dreams of the collective must be laid to rest until that day when we will all enjoy eternal peace.

Nietzsche: The Will to Power

Like Kierkegaard, Friedrich Nietzsche (1844–1900) was a great solitary figure. He, too, stood in opposition to his time and, through his restless negativity, provoked his own exclusion—his friends deserted him one by one, his books were unread, the intellectual community excluded him. Also like Kierkegaard, he had an excruciating insight into the frailty of the finite, but while Kierkegaard had a faith in Christ that enabled him to stand on firm ground, albeit alone, Nietzsche, unable to stand the frail structure of the finite, shifted about constantly and never achieved any real identity. He was condemned never to *be* but always to *become*. The famous existentialist slogan, "existence precedes essence," finds here its psychological origin: man is mobility, and there is no way of holding him within a stable nature, no hope of his finding solutions, definitions, or any final rest. Unable to

---

[5] It is highly debatable whether or not Kierkegaard always understood Hegel. The young Hegel, for example, left a large margin to the irrational; and in the beautiful analysis of "the unhappy consciousness," the sense of mystery is accepted, for, as Jaspers suggests, it contains the night no less than the day.

discover an absolute and desperately in need of one, Nietzsche ultimately ended his life in madness.

The man who in our times perhaps best understands Nietzsche is Karl Jaspers (b. 1883). Jaspers was prepared to understand him because in his vision the unique was not only accepted but welcomed; a man like Nietzsche and his ideas could be treated with kindness and even with respect, without being wholly approved. "Only in the light of the exception can we find our way back without deception to a universality in the history of Philosophy, which thereby once again becomes transformed." [6]

Nietzsche's philosophy is a dynamic and creative one. His intellect was constantly on the move in unrelenting pursuit of a definition of man and his ethics. The attempt to get hold of that which is by itself capable of endless explanation can be never-ending and eventually self-destructive; for Nietzsche dissatisfaction necessarily follows upon definition. Unable for this reason ever to achieve a coherent and systematic presentation, he remains the model *par excellence* of the *irrequieti*. The model can be inspiring—one cannot help but admire the power of the incessant creation—but it can also be dangerous, and there is no need to follow him to the point of his devaluation of all values (*Umsturz aller Werte*). Jaspers suggests a way to complete Nietzsche, whose assertions are by themselves incomplete, extreme, and immature: "What Nietzsche ultimately is or will be depends upon what others make of him." [7]

The Ethics of Dionysus

While Nietzsche was a university professor in Basel, he published his first book, *The Birth of Tragedy* (1872). Although this is not his best work, it does contain some of his basic ideas. It is in this work, for example, that we find his famous Dionysian-Apollonian antithesis. According to Nietzsche, the core of all esthetic productivity lies in the synthesis of the Dionysian principle (representing the power of life) and the Apollonian principle (the element of clarity and intelligibility). However necessary the restraint exerted by the Apollonian element may be, it is to the Dionysian that Nietzsche turned his greatest attention and admiration. At first merely the obscure, underlying element that is opposed to Apollo, Dionysus becomes, when all the consideration of man is ignored, the *total* dimension of the universe, a universe that is power and life, unrestrained, and boundless. The cosmos *is* Dionysus and is thus "beyond good and evil." "Good" and "evil" are merely categories imposed upon our world by these who gradually emerged from its depths. They are creations of man, and, as such, they have nothing eternal or stable about them but change with the alterations of the image of man himself. This distinction is an essential point for the understanding of Nietzsche. He elaborated at length upon it in his two

[6] Karl Jaspers, *Reason and Existenz*, trans. by William Earle (New York: Farrar, Straus & Giroux, 1955), p. 130.
[7] *Ibid.*, p. 110.

best works, *Beyond Good and Evil* (1886) and *The Genealogy of Morals* (1887). *Thus Spake Zarathustra* (1883–85) is perhaps better known, but contains little that is not given in his two other works, which are more philosophical but equally well written.

Beyond Good and Evil was written in Italy, where Nietzsche spent most of his time after his retirement from teaching in 1879. Although written in the aphoristic style characteristic of Nietzsche, it has much more unity than at first appears. It is an essay toward a concept of truth; in it Nietzsche discovered that there is no will to truth among philosophers but merely will to power. Philosophy "creates the world in its own image; it cannot do otherwise; philosophy is this tyrannical impulse itself, the most spiritual Will to Power, the will 'to creation of the world,' the will to the *causa prima.*" [8] With this the foundation for relativism is laid, and henceforth neither religion nor ethics will be able to offer a dwelling where man is *absolutely* safe; everything will be relative and provisional. Nietzsche's "free spirit," well aware of this twilight of the idols, builds his nest among the eagles, from whence he looks down upon those poor mortals who are still credulous.

Yet Nietzsche did not deny that religion (together with its ethics) has been used successfully as an instrument; he wondered whether or not "all this violence, arbitrariness, severity, dreadfulness, and unreasonableness of the Church and Christianity has proved itself the disciplinary means whereby the European spirit has attained its strength, its remorseless curiosity and subtle mobility. . . ." [9] Nature or life needs its own restraint in order to survive; ethics provides such a protection with its restraint upon the instincts of man. It is undeniable that silence, self-control, and solitude are instruments of value in this respect, but their origin and purpose are purely natural, and the fact that they are part of Christian ethics is of no importance. There is no supernatural. All that counts is life, that magnificent force that carries within itself both the rational and irrational, the restrained and unrestrained.

Master-Slave Morality

Later in the same work Nietzsche traced the origin of Christian ethics to what he called "Jewish resentment." [10] It was the Jew who, inverting the deeper values of the Greeks and the Romans, began to call "ugly" what was beautiful and "world" what was in fact the power of Rome and the splendor of Greece. This inversion of values was in itself a Will to Power or, better still, it was a self-defense of the slaves. At this point Nietzsche introduced his famous distinction between master morality and slave

---

[8] Friedrich Nietzsche, *The Philosophy of Nietzsche,* trans. by T. Common, H. Zimmern, and C. P. Fadiman, and with Introd. by W. H. Wright (New York: Random House, 1954), p. 389.

[9] *Ibid.,* p. 477.

[10] *Ibid.,* p. 485.

morality. The truthful, the noble, the proud are "good" in the Nietzschean sense of the word, while the humble, the self-abasing, the patient—in short, all those who follow the spirit of the Beatitudes—are despicable.

Neither *The Birth of Tragedy* nor *Beyond Good and Evil* devotes much comment to the concept of the Superman, a concept that attracted more fame for its author than he could have wished and from quarters he might not altogether have acknowledged.[11] In fact, Nietzsche did not define the term "Superman" with precision in any of his works. In the *Genealogy* Napoleon is considered to be the incarnation of the aristocratic ideal, "that synthesis of Monster and Superman." Cesare Borgia is mentioned with more than usual tolerance in *Beyond Good and Evil* as a beast of prey, but he is still not a Superman. Even Julius Caesar and Leonardo da Vinci, although described as "those marvelously incomprehensible beings," are not given the epithet.[12] In *Thus Spake Zarathustra* and *The Will to Power* (1901) the Superman is considered ethically as an ideal of the present-day man still to be fulfilled in the remote future. Walter Kaufmann favors the term "Overman" for this being of the future, since in certain texts he is the one who "overcomes" himself in transcending his mediocrity and in disciplining his impulses and lower desires.[13] There is in this interpretation an undeniable note of asceticism: the Superman subdues himself as well as others. If some form of asceticism is present, however, it should definitely not be understood as one with spiritual implications, for the *Ubermensch* is not merely godless but is the god of the future: "Dead are all the gods, now we desire the Superman to live." [14]

Sartre: An Ethics of Ambiguity

A certain parallelism exists between Nietzsche and Jean-Paul Sartre (b. 1905), but it should be neither overstressed nor ignored. Both men have denied the supernatural and see man and man only as the supreme value. Nietzsche considered value-creation as dependent upon the structure of man himself, while Sartre believes in a *projet fondamental* according to which

---

[11] Nazi theoreticians, for example, attempted to claim Nietzsche for their own. However, they themselves were well aware of Nietzsche's half-hearted backing of their position and confessed so with great regret. While applauding his Pan-European ideas, his anti-English attitude, his appraising words for *war* as a "freemaking value," his expectation of an ultimate agreement between Germans and Russians, they regretted his distinction between slave morality and the morality of the strong man, his "aristocratic" divorce from the people, and his contempt for state and nation, ideas that a real National Socialist should not have. See Karl J. Obenauer, *Friedrich Nietzsche und die Deutsche Gegenwart* (Bonn: Gebr. Scheur, 1940), p. 10; Heinrich Haertle, *Nietzsche und der Nationalsozialismus* (Munich: Zentralverlag der NSDAP, 1937).
[12] Nietzsche, p. 665.
[13] *Nietzsche: Philosopher, Psychologist, AntiChrist* (Princeton, N.J.: Princeton University Press, 1951), p. 274.
[14] Nietzsche, p. 83.

every individual chooses himself and his world. Nietzsche considered it the prerogative of the very few to be independent, or, in his own words, "it is a privilege of the strong";[15] for Sartre every man is free, whoever or wherever he may be. As we have seen, the Will to Power is for Nietzsche the great impulse of life and of every accomplishment within life, even of our search for truth. For Sartre nothing counts but *praxis*, the free deed, which in its very execution has cognitive value. To act is already a way of understanding. Understanding itself and all intellectual activity, even culture, stand in service of a cause. There is no speculation for its own sake.

Sartre, no less than Nietzsche, protects the individual self. As is wellknown to the reader of *Being and Nothingness* (1943), man is sovereign, and it is the self which through its very presence reveals a world, stands as a center of its creation, desires and wishes, evaluates and judges. A similar trend is present in Sartre's second major philosophical work, *Critique de la raison dialectique* (1960), which, while purporting to be a sociological study, still gives full sway to the activity of the individual man.[16] To quote from my recent study of Sartre:

> What (according to Sartre) makes the group? The individual. What moves the inert? disturbs the sociological strata? starts the revolution? expels the king? The individual once more. Neither God nor devil, neither State nor society, only man is responsible for man, only the individual man makes and assembles the totality through *praxis*. There is nothing but the individual self and its unexplained and unexplainable power of synthesis.[17]

This enormous stress upon the self has a double implication. First, Sartre's self is free, supremely free. This was and still is Sartre's great contribution, for whatever may be the limitations of his line of thought, more than anyone else he has defended this supreme quality. It is regrettable that his virulent opponents have not seen or sufficiently appreciated his defense of man's freedom and its concomitant, man's dignity. Nor have they seen his incessant attempts to show man as fully responsible for his own actions. Human consciousness is not the world of "matter" that it reveals; hence it moves outside a world where determinism reigns supreme.

Unfortunately, and this is the second implication, a self as free as that envisioned by Sartre theoretically escapes all control. Since there is no God and no stable concept of man, it becomes difficult to discover a definite element that is "immobile and might be considered to be an entity englobing the individual man."[18] Although Sartre has no clear norm of ethics, he has always shown a profound interest in the poor and the underdog; this interest was evident in the young lycée professor and is still present in the

---

[15] *Ibid.,* p. 414.
[16] Jean-Paul Sartre, *Critique de la raison dialectique* (Paris: Gallimard, 1960), vol. 1.
[17] Wilfrid Desan, *The Marxism of Jean-Paul Sartre* (Garden City, N.Y.: Doubleday & Co., 1965), p. 284.
[18] *Ibid.,* p. 270.

aging, somewhat disillusioned *homme de lettres*. According to Sartre, one has to consult the poor in order to know what to do; their look is both a testimony and an accusation, for in it we see both what the social order is and what it should be.

Undoubtedly this attitude reflects the Marxist influence upon Sartre. Marx, it should be noted, had no direct interest in formulating an ethics. What mattered for him was the success of the proletarian revolution. However, after a while it became apparent that the phenomenon of ethics needed some explanation, which Marx gave in his well-known distinction between the infrastructure, the material situation, and the suprastructure, the ideological framework resulting from the material situation. Ethics is part of the suprastructure and is grounded in economics. A feudal system has a feudal ethics, a capitalistic world has a moral system fitted to its demands, and a proletarian world will someday have its own ethics. What sort of ethics this is or will be has never been clarified.

One thing is clear, such an approach in ethics can only lead to relativism. On this most Marxists would agree, and, although Sartre has expressed some reservations concerning the relation of the suprastructure and the infrastructure, he would agree with Marx in rejecting any absolute norm in ethics.[19] What matters also for Sartre as well as Marx is the triumph of the proletarian revolution. Any "ought" is provisional and will have to be modified once the revolution has achieved its ultimate purpose. The ought as embodied in certain values of the present stems from a bourgeois ethics, which teaches obedience, submissiveness, and other "virtues" that serve only to keep the present state of affairs as it is. It is not surprising that in the *Critique* Sartre condones or at least tolerates dictatorial regimes and even certain forms of violence as long as they serve the ends of "liberation" or "revolution." This explains Sartre's otherwise perplexing views on current affairs. For, "one fact appears more and more distinctly, that the Revolution seems to be devoid of all moral obligations save one, and that is to succeed." [20]

Marcel: The Dignity of Man

Gabriel Marcel (b. 1889) brings a more hopeful note to existentialism. Half-Jewish and half-Christian by origin, Marcel grew up in a milieu that was totally indifferent to religion. During World War I when he served as an army nurse, his attention was focused again and again upon the problem of immortality, since it was his sad function to inform the families of the

---

[19] Sartre agrees with Marx that "matter" shapes history, hence all culture as well, but in Sartre's view it is "matter" as shaped by free men. Only a free being can make "values," for a value in the Sartrian semantics presumes a choice and a preference. On that topic, see Desan, p. 263.

[20] *Ibid.*, p. 265.

deceased. Around that time he started a diary entitled *Journal méta-physique*. This penetrating and slow analysis was for all practical purposes the journal of his conversion. He worked at it for many years and had it published in the year of his conversion (1927). By that time nothing else was left to do. *"Vous êtes un des nôtres,"* said François Mauriac, who knew him well and was acquainted with his thought.

Marcel spent his whole life in Paris, where he taught intermittently and wrote drama criticism, as well as a great number of books. Scattered throughout his books are ethical implications, but he does not develop them into any system. The reader of Gabriel Marcel will find that he wanders around endlessly, drifts away from the topic, yet somehow manages to develop the most penetrating insights and the most cogent conclusions. In *Man Against Mass Society* (1951) certain passages seem to keep within bounds material that was spread open in other writings. The predominant themes—the dignity of man, the reaction against standardization, the value of the concrete—are not Marcel's exclusively, but the delicate and nuanced way in which he handles them definitely is.

Reaction Against Technology

Marcel is concerned still more than Sartre with the menace of modern technology. Although technique is in itself neutral, or can even be called good to the extent of its usefulness, it poses a threat to the spiritual value in man because of its emphasis upon the priority of matter. The inventor displays sharp insight, but the average consumer, playing no part in the product, merely looks for comfort. His mental activity falls behind in the rush towards the material pleasures of life. Self-mastery, in the opinion of Marcel, has not kept up with mastery of the earth.

Technique can be even more perilous when the attempt is made to apply its principles and method to man himself, for when man is treated as an "object," he is no longer respected in his freedom and uniqueness. Here freedom means not merely possibility of choice, but it presumes a certain power of creation. For Marcel, as for the other existentialists (although in a somewhat different way), freedom implies a production of the new, a spontaneity that results not in a mere repetition of the past but in an assertion of the self that is unique and irreplaceable. Freedom thus conceived suffers even more drastically when man is conditioned as a robot and equalized with his fellowmen.

There is a movement of the soul, however, to escape this objectification, which consists in what Marcel calls *"participation ontologique."* This ontological participation requires Marcel's form of intersubjectivity, which takes place when I acknowledge the other as a living "subject" and he in return recognizes me in the same way. *I* become fully myself in recognizing *you*, and the reverse is equally true.[21] Clearly, it is not through egotism

---

[21] Gabriel Marcel, *Journal métaphysique* (Paris: Gallimard, 1927), p. 145.

that the self is born but through the recognition of the other as a person and as a subject. There can, of course, never be a response between me and a flower, nor can there be a response between me and the individual who is merely an object of inquiry or information. But once *I* am interested in *you* as a person and show this in my attitude and my dialogue, then I start considering you as a subject: we are "co-present." If this state of being co-present does not result in moral improvement, it does not exist.

It is important to notice that this is the Marcellian way of *existing:* one *is* through love and charity. The art of living consists in remaining faithful to this form of encounter and communion. Fidelity, as Marcel calls it, is not an easy virtue and requires prayer for its growth. This is true for any real friendship or conjugal love, but as it is extended beyond these limits it becomes charity, and presumes an attitude of brotherhood toward one's fellow men, founded upon an awareness of common origin and common destiny. This is naturally easier to practice within the orbit of Christian faith and convictions.

The question may be asked whether Marcel's argument presumes Christian faith or, if it does not, whether it leads to it.[22] His answer is that charity is present among non-Christians, but that it comes to its full growth within the orbit of Christian life. In a more general way, the French Catholic existentialist has confessed that his brand of philosophy is totally unacceptable to anyone who is not in some way religious.

The problem of God is more central in the philosophy of Gabriel Marcel than one is generally inclined to believe. His own words summarize his position very well. "Without doubt I am to the extent that God is more for me . . ."[23] God cannot, however, be approached as an *object;* he cannot be reached through a syllogism. God is *"l'Absolu invérifiable,"* and the only attitude is one of faith. *Credo in Te.* In this act of faith, God exists for me, that is, I enter into communion with Him as I do with the Supreme Subject.[24] We have already seen that only the encounter with another subject results in the birth of the self. It can now be added that I become *fully* myself only when I encounter a Thou of divine size. This acceptance of God is fulfilled in the *Credo in Te,* which is a free act, as spontaneous and autonomous as the *Cogito.* God is reached in freedom as the supreme Thou, but this particular movement of the soul also gives the human individual his highest status and dignity. Recognition of the Transcendent Being is necessary to Marcel's ethics, for it is in and through this acceptance that the individual subject reaches his most sublime dignity, the broth-

---

[22] Several of the ideas presented in this section I obtained from Marcel himself, either during his visits to the United States or in meetings with him in Paris. The question and answer mentioned in the text were exchanged during a personal interview. The reader will note that I also quote from the *Journal métaphysique,* which, from a philosophical point of view, is his best work, although it does not contain his entire moral philosophy.

[23] Marcel, p. 206.

[24] *Ibid.,* p. 33.

erhood of men is confirmed, and man himself is protected against the menace of matter and technique.

It may appear that here we are far removed from the ethics of Sartre, yet we should not overlook the fact that both Sartre and Marcel stress the concrete against the world of speculation and logical deduction, both believe in freedom and spontaneity, and both defend the individual and the unique. One might say that Sartre's search for the intersubjective has failed,[25] while Marcel, although less vigorous and systematic in approach, seems to have come closer to a solution. In later years Marcel's thought is becoming increasingly anti-Cartesian: the self is not enclosed in itself but attempts to communicate with others. Marcel's effort to build up the collective may be said to be more on a religious than on a philosophical basis.[26] But whatever his method, it results in a breaking away from the "insularity" of the individual self and in the discovery of an existential link between men. Gone is Valery's *"oeil pur, pur regard"* (I am only knowledge, only will to knowledge, and within its circle I englobe all men). Of this Marcel cannot approve. The link with other men is more than mere noesis.

Camus: Reaction to Unlimited Freedom

Albert Camus was born in Algeria in 1913. He held a succession of jobs —first journalist in Algeria, later director of the French theater group *l'Equipe* (1935–38), and still later editor of *Combat,* the most famous newspaper of the French Resistance—all of which furthered his vocation as a writer. He was a close associate of Sartre in the postwar movement, but their differences of thought, clearly manifest upon the publication of *The Rebel* (1954), resulted in a definitive split. *L'homme révolté* was reviewed in Sartre's *Les Temps Modernes* under the title *"Camus, ou l'Ame révoltée."* The title was ironical, and it clearly betrayed Sartre's disapproval. Although Sartre wrote a moving eulogy upon the announcement of Camus' accidental death in 1960, the two old friends were never really reconciled.

From an ethical point of view *The Plague* (1948) and *The Rebel* are among Camus' more important books. His ethical position, which is characterized above all by an emphasis upon action rather than speculation, is evident in *The Plague.* This novel narrates what happens to a modern city when it is suddenly hit by the plague and describes how people react to the calamity. Camus' own position is clearly identified with that of Rieux, the the medical doctor, who persistently but without ostentation performs his nightmarish duty. Father Paneloux, on the contrary, wants to offer a metaphysical explanation of the problem of evil, claiming that the inhabitants of

---

[25] See Desan, pp. 278 ff.
[26] See Marcel, pp. 64–67.

Oran are being punished for some unknown crime. That evil is penance is unconvincing to Camus, for in his understanding evil is *absurd,* and any effort of the human mind to explain the irrationality of its surroundings is part of the *nostalgie humaine;* one tries but with no result. It should be added, however, that the attitude of the Jesuit priest is not presented as being merely one of speculation and inaction; he himself becomes one of the most devoted helpers in the desperate struggle against the endless suffering. A child dies, and the agony of the boy is one of the most moving passages of the whole book. A few seconds before his death, "slowly the lips parted and from them rose a long, incessant scream, hardly varying with his respiration, and filling the ward with a fierce, indignant protest, so little childish that it seemed like a collective voice issuing from all the sufferers there." [27] This was the angry death-cry of protest that has sounded through the ages of mankind. To this provocation of suffering there is no other answer but action.

For Camus action is essentially a "revolt," which actually constitutes the theme of *The Rebel.* The man in revolt is a man "who says no but whose refusal does not imply a renunciation." [28] His attitude is a part of Western man wherever he is: it is permanent, to the extent that suffering in this world is permanent; it is blind, in that there is no rational explanation of the suffering; but it is nonetheless free, for it is a revolt against destiny.

Camus, more than Sartre, loved humanity. Sartre is no doubt sincerely devoted to the alleviation of suffering, but fundamentally Camus had more trust in the goodness of man, and his revolt subsequently had a sense of moderation. "In order to exist, man must rebel, but rebellion must respect the limit it discovers in itself—a limit where minds meet and in meeting, begin to exist." [29] His revolt is seen to be a collective one. "We're working side by side for something that unites us—beyond blasphemy and prayers. And it is the only thing that matters. . . . ," says Rieux to the Jesuit.[30] More than Sartre, Camus had a sense of the solidarity of mankind; it is precisely this that gives his individuals a sense of eternity, for the individual who accepts death as a result of his rebellion demonstrates that he is willing to sacrifice himself for the sake of the common good. In the act of rebellion and in the death that may result, man surpasses himself. His act is an identification with the totality of men as such. *"I rebel"* implies that *"we exist."*

Camus' rebel, like Camus himself, is not a believer. Indeed, he made clear that rebellion ignores the sacred. Although at one time two explana-

---

[27] Albert Camus, *The Plague,* trans. by Stuart Gilbert (New York: Alfred A. Knopf, 1948), p. 194.
[28] Camus *The Rebel,* trans. by Anthony Bower (New York: Alfred A. Knopf, 1954), p. 14.
[29] *Ibid.,* p. 22.
[30] *The Plague,* p. 197.

tions of the problem of suffering were open to man, that offered by religion and that by reason, neither is acceptable today. In a universe dominated by the absurd, rebellion is the only answer.

To quite a few of us, this may appear to be a hasty conclusion. It is not obvious that the sacred and the religious are disappearing, as Camus believed. Nor must the alternatives he offered mutually exclude one another: the sacred does not necessarily rule out rebellion. Nor is it evident that rebellion finds itself at odds with the rational, since more than one rationalist has found himself among the rebels. Nevertheless, one cannot deny Camus' positive contribution. He was one of the rare atheists who did not profess to be a pessimist. Believing in the absurd, he still did not indict man for his efforts; defending the individual, he still dared to submit to *"la solidarité."*

Teilhard de Chardin: Toward the Collectivist View

Summary of Existentialist Ethics

Our examination of ethics in existential philosophy has revealed that none of the philosophers considered had a systematic moral philosophy, yet all were strangely obsessed by ethical problems. Notwithstanding their unwillingness to present things in an orderly fashion, they nevertheless have left a mark upon ethical thought as a whole. This obsession with ethics is actually linked with their principal concern, which is man himself. *"Ce qui m'interesse, c'est l'homme,"* Sartre once said. This is a very honest statement, and every one of the philosophers could repeat it: they are interested in ethics because they are interested in *man*. This interest of course has led them in diversified directions. Kierkegaard was *the* individualist for whom ethical fulfillment was of far greater importance than any systematic speculation. Yet he was ignorant of the values and the assets of the collective and strangely uninterested in the problem of the intersubjective. Nietzsche was no less concerned with the individual, but his concern was selective, and only the individual few deserved his attention. While regretting his contempt for the masses, his one-sidedness, and his fanaticism, one must admit that at times he had a sense of the unique: "Let us not level, let us make it clear how expensive and rare virtue is: let us insist that Virtue (or talent) is not something moderately desirable but is in fact a noble folly, a beautiful exception and the privilege of becoming great." [31]

Nietzsche's Will to Power was replaced by Sartre's Will to Freedom. Nowhere in the history of philosophy can we find individual freedom estimated so highly, and man condemned so forcefully to become the maker of

---

[31] Nietzsche, *Wille zur Macht*, IV, 805, Musarion ausgabe, XIX, p. 265. Excerpt trans. by Wilfrid Desan.

his own destiny. But Sartre had dreams of a better society for mankind, and when he attempted to give them a philosophical basis, the very importance attached to individual freedom became an obstacle to a sound philosophy of the collective. His philosophical answer failed but not his flair for things to come: he senses the urge to the collective in the air.

Neither Marcel nor Camus have Sartre's technical power of mind or his immense intellectual energy, but both take a more positive stand in the realm of the intersubjective and the collective. Marcel analyzed with deep penetration the value and need of human relationship; his approach has given a spirit of hope and tranquil optimism to the existentialist movement. Camus in turn never was caught up in the absurd to the extreme degree that Sartre was in his early years. Camus had a greater sense of moderation, yet his novels always revealed a sense of the tragedy of life. They are profoundly genuine but not desperate. His negation or rebellion has positive implications, and unlike Nietzsche he had no desire to become an iconoclast. Camus' thought is constructive; his rebel wants to build a world with others.

The Post-Existenialist

From this summary, one thing appears clear: the emphasis upon the subjective, so characteristic of this age, is veering toward the collective. It is to show that trend that Pierre Teilhard de Chardin has been chosen to close the series.

Although older than those belonging to the contemporary existentialist movement, Teilhard (1881–1955) in many ways seems younger. He belongs to a future as yet unaccomplished: even though his prophecies of collectivization are still far from their fulfillment, many of his ideas become more and more modern. I am not referring here to his speculation on the Omega point or to his scientific theories on the origin of life, but rather to his ideas on collectivization and on love, those which point to a particular ethical position. Two lines of thought seem to have dominated Teilhard's ethics: a profound love for the earth and an all-encompassing love for his fellowmen.

Teilhard's love for the earth pervades his philosophy. Since God has created a world whose destiny is one of convergent growth, the inorganic is not something radically divorced from the organic but is in itself a form of "prelife" that later becomes life. Life itself has not stood forever remote from consciousness but has grown into consciousness, while consciousness, in turn, is destined to achieve a still higher form of spiritualization, especially through the medium of Christian love. If, then, our universe is this unified ensemble, with each part growing into a new dimension, it can be easily understood that Teilhard's love will include matter. As a little boy who walked with his father through the countryside of Auvergne and collected mineral and botanical specimens along the way, Teilhard de Chardin showed his love for the earth. More than anything else he seized upon pieces of iron because they were hard and durable, and his most cherished possession was a plough spanner, which he called his God of iron.[32] He was soon to discover that this piece of iron was not a god, yet his childish experience betrayed an unconscious desire to spiritualize matter. His essay on the spiritualization of matter published in this anthology might be considered an adult correction and elaboration of this earlier impulse. His mature views avoid extremes. On the one hand he rejected all Manicheism, for matter is not evil; on the other, he never succumbed to any form of idolatry. If matter does not deserve the utter contempt of a distorted asceticism, neither does it merit the adoration of the pantheist. Matter must be used, not abused. Teilhard could not preach *detachment* from the earth but only *attachment* with the right intention. The earth must be brought in touch with God and not opposed to him.

It is not just matter that has evolved into consciousness. The existentialists would stop here, but Teilhard went a step farther and stated that the human species gradually has evolved into a more complex phase of social organization, with the individual discovering that the center of gravity has been transferred to, or at least aligned with, that of the national or ethnic group to which he belongs. The immense disturbances that upset the world of today signify that mankind as a whole proceeds to a still more intense socialization. Teilhard believed that this evolution must be looked upon with optimism and furthered by each one of us through our positive contributions of love and charity. Love does not level man. On the contrary, it arouses his sense of uniqueness and his creative powers. Love and charity are the greatest virtues, for they are instrumental in the survival of the species. If this is Teilhard's ethics, it is only natural that for him Christianity take the lead in the realm of morality, for it has personalized in Christ the concept of love and immortalized in the gospel the harmfulness of egocentrism and magnificence of charity.

Glossary

BEING FOR ITSELF:
   Part of the peculiarly Sartrian semantics used to denote the human consciousness. It is not a substance or a person in the metaphysical sense of the word; it is the individual consciousness as complete translucidity and pure freedom as well as the negation of what it is not. It is the absence of "Being in itself." Sometimes simply called "For itself" or *pour-soi*.

BEING IN ITSELF:
   A Sartrian term that can be defined as all that is not human consciousness,

---

[32] Pierre Teilhard de Chardin, *Le Milieu Divin: An Essay on the Interior Life* (London: Fontana Books, 1964), pp. 17–18.

the massive or full being. The terms "being for itself" and "being in itself" are correlative and must be defined one through the other. The for itself is not a thing; it can only be considered as the revelation and the desire for a thing (or for the in itself). Sometimes called "In itself" or *en-soi*.

FACTICITY:

Another term belonging to the Sartrian vocabulary denoting the whole set of obstacles that freedom has to face. In Sartre's view this includes my *place*, my *past*, my *surroundings*, my *fellowmen*, and *my death*. It is, however, part of the Sartrian thesis to show that there is *no* absolute obstacle, but that an obstacle reveals its coefficients of adversity and resistance in proportion to my means and decision to surmount adversity.

ONTOLOGICAL PARTICIPATION:

In Marcellian terminology, that mutual recognition between two persons who, by virtue of this act, become subjects.

PANTECHNICISM:

That stage where techniques have emancipated themselves from all restraint and totally regulate our social and individual lives. Technique then has become *aim* instead of *instrument*.

THE IMMANENT:

Used by Marcel to indicate a world view that rejects the meta-empirical. Such views constitute the core of a philosophy of *immanence*. Marcel extends the customary definition of the immanent ("confined to consciousness or to the mind") to cover a philosophical position.

THE TRANSCENDENT:

Denotes the existence in one form or another of that which is beyond the merely empirical. When we are compelled or conditioned to certain deeds, we still have the conviction, Marcel maintains, that there is a world beyond this visible world of coercion to which our "real selves" belong.

TO EXIST:

According to Marcel, "to exist" is to be with other subjects in a form of encounter and communion: to be "co-present."

Søren Kierkegaard

The Balance Between
the Aesthetical and the Ethical

My Friend,

What I have so often said to you I say now once again, or rather I shout it: Either/or, *aut/aut.* For a single *aut* adjoined as a rectification does not make the situation clear, since the question here at issue is so important that one cannot rest satisfied with a part of it, and in itself it is too coherent to be possessed partially. There are situations in life where it would be ridiculous or a species of madness to apply an either/or; but also, there are men whose souls are too dissolute (in the etymological sense of the word) to grasp what is implied in such a dilemma, whose personalities lack the energy to say with pathos, Either/or. Upon me these words have always made a deep impression, and they still do, especially when I pronounce them absolutely and without specific reference to any objects, for this use of them suggests the possibility of starting the most dreadful contrasts into action. They affect me like a magic formula of incantation, and my soul becomes exceeding serious, sometimes almost harrowed. I think of my early youth, when without clearly comprehending what it is to make a choice I listened with childish trust to the talk of my elders and the instant of choice was solemn and venerable, although in choosing I was only following the instructions of another person. I think of the occasions in my later life when I stood at the crossways, when my soul was matured in the

From pp. 85–95 of Søren Kierkegaard, *Either/Or,* vol. I, translated by David F. and Lillian M. Swenson. Reprinted by permission of Princeton University Press. Copyright 1959.

hour of decision. I think of the many occasions in life less important but by no means indifferent to me, when it was a question of making a choice. For although there is only one situation in which either/or has absolute significance, namely, when truth, righteousness and holiness are lined up on one side, and lust and base propensities and obscure passions and perdition on the other; yet, it is always important to choose rightly, even as between things which one may innocently choose; it is important to test oneself, lest some day one might have to beat a painful retreat to the point from which one started, and might have reason to thank God if one had to reproach oneself for nothing worse than a waste of time. In common parlance I use these words as others use them, and it would indeed be a foolish pedantry to give up using them. But sometimes it occurs, nevertheless, that I become aware of using them with regard to things entirely indifferent. Then they lay aside their humble dress, I forget the insignificant thoughts they discriminated, they advance to meet me with all their dignity, in their official robes. As a magistrate in common life may appear in plain clothes and mingle without distinction in the crowd, so do these words mingle in common speech—when, however, the magistrate steps forward with authority he distinguishes himself from all. Like such a magistrate whom I am accustomed to see only on solemn occasions, these words appear before me, and my soul always becomes serious. And although my life now has to a certain degree its either/or behind it, yet I know well that it may still encounter many a situation where the either/or will have its full significance. I hope, however, that these words may find me in a worthy state of mind when they check me on my path, and I hope that I may be successful in choosing the right course; at all events, I shall endeavor to make the choice with real earnestness, and with that I venture, at least, to hope that I shall the sooner get out of the wrong path. . . .

But now mark well what I would say to you, young man—for though you are not young, one is always compelled to address you as such. Now what did you do in this case? You acknowledged, as ordinarily you are not willing to do, the importance of an either/or. And why? Because your soul was moved by love for the young man. And yet in a way you deceived him, for he will, perhaps, encounter you at another time when it by no means suits your convenience to acknowledge this importance. Here you see one of the sorry consequences of the fact that a man's nature cannot harmoniously reveal itself. You thought you were doing the best for him, and yet perhaps you have harmed him; perhaps he would have been better able to maintain himself over against your distrust of life than to find repose in the subjective, deceitful trust you conveyed to him. Imagine that after the lapse of several years you again encountered him; he was lively, witty, intellectual, daring in his thought, bold in his expression, but your ear easily detected doubt in his soul, you conceived a suspicion that he had acquired the questionable wisdom: I say merely either/or. It is true, is it not, that you would be sorry for him, would feel that he had lost something, and something very essential. But for yourself you will not sorrow, you are content with your ambiguous wisdom, yea, proud of it, so proud that you will not suffer another to share it, since you wish to be alone with it. And yet you find it deplorable in another connection, and it is your sincere opinion that it was deplorable for the young man to have reached the same wisdom. What a monstrous contradiction. Your whole nature contradicts itself. But you can only get out of this contradiction by an either/or, and I, who love you more sincerely than you loved this young man, I, who in my life have experienced the significance of choice, I congratulate you upon the fact that you are still so young, that even though you always will be sensible of some loss, yet, if you have, or rather if you will to have the requisite energy, you can win what is the chief thing in life, win yourself, acquire your own self.

Now in case a man were able to maintain himself upon the pinnacle of the instant of choice, in case he could cease to be a man, in case he were in his inmost nature only an airy thought, in case personality meant nothing more than to be a kobold, which takes part, indeed, in the movements but nevertheless remains unchanged; in case such were the situation, it would be foolish to say that it might ever be too late for a man to choose, for in a deeper sense there could be no question of a choice. The choice itself is decisive for the content of the personality, through the choice the personality immerses itself in the thing chosen, and when it does not choose it withers away in consumption. For an instant it is so, for an instant it may seem as if the things between which a choice is to be made lie outside of the chooser, that he stands in no relationship to it, that he can preserve a state of indifference over against it. This is the instant of deliberation, but this, like the Platonic instant, has no existence, least of all in the abstract sense in which you would hold it fast, and the longer one stares at it the less it exists. That which has to be chosen stands in the deepest relationship to the chooser, and when it is a question of a choice involving a life problem the individual must naturally be living in the meantime, and hence, it comes about that the longer he postpones the choice the easier it is for him to alter its character, notwithstanding that he is constantly deliberating and deliberating and believes that thereby he is holding the alternatives distinctly apart. When life's either/or is regarded in this way one is not easily tempted to jest with it. One sees, then, that the inner drift of the personality leaves no time for thought experiments, that it constantly hastens onward and in one way or another posits this alternative or that, making the choice more difficult the next instant because what has thus been posited must be revoked. Think of the captain on his ship at the instant when it has to come about. He will perhaps be able to say, "I can either do this or that"; but in case he is not a pretty poor navigator, he will be aware at the same time that the ship is all the while making its usual headway, and that therefore it is only an instant when it is indifferent whether he does this or that. So it is with a man. If he forgets to take account of the headway, there comes at last an instant when there no longer is any question of an either/or, not because he has chosen but because he has neglected to choose, which is equivalent to saying, because others have chosen for him, because he has lost his self.

You will perceive also in what I have just been saying how essentially my view of choice differs from yours (if you can properly be said to have any view), for yours differs precisely in the fact that it prevents you from choosing. For me the instant of choice is very serious, not so much on account of the rigorous cogitation involved in weighing the alternatives, not on account of the multiplicity of thoughts which attach themselves to every link in the chain, but rather because there is danger afoot, danger that the next instant it may not be equally in my power to choose, that something already has been lived which must be lived over again. For to think that for an instant one can keep one's personality a blank, or that strictly speaking one can break off and bring to a halt the course of the personal life, is a delusion. The personality is already interested in the choice before one chooses, and when the choice is postponed the personality chooses unconsciously, or the choice is made by obscure powers within it. So when at last the choice is made one discovers (unless, as I remarked before, the personality has been completely volatilized) that there is something which must be done over again, something which must be revoked, and this is often very difficult. We read in fairy tales about human beings whom mermaids and mermen enticed into their power by means of demoniac music. In order to break the enchantment it was necessary in the fairy tale for the person who was under the spell to play the same piece of music backwards without making a single mistake. This is very profound, but very difficult to perform, and yet so it is: the errors one has taken into oneself one must eradicate in this way, and every time one makes a mistake one must begin all over. Therefore, it is important to choose and to choose in time. You, on the contrary, have another method—for I know very well that the polemical side you turn towards the world is not your true nature. Yea, if to deliberate were the proper task for a human life, you would be pretty close to perfection. I will adduce an example. To fit your case the contrasts must be bold: either a parson/or an actor. Here is the dilemma. Now all your passionate energy is awakened, reflection with its hundred arms lays hold of the thought of being a parson. You find no repose, day and night you think about it, you read all the books you can lay your hands on, you go to church three times every Sunday, pick up acquaintance with parsons, write sermons yourself, deliver them to yourself; for half a year you are dead to the whole world. You can now talk of the clerical calling with more insight and apparently with more experience than many who have been parsons for twenty years. When you encounter such men it arouses your indignation that they do not know how to get the thing off their chests with more eloquence. "Is this enthusiasm?" you say. "Why I who am not a parson, who have not consecrated myself to this calling, speak with the voice of angels as compared with them." That, perhaps, is true enough, but nevertheless, you have not become a parson. Then you act in the same way with respect to the other task, and your enthusiasm for art almost surpasses your clerical eloquence. Then you are ready to choose. However, one may be sure that in the prodigious thought-production you were engaged in there must have been lots of waste products, many incidental reflections and observations. Hence, the instant you have to choose, life and animation enter into this waste mass, a new either/or presents itself—jurist, perhaps advocate, this has something in common with both the other alternatives. Now you are lost. For that same moment you are at once advocate enough to be able to prove the reasonableness of taking the third possibility into account. So your life drifts on.

After you have wasted a year and a half on such deliberations, after you have with admirable energy exerted to the utmost the powers of your soul, you have not got one step further. You break the thread of thought, you become impatient, passionate, scolding and storming, and then you continue: "Either hairdresser/or bank teller; I say merely either/or." What wonder, then, that this saying has become for you an offense and foolishness, that it seems, as you say, as if it were like the arms attached to the iron maiden whose embrace was the death penalty. You treat people superciliously, you make sport of them, and what you have become is what you most abhor: a critic, a universal critic in all faculties. Sometimes I cannot help smiling at you, and yet it is pitiful to see how your really excellent intellectual gifts are thus dissipated. But here again there is the same contradiction in your nature; for you see the ludicrous very clearly, and God help him who falls into your hands if his case is similar to yours. And yet the whole difference is that he perhaps becomes downcast and broken, while you on the contrary become light and erect and merrier than ever, making yourself and others blissful with the gospel: *vanitas vanitatum vanitas,* hurrah! But this is no choice, it is what we call in Danish letting it go, or it is mediation like letting five count as an even number. Now you feel yourself free, you say to the world, farewell.

> *So zieh' ich hin in alle Ferne,*
> *Ueber meiner Mütze nur die Sterne.*[1]

Therewith you have chosen . . . not to be sure, as you yourself will admit, the better part. But in reality you have not chosen at all, or it is in an improper sense of the word you have chosen. Your choice is an aesthetic choice, but an aesthetic choice is no choice. The act of choosing is essentially a proper and stringent expression of the ethical. Whenever in a stricter sense there is question of an either/or, one can always be sure that

---

[1] Goethe, *West-östlicher Divan,* "Freiheit." The meaning of the couplet may be suggested by a free translation:

I give myself up to infinite space.
And nothing but the stars are above my head.   [S.K.]

the ethical is involved. The only absolute either/or is the choice between good and evil, but that is also absolutely ethical. The aesthetic choice is either entirely immediate and to that extent no choice, or it loses itself in the multifarious. Thus, when a young girl follows the choice of her heart, this choice, however beautiful it may be, is in the strictest sense no choice, since it is entirely immediate. When a man deliberates aesthetically upon a multitude of life's problems, as you did in the foregoing, he does not easily get one either/or, but a whole multiplicity, because the self-determining factor in the choice is not ethically accentuated, and because when one does not choose absolutely one chooses only for the moment, and therefore can choose something different the next moment. The ethical choice is therefore in a certain sense much easier, much simpler, but in another sense it is infinitly harder. He who would define his life task ethically has ordinarily not so considerable a selection to choose from; on the other hand, the act of choice has far more importance for him. If you will understand me aright, I should like to say that in making a choice it is not so much a question of choosing the right as of the energy, the earnestness, the pathos with which one chooses. Thereby the personality announces its inner infinity, and thereby, in turn, the personality is consolidated. Therefore, even if a man were to choose the wrong, he will nevertheless discover, precisely by reason of the energy with which he chose, that he had chosen the wrong. For the choice being made with the whole inwardness of his personality, his nature is purified and he himself brought into immediate relation to the eternal Power whose omnipresence interpenetrates the whole of existence. This transfiguration, this higher consecration, is never attained by that man who chooses merely aesthetically. The rhythm in that man's soul, in spite of all its passion, is only a *spiritus lenis*.

So, like a Cato I shout at you my either/or, and yet not like a Cato, for my soul has not yet acquired the resigned coldness which he possessed. But I know that only this incantation, if I have the strength for it, will be capable of rousing you, not to an activity of thought, for of that you have no lack, but to earnestness of spirit. Perhaps you will succeed without that in accomplishing much, perhaps even in astonishing the world (for I am not niggardly), and yet you will miss the highest thing, the only thing which truly gives meaning to life; perhaps you will gain the whole world and lose your own self.

What is it, then, that I distinguish in my either/or? Is it good and evil? No, I would only bring you up to the point where the choice between the evil and the good acquires significance for you. Everything hinges upon this. As soon as one can get a man to stand at the crossways in such a position that there is no recourse but to choose, he will choose the right. Hence, if it should chance that, while you are in the course of reading this somewhat lengthy dissertation, which again I send you in the form of a letter, you were to feel that the instant for choice had come, then throw the rest of this away, never concern yourself about it, you have lost nothing

—but choose and you shall see what validity there is in this act, yea, no young girl can be so happy with the choice of her heart as is a man who knows how to choose. So then, one either has to live aesthetically or one has to live ethically. In this alternative, as I have said, there is not yet in the strictest sense any question of a choice; for he who lives aesthetically does not choose, and he who after the ethical has manifested itself to him chooses the aesthetical is not living aesthetically, for he is sinning and is subject to ethical determinants even though his life may be described as un-ethical. Lo, this is, as it were, a *character indelebilis* impressed upon the ethical, that though it modestly places itself on a level with the aesthetical, it is nevertheless that which makes the choice a choice. And this is the piti-ful thing to one who contemplates human life, that so many live on in a quiet state of perdition; they outlive themselves, not in the sense that the content of life is successively unfolding and now is possessed in this ex-panded state, but they live their lives, as it were, outside of themselves, they vanish like shadows, their immortal soul is blown away, and they are not alarmed by the problem of its immortality, for they are already in a state of dissolution before they die. They do not live aesthetically, but neither has the ethical manifested itself in its entirety, so they have not ex-actly rejected it either, they therefore are not sinning, except in so far as it is sin not to be either one thing or the other; neither are they ever in doubt about their immortality, for he who deeply and sincerely is in doubt of it on his own behalf will surely find the right. *On his own behalf,* I say, and surely it is high time to utter a warning against the great-hearted, heroic objectivity with which many thinkers think on behalf of others and not on their own behalf. If one would call this which I here require selfishness, I would reply that this comes from the fact that people have no conception of what this "self" is, and that it would be of very little use to a man if he were to gain the whole world and lose himself, and that it must necessarily be a poor proof which does not first of all convince the man who presents it.

My either/or does not in the first instance denote the choice between good and evil; it denotes the choice whereby one chooses good *and* evil/or excludes them. Here the question is under what determinants one would contemplate the whole of existence and would himself live. That the man who chooses good and evil chooses the good is indeed true, but this be-comes evident only afterwards; for the aesthetical is not the evil but neu-trality, and that is the reason why I affirmed that it is the ethical which constitutes the choice. It is, therefore, not so much a question of choosing between willing the good *or* the evil, as of choosing to will, but by this in turn the good and the evil are posited. He who chooses the ethical chooses the good, but here the good is entirely abstract, only its being is posited, and hence it does not follow by any means that the chooser cannot in turn choose the evil, in spite of the fact that he chose the good. Here you see again how important it is that a choice be made, and that the crucial thing is not deliberation but the baptism of the will which lifts up the choice into the ethical. The longer the time that elapses, the more difficult it is to choose, for the soul is constantly attached to one side of the dilemma, and it becomes more and more difficult, therefore, to tear oneself loose. And yet this is necessary if one is to choose and is therefore of the utmost importance if a choice signifies something. . . .

The Task of Becoming Subjective

Objectively we consider only the matter at issue, subjectively we have regard to the subject and his subjectivity; and behold, precisely this subjectivity is the matter at issue. This must constantly be borne in mind, namely, that the subjective problem is not something about an objective issue, but is the subjectivity itself. For since the problem in question poses a decision, and since all decisiveness inheres in subjectivity, it is essential that every trace of an objective issue should be eliminated. If any such trace remains, it is at once a sign that the subject seeks to shirk something of the pain and crisis of the decision; that is, he seeks to make the problem to some degree objective. If the Introduction still awaits the appearance of another work before bringing the matter up for judgment, if the System still lacks a paragraph, if the speaker has still another argument up his sleeve, it follows that the decision is postponed. Hence we do not here raise the question of the truth of Christianity in the sense that when this has been determined, the subject is assumed ready and willing to accept it. No, the question is as to the mode of the subject's acceptance; and it must be regarded as an illusion rooted in the demoralization which remains ignorant of the subjective nature of the decision, or as an evasion springing from the disingenuousness which seeks to shirk the decision by an objective mode of approach, wherein there can in all eternity be no decision, to assume that the transition from something objective to the subjective acceptance is a direct transition, following upon the objective deliberation as a matter of course. On the contrary, the subjective acceptance is precisely the decisive factor; and an objective acceptance of Christianity (*sit venia verbo*) is paganism or thoughtlessness. . . .

The objective tendency, which proposes to make everyone an observer, and in its maximum to transform him into so objective an observer that he becomes almost a ghost, scarcely to be distinguished from the tremendous spirit of the historical past—this tendency naturally refuses to know or lis-

From pp. 115–17 of Søren Kierkegaard, *Concluding Unscientific Postscript,* translated by David F. Swenson and Walter Lowrie. Reprinted by permission of Princeton University Press. Copyright 1941.

ten to anything except what stands in relation to itself. If one is so fortunate as to be of service within the given presupposition, by contributing one or another item of information concerning a tribe perhaps hitherto unknown, which is to be provided with a flag and given a place in the paragraph parade; if one is competent within the given presupposition to assign China a place different from the one it has hitherto occupied in the systematic procession,—in that case one is made welcome. But everything else is divinity-school prattle. For it is regarded as a settled thing, that the objective tendency in direction of intellectual contemplation, is, in the newer linguistic usage, the *ethical* answer to the question of what I *ethically* have to do; and the task assigned to the contemplative nineteenth century is world history. The objective tendency is the way and the truth; the ethical is, becoming an observer! That the individual must become an observer, is the *ethical* answer to the problem of life—or else one is compelled to assume that there is no ethical question at all, and in so far no ethical answer.

Let us here in all simplicity seek to bring clearly before our minds a little subjective doubt with respect to the tendency toward objectivity. Just as the *Fragments* called attention to an introductory consideration, which might suitably be reflected upon before proceeding to exhibit in the concrete the world-historic progress of the Idea, so I now propose to dwell a bit upon a little introductory consideration bearing upon the objective tendency. The question I would ask is this: *What conclusion would inevitably force itself upon Ethics, if the becoming a subject were not the highest task confronting a human being?* And to what conclusion would Ethics be forced? Aye, it would, of course, be driven to despair. But what does the System care about that? It is consistent enough not to include an Ethic in its systematic scheme.

The Idea of a universal history tends to a greater and greater systematic concentration of everything. A Sophist has said that he could carry the whole world in a nutshell, and this is what modern surveys of world history seem to realize: the survey becomes more and more compendious. It is not my intention to show how comical this is, but rather to try to make it clear, through the elaboration of several different thoughts all leading to the same end, what objection Ethics and the ethical have to raise against this entire order of things. For in our age it is not merely an individual scholar or thinker here and there who concerns himself with universal history; the whole age loudly demands it. Nevertheless, Ethics and the ethical, as constituting the essential anchorage for all individual existence, have an indefeasible claim upon every existing individual; so indefeasible a claim, that whatever a man may accomplish in the world, even to the most astonishing of achievements, it is none the less quite dubious in its significance, unless the individual has been ethically clear when he made his choice, has ethically clarified his choice to himself. The ethical quality is jealous for its own integrity, and is quite unimpressed by the most astounding quantity.

It is for this reason that Ethics looks upon all world-historical knowledge with a degree of suspicion, because it may so easily become a snare, a demoralizing aesthetic diversion for the knowing subject, in so far as the distinction between what does or does not have historical significance obeys a quantitative dialectic. As a consequence of this fact, the absolute ethical distinction between good and evil tends for the historical survey to be neutralized in the aesthetic-metaphysical determination of the great and significant, to which category the bad has equal admittance with the good. In the case of what has world-historic significance, another set of factors plays an essential rôle, factors which do not obey an ethical dialectic: accidents, circumstances, the play of forces entering into the historic totality that modifyingly incorporates the deed of the individual so as to transform it into something that does not directly belong to him. Neither by willing the good with all his strength, nor by satanic obduracy in willing what is evil, can a human being be assured of historical significance. Even in the case of misfortune the principle holds, that it is necessary to be fortunate in order that one's misfortune may obtain world-historical significance. How then does an individual acquire historical significance? By means of what from the ethical point of view is accidental. But Ethics regards as unethical the transition by which an individual renounces the ethical quality in order to try his fortune, longingly, wishingly, and so forth, in the quantitative and non-ethical.

An age or an individual may be immoral in many different ways. It is also a form of immorality, or at any rate constitutes a temptation, for an individual to practise too assiduous an intercourse with the historical, since this may readily lead him to crave world-historical significance when the time comes for him to act for himself. Through an absorption in constant contemplation of the accidental, of that *accessorium* through which historical figures become historical, one may easily be misled into confusing this with the ethical; and instead of concerning oneself infinitely with the ethical, one may existentially be betrayed into developing an unwholesome, frivolous and cowardly concern for the accidental. This is possibly the reason why the contemporary age is seized with discontent when it confronts the necessity of action, because it has been spoiled by the habit of contemplation; and from this proceed, perhaps, the many sterile attempts to count for more than one by socially clubbing together, hoping thus numerically to overawe the spirit of history. Demoralized by too assiduous an absorption in world-historical considerations, people no longer have any will for anything except what is world-historically significant, no concern for anything but the accidental, the world-historical outcome, instead of concerning themselves solely with the essential, the inner spirit, the ethical, freedom. . . .

For the study of the ethical, every man is assigned to himself. His own self is as material for this study more than sufficient; aye, this is the only place where *he* can study it with any assurance of certainty. Even another human being with whom he lives can reveal himself to his observation only through the external; and in so far the interpretation is necessarily affected with ambiguities. But the more complicated the externality in which the ethical inwardness is reflected, the more difficult becomes the problem of observation, until it finally loses its way in something quite different, namely, in the aesthetic. The apprehension of the historical process therefore readily becomes a half poetic contemplative astonishment, rather than a sober ethical perspicuity. It becomes more and more difficult even for a judge to find a clear way through the mazes of his case, the more significant the parties involved. And yet the judge does not have the responsibility of passing an ethical judgment, but merely a legal one, where guilt and innocence are subject to a dialectic which takes a quantitative account of the greater or the lesser in the circumstances, and is partly determined by an accidental reference to the consequences. There is a far wider scope for confusion in connection with the contemplation of the world-process, where it often seems as if good and evil were subject to a quantitative dialectic, and that there is a certain magnitude of crime and cunning, affecting millions of individuals and entire peoples, where the ethical becomes as shy and diffident as a sparrow in a dance of cranes. . . .

Teleological Suspension of the Ethical

The ethical as such is the universal, and as the universal it applies to everyone, which may be expressed from another point of view by saying that it applies every instant. It reposes immanently in itself, it has nothing without itself which is its *telos*,[1] but is itself *telos* for everything outside it, and when this has been incorporated by the ethical it can go no further. Conceived immediately as physical and psychical, the particular individual is the individual who has his *telos* in the universal, and his ethical task is to express himself constantly in it, to abolish his particularity in order to become the universal. As soon as the individual would assert himself in his

---

[1] A Greek word meaning end or goal—which S.K. writes with Greek letters but I transliterate because it is of such common occurrence, and also because it is in the way of becoming an English word. [w.l.]

From pp. 79–92 of Søren Kierkegaard, *Fear and Trembling,* translated by Walter Lowrie. Reprinted by permission of Princeton University Press. Copyright 1941.

particularity over against the universal he sins, and only by recognizing this can he again reconcile himself with the universal. Whenever the individual after he has entered the universal feels an impulse to assert himself as the particular, he is in temptation (*Anfechtung*), and he can labor himself out of this only by penitently abandoning himself as the particular in the universal. If this be the highest thing that can be said of man and of his existence, then the ethical has the same character as man's eternal blessedness, which to all eternity and at every instant is his *telos,* since it would be a contradiction to say that this might be abandoned (i.e. teleologically suspended), inasmuch as this is no sooner suspended than it is forfeited, whereas in other cases what is suspended is not forfeited but is preserved precisely in that higher thing which is its *telos.*[2]

If such be the case, then Hegel is right when in his chapter on "The Good and the Conscience," [3] he characterizes man merely as the particular and regards this character as "a moral form of evil" which is to be annulled in the teleology of the moral, so that the individual who remains in this stage is either sinning or subjected to temptation (*Anfechtung*). On the other hand, Hegel is wrong in talking of faith, wrong in not protesting loudly and clearly against the fact that Abraham enjoys honor and glory as the father of faith, whereas he ought to be prosecuted and convicted of murder.

For faith is this paradox, that the particular is higher than the universal—yet in such a way, be it observed, that the movement repeats itself, and that consequently the individual, after having been in the universal, now as the particular isolates himself as higher than the universal. If this be not faith, then Abraham is lost, then faith has never existed in the world . . . because it has always existed. For if the ethical (i.e. the moral) is the highest thing, and if nothing incommensurable remains in man in any other way but as the evil (i.e. the particular which has to be expressed in the universal), then one needs no other categories besides those which the Greeks possessed or which by consistent thinking can be derived from them. This fact Hegel ought not to have concealed, for after all he was acquainted with Greek thought.

One not infrequently hears it said by men who for lack of losing themselves in studies are absorbed in phrases that a light shines upon the Christian world whereas a darkness broods over paganism. This utterance has always seemed strange to me, inasmuch as every profound thinker and every serious artist is even in our day rejuvenated by the eternal youth of the Greek race. Such an utterance may be explained by the consideration

---

[2] This is the conception of the ethical which is stressed in the Second Part of *Either/Or.* Perhaps Schrempf is right in affirming that what caused S.K. unnecessary agony was his acceptance of the Hegelian notion of the relation between the universal and the particular. [w.l.]

[3] Cf. *Philosophie des Rechts,* 2nd ed. (1840) §§129–141 and Table of Contents p. xix. [w.l.]

that people do not know what they ought to say but only that they must say something. It is quite right for one to say that paganism did not possess faith, but if with this one is to have said something, one must be a little clearer about what one understands by faith, since otherwise one falls back into such phrases. To explain the whole of existence and faith along with it, without having a conception of what faith is, is easy, and that man does not make the poorest calculation in life who reckons upon admiration when he possesses such an explanation. . . .

Faith is precisely this paradox, that the individual as the particular is higher than the universal, is justified over against it, is not subordinate but superior—yet in such a way, be it observed, that it is the particular individual who, after he has been subordinated as the particular to the universal, now through the universal becomes the individual who as the particular is superior to the universal, for the fact that the individual as the particular stands in an absolute relation to the absolute. This position cannot be mediated, for all mediation comes about precisely by virtue of the universal; it is and remains to all eternity a paradox, inaccessible to thought. And yet faith is this paradox—or else (these are the logical deductions which I would beg the reader to have *in mente* at every point, though it would be too prolix for me to reiterate them on every occasion)—or else there never has been faith . . . precisely because it always has been. In other words, Abraham is lost.

That for the particular individual this paradox may easily be mistaken for a temptation (*Anfechtung*) is indeed true, but one ought not for this reason to conceal it. That the whole constitution of many persons may be such that this paradox repels them is indeed true, but one ought not for this reason to make faith something different in order to be able to possess it, but ought rather to admit that one does not possess it, whereas those who possess faith should take care to set up certain criteria so that one might distinguish the paradox from a temptation (*Anfechtung*).

Now the story of Abraham contains such a teleological suspension of the ethical. There have not been lacking clever pates and profound investigators who have found analogies to it. Their wisdom is derived from the pretty proposition that at bottom everything is the same. If one will look a little more closely, I have not much doubt that in the whole world one will not find a single analogy (except a later instance which proves nothing), if it stands fast that Abraham is the representative of faith, and that faith is normally expressed in him whose life is not merely the most paradoxical that can be thought but so paradoxical that it cannot be thought at all. He acts by virtue of the absurd, for it is precisely absurd that he as the particular is higher than the universal. This paradox cannot be mediated; for as soon as he begins to do this he has to admit that he was in temptation (*Anfechtung*), and if such was the case, he never gets to the point of sacrificing Isaac, or, if he has sacrificed Isaac, he must turn back repentantly to the universal. By virtue of the absurd he gets Isaac again. Abraham is therefore at no instant a tragic hero but something quite different, either a murderer or a believer. The middle term which saves the tragic hero, Abraham has not. Hence it is that I can understand the tragic hero but cannot understand Abraham, though in a certain crazy sense I admire him more than all other men.

Abraham's relation to Isaac, ethically speaking, is quite simply expressed by saying that a father shall love his son more dearly than himself. Yet within its own compass the ethical has various gradations. Let us see whether in this story there is to be found any higher expression for the ethical such as would ethically explain his conduct, ethically justify him in suspending the ethical obligation toward his son, without in this search going beyond the teleology of the ethical.

When an undertaking in which a whole nation is concerned is hindered,[4] when such an enterprise is brought to a standstill by the disfavor of heaven, when the angry deity sends a calm which mocks all efforts, when the seer performs his heavy task and proclaims that the deity demands a young maiden as a sacrifice—then will the father heroically make the sacrifice. He will magnanimously conceal his pain, even though he might wish that he were "the lowly man who dares to weep," [5] not the king who must act royally. And though solitary pain forces its way into his breast, he has only three confidants among the people, yet soon the whole nation will be cognizant of his pain, but also cognizant of his exploit, that for the welfare of the whole he was willing to sacrifice her, his daughter, the lovely young maiden. O charming bosom! O beautiful cheeks! O bright golden hair! (v.687). And the daughter will affect him by her tears, and the father will turn his face away, but the hero will raise the knife.—When the report of this reaches the ancestral home, then will the beautiful maidens of Greece blush with enthusiasm, and if the daughter was betrothed, her true love will not be angry but be proud of sharing in the father's deed, because the maiden belonged to him more feelingly than to the father.

When the intrepid judge [6] who saved Israel in the hour of need in one breath binds himself and God by the same vow, then heroically the young maiden's jubilation, the beloved daughter's joy, he will turn to sorrow, and with her all Israel will lament her maiden youth; but every free-born man will understand, and every stout-hearted woman will admire Jephtha, and every maiden in Israel will wish to act as did his daughter. For what good would it do if Jephtha were victorious by reason of his vow if he did not keep it? Would not the victory again be taken from the nation?

---

[4] The Trojan war. When the Greek fleet was unable to set sail from Aulis because of an adverse wind the seer Calchas announced that King Agamemnon had offended Artemis and that the goddess demanded his daughter Iphigenia as a sacrifice of expiation. [W.L.]

[5] See Euripides, *Iphigenia in Aulis*, v. 448 in Wilster's translation. Agamemnon says, "How lucky to be born in lowly station where one may be allowed to weep." The confidants mentioned below are Menelaus, Calchas and Ulysses. Cf. v. 107. [W.L.]

[6] Jephtha. Judges 11:30–40. [W.L.]

When a son is forgetful of his duty,[7] when the state entrusts the father with the sword of justice, when the laws require punishment at the hand of the father, then will the father heroically forget that the guilty one is his son, he will magnanimously conceal his pain, but there will not be a single one among the people, not even the son, who will not admire the father, and whenever the law of Rome is interpreted, it will be remembered that many interpreted it more learnedly, but none so gloriously as Brutus.

If, on the other hand, while a favorable wind bore the fleet on with swelling sails to its goal, Agamemnon had sent that messenger who fetched Iphigenia in order to be sacrificed; if Jephtha, without being bound by any vow which decided the fate of the nation, had said to his daughter, "Bewail now thy virginity for the space of two months, for I will sacrifice thee"; if Brutus had had a righteous son and yet would have ordered the lictors to execute him—who would have understood them? If these three men had replied to the query why they did it by saying, "It is a trial in which we are tested," would people have understood them better?

When Agamemnon, Jephtha, Brutus at the decisive moment heroically overcome their pain, have heroically lost the beloved and have merely to accomplish the outward sacrifice, then there never will be a noble soul in the world who will not shed tears of compassion for their pain and of admiration for their exploit. If, on the other hand, these three men at the decisive moment were to adjoin to their heroic conduct this little word, "But for all that it will not come to pass," who then would understand them? If as an explanation they added, "This we believe by virtue of the absurd," who would understand them better? For who would not easily understand that it was absurd, but who would understand that one could then believe it?

The difference between the tragic hero and Abraham is clearly evident. The tragic hero still remains within the ethical. He lets one expression of the ethical find its *telos* in a higher expression of the ethical; the ethical relation between father and son, or daughter and father, he reduces to a sentiment which has its dialectic in its relation to the idea of morality. Here there can be no question of a teleological suspension of the ethical itself.

With Abraham the situation was different. By his act he overstepped the ethical entirely and possessed a higher *telos* outside of it, in relation to which he suspended the former. For I should very much like to know how one would bring Abraham's act into relation with the universal, and whether it is possible to discover any connection whatever between what Abraham did and the universal . . . except the fact that he transgressed it. It was not for the sake of saving a people, not to maintain the idea of the state, that Abraham did this, and not in order to reconcile angry deities. If there could be a question of the deity being angry, he was angry only with

---

[7] The sons of Brutus, while their father was Consul, took part in a conspiracy to restore the king Rome had expelled, and Brutus ordered them to be put to death. [W.L.]

Abraham, and Abraham's whole action stands in no relation to the universal, is a purely private undertaking. Therefore, whereas the tragic hero is great by reason of his moral virtue, Abraham is great by reason of a purely personal virtue. In Abraham's life there is no higher expression for the ethical than this, that the father shall love his son. Of the ethical in the sense of morality there can be no question in this instance. In so far as the universal was present, it was indeed cryptically present in Isaac, hidden as it were in Isaac's loins, and must therefore cry out with Isaac's mouth, "Do it not! Thou art bringing everything to naught."

Why then did Abraham do it? For God's sake, and (in complete identity with this) for his own sake. He did it for God's sake because God required this proof of his faith; for his own sake he did it in order that he might furnish the proof. The unity of these two points of view is perfectly expressed by the word which has always been used to characterize this situation: it is a trial, a temptation (*Fristelse*).[8] A temptation—but what does that mean? What ordinarily tempts a man is that which would keep him from doing his duty, but in this case the temptation is itself the ethical . . . which would keep him from doing God's will. But what then is duty? Duty is precisely the expression for God's will.

Here is evident the necessity of a new category if one would understand Abraham. Such a relationship to the deity paganism did not know. The tragic hero does not enter into any private relationship with the deity, but for him the ethical is the divine, hence the paradox implied in his situation can be mediated in the universal.

Abraham cannot be mediated, and the same thing can be expressed also by saying that he cannot talk. So soon as I talk I express the universal, and if I do not do so, no one can understand me. Therefore if Abraham would express himself in terms of the universal, he must say that his situation is a temptation (*Anfechtung*), for he has no higher expression for that universal which stands above the universal which he transgresses.

Therefore, though Abraham arouses my admiration, he at the same time appalls me. He who denies himself and sacrifices himself for duty gives up the finite in order to grasp the infinite, and that man is secure enough. The tragic hero gives up the certain for the still more certain, and the eye of the beholder rests upon him confidently. But he who gives up the universal in order to grasp something still higher which is not the universal —what is he doing? Is it possible that this can be anything else but a temptation (*Anfechtung*)? And if it be possible . . . but the individual was mistaken—what can save him? He suffers all the pain of the tragic hero, he

---

[8] This is temptation in the sense we ordinarily attach to the word. For temptation in a higher sense (*Anfaegtelse*) I have in the translation of other books used the phrase "trial of temptation." Professor Swenson, in an important passage in the *Postscript*, preferred to use the German word *Anfechtung*. In this work I have used "temptation" and added the German word in parenthesis. The distinction between the two sorts of temptation is plainly indicated by S.K. in this paragraph. [W.L.]

brings to naught his joy in the world, he renounces everything . . . and perhaps at the same instant debars himself from the sublime joy which to him was so precious that he would purchase it at any price. Him the beholder cannot understand nor let his eye rest confidently upon him. Perhaps it is not possible to do what the believer proposes, since it is indeed unthinkable. Or if it could be done, but if the individual had misunderstood the deity—what can save him? The tragic hero has need of tears and claims them, and where is the envious eye which would be so barren that it could not weep with Agamemnon; but where is the man with a soul so bewildered that he would have the presumption to weep for Abraham? The tragic hero accomplishes his act at a definite instant in time, but in the course of time he does something not less significant, he visits the man whose soul is beset with sorrow, whose breast for stifled sobs cannot draw breath, whose thoughts pregnant with tears weigh heavily upon him, to him he makes his appearance, dissolves the sorcery of sorrow, loosens his corslet, coaxes forth his tears by the fact that in his sufferings the sufferer forgets his own. One cannot weep over Abraham. One approaches him with a *horror religiosus,* as Israel approached Mount Sinai.—If then the solitary man who ascends Mount Moriah, which with its peak rises heaven-high above the plain of Aulis, if he be not a somnambulist who walks securely above the abyss while he who is stationed at the foot of the mountain and is looking on trembles with fear and out of reverence and dread dare not even call to him—if this man is disordered in his mind, if he had made a mistake! Thanks and thanks again to him who proffers to the man whom the sorrows of life have assaulted and left naked—proffers to him the figleaf of the word with which he can cover his wretchedness. Thanks be to thee, great Shakespeare, who art able to express everything, absolutely everything, precisely as it is—and yet why didst thou never pronounce this pang? Didst thou perhaps reserve it to thyself—like the loved one whose name one cannot endure that the world should mention? For the poet purchases the power of words, the power of uttering all the dread secrets of others, at the price of a little secret he is unable to utter . . . and a poet is not an apostle, he casts out devils only by the power of the devil.

But now when the ethical is thus teleologically suspended, how does the individual exist in whom it is suspended? He exists as the particular in opposition to the universal. Does he then sin? For this is the form of sin, as seen in the idea. Just as the infant, though it does not sin, because it is not as such yet conscious of its existence, yet its existence is sin, as seen in the idea, and the ethical makes its demands upon it every instant. If one denies that this form can be repeated [in the adult] in such a way that it is not sin, then the sentence of condemnation is pronounced upon Abraham. How then did Abraham exist? He believed. This is the paradox which keeps him upon the sheer edge and which he cannot make clear to any other man, for the paradox is that he as the individual puts himself in an absolute relation to the absolute. Is he justified in doing this? His justification is once more the paradox; for if he is justified, it is not by virtue of anything universal, but by virtue of being the particular individual.

How then does the individual assure himself that he is justified? It is easy enough to level down the whole of existence to the idea of the state or the idea of society. If one does this, one can also mediate easily enough, for then one does not encounter at all the paradox that the individual as the individual is higher than the universal—which I can aptly express also by the thesis of Pythagoras, that the uneven numbers are more perfect than the even. If in our age one occasionally hears a rejoinder which is pertinent to the paradox, it is likely to be to the following effect: "It is to be judged by the result." A hero who has become a *skandalon* [9] to his contemporaries because they are conscious that he is a paradox who cannot make himself intelligible, will cry out defiantly to his generation, "The result will surely prove that I am justified!" In our age we hear this cry rather seldom, for as our age, to its disadvantage, does not produce heroes, it has also the advantage of producing few caricatures. When in our age one hears this saying, "It is to be judged according to the result," a man is at once clear as to who it is he has the honor of talking with. Those who talk thus are a numerous tribe, whom I will denominate by the common name of *Docents*. [10] In their thoughts they live secure in existence, they have a *solid* position and *sure* prospects in a well-ordered state, they have centuries and even millenniums between them and the concussions of existence, they do not fear that such things could recur—for what would the police say to that! and the newspapers! Their lifework is to judge the great, and to judge them according to the result. Such behavior toward the great betrays a strange mixture of arrogance and misery: of arrogance because they think they are called to be judges; of misery because they do not feel that their lives are even in the remotest degree akin to the great. Surely a man who possesses even a little *erectioris ingenii* [of the higher way of thinking] has not become entirely a cold and clammy mollusk, and when he approaches what is great it can never escape his mind that from the creation of the world it has been customary for the result to come last, and that, if one would truly learn anything from great actions, one must pay attention precisely to the beginning. In case he who should act were to judge himself according to the result, he would never get to the point of beginning. Even though the result may give joy to the whole world, it cannot help the hero, for he would get to know the result only when the whole thing was over, and it was not by this he became a hero, but he was such for the fact that he began.

Moreover, the result (inasmuch as it is the answer of finiteness to the infinite query) is in its dialectic entirely heterogeneous with the existence of

---

[9] This is the Scriptural word which we translate by "offense" or "stumbling block." Only Mr. Dru has preferred to use the identical word "scandal." [W.L.]

[10] *Docents* and *Privatdocents* (both of them German titles for subordinate teachers in the universities) were very frequently the objects of S.K.'s satire. He spoke more frequently of "the professor" after Martensen had attained that title. [W.L.]

the hero. Or is it possible to prove that Abraham was justified in assuming the position of the individual with relation to the universal . . . for the fact that he got Isaac by *miracle?* If Abraham had actually sacrificed Isaac, would he then have been less justified?

But people are curious about the result, as they are about the result in a book—they want to know nothing about dread, distress, the paradox. They flirt aesthetically with the result, it comes just as unexpectedly but also just as easily as a prize in the lottery; and when they have heard the result they are edified. And yet no robber of temples condemned to hard labor behind iron bars, is so base a criminal as the man who pillages the holy, and even Judas who sold his Master for thirty pieces of silver is not more despicable than the man who sells greatness.

It is abhorrent to my soul to talk inhumanly about greatness, to let it loom darkly at a distance in an indefinite form, to make out that it is great without making the human character of it evident—wherewith it ceases to be great. For it is not what happens to me that makes me great, but it is what I do, and there is surely no one who thinks that a man became great because he won the great prize in the lottery. Even if a man were born in humble circumstances, I would require of him nevertheless that he should not be so inhuman toward himself as not to be able to think of the King's castle except at a remote distance, dreaming vaguely of its greatness and wanting at the same time to exalt it and also to abolish it by the fact that he exalted it meanly. I require of him that he should be man enough to step forward confidently and worthily even in that place. He should not be unmanly enough to desire impudently to offend everybody by rushing straight from the street into the King's hall. By that he loses more than the King. On the contrary, he should find joy in observing every rule of propriety with a glad and confident enthusiasm which will make him frank and fearless. This is only a symbol, for the difference here remarked upon is only a very imperfect expression for spiritual distance. I require of every man that he should not think so inhumanly of himself as not to dare to enter those palaces where not merely the memory of the elect abides but where the elect themselves abide. He should not press forward impudently and impute to them kinship with himself; on the contrary, he should be blissful every time he bows before them, but he should be frank and confident and always be something more than a charwoman, for if he will not be more, he will never gain entrance. And what will help him is precisely the dread and distress by which the great are tried, for otherwise, if he has a bit of pith in him, they will merely arouse his justified envy. And what distance alone makes great, what people would make great by empty and hollow phrases, that they themselves reduce to naught.

Who was ever so great as that blessed woman, the Mother of God, the Virgin Mary? And yet how do we speak of her? We say that she was highly favored among women. And if it did not happen strangely that those who hear are able to think as inhumanly as those who talk, every young girl might well ask, "Why was not I too the highly favored?" And if I had nothing else to say, I would not dismiss such a question as stupid, for when it is a matter of favor, abstractly considered, everyone is equally entitled to it. What they leave out is the distress, the dread, the paradox. My thought is as pure as that of anyone, and the thought of the man who is able to think such things will surely become pure—and if this be not so, he may expect the dreadful; for he who once has evoked these images cannot be rid of them again, and if he sins against them, they avenge themselves with quiet wrath, more terrible than the vociferousness of ten ferocious reviewers. To be sure, Mary bore the child miraculously, but it came to pass with her after the manner of women, and that season is one of dread, distress and paradox. To be sure, the angel was a ministering spirit, but it was not a servile spirit which obliged her by saying to the other young maidens of Israel, "Despise not Mary. What befalls her is the extraordinary." But the Angel came only to Mary, and no one could understand her. After all, what woman was so mortified as Mary? And is it not true in this instance also that one whom God blesses He curses in the same breath? This is the spirit's interpretation of Mary, and she is not (as it shocks me to say, but shocks me still more to think that they have thoughtlessly and coquettishly interpreted her thus)—she is not a fine lady who sits in state and plays with an infant god. Nevertheless, when she says, "Behold the handmaid of the Lord"—then she is great, and I think it will not be found difficult to explain why she became the Mother of God. She has no need of worldly admiration, any more than Abraham has need of tears, for she was not a heroine, and he was not a hero, but both of them became greater than such, not at all because they were exempted from distress and torment and paradox, but they became great through these.[11]

It is great when the poet, presenting his tragic hero before the admiration of men, dares to say, "Weep for him, for he deserves it." For it is great to deserve the tears of those who are worthy to shed tears. It is great that the poet dares to hold the crowd in check, dares to castigate men, requiring that every man examine himself whether he be worthy to weep for the hero. For the waste-water of blubberers is a degradation of the holy.—But greater than all this it is that the knight of faith dares to say even to the noble man who would weep for him, "Weep not for me, but weep for thyself."

One is deeply moved, one longs to be back in those beautiful times, a sweet yearning conducts one to the desired goal, to see Christ wandering in the promised land. One forgets the dread, the distress, the paradox. Was it so easy a matter not to be mistaken? Was it not dreadful that this man who walks among the others—was it not dreadful that He was God? Was it not

---

[11] It would be interesting and edifying to make an anthology of the passages in which S.K. speaks of the Blessed Virgin; for surely no Protestant was ever so much engrossed in this theme, and perhaps no Catholic has appreciated more profoundly the unique position of Mary. [W.L.]

dreadful to sit at table with Him? Was it so easy a matter to become an Apostle? But the result, eighteen hundred years—that is a help, it helps to the shabby deceit wherewith one deceives oneself and others. I do not feel the courage to wish to be contemporary with such events, but hence I do not judge severely those who were mistaken, nor think meanly of those who saw aright.

I return, however, to Abraham. Before the result, either Abraham was every minute a murderer, or we are confronted by a paradox which is higher than all mediation.

The story of Abraham contains therefore a teleological suspension of the ethical. As the individual he became higher than the universal. This is the paradox which does not permit of mediation. It is just as inexplicable how he got into it as it is inexplicable how he remained in it. If such is not the position of Abraham, then he is not even a tragic hero but a murderer. To want to continue to call him the father of faith, to talk of this to people who do not concern themselves with anything but words, is thoughtless. A man can become a tragic hero by his own powers—but not a knight of faith. When a man enters upon the way, in a certain sense the hard way of the tragic hero, many will be able to give him counsel; to him who follows the narrow way of faith no one can give counsel, him no one can understand. Faith is a miracle, and yet no man is excluded from it; for that in which all human life is unified is passion,[12] and faith is a passion.

QUESTIONS FOR STUDY AND DISCUSSION

1. What is the difference between the aesthetic and the ethical? Which one is considered by Kierkegaard to be a "real" choice, and why?
2. What purpose does an either/or choice serve in Kierkegaard's philosophy?
3. Must ethics be completely interiorized for the "subjective thinker"? If so, does this result in mere subjectivism?
4. Why is Abraham considered to be a "Knight of Faith" rather than a murderer or a tragic hero? Can his conduct be ethically justified?

---

[12] Lessing has somewhere given expression to a similar thought from a purely aesthetic point of view. What he would show expressly in this passage is that sorrow too can find a witty expression. To this end he quotes a rejoinder of the unhappy English king, Edward II. In contrast to this he quotes from Diderot a story of a peasant woman and a rejoinder of hers. Then he continues: "That too was wit, and the wit of a peasant at that; but the situation made it inevitable. Consequently one must not seek to find the excuse for the witty expressions of pain and of sorrow in the fact that the person who uttered them was a superior person, well educated, intelligent, and witty withal, *for the passions make all men again equal*—but the explanation is to be found in the fact that in all probability everyone would have said the same thing in the same situation. The thought of a peasant woman a queen could have had and must have had, just as what the king said in that instance a peasant too would have been able to say and doubtless would have said." Cf. *Sämtliche Werke,* XXX. p. 223. [S.K.]

Friedrich Nietzsche

FRIEDRICH NIETZSCHE, the son and grandson of Protestant clergymen, was
born in 1844 in the Prussian province of Saxony. He entered the University of Bonn in 1864 as a student of theology and classical philology; he
soon abandoned theology, however, and devoted himself exclusively to
philological studies both at Bonn and at the University of Leipzig. In 1868
he received an appointment to the University of Basle but was forced to
retire from teaching in 1879 because of ill health. The next ten years were
spent in solitude, during which time he produced his major works, including *Thus Spake Zarathustra* (1883–85), *Beyond Good and Evil* (1886),
and *The Will to Power* (published posthumously in 1901). In 1889 he
suffered a mental breakdown, and he died in 1900.

Atheism and Its Results

The Madman. Have you not heard of that madman who lit a lantern in the
bright morning hours, ran to the market place, and cried incessantly, "I
seek God! I seek God!" As many of those who did not believe in God were
standing around just then, he provoked much laughter. Why, did he get
lost? said one. Did he lose his way like a child? said another. Or is he hiding? Is he afraid of us? Has he gone on a voyage? or emigrated? Thus they
yelled and laughed. The madman jumped into their midst and pierced them
with his glances.

"Whither is God" he cried. "I shall tell you. *We have killed him*—you
and I. All of us are his murderers. But how have we done this? How were
we able to drink up the sea? Who gave us the sponge to wipe away the
entire horizon? What did we do when we unchained this earth from its sun?
Whither is it moving now? Whither are we moving now? Away from all
suns? Are we not plunging continually? Backward, sideward, forward, in
all directions? Is there any up or down left? Are we not straying as through
an infinite nothing? Do we not feel the breath of empty space? Has it not
become colder? Is not night and more night coming on all the while? Must
not lanterns be lit in the morning? Do we not hear anything yet of the noise
of the gravediggers who are burying God? Do we not smell anything yet of

God's decomposition? Gods too decompose. God is dead. God remains dead. And we have killed him. How shall we, the murderers of all murderers, comfort ourselves? What was holiest and most powerful of all that the world has yet owned has bled to death under our knives. Who will wipe this blood off us? What water is there for us to clean ourselves? What festivals of atonement, what sacred games shall we have to invent? Is not the greatness of this deed too great for us? Must not we ourselves become gods simply to seem worthy of it? There has never been a greater deed; and whoever will be born after us—for the sake of this deed he will be part of a higher history than all history hitherto."

Here the madman fell silent and looked again at his listeners; and they too were silent and stared at him in astonishment. At last he threw his lantern on the ground, and it broke and went out. "I come too early," he said then; "my time has not come yet. This tremendous event is still on its way, still wandering—it has not yet reached the ears of man. Lightning and thunder require time, the light of the stars requires time, deeds require time even after they are done, before they can be seen and heard. This deed is still more distant from them than the most distant stars—*and yet they have done it themselves.*"

It has been related further that on that same day the madman entered divers churches and there sang his *requiem aeternam deo.* Led out and called to account, he is said to have replied each time, "What are these churches now if they are not the tombs and sepulchers of God?"

Truth and Its Origin

You desire to *live* "according to Nature"? Oh, you noble Stoics, what fraud of words! Imagine to yourselves a being like Nature, boundlessly extravagant, boundlessly indifferent, without purpose or consideration, without pity or justice, at once fruitful and barren and uncertain: imagine to yourselves *indifference* as a power—how *could* you live in accordance with such indifference? To live—is not that just endeavouring to be otherwise than this Nature? Is not living valuing, preferring, being unjust, being limited, endeavouring to be different? And granted that your imperative, "living according to Nature," means actually the same as "living according to life"—how could you do *differently?* Why should you make a principle out of what you yourselves are, and must be? In reality, however, it is quite otherwise with you: while you pretend to read with rapture the canon of your law in Nature, you want something quite the contrary, you extraordi-

From pp. 388–89 of Friedrich Nietzsche, *Beyond Good and Evil,* translated by Helen Zimmern, in *The Philosophy of Nietzsche.* Copyright 1954 by Random House, Inc. Reprinted by permission of George Allen and Unwin Ltd., London.

nary stage-players and self-deluders! In your pride you wish to dictate your morals and ideals to Nature, to Nature herself, and to incorporate them therein; you insist that it shall be Nature "according to the Stoa," and would like everything to be made after your own image, as a vast, eternal glorification and generalism of Stoicism! With all your love for truth, you have forced yourselves so long, so persistently, and with such hypnotic rigidity to see Nature *falsely,* that is to say, Stoically, that you are no longer able to see it otherwise—and to crown all, some unfathomable super-ciliousness gives you the Bedlamite hope that *because* you are able to tyrannise over yourselves—Stoicism is self-tyranny—Nature will also allow herself to be tyrannised over: is not the Stoic a *part* of Nature? . . . But this is an old and everlasting story: what happened in old times with the Stoics still happens today, as soon as ever a philosophy begins to believe in itself. It always creates the world in its own image; it cannot do otherwise; philosophy is this tyrannical impulse itself, the most spiritual Will to Power, the will to "creation of the world," the will to the *causa prima.*

Evaluation of Religion

The philosopher, as *we* free spirits understand him—as the man of the greatest responsibility, who has the conscience for the general development of mankind,—will use religion for his disciplining and educating work, just as he will use the contemporary political and economic conditions. The selecting and disciplining influence—destructive, as well as creative and fashioning—which can be exercised by means of religion is manifold and varied, according to the sort of people placed under its spell and protection. For those who are strong and independent, destined and trained to command, in whom the judgment and skill of a ruling race is incorporated, religion is an additional means for overcoming resistance in the exercise of authority—as a bond which binds rulers and subjects in common, betraying and surrendering to the former the conscience of the latter, their inmost heart, which would fain escape obedience. And in the case of the unique natures of noble origin, if by virtue of superior spirituality they should incline to a more retired and contemplative life, reserving to themselves only the more refined forms of government (over chosen disciples or members of an order), religion itself may be used as a means for obtaining peace from the noise and trouble of managing *grosser* affairs, and for securing immunity from the *unavoidable* filth of all political agitation. The Brahmins, for instance, understood this fact. With the help of a religious

From pp. 446–50 and 476–79 of Friedrich Nietzsche, *Beyond Good and Evil,* translated by Helen Zimmern, in *The Philosophy of Nietzsche.* Copyright 1954 by Random House, Inc. Reprinted by permission of George Allen and Unwin Ltd., London.

organisation, they secured to themselves the power of nominating kings for the people, while their sentiments prompted them to keep apart and outside, as men with a higher and super-regal mission. At the same time religion gives inducement and opportunity to some of the subjects to qualify themselves for future ruling and commanding: the slowly ascending ranks and classes, in which, through fortunate marriage customs, volitional power and delight in self-control are on the increase. To them religion offers sufficient incentives and temptations to aspire to higher intellectuality, and to experience the sentiments of authoritative self-control, of silence, and of solitude. Asceticism and Puritanism are almost indispensable means of educating and ennobling a race which seeks to rise above its hereditary baseness and work itself upward to future supremacy. And finally, to ordinary men, to the majority of the people, who exist for service and general utility, and are only so far entitled to exist, religion gives invaluable contentedness with their lot and condition, peace of heart, ennoblement of obedience, additional social happiness and sympathy, with something of transfiguration and embellishment, something of justification of all the commonplaceness, all the meanness, all the semi-animal poverty of their souls. Religion, together with the religious significance of life, sheds sunshine over such perpetually harassed men, and makes even their own aspect endurable to them; it operates upon them as the Epicurean philosophy usually operates upon sufferers of a higher order, in a refreshing and refining manner, almost *turning* suffering *to account,* and in the end even hallowing and vindicating it. There is perhaps nothing so admirable in Christianity and Buddhism as their art of teaching even the lowest to elevate themselves by piety to a seemingly higher order of things, and thereby to retain their satisfaction with the actual world in which they find it difficult enough to live—this very difficulty being necessary.

To be sure—to make also the bad counter-reckoning against such religions, and to bring to light their secret dangers—the cost is always excessive and terrible when religions do *not* operate as an educational and disciplinary medium in the hands of the philosopher, but rule voluntarily and *paramountly,* when they wish to be the final end, and not a means along with other means. Among men, as among all other animals, there is a surplus of defective, diseased, degenerating, infirm, and necessarily suffering individuals; the successful cases, among men also, are always the exception; and in view of the fact that man is *the animal not yet properly adapted to his environment,* the rare exception. But worse still. The higher the type a man represents, the greater is the improbability that he will *succeed;* the accidental, the law of irrationality in the general constitution of mankind, manifests itself most terribly in its destructive effect on the higher orders of men, the conditions of whose lives are delicate, diverse, and difficult to determine. What, then, is the attitude of the two greatest religions abovementioned to the *surplus* of failures in life? They endeavour to preserve and keep alive whatever can be preserved; in fact, as the religions *for sufferers,* they take the part of these upon principle; they are always in favour of those who suffer from life as from a disease, and they would fain treat every other experience of life as false and impossible. However highly we may esteem this indulgent and preservative care (inasmuch as in applying to others, it has applied, and applies also to the highest and usually the most suffering type of man), the hitherto *paramount* religions—to give a general appreciation of them—are among the principal causes which have kept the type of "man" upon a lower level—they have preserved too much *that which should have perished.* One has to thank them for invaluable services; and who is sufficiently rich in gratitude not to feel poor at the contemplation of all that the "spiritual men" or Christianity have done for Europe hitherto! But when they had given comfort to the sufferers, courage to the oppressed and despairing, a staff and support to the helpless, and when they had allured from society into convents and spiritual penitentiaries the broken-hearted and distracted: what else had they to do in order to work systematically in that fashion, and with a good conscience, for the preservation of all the sick and suffering, which means, in deed and in truth, to work for *the deterioration of the European race?* To *reverse* all estimates of value—*that* is what they had to do! And to shatter the strong, to spoil great hopes, to cast suspicion on the delight in beauty, to break down everything autonomous, manly, conquering, and imperious—all instincts which are natural to the highest and most successful type of "man"—into uncertainty, distress of conscience, and self-destruction; forsooth, to invert all love of the earthly and of supremacy over the earth, into hatred of the earth and earthly things—*that* is the task the Church imposed on itself, and was obliged to impose, until, according to its standard of value, "unworldliness," "unsensuousness," and "higher man" fused into one sentiment. If one could observe the strangely painful, equally coarse and refined comedy of European Christianity with the derisive and impartial eye of an Epicurean god, I should think one would never cease marvelling and laughing; does it not actually seem that some single will has ruled over Europe for eighteen centuries in order to make a *sublime abortion* of man? He, however, who, with opposite requirements (no longer Epicurean) and with some divine hammer in his hand, could approach this almost voluntary degeneration and stunting of mankind, as exemplified in the European Christian (Pascal, for instance), would he not have to cry aloud with rage, pity, and horror; "Oh, you bunglers, presumptuous pitiful bunglers, what have you done! Was that a work for your hands? How you have hacked and botched my finest stone! What have *you* presumed to do!"—I should say that Christianity has hitherto been the most portentous of presumptions. Men, not great enough, nor hard enough, to be entitled as artists to take part in fashioning *man;* men, not sufficiently strong and farsighted to *allow,* with sublime self-constraint, the obvious law of the thousandfold failures and perishings to prevail; men, not sufficiently noble to see the radically different grades of rank and intervals of rank that separate man from man:—*such* men, with their "equality before God," have hitherto swayed the destiny of Europe; until at last a dwarfed, almost ludicrous species has been produced, a gregarious animal, something obliging, sickly, mediocre, the European of the present day.

In contrast to *laisser-aller,* every system of morals is a sort of tyranny against "nature" and also against "reason"; that is, however, no objection, unless one should again decree by some system of morals, that all kinds of tyranny and unreasonableness are unlawful. What is essential and invaluable in every system of morals, is that it is a long constraint. In order to understand Stoicism, or Port-Royal, or Puritanism, one should remember the constraint under which every language has attained to strength and freedom—the metrical constraint, the tyranny of rhyme and rhythm. How much trouble have the poets and orators of every nation given themselves!—not excepting some of the prose writers of today, in whose ear dwells an inexorable conscientiousness—"for the sake of a folly," as utilitarian bunglers say, and thereby deem themselves wise—"from submission to arbitrary laws," as the anarchists say, and thereby fancy themselves "free," even free-spirited. The singular fact remains, however, that everything of the nature of freedom, elegance, boldness, dance, and masterly certainty, which exists or has existed, whether it be in thought itself, or in administration, or in speaking and persuading, in art just as in conduct, has only developed by means of the tyranny of such arbitrary law; and in all seriousness, it is not at all improbable that precisely this is "nature" and "natural"—and *not laisser-aller!* Every artist knows how different from the state of letting himself go, is his "most natural" condition, the free arranging, locating, disposing, and constructing in the moments of "inspiration"—and how strictly and delicately he then obeys a thousand laws, which, by their very rigidness and precision, defy all formulation by means of ideas (even the most stable idea has, in comparison therewith, something floating, manifold, and ambiguous in it). The essential thing "in heaven and in earth" is, apparently (to repeat it once more), that there should be long *obedience* in the same direction; there thereby results, and has always resulted in the long run, something which has made life worth living; for instance, virtue, art, music, dancing, reason, spirituality—anything whatever that is transfiguring, refined, foolish, or divine. The long bondage of the spirit, the distrustful constraint in the communicability of ideas, the discipline which the thinker imposed on himself to think in accordance with the rules of a church or a court, or conformable to Aristotelian premises, the persistent spiritual will to interpret everything that happened according to a Christian scheme, and in every occurrence to rediscover and justify the Christian God:—all this violence, arbitrariness, severity, dreadfulness, and unreasonableness, has proved itself the disciplinary means whereby the European spirit has attained its strength, its remorseless curiosity and subtle mobility; granted also that much irrecoverable strength and spirit had to be stifled, suffocated, and spoiled in the process (for here, as everywhere, "nature" shows herself as she is, in all her extravagant and *indifferent* magnificence, which is shocking, but nevertheless noble). That for centuries European thinkers only thought in order to prove something—nowadays, on the contrary, we are suspicious of every thinker who "wishes to prove something"—that it was always settled beforehand what *was to be* the result of their strictest thinking, as it was perhaps in the Asiatic astrology of former times, or as it is still at the present day in the innocent, Christian-moral explanation of immediate personal events "for the glory of God," or "for the good of the soul":—this tyranny, this arbitrariness, this severe and magnificent stupidity, has *educated* the spirit; slavery, both in the coarser and the finer sense, is apparently an indispensable means even of spiritual education and discipline. One may look at every system of morals in this light: it is "nature" therein which teaches to hate the *laisser-aller,* the too great freedom, and implants the need for limited horizons, for immediate duties—it teaches the *narrowing of perspectives,* and thus, in a certain sense, that stupidity is a condition of life and development. "Thou must obey some one, and for a long time; *otherwise* thou wilt come to grief, and lose all respect for thyself"—this seems to me to be the moral imperative of nature, which is certainly neither "categorical," as old Kant wished (consequently the "otherwise"), nor does it address itself to the individual (what does nature care for the individual!), but to nations, races, ages, and ranks, above all, however, to the animal "man" generally, to *mankind.*

Industrious races find it a great hardship to be idle: it was a master stroke of *English* instinct to hallow and begloom Sunday to such an extent that the Englishman unconsciously hankers for his week- and work-day again: —as a kind of cleverly devised, cleverly intercalated *fast,* such as is also frequently found in the ancient world (although, as is appropriate in southern nations, not precisely with respect to work). Many kinds of fasts are necessary; and wherever powerful influences and habits prevail, legislators have to see that intercalary days are appointed, on which such impulses are fettered, and learn to hunger anew. Viewed from a higher standpoint, whole generations and epochs, when they show themselves infected with any moral fanaticism, seem like those intercalated periods of restraint and fasting, during which an impulse learns to humble and submit itself—at the same time also to *purify* and *sharpen* itself; certain philosophical sects likewise admit of a similar interpretation (for instance, the Stoa, in the midst of Hellenic culture, with the atmosphere rank and overcharged with Aphrodisiacal odours).—Here also is a hint for the explanation of the paradox, why it was precisely in the most Christian period of European history, and in general only under the pressure of Christian sentiments, that the sexual impulse sublimated into love (*amour-passion*).

Master and Slave Morality

Corruption—as the indication that anarchy threatens to break out among the instincts, and that the foundation of the emotions, called "life," is convulsed—is something radically different according to the organisation in which it manifests itself. When, for instance, an aristocracy like that of France at the beginning of the Revolution, flung away its privileges with sublime disgust and sacrificed itself to an excess of its moral sentiments, it was corruption:—it was really only the closing act of the corruption which had existed for centuries, by virtue of which that aristocracy had abdicated step by step its lordly prerogatives and lowered itself to a *function* of royalty (in the end even to its decoration and parade-dress). The essential thing, however, in a good and healthy aristocracy is that it should *not* regard itself as a function either of the kingship or the commonwealth, but as the *significance* and highest justification thereof—that it should therefore accept with a good conscience the sacrifice of a legion of individuals, who, *for its sake,* must be suppressed and reduced to imperfect men, to slaves and instruments. Its fundamental belief must be precisely that society is *not* allowed to exist for its own sake, but only as a foundation and scaffolding, by means of which a select class of beings may be able to elevate themselves to their higher duties, and in general to a higher *existence*: like those sun-seeking climbing plants in Java—they are called *Sipo Matador,*—which encircle an oak so long and so often with their arms, until at last, high above it, but supported by it, they can unfold their tops in the open light, and exhibit their happiness.

To refrain mutually from injury, from violence, from exploitation, and put one's will on a par with that of others: this may result in a certain rough sense in good conduct among individuals when the necessary conditions are given (namely, the actual similarity of the individuals in amount of force and degree of worth, and their co-relation within one organisation). As soon, however, as one wished to take this principle more generally, and if possible even as *the fundamental principle of society,* it would immediately disclose what it really is—namely, a Will to the *denial* of life, a principle of dissolution and decay. Here one must think profoundly to the very basis and resist all sentimental weakness: life itself is *essentially* appropriation, injury, conquest of the strange and weak, suppression, severity, obtrusion of peculiar forms, incorporation, and at the least, putting it mild-

From pp. 577–82 of Friedrich Nietzsche, *Beyond Good and Evil,* translated by Helen Zimmern, in *The Philosophy of Nietzsche.* Copyright 1954 by Random House, Inc. Reprinted by permission of George Allen and Unwin Ltd., London.

est, exploitation;—but why should one for ever use precisely these words on which for ages a disparaging purpose has been stamped? Even the organisation within which, as was previously supposed, the individuals treat each other as equal—it takes place in every healthy aristocracy—must itself, if it be a living and not a dying organisation, do all that towards other bodies, which the individuals within it refrain from doing to each other: it will have to be the incarnated Will to Power, it will endeavour to grow, to gain ground, attract to itself and acquire ascendency—not owing to any morality or immorality, but because it *lives,* and because life *is* precisely Will to Power. On no point, however, is the ordinary consciousness of Europeans more unwilling to be corrected than on this matter; people now rave everywhere, even under the guise of science, about coming conditions of society in which "the exploiting character" is to be absent:—that sounds to my ears as if they promised to invent a mode of life which should refrain from all organic functions. "Exploitation" does not belong to a depraved, or imperfect and primitive society: it belongs to the *nature* of the living being as a primary organic function; it is a consequence of the intrinsic Will to Power, which is precisely the Will to Life.—Granting that as a theory this is a novelty—as a reality it is the *fundamental fact* of all history: let us be so far honest towards ourselves!

In a tour through the many finer and coarser moralities which have hitherto prevailed or still prevail on the earth, I found certain traits recurring regularly together, and connected with one another, until finally two primary types revealed themselves to me, and a radical distinction was brought to light. There is *master-morality* and *slave-morality;*—I would at once add, however, that in all higher and mixed civilisations, there are also attempts at the reconciliation of the two moralities; but one finds still oftener the confusion and mutual misunderstanding of them, indeed, sometimes their close juxtaposition—even in the same man, within one soul. The distinctions of moral values have either originated in a ruling caste, pleasantly conscious of being different from the ruled—or among the ruled class, the slaves and dependents of all sorts. In the first case, when it is the rulers who determine the conception "good," it is the exalted, proud disposition which is regarded as the distinguishing feature, and that which determines the order of rank. The noble type of man separates from himself the beings in whom the opposite of this exalted, proud disposition displays itself: he despises them. Let it at once be noted that in this first kind of morality the antithesis "good" and "bad" means practically the same as "noble" and "despicable";—the antithesis "good" and *"evil"* is of a different origin. The cowardly, the timid, the insignificant, and those thinking merely of narrow utility are despised; moreover, also, the distrustful, with their constrained glances, the self-abasing, the dog-like kind of men who let themselves be abused, the mendicant flatterers, and above all the liars:—it is a fundamental belief of all aristocrats that the common people are untruthful. "We truthful ones"—the nobility in ancient Greece called themselves. It is obvious that everywhere the designations of moral value were at first applied to *men,* and were only derivatively and at a later period applied to *actions;* it is a gross mistake, therefore, when historians of morals start questions like, "Why have sympathetic actions been praised?" The noble type of man regards *himself* as a determiner of values; he does not require to be approved of; he passes the judgment: "What is injurious to me is injurious in itself"; he knows that it is he himself only who confers honour on things; he is a *creator of values.* He honours whatever he recognises in himself: such morality is self-glorification. In the foreground there is the feeling of plenitude, of power, which seeks to overflow, the happiness of high tension, the consciousness of a wealth which would fain give and bestow:—the noble man also helps the unfortunate, but not—or scarcely —out of pity, but rather from an impulse generated by the super-abundance of power. The noble man honours in himself the powerful one, him also who has power over himself, who knows how to speak and how to keep silence, who takes pleasure in subjecting himself to severity and hardness, and has reverence for all that is severe and hard. "Wotan placed a hard heart in my breast," says an old Scandinavian Saga: it is thus rightly expressed from the soul of a proud Viking. Such a type of man is even proud of *not* being made for sympathy; the hero of the Saga therefore adds warningly: "He who has not a hard heart when young, will never have one." The noble and brave who think thus are the furthest removed from the morality which sees precisely in sympathy, or in acting for the good of others, or in *désintéressement,* the characteristic of the moral; faith in oneself, pride in oneself, a radical enmity and irony towards "selflessness," belong as definitely to noble morality, as do a careless scorn and precaution in presence of sympathy and the "warm heart."—It is the powerful who *know* how to honour, it is their art, their domain for invention. The profound reverence for age and for tradition—all law rests on this double reverence,—the belief and prejudice in favour of ancestors and unfavourable to newcomers, is typical in the morality of the powerful; and if, reversely, men of "modern ideas" believe almost instinctively in "progress" and the "future," and are more and more lacking in respect for old age, the ignoble origin of these "ideas" has complacently betrayed itself thereby. A morality of the ruling class, however, is more especially foreign and irritating to present-day taste in the sternness of its principle that one has duties only to one's equals; that one may act towards beings of a lower rank, towards all that is foreign, just as seems good to one, or "as the heart desires," and in any case "beyond good and evil": it is here that sympathy and similar sentiments can have a place. The ability and obligation to exercise prolonged gratitude and prolonged revenge—both only within the circle of equals,—artfulness in retaliation, *raffinement* of the idea in friendship, a certain necessity to have enemies (as outlets for the emotions of envy, quarrelsomeness, arrogance—in fact, in order to be a good *friend*):

all these are typical characteristics of the noble morality, which, as has been pointed out, is not the morality of "modern ideas," and is therefore at present difficult to realise, and also to unearth and disclose.—It is otherwise with the second type of morality, *slave-morality*. Supposing that the abused, the oppressed, the suffering, the unemancipated, the weary, and those uncertain of themselves, should moralise, what will be the common element in their moral estimates? Probably a pessimistic suspicion with regard to the entire situation of man will find expression, perhaps a condemnation of man, together with his situation. The slave has an unfavourable eye for the virtues of the powerful; he has a scepticism and distrust, *a refinement* of distrust of everything "good" that is there honoured—he would fain persuade himself that the very happiness there is not genuine. On the other hand, *those* qualities which serve to alleviate the existence of sufferers are brought into prominence and flooded with light; it is here that sympathy, the kind, helping hand, the warm heart, patience, diligence, humility, and friendliness attain to honour for here these are the most useful qualities, and almost the only means of supporting the burden of existence. Slave-morality is essentially the morality of utility. Here is the seat of the origin of the famous antithesis "good" and "evil":—power and dangerousness are assumed to reside in the evil, a certain dreadfulness, subtlety, and strength, which do not admit of being despised. According to slave-morality, therefore, the "evil" man arouses fear; according to master-morality, it is precisely the "good" man who arouses fear and seeks to arouse it, while the bad man is regarded as the despicable being. The contrast attains its maximum when, in accordance with the logical consequences of slave-morality, a shade of depreciation—it may be slight and well-intentioned—at last attaches itself to the "good" man of this morality; because, according to the servile mode of thought, the good man must in any case be the *safe* man: he is good natured, easily deceived, perhaps a little stupid, *un bonhomme*. Everywhere that slave-morality gains the ascendency, language shows a tendency to approximate the significations of the words "good" and "stupid."—At last fundamental difference: the desire for *freedom,* the instinct for happiness and the refinements of the feeling of liberty belong as necessarily to slave-morals and morality, as artifice and enthusiasm in reverence and devotion are the regular symptoms of an aristocratic mode of thinking and estimating.—Hence we can understand without further detail why love *as a passion*—it is our European specialty —must absolutely be of noble origin; as is well known, its invention is due to the Provençal poet-cavaliers, those brilliant, ingenious men of the *"gai saber,"* to whom Europe owes so much, and almost owes itself.

Considerations on the Origin of Morals

My thoughts concerning the *genealogy* of our moral prejudices—for they constitute the issue in this polemic—have their first, bald, and provisional expression in that collection of aphorisms entitled *Human, all-too-Human, a Book for Free Minds,* the writing of which was begun in Sorrento, during a winter which allowed me to gaze over the broad and dangerous territory through which my mind had up to that time wandered. This took place in the winter of 1876–77; the thoughts themselves are older.

They were in their substance already the same thoughts which I take up again in the following treatises:—we hope that they have derived benefit from the long interval, that they have grown riper, clearer, stronger, more complete. The fact, however, that I still cling to them even now, that in the meanwhile they have always held faster by each other, have, in fact, grown out of their original shape and into each other, all this strengthens in my mind the joyous confidence that they must have been originally neither separate, disconnected, capricious nor sporadic phenomena, but have sprung from a common root, from a fundamental *"fiat"* of knowledge, whose empire reached to the soul's depth, and that ever grew more definite in its voice, and more definite in its demands. That is the only state of affairs that is proper in the case of a philosopher.

We have no right to be *"disconnected"*; we must neither err "disconnectedly" nor strike the truth "disconnectedly." Rather with the necessity with which a tree bears its fruit, so do our thoughts, our values, our Yes's and No's and If's and Whether's, grow connected and interrelated, mutual witnesses of *one* will, *one* health, *one* kingdom, *one* sun—as to whether they are to *your* taste, these fruits of ours?—But what matters that to the trees? What matters that to us, us the philosophers?

Owing to a scrupulosity peculiar to myself, which I confess reluctantly,—it concerns indeed *morality,*—a scrupulosity, which manifests itself in my life at such an early period, with so much spontaneity, with so chronic a persistence and so keen an opposition to environment, epoch, precedent, and ancestry that I should have been almost entitled to style it my *"a priori"*—my curiosity and my suspicion felt themselves betimes bound to halt at the question, of what in point of actual fact was the *origin* of our "Good" and of our "Evil." Indeed, at the boyish age of thirteen the problem of the origin of Evil already haunted me: at an age "when games and God divide

From pp. 622–24 and 628–29 of Friedrich Nietzsche, *The Genealogy of Morals,* translated by Horace B. Samuel, in *The Philosophy of Nietzsche.* Copyright 1954 by Random House, Inc. Reprinted by permission of George Allen and Unwin Ltd., London.

one's heart," I devoted to that problem my first childish attempt at the literary game, my first philosophic essay—and as regards my infantile solution of the problem, well, I gave quite properly the honour to God, and made him the *father* of evil. Did my own *"a priori"* demand that precise solution from me? that new, immoral, or at least "amoral" *"a priori"* and that "categorical imperative" which was its voice (but, oh! how hostile to the Kantian article, and how pregnant with problems!), to which since then I have given more and more attention, and indeed what is more than attention. Fortunately I soon learned to separate theological from moral prejudices, and I gave up looking for a *supernatural* origin of evil. A certain amount of historical and philological education, to say nothing of an innate faculty of psychological discrimination *par excellence* succeeded in transforming almost immediately my original problem into the following one:— Under what conditions did Man invent for himself those judgments of values, "Good" and "Evil"? *And what intrinsic value do they possess in themselves?* Have they up to the present hindered or advanced human wellbeing? Are they a symptom of the distress, impoverishment, and degeneration of Human Life? Or, conversely, is it in them that is manifested the fullness, the strength, and the will of Life, its courage, its self-confidence, its future? On this point I found and hazarded in my mind the most diverse answers, I established distinctions in periods, peoples, and castes, I became a specialist in my problem, and from my answers grew new questions, new investigations, new conjectures, new probabilities; until at last I had a land of my own and a soil of my own, a whole secret world growing and flowering, like hidden gardens of whose existence no one could have an inkling—oh, how happy are we, we finders of knowledge, provided that we know how to keep silent sufficiently long.

This problem of the value of pity and of the pity-morality (I am an opponent of the modern infamous emasculation of our emotions) seems at the first blush a mere isolated problem, a note of interrogation for itself; he, however, who once halts at this problem, and learns how to put questions, will experience what I experienced:—a new and immense vista unfolds itself before him, a sense of potentiality seizes him like a vertigo, every species of doubt, mistrust, and fear springs up, the belief in morality, nay, in all morality, totters,—finally a new demand voices itself. Let us speak out this *new demand:* we need a *critique* of moral values, *the value of these values* is for the first time to be called into question—and for this purpose a knowledge is necessary of the conditions and circumstances out of which these values grew, and under which they experienced their evolution and their distortion (morality as a result, as a symptom, as a mask, as Tartuffism, as disease, as a misunderstanding; but also morality as a cause, as a remedy, as a stimulant, as a fetter, as a drug), especially as such a knowledge has neither existed up to the present time nor is even now generally desired. The value of these "values" was taken for granted as an indisputable fact, which was beyond all question. No one has, up to the present, exhibited the faintest doubt or hesitation in judging the "good man" to be of a higher value than the "evil man," of a higher value with regard specifically to human progress, utility, and prosperity generally, not forgetting the future. What? Suppose the converse were the truth! What? Suppose there lurked in the "good man" a symptom of retrogression, such as a danger, a temptation, a poison, a *narcotic,* by means of which the present *battened on the future!* More comfortable and less risky perhaps than its opposite, but also pettier, meaner! So that morality would really be saddled with the guilt, if the *maximum potentiality of the power and splendour* of the human species were never to be attained? So that really morality would be the danger of dangers?

Resentment and Its Implications

The revolt of the slaves in morals begins in the very principle of *resentment* becoming creative and giving birth to values—a resentment experienced by creatures who, deprived as they are of the proper outlet of action, are forced to find their compensation in an imaginary revenge. While every aristocratic morality springs from a triumphant affirmation of its own demands, the slave morality says "no" from the very outset to what is "outside itself," "different from itself," and "not itself": and this "no" is its creative deed. This volte-face of the valuing standpoint—this *inevitable* gravitation to the objective instead of back to the subjective—is typical of "resentment": the slave-morality requires as the condition of its existence an external and objective world, to employ physiological terminology, it requires objective stimuli to be capable of action at all—its action is fundamentally a reaction. The contrary is the case when we come to the aristocrat's system of values: it acts and grows spontaneously, it merely seeks its antithesis in order to pronounce a more grateful and exultant "yes" to its own self;—its negative conception, "low," "vulgar," "bad," is merely a pale late-born foil in comparison with its positive and fundamental conception (saturated as it is with life and passion), of "we aristocrats, we good ones, we beautiful ones, we happy ones."

When the aristocratic morality goes astray and commits sacrilege on reality, this is limited to that particular sphere with which it is *not* sufficiently acquainted—a sphere, in fact, from the real knowledge of which it disdainfully defends itself. It misjudges, in some cases, the sphere which it despises, the sphere of the common vulgar man and the low people: on the

From pp. 647–54 of Friedrich Nietzsche, *The Genealogy of Morals,* translated by Horace B. Samuel, in *The Philosophy of Nietzsche.* Copyright 1954 by Random House, Inc. Reprinted by permission of George Allen and Unwin Ltd., London.

other hand, due weight should be given to the consideration that in any case the mood of contempt, of disdain, of superciliousness, even on the supposition that it *falsely* portrays the object of its contempt, will always be far removed from that degree of falsity which will always characterise the attacks—in effigy, of course—of the vindictive hatred and revengefulness of the weak in onslaughts on their enemies. In point of fact, there is in contempt too strong an admixture of nonchalance, of casualness, of boredom, of impatience, even of personal exultation, for it to be capable of distorting its victim into a real caricature or a real monstrosity. Attention again should be paid to the almost benevolent *nuances* which, for instance, the Greek nobility imports into all the words by which it distinguishes the common people from itself; note how continuously a kind of pity, care, and consideration imparts its honeyed *flavour,* until at last almost all the words which are applied to the vulgar man survive finally as expressions for "unhappy," "worthy of pity" . . . —and how, conversely, "bad," "low," "unhappy" have never ceased to ring in the Greek ear with a tone in which "unhappy" is the predominant note: this is a heritage of the old noble aristocratic morality, which remains true to itself even in contempt. . . . The "well-born" simply *felt* themselves the "happy"; they did not have to manufacture their happiness artificially through looking at their enemies, or in cases to talk and lie themselves into happiness (as is the custom with all resentful men); and similarly, complete men as they were, exuberant with strength, and consequently *necessarily* energetic, they were too wise to dissociate happiness from action—activity becomes in their minds necessarily counted as happiness . . . —all in sharp contrast to the "happiness" of the weak and the oppressed, with their festering venom and malignity, among whom happiness appears essentially as a narcotic, a deadening, a quietude, a peace, a "Sabbath," an enervation of the mind and relaxation of the limbs,—in short, a purely *passive* phenomenon. While the aristocratic man lived in confidence and openness with himself, . . . the resentful man, on the other hand, is neither sincere nor naïf, nor honest and candid with himself. His soul *squints;* his mind loves hidden crannies, tortuous paths and backdoors, everything secret appeals to him as *his* word, *his* safety, *his* balm; he is past master in silence, in not forgetting, in waiting, in provisional self-depreciation and self-abasement. A race of such *resentful* men will of necessity eventually prove more *prudent* than any aristocratic race, it will honour prudence on quite a distinct scale, as, in fact, a paramount condition of existence, while prudence among aristocratic men is apt to be tinged with a delicate flavour of luxury and refinement; so among them it plays nothing like so integral a part as that complete certainty of function of the governing *unconscious* instincts, or as indeed a certain lack of prudence, such as a vehement and valiant charge, whether against danger or the enemy, or as those ecstatic bursts of rage, love, reverence, gratitude, by which at all times noble souls have recognised each other. When the resentment of the aristocratic man manifests

itself, it fulfils and exhausts itself in an immediate reaction, and consequently instills no *venom:* on the other hand, it never manifests itself at all
in countless instances, when in the case of the feeble and weak it would be
inevitable. An inability to take seriously for any length of time their enemies, their disasters, their *misdeeds*—that is the sign of the full strong
natures who possess a superfluity of moulding plastic force, that heals
completely and produces forgetfulness: a good example of this in the modern world is Mirabeau, who had no memory for any insults and meannesses
which were practised on him, and who was only incapable of forgiving because he forgot. Such a man indeed shakes off with a shrug many a worm
which would have buried itself in another; it is only in characters like these
that we see the possibility (supposing, of course, that there is such a possibility in the world) of the real *"love* of one's enemies." What respect for
his enemies is found, forsooth, in an aristocratic man—and such a reverence is already a bridge to love! He insists on having his enemy to himself
as his distinction. He tolerates no other enemy but a man in whose character there is nothing to despise and *much* to honour! On the other hand,
imagine the "enemy" as the resentful man conceives him—and it is here
exactly that we see his work, his creativeness; he has conceived "the evil
enemy," the "evil one," and indeed that is the root idea from which he now
evolves as a contrasting and corresponding figure a "good one," himself—
his very self!

The method of this man is quite contrary to that of the aristocratic man,
who conceives the root idea "good" spontaneously and straight away, that
is to say, out of himself, and from that material then creates for himself a
concept of "bad"! This "bad" of aristocratic origin and that "evil" out of
the cauldron of unsatisfied hatred—the former an imitation, an "extra,"
an additional nuance; the latter, on the other hand, the original, the beginning, the essential act in the conception of a slave-morality—these two
words "bad" and "evil," how great a difference do they mark, in spite of
the fact that they have an identical contrary in the idea "good." But the
idea "good" is *not* the same: much rather let the question be asked, "Who
is really evil according to the meaning of the morality of resentment?" In
all sternness let it be answered thus:—*just* the good man of the other
morality, just the aristocrat, the powerful one, the one who rules, but who
is distorted by the venomous eye of resentfulness, into a new colour, a new
signification, a new appearance. This particular point we would be the last
to deny: the man who learned to know those "good" ones only as enemies,
learned at the same time not to know them only as *"evil enemies,"* and the
same men who *inter pares* were kept so rigorously in bounds through convention, respect, custom, and gratitude, though much more through mutual
vigilance and jealousy *inter pares,* these men who in their relations with
each other find so many new ways of manifesting consideration, self-
control, delicacy, loyalty, pride, and friendship, these men are in reference

And now look at the other side, at those rare cases, of which I spoke, the most supreme idealists to be found nowadays among philosophers and scholars. Have we, perchance, found in them the sought-for *opponents* of the ascetic ideal, its *anti-idealists?* In fact, they *believe* themselves to be such, these "unbelievers" (for they are all of them that): it seems that this idea is their last remnant of faith, the idea of being opponents of this ideal, so earnest are they on this subject, so passionate in word and gesture;—but does it follow that what they believe must necessarily be *true?* We "knowers" have grown by degrees suspicious of all kinds of believers, our suspicion has step by step habituated us to draw just the opposite conclusions to what people have drawn before; that is to say, wherever the strength of a belief is particularly prominent to draw the conclusion of the difficulty of proving what is believed, the conclusion of its actual *improbability.* We do not again deny that "faith produces salvation": *for that very reason* we do deny that faith *proves* anything,—a strong faith, which produces happiness, causes suspicion of the object of that faith, it does not establish its "truth," it does establish a certain probability of—*illusion.* What is now the position in these cases? These solitaries and deniers of to-day; these fanatics in one thing, in their claim to intellectual cleanness; these hard, stern, continent, heroic spirits, who constitute the glory of our time; all these pale atheists, anti-Christians, immoralists, Nihilists; these sceptics, "ephectics," and "hectics" of the intellect (in a certain sense they are the latter, both collectively and individually); these supreme idealists of knowledge, in whom alone nowadays the intellectual conscience dwells and is alive—in point of fact they believe themselves as far away as possible from the ascetic ideal, do these "free, very free spirits": and yet, if I may reveal what they themselves cannot see—for they stand too near themselves: this ideal is simply *their* ideal, they represent it nowadays and perhaps no one else, they themselves are its most spiritualised product, its most advanced picket of skirmishers and scouts, its most insidious, delicate and elusive form of seduction.—If I am in any way a reader of riddles, then I will be one with this sentence: for some time past there have been no *free spirits; for they still believe in truth.* When the Christian Crusaders in the East came into collision with that invincible order of assassins, that order of free spirits *par excellence,* whose lowest grade lives in a state of discipline such as no order of monks has ever attained, then in some way or other they managed to get an inkling of that symbol and tally-word, that was reserved for the highest grade alone as their *secretum,* "Nothing is true, everything is allowed,"—in sooth, *that* was *freedom* of thought, thereby was *taking leave* of the very belief in truth. Has indeed any European, any Christian freethinker, ever yet wandered into this proposition and its labyrinthine *consequences?* Does he know *from experience* the Minotauros of this den?—I doubt it—nay, I know otherwise. Nothing is more really alien to these "monofanatics," these *so-called* "free spirits," than freedom and unfettering in that sense; in no respect are they more closely tied, the absolute fanaticism of their belief in truth is unparalleled. I know all this perhaps too much from experience at close quarters—that dignified philosophic abstinence to which a belief like that binds its adherents, that stoicism of the intellect, which eventually vetoes negation as rigidly as it does affirmation, that *wish* for standing still in front of the actual, the *factum brutum,* that fatalism in *"petits faits"* (*ce petit fatalisme,* as I call it), in which French Science now attempts a kind of moral superiority over German, this renunciation of interpretation generally (that is, of forcing, doctoring, abridging, omitting, suppressing, inventing, falsifying, and all the other *essential* attributes of interpretation)—all this, considered broadly, expresses the asceticism of virtue, quite as efficiently as does any repudiation of the senses (it is at bottom only a *modus* of that repudiation). But what forces it into that unqualified will for truth is the faith *in the ascetic ideal itself,* even though it take the form of its unconscious imperatives,—make no mistake about it, it is the faith, I repeat, in a *metaphysical* value, an *intrinsic* value of truth, of a character which is only warranted and guaranteed in this ideal (it stands and falls with that ideal). Judged strictly, there does not exist a science without its "hypotheses," the thought of such a science is inconceivable, illogical: a philosophy, a faith, must always exist first to enable science to gain thereby a direction, a meaning, a limit and method, *a right* to existence. (He who holds a contrary opinion on the subject—he, for example, who takes it upon himself to establish philosophy "upon a strictly scientific basis"—has first got to "turn upside-down" not only philosophy but also truth itself—the gravest insult which could possibly be offered to two such respectable females!) Yes, there is no doubt about it—and here I quote my *Joyful Wisdom,* cf. Book V. Aph. 344: "The man who is truthful in that daring and extreme fashion, which is the presupposition of the faith in science, *asserts thereby a different world* from that of life, nature, and history; and in so far as he asserts the existence of that different world, come, must he not similarly repudiate its counterpart, this world, *our* world? The belief on which our faith in science is based has remained to this day a metaphysical belief—even we knowers of today, we godless foes of metaphysics, we, too, take our fire from that conflagration which was kindled by a thousand-year-old faith, from that Christian belief, which was also Plato's belief, the belief that God is truth, that truth is *divine.* . . . But what if this belief becomes more and more incredible, what if nothing proves itself to be divine, unless it be error, blindness, lies—what if God Himself proved Himself to be our *oldest lie?"*—It is necessary to stop at this point and to consider the situation carefully. Science itself now *needs* a justification (which is not for a minute to say that there is such a justification). Turn in this context to the most ancient and the most modern philosophers: they all fail to realise the extent of the need of a justification on the part of the Will for Truth—here is a gap in every philosophy—what is it caused by? Because up to the present the ascetic ideal dominated all philosophy, because Truth was fixed as Being, as God, as the Supreme Court of Appeal, because Truth was not allowed to be a problem. Do you understand this "allowed"? From the minute that the belief in the God of the ascetic ideal is repudiated, there exists *a new problem:* the problem of the value of truth. The Will for Truth needed a critique—let us define by these words our own task—the value of truth is tentatively *to be called in question.* . . . (If this seems too laconically expressed, I recommend the reader to peruse again that passage from the *Joyful Wisdom* which bears the title, "How far we also are still pious," Aph. 344, and best of all the whole fifth book of that work, as well as the preface to *The Dawn of Day.*)

No! You can't get around me with science, when I search for the natural antagonists of the ascetic ideal, when I put the question: *"Where* is the opposed will in which the *opponent ideal* expresses itself?" Science is not, by a long way, independent enough to fulfil this function; in every department science needs an ideal value, a power which creates values, and in whose *service* it *can believe* in itself—science itself never creates values. Its relation to the ascetic ideal is not in itself antagonistic; speaking roughly, it rather represents the progressive force in the inner evolution of that ideal. Tested more exactly, its opposition and antagonism are concerned not with the ideal itself, but only with that ideal's outworks, its outer garb, its masquerade, with its temporary hardening, stiffening, and dogmatising—it makes the life in the ideal free once more, while it repudiates its superficial elements. These two phenomena, science and the ascetic ideal, both rest on the same basis—I have already made this clear—the basis, I say, of the same over-appreciation of truth (more accurately the same belief in the *impossibility* of valuing and of criticising truth), and consequently they are *necessarily* allies, so that, in the event of their being attacked, they must always be attacked and called into question together. A variation of the ascetic ideal inevitably entails a valuation of science as well; lose no time in seeing this clearly, and be sharp to catch it (*Art,* I am speaking provisionally, for I will treat it on some other occasion in greater detail,—art, I repeat, in which lying is sanctified and the *will for deception* has good conscience on its side, is much more fundamentally opposed to the ascetic ideal than is science: Plato's instinct felt this—Plato, the greatest enemy of art which Europe has produced up to the present. Plato *versus* Homer, that is the complete, the true antagonism—on the one side, the wholehearted "transcendental," the great defamer of life; on the other, its involuntary panegyrist, the *golden* nature. An artistic subservience to the service of the ascetic ideal is consequently the most absolute artistic *corruption* that there can be, though unfortunately it is one of the most frequent phases, for nothing is more corruptible than an artist.) Considered physiologically, moreover, science rests on the same basis as does the ascetic ideal: a certain *impoverishment of life* is the presupposition of the latter as of the former—add frigidity of the emotions, slackening of the *tempo,* the substitution of dialectic for instinct, *seriousness* impressed on mien and gesture (seriousness, that most unmistakable sign of strenuous metabolism, of struggling, toiling life). Consider the periods in a nation in which the learned man comes into prominence; they are the periods of exhaustion, often of sunset, of decay—the effervescing strength, the confidence in life, the confidence in the future are no more. The preponderance of the mandarins never signifies any good, any more than does the advent of democracy, or arbitration instead of war, equal rights for women, the religion of pity, and all the other symptoms of declining life. (Science handled as a problem! what is the meaning of science?—upon this point the Preface to the *Birth of Tragedy*.) No! this "modern science"—mark you this well—is at times the *best* ally for the ascetic ideal, and for the very reason that it is the ally which is most unconscious, most automatic, most secret, and most subterranean! They have been playing into each other's hands up to the present, have these "poor in spirit" and the scientific opponents of that ideal (take care, by the bye, not to think that these opponents are the antithesis of this ideal, that they are the *rich* in spirit—that they are *not;* I have called them the *hectic* in spirit). As for these celebrated *victories* of science; there is no doubt that they are victories—but victories over what? There was not for a single minute any victory among their list over the ascetic ideal, rather was it made stronger, that is to say, more elusive, more abstract, more insidious, from the fact that a wall, an outwork, that had got built on to the main fortress and disfigured its appearance, should from time to time be ruthlessly destroyed and broken down by science. Does any one seriously suggest that the downfall of the theological astronomy signified the downfall of that ideal?—Has, perchance, man grown *less in need* of a transcendental solution of his riddle of existence, because since that time his existence has become more random, casual, and superfluous in the *visible* order of the universe? Has there not been since the time of Copernicus an unbroken progress in the self-belittling of man and his *will* for belittling himself? Alas, his belief in his dignity, his uniqueness, his irreplaceableness in the scheme of existence, is gone—he has become animal, literal, unqualified, and unmitigated animal, he who in his earlier belief was almost God ("child of God," "demi-God"). Since Copernicus man seems to have fallen on to a steep plane—he rolls faster and faster away from the centre—whither? into nothingness? *into the "thrilling sensation of his own nothingness"?*—Well! this would be the straight way—to the *old* ideal?— *All* science (and by no means only astronomy, with regard to the humiliating and deteriorating effect of which Kant has made a remarkable confession, "it annihilates my own importance"), all science, natural as much as *unnatural*—by unnatural I mean the self-critique of reason—nowadays sets out to talk man out of his present opinion of himself, as though that opinion had been nothing but a bizarre piece of conceit; you might go so far as to say that science finds its peculiar pride, its peculiar bitter form of stoical ataraxia, in preserving man's *contempt of himself,* that state which it took so much trouble to bring about, as man's final and most serious claim to self-appreciation (rightly so, in point of fact, for he who despises is always "one who has not forgotten how to appreciate"). But does all this involve any real effort to *counteract* the ascetic ideal? Is it really seriously suggested that Kant's *victory* over the theological dogmatism about "God," "Soul," "Freedom," "Immortality," has damaged that ideal in any way (as the theologians have imagined to be the case for a long time past)?—And in this connection it does not concern us for a single minute, if Kant himself intended any such consummation. It is certain that from the time of Kant every type of transcendentalist is playing a winning game—they are emancipated from the theologicans; what luck!—he has revealed to them that secret art, by which they can now pursue their "heart's desire" on their own responsibility, and with all the respectability of science. Similarly, who can grumble at the agnostics, reverers, as they are, of the unknown and the absolute mystery, if they now worship *their very query* as God? (Xaver Doudan talks somewhere of the *ravages* which *l'habitude d'admirer l'inintelligible au lieu de rester tout simplement dans l'inconnu* has produced—the ancients, he thinks, must have been exempt from those ravages.) Supposing that everything, "known" to man, fails to satisfy his desires, and on the contrary contradicts and horrifies them, what a divine way out of all this to be able to look for the responsibility, not in the "desiring" but in "knowing!"—"There is no knowledge. *Consequently*—there is a God"; what a novel *elegantia syllogismi!* what a triumph for the ascetic ideal!

If you except the ascetic ideal, man, the *animal* man had no meaning. His existence on earth contained no end; "What is the purpose of man at all?" was a question without an answer; the *will* for man and the world was lacking; behind every great human destiny rang as a refrain a still greater "Vanity!" The ascetic ideal simply means this: that something *was lacking,* that a tremendous *void* encircled man—he did not know how to justify himself, to explain himself, to affirm himself, he *suffered* from the problem of his own meaning. He suffered also in other ways, he was in the main a *diseased* animal; but his problem was not suffering itself, but the lack of an answer to that crying question, *"To what purpose* do we suffer?" Man, the bravest animal and the one most inured to suffering, does *not* repudiate suffering in itself: he *wills* it, he even seeks it out, provided that he is shown a meaning for it, a *purpose* of suffering. *Not* suffering, but the senselessness of suffering was the curse which till then lay spread over humanity—*and the ascetic ideal gave it a meaning!* It was up till then the only meaning; but any meaning is better than no meaning; the ascetic ideal was in that connection the *"faute de mieux"* par excellence that existed at that time. In that ideal suffering *found an explanation;* the tremendous gap seemed filled; the door to all suicidal Nihilism was closed. The explanation—there is no doubt about it—brought in its train new suffering, deeper, more penetrating, more venomous, gnawing more brutally into life: it brought all suffering under the perspective of *guilt;* but in spite of all that—man was *saved* thereby, he had a *meaning,* and from henceforth was no more like a leaf in the wind, a shuttle-cock of chance, of nonsense, he could now "will" something—absoutely immaterial to what end, to what purpose, with what means he wished: *the will itself was saved.* It is absolutely impossible to disguise *what* in point of fact is made clear by every complete will that has taken its direction from the ascetic ideal: this hate of the human, and even more of the animal, and more still of the material, this horror of the senses, of reason itself, this fear of happiness and beauty, this desire to get right away from all illusion, change, growth, death, wishing and even desiring— all this means—let us have the courage to grasp it—a will for Nothingness, a will opposed to life, a repudiation of the most fundamental conditions of life, but it is and remains *a will!*—and to say at the end that which I said at the beginning—man will wish *Nothingness* rather than not wish *at all.*

QUESTIONS FOR STUDY AND DISCUSSION

1. Explain the Dionysian-Appollonian antithesis in Nietzsche.
2. In what sense should Nietzsche's concept of the Superman be understood? Support your views by referring to the text.
3. What is the meaning of the scene of "The Madman"?
4. Where, according to Nietzsche, lies the orgin of truth?
5. What is Nietzsche's evaluation of Christianity? Critically examine his position.
6. Concerning Nietzsche's famous dualism, master-morality and slave-morality, how does he trace the "origin" of these ethical positions? What are their implications and results?
7. What does resentment mean in Nietzsche's use of the term and what are its consequences?

Jean-Paul Sartre

JEAN-PAUL SARTRE was born in Paris in 1905. He studied at the Ecole
Normale Supérieure, from which he graduated in 1929, and taught for
several years at lycées in Le Havre and Paris. He joined the French army
in 1939; after being a prisoner of war for a year, he was active in the
French Resistance movement from 1941 to 1944. Since the war he has devoted himself to writing and to editing the journal he founded, *Les Temps
Modernes*. A brilliant stylist, he received the Nobel prize for literature in
1964, but he rejected the award, fearing that his work would be judged as
that of a Nobel prize winner rather than for itself. Numbered among his
essays, novels, plays, and reviews are two very important philosophical
works, *Being and Nothingness* (1943) and *Critique de la raison dialectique* (1960).

A New Individualism

Introduction to *Les Temps Modernes*

Any writer of bourgeois origin has faced the temptation of irresponsibility.
It has been a tradition in the career of letters for more than a century. The
author rarely connects his work with the payment for it. On the one hand,
he writes, he sings, he sighs; on the other hand, he is given money. They
are two facts with no apparent relation; the best he can do is to tell himself
that he is paid for sighing. So he considers himself more like a student who
has been granted a scholarship than a worker who receives the price of his
toil. The theoreticians of the Aesthetic and Realist schools confirmed him
in this opinion. Has it been noticed that they have the same aims and the
same origin? The main concern of the author who follows the principles of
the former is to write useless works. Provided they are gratuitous, absolutely rootless, he is not far from thinking that they are beautiful. Thus he
puts himself outside of society, or rather he agrees to belong to it only as a
consumer, precisely like the scholar. The Realist, too, likes to consume. As
for producing, it is another story. He has been told that science does not
care about the useful and he aims at the sterile impartiality of the scientist.
How many times have we been told that he "bent" his attention to the

Reprinted by permission of *Les Temps Modernes,* Paris.

milieus he wanted to describe! He bent his attention! Where was he then? Up in the air? The truth is that, uncertain about his social position, too timid to stand against the bourgeoisie who pay him, too lucid to accept it without restrictions, he chose to judge his century and convinced himself through this means that he remained outside of it, as the experimentalist is outside of the experimental system. Thus the indifference of pure science comes near the gratuity of Art for Art's Sake. It is not by chance that Flaubert is at the same time a pure stylist, reverent of form, and the father of naturalism; it is not by chance that the Goncourts pride themselves at the same time on their keen observation and on their artistic writing.

This inherited irresponsibility troubles many minds. They suffer from a literary bad conscience and no longer know whether writing is admirable or grotesque. The poet used to take himself for a prophet, it was honorable; later, he became an accursed social outcast, it was still all right. But today he has fallen into the ranks of specialists, and it is not without a certain uneasiness that he mentions the profession of *homme de lettres* after his name when he signs in a hotel. *Homme de lettres:* this association of words is enough, by itself, to cause anyone to shun writing; one thinks of an Ariel, a Vestal, an *enfant terrible;* also of a harmless maniac, related to weight-lifters or numismatists. All this is rather ridiculous. The man of letters writes while the others fight. One day, he is proud of it, he feels like the scholar guarding ideal values; the next day, he is ashamed of it, he finds that literature is very much like a kind of special affection. With the bourgeois who read him, he is aware of his dignity; but in front of the workers, who do not read him, he suffers from an inferiority complex, as it has been seen in 1936, at the *Maison de la Culture*. This complex is undoubtedly at the origin of what Paulhan calls *terrorism*. It led the Surrealists to scorn the literature on which they lived. After the First World War, it produced a particular lyricism. The best writers, the purest, publicly confessed what might humiliate them most and were satisfied when they had brought bourgeois disapproval upon themselves. They had written something which somewhat resembled an act because of its consequences. These isolated experiments could not prevent words from depreciating more and more. There was a crisis in rhetoric, then a crisis in language. Just before the Second World War, most literary men had resigned themselves to be only nightingales. Some authors went to extremes in their disgust for writing: outdoing their elders, they judged that it would not be enough to publish a merely useless book, they maintained that the secret aim of literature is to destroy language, and that the only way to attain it was to speak without saying anything. This unending silence was the fashion for a time, and the distribution service of *Hachette* sent condensed silence in the form of bulky novels to the station libraries. Today, things have gone so far that some writers, blamed or punished for renting their pen to the Germans, are seen to show painful surprise. "What," they say, "does what you write commit you?"

We do not want to be ashamed of writing and we do not feel like speaking to say nothing. Besides, should we wish it, we would not succeed. No one can succeed in this. Anything written has a meaning, even if this meaning is very far from the one intended by the author. For us, the writer is neither a Vestal nor an Ariel. He is "in it," whatever he does marked compromised, even in the farthest refuge. If at certain times he applies his art to forging trifles of sonorous inanity, it is a sign. It is because there is a crisis in letters, and probably in society, or because the power classes have directed him towards an activity of luxury without his knowing it, for fear he might join revolutionary troops. Who is Flaubert for us but a talented coupon-clipper, he who has been so violent against the bourgeois and thought he had withdrawn from the social machine? And does his minute art not imply the comfort of Croisset, the tender care of a mother or a niece, an orderly life, a successful business, dividends to cash regularly? It takes only a few years for a book to become a social fact that one questions like an institution or lists in statistics like a thing; it takes little time for it to blend with the furniture of a certain time, with its clothes, its hats, its means of transportation and its food. A historian will say about us: "They ate this, read that, dressed thus." The first railways, cholera, the Canuts rebellion, the novels of Balzac, the rapid growth of industry, equally contribute in characterizing the *Monarchie de Juillet*. All this has been said over and over again since Hegel. We want to draw from it practical conclusions. Since the writer has no means to escape, we want him tightly to embrace his time; it is his unique chance: it made itself for him and he is made for it. One regrets Balzac's indifference to the 1848 Revolution, Flaubert's frightened incomprehension of the Commune. One regrets it for *them*. There is something there that they missed forever. We do not want to miss anything in our time. There may be some more beautiful, but this one is our own. We have only *this* life to live, in the middle of *this* war, of *this* revolution perhaps. Let us not draw the conclusion that we speak for a kind of populism. It is quite the contrary. Populism is the child of old parents, the dull offspring of the last Realists. It is another attempt to get out of the game unharmed. We are convinced, on the contrary, that one *cannot* get out of the game unharmed. Should we be mute and quiet as stones, our very passivity would be an action. The abstention of the man who would devote his life to writing novels about the Hittites would be, in itself, taking up a position. The writer is *situated* in his time. Every word has consequences. Every silence, too. I hold Flaubert and Goncourt responsible for the repression which followed the Commune because they did not write one line to prevent it. One might say that it was not their business. But was the Calas trial Voltaire's business? Dreyfus' condemnation Zola's? the administration of the Congo, Gide's? Each of these authors, in a special circumstance of his life, measured his responsibility as a writer. The Occupation taught us ours. Since we act on our time by our very existence, we decide that this action will be deliberate. Still we have to make it more precise. A writer ordinarily wants to make his modest contribution to prepare the future. But there is a vague and conceptual future which concerns all humanity and about which we know nothing: Will history have an end? Will the sun go out? What will be the condition of man in the socialist regime of the year 3,000? We leave these dreams to the writers of science fiction. It is the future of *our* time that we must care about: a limited future, hardly to be distinguished from it—for a time, like a man, is first a future. It is made of its works in process, its enterprises, its immediate or long-range plans, its rebellions, its fights, its hopes. When will the war end? How will the country be re-equipped? How will international relations be handled? What will social reforms be? Will reactionary forces triumph? Will there be a revolution and which will it be? We make this future ours and we do not want any other. Certainly, some authors care less about the present and have shorter views. They wander among us as if they were absent. Where are they then? With their grand-nephews, they turn back to appreciate this dead era that was ours, of which they are the only survivors. But their idea is bad. Posthumous glory is always based on a misunderstanding. What do they know of these grand-nephews who will dig them out! Immortality is a terrible alibi. It is not easy to live with one foot on this side of the grave and the other on the other side. How to deal with current matters when one looks at them from so far away! How to get excited about a fight, how to enjoy the victory! All is equivalent. They look at us without seeing us. We are already dead for them—and they go back to the novel they write for people whom they will never see. They let immortality steal their lives from them. We write for our contemporaries, we do not want to look at our world with our future eyes—it would be the surest way to kill it—but with our living eyes, our real, perishable eyes. We do not wish to win our case on appeal and we have no use for a rehabilitation after our death. It is here and while we are still living that cases are won or lost.

However, we do not think of setting up a literary relativism. We care little about the purely historical. Besides, does the purely historical exist except in M. Seignobos' books? Each time discovers an aspect of human fate; in each time man chooses himself when confronted with others, with love, death, the world; and when parties argue over the disarmament of the *F.F.I.* [resistance forces] or the aid to the Spanish Republicans, it is this metaphysical choice, this singular and absolute project which is involved. Thus, by taking sides in the singularity of our time, we finally reach eternity, and it is our duty as writers to make one aware of the eternal values implied in these social and political debates. But we do not want to look for them in an intelligible heaven: they are only interesting in their present manifestations. Far from being relativists, we highly proclaim that man is an absolute. But he is so in his time, his milieu, on his earth. What is absolute, what a thousand years of history cannot destroy, is *this* irreplaceable, incomparable decision he makes at this moment about these circumstances.

Descartes is the absolute, the man who escapes us because he is dead, who lived in his time, who thought it out day after day with the only means he had, who formed his doctrine from a certain state of sciences, who knew Gassendi, Caterus and Mersenne, who loved a cross-eyed girl when he was a youth, who fought in war and who got a servant with child, who attacked not the principle of authority in general, but Aristotle's authority in particular, and who stands in his time, disarmed but not defeated, like a milestone. Cartesianism is the relative, this strolling philosophy passing from one century to another in which everyone finds what he puts in it. It is not by running after immortality that we shall become eternal: we shall not be absolutes for reflecting in our work some skinny principles, empty and worthless enough to pass through the centuries, but for passionately fighting in our time, for passionately loving it, and for electing to die entirely with it.

To sum it up, our intention is to participate in bringing forth certain changes in our society. By this, we do not mean a change in the souls: we gladly leave the direction of souls to authors who have a specialised *clientèle*. We who, without being materialist, have never differentiated the soul from the body and who only know an indecomposable reality: human reality, we side with those who want to change both the social condition of man and his conception of himself. Therefore, *à propos* of the coming social and political events, our review will take a stand in each case. It will not do it *politically,* that is to say it will not serve any party; but it will strive to isolate the conception of man on which the theses involved will be based, and it will give its opinion according to the conception it upholds. If we are able to keep to our intentions, if we are able to make some readers share our views, we will not feel over-proud; we simply will be glad to have regained a professional good conscience and to know that, at least for us, literature will have become again what it should never have ceased to be: a social function.

And, one will ask, what is this conception of man that you pretend to reveal to us? We will answer that it is a very common one and that we do not pretend to reveal it, but only to help in defining it. I will call this conception totalitarian. But, as the word may seem unfortunate, as it has been very unpopular lately, as it has been used to designate a type of oppressive and anti-democratic State and not the human person, some explanations ought to be given.

The bourgeois class, it seems to me, may intellectually be defined by its use of the analytic turn of mind, the initial postulate of which is that compounds necessarily are only a pattern of simple elements. In its hands, this postulate once was an offensive weapon which was used to dismantle the bulwarks of the Ancien Régime. Everything was analysed; in the same way, one reduced air and water to their elements, the mind to the sum of the impressions that compose it, society to the sum of the individuals who constitute it. The wholes vanished: they became abstract summations due to the chance of combinations. Reality took refuge in the ultimate terms of decomposition. These unvaryingly retain their essential properties—it is the second postulate of the analysis—whether they are one component in a compound or they exist in the free state. There was an immutable nature of oxygen, hydrogen, nitrogen, of the elementary impressions which make up our mind, there was an immutable nature of man. Man was man as a circle is a circle: once and for all; the individual, whether on the throne or in utter poverty, remained absolutely identical with himself because he was conceived after the pattern of an oxygen atom, which can combine with hydrogen to become water, with nitrogen to become air, without changing its inner structure. These principles presided over the Declaration of the Rights of Man. In the society conceived by the analytical mind, the individual, a solid and permanent particle, a vehicle of human nature, lives like one pea in a can of peas: he is all round, closed within himself, incommunicable. All men are *equal:* they all participate equally of the essence of man. All men are *brothers:* fraternity is a passive link between distinct molecules, instead of a solidarity of class or action that the analytical turn of mind cannot even conceive. It is a relation entirely external and purely sentimental which hides the simple juxtaposition of the individuals in the analytical society. All men are *free:* free to *be men,* of course. Which means that the action of the politician must be negative: he has nothing to do with human nature; his task is to remove any obstacle to its thriving. Thus, wishing to destroy the divine law, the right of birth and blood, birthright, all these rights based on the idea that there are differences in nature between people, the bourgeoisie blended its cause with the cause of analysis and built up the myth of the universal for its own use. Unlike the contemporary revolutionaries, it carried out its claims only by shedding its class conscience: the members of the Third Estate at the Constituent Assembly were bourgeois insofar as they looked at themselves simply as men.

After a hundred and fifty years, the analytical turn of mind remains the official doctrine of the bourgeois democracy, only it has become a defensive weapon. The interest of the bourgeoisie is still to deceive itself about classes as it used to about the synthetic reality of the institutions of the old régime. It persists in seeing only men, in proclaiming the identity of human nature through all the varieties of situation: but it is against the proletariat that it proclaims it. For it, a worker is first a man—a man like the others. If the Constitution grants to this man the right to vote and the freedom of opinion, he manifests his human nature as much as a bourgeois. A controversial literature too often has represented the bourgeois as a scheming and gloomy mind whose only care is to protect his privileges. In fact, one *becomes bourgeois* by choosing, once and for all, a certain vision of the analytical world, that one tries to impose upon every man and which blinds one from collective realities. Thus, the bourgeois defense is permanent in a way and is one with the bourgeoisie itself; but it does not reveal itself by scheming; within the world it has built for itself, there is room for virtues of lightheartedness, altruism, even generosity; only, bourgeois good deeds are individual acts addressed to universal human nature as embodied in an individual. In this sense, they are as efficient as a shrewd propaganda, for the beneficiary is forced to receive these marks of kindness as they are offered to him; that is to say, as a human being alone in front of another human being. Bourgeois charity fosters the myth of fraternity.

But there is another propaganda in which we are more particularly interested here, since we are writers, and writers are unwittingly the agents of it. This legend of the poet's irresponsibility that we denounced a moment ago, springs from the analytical mind. Since the bourgeois authors consider themselves as peas in a can, the solidarity which unites them with other people seems strictly mechanical to them, i.e., a mere juxtaposition. Even if they feel strongly about their literary mission, they think they have done enough when they have described their own nature or that of their friends. Since all men are alike, they will have helped all of them by enlightening everyone about himself. And as they start from the same postulate as analysis, it seems very simple to them to use the analytical method to know themselves. Such is the origin of intellectualist psychology, the perfect example of which we find in Proust's works. A paederast, Proust thought he could use his homosexual experience to describe Swann's love for Odette; a bourgeois, he presents this sentiment of a rich, idle bourgeois for a kept woman as the prototype of love. It is then that he believes in the existence of universal passions, the mechanism of which does not vary much when one modifies the sexual characters, the social condition, the nation or the time of the individuals who feel them. After thus "isolating" these unalterable affections, he will be able to start converting them, in their turn, into elementary particles. Abiding by the postulates of the analytical mind, he does not even think that there may be a dialectic in sentiments, but only a mechanism. Thus social atomism, the position of retreat for the contemporary bourgeoisie, brings about psychological atomism. Proust has *chosen to be a bourgeois,* he has made himself the accomplice of the bourgeois propaganda, since his work contributes in spreading the myth of human nature.

We are convinced that the analytical approach is dead and that its unique role today is to trouble the revolutionary conscience and isolate men in favor of the privileged classes. We do not believe any more in the intellectualist psychology of Proust and we consider it harmful. Since we chose his analysis of passionate love as an example, we will probably enlighten the reader by mentioning the essential points on which we disagree with him entirely.

First, we do not accept *a priori* the idea that passionate love is an affection constitutive of the human mind. It could very well have, as Denis de Rougemont suggested, a historical origin related to Christian ideology.

More generally, we think that a sentiment is always the expression of a certain way of life and a certain conception of the world, common to a whole class or time, and that its evolution is not caused by I know not what inner mechanism but by these historical and social factors.

Secondly, we cannot admit that a human affection is composed of molecular elements which juxtapose without modifying one another. We consider it to be not a well adjusted machine but an organised form. We do not conceive the possibility of *analysing* love because the evolution of this sentiment, as of all others, is *dialectic*.

Thirdly, we refuse to believe that a homosexual's love has the same characters as a heterosexual's. The secret, forbidden character of the former, its aspect of black magic, the existence of a homosexual freemasonry, and this damnation to which the invert is aware of dragging his partner with him: it seems to us that all these facts influence the whole sentiment to the very details of its evolution. We maintain that a person's various sentiments are not juxtaposed but that there is a synthetic unity of emotional functions and that each individual moves within an emotional world which is his own.

Fourthly, we deny the individual's origin, class, milieu, nation, to be mere concurrents in his sentimental life. On the contrary, we think that every affection, as any other form of his psychic life, *manifests* his social situation. This worker, who gets a salary, who does not own his working tools, who is isolated by his work from the substance of his material, and who protects himself from being oppressed by becoming conscious of his class, would not feel, under any circumstances, like this analytical-minded bourgeois, who, because of his profession, entertains polite relations with other bourgeois.

So, against the analytical mind, we turn to a synthetic conception of reality, the principle of which is that a whole, whatever it is, is different, by nature, from the sum of its parts. For us, what men have in common is not a nature, it is a metaphysical condition; and by this, we mean all the constraints which limit them *a priori,* the necessity of being born and dying, of being *finite,* and existing in the world among other men. For the rest, they constitute indecomposable wholes, whose ideas, moods and acts are secondary and dependent structures, and whose essential character is to be *situated,* and they differ from each other as their situations differ. The unity of these significant wholes is the meaning they manifest. Whether he writes or works on a production line, whether he chooses a wife or a tie, man always manifests: he manifests his professional milieu, his family, class, and finally, as he is situated in relation to the whole world, it is the world he manifests. A man is the whole earth. He is present everywhere, he acts everywhere, he is responsible for everything, and it is everywhere, in Paris, Potsdam, Vladivostok, that his destiny is at stake. We adhere to these views because they seem true, because they seem socially useful at the present time, and because most people seem to anticipate and call for them. Our review would like to contribute, for its modest part, to the constitution of a synthetic anthropology. But we repeat, we do not want only to prepare a progress in the field of pure knowledge; the distant purpose we give ourselves is a *liberation.* Since man is a whole, it is not enough to give him the right to vote, without touching the other factors which constitute him: he must free himself entirely, that is to say become *other,* by working on his biological constitution as well as on his economical conditioning, on his sexual complexes as well as on the political data of his situation.

However, this synthetic view is very dangerous: if the individual is an arbitrary selection made by the analytical mind, don't we risk substituting the reign of collective conscience for the reign of the person, by giving up the analytical conceptions? One does not give the proper share to the synthetic approach. While hardly born, the *total-man* is going to disappear, engulfed by the class; only the class exists, it alone should be freed. But, one will say, by freeing the class, do you not free the men who belong to it? Not necessarily: would the triumph of Hitlerian Germany have been the triumph of each German? Besides, where will the synthesis stop? Tomorrow we will be told that the class is a secondary structure, depending on a bigger whole which will be, for instance, the nation. If Nazism attracted some people from the left, it is probably because it carried the totalitarian conception to the absolute: its theoreticians, too, denounced the harm done by analysis, the abstract character of democratic liberties; also, its propaganda promised to forge a new man, it retained the words Revolution and Liberation: only, for the class proletariat, a proletariat of nations was substituted. The individuals became only functions depending on the class, classes became only functions depending on the nation, the nations became only functions depending on the European continent. If, in the occupied countries, the working class fought against the invaders, it was certainly because it felt itself wounded in its revolutionary yearnings, but also because it was invincibly reluctant to let the person be dissolved in the collectivity.

Thus the contemporary conscience seems to be torn by an antinomy. Those who are attached, above all, to the dignity of the human person, his liberty, his imprescriptible rights, tend because of this to think according to the analytical mind which conceives individuals out of their real conditions of existence, which grants them an immutable and abstract nature, which isolates them and deceives itself about their solidarity. Those who strongly feel that man is rooted in collectivity and who want to stress the importance of economical, technical and historical factors, turn to the synthetical mind which, unconcerned with persons, sees only groups. This antinomy is found, for instance, in the widespread belief that socialism is completely averse to individual freedom. Thus, those who believe in the person's autonomy would be condemned to a capitalist liberalism, which we know to be harmful. Those who want a socialist organisation of the economy should turn for it I know not to what totalitarian authoritarianism. The present uneasiness springs from the fact that no one can accept the extreme consequences of these principles: there is a "synthetic" component in democrats of good will; there is an analytical component in the socialists. Remember, for instance, what the Radical Party was in France. One of its theoreticians published a book entitled: *The Citizen Against the Powers.* This title well shows how he conceived politics: everything would be better if the isolated citizen, a molecular representative of human nature, controlled his elected officials and, if need be, used his free judgment against them. But precisely, the Radicals had to admit their failure; this great party had no longer, in 1939, either will, program or ideology; it fell into opportunism: this because it wanted to solve politically problems which could not have a political solution. The best minds seemed surprised by this: if man is a political animal, how come his fate has not been settled once and for all by giving him political freedom? How come the free play of parliamentary institutions did not succeed in suppressing poverty, unemployment, the oppression of the trusts? How come there is a class conflict beyond the parties' brotherly oppositions? One did not have to go much farther to see the limits of the analytical approach. The fact that radicalism constantly sought the alliance of parties of the Left clearly shows the trend it wanted to take because of its sympathies and confused aspirations, but it lacked the intellectual technique which would have enabled it not only to solve, but also to formulate the problems it felt obscurely.

On the other side, there is no less uneasiness. The working class has inherited the democratic traditions. It is in the name of democracy that it claims its liberation. Now, we saw that the democratic ideal historically takes the form of a social contract between free individuals. Thus, Rousseau's analytical claims often interfere in people's consciences with the synthetic claims of Marxism. Besides, the worker's technical education develops in him an analytical mind. Like the scientist, he must solve the problem of matter by analysis. If he turns towards persons, he tends, in order to understand them, to appeal to the way of thinking he uses in his work; thus, he applies to human behavior an analytical psychology similar to the one of the French seventeenth century.

The simultaneous existence of these two types of explanation reveals a certain hesitation; this constant use of "as if . . ." clearly shows that Marxism has not yet at its disposal a synthetic psychology fit for its totalitarian conception of the class.

As for us, we refuse to let ourselves be torn between thesis and antithesis. We conceive with no difficulty that a man may be a center of irreducible indetermination, although his situation conditions him totally. This unforeseen area which stands out of the social field, is what we call freedom and the person is nothing else but his freedom. This freedom should not be considered as a metaphysical power of human "nature"; neither is it the license to do everything we want, nor is it a kind of inner refuge which we could enjoy even while enchained. We do not do what we want; however, we are responsible for what we are: this is the fact. Man, simultaneously explained by so many causes, is still alone to bear the burden of himself. In this sense, freedom could be considered as a curse, it is a curse. But it also is the unique source of human grandeur. On this fact, the Marxists will agree with us in spirit if not in the letter, because they do not hesitate, as far as I know, to express moral condemnations. It remains to explain it: but it is the philosophers' business, not ours. We will only point out that, if society makes the person, the person, by a process similar to what Auguste Comte called the passage to subjectivity, makes society. Without its future, a society is only a heap of material, but its future is only the self-projects made, beyond the present state of things, by the millions of men who compose it. Man is only a situation: a worker is not *free* to think or to feel like a bourgeois; but in order that this situation should become *a man,* a whole man, it should be lived and left behind on the way towards a particular aim. In itself, it remains indifferent as long as a human freedom does not give it a meaning: it is neither tolerable nor unbearable as long as a freedom does not accept it, does not rebel against it, that is to say as long as a man does not choose himself in it, by choosing its significance. Then only, within this free choice, it becomes determinant because it is over-determined. No, a worker cannot live as a bourgeois; in the social organization of today, he must suffer to the end his condition of salaried worker; no escape is possible, there is nothing to do about it. But a man does not exist in the same way as a tree or a stone: he must *make himself* a worker. Totally conditioned by his class, his salary, the nature of his work, conditioned even to his feelings, his thoughts, he is the one to decide the meaning of his condition and that of his companions, he is the one who, freely, gives to the proletariat a future of endless humiliation or of conquest and victory, whether he chooses himself to be resigned or revolutionary. And he is responsible for this choice. Not free not to choose: he is committed, he must wager, abstention is a choice. But free to choose, by one and the same decision, his destiny, the destiny of all men, and the value to attribute to mankind. Thus, he chooses himself to be both worker and man, while giving a meaning to the proletariat. Such is man as we conceive him: a total man. Totally committed and totally free. However, it is this free man who must be *delivered,* by widening his possibilities of choice. In certain situations, there is only room for one alternative, one term of which is death. It must be so that man can choose life, in any circumstances.

Freedom and Responsibility

Although the considerations which are about to follow are of interest primarily to the ethicist, it may nevertheless be worthwhile after these descriptions and arguments to return to the freedom of the for-itself and to try to understand what the fact of this freedom represents for human destiny.

The essential consequence of our earlier remarks is that man being condemned to be free carries the weight of the whole world on his shoulders; he is responsible for the world and for himself as a way of being. We are taking the word "responsibility" in its ordinary sense as "consciousness (of) being the incontestable author of an event or of an object." In this sense the responsibility of the for-itself is overwhelming since he [1] is the one by whom it happens that *there is* a world; since he is also the one who makes himself be, then whatever may be the situation in which he finds himself, the for-itself must wholly assume this situation with its peculiar coefficient of adversity, even though it be insupportable. He must assume the situation with the proud consciousness of being the author of it, for the very worst disadvantages or the worst threats which can endanger my person have meaning only in and through my project; and it is on the ground of the engagement which I am that they appear. It is therefore senseless to think of complaining since nothing foreign has decided what we feel, what we live, or what we are.

Furthermore this absolute responsibility is not resignation; it is simply the logical requirement of the consequences of our freedom. What happens to me happens through me, and I can neither affect myself with it nor revolt against it nor resign myself to it. Moreover everything which happens to me is *mine*. By this we must understand first of all that I am always equal to what happens to me *qua* man, for what happens to a man through other men and through himself can be only human. The most terrible situations of war, the worst tortures do not create a non-human state of things; there is no non-human situation. It is only through fear, flight, and recourse to magical types of conduct that I shall decide on the non-human, but this decision is human, and I shall carry the entire responsibility for it. But in

---

[1] I am shifting to the personal pronoun here since Sartre is describing the for-itself in concrete personal terms rather than as a metaphysical entity. Strictly speaking, of course, this is his position throughout, and the French "*il*" is indifferently "he" or "it." [H.E.B.]

From pp. 553–56 of Jean-Paul Sartre, *Being and Nothingness,* translated by Hazel E. Barnes. Copyright, Philosophical Library, Inc., 1956. Reprinted by permission of the publisher.

addition the situation is *mine* because it is the image of my free choice of myself, and everything which it presents to me is *mine* in that this represents me and symbolizes me. Is it not I who decide the coefficient of adversity in things and even their unpredictability by deciding myself?

Thus there are no *accidents* in a life; a community event which suddenly bursts forth and involves me in it does not come from the outside. If I am mobilized in a war, this war is *my* war; it is in my image and I deserve it. I deserve it first because I could always get out of it by suicide or by desertion; these ultimate possibles are those which must always be present for us when there is a question of envisaging a situation. For lack of getting out of it, I have *chosen* it. This can be due to inertia, to cowardice in the face of public opinion, or because I prefer certain other values to the value of the refusal to join in the war (the good opinion of my relatives, the honor of my family, etc.). Anyway you look at it, it is a matter of a choice. This choice will be repeated later on again and again without a break until the end of the war. Therefore we must agree with the statement by J. Romains, "In war there are no innocent victims." If therefore I have preferred war to death or to dishonor, everything takes place as if I bore the entire responsibility for this war. Of course others have declared it, and one might be tempted perhaps to consider me as a simple accomplice. But this notion of complicity has only a juridical sense, and it does not hold here. For it depended on me that for me and by me this war should not exist, and I have decided that it does exist. There was no compulsion here, for the compulsion could have got no hold on a freedom. I did not have any excuse; for as we have said repeatedly in this book, the peculiar character of human-reality is that it is without excuse. Therefore it remains for me only to lay claim to this war.

But in addition the war is *mine* because by the sole fact that arises in a situation which I cause to be and that I can discover it there only by engaging myself for or against it, I can no longer distinguish at present the choice which I make of myself from the choice which I make of the war. To live this war is to choose myself through it and to choose it through my choice of myself. There can be no question of considering it as "four years of vacation" or as a "reprieve," as a "recess," the essential part of my responsibilities being elsewhere in my married, family, or professional life. In this war which I have chosen I choose myself from day to day, and I make it mine by making myself. If it is going to be four empty years, then it is I who bear the responsibility for this.

Finally, as we pointed out earlier, each person is an absolute choice of self from the standpoint of a world of knowledges and of techniques which this choice both assumes and illumines; each person is an absolute upsurge at an absolute date and is perfectly unthinkable at another date. It is therefore a waste of time to ask what I should have been if this war had not broken out, for I have chosen myself as one of the possible meanings of the epoch which imperceptibly led to war. I am not distinct from this same epoch; I could not be transported to another epoch without contradiction. Thus *I am* this war which restricts and limits and makes comprehensible the period which preceded it. In this sense we may define more precisely the responsibility of the for-itself if to the earlier quoted statement, "There are no innocent victims," we add the words, "We have the war we deserve." Thus, totally free, undistinguishable from the period for which I have chosen to be the meaning, as profoundly responsible for the war as if I had myself declared it, unable to live without integrating it in *my* situation, engaging myself in it wholly and stamping it with my seal, I must be without remorse or regrets as I am without excuse; for from the instant of my upsurge into being, I carry the weight of the world by myself alone without anything or any person being able to lighten it.

Yet this responsibility is of a very particular type. Someone will say, "I did not ask to be born." This is a naive way of throwing greater emphasis on our facticity. I am responsible for everything, in fact, except for my very responsibility, for I am not the foundation of my being. Therefore everything takes place as if I were compelled to be responsible. I am *abandoned* in the world, not in the sense that I might remain abandoned and passive in a hostile universe like a board floating on the water, but rather in the sense that I find myself suddenly alone and without help, engaged in a world for which I bear the whole responsibility without being able, whatever I do, to tear myself away from this responsibility for an instant. For I am responsible for my very desire of fleeing responsibilities. To make myself passive in the world, to refuse to act upon things and upon Others is still to choose myself, and suicide is one mode among others of being-in-the-world. Yet I find an absolute responsibility for the fact that my facticity (here the fact of my birth) is directly inapprehensible and even inconceivable, for this fact of my birth never appears as a brute fact but always across a projective reconstruction of my for-itself. I am ashamed of being born or I am astonished at it or I rejoice over it, or in attempting to get rid of my life I affirm that I live and I assume this life as bad. Thus in a certain sense I *choose* being born. This choice itself is integrally affected with facticity since I am not able not to choose, but this facticity in turn will appear only in so far as I surpass it toward my ends. Thus facticity is everywhere but inapprehensible; I never encounter anything except my responsibility. That is why I can not ask, *"Why* was I born?" or curse the day of my birth or declare that I did not ask to be born, for these various attitudes toward my birth—i.e., toward the *fact* that I realize a presence in the world—are absolutely nothing else but ways of assuming this birth in full responsibility and of making it *mine*. Here again I encounter only myself and my projects so that finally my abandonment—i.e., my facticity—consists simply in the fact that I am condemned to be wholly responsible for myself. I am the being which *is* in such a way that in its being its being is in question. And this "is" of my being *is* as present and inapprehensible.

Under these conditions since every event in the world can be revealed to me only as *opportunity* (an opportunity made use of, lacked, neglected, etc.), or better yet since everything which happens to us can be considered as a chance (i.e., can appear to us only as a way of realizing this being which is in question in our being) and since others as transcendences-transcended are themselves only *opportunities* and *chances,* the responsibility of the for-itself extends to the entire world as a peopled-world. It is precisely thus that the for-itself apprehends itself in anguish; that is, as a being which is neither the foundation of its own being nor of the Other's being nor of the in-itselfs which form the world, but a being which is compelled to decide the meaning of being—within it and everywhere outside of it. The one who realizes in anguish his condition as *being* thrown into a responsibility which extends to his very abandonment has no longer either remorse or regret or excuse; he is no longer anything but a freedom which perfectly reveals itself and whose being resides in this very revelation. But as we pointed out at the beginning of this work, most of the time we flee anguish in bad faith.

QUESTIONS FOR STUDY AND DISCUSSION

1. Sartre's obsession in "A New Individualism" seems to be "the writer" as a committed man. To what is he committed? How is he committed? Does Sartre consider himself a relativist? If not, what is his position?
2. How does Sartre in this first selection oppose the systematic versus the analytical mind? How does he attempt to combine individual choice with the power of the group?
3. Does Sartre have an ethics? If so, in what sense?
4. Define responsibility according to Sartre. How far does it reach?
5. In what sense do "I *choose* being born"?

Gabriel Marcel

GABRIEL MARCEL was born in Paris in 1889. His father was active in French diplomatic and artistic worlds, which enabled him to acquire a broad and rich cultural education. Marcel taught intermittently at French lycées from 1911 until 1922, and again from 1939 to 1941. Distinguished author, playwright, and critic, he has been the recipient of many literary awards, and in 1952 was appointed to the French Academy. Generally regarded as the chief representative of Christian existentialism, Marcel became a convert to Catholicism in 1927. Among his outstanding works are *Being and Having* (1935), *The Mystery of Being* (1951), and *Man Against Mass Society* (1951).

What Is a Free Man?

A problem such as the one we are dealing with in this chapter, "What is a free man?" cannot, or so it seems to me, be usefully discussed in the abstract. It cannot be discussed, that is, out of the context of historical situations, considered in their concrete fullness; it is, for that matter, of the very essence of the human lot that man always is in a situation of some sort or other, and this is what a too abstract kind of humanism always runs the risk of forgetting. We are not therefore here asking ourselves what a free man is *in se,* what the essential notion of a free man is; for that question very possibly has no meaning at all. But we are asking ourselves how in an historical situation which is *our* situation, which we have to face here and now, man's freedom can be conceived, and how we can bear witness to it.

About seventy-five years ago, Nietzsche asserted: "God is dead." Today, we can hear, not so much boldly asserted as muttered in anguish, a statement that seems to echo that of Nietzsche: "Man is in his death-throes." Let us make ourselves clear; this statement, by those who make it sincerely, is not intended to have the force of prophecy; at the level of reflective awareness (and it is at this level that the statement is made) we cannot make any sort of pronouncement at all on coming events, we are in fact even forced to acknowledge our ignorance of the future. And there is a sense in which we ought even to rejoice in that ignorance, for it is that ignorance alone which makes possible that perpetual hopeful betting on the

From pp. 13–25 of Gabriel Marcel, *Man Against Mass Society,* translated by G. S. Fraser. © 1962 by Henry Regnery Company. Reprinted by permission of the publisher.

future without which human activity, as such, would find itself radically inhibited. To say that man is in his death-throes is only to say that man today finds himself facing, not some external event, such as the annihilation of our planet, for instance, which might be the consequence of some catastrophe in the heavens, but rather possibilities of complete self-destruction inherent in himself. These possibilities, always latent, become patent from the moment in which man makes a bad use, or rather an impious use, of the powers that constitute his nature. I am thinking here both of the atomic bomb and of techniques of human degradation, as these have been put into effect in all totalitarian states without exception. Between the physical destruction wrought by the atomic bomb and the spiritual destruction wrought by techniques of human degradation there exists, quite certainly, a secret bond; it is precisely the duty of reflective thinking to lay bare that secret.

The relationship which can exist between the two statements, "God is dead," "Man is in his death-throes," is not only a complex relationship, but an ambiguous one. We can ask ourselves, for instance, whether Nietzsche's cry of exultation or pain did not, just like the modern cry of mere pain, presuppose a concrete historical situation; linked itself, like our situation, to a preliminary misuse of human powers, of which men at that time had been guilty. No doubt we ought to recognize that the relationship between the two statements, "God is dead," and "Man is in his death-throes," is concrete and existential, not logical: it is quite impossible to extract from Nietzsche's statement about God by any method of analysis the other statement about man, though Nietzsche perhaps would have accepted the statement about man, at least during the ultimate or penultimate period of his working life. Even if he had accepted it, however, he would probably not have perceived all the overtones in the statement, "Man is in his death-throes," which we can perceive to-day. Also (this is a strange reflection, but a true one) it is perhaps by starting from the statement, "Man is in his death-throes," that we may be able to question once more the statement, "God is dead," and to discover that God is living after all. It is, as the reader will soon discover, towards the latter conclusion that the whole of my subsequent argument tends.

But what we have to ask ourselves first is the following question: what becomes of freedom in a world in which man, or at least man at a certain level of self-awareness, is forced to recognize that he has entered into his death-throes?

At this point, however, we may be faced with a preliminary objection. It is one which presents itself readily to the mind. Might it not be convenient to say that the question, "What is a free man?" can only receive a positive answer in a country which has itself remained a free country?

However, the very notion of a free country or a free people, on a little analysis, appears to be a much less distinct notion than we should be tempted to think it at first. I shall take two examples: Switzerland, as the sequel to a process of political blackmail, found itself under the necessity of putting its factories to work for the benefit of Nazi Germany—was Switzerland still a free country? Sweden, at the end of the war, was obliged to conclude with Soviet Russia a very burdensome trade treaty, which had the effect of throttling her economic life. Ought not Sweden to have admitted to herself that—at the level of facts, if not at the level of words—she was no longer a free country? If the freedom of a people or a country be defined as *absolute independence,* is it not obvious that in a world like ours freedom cannot exist, not only because of inevitable economic interdependences, but because of the part played by pressure, or, less politely, by blackmail, at all levels of international intercourse?

Following out this line of thought, we should be led to acknowledge that the individual himself, in any country whatsoever, not only finds himself dependent but finds himself, in a great many cases, obliged to carry out actions which his conscience disapproves. (We have only to think, for instance, of military conscription and its consequences to become aware of this fact.) All that we can say is that in countries where there is still a recognition of what we can call in a very general fashion the rights of the human person, a certain number of guarantees of freedom survive: but we ought immediately to add that such guarantees are becoming less and less numerous and that, failing a very improbable reversal of the present general tendency of things, there will be a continuing demand for their further reduction. It would be contrary to the facts of the case to assert that men, in what we broadly call "the free countries," enjoy absolute independence. That does not matter so much, for, except to a pedantic type of anarchist, such absolute independence is inconceivable. But it would also be contrary to the facts to assert that men in free countries to-day generally possess the power to square their conduct with their consciences.

This is the point at which we ought to pass to the extreme case and ask ourselves what becomes of the freedom of the individual, even of what we call his inner freedom, in a totalitarian country. Here, I believe, we shall find ourselves forced to recognize an exceptionally important fact: Stoicism (and I am thinking less of an abstract philosophical doctrine than of a spiritual attitude) has been to-day, I shall not say refuted by the facts, but uprooted by them from the soil which used to nourish it. This ancient and respectable attitude rested on the distinction made so forcibly and severely by such writers as Epictetus, Seneca, and Marcus Aurelius: the distinction between what depends on my will, and what does not depend on it. Stoic thought, in so far as it was not merely formulated in abstract terms but adopted with dauntless courage as a way of life, implied a belief in the inner tribunal of conscience: a tribunal unviolated, and indeed inviolable, by any intrusion of external power. There can be no Stoicism without a belief in an inalienable inner sovereignty, an absolute possession of the self by the self.

However, the very essence of those modern techniques of degradation, to which I made an earlier allusion, consists precisely in putting the individual into a situation in which he loses touch with himself, in which he is literally beside himself, even to the point of being able sincerely to disavow acts into which nevertheless he had put sincerely his whole heart, or on the other hand of being able to confess to acts which he had not committed. I shall not attempt at this point to define the *kind* of sincerity, obviously a factitious and artificial kind, that we are talking of. I shall note merely that, though in recent years such techniques of degradation have been brought to an almost unimaginable degree of refinement, they were already in use in periods much earlier than ours. I was told recently that during the trial of the Knights Templars under Philip the Fair confessions were obtained by processes which cannot have consisted merely of physical torture; since later on, during a second and last retractation of their original confessions, the accused, once more in possession of their faculties, declared that they had originally *sincerely* accused themselves of acts which they *had not committed.* Physical torture by itself seems incapable of producing such sincerity; it can be evoked only by those abominable methods of *psychological* manipulation to which so many countries, in such various latitudes, have in recent years had recourse.

Given these conditions, the situation that each one of us must face to-day is as follows: (I say *each one of us,* supposing that we do not want to lie to ourselves or to commit the sin of unwarranted presumption; given that supposition, we must admit that there are real and practical methods that can be applied to any of us to-morrow with the effect of depriving us of self-sovereignty or, less grandiosely, of self-control: even though in another age we should have had sound reasons for regarding that self-sovereignty as infrangible and inviolable). Our situation, then, is this: we ought not even to say, as the Stoics said, that even at the very worst there remains for us the possibility of suicide, as a happy way out. That is no longer a true statement of the case. A man to-day can be put into a situation in which he *will no longer want to kill himself;* in which suicide will appear to him as an *illicit* or *unfair* way out; in which he will think of himself as under an obligation not merely to suffer, but to wish for, the punishment appropriate to crimes which he will impute to himself *without having committed them.*

It may be objected here that the mere mention of such horrible possibilities is itself dangerous, almost criminal. Certainly, if I were addressing myself to a class of schoolboys or students, it might be proper to leave this aspect of my subject in the shadow. But I am addressing myself to mature minds, minds I assume already capable of higher reflection; and on such minds, just because of their maturity, a real responsibility rests.

What we have to recognize is this. Thanks to the techniques of degradation it is creating and perfecting, a materialistic mode of thought, in our time, is showing itself capable of bringing into being a world which more and more *tends to verify its own materialistic postulates.* I mean that a human being who has undergone a certain type of psychological manipulation tends progressively to be reduced to the status of a mere *thing;* a psychic thing, of course, but nevertheless a thing which falls quite tidily within the province of the theories elaborated by an essentially materialistic psychology. This assertion of mine is, of course, obviously ambiguous; it does not mean that this materialistic psychology, with however startling powers of reductive transformation it may become endowed, will ever be of a nature to grasp and reveal to us reality as it is in itself. Rather, my assertion emphasizes the fact that there is nothing surprising for a philosophy like my own, a philosophy of man as a being in a situation, in the fact that man depends, to a very great degree, on the idea he has of himself and that this idea cannot be degraded without at the same time degrading man. This is one more reason, and on the face of things the most serious and imperative reason, for condemning materialistic thinking, root and branch. And it is relevant to note here that in our day the materialistic attitude has acquired a virulence and a cohesion which it was far from possessing in the last century. It was a common spectacle then to see thinkers who regarded themselves as thoroughly imbued with materialistic principles showing in their personal lives all the scrupulosity of Kantian rigorists.

It may seem that I am rather straying here from the question which I set out to answer at the beginning of this chapter, "What is a free man?" But this is not in fact by any means the case, for it is very important for us to recognize, whatever fancies certain thinkers incapable of the least coherence may have had about this question, that a materialistic conception of the universe is radically incompatible with the idea of a free man: more precisely, that, in a society ruled by materialistic principles, freedom is transmuted into its opposite, or becomes merely the most treacherous and deceptive of empty slogans.

Theoretically, of course, we can imagine the possibility of man's preserving a minimum of independence even in a society ruled on materialistic principles; but, as we ought to be immediately aware, this possibility is an evanescent one, implying contradictions: for freedom in such a society would consist, if I may put it so, in rendering oneself sufficiently insignificant to escape the attention of the men in power. But is it not fairly obvious that this wish for insignificance, supposing even that it is a wish that can be put into effect, is already in a sense a suicidal wish? In such a society, the mere keeping, for instance, of an intimate diary might be a capital crime, and one does not see why, by the use of tape recorders and tapped telephones, as well as by various quite conceivable extensions of the use of radio, it should not be quite possible to keep the police well informed about the thoughts and the feelings of any individual whatsoever. From the point of view of the individual in such a society, there is no conceivable way out at all: private life, as such, does not exist any more.

But let us imagine, then, the situation of our own country immediately after a *putsch* or a *coup d'état:* if rebellion is futile, and a retreat into insignificance impracticable, what, supposing that we are fully aware of our situation, does there remain for us to do? At the risk of discontenting and even of shocking those who still tend to think of solutions for political problems in terms of positive action, I shall say that in that region all the ways of escape seem to me to be barred. Our only recourse can be to the Transcendent: but what does that mean? "The transcendent," "transcendence," these are words which among philosophers and intellectuals, for a good many years past, have been strangely misused. When I myself speak here of a recourse to the transcendent, I mean, as concretely as possible, that our only chance in the sort of horrible situation I have imagined is to appeal, I should perhaps *not* say to a power, but rather to a level of being, an order of the spirit, which is also the level and order of grace, of mercy, of charity; and to proclaim, while there is still time, that is to say before the state's psychological manipulations have produced in us the alienation from our true selves that we fear, that we repudiate *in advance* the deeds and the acts that may be obtained from us by any sort of constraint whatsoever. We solemnly affirm, by this appeal to the transcendent, that the reality of our selves lies *beyond* any such acts and any such words. It will be said, no doubt, that by this gesture we are giving ourselves a very ideal, a very unreal, sort of satisfaction; but to say so is to fail to recognize the real nature of the thought which I am groping to put into shape. What we have to do is to proclaim that we do *not* belong entirely to the world of objects to which men are seeking to assimilate us, in which they are straining to imprison us. To put it very concretely indeed, we have to proclaim that this life of ours, which it has now become technically possible to make into a hideous and grimacing parody of all our dreams, may in reality be only the most insignificant aspect of a grand process unfolding itself far beyond the boundaries of the visible world. In other words, this amounts to saying that *all philosophies of immanence have had their day,* that in our own day they have revealed their basic unreality or, what is infinitely more serious, their complicity with those modern idolatries which it is our duty to denounce without pity: the idolatry of race, the idolatry of class. I should add here that even the authentic religions may become similarly degraded in their very principle of being. They too can degenerate into idolatries; especially where the will to power is waiting to corrupt them; and this, alas, is almost invariably the case when the Church becomes endowed with temporal authority.

But we are now on the road towards a number of pretty positive conclusions. I should formulate them as follows: a man cannot be free or remain free, except in the degree to which he remains linked with that which transcends him, whatever the particular form of that link may be: for it is pretty obvious that the form of the link need not reduce itself to official and canonical prayers. I should say that in the case particularly of the true artist in paint, or stone, or music, or words, this relationship to the transcendent is something that is experienced in the most authentic and profound way. I am supposing, of course, that he does not yield to the innumerable temptations to which the artist is exposed to-day: the temptation to startle, to innovate at all costs, to shut oneself up in a private world leaving as few channels as possible open for communication with the world of eternal forms: and so on. But nothing could be falser and more dangerous than to base on these observations of mine some sort of neo-aestheticism. We have to recognize that there are modes of creation which do not belong to the aesthetic order, and which are within the reach of everybody; and it is in so far as he is a creator, at however humble a level, that any man at all can recognize his own freedom. It would be necessary, moreover, to show that the idea of being creative, taken in this quite general sense, always implies the idea of being open towards others: that openness I have called in my Gifford Lectures, intersubjectivity, whether that is conceived as *agape* (charity) or *philia* (attachment): these two notions, in any case, I think, tend ultimately to converge. But what must be stated as forcibly as possible is that societies built on a materialistic basis, whatever place they tactfully leave for a collective and at bottom purely animal exaltation, sin radically against intersubjectivity; they exclude it in principle; and it is because they exclude it, that they grub up every possible freedom by its roots.

It is quite conceivable—and I put this idea forward not as an abstract hypothesis but as a familiar fact—that in a country enslaved by a totalitarian power, a man might find himself constrained, not merely in order to live but in order to withdraw his dependants from a state of absolute wretchedness, to accept, for instance, a job with the security police: a job which might compel him to carry out acts absolutely repugnant to his conscience. Is mere refusal to carry out such acts a solution to his problem? We may doubt this, for the very reason that such a refusal might entail direful consequences not only for the man himself but for his innocent dependants. But it could happen that the man who accepted such a job might make a religious vow to use the share of power which he has been given so much as possible to help the very people of whom he was officially the persecutor. Such a vow, with the creative power that it re-bestows on him who makes it, is a concrete example of that recourse to the transcendent of which I spoke earlier on. But it is obvious that there is nothing in such an extremely particular case out of which any general rule can be framed. A rigoristic moral formalism, an attempt to bring all human acts under very general rules, ceases almost entirely to be acceptable as soon as one becomes aware of that element of the unique and the incommensurable which is the portion of every concrete being, confronted with a concrete situation. No two beings, and no two situations, are really commensurable with each other. To become aware of this fact is to undergo a sort of crisis. But it is with this crisis in our moral awareness as a starting-point, that there becomes possible that cry from us towards the creative principle, and that demand by it on us, which each must answer in his own way, if he does not wish to become an accomplice of what Simone Weil called "the gross beast." In our world as it is to-day there can be hardly any set of circumstances in which we may not be forced to ask ourselves whether, through our free choice, through our particular decisions, we are not going to make ourselves guilty of just such a complicity.

Techniques of Degradation

In this chapter, then, we have started by considering techniques of degradation at their most deliberate and systematic, the techniques which aim at degrading some given category of men—of degrading them *in their own eyes*. It is easy to see that it is only possible to make use of such techniques in a world in which universal values are being systematically trampled underfoot; and by "universal values" here, I do not wish to emphasize particularly notions like "goodness as such," "truth as such"—that is a type of Platonism of which I am hardly an adherent. It is not a matter merely of the *idea* of the good or the true being trampled on, but of these values being trampled on in their living scope and actual relations: being trampled on in so far as they confer on human existence its proper dignity —in so far as they confer that on *every* human existence. In this connection, I should notice in passing, it is quite impossible to acquit Nietzsche of a certain at least indirect responsibility for the horrors of which we have been, and still are, the witnesses. We ought not, of course, to be deceived by a philosopher's special vocabulary; and when Nietzsche talked about getting "beyond good and evil," we should recognize that he wanted to lay the foundations for a higher kind of good. It is none the less true—and either Nietzsche failed to perceive this, or he was very wrong in thinking himself not bound to take it into consideration—that, at the level of experience, Nietzsche's "beyond" becomes a "beneath"; his way up is, in practice, a way down: not a transcendence of ordinary moral categories but, to use a word coined by Jean Wahl, a transdescendence from them.

Whatever we may think in the long run of Nietzsche's contrast between the morality of slaves and that of masters, even admitting that there is a context in which it might make good sense, it is quite obvious that, given a crude historical application, that antithesis could only itself become degraded and give rise to worse aberrations than itself. As soon as one cynically postulates that, whether for reasons of race or class, a certain category of human beings can have no share in certain human values—as soon as one has done that, so soon one finds, by a kind of reactive shock, that it

From pp. 66–75 of Gabriel Marcel, *Man Against Mass Society,* translated by G. S. Fraser. © 1962 by Henry Regnery Company. Reprinted by permission of the publisher.

is the values one imagines oneself to be defending that one is making unreal. In another vocabulary, but in one with many affinities to the previous one, we might say that these abominable techniques of degradation can be put into operation only if one refuses to regard man as being made in the image of God; or one might even say quite simply, when one refuses to regard man as a created being. All this is too obvious to be worth insisting on. On the other hand, the converse of the above proposition seems to me extremely significant and, at the moment of history at which we have now arrived, deserving of deep consideration: *so soon as man denies to himself that he is a created being,* a double peril faces him: on the one hand he will be led—and this is exactly what we see in Sartre's type of existentialism —to claim for himself a kind of *self-dependence* which caricatures that of the Deity. He will be led, that is, to consider himself as a being who makes himself and *is* only what he makes of himself; for if there is nobody who can destroy his self-sufficiency, similarly there is no gift which can be made to that sufficiency; a being conceived as Sartre conceives man is utterly incapable of receiving anything. But from another point of view, and yet in a closely connected way, the man who conceives himself as Sartre conceives man will be led to think of himself as a sort of waste product of a universe which is, for that matter, an inconceivable universe—so that we see such a man, at the same time and for the same set of reasons, exalting and abasing himself beyond all just measure. For that matter, we ought to add that, strange as it may seem, this self-abasement will have an exhilarating effect; it will enable our Sartrian man to procure a kind of joy for himself, just as having themselves whipped, for some people, is a condition of erotic pleasure . . . I have spoken, however, of this Sartrian self-exaltation and self-abasement as being *beyond all just measure:* it may be asked, where are we to get our measure from: to what other levels of being can man, after all, be properly related or compared? Will it be said that we must come back, quite simply, to the formula of the Greek sophist: "man is the measure of all things." That, in fact, is a possibility. But the formula itself is a strangely ambiguous one, for it throws no light at all on just how man comes to understand himself and judge himself. But we can also perhaps say with considerable plausibility that the moral relativism implied in the formula, "Man is the measure of all things," puts us on a path that will in the long run lead us to a degraded kind of humanism: a humanism that is parasitic on nature, as moss is parasitic on a tree.

Our first theme, in this chapter, then, was modern techniques of degradation at their most systematic and deliberate; we were led to consider, thereafter, such a technique as propaganda, which can only in fact degrade those on whom it is exercised, and which presupposes, in those who exercise it, an utter contempt for those on whom it is exercised. In a word, every kind of propaganda implies a claim to have the right to manipulate other men's consciences. Following on the heels of the abject ferocity of the concentration camps, what we here witness is the spirit of imposture. We should notice, also, the inevitable connection between these two aspects of a single scourge. For how would it be possible not to take the most severe, the most inhuman steps against those who refuse to let themselves be indoctrinated and who become, consequently, opponents who must be put down by any means available? Propaganda is a cynical refusal to recognize that ordering of man's awareness in subordination to truth which it is the imperishable glory of the great rationalist philosophers, whatever may have been their metaphysical errors, to set in the clearest light. But what is truth? That is the question that may be asked with insulting irony by the man who, as a propagandist, is a past master in the art of shaping opinion according to his fancy. It is obvious that this Machiavellian attitude, in all its forms, implies that refusal to recognize the claims of Socrates and of all his philosophical posterity—the eternal claim to seek truth, and nothing but truth. And in this fact, or so it seems to me, we can find a grave and solemn warning to all who, in the name of class prejudice or race prejudice, have repudiated the very notion of universality: a warning even, at a much deeper level of significance, to those who claim to substitute (and at some periods in my life this has perhaps been my own case) for the traditional philosophical categories that have been organized round the notion of truth, new tragic categories, like those of self-commitment, belief as a wager, life as the taking of a risk. Obviously, the intrinsic value of these existential notions is not something that can be denied: but only on condition that they are kept in their place, in the place that can be properly assigned to them, that is to say in subordination to grander structures which ought not, themselves, to be called into question. For there will always be a danger that what, for exceptional individualities, presents itself as a tragic philosophy, with its own undeniable grandeur, may become at the mass level a mere pragmatism for the use of middlemen and adventurers.

After dealing with these points, I was led, in this chapter, into raising an extremely general problem, a problem bearing on the spiritual and intellectual crimes attributable to what one might call a sort of *pantechnicism,* or possibly a general emancipation of techniques. Once again, this is not a matter of attributing criminality to techniques considered in themselves. For where techniques fulfil their proper functions, they are subordinated to something higher; there is no such thing, at the proper level of technical function, as a technique *in se.* The idea of the nature of something *in itself* is not relevant when we are talking of something, such as a technical process, which exists for purposes *outside itself.* But the case is radically altered when technical knowledge begins to claim a sort of primacy in relation to modes of thinking, like my own, that concentrate on being rather than doing. It should be clear to readers who have followed my work for some time that these remarks are a development of those I made, more than ten years ago, about the notion of *function,* in so far as this contrasts with that of an actual grip on being, of any sort. In the claims of technical knowledge to primacy and in the way in which a concentration on mere technical functioning is opposed to an actual grasp of reality we have, no doubt, two manifestations of the same evil, the same flinching of the human spirit. But what ought to strike us more than anything else about what I have called the emancipation of techniques is the fact that what starts off as a collection of means put together to serve an end outside itself tends, after all, in the long run to be valued and cultivated for its own sake; and in consequence to become the centre, the focus, of an obsessive cult. It is in this way that the abuse of technical knowledge and technical processes is in danger, as I have already indicated in passing, of giving rise to an actual idolatry: an idolatry which, to be sure, is not recognized as such, its very nature excluding any such recognition.

The purpose of such evidence on this topic as I have endeavoured to assemble here is to help us to get our bearings in an investigation into the conditions which are undoubtedly likely to prevail in a world more and more completely given over to technical processes. Obviously, this world will require a growingly extended human agreement about its desirability; it is clear enough that no technical process can flourish independently of other technical processes. And at a first glance, this observation might seem of a sort to encourage us in a kind of optimism about the progress of human solidarity. But, to be honest, it does not seem to me that more prolonged reflection will be able to justify such optimism. What we have to fear, in fact, is that it is not among *men* that this solidarity is fated to be established, but rather among *submen*. It will be established, I mean, among beings who tend more and more to be reduced to their own strict function in a mechanized society, though with a margin of leisure reserved for amusements from which the imagination will be more and more completely banished. With this in mind, we might be tempted to ask what is, I agree, a rather paradoxical question. Observers have noted that in many countries to-day the majority of those whose tasks are purely functional seem to be suffering from a severe attack of laziness, or apathy. Is it not possible that this laziness may correspond to an obscure but necessary impulse of self-defence—of self-defence against a mortal danger to which most factory hands, for instance, exposed themselves quite light-heartedly when they first became cogs in the wheel?

I am far from asserting that such tasks involve, for every individual engaged in them, a *necessary* degradation. But what we can say is that it becomes less and less probable, in a world given over to techniques, that the individual will be able to free himself from a set of constraints, of which many appear, at first, less as constraints than as seductions; that is strictly the case, for instance, not only in relation to propaganda, but in relation to all its ancillary operations at the level of publicity or psuedo-art. And that is not the whole story; for in such a world the proper domain of truth is more and more ignored and abandoned, and so quite naturally, as we have seen, imposture tends to proliferate like a fungus, with the help of these technical methods which every quack, to-day, can use to sell his elixirs to the gullible. But there are other points we ought to emphasize here. I am thinking especially of the extraordinary degradation in our time of discussion, the very bases of discussion; a degradation to which each succeeding day, in France, bears melancholy witness. To dispose of your opponent, or to put him down for the count, it is enough, in France to-day, to stick an obnoxious label on him and then to fling in his face, as one might a bottle of acid, some gross accusation to which it is impossible for him to reply; your opponent being completely confounded by such tactics, it will be said that he admits your case and capitulates. Thus, in certain circles in France to-day, it would be impossible to utter a balanced judgment on certain historical figures of our time and the intentions they may have started out with, without being automatically classed among those who approve of the methods of Buchenwald and Auschwitz. That, however, is just one example, among many possible other ones, of the sort of thing I am talking of. What is glaringly obvious is that this sense of the fine shades of truth, so inseparable from the sense of truth itself, is being literally stifled to-day by partisan passions. To be sure, a rather long analysis would be necessary if we were to attempt to show in detail how inevitable it is, in such a world as I have described, that these passions should spawn and multiply: but it cannot escape anyone that there does exist between partisan passions and propaganda a reciprocal solidarity, the reciprocal solidarity almost of premisses and conclusions in a viciously circular argument. The propaganda incites the passions, the passions in their turn justify the excesses of the propaganda.

At all events, any man who puts himself under the influence of that spirit of imposture, which is the spirit of propaganda, will gradually be contaminated to the point at which, even in his own proper sphere of activity, he is ready to participate in deception. What one can say, no doubt, is that novices in imposture are generally not in a state to become aware of how far they are deliberately deceiving themselves and others, but this very fact makes their situation almost desperate: how, in fact, can we hope to cure them of a malady whose early symptoms they are incapable of discovering?

At this point we ought to make a strict synthesis of all our observations so far, and we ought to show, in particular, how the spirit of imposture almost invariably thrives best in a world given over to resentment. Obviously, between the growth in men of a mood of resentment and that general emancipation of techniques that we have been describing, it is not possible, at a first glance, to grasp any direct connection. But what ought to be understood is that technical man (if I may call him so), having in the deepest sense lost his awareness of himself—having lost, above all, that is, his awareness of these transcendental laws which allow him to guide his behaviour and direct his intentions—is becoming more and more completely disarmed in the face of the powers of destruction unleashed around him and in the face, also, of the spirit of complicity which these powers encounter in the depths of his own nature.

For in the long run all that is not done through Love and for Love must invariably end by being done against Love. The human being who denies his nature as a created being ends up by claiming for himself attributes which are a sort of caricature of those that belong to the Uncreated. But how should this pretended or parodic human autarchy that modern man usurps for himself not degenerate into a resentment turned back on the very self for which absurd claims are made? And that resentment flows out into the techniques of degradation. There is a road that could be marked out by a succession of signposts leading from the abortionists to the death camps where torturers rage and sate themselves on a population of defenceless victims.

The Crisis of Values

All this, however, has only taken us up to the entrance of our subject, under a sort of portico which we must now pass through. But we can all pass through it on condition that we make a direct attack on the very idea of value: only, *is* value really an idea? In all that follows, I shall start from the hypothesis that something was irremediably compromised, if not actually lost for good, from the moment when the very notion of value made its appearance in philosophy. I emphasize the words "in philosophy": I am not thinking here of Political Economy which, of course, could not fail to imply a technical investigation into the nature of values. But has the mistake of philosophers not been that of transferring, by a process of illicit extrapolation, into the realm of essences or of being a notion which in reality only properly relates to the empirical cycle of production, distribution, and consumption? And was their mistake not also that of assimilating, sometimes cynically, sometimes hypocritically, the man who devotes himself, for instance, to the quest for truth or the practice of goodness to the man whose place is somewhere on that economic circuit? Of course, if one keeps to the empirical data themselves, that assimilation can appear not only justified but almost inevitable. It can be truly said that Vermeer or Mozart have flung on the market material which has become wealth or a source of profit for picture dealers, exhibition organizers, editors, performers, impresarios, and so on. But everything is lost if we do not retain the sharpest possible awareness of the absolute transcendence of the "View of

From pp. 168–92 of Gabriel Marcel, *Man Against Mass Society,* translated by G. S. Fraser. © 1962 by Henry Regnery Company. Reprinted by permission of the publisher.

Delft," "The Woman in the Turban," the "Symphony in C Minor" or one of the quartets, in relation to this possible economic exploitation of such works of art. However, as soon as we start using the term "value" in strictly philosophical discourse, there is every reason to fear that the way is being paved towards such sinister confusions. I am thus led to make the no doubt paradoxical assertion that the introduction of the idea of value into philosophy, an idea almost foreign to the great metaphysicians of the past, is, as it were, a symptom of a kind of fundamental devaluation, a devaluation of reality itself. As often happens, the idea and the word together make their appearance as the marks of a kind of internal collapse, and what the word really seeks to indicate is the place where the collapse has taken place.

This becomes particularly clear when truth itself, as in Nietzsche, is treated as a value. But I should like to cite another kind of example of this very general phenomenon. It seems to me that the development in philosophy of what is called "personalism"—the very word has become insupportable—would only have been possible in an increasingly dehumanized world, in which the reality of what one means by "the person" is every day trampled underfoot.

It would be permissible, I think, to suppose that we are here in the presence of some process of compensation: an almost entirely illusory process, to be sure, since it seeks to reconstitute at the level of the ideal—or fundamentally at the level of the imaginary—what at the level of the real is tending on the contrary to be destroyed. People would not bother to appeal to the idea of "the person" so constantly if human personality were not on the way towards its disappearance. At the political level, this sort of thing is just as striking; one example will be enough for me, that of the use made of the word "democracy" by men who have made themselves the champions of a political system, Marxist Communism, which implies the suppression of all the liberties that give the word "democracy" its only valuable associations. Of course, we should be within our rights here if we talked of imposture; but we ought to have the courage to recognize that, except in the cases of a few real scoundrels, this imposture is not really recognized as imposture by those who are guilty of it; what we are dealing with is, rather, really an illusion but one so deeply rooted that it would be chimerical, at least for the time being, to dream of making the man who feeds on the illusion aware that he is deceived.

On the basis of such observations, our problem changes its appearance; it can no longer be a question of substituting one system of values for another, as one might replace, for instance, one coinage by another, or one system of measurement by another. Such comparisons are basically wrong; and it is on this radical difference of kind between such notions of measurement and exchange on the one hand, and whatever recent philosophers have been trying to get at when they talked about "values" on the other, that we ought now to insist. When we talk of a system of measures we imply at the same time that there is something to be measured; and that correlation, and that contrast, constitute our whole realm of discourse. It is too clear to need emphasizing that a system of measurement is essentially relative, since it is the object of an initial choice. But, whatever Sartre, for instance, may have imagined to the contrary—and this no doubt is a very serious error in his philosophy, one fraught with consequences—what philosophers call "value" is essentially something which *does not allow itself to be chosen.* Or let us be more precise: why philosophers were wrong to use the word "value" is that it does irresistibly evoke the ideas of objective measurement and prior choice, and yet what they sought to designate by the word is really something at a quite different level. It is on the essential nature of this "something" that we now ought to concentrate our attention, though of course we must resist the temptation to think of it as really an object or a thing at all. There *is* a central point of view from which whatever it is that we improperly designate by the word "value" ought to be considered; but we must arrive at that central point of view itself.

The "View of Delft" of Vermeer and the "Thirteenth Quartet" of Beethoven cannot be thought of except as responses to a sort of appeal. The appeal, however, hardly becomes aware of itself as such except according to the distinctness with which the responses develop; and yet the responses, at the same time, tend to mask the appeal. In this sense, I should tend to say that an appeal has proper existence only for metaphysical reflection. That, above all, means that it cannot be compared to an empirical and identifiable appeal—to some known person calling out to me aloud. There is literally no point at all in asking *who* made such an appeal: we are above the "who" level—above, not below, I insist, and we certainly ought to distinguish carefully this suprapersonal level from the infrapersonal level, which is mere abstraction. I am thinking, for instance, of the infrapersonal level of official notices: "It is forbidden to . . . ," "It is requested that . . . ," and so on. There does exist a permanent and sinister temptation, which sociologists, for instance, can seldom resist, to identify or confuse the suprapersonal and infrapersonal levels.

Let us notice, however, that it is from every point of view extremely difficult for thought to grasp the suprapersonal directly: in seeking to make a concept of it, we convert it into an impersonal abstraction. As always in such cases, we must have recourse to second-level reflection: to a kind of thinking that becomes aware that our first attempt to grasp the suprapersonal in thought has involved a degradation of what we were trying to think about and, by becoming aware of this, frees itself from that degradation. The way is thus made clear for a discipline thanks to which we are permitted to turn back towards the principle of whatever it is that we mean by value, which principle can only be *being.* But all too certainly a very great danger threatens us here. It is that of substituting a mere word, a mouth-filling sonority, for the rich and palpitating experience of what we call, in our defective philosophical vocabulary, moral and aesthetic values. Merely to point out such a danger is, however, in some sense already to conjure it away: for we cannot really lose ourselves in abstract discussions about the intrinsic characteristics of Being—as if Being were a *thing,* capable of being contrasted with other things, which are only its appearances and manifestations. From this point of view, the philosophical term Ontology, the Science of Being, is an unsatisfactory one and runs the risk of encouraging regrettable misunderstandings. For Being is, quite fundamentally, not something which one can discuss. We can discuss only that which is *not* Being and thus, indirectly and humbly, map and mark out the tracks that led towards Being, so long, that is, as we ourselves are still able to climb back by these tracks towards Being; for it is just as true to say of them that they put a distance between Being and ourselves or lead us away from Being.

I would sum up all this by saying that a philosophy of values, in so far as it becomes aware of itself and of the confusions to which it has given birth, and also of the secret, urgent, inner need that animates it, is capable both of transcending itself and of pointing towards that which transcends it infinitely.

But one must add at once—and here we are touching the living nerve of our subject—that common thought to-day is setting its course in a precisely opposite direction. In particular, it often lets itself be fascinated by the categories which lie at the *lower limit* of that scale of degradation (and of possible re-ascension) to which I have just referred. It is at that lower limit, for instance, that the notions of function and output, in particular, lie. But one should make a preliminary distinction here: there would be no point in considering the notion of function, or even that of output as such, as evil notions in themselves. What we have to do with here are rather deviations or perversions of these ideas. An expression which is current in the United States may help us to get our bearings. It is a common saying there that some man or other is "worth so many dollars." Maurice Sachs in his *Sabbat* tells us that when he was giving a lecture at San Diego, on the Mexican frontier, the chairwoman introduced him in more or less the following terms: "Ladies, I flatter myself that I have been able to introduce to you some of the greatest lecturers of our age, at the times in their lives before they had grown too wealthy and cost too much. For instance, we had Mr. Sinclair Lewis, who is worth a thousand dollars a lecture to-day, at the time when he was only worth a hundred. And just so with Mr. Dreiser . . . Today, I have the honour of presenting Mr. Sachs to you, whose lectures are worth only a hundred dollars each to him to-day, but I hope for his sake they will soon be worth a thousand; I say, for *his* sake, for we won't be rich enough to have him then." Sachs adds, "I was no longer in public, I was exposed on a shop counter." We should emphasize here that the English word "worth" really has the sense of "value" and is directly related to the word *wert,* which in German is even the technical term for "value." Let us suppose that the lecturer in this anecdote gradually loses his voice, his value will diminish, and finally he will be "worth nothing." But value conceived in this way has obviously its place alongside the ideas of output and function.

Let us note also that, at least in the United States, a man can be "worth a hundred thousand dollars," even if as a man he is worth nothing, so long as he can still sign a cheque for a hundred thousand dollars. Let us be accurate, however: it is not a matter of the physical possibility of tracing certain symbols on the paper, but of the fact that the paper on which these symbols are traced will be honoured by the bank. It would be useful to ponder at length on the type of relationship between moral and economic concepts, to all appearances a degraded one, that the word "worth," the term "value," masks in such extreme cases. The French technical term *actif,* meaning one's credit balance in contrast to *passif,* one's debit balance, is rather suggestive in this connection, since it seems to indicate an intimate or dynamic relationship between a man and the sum of money which he has it in his power to dispose of as he pleases (for if the money is in the hands of a trustee pending litigation I think one ought no longer strictly to speak of the credit balance as an *actif*).

Now, whatever appearances there may be to the contrary, there does not really exist any fundamental difference between the kind of attitude I have been evoking and that which consists of identifying a man's value or worth with his possible output. In this connection I recall a scarcely credible fact: as part of the carrying out of some administrative regulations, citizens in France filling in certain papers connected with their taxes were asked, at least in certain regions, to evaluate their own intellectual capital. For instance, it was supposed that an artist or a writer, basing himself on what he had earned in previous years, could make an accurate estimate of what he was likely to earn over several years to come. Let us notice that this request may, strictly speaking, have had some meaning in the case of those who write, so to say, to eat; and who in bad years and good years, unless they are interrupted by a serious illness, pound out their steady three sex shockers or detective thrillers; but as soon as the artistic conscience, the creative impulse, in any form at all, comes into the picture, the request does cease to have meaning; and what is sinister in the world that is taking shape before our eyes is this claim to measure the case of the superior by that of the inferior, to reduce the superior to the level of the inferior. Here as elsewhere the techniques of degradation are in the ascendant.

But let us now ask directly just what this reduction of the value of the individual to his probable output implies. It implies that the individual has no dignity of his own, as he would have, for example, if he were considered in relation to a God, a Creator, in whose image he was made. Man is no longer thought of except as a set of possibilities, among which, moreover, a choice must be made; do not let us entangle ourselves in the metaphysical but very real difficulty about who is to make this choice; for we shall not really clear up anything by bringing out the word "freedom." Is freedom merely one human possibility among others? To deny this, that is to say to recognize in man's freedom a kind of specific reality, a priority in relation to the carrying out of his possibilities, is to reintegrate, though in a rather uncertain and timid form, a metaphysical principle which those who think in this way originally intended to do without. It hardly seems possible, on the other hand, simply to include freedom among possibilities; in other words, to say that I can be free or not; or at least this way of expressing things would imply a complete change in the point of view. The finally almost irresistible temptation will now be to make a clean sweep of freedoms, and to place *in things,* in circumstances themselves, the conditions that will ensure that one possibility rather than another becomes actual.

All that argument may look abstract, but it is in reality very simple. It will be held that if a given individual may, starting off in life, become either a great artist or a great criminal, still there is no point in imagining an inner freedom in him that would decide his development in one direction or the other: what we have to take account of is these external conditions of existence that in the long run may turn him into either a Debussy or a Landru. Of course, from this point of view, it does look as if the notion of possibility ought in the end to suffer the same fate as that of freedom, and leave us with a radical fatalism. But the acceptance of such a fatalism, is, let us note carefully, possible only if we totally deny the competence of the evidence of the human conscience for which choices, that is to say, possibilities, do exist. However, from this very point of view, the evidence of conscience—or, in a wider sense, of consciousness—will tend to be treated more and more as a negligible factor; and I may remark in passing that psychoanalysis will frequently be called in as an ally to reinforce the plea which it has been decided to make against conscience. Unless, indeed, as in the case of the author of *L'Etre et le néant,* one sets out to demonstrate that man's conscience, or consciousness, is always insincere, even, and perhaps above all, when it develops what looks to itself like a will to sincerity.

But to whose credit are we going to pay in what we have thus withdrawn from consciousness and in the long run also from freedom? For Sartre's attempt seems to me condemned to failure; it does not seem that it can resist the assaults of contemporary materialism and, above all, of Marxism. I use that phrase "to whose credit," that image from banking, deliberately. At this point in our argument, this is the aptest kind of comparison to hand. We are in the same sort of position as an accountant studying a balance-sheet, observing that a certain sum has been withdrawn from the credit column, and asking what has become of it, since even in that case it cannot have simply disappeared: and we have to note that the answer to our analogous question is of an incredible poverty. A kind of humanism, which owes its origins if not its essence to Nietzsche, sought to transfer to man certain attributes that formerly belonged to a God now declared to be dead: but is it still merely to man that these gifts are being transferred? It is at this point that there surges up, under its most tragic aspect, the central problem around which all these reflections of mine are poised. If we have the courage to pierce below the surface, below, that is especially to say, a sort of flattering verbiage, are we not induced to recognize that it is man himself, the very idea of man, that is decomposing before our eyes? To grasp this, all we have to do is to bring this long parenthesis to a close, and to develop what we have already been saying about function and output. Everything tends to show that, in what is very pretentiously called present-day civilization, it is the man whose output can be objectively calculated—as I showed just now, when dealing with the special case of the taxable earnings of the artist or man of letters—who is taken as the archetype: that is to say (and let us note this carefully) the man who by this type of activity seems to be most directly comparable to a kind of machine. One might say that it is starting with the machine, and in some sense on the model of the machine, that man at the present time is more and more commonly thought of, and one should remember that this is true also of, and is perhaps the essential truth about, Marxism: even though Marxism has undoubtedly its origins in a rebellious protest against the human condition in an industrialized world. Yet Marxism seems to have shown itself incapable of resisting the fascination exercised on it by the spectacle of this very world against which it first revolted. It is therefore quite as one would expect that, given such conditions, the genuinely creative man who sees things in terms of quality should find himself out of favour and even actively discredited.

But the evil is greater than this and has deeper roots. After all the producer, whether he is a miner or a metallurgist, does make a positive and necessary contribution to the human world. It is not so—at least, in the limiting case it is not so—for the clerk, the official, and this because of the unhealthy and in some sense cancerous conditions of the proliferation of officialdom in our day. The government official is beginning to seem more and more like something parasitic or verminous that is being bred out of society's decay. Everything to-day seems to tend towards a state of affairs in which the individual will not only be pestered by this officialdom, but, what is still more serious, caught up in it, asked, under the pressure of threats, to take his share in it. It is enough to think of the number of forms about taxes, insurance, compensation, and so on, that everybody now has to fill up every year, to recognize that we have been literally conscripted into an auxiliary bureaucracy. That is a strangely significant fact. If we think about it seriously, this is perhaps the only form in which what chimerical minds would regard as a progress towards unity has been really brought about. Under the German occupation, for that matter, we in France have been able to see just how far this process can be pushed, every individual being seemingly more and more easily reducible to an index card that can be sent to a central office and whose entries will determine the further treatment of the individual. A sanitary file, a judicial file, a file on payment of taxes, to be completed to-morrow perhaps by an estimate of character derived from handwriting analysis or facial measurements—in what is called an "organized" society such papers will be sufficient to decide the final disposal of the individual, without any account being taken of his family ties, his deepest attachments, his spontaneous tastes, his sense of vocation. For that matter, the very word "vocation" like the word "heritage" will be more and more devaluated and finally no doubt the authorities will refuse to recognize anything in the words at all except the residual validity of a surviving superstition.

It seems to me very important to notice that the methods which our enemies used during the war in dealing with inhabitants of occupied countries, labour conscripts, or deportees, should be looked at from this point of view, and not as the monstrous and unnatural expression of a demoniac will. These methods were, rather, the premature but at bottom rigorously logical expression of a state of mind which all around us we can see becoming more and more general, and that, moreover, in countries where the majority must be thought free of that madness which is itself, nevertheless —as Chesterton for instance saw so clearly—only a rationality that has broken out of its proper bounds. The only thing that appears as in some sense superfluous, as implying an excess of horror, inexplicable in itself, and not fitting neatly into a logical system, is the sadism of certain kinds of torture. But this, again, may be only a superficial view; we have certainly no clear notion of the conditions in which the sadistic mentality is developed; it may after all represent a kind of explosion of the irrational in a world of false rationality. But the fact, for instance, that certain poor wretches whose output had fallen below a given minimum were hurried away to the crematorium does not appear at all an irrational fact, if we start with certain premises. If man is thought of on the model of a machine, it is quite according to the rules and it conforms to the principles of a healthy economy that when his output falls below the cost of his maintenance and when he is "not worth repairing" (that is, not worth sending to hospital) because the cost of patching him up would be too much of a burden in proportion to any result to be expected from it, it is quite logical that he should be sent to the scrap heap like a worn-out car, thus allowing any still useful parts of him to be salvaged (as, if I am not mistaken, the Third Reich in wartime salvaged the fatty elements of corpses). If such attitudes and methods still appear monstrous and absurd to us, it is because we refuse to acknowledge that man really can be thought of on the model of a machine; that is a premise which we reject spontaneously and with horror; and it is well that we should do so, but a purely emotional reaction is not enough; we have to ask ourselves if we can translate our emotional reaction into terms of thought, for otherwise it will be all too easy for the doctrinaires of the new rationality to see in this emotional reaction only the residual life, the last kick, of an out-of-date and exhausted attitude of mind.

Besides all this, the question really has an extraordinary practical relevance. When I had a radio discussion with two biologists of a more or less materialist tendency, M. Jean Rostand and M. Marcel Prenant, I had a very strong and definite feeling that they either could not or would not state this problem. The lack of agreement between their emotional reactions and their mode of thinking did not seem to worry them, and I think that they were even unable to perceive it. One ought to bring in here, of course, that notion of insincerity or bad faith, which Sartre has done such good work in underlining, without necessarily being free from the fault himself. People of materialist tendencies do in fact refuse to recognize that if certain acts or practices still appear to us as open to condemnation, that is because we are living on a moral capital of feelings which for some time survive the positive ideas and beliefs which originally justified them. But we ought not to imagine that such a state of affairs has the least chance of lasting for very long. There is every indication that these feelings, deprived in some sense of their traditional function, like a church turned into a museum, are bound to disappear. This, for instance, is what is happening to the peasantry of certain regions of the centre and south-east of France, whose old manners and customs, as Gustave Thibon has shown in a forcible and gripping fashion, are undergoing actual destruction. I have noted down the terrifying evidence of a young priest who lives in one of these regions and who said to me, "Nothing counts any more for the peasants except money and pleasures, they have become mere automata at the service of money and pleasure." I observed to him that one had no right to speak of men as automata when they were undertaking anything as toilsome and arduous as labour on the land. But I immediately added, "The fascination exercised by the towns and by office jobs on the peasantry can, alas, perhaps be partly explained by the almost wholly automatized character of such jobs, of such lives."

For the rest, one can ask oneself whether this apparent obsession with money and pleasure which my friend spoke of was not, above all, a phenomenon resulting from fatigue. And here we touch on an idea which strikes me as one of the most important among all those which I am offering for the reader's consideration.

There is every reason to suppose that the extraordinary growth of the spirit of negation which we have witnessed in recent years, among men who quite literally no longer believe in anything, and—this is the point I want specially to emphasize—who are not tied to anything except money (and this at the very moment when the value of money is obviously becoming a fantasy value), there is every reason, I say, to suppose that this spirit of negation can be very largely explained by the inhuman conditions of work and living to which such men have been submitted since the two World Wars: conditions, of course, which have their repercussions on their families. On a scale without historical precedent, men in this century have experienced destruction and have also experienced the apparent uselessness of superhuman sacrifices: given these conditions, unless a man still adheres to some positive religious faith, on what is he going to lean, where is he going to rest his hope? It seems as if the very idea of a future were being abolished; one does not know whether one may not be wiped out tomorrow. In such a situation, *"Carpe diem"* becomes the universal imperative; but it is all too easy to imagine what *"Carpe diem"* implies at the level of a society which no longer knows anything of the refinements of ancient Epicureanism. The reduction of life to what is immediately lived—and that in a world in which technique is triumphing in the form of the radio, the cinema, and so on—can lead only to an almost unprecedented coarseness and vulgarity.

Here, of course, we ought to correct our general picture with plenty of specific, and no doubt often contrasting, examples. Let us take for instance, the peasant: it is the normal thing that his existence *should* have its bearings set towards the future, towards the harvest. So there is a growingly deep divorce, a violent disjunction, between what is implied in his traditional mode of life and the new attitudes and habits he is now acquiring. We ought to ask ourselves whether the progress of Communism in the French countryside is not the almost feverish expression of this living contradiction between the peasant's old traditions and his new desires, a contradiction which, at his level, is not likely to become easily aware of itself. But further analysis would enable us to recognize two separate elements in this unrest: on the one hand, among a chosen few, what is in itself a touching aspiration towards a better existence, a more worthy and as it were a renewed life; and on the other hand, and above all, resentment, envy. The condition of life of a workman or of many clerks and other subordinate employees would provide material for similar analyses. In particular, it would be very interesting to discover under what forms the future impinges on the consciousness of the clerk or the petty official; it is all too obvious that, apart from a few ambitious exceptions, the idea of eventually retiring with a small pension has come to replace that of a task to be accomplished. But it is doubtful whether one can exaggerate the impact of this idea of retirement on a man's very way of life, of conceiving the relation between himself and his life. Living is in danger of becoming a mere marking time while one is waiting—something petty and cautious, a diminished life. The mentality appropriate to the retirement one is looking forward to anticipates itself. The so-called active citizen is in virtual retirement already. It would, however, show a deep lack of understanding to treat such an attitude only in an ironical way, or to use it as a target for one's satirical gusto. For I think that such attitudes are, above all if one understands the very depths of them, of a nature to awaken a strong sense of pity. Let us leave aside the question of an actual wretchedness of poverty, which cannot be tolerated, and in fact probably will be tolerated less and less: for I do not believe that one is sinning by an excess of optimism in believing that, except in the event of some new disaster, such wretchedness is bound in the long run to disappear. Yet, even leaving actual wretchedness out of the argument, the condition of the majority of men does appear, to the reflective mind, pitiable in the extreme, from the moment when their horizon no longer stretches beyond the limits of this earthly life. And from this point of view we cannot be too severe in judging those who in the depths of their hearts have set themselves systematically to darken the human sky. But this whole theme would need a long elaboration, and we should have to emphasize, particularly, the impoverishment and even the adulteration which, for centuries past, the notion of truth has suffered.

The combined effect of all the remarks I have just been making is to show us that the human world to-day—a world some at least of whose principal characteristics Kafka has surely correctly grasped—is a world in great part given over to fatigue, and one suffering from a distress so deep that it no longer even recognizes itself as such. But at the same time—and this is the most terrible thing—a parasitic mode of thought finds very plausible ways of justifying this world: this mode of thought rests, at bottom, on a kind of idolatry of the masses and of the man who is at home in the masses: it lulls itself with the hope of seeing these masses, this man at the service of the masses, attaining a happiness which so far has been unknown and which, moreover, in its fulfilment will coincide with the fulfilment of social duty. Here again we have a formula of ancient philosophy rising up into new life; but it is no longer like *"Carpe diem"* an injunction for immediate application, it is on the contrary the expression of a hope for which a long-term credit must be allowed: the hope that virtue and happiness are ultimately identical. Unhappily, experience must be our teacher here; what we can watch growing up around is in fact a mode of life in which the words "virtue" and "happiness" are tending to become emptied of all meaning. In a termite colony, for instance, there is no reason to suppose that there is anything which merits either of these names. But recently I have quite often had occasion to say that here we have what does seem to me a real possibility of choice for man: *between the termite colony and the Mystical Body:* and the gravest error that anybody could commit would be to confuse the one with the other. Yet, for a mind which is not at home with the terms of Christian mysticism, the expression "Mystical Body" no doubt seems an almost meaningless one, and we shall have to make clear by concrete examples what we have in mind when we use this phrase.

At a level which is not the mere level of passing events, of news, the dominant fact about our world to-day is that life is no longer loved. Fundamentally, nothing can less resemble the love of life than can unhealthy taste for immediate enjoyment: in the indulgence of that taste, as I have said elsewhere, it is as if a kind of marriage tie between man and life had been broken. Moreover, it is extremely interesting to observe that the breaking of this tie coincided in history with the progressive establishment of biology as a science. And one may say, moreover, that the rupture between man and life has been observable in every circle in which a certain sense of the supernatural has not been preserved. For it is clear to-day that Nietzsche was guilty of a colossal error on this matter: that, I mean, of believing that Christians hate life, where, apart from certain heretical exceptions—I am thinking above all of Jansenism—it is exactly the opposite that is true. In particular, Nietzsche completely misconceived the meaning of the Christian belief in original sin: our awareness of original sin is our awareness of a principle of death that has found its way into the heart of our true life: redemption is the act by which God has grafted a new life—Life itself—on a life attacked by death, and which, without that grafting, would certainly be damned. The dominant question today is how these ties between man and life can be renewed, how the love of life can be rekindled in beings who no longer seem to have any feeling of it. But at this point we must avoid being the victims of certain very dangerous illusions. For it is obvious that our problem is not, fundamentally, that of reawakening a taste for life in a sick man by creating amusements for him. It is a much deeper, a more radical problem, and amusements and distractions are a completely inadequate solution; there is every reason on the contrary to suppose that current types of amusement, above all the cinema and the radio, where they are not guided by a higher principle, play into the hands of despair and death. Incidentally, let me add here, since I have brought up this idea of diversion, that Pascal, if we take him literally, seems to me on this subject an extremely dangerous guide.

It is not, therefore, in terms of value but only in terms of love that one can succeed in even stating this fundamental problem. But love is substantial, love is rooted in being, love is not commensurate with anything on which a value can be set or with anything "marketable," as the English say; and possibly it is only a sufficiently deep reflection on the nature of love that will enable one to recognize what an impossibility a philosophy of values is. For love is not a value itself and yet, on the other hand, there is not and cannot be any value without love. But a metaphysic of love, allowing that it brings in, though no doubt without making it an absolute, the distinction which so many contemporary theologians have borrowed from the Swedish thinker, Nygren, between *eros* and *agape,* cannot fail to culminate in a doctrine of the Mystical Body.

I have now reached the end of the task which I set myself in this chapter and I must confine myself in conclusion to making what seem to me a few essentially relevant remarks.

In the first place it would be absurd, not to say crazy, to suppose that there exists some technique, that is, some combination of methods which can be defined in abstract terms, by means of which we could reawaken love in souls that appear dead. Quite summarily, we have to say that such a reawakening can only be the work of grace, that is, of something which is at the opposite pole to any sort of technique. But this observation ought not to lead us to despair or, what comes to the same thing, to shut ourselves up within a sort of quietism, that is to say, to put a grinding brake on the dynamic impulse that leads us to act, to will, to bring remedies. In fact, an objection to my argument that is based on the fear of this sort of quietism seems to me to imply the falsest possible notion of grace and the ties that bind grace to man's freedom. Here again, we ought to denounce the errors of Sartre and his school. But, in fact, these errors are more or less common to all contemporary non-Christian philosophers; and for this fact the old rationalist philosophies bear a heavy load of responsibility. In fact, as soon as I think of grace, of the transcendency of grace, that thought itself tends to be transmuted into a freedom at the service of grace. "At the service," I say: but there is another word whose meaning is no longer understood. Through an incredible aberration, every kind of obedience tends to-day to be thought of in terms of passivity. Yet to serve means to expend oneself on behalf of something: the soul of service is generosity. The servant is the opposite of the slave. But our contemporary word-battle confounds these two terms. Here I can only point to the path on which that type of reflection which aims at reconstruction ought to set out; without this type of reflection, there is no philosophy worthy of the name. What we ought to ask ourselves is in what conditions freedom really can be exercised in the service of grace. There are two possibilities that we can immediately reject. In the first place, nobody can any longer accept the atomic individualism that was fashionable in the last century. This fact is too obvious to need insisting on. But the other possibility should be explored, mapped, and denounced with great care: I am speaking of the possibility of immersing oneself in the masses.

There is every reason to believe that it is only within very restricted groups, very small communities, that freedom can really be exercised in the service of grace. Such communities may assume very different forms: a parish, certainly, but also some straightforward business or professional undertaking, a school, for instance, but also for all I know an inn . . . . One should add also that these groups should not be "closed communities" in the Bergsonian sense, but on the contrary open to each other, and linked by tactful intermediaries, perhaps travelling from one community to another. Between these groups ties should grow up giving them the unity of grains in an ear of corn, but certainly not that of the mere elements lumped together in an aggregate. What we have to recreate is the living tissue. Not merely the national tissue. For we have got, I think, to look much further than the nation. It is not for that matter demonstrable that the nation, as such, can still constitute a quite living unity in the huge collective context we see around us. As Arnold Sandieu—in some matters truly a prophet— saw with penetrating clarity, we have to keep our eyes both on what lies on the far side and what lies on the near side of the national horizon.

These remarks, I can foresee, will provoke reactions of annoyance: among which I shall mention only this one—it will be said to me, "We have no time, disaster threatens us." I quite agree, disaster may be imminent. But no general scheme of action will enable us to conjure it away. Whether it must or must not happen, we should look further, beyond the possible deluge. And in this case, as in Noah's, it is only the rainbow of reconciliation that can bring salvation to us—though it may, of course, be salvation elsewhere: salvation far beyond our earthly limits, far beyond the unavoidable yet only apparent bankruptcy of our earthly deaths: in eternity: in an eternity whose call upon us becomes irresistible as soon as we have laid bare the mechanism of the triple illusion practised on us by the object, by number, and by value.

QUESTIONS FOR STUDY AND DISCUSSION

1. In Marcel's view, what is the conflict between man and technique?
2. What is Marcel's understanding of God and his appreciation of the traditional proofs?
3. How does Marcel conceive the free man?
4. What are the techniques of degradation and in what way could these be remedied?
5. According to Marcel, how does value judgment in present day society hamper freedom and responsibility?

Albert Camus

ALBERT CAMUS was born in Mondovi, Algeria, in 1913. He spent the early years of his life in North Africa, where he began writing and working in the theater. During World War II he was one of the leading writers in the French Resistance movement in Paris and editor of *Combat,* an important underground paper. A distinguished essayist, novelist, and playwright, Camus was awarded the Nobel prize for literature in 1957. He died in an automobile accident in 1960. *The Plague* (1948) and *The Rebel* (1954) are among his most widely read books.

The Rebel: A Definition

What is a rebel? A man who says no, but whose refusal does not imply a renunciation. He is also a man who says yes, from the moment he makes his first gesture of rebellion. A slave who has taken orders all his life suddenly decides that he cannot obey some new command. What does he mean by saying "no"?

He means, for example, that "this has been going on too long," "up to this point yes, beyond it no," "you are going to far," or, again, "there is a limit beyond which you shall not go." In other words, his no affirms the existence of a borderline. The same concept is to be found in the rebel's feeling that the other person "is exaggerating," that he is exerting his authority beyond a limit where he begins to infringe on the rights of others. Thus the movement of rebellion is founded simultaneously on the categorical rejection of an intrusion that is considered intolerable and on the confused conviction of an absolute right which, in the rebel's mind, is more precisely the impression that he "has the right to . . . ." Rebellion cannot exist without the feeling that, somewhere and somehow, one is right. It is in this way that the rebel slave says yes and no simultaneously. He affirms that there are limits and also that he suspects—and wishes to preserve—the existence of certain things on this side of the borderline. He demonstrates, with obstinacy, that there is something in him which "is worth while . . . ." and which must be taken into consideration. In a certain way, he confronts an order of things which oppresses him with the insistence on a kind of right not to be oppressed beyond the limit that he can tolerate.

In every act of rebellion, the rebel simultaneously experiences a feeling of revulsion at the infringment of his rights and a complete and spontaneous loyalty to certain aspects of himself. Thus he implicitly brings into play a standard of values so far from being gratuitous that he is prepared to support it no matter what the risks. Up to this point he has at least remained silent and has abandoned himself to the form of despair in which a condition is accepted even though it is considered unjust. To remain silent is to give the impression that one has no opinions, that one wants nothing, and in certain cases it really amounts to wanting nothing. Despair, like the absurd, has opinions and desires about everything in general and nothing in particular. Silence expresses this attitude very well. But from the moment that the rebel finds his voice—even though he says nothing but "no"—he begins to desire and to judge. The rebel, in the etymological sense, does a complete turnabout. He acted under the lash of his master's whip. Suddenly he turns and faces him. He opposes what is preferable to what is not. Not every value entails rebellion, but every act of rebellion tacitly invokes a value. Or is it really a question of values?

Awareness, no matter how confused it may be, develops from every act of rebellion: the sudden, dazzling perception that there is something in man with which he can identify himself, even if only for a moment. Up to now this identification was never really experienced. Before he rebelled, the slave accepted all the demands made upon him. Very often he even took orders, without reacting against them, which were far more conducive to insurrection than the one at which he balks. He accepted them patiently, though he may have protested inwardly, but in that he remained silent he was more concerned with his own immediate interests than as yet aware of his own rights. But with loss of patience—with impatience—a reaction begins which can extend to everything that he previously accepted, and which is almost always retroactive. The very moment the slave refuses to obey the humiliating orders of his master, he simultaneously rejects the condition of slavery. The act of rebellion carries him far beyond the point he had reached by simply refusing. He exceeds the bounds that he fixed for his antagonist, and now demands to be treated as an equal. What was at first the man's obstinate resistance now becomes the whole man, who is identified with and summed up in this resistance. The part of himself that he wanted to be respected he proceeds to place above everything else and proclaims it preferable to everything, even to life itself. It becomes for him the supreme good. Having up to now been willing to compromise, the slave suddenly adopts ("because this is how it must be. . . .") an attitude of All or Nothing. With rebellion, awareness is born.

But we can see that the knowledge gained is, at the same time, of an "all" that is still rather obscure and of a "nothing" that proclaims the possibility of sacrificing the rebel to this "All." The rebel himself wants to be "all"—to identify himself completely with this good of which he has suddenly become aware and by which he wants to be personally recognized and acknowledged—or "nothing"; in other words, to be completely destroyed by the force that dominates him. As a last resort, he is willing to accept the final defeat, which is death, rather than be deprived of the personal sacrament that he would call, for example, freedom. Better to die on one's feet than to live on one's knees.

Values, according to good authorities, "most often represent a transition from facts to rights, from what is desired to what is desirable (usually through the intermediary of what is generally considered desirable)." [1] The transition from facts to rights is manifest, as we have seen, in rebellion. So is the transition from "this must be" to "this is how I should like things to be," and even more so, perhaps, the idea of the sublimation of the individual in a henceforth universal good. The sudden appearance of the concept of "All or Nothing" demonstrates that rebellion, contrary to current opinion, and though it springs from everything that is most strictly individualistic in man, questions the very idea of the individual. If the individual, in fact, accepts death and happens to die as a consequence of his act of rebellion, he demonstrates by doing so that he is willing to sacrifice himself for the sake of a common good which he considers more important than his own destiny. If he prefers the risk of death to the negation of the rights that he defends, it is because he considers these rights more important than himself. Therefore he is acting in the name of certain values which are still indeterminate but which he feels are common to himself and to all men. We see that the affirmation implicit in every act of rebellion is extended to something that transcends the individual in so far as it withdraws him from his supposed solitude and provides him with a reason to act. But it is already worth noting that this concept of values as pre-existent to any kind of action contradicts the purely historical philosophies, in which values are acquired (if they are ever acquired) after the action has been completed. Analysis of rebellion leads at least to the suspicion that, contrary to the postulates of contemporary thought, a human nature does exist, as the Greeks believed. Why rebel if there is nothing permanent in oneself worth preserving? It is for the sake of everyone in the world that the slave asserts himself when he comes to the conclusion that a command has infringed on something in him which does not belong to him alone, but which is common ground where all men—even the man who insults and oppresses him —have a natural community.[2]

Two observations will support this argument. First, we can see that an act of rebellion is not, essentially, an egoistic act. Of course, it can have egoistic motives. But one can rebel equally well against lies as against oppression. Moreover, the rebel—once he has accepted the motives and at the moment of his greatest impetus—preserves nothing in that he risks

---

[1] Lalande: *Vocabulaire philosophique*. [A.C.]

[2] The community of victims is the same as that which unites victim and executioner. But the executioner does not know this. [A.C.]

everything. He demands respect for himself, of course, but only in so far as he identifies himself with a natural community.

Then we note that rebellion does not arise only, and necessarily, among the oppressed, but that it can also be caused by the mere spectacle of oppression of which someone else is the victim. In such cases there is a feeling of identification with another individual. And it must be pointed out that this is not a question of psychological identification—a mere subterfuge by which the individual imagines that it is he himself who has been offended. On the contrary, it can often happen that we cannot bear to see offenses done to others which we ourselves have accepted without rebelling. The suicides of the Russian terrorists in Siberia as a protest against their comrades' being whipped is a case in point. Nor is it a question of the feeling of a community of interests. Injustices done to men whom we consider enemies can, actually, be profoundly repugnant to us. There is only identification of one's destiny with that of others and a choice of sides. Therefore the individual is not, in himself alone, the embodiment of the values he wishes to defend. It needs all humanity, at least, to comprise them. When he rebels, a man identifies himself with other men and so surpasses himself, and from this point of view human solidarity is metaphysical. But for the moment we are only talking of the kind of solidarity that is born in chains.

It would be possible for us to define the positive aspect of the values implicit in every act of rebellion by comparing them with a completely negative concept like that of resentment as defined by Scheler. Rebellion is, in fact, much more than pursuit of a claim, in the strongest sense of the word. Resentment is very well defined by Scheler as an autointoxication—the evil secretion, in a sealed vessel, of prolonged impotence. Rebellion, on the contrary, breaks the seal and allows the whole being to come into play. It liberates stagnant waters and turns them into a raging torrent. Scheler himself emphasizes the passive aspect of resentment and remarks on the prominent place it occupies in the psychology of women who are dedicated to desire and possession. The fountainhead of rebellion, on the contrary, is the principle of superabundant activity and energy. Scheler is also right in saying that resentment is always highly colored by envy. But one envies what one does not have, while the rebel's aim is to defend what he is. He does not merely claim some good that he does not possess or of which he was deprived. His aim is to claim recognition for something which he has and which has already been recognized by him, in almost every case, as more important than anything of which he could be envious. Rebellion is not realistic. According to Scheler, resentment always turns into either unscrupulous ambition or bitterness, depending on whether it is implanted in a strong person or a weak one. But in both cases it is a question of wanting to be something other than what one is. Resentment is always resentment against oneself. The rebel, on the contrary, from his very first step, refuses to allow anyone to touch what he is. He is fighting for the integrity of one part of his being. He does not try, primarily, to conquer, but simply to impose.

Finally, it would seem that resentment takes delight, in advance, in the pain that it would like the object of its envy to feel. Nietzsche and Scheler are right in seeing an excellent example of this in the passage where Tertullian informs his readers that one of the greatest sources of happiness among the blessed will be the spectacle of the Roman emperors consumed in the fires of hell. This kind of happiness is also experienced by the decent people who go to watch executions. The rebel, on the contrary, limits himself, as a matter of principle, to refusing to be humiliated without asking that others should be. He will even accept pain provided his integrity is respected.

It is therefore hard to understand why Scheler completely indentifies the spirit of rebellion with resentment. His criticism of the resentment to be found in humanitarianism (which he treats as the non-Christian form of love for mankind) could perhaps be applied to certain indeterminate forms of humanitarian idealism, or to the techniques of terror. But it rings false in relation to man's rebellion against his condition—the movement that enlists the individual in the defense of a dignity common to all men. Scheler wants to demonstrate that humanitarian feelings are always accompanied by a hatred of the world. Humanity is loved in general in order to avoid having to love anybody in particular. This is correct, in some cases, and it is easier to understand Scheler when we realize that for him humanitarianism is represented by Bentham and Rousseau. But man's love for man can be born of other things than a mathematical calculation of the resultant rewards or a theoretical confidence in human nature. In face of the utilitarians, and of Émile's preceptor, there is, for example, the kind of logic, embodied by Dostoievsky in Ivan Karamazov, which progresses from an act of rebellion to metaphysical insurrection. Scheler is aware of this and sums up the concept in the following manner: "There is not enough love in the world to squander it on anything but human beings." Even if this proposition were true, the appalling despair that it implies would merit anything but contempt. In fact, it misunderstands the tortured character of Karamazov's rebellion. Ivan's drama, on the contrary, arises from the fact that there is too much love without an object. This love finding no outlet and God being denied, it is then decided to lavish it on human beings as a generous act of complicity.

Nevertheless, in the act of rebellion as we have envisaged it up to now, an abstract ideal is not chosen through lack of feeling and in pursuit of a sterile demand. We insist that the part of man which cannot be reduced to mere ideas should be taken into consideration—the passionate side of his nature that serves no other purpose than to be part of the act of living. Does this imply that no rebellion is motivated by resentment? No, and we know it only too well in this age of malice. But we must consider the idea of rebellion in its widest sense on pain of betraying it; and in its widest sense rebellion goes far beyond resentment. When Heathcliff, in *Wuthering Heights,* says that he puts his love above God and would willingly go to hell in order to be reunited with the woman he loves, he is prompted not only by youth and humiliation but by the consuming experience of a whole lifetime. The same emotion causes Eckart, in a surprising fit of heresy, to say that he prefers hell with Jesus to heaven without Him. This is the very essence of love. Contrary to Scheler, it would therefore be impossible to overemphasize the passionate affirmation that underlies the act of rebellion and distinguishes it from resentment. Rebellion, though apparently negative, since it creates nothing, is profoundly positive in that it reveals the part of man which must always be defended.

But, to sum up, are not rebellion and the values that it implies relative? Reasons for rebellion do seem to change, in fact, with periods and civilizations. It is obvious that a Hindu pariah, an Inca warrior, a primitive native of central Africa, and a member of one of the first Christian communities had not at all the same ideas about rebellion. We could even assert, with considerable assurance, that the idea of rebellion has no meaning in these particular cases. However, a Greek slave, a serf, a *condottiere* of the Renaissance, a Parisian bourgeois during the Regency, a Russian intellectual at the beginning of the twentieth century, and a contemporary worker would undoubtedly agree that rebellion is legitimate, even if they differed about the reasons for it. In other words, the problem of rebellion seems to assume a precise meaning only within the confines of Western thought. It is possible to be even more explicit by remarking, like Scheler, that the spirit of rebellion finds few means of expression in societies where inequalities are very great (the Hindu caste system) or, again, in those where there is absolute equality (certain primitive societies). The spirit of rebellion can exist only in a society where a theoretical equality conceals great factual inequalities. The problem of rebellion, therefore, has no meaning except within our own Western society. One might be tempted to affirm that it is relative to the development of individualism if the preceding remarks had not put us on our guard against this conclusion.

On the basis of the evidence, the only conclusion that can be drawn from Scheler's remark is that, thanks to the theory of political freedom, there is, in the very heart of our society, an increasing awareness in man of the idea of man and, thanks to the application of this theory of freedom, a corresponding dissatisfaction. Actual freedom has not increased in proportion to man's awareness of it. We can only deduce from this observation that rebellion is the act of an educated man who is aware of his own rights. But there is nothing which justifies us in saying that it is only a question of individual rights. Because of the sense of solidarity we have already pointed out, it would rather seem that what is at stake is humanity's gradually increasing self-awareness as it pursues its course. In fact, for the Inca and the pariah the problem never arises, because for them it had been solved by a tradition, even before they had had time to raise it—the answer being that tradition is sacred. If in a world where things are held sacred the problem of rebellion does not arise, it is because no real problems are to be found in such a world, all the answers having been given simultaneously. Metaphysic is replaced by myth. There are no more questions, only eternal answers and commentaries, which may be metaphysical. But before man accepts the sacred world and in order that he should be able to accept it—or before he escapes from it and in order that he should be able to escape from it—there is always a period of soul-searching and rebellion. The rebel is a man who is on the point of accepting or rejecting the sacred and determined on laying claim to a human situation in which all the answers are human—in other words, formulated in reasonable terms. From this moment every question, every word, is an act of rebellion while in the sacred world every word is an act of grace. It would be possible to demonstrate in this manner that only two possible worlds can exist for the human mind: the sacred (or, to speak in Christian terms, the world of grace [3]) and the world of rebellion. The disappearance of one is equivalent to the appearance of the other, despite the fact that this appearance can take place in disconcerting forms. There again we rediscover the *All or Nothing*. The present interest of the problem of rebellion only springs from the fact that nowadays whole societies have wanted to discard the sacred. We live in an unsacrosanct moment in history. Insurrection is certainly not the sum total of human experience. But history today, with all its storm and strife, compels us to say that rebellion is one of the essential dimensions of man. It is our historic reality. Unless we choose to ignore reality, we must find our values in it. Is it possible to find a rule of conduct outside the realm of religion and its absolute values? That is the question raised by rebellion.

We have already noted the confused values that are called into play by incipient rebellion. Now we must inquire if these values are to be found again in contemporary forms of rebellious thought and action, and if they are, we must specify their content. But, before going any farther, let us note that the basis of these values is rebellion itself. Man's solidarity is founded upon rebellion, and rebellion, in its turn, can only find its justification in this solidarity. We have, then, the right to say that any rebellion which claims the right to deny or destroy this solidarity loses simultaneously its right to be called rebellion and becomes in reality an acquiescence in murder. In the same way, this solidarity, except in so far as religion is concerned, comes to life only on the level of rebellion. And so the real drama of revolutionary thought is announced. In order to exist, man must rebel, but rebellion must respect the limit it discovers in itself—a limit

---

[3] There is, of course, an act of metaphysical rebellion at the beginning of Christianity, but the resurrection of Christ and the annunciation of the kingdom of heaven interpreted as a promise of eternal life are the answers that render it futile. [A.C.]

where minds meet and, in meeting, begin to exist. Rebellious thought, therefore, cannot dispense with memory: it is a perpetual state of tension. In studying its actions and its results, we shall have to say, each time, whether it remains faithful to its first noble promise or if, through indolence or folly, it forgets its original purpose and plunges into a mire of tyranny or servitude.

Meanwhile, we can sum up the initial progress that the spirit of rebellion provokes in a mind that is originally imbued with the absurdity and apparent sterility of the world. In absurdist experience, suffering is individual. But from the moment when a movement of rebellion begins, suffering is seen as a collective experience. Therefore the first progressive step for a mind overwhelmed by the strangeness of things is to realize that this feeling of strangeness is shared with all men and that human reality, in its entirety, suffers from the distance which separates it from the rest of the universe. The malady experienced by a single man becomes a mass plague. In our daily trials rebellion plays the same role as does the *"cogito"* in the realm of thought: it is the first piece of evidence. But this evidence lures the individual from his solitude. It founds its first value on the whole human race. I rebel—therefore we exist.

Moderation and Excess

The errors of contemporary revolution are first of all explained by the ignorance or systematic misconception of that limit which seems inseparable from human nature and which rebellion reveals. Nihilist thought, because it neglects this frontier, ends by precipitating itself into a uniformly acclerated movement. Nothing any longer checks it in its course and it reaches the point of justifying total destruction or unlimited conquest. We now know, at the end of this long inquiry into rebellion and nihilism, that rebellion with no other limits but historical expediency signifies unlimited slavery. To escape this fate, the revolutionary mind, if it wants to remain alive, must therefore return again to the sources of rebellion and draw its inspiration from the only system of thought which is faithful to its origins: thought that recognizes limits. If the limit discovered by rebellion transfigures everything, if every thought, every action that goes beyond a certain point negates itself, there is, in fact, a measure by which to judge events and men. In history, as in psychology, rebellion is an irregular pendulum, which swings in an erratic arc because it is looking for its most perfect and profound rhythm. But its irregularity is not total: it functions around a pivot. Rebellion, at the same time that it suggests a nature common to all men, brings to light the measure and the limit which are the very principle of this nature.

Every reflection today, whether nihilist or positivist, gives birth, sometimes without knowing it, to standards that science itself confirms. The quantum theory, relativity, the uncertainty of interrelationships, define a world that has no definable reality except on the scale of average greatness, which is our own. The ideologies which guide our world were born in the time of absolute scientific discoveries. Our real knowledge, on the other hand, only justifies a system of thought based on relative discoveries. "Intelligence," says Lazare Bickel, "is our faculty for not developing what we think to the very end, so that we can still believe in reality." Approximative thought is the only creator of reality.[1]

The very forces of matter, in their blind advance, impose their own limits. That is why it is useless to want to reverse the advance of technology. The age of the spinning-wheel is over and the dream of a civilization of artisans is vain. The machine is bad only in the way that it is now employed. Its benefits must be accepted even if its ravages are rejected. The truck, driven day and night, does not humiliate its driver, who knows it inside out and treats it with affection and efficiency. The real and inhuman excess lies in the division of labor. But by dint of this excess, a day comes when a machine capable of a hundred operations, operated by one man, creates one sole object. This man, on a different scale, will have partially rediscovered the power of creation which he possessed in the days of the artisan. The anonymous producer then more nearly approaches the creator. It is not certain, naturally, that industrial excess will immediately embark on this path. But it already demonstrates, by the way it functions, the necessity for moderation and gives rise to reflections on the proper way to organize this moderation. Either this value of limitation will be realized, or contemporary excesses will only find their principle and peace in universal destruction.

This law of moderation equally well extends to all the contradictions of rebellious thought. The real is not entirely rational, nor is the rational entirely real. As we have seen in regard to surrealism, the desire for unity not only demands that everything should be rational. It also wishes that the irrational should not be sacrificed. One cannot say that nothing has any meaning, because in doing so one affirms a value sanctified by an opinion; nor that everything has a meaning, because the word everything has no meaning for us. The irrational imposes limits on the rational, which, in its

---

[1] Science today betrays its origins and denies its own acquisitions in allowing itself to be put to the service of State terrorism and the desire for power. Its punishment and its degradation lie in only being able to produce, in an abstract world, the means of destruction and enslavement. But when the limit is reached, science will perhaps serve the individual rebellion. This terrible necessity will mark the decisive turning-point. [A.C.]

turn, gives it its moderation. Something has a meaning, finally, which we must obtain from meaninglessness. In the same way, it cannot be said that existence takes place only on the level of essence. Where could one perceive essence except on the level of existence and evolution? But nor can it be said that being is only existence. Something that is always in the process of development could not exist—there must be a beginning. Being can only prove itself in development, and development is nothing without being. The world is not in a condition of pure stability; nor is it only movement. It is both movement and stability. The historical dialectic, for example, is not in continuous pursuit of an unknown value. It revolves around the limit, which is its prime value. Heraclitus, the discoverer of the constant change of things, nevertheless set a limit to this perpetual process. This limit was symbolized by Nemesis, the goddess of moderation and the implacable enemy of the immoderate. A process of thought which wanted to take into account the contemporary contradictions of rebellion should seek its inspiration from this goddess.

As for the moral contradictions, they too begin to become soluble in the light of this conciliatory value. Virtue cannot separate itself from reality without becoming a principle of evil. Nor can it identify itself completely with reality without denying itself. The moral value brought to light by rebellion, finally, is no farther above life and history than history and life are above it. In actual truth, it assumes no reality in history until man gives his life for it or dedicates himself entirely to it. Jacobin and bourgeois civilization presumes that values are above history, and its formal virtues then lay the foundation of a repugnant form of mystification. The revolution of the twentieth century decrees that values are intermingled with the movement of history and that their historical foundations justify a new form of mystification. Moderation, confronted with this irregularity, teaches us that at least one part of realism is necessary to every ethic: pure and unadulterated virtue is homicidal. And one part of ethics is necessary to all realism: cynicism is homicidal. That is why humanitarian cant has no more basis than cynical provocation. Finally, man is not entirely to blame; it was not he who started history; nor is he entirely innocent, since he continues it. Those who go beyond this limit and affirm his total innocence end in the insanity of definitive culpability. Rebellion, on the contrary, sets us on the path of calculated culpability. Its sole but invincible hope is incarnated, in the final analysis, in innocent murderers.

At this limit, the "We are" paradoxically defines a new form of individualism. "We are" in terms of history, and history must reckon with this "We are," which must in its turn keep its place in history. I have need of others who have need of me and of each other. Every collective action, every form of society, supposes a discipline, and the individual, without this discipline, is only a stranger, bowed down under the weight of an inimical collectivity. But society and discipline lose their direction if they deny the "We are." I alone, in one sense, support the common dignity that

I cannot allow either myself or others to debase. This individualism is in no sense pleasure; it is perpetual struggle, and, sometimes, unparalleled joy when it reaches the heights of proud compassion.

THOUGHT AT THE MERIDIAN

As for knowing if such an attitude can find political expression in the contemporary world, it is easy to evoke—and this is only an example—what is traditionally called revolutionary trade-unionism. Cannot it be said that even this trade-unionism is ineffectual? The answer is simple: it is this movement alone that, in one century, is responsible for the enormously improved condition of the workers from the sixteen-hour day to the forty-hour week. The ideological Empire has turned socialism back on its tracks and destroyed the greater part of the conquests of trade-unionism. It is because trade-unionism started from a concrete basis, the basis of professional employment (which is to the economic order what the commune is to the political order), the living cell on which the organism builds itself, while the Cæsarian revolution starts from doctrine and forcibly introduces reality into it. Trade-unionism, like the commune, is the negation, to the benefit of reality, of bureaucratic and abstract centralism.[2] The revolution of the twentieth century, on the contrary, claims to base itself on economics, but is primarily political and ideological. It cannot, by its very function, avoid terror and violence done to the real. Despite its pretensions, it begins in the absolute and attempts to mold reality. Rebellion, inversely, relies on reality to assist it in its perpetual struggle for truth. The former tries to realize itself from top to bottom, the latter from bottom to top. Far from being a form of romanticism, rebellion, on the contrary, takes the part of true realism. If it wants a revolution, it wants it on behalf of life, not in defiance of it. That is why it relies primarily on the most concrete realities—on occupation, on the village, where the living heart of things and of men is to be found. Politics, to satisfy the demands of rebellion, must submit to the eternal verities. Finally, when it causes history to advance and alleviates the sufferings of mankind, it does so without terror, if not without violence, and in the most dissimilar political conditions.[3]

But this example goes farther than it seems. On the very day when the Cæsarian revolution triumphed over the syndicalist and libertarian spirit, revolutionary thought lost, in itself, a counterpoise of which it cannot, without decaying, deprive itself. This counterpoise, this spirit which takes the measure of life, is the same that animates the long tradition that can be

---

[2] Tolain, the future Communard, wrote: "Human beings emancipate themselves only on the basis of natural groups." [A.C.]

[3] Scandinavian societies today, to give only one example, demonstrate how artificial and destructive are purely political opposites. The most fruitful form of trade-unionism is reconciled with constitutional monarchy and achieves an approximation of a just society. The first preoccupation of the historical and natural State has been, on the contrary, to crush forever the professional nucleus and communal autonomy. [A.C.]

called solitary thought, in which, since the time of the Greeks, nature has always been weighed against evolution. The history of the First International, when German Socialism ceaselessly fought against the libertarian thought of the French, the Spanish, and the Italians, is the history of the struggle of German ideology against the Mediterranean mind.[4] The commune against the State, concrete society against absolutist society, deliberate freedom against rational tyranny, finally altruistic individualism against the colonization of the masses, are, then, the contradictions that express once again the endless opposition of moderation to excess which has animated the history of the Occident since the time of the ancient world. The profound conflict of this century is perhaps not so much between the German ideologies of history and Christian political concepts, which in a certain way are accomplices, as between German dreams and Mediterranean traditions, between the violence of eternal adolescence and virile strength, between nostalgia, rendered more acute by knowledge and by books and courage reinforced and enlightened by the experience of life—in other words, between history and nature. But German ideology, in this sense, has come into an inheritance. It consummates twenty centuries of abortive struggle against nature, first in the name of a historic god and then of a deified history. Christianity, no doubt, was only able to conquer its catholicity by assimilating as much as it could of Greek thought. But when the Church dissipated its Mediterranean heritage, it placed the emphasis on history to the detriment of nature, caused the Gothic to triumph over the romance, and, destroying a limit in itself, has made increasing claims to temporal power and historical dynamism. When nature ceases to be an object of contemplation and admiration, it can then be nothing more than material for an action that aims at transforming it. These tendencies—and not the concepts of mediation, which would have comprised the real strength of Christianity—are triumphing in modern times, to the detriment of Christianity itself, by an inevitable turn of events. That God should, in fact, be expelled from this historical universe and German ideology be born where action is no longer a process of perfection but pure conquest, is an expression of tyranny.

But historical absolutism, despite its triumphs, has never ceased to come into collision with an irrepressible demand of human nature, of which the Mediterranean, where intelligence is intimately related to the blinding light of the sun, guards the secret. Rebellious thought, that of the commune or of revolutionary trade-unionism, has not ceased to deny this demand in the presence of bourgeois nihilism as well as of Cæsarian socialism. Authoritarian thought, by means of three wars and thanks to the physical destruction of a revolutionary elite, has succeeded in submerging this libertarian tradition. But this barren victory is only provisional; the

[4] See Marx's letter to Engels (July 20, 1870) hoping for the victory of Prussia over France: "The preponderance of the German proletariat over the French proletariat would be at the same time the preponderance of our theory over Proudhon's." [A.C.]

battle still continues. Europe has never been free of this struggle between darkness and light. It has only degraded itself by deserting the struggle and eclipsing day by night. The destruction of this equilibrium is today bearing its bitterest fruits. Deprived of our means of mediation, exiled from natural beauty, we are once again in the world of the Old Testament, crushed between a cruel Pharaoh and an implacable heaven.

In the common condition of misery, the eternal demand is heard again; nature once more takes up the fight against history. Naturally, it is not a question of despising anything, or of exalting one civilization at the expense of another, but of simply saying that it is a thought which the world today cannot do without for very much longer. There is, undoubtedly, in the Russian people something to inspire Europe with the potency of sacrifice, and in America a necessary power of construction. But the youth of the world always find themselves standing on the same shore. Thrown into the unworthy melting-pot of Europe, deprived of beauty and friendship, we Mediterraneans, the proudest of races, live always by the same light. In the depths of the European night, solar thought, the civilization facing two ways awaits its dawn. But it already illuminates the paths of real mastery.

Real mastery consists in refuting the prejudices of the time, initially the deepest and most malignant of them, which would reduce man, after his deliverance from excess, to a barren wisdom. It is very true that excess can be a form of sanctity when it is paid for by the madness of Nietzsche. But is this intoxication of the soul which is exhibited on the scene of our culture always the madness of excess, the folly of attempting the impossible, of which the brand can never be removed from him who has, once at least, abandoned himself to it? Has Prometheus ever had this fanatical or accusing aspect? No, our civilization survives in the complacency of cowardly or malignant minds—a sacrifice to the vanity of aging adolescents. Lucifer also has died with God, and from his ashes has arisen a spiteful demon who does not even understand the object of his venture. In 1950, excess is always a comfort, and sometimes a career. Moderation, on the one hand, is nothing but pure tension. It smiles, no doubt, and our Convulsionists, dedicated to elaborate apocalypses, despise it. But its smile shines brightly at the climax of an interminable effort: it is in itself a supplementary source of strength. Why do these petty-minded Europeans who show us an avaricious face, if they no longer have the strength to smile, claim that their desperate convulsions are examples of superiority?

The real madness of excess dies or creates its own moderation. It does not cause the death of others in order to create an alibi for itself. In its most extreme manifestations, it finds its limit, on which, like Kaliayev, it sacrifices itself if necessary. Moderation is not the opposite of rebellion. Rebellion in itself is moderation, and it demands, defends, and re-creates it throughout history and its eternal disturbances. The very origin of this value guarantees us that it can only be partially destroyed. Moderation, born of rebellion, can only live by rebellion. It is a perpetual conflict, continually created and mastered by the intelligence. It does not triumph either in the impossible or in the abyss. It finds its equilibrium through them. Whatever we may do, excess will always keep its place in the heart of man, in the place where solitude is found. We all carry within us our places of exile, our crimes and our ravages. But our task is not to unleash them on the world; it is to fight them in ourselves and in others. Rebellion, the secular will not to surrender of which Barrès speaks, is still today at the basis of the struggle. Origin of form, source of real life, it keeps us always erect in the savage, formless movement of history.

Beyond Nihilism

There does exist for man, therefore, a way of acting and of thinking which is possible on the level of moderation to which he belongs. Every undertaking that is more ambitious than this proves to be contradictory. The absolute is not attained nor, above all, created through history. Politics is not religion, or if it is, then it is nothing but the Inquisition. How would society define an absolute? Perhaps everyone is looking for this absolute on behalf of all. But society and politics only have the responsibility of arranging everyone's affairs so that each will have the leisure and the freedom to pursue this common search. History can then no longer be presented as an object of worship. It is only an opportunity that must be rendered fruitful by a vigilant rebellion.

"Obsession with the harvest and indifference to history," writes René Char admirably, "are the two extremities of my bow." If the duration of history is not synonymous with the duration of the harvest, then history, in effect, is no more than a fleeting and cruel shadow in which man has no more part. He who dedicates himself to this history dedicates himself to nothing and, in his turn, is nothing. But he who dedicates himself to the duration of his life, to the house he builds, to the dignity of mankind, dedicates himself to the earth and reaps from it the harvest that sows its seed and sustains the world again and again. Finally, it is those who know how to rebel, at the appropriate moment, against history who really advance its interests. To rebel against it supposes an interminable tension and the agonized serenity of which René Char also speaks. But the true life is present in the heart of this dichotomy. Life is this dichotomy itself, the mind soaring over volcanoes of light, the madness of justice, extenuating intransigence of moderation. The words that reverberate for us at the confines of this long adventure of rebellion are not formulas for optimism, for which we have no possible use in the extremities of our unhappiness, but words of courage and intelligence which, on the shores of the eternal seas, even have the qualities of virtue.

No possible form of wisdom today can claim to give more. Rebellion indefatigably confronts evil, from which it can only derive a new impetus. Man can master in himself everything that should be mastered. He should rectify in creation everything that can be rectified. And after he has done so, children will still die unjustly even in a perfect society. Even by his greatest effort man can only propose to diminish arithmetically the sufferings of the world. But the injustice and the suffering of the world will remain and, no matter how limited they are, they will not cease to be an outrage. Dimitri Karamazov's cry of "Why?" will continue to resound; art and rebellion will die only with the last man.

There is an evil, undoubtedly, which men accumulate in their frantic desire for unity. But yet another evil lies at the roots of this inordinate movement. Confronted with this evil, confronted with death, man from the very depths of his soul cries out for justice. Historical Christianity has only replied to this protest against evil by the annunciation of the kingdom and then of eternal life, which demands faith. But suffering exhausts hope and faith and then is left alone and unexplained. The toiling masses, worn out with suffering and death, are masses without God. Our place is henceforth at their side, far from teachers, old or new. Historical Christianity postpones to a point beyond the span of history the cure of evil and murder, which are nevertheless experienced within the span of history. Contemporary materialism also believes that it can answer all questions. But, as a slave to history, it increases the domain of historic murder and at the same time leaves it without any justification, except in the future—which again demands faith. In both cases one must wait, and meanwhile the innocent continue to die. For twenty centuries the sum total of evil has not diminished in the world. No paradise, whether divine or revolutionary, has been realized. An injustice remains inextricably bound to all suffering, even the most deserved in the eyes of men. The long silence of Prometheus before the powers that overwhelmed him still cries out in protest. But Prometheus, meanwhile, has seen men rail and turn against him. Crushed between human evil and destiny, between terror and the arbitrary, all that remains to him is his power to rebel in order to save from murder him who can still be saved, without surrendering to the arrogance of blasphemy.

Then we understand that rebellion cannot exist without a strange form of love. Those who find no rest in God or in history are condemned to live for those who, like themselves, cannot live: in fact, for the humiliated. The most pure form of the movement of rebellion is thus crowned with the heart-rendering cry of Karamazov: if all are not saved, what good is the salvation of one only? Thus Catholic prisoners, in the prison cells of Spain, refuse communion today because the priests of the regime have made it obligatory in certain prisons. These lonely witnesses to the crucifixion of innocence also refuse salvation if it must be paid for by injustice and oppression. This insane generosity is the generosity of rebellion, which unhesitatingly gives the strength of its love and without a moment's delay refuses injustice. Its merit lies in making no calculations, distributing everything it possesses to life and to living men. It is thus that it is prodigal in its gifts to men to come. Real generosity toward the future lies in giving all to the present.

Rebellion proves in this way that it is the very movement of life and that it cannot be denied without renouncing life. Its purest outburst, on each occasion, gives birth to existence. Thus it is love and fecundity or it is nothing at all. Revolution without honor, calculated revolution which, in preferring an abstract concept of man to a man of flesh and blood, denies existence as many times as is necessary, puts resentment in the place of love. Immediately rebellion, forgetful of its generous origins, allows itself to be contaminated by resentment; it denies life, dashes toward destruction, and raises up the grimacing cohorts of petty rebels, embryo slaves all of them, who end by offering themselves for sale, today, in all the marketplaces of Europe, to no matter what form of servitude. It is no longer either revolution or rebellion but rancor, malice, and tyranny. Then, when revolution in the name of power and of history becomes a murderous and immoderate mechanism, a new rebellion is consecrated in the name of moderation and of life. We are at that extremity now. At the end of this tunnel of darkness, however, there is inevitably a light, which we already divine and for which we only have to fight to ensure its coming. All of us, among the ruins, are preparing a renaissance beyond the limits of nihilism. But few of us know it.

Already, in fact, rebellion, without claiming to solve everything, can at least confront its problems. From this moment high noon is borne away on the fast-moving stream of history. Around the devouring flames, shadows writhe in mortal combat for an instant of time and then as suddenly disappear, and the blind, fingering their eyelids, cry out that this is history. The men of Europe, abandoned to the shadows, have turned their backs upon the fixed and radiant point of the present. They forget the present for the future, the fate of humanity for the delusion of power, the misery of the slums for the mirage of the eternal city, ordinary justice for an empty promised land. They despair of personal freedom and dream of a strange freedom of the species; reject solitary death and give the name of immortality to a vast collective agony. They no longer believe in the things that exist in the world and in living man; the secret of Europe is that it no longer loves life. Its blind men entertain the puerile belief that to love one single day of life amounts to justifying whole centuries of oppression. That is why they wanted to efface joy from the world and to postpone it until a much later date. Impatience with limits, the rejection of their double life, despair at being a man, have finally driven them to inhuman excesses. Denying the real grandeur of life, they have had to stake all on their own excellence. For want of something better to do, they deified themselves and their misfortunes began; these gods have had their eyes put out. Kaliayev, and his brothers throughout the entire world, refuse, on the contrary, to be deified in that they refuse the unlimited power to inflict death. They choose, and give us as an example the only original rule of life today: to learn to live and to die, and, in order to be a man, to refuse to be a god.

At this meridian of thought, the rebel thus rejects divinity in order to share in the struggles and destiny of all men. We shall choose Ithaca, the faithful land, frugal and audacious thought, lucid action, and the generosity of the man who understands. In the light, the earth remains our first and our last love. Our brothers are breathing under the same sky as we; justice is a living thing. Now is born that strange joy which helps one live and die, and which we shall never again postpone to a later time. On the sorrowing earth it is the unresting thorn, the bitter brew, the harsh wind off the sea, the old and the new dawn. With this joy, through long struggle, we shall remake the soul of our time, and a Europe which will exclude nothing. Not even that phantom Nietzsche, who for twelve years after his downfall was continually invoked by the West as the blasted image of its loftiest knowledge and its nihilism; nor the prophet of justice without mercy who lies, by mistake, in the unbelievers' plot at Highgate Cemetery; nor the deified mummy of the man of action in his glass coffin; nor any part of what the intelligence and energy of Europe have ceaselessly furnished to the pride of a contemptible period. All may indeed live again, side by side with the martyrs of 1905, but on condition that it is understood that they correct one another, and that a limit, under the sun, shall curb them all. Each tells the other that he is not God; this is the end of romanticism. At this moment, when each of us must fit an arrow to his bow and enter the lists anew, to reconquer, within history and in spite of it, that which he owns already, the thin yield of his fields, the brief love of this earth, at this moment when at last a man is born, it is time to forsake our age and its adolescent furies. The bow bends; the wood complains. At the moment of supreme tension, there will leap into flight an unswerving arrow, a shaft that is inflexible and free.

QUESTIONS FOR STUDY AND DISCUSSION

1. In what sense is rebellion a retroactive expression?
2. Is the act of rebellion individualistic in the sense that it attempts to defy the universal order? Explain your answer fully.
3. What role, if any, does resentment play in rebellion?
4. How does "I rebel" imply that "we exist"?

Pierre Teilhard de Chardin

PIERRE TEILHARD DE CHARDIN, a leading exponent of the collectivist or post-existentialist trend in contemporary philosophy, was born in Auvergne, France, in 1882. An ordained member of the Society of Jesus, he held positions as professor of Geology at the Catholic Institute in Paris, director of the National Geologic Survey of China, and director of the National Research Center of France. He died in New York in 1955. Two of his outstanding published works are *The Phenomenon of Man* (1959) and *The Divine Milieu* (1960).

The Spiritual Power of Matter

The same beam of light which christian spirituality, rightly and fully understood, directs upon the Cross to humanise it (without veiling it) is reflected on matter so as to spirtualise it.

In their struggle towards the mystical life, men have often succumbed to the illusion of crudely contrasting soul and body, spirit and flesh, as good and evil. But despite certain current expressions, this Manichean tendency has never had the Church's approval. And, in order to prepare the way for our final view of the divine *milieu,* perhaps we may be allowed to vindicate and exalt that aspect of it which the Lord came to put on, save and consecrate: *holy matter.*

From the mystical and ascetic point of view adopted in these pages, matter is not exactly any of the abstract entities defined under that name by science and philosophy. It is certainly the same *concrete* reality, for us, as it is for physics and metaphysics, having the same basic attributes of plurality, perceivability and inter-connection. But here we want to embrace that reality as a whole in its widest possible sense: to give it its full abundance as it reacts not only to our scientific or analytical investigations, but to all our practical activities. Matter, as far as we are concerned, is the assemblage of things, energies and creatures which surround us in so far as these are palpable, sensible and "natural" (in the theological sense of the word). Matter is the common, universal, tangible setting, infinitely shifting and varied, in which we live.

How, then, does the thing thus defined present itself to us to be acted upon? Under the enigmatic features of a two-sided power.

On the one hand matter is the burden, the fetters, the pain, the sin and the threat to our lives. It weighs us down, suffers, wounds, tempts and grows old. Matter makes us heavy, paralysed, vulnerable, guilty. Who will deliver us from this body of death?

But at the same time matter is physical exuberance, ennobling contact, virile effort and the joy of growth. It attracts, renews, unites and flowers. By matter we are nourished, lifted up, linked to everything else, invaded by life. To be deprived of it is intolerable. *Non exui volumnus sed superindui* (2 Cor. v, 4). Who will give us an immortal body?

Asceticism deliberately looks no further than the first aspect, the one which is turned towards death; and it recoils, exclaiming "Flee!" *But what would our spirits be, O God, if they did not have the bread of earthly things to nourish them, the wine of created beauties to intoxicate them, and the conflicts of human life to fortify them? What feeble powers and blood-less hearts your creatures would bring you if they were to succeed in cutting themselves off prematurely from the providential setting in which you have placed them! Teach us, Lord, how to contemplate the sphinx without succumbing to its spell; how to grasp the hidden mystery in the womb of death, not by a refinement of human doctrine, but in the simple concrete act by which you plunged yourself into matter in order to redeem it. By the virtue of your suffering incarnation disclose to us, and then teach us to harness jealousy for you, the spiritual power of matter.*

Let us take a comparison as our starting point. Imagine a deep-sea diver trying to get back from the seabed to the clear light of day. Or imagine a traveller on a fog-bound mountain-side climbing upward towards the summit bathed in light. For each of these men space is divided into two zones marked with opposing properties: the one behind and beneath appears ever darker, while the one in front and above becomes ever lighter. Both diver and climber can succeed in making their way towards the second zone only if they use everything around and about them as points of leverage. Moreover, in the course of their task, the light above them grows brighter with each advance made; and at the same time the area which has been traversed, as it is traversed, ceases to hold the light and is engulfed in darkness. Let us remember these stages, for they express symbolically all the elements we need in order to understand how we should touch and handle matter with a proper sense of reverence.

Above all matter is not just the weight that drags us down, the mire that sucks us in, the bramble that bars our way. In itself, and before we find ourselves where we are, and before we choose, it is simply the slope on which we can go up just as well as go down, the medium that can uphold or give way, the wind that can overthrow or lift up. Of its nature, and as a result of original sin, it is true that it represents a perpetual impulse towards failure. But by nature too, and as a result of the Incarnation, it contains the spur or the allurement to be our accomplice towards heightened being, and this counter-balances and even dominates the *fomes peccati*. The full truth of our situation is that, here below, and by virtue of our immersion in the universe, we are each one of us placed within its layers or on its slopes, at a specific point defined by the present moment in the history of the world, the place of our birth, and our individual vocation. And *from that starting point,* variously situated at different levels, the task assigned to us is to climb towards the light, passing through, so as to attain God, *a given series of created things* which are not exactly obstacles but rather foot-holds, intermediaries to be made use of, nourishment to be taken, sap to be purified and elements to be associated with us and borne along with us.

That being so, and still as a result of our initial position among things, and also as a result of each position we subsequently occupy in matter, matter falls into two distinct zones, differentiated according to our effort: the zone already left behind or arrived at, to which we should not return, or at which we should not pause, lest we fall back—this is the zone of matter *in the material and carnal sense;* and the zone offered to our renewed efforts towards progress, search, conquest and "divinisation," the zone of matter *taken in the spiritual sense;* and the frontier between these two zones is essentially relative and shifting. That which is good, sanctifying and spiritual for my brother below or beside me on the mountainside, can be material, misleading or bad for me. What I rightly allowed myself yesterday, I must perhaps deny myself today. And conversely, actions which would have been a grave betrayal in a St. Aloysius Gonzaga or a St. Anthony, may well be models for me if I am to follow in the footsteps of these saints. In other words, the soul can only rejoin God after having traversed *a specific path* through matter—which path can be seen as the distance which separates, but it can also be seen as the road which links. Without certain possessions and certain victories, no man exists as God wishes him to be. Each one of us has his Jacob's ladder, whose rungs are formed of a series of objects. Thus it is not our business to withdraw from the world before our time; rather let us learn to orientate our being in the flux of things; then, instead of the force of gravity which drags us down to the abyss of self-indulgence and selfishness, we shall feel a salutary "component" emerge from created things which, by a process we have already described, will enlarge our horizons, will snatch us away from our pettinesses and impel us imperiously towards a widening of our vision, towards the renunciation of cherished pleasure, towards the desire for ever more spiritual beauty. Matter, which at first seemed to counsel us towards the maximum pleasure and the minimum effort, emerges as the principle of minimum pleasure and maximum effort.

In this case, too, the law which applies to the individual would seem to be a small-scale version of the law which applies to the whole. It would surely not be far wrong to suggest that, in its universality, the world too has a prescribed path to follow before attaining its consummation. There can really be no doubt of it. If the material totality of the world includes energies, which cannot be made use of, and if, more unfortunately, it contains perverted energies and elements which are slowly separated from it, it is still more certain that it contains *a certain quantity of spiritual power* of which the progressive sublimation, *in Christo Jesu,* is, for the Creator, the fundamental operation taking place. At the present time this power is still diffused almost everywhere: nothing, however insignificant or crude it may appear, is without some trace of it. And the task of the body of Christ, living in his faithful, is patiently to sort out those heavenly forces—to extract, without letting any of it be lost, that chosen substance. Little by little, we may rest assured, the work is being done. Thanks to the multitude of individuals and vocations, the Spirit of God insinuates itself everywhere and is everywhere at work. It is the great tree we spoke of a moment ago, whose sunlit branches refine and turn to flowers the sap extracted by the humblest of its roots. As the work progresses, certain zones, no doubt, become worked out. Within each individual life, as we have noted, the frontier between spiritual matter and carnal matter is constantly moving upward. And in the same way, in proportion as humanity is christianised, it feels less and less need for certain earthly nourishment. Contemplation and chastity should thus tend, quite legitimately, to gain mastery over anxious work and direct possession. This is the *general "drift" of matter* towards spirit. This movement must have its term: one day the whole divinisable substance of matter will have passed into the souls of men; all the chosen dynamisms will have been recovered: and then our world will be ready for the Parousia.

Who can fail to perceive the great symbolic gesture of baptism in this general history of matter? Christ immerses himself in the waters of Jordan, symbol of the forces of the earth. These he sanctifies. And as he emerges, in the words of St. Gregory of Nyssa, with the water which runs off his body he elevates the whole world.

Immersion and emergence; participation in things and sublimation; possession and reunuciation; crossing through and being borne onwards— that is the twofold yet single movement which answers the challenge of matter in order to save it.[1]

---

[1] The sensual mysticisms and certain neo-pelagianisms (such as Americanism), by paying too much attention to the first of these phases, have fallen into the error of seeking divine love and the divine kingdom *on the same level* as human affections and human progress. Conversely, by concentrating too much on the second phase, some exaggerated forms of Christianity conceive perfection as built upon the destruction of "nature." The true christian supernatural, frequently defined by the Church, neither leaves the creature where he is, on his own plane, nor suppresses him; it "sur-animates" him. It must surely be obvious that, however transcendent and

Matter, you in whom I find both seduction and strength, you in whom I find blandishment and virility, you who can enrich and destroy, I surrender myself to your mighty layers, with faith in the heavenly influences which have sweetened and purified your waters. The virtue of Christ has passed into you. *Let your attractions lead me forward, let your sap be the food that nourishes me; let your resistance give me toughness; let your robberies and inroads give me freedom. And finally, let your whole being lead me towards Godhead.*

Can Harmony Be Realized on Earth?

How depressing is the spectacle of the scattered human mass! A turbulent ant-hill of separate elements whose most evident characteristic, excepting certain limited cases of deep affinity (married couples, families, the team, the mother country) seems to be one of mutual repulsion, whether between individuals or groups. Yet we nurse in the depths of our hearts the conviction that it could be otherwise, that the chaos and disorder are "against nature" inasmuch as they prevent the realisation, or delay the coming, of a state of affairs which would multiply as though to infinity our human powers of thought, feeling and action.

Is the situation really desperate, or are there reasons for believing, despite appearances to the contrary, that Mankind as a whole is not only capable of unanimity but is actually in process of becoming unanimised? Do there exist, in other words, certain planetary energies which, overcoming the forces of repulsion that seem to be incurably opposed to human harmony, are tending inexorably to bring together and organise upon itself (unbelievable though this may seem) the terrifying multitude of milliards of thinking consciousnesses which forms the "reflective layer" of the earth?

My object here is to show that such energies do exist.

They are of two kinds: forces of compression, which by external and

---

creative they may be, God's love and ardour could only fall upon the *human* heart, that is to say upon an object prepared (from near or from afar) by means of all the nourishments of the earth. It is astonishing that so few minds should succeed, in this as in other cases, in grasping the notion of transformation. Sometimes the thing transformed seems to them to be the old thing unchanged; at other times they see in it only the entirely new. In the first case it is the spirit that eludes them; in the second case, it is the matter. Though not so crude as the first excess, the second is shown by experience to be no less destructive of the equilibrium of mankind. [P.T. DE C.]

From pp. 281–288 of *The Future of Man* by Pierre Teilhard de Chardin. Translated from the French, *L'Avenir de l'homme,* first published by Editions du Seuil and copyright 1959 by Editions du Seuil. © 1964 in the English translation by William Collins Sons & Company Ltd., London, and Harper & Row, Publishers. Reprinted by permission of Harper & Row, Publishers, and William Collins Sons & Company Ltd.

internal determinisms bring about a first stage of enforced unification; and subsequently forces of attraction, which through the action of internal affinity effect a genuine unanimisation by free consent.

Let us look in turn at these two processes which so pervade the human atmosphere that like light and air, we tend to ignore them, although they envelop us so closely that no act of ours can escape them.

ENFORCED UNIFICATION: OR THE GEOGRAPHICAL AND MENTAL CURVATURE OF COMPRESSION

The Geographical Curvature

Biologically speaking the human zoological group is developing on a closed surface. More exactly, since although the world population has already virtually filled the continents to saturation-point it shows no sign of levelling out but continues to increase at an ever-growing rate, the group behaves as though it were developing in a world that is shrinking, so that it becomes ever more tightly compressed upon itself.

The first and obvious effect of this ethnic compression is to bring bodies together. But the growing density of human matter, however material its origin, is also having a profound effect on human souls. In order to adapt itself in a vital sense to the increasing pressure, to survive and live in comfort, the multitude of thinking beings reacts naturally by arranging itself as well as possible, economically and technologically, upon itself. This automatically compels it to be constantly *inventing* new systems of mechanical equipment and social organisation. In other words it is forced to reflect; and this causes it to reflect a little more upon itself—to turn inward, that is to say, and further develop in itself those qualities which are specifically and in a higher sense human.

It is a profoundly instructive and mysterious phenomenon. The human mass is spiritually warmed and illumined by the iron grip of planetary compression; and the warming, whereby the rays of individual interaction expand, induces a further increase, in a kind of recoil, of the compression which was its cause . . . and so on, in a chain-reaction of increasing rapidity.

Out of this there arises first an irresistible grouping principle which, in its impact on the intelligence, almost automatically overrules the egoistical and mutually repulsive tendencies of the individual.

But that is not all: for to this first geographical compression there is rapidly added a tightening effect, due this time to the emergence and influence of a curvature which is not mechanical but *mental,* and which I must now explain.

The Mental Curvature

In the "humanising" chain of events which we have described, the mind, which at first seemed to be no more than a "device" for confronting and resisting planetary compression, is swiftly transformed into a "reason" of existence. We think first in order to survive, and then we live in order to think: such is the fundamental law of anthropogenesis which emerges. But Thought, once it is let loose, displays an extraordinary power of self-protraction and extension, as though it were an independent organism which, being once born, cannot be restrained from growing and propagating itself and absorbing everything into its network. All history bears witness to the fact that nothing has ever been able to prevent an idea from growing and spreading and finally becoming universal. The reflective, psychic environment which surrounds us is so constituted that we cannot remain in it without moving forward; and we cannot advance except by drawing closer and rubbing shoulders with one another. It is as though all our individual strivings after truth soared upward into a mental "cupola" whose closed walls inexorably compel our minds to mingle!

An enforced coalescence of all Thought in the sum total of itself . . .

The increasingly apparent growth, overriding the monstrous and chaotic human dispersal which so distresses us, of this force of auto-unification emerging from the psychic energies released by our technico-social mastery of the earth: this surely is a guarantee that, within our universe, the impulse of totalisation must eventually triumph over the impulses of dispersal.

But on one condition. Under the influence of economic forces and the intellectual reasons invoked to break down the barriers behind which our egotism shelters, there must emerge, since this alone can be completely unanimising, the sense of a single fundamental aspiration.

FREE UNIFICATION THROUGH ATTRACTION.
A POINT OF UNIVERSAL CONVERGENCE ON THE HORIZON

Despite the compulsions, both geographical and psychic, which oblige men to live and think in an ever closer community, they do not necessarily love each other the more on that account. The two greatest scientists in the world, being preoccupied with the same problem, may none the less detest each other. This is a sad fact of which we are all aware, and because of this separation of head and heart we are bound to conclude that, however social necessity and logic may impel it from behind, the human mass will only become thoroughly unified under the influence of some form of *affective* energy which will place the human particles in the happy position of being unable to love and fulfil themselves individually except by contributing in some degree to the love and fulfilment of all; to the extent, that is to say, that all are equal and integral parts of a single universe that is vitally converging. A "pull," in other words, must be born of the "push." But amid the politico-social crisis which now besets us, have we valid, objective reasons for believing in the possibility of this hopeful state of affairs, even to the point of discerning its first indications?

I believe we have, on the following grounds.

If we look for the principal outcome, "Result No. 1," of the ineluctable unification of our scientific intelligence during the past century, we must quickly perceive that the gain consists far less in our securing control of any particular source of natural energy than in the general awakening of our consciousness to the vast and extreme organicity of the universe as a whole, considered in terms of its internal forces of development. We see more clearly with every increase in our knowledge that we are, all of us, participants in a process (Cosmogenesis culminating in Anthropogenesis) upon which our ultimate fulfilment—one might even say, our beatification—obscurely depends. And whence can it arise, this accumulation of evidence that the extreme point of each of us (our ultra-ego, it might be termed) coincides with some common fulfilment of the evolutionary process, a common super-ego, except out of the principle of attraction which we have postulated as being necessary to bring together the rebellious seeds of our individualities, uniting them from within and unanimising them at the heart?

Thus, superimposed on the twofold tightening action of what I have called the geometrical and mental curvature of the human earth—superimposed yet *emanating* from them—we have a third and final unifying influence brought to bear in regulating the movements of the Noosphere, that of a destiny that is supremely attractive, the same for all at the same time. A total community of desire, which makes of it a third force as planetary in its dimensions as the other two, but operating, no matter how irresistibly, in the manner of seduction—that is to say, by free consent.

It would be premature to assert that this new force as yet plays any very explicit part in the course of political or social events. Yet may we not claim, observing the precipitate growth of democracies and totalitarian regimes during the past hundred and fifty years, that it is the *Sense of Species,* which for a time seemed to have vanished from human hearts, dispelled in some sort by the growth of Reflection, that is now gradually resuming its place and reasserting its rights over narrow individualism? Sense of Species interpreted in the new, grand human manner: not, as formerly, a shoot which merely seeks to prolong itself until it bears its fruit, but the fruit itself, gathering and growing upon itself in the expectation of eventual ripeness.

But if the hope of this maturing of the Species, and the belief in its coming, are to illuminate and truly unanimise our hearts, we must endow it with certain positive attributes. It is here that opinions are divided.

Those who think on Marxist lines believe that all that is necessary to inspire and polarise the human molecules is that they should look forward to an eventual state of *collective* reflection and sympathy, at the culmination of anthropogenesis, from which all will benefit through *participation:* as it were, a vault of intermingled thoughts, a closed circuit of attachments in which the individual will achieve intellectual and affective wholeness to the extent that he is one with the whole system.

But in the Christian view only the eventual appearance, at the summit and in the heart of the unified world, of an autonomous centre of congregation is structurally and functionally capable of inspiring, preserving and fully releasing, within a human mass still spiritually dispersed, the looked-for forces of unanimisation. By this hypothesis only a veritable *super-love,* the attractive power of a veritable "super-being," can of psychological necessity dominate, possess and synthesise the host of earthly loves. Failing such a centre of universal coherence, not metaphorical or theoretical but *real,* there can be no true union among totalised Mankind, and therefore no true substance. A world culminating in the Impersonal can bring us neither the warmth of attraction nor the hope of irreversibility (immortality) without which individual egotism will always have the last word. A veritable *Ego* at the summit of the world is needed for the consummation, without confounding them, of all the elemental *egos* of Earth . . . I have talked of the "Christian view," but this idea is gaining ground in other circles. Was it not Camus who wrote in *Sisyphe,* "If Man found that the Universe could love he would be reconciled"? And did not Wells, through his exponent the humanitarian biologist Steele in *The Anatomy of Frustration,* express his need to find, above and beyond humanity, a "universal lover"?

Let me recapitulate and conclude.

Essentially, in the twofold irresistible embrace of a planet that is visibly shrinking, and Thought that is more and more rapidly coiling in upon itself, the dust of human units finds itself subjected to a formidable pressure of coalescence, far stronger than the individual or national repulsions that so alarm us. But despite the closing of this vise nothing seems finally capable of guiding us into the natural sphere of our inter-human affinities except the emergence of a powerful field of internal attraction, in which we shall find ourselves caught *from within.* The rebirth of the Sense of Species, rendered virtually inevitable by the phase of compressive and totalising socialisation which we have now entered, affords a first indication of the existence of such a field of unanimisation and a clue to its nature.

Nevertheless, however efficacious this newly born faith of Man in the ultra-human may prove to be, it seems that Man's urge towards *Some Thing* ahead of him cannot achieve its full fruition except by combining with another and still more fundamental aspiration—one from above, urging him towards *Some One.*

QUESTIONS FOR STUDY AND DISCUSSION

1. Analyze Teilhard's double approach to the concept of matter.
2. What are the two kinds of energy the author claims he discovers in the general evolution of the earth and its inhabitants?
3. What role does the reflective element (love) play in Teilhard's ethical philosophy?

TOPICS FOR DISCUSSION AND TERM PAPERS

A.

1. When Abraham set forth to sacrifice his son he suspended the ethical. He was at that moment "the particular who becomes higher than the universal." In your opinion, can Abraham ever return to the universal or must he forever remain outside it?
2. Can Nietzsche be called a materialist?
3. Nietzsche has often been condemned, and with reason, for being anti-Christian. Does this imply that he has unlimited faith in the empirical and the scientific? Discuss his attitude.
4. Discuss the relation between Camus' *The Rebel* and *The Plague*.

B.

1. Analyze and compare Nietzsche's *The Madman* with Marcel's comment on Nietzsche's phrase "God is dead."
2. Compare Nietzsche and Marcel on ethical values. (See especially Nietzsche, *"Master and Slave Morality,"* and Marcel, *"Techniques of Degradation."*)
3. Sketch a comparison between Sartre and Nietzsche.
4. Compare Teilhard de Chardin's approach to matter with St. Augustine's understanding of the same. Examine the ethical implications of their respective positions.
5. St. Thomas accepts an evolution of man's creative freedom within the fundamental framework of a permanent human nature. Sartre, basing himself upon the principle that "existence precedes essence and that man makes himself incessantly," does not seem to defend any permanent concept of man or unchangeable norm of ethics. Is there a resolution for this apparent conflict in thought?

RECOMMENDED READINGS

Primary Sources

Camus, Albert. *The Fall*. Trans. by Justin O'Brien. New York: Alfred A. Knopf, 1957. A critique of modern times to the extent that they dehumanize man. The main personage is a perverted man, a result of the abuses of the age.

———. *The Myth of Sisyphus*. Trans. by Justin O'Brien. New York: Alfred A. Knopf, 1955. This and *The Stranger* are early works; they are very Sartrian and stress the absurd. Happiness is a stoical confrontation with destiny. There is no real love but a commitment toward one self.

———. *The Plague*. New York: Alfred A. Knopf, 1948. Camus' best novel. It discusses the problem of evil and describes the reactions of a certain number of people living in a plague-ridden city.

———. *The Stranger*. Trans. by Stuart Gilbert. New York: Alfred A. Knopf, 1946.

Kierkegaard, Søren. *Concluding Unscientific Postscript*. Trans. by David F.

Swenson and Walter Lowrie. Princeton, N.J.: Princeton University Press, 1941. A reaction to Hegel and to all systematic and rationalistic thought.

Kierkegaard, Søren. *Either/Or.* 2 vols. Trans. by David F. and Lillian M. Swenson and Walter Lowrie. Also presents Kierkegaard's anti-Hegelian stand. The book clearly denotes his hatred of the "synthesis," which includes *both* "thesis" and "antithesis."

————. *Fear and Trembling, and Sickness unto Death.* Trans. by Walter Lowrie. New York: Doubleday & Co., 1964. In the opinion of some commentators, these books, published in one volume, constitute Kierkegaard's most important work. The first one developed from his own experience and has direct relation to his break with Regina. Yet this concrete and individual case gains a universal dimension in this volume. *Sickness unto Death* is an investigation into the corruption of human nature and the despair that results from it.

————. *A Kierkegaard Anthology.* Ed. by Robert Bretall. Princeton, N.J.: Princeton University Press, 1951. A first-class selection from Kierkegaard's works.

————. *Philosophical Fragments.* Princeton, N.J.: Princeton University Press, 1962. This work is a discussion of why and how Christ is the teacher *par excellence.*

Marcel, Gabriel. *Creative Fidelity.* Trans. and with Introd. by Robert Rosthal. New York: Farrar, Straus & Giroux, 1964.

————. *Homo Viator.* Trans. by E. Craufurd. London: Gollancz, 1951. Both this and *Creative Fidelity* contain a series of articles and lectures on such topics as Hope, Fidelity, Faith, and the Existence of God. The presentation is always penetrating and thorough, rarely systematic or synthetic.

————. *Journal métaphysique.* Paris: Gallimard, 1927. A very penetrating philosophical work, written in the form of a diary and culminating in Marcel's conversion to Catholicism.

————. *Man Against Mass Society.* Trans. by G. S. Fraser. La Salle, Ill.: Henry Regnery Co., 1962. A protest against man's dehumanization through modern techniques.

————. *The Mystery of Being.* 2 vols. La Salle, Ill.: Henry Regnery Co., 1960. Written record of the Gifford Lectures given by the author at Aberdeen, 1949–50. It presents his philosophy in a systematic way.

Nietzsche, Friedrich. *The Philosophy of Nietzsche.* Trans. by T. Common, H. Zimmern, and C. P. Fadiman, and with Introd. by W. H. Wright. New York: Random House, 1954. Excellent collection of Nietzsche's best-known works, although *The Will to Power* is missing. The translation on the whole is somewhat pedantic.

————. *The Portable Nietzsche.* Ed. and trans. by Walter Kaufmann. New York: Viking Press, 1954. A translation of some of Nietzsche's work into a fresh and modern English. Unfortunately some of his best efforts such as *Beyond Good and Evil* and *The Genealogy of Morals* are not included.

Sartre, Jean-Paul. *Being and Nothingness.* Trans. and with Introd. by Hazel E. Barnes. New York: Philosophical Library, 1956. One of Sartre's two major philosophical works. The author himself calls it an ontology based upon a phenomenological or descriptive method.

————. *Literary and Philosophical Essays.* New York: Collier Books, 1962. Excellent selection of some of Sartre's articles published in his periodical, *Les Temps Modernes,* including his now famous "Materialism and Revolution."

Sartre, Jean-Paul. *Nausea*. Trans. by Lloyd Alexander. New York: New Directions, 1949. Sartre's best novel so far. Written in the form of a diary, it narrates in a very striking way the tribulations of a French prewar intellectual.

―――――. *No Exit, and Three Other Plays*. Trans. by Stuart Gilbert. New York: Alfred A. Knopf, 1946. A collection of plays written by the young Sartre. They have great originality and are forceful and incisive. Each one carries an ethical message.

―――――. *Search for a Method*. New York: Alfred A. Knopf, 1963. A translation of Sartre's Introduction to the *Critique de la raison dialectique,* his second major philosophical opus.

Teilhard de Chardin, Pierre. *The Divine Milieu*. New York: Harper & Row, 1960. An interesting and readable publication, containing a series of articles concerning Teilhard's ethical and ascetical stand.

―――――. *The Future of Man*. Trans. by Norman Denny. New York: Harper & Row, 1964. A series of articles on the philosophical and sociological implications of an evolving mankind.

―――――. *The Phenomenon of Man*. Trans. by Bernard Wall and with Introd. by Julian Huxley. New York: Harper & Row, 1959. Considered by most to be Teilhard's best work. It lays the scientific groundwork for his theory of evolution and the ensuing philosophical and theological speculations.

Commentaries

Brée, Germaine. *Albert Camus*. New York: Columbia University Press, 1964.

Collins, James. *The Mind of Kierkegaard*. La Salle, Ill.: Henry Regnery Co., 1953. A penetrating analysis of Kierkegaard's philosophical position and an excellent introduction to his writings.

Desan, Wilfrid. *The Marxism of Jean-Paul Sartre*. Garden City, N.Y.: Doubleday & Co., 1965. A critical analysis of *Critique de la raison dialectique,* vol. I, which itself is an attempt to construct a synthesis between existentialism and Marxism.

―――――. *The Tragic Finale: An Essay on the Philosophy of Jean-Paul Sartre*. New York: Harper & Row, 1960. An exposition of Sartre's most important work, *Being and Nothingness*.

Dupré, Louis. *Kierkegaard as Theologian*. New York: Sheed and Ward, 1963. More on the theological level than Collins' work but eminently worthwhile reading.

Gallagher, Kenneth T. *The Philosophy of Gabriel Marcel*. New York: Fordham University Press, 1962. Good synthesis; at times inclined to keep too closely to Marcellian semantics.

Jaspers, Karl. *Nietzsche*. Tucson: University of Arizona Press, 1965. Although very difficult and unsystematic, this is perhaps the most penetrating work on Nietzsche.

Kaufmann, Walter. *Nietzsche: Philosopher, Psychologist, AntiChrist*. New York: Meridian Books, 1956. Erudite, attractive, and pictorial approach. Should be read by any Nietzsche student, although all of its theses are not equally convincing.

Lowrie, Walter. *A Short Life of Kierkegaard*. Princeton, N.J.: Princeton University Press, 1942. Extremely useful for any Kierkegaard student.

Mooney, Christopher F. *Teilhard de Chardin and the Mystery of Christ.* New York: Harper & Row, 1966. The best on Teilhard, with special emphasis on the theological aspect, within reach of the college student.

Murdoch, J. *Sartre: Romantic Rationalist.* New Haven: Yale University Press, 1953.

Thody, Philip. *Albert Camus, 1913–1960,* New York: Macmillan Co., 1962. Both this work and the one by Brée give an interesting and lively account of Camus and his work. Brée is perhaps a little more literary in her expression, while Thody has a more factual approach. See Brée, Ch. 14, on *The Plague,* and compare it with Thody, Ch. 12.

———. *Jean-Paul Sartre: A Literary and Political Study.* New York: Macmillan Co., 1961. A penetrating study, within the limits indicated by the title.

A 6
B 7
C 8
D 9
E 0
F 1
G 2
H 3
I 4
J 5

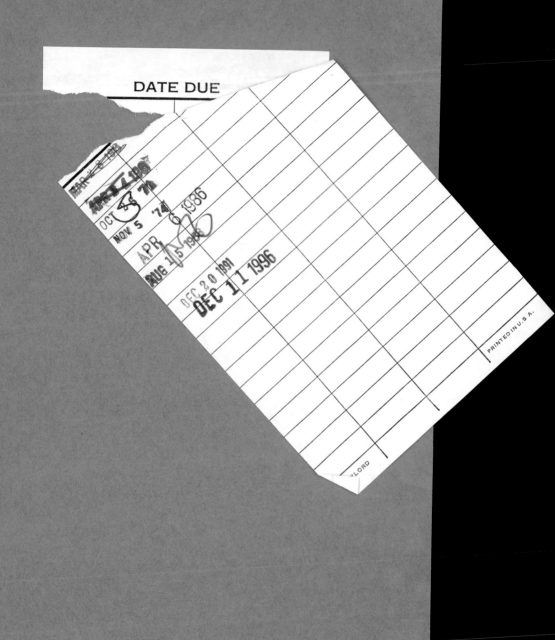

DATE DUE